LITERARY DISCOURSE:
A SEMIOTIC-PRAGMATIC APPROACH TO LITERATURE

JØRGEN DINES JOHANSEN

Literary Discourse

A Semiotic-Pragmatic Approach to Literature

UNIVERSITY OF TORONTO PRESS
Toronto Buffalo London

© University of Toronto Press Incorporated 2002
Toronto Buffalo London
Printed in Canada

ISBN 0-8020-3577-9

Printed on acid-free paper

Toronto Studies in Semiotics and Communication
Editors: Marcel Danesi, Umberto Eco, Paul Perron, Thomas Sebeok,
and Peter Schulz

National Library of Canada Cataloguing in Publication Data

Johansen, Jørgen Dines
  Literary discourse : a semiotic-pragmatic approach to
  literature

  (Toronto studies in semiotics and communication)
  Includes bibliographical references and index.
  ISBN 0-8020-3577-9

  1. Semiotics and literature.   2. Literature – Philosophy.
  I. Title.   II. Series.

  P302.5.J64 2002   801'.95   C2001-903577-9

This book has been published with the help of a grant from the
University of Southern Denmark.

University of Toronto Press acknowledges the financial assistance to
its publishing program of the Canada Council for the Arts and the
Ontario Arts Council.

University of Toronto Press acknowledges the financial support for
its publishing activities of the Government of Canada through the
Book Publishing Industry Development Program (BPIDP).

For Helle,

and Morten, Ditte, Thomas, and Rasmus

Contents

Preface   xi

Introduction: Literature?   3
1 Trouble with Genres: The Instability of Categories   4
2 The Todorov Hypothesis   10
3 Exemplars and Contests   14

PART 1   SIGN, DIALOGUE, DISCOURSE

Chapter 1   From Sign to Dialogue   25

1.1 Representation   26
1.2 Immediate and Dynamical Object   26
1.3 Icons, Indices, and Symbols   29
    1.3.1 Iconic Signs   30
        1.3.1.1 Images   30
        1.3.1.2 Diagrams   31
        1.3.1.3 Metaphors   33
    1.3.2 Indexical Signs   35
        1.3.2.1 Reagents   35
        1.3.2.2 Designations   37
    1.3.3 The Symbolic Sign   38
1.4 The Uses of Iconic, Indexical, and Symbolic Signs   40
1.5 The Interpretants   42
    1.5.1 Emotional, Energetic, and Logical Interpretants   43
    1.5.2 Immediate, Dynamical, and Final Interpretants   44
1.6 Interpretant and Dialogue   46
1.7 Utterer and Addresser, Addressee and Interpreter   49

- 1.8 The Semiotic Pyramid 54
- 1.9 The Interrelations of the Immediate Interpretants 58
- 1.10 Language 63
- 1.11 From Language to Text: The Three Levels of Linguistic Communication 66

Chapter 2 Discourse and Text 74

- 2.1 Two Concepts of Discourse: Foucault and Habermas 74
- 2.2 Discourse and Text 87
- 2.3 The Four Discourses 89
- 2.4 Literary Discourse 97
- 2.5 Literature Becoming Literature 100
    - 2.5.1 After Dark 101
    - 2.5.2 Literature and Other Discourses 103

PART 2 THE FOUR DIMENSIONS OF THE LITERARY TEXT

Chapter 3 Mimesis: Literature as Imitation and Model 113

- 3.1 Literature as Representation and Fiction 114
- 3.2 Signs and Universes 116
- 3.3 Ten Features of a Fictional Universe 122
- 3.4 The Relation of Fictional and Historical Universes 124
    - 3.4.1 Contiguity: The Magic Map 124
    - 3.4.2 Conventions of Embedding and Representation 135
    - 3.4.3 Improving the Universe 143
- 3.5 Similarity 146
    - 3.5.1 Iconic Relationship between Sign and Object 147
    - 3.5.2 The Text-mediated Relation between Literature and the Historical Universe 149
    - 3.5.3 Figurative Representation in Literature 153
- 3.6 Literature and the Claim to Truth 157
- 3.7 Fiction, Model, and Lifeworld 162
    - 3.7.1 Literary Representation: Model and Exemplification 170

Chapter 4 Self-representation and Analogy in Literature 174

- 4.1 Repetition as a Proto-aesthetic Phenomenon 176
- 4.2 Repetition, Analogy, and Poeticity 177
- 4.3 Analogy as a Cognitive and Textual Structural Principle 185
- 4.4 Analogy and Metaphor 191

4.5 From Repetition to Metaphor   199
4.6 The Self-representation of Narrative   203
    4.6.1 The Crisis of Adolescence in Fairy Tales   206
    4.6.2 Family Business: The Fateful Square   211
4.7 Literature and the Existential Analogy   221

Chapter 5 Literature as Self-expression: Subjectivity and Imagination   228

5.1 Self-representation and Self-expression   230
5.2 Subject, Subjectivity, and Self-expression   233
5.3 The Subject in Literature and Fiction   240
5.4 The Subjective Thematics of Literature   248
5.5 Desire and Fiction: Persinna's Confession   259
5.6 Language, Materiality, and Repetition in Literature   264
5.7 Naming and Enumeration   275
5.8 Plenitude, Variety, Lack   279
5.9 *Non omnis moriar*   284

Chapter 6 The Interpreters   289

6.1 Literature as an Institution   290
6.2 The Interpellation: *Plaudite*   303
6.3 Mistrusting the Author   308
6.4 Vitally Important Subjects   313
6.5 Such stuff as dreams are made of   322
6.6 Reading as Iconizing   326
    6.6.1 Three Ways of Iconizing the Literary Text   327
        6.6.1.1 Imaginization   328
        6.6.1.2 Diagrammatization   332
        6.6.1.3 Allegorization   334
    6.6.2 Reading as Iconization   338
6.7 A Space of One's Own   341
6.8 Complexity and Ambiguity in the Communication of Literature   346

PART 3 ON INTERPRETATION

Chapter 7 Interpreting Literature   353

7.1 Interpretation as Semiosis   354
7.2 Interpretation as Prediction and Reconstruction   361

7.3 Reconstruction and/vs. Recontextualization 364
7.4 Interpretation as Abduction and Rational Reconstruction 366
7.5 The Practice and Predicaments of the Literary Interpretation 371
    7.5.1 The Sensitivity of Listening: The Reader and the Dialogical Principle 372
    7.5.2 The Text as Dynamical Structure 376
    7.5.3 The Text as a Set of Traces and Clues 380
7.6 Interpretation by Analogy 388
7.7 Interpreting the Text as Enunciation and Utterance 392
7.8 Contextualization: Exclusivity or Integration? 400
7.9 Infinite (Re)interpretation? 407

CONCLUSION

Conclusion: Literature! 415

8.1 Literature's Heterogeneity 416
8.2 Other-representation and Self-representation 418
8.3 Eight Paradoxes of Literature 423
8.4 Literature! 430

Notes 433

Bibliography 457

Index 475

Preface

This book is an attempt to approach the study of literature from a semiotic-pragmatic point of view; more specifically, the semiotics and pragmatics of C.S. Peirce and the universal pragmatics of Jürgen Habermas. Thus it owes its framework, its architecture, to speak with Peirce, to his conception of the sign as I understand it and to my understanding and use of Habermas's concept of discourse.

In the introduction some problems concerning the categorization of literature are discussed, those dealing with the distinction between literature and non-literature and those dealing with distinctions between the different literary genres. An attempt is made to explain the fuzzy boundaries and the internal heterogeneity of literature by pointing out (with Gallie) that literature is inherently unruly and agonistic. Consequently, it seems impossible to give a universally valid definition of it. Instead, it should be studied and described in relation to its functions within a historical and communicative context.

The first part, 'Sign, Dialogue, Discourse' (chapters 1–2), expounds the general theoretical framework of this approach. The first chapter is on Peircean semiotics: on his concepts of sign and semiosis, and on communication from a semiotic perspective. In the second chapter, the point of departure is the two different concepts of discourse of Foucault and Habermas. This discussion, following Habermas, leads to the hypothesis that four basic discourses are needed for a community, and a culture, to survive. I further argue that a fifth should be added, that of literary discourse. This chapter ends with a brief sketch of the status of fictional literature at different times in European literary history. I further attempt a heterogeneous definition of literature using a cluster of often encountered features that are related to different dimensions of communicative semiosis (the semiotic pyramid).

This introductory section on semiotics in general and the concept of discourse is necessitated by my conviction that literature is firmly entrenched in communication within the lifeworld of communities, where it fulfils a number of important functions. Thus, to approach what is specific to literature as a mode of communication, and as an institution, presupposes an awareness of what different kinds of human sign production and interpretation have in common.

The second and central part of the book, 'The Four Dimensions of the Literary Text' (chapters 3–6) treats the mimetic, formal, subjective, and communicative dimensions of literature, respectively. The design of this part follows from the ideas of a communicative semiotics presented in chapters 1 and 2. However, even if the perspective is most certainly semiotic, I hope that it also will become evident that the person writing is a literary scholar who likes his trade. Theory should further, not hinder, the dialogue with, and interpretation of, literary texts. And it seems to me that literary theory is important because literature matters very much. Although interpretation is by necessity both reductive and amplificatory – it always says less and more than the text it interprets – I firmly believe that theoretical approaches to any field should, as far as possible, respect the heterogeneity of their object. And literature both is structurally complex and fulfils several functions at the same time.

Semiotics, in my understanding, offers a valuable perspective applicable to many fields, namely, that of seeing them as sign processes, as the production and interpretation of meanings. Indeed, I suppose that the study of meaning is ultimately what semiotics is all about. From such a perspective excellent work has been done in fields ranging from biosemiotics to the semiotics of literature. However, in order to be a biosemiotician one must have studied biology, and to be a literary semiotician one must know about the history and the theories of literature other than those called semiotic. Semiotics offers a indispensable perspective and a method of investigation. Nevertheless, as regards literature, semioticians must also respect the fact that they deal with a highly structured artefact, the product of a craft with a long tradition, and that much valuable knowledge about it is produced by scholars who do not consider themselves semioticians.

As regards literature, its heterogeneity stems from the fact that literary texts are linguistic utterances communicated from an author to a readership at a given time under specific social and cultural conditions and within, or in relation to, the literary institution. Thus, literary texts should be studied as texts that are rule-governed at different levels –

but that are also rule-breaking and rule-creating. Further, as utterances they are intentional and motivated; the author wants to represent and insist on something in addressing his or her listeners or readers, although what is said transcends what has been intended. Literary texts, even more than texts related to everyday business, seem to contain a surplus of meaning. The matter of literature is, broadly speaking, the human condition as it is seen – or in the case of literature, just as much imagined – by the uttering subject. Since such a perspective is grounded in time and space, the historical context of uttering is important to the understanding of the texts. Not taking this fact into account makes eminent the danger of reducing texts from different times and places to saying more or less the same things.

Literature, as one discourse among others, has somehow always been institutionalized, at least in a minimal way, but the literary institution has grown and changed over time, and the texts that have been categorized as literary has also changed. The offices and functions that literature has been thought to fulfil – by the poets, by authorities, and by readerships – have changed as well. And these, perhaps conflicting, self-understandings (e.g., the prescriptive and descriptive poetics – always a part of the literary institution) are not external to its texts.

Obviously, the individual literary scholar must have his or her own field of interest and study. Without such division of labour, the establishment of scholarship would be impossible. However, as regards literary theory, semiotic or non-semiotic, it seems important that it not be narrowly conceived according to special interests and fashionable points of view – *vestigia terrent*. This argument I have attempted to make in the third part of the book, 'On Interpretation,' where chapter 7 deals with the problems of hermeneutics from a semiotic perspective. Finally, in the Conclusion, I attempt to point to certain paradoxes that characterize literature as institutionalized communication.

I have tried to write a non-polemic book. Consequently, since this book is written from a semiotic-pragmatic perspective, I have refrained from taking up, and objecting to, points of view argued by other schools or movements, even when they question the point of view put forward here. The decisive reason for abstaining from such confrontation is that it would have made a much longer book. Instead, I have tried to argue my own points of view as best I could.

However, one's own ideas are the result of an ongoing dialogue with those of others, and of reflecting on and taking a stand on issues viewed differently by different scholars. Thus, Peirce more than Saussure,

Jakobson more than Hjelmslev, and Habermas more than Foucault have been the main sources of inspiration for the semiotic-pragmatic approach to literature contained in this book. And, going back to the first fully developed philosophical debate on literature, Aristotle, more than Plato, has influenced my views. The reason for pointing this out is not to inform the reader of something difficult to detect, because I trust that even the most cursory reading of the book will make these influences very clear. There is often, however, a complementarity between differing views. In spite of the fact that they cannot, at the same time, both be used as points of departure and as general frameworks for approaching literary texts, the one not chosen may supplement the chosen one.

For instance, in my opinion, the dynamism, generality, dialogic nature, and inclusiveness of Peirce's view makes it better suited to function as the general framework for the semiotic-pragmatic approach to literature. Within this framework questions may be asked that are not easily raised (or whose answer is deferred by referring to the fact that this part of the theory is not yet established) within the Continental tradition (mainly those concerning reference, communication and use – i.e., fields later taken up by linguistic pragmatics). However, even if the dethronement of structuralism in the 1970s was necessary, this does not mean that it did not possess (and does not still) real merit because of its valid and valuable insight into the ways in which significations are connected within what Greimas called semantic micro-universes. After all, structuralism was a linguistic semiotics, and thus close to spoken and written texts. Parts of chapter 4 draw on this tradition.

The other viewpoints that are contrasted here, the other 'less thans,' also make important points. Constructions of fields of inquiry that one may find unsuitable as general frameworks of research may prove useful for investigating phenomena of a more local nature. This is especially valid as regards literature, because literary texts are the products of complex human action and are thus overdetermined. The theoretical perspective through which they are seen should allow for supplementary points of view, not preclude them. And I have attempted to allow for such supplementarity in this book.

What follows is an attempt to apply the general semiotic viewpoints of my book *Dialogic Semiosis: An Essay on Signs and Meaning* (1993) to literature. In that book I studied semiosis, sign action, and sign interpretation in general, and I attempted to establish a comprehensive and coherent approach to the study of meaning. However, I have been trained as a literary scholar, and it has always been my goal to make semiotics fruitful for the study of literature. The present book is an attempt to fulfil this ambition.

The work on this book was begun by my teaching a seminar on the subject while I was a Fulbright professor in the Scandinavian department at University of California, Berkeley, 1994/95. The department generously gave me time for research, and the discussions with graduate students and my colleagues proved inspiring. That year was a very good start. In the spring of 1997 I was a fellow at the Northrop Frye Centre in Victoria College of the University of Toronto. During those months I was able to create the general outline of the book, and I profited much from discussions with literary scholars Eva Kushner, Roseann Runte, and Mario Valdés and with semioticians Paul Buissac and Marcel Danesi. In 1998/99 I had a sabbatical year from the University of Southern Denmark, and spent October 1998 as a guest professor in the General and Comparative Literature Section at the University of Oslo, lecturing on the subject of this book and giving final form to chapters 6 and 7. However, I owe an equal debt to students and colleagues at my own university for inspiration and to other of its divisions for other kinds of support.

I am happy that University of Toronto Press was able to get the permission to reproduce the painting of Magritte, *La tentative de l'impossible* (1928, Attempting the Impossible) on the cover of this book. Although a painting, it is also a commentary on literature. First, it shows that what is represented is created by the artist. Second, it intimates that such creation is also an act of desire. Third, although it can be known only through contextualization, the female figure is, in fact, a representation of Georgette Magritte, the artist's wife, and the painter on the canvas is a self-portrait. Thus, the painting has its models, and model and artist are themselves present in the artwork. Fourth, nobody would, in spite of its close relation to the couple's lifeworld, take the painting for an accurate representation of reality. I think that these four points characterize literature as well as painting.

Flemming G. Andersen, dean of the humanities at the University of Southern Denmark, graciously relieved me from serving on the executive board of the faculty during 1998/99. I don't think that I could have completed the book while being involved in administration and university politics. Second, in the critical period when I was constantly carrying discs back and forth between my home and the university, the head of the IT division at our faculty, Jørn Erik Wennerstrøm, generously provided me with a home computer that matched the powerful text program of the one in my office. Everybody knows that matching computers are bliss. My colleague Professor Morten Nøjgaard of the Institute of Literature, Culture, and Media in my own university has taken the trouble of reading the entire manuscript of the book, and I have profited much from his comments and suggestions. I also thank Professor Marianne Innis at University of Massachusetts, Lowell, for revising and correcting my English.

Last but not least, I thank my wife – for being my wife, and for her support and encouragement; for putting up with the long hours and for urging me to get the job done. This is why I dedicate this book to her – and to my children, who have given me peace of mind and made me happy by turning into affectionate, responsible, and independent grown-ups while this book was being written.

Introduction

Introduction: Literature?

Owing to the necessity of making theories far more simple than the real facts, we are obliged to be cautious in accepting any extreme consequences of them, and to be also upon our guard against apparent refutations of them based upon such extreme consequences.
(C.S. Peirce, CP 7.96)[1]

What follows is an inquiry into what, to use a somewhat old-fashioned expression, is called the nature of literature, but which I prefer to see as something less pretentious, namely, as an investigation of the dimensions and features that are – rightfully, I think – thought to be general characteristics of the literary texts. Such a generality, however, should not be understood as a claim that every individual text deemed to be literature must possess all of them, because clearly each does not. It is, rather, the thesis of this book that it would be a sound analytic strategy to scan, as it were, literary texts to see whether they possess the features and dimensions mentioned below.

As a point of departure, transhistorical and static – that is, exclusively structural – definitions may be valuable, since they underscore structures and features that are often pertinent to literature. They are insufficient, however, because they neglect literature as discourse, that is, as one kind of cognition and communication among others, and the fact that literature fulfils multiple functions within a community. In this introductory chapter some of the difficulties in categorizing literature as specific kind of texts with stable properties will be confronted.

Thus, I share most literary scholars' belief in the historical reality of literature. Texts certainly exist that, at a given point in time and at a given place, are referred to as literature (or some other term that we would translate as literature). Furthermore, such texts would be incorrectly categorized as, for instance, texts of sacred or profane history, technical descriptions, or legal treatises.

1. Trouble with Genres: The Instability of Categories

To doubt the possibility of delimiting a class of texts that all fulfil a set of criteria that univocally will allow us to distinguish them from other texts is not new. Classical categorization, distinguishing between classes on the basis of an eternal set of properties valid for every member, has been under fire from Wittgenstein through Rosch to Lakoff. Lakoff has even argued that no objective criterion exists for dividing the animal kingdom into species (Lakoff 1987: 187–95); just as the study of genes reveals that plants, for instance, are genetically related to each other in quite other ways that supposed in Linnaeus's categorization.

Within the study of literature the question of genre parallels that of natural kinds within zoology and biology. And from Aristotle (cf. *Poetics* 1449a) to Brunetière (1924, influenced by Darwin) this metaphor has played a role in literary scholarship. However, neither Aristotle's idea that a genre can be defined by a set of properties that are unfolded in a teleological process nor the idea of a development of genre similar to evolution in nature have many supporters today. In my own study of the concept of the *novelle* in postwar literary scholarship (Johansen 1970), I pointed out that even as regards this epic subgenre neither a transhistorical nor an intrinsic teleological definition is possible. In fact, the way in which the *novelle* is defined and distinguished in relation to other epic subgenera – such as, for instance, anecdote, story, short story, tale, folk tale, narrative, sketch, romance, and novel – is both fuzzy and historically variable. In this study I also suggest that literary genres, and individual literary texts themselves, are related to each other in the way Wittgenstein describes the relationship between games (see Wittgenstein 1963: 31–4, §§ 66–71), that is, by family resemblances.

A certain kind of literary text, such as the *novelle*, may at a given time, t, be characterized by a set of properties, A. At another time, t + 1, it may be characterized by a different, but partly identical, set B. And through a series of intermediary stages, at a much later stage, the kind of text may be characterized by a set of properties, Z, that have no properties in common with set A.[2]

In mentioning the *novelle* as one example from a group of literary texts that have no transhistorical properties in common (other than being narratives), it may be objected that at least it is always their common property to be short. For two reasons this objection is invalid: first, shortness is a relational concept, that is, the question immediately arises, Shorter than what? Normally the answer is, Shorter than the novel. In many cases this answer seems sensible. Certainly, Dickens's *Martin Chuzzlewitt* is much longer than *George Silverman's Explanation* and Joyce's *Ulysses* is much longer than 'The Dead.' The point is, however, that being short or long is both a relational and a relative property; we could talk about long short stories and short novels. Obviously, in some cases we might just as well call a given text a long short story as a short novel. Since the criterion is quantitative, we have opposition by scale and not by cut, as Ogden says (cf. Ogden 1932). Opposition by scale, however, does not do very well as a *differentia specifica*, and this is why literary theorists have often tried to point to other, qualitative, differences between the *novelle* and a number of other narrative forms. In calling a given text *novelle* it seems that writers, readers, and literary scholars use a multiplicity of fallible criteria. Some of these criteria are used consciously, others unconsciously. The point is, however, that neither party uses them consistently and automatically.

Among the qualitative criteria one has become especially famous because of Goethe; namely, the definition of the *novelle* as a narrative concentrated on a single, extraordinary event (in Goethe's words, 'eine sich ereignete, unerhörte Begebenheit').[3] The novel, by contrast, presents, according to this theory, a much longer period of time, indeed, often the whole life of a character. The trouble is, however, that what we normally call *novelle* and novel do not generally conform to this formula. In fact, on this definition it could plausibly be argued that Joyce's *Ulysses* is a *novelle*, because it concentrates on one extraordinary event, namely, the meeting of Stephen and Bloom.[4]

In addition to being imprecise, the shortness criterion is also insufficient, because it is not systematically related to qualitative criteria and their relative weight in different cases. In one case a criterion, A, may outweigh criterion B plus other criteria, while in another case it is the other way around. Reluctance, to say the least, to calling *Ulysses* a *novelle* is probably first of all due to its sheer length and, linked with this, to its abundance of detail, its variety of style, and so forth. In this case, then, length overrules narrative unity as the different specific. Flaubert's *Un coeur simple*, on the other hand, tells the life of a poor maidservant, but on account of its relative shortness, and because Flaubert himself called it a *conte*, it is classified as a *novelle*.

Notice, however, that Flaubert did not call *Un coeur simple* a *novelle*, or *nouvelle* in French, but a *conte*. This points to another bewildering fact about the use of genre terminology, namely, that different languages have different labels for literary genres, and that very often these labels are used to carve the text body differently – the distinction *conte/nouvelle* certainly makes no clear cut either. Consequently, no uniform translation of genre terminology is possible. I have consistently used here the Scandinavico-German term *novelle*, which is unfamiliar in English and has a foreign and/or technical ring (thus the italics). I could not use *novella* because it is more specific, connoting a longer narrative, which is, however, not quite as long as a novel, and I have not used *short story*, because this term lacks the historical dimension inherent in *novelle*. However, the demarcation problems in German between, for instance, *Novelle*, *Erzählung*, and *Geschichte*, and in Danish between *novelle*, *fortælling*, and *historie* are no less than those in English and French terminology.

Even if what has been said till now about short versus long narrative is accepted, it might be objected that prose narrative is special. The different kinds of epic prose fiction have always been an unruly mess that honest people and aestheticians frowned upon until the eighteenth century, and even then ...

Drama, for instance, might prove different. Indeed, the distinction between tragedy and comedy, as it is conceived from Aristotle onwards, suggests that clear-cut differences exist that allow us to distinguish unmistakably between texts belonging to one or the other genre. In Aristotle the most important distinction between them concerns their respective objects of imitation:

> Since living persons are the objects of representation, these must necessarily be either good men or inferior ... that is to say either better than ourselves, or worse, or much as we are. It is the same with painters. Polygnotus depicted men as better than they are and Pausan worse, while Dionysius made likenesses ... It is just in this respect that tragedy differs from comedy. The latter sets out to represent people as worse than they are to-day, the former as better. (Aristotle 1927: 9–11, 1448a)

According to Aristotle, this difference is also valid for the origins of the two opposite kinds of texts that later develop into tragedy and comedy, because they depend upon the character of their producers: 'the more serious poets represented fine doings and the doings of fine men, while those of a less exalted nature represented the actions of inferior men' (ibid.: 15, 1448b). Aristotle did not heed Socrates' insistence to Agathon and Aristophanes in *Symposion* that the genius of comedy is the same as that of tragedy and that the dramatic writer should write both. The difference between tragedy and comedy is further described as follows: 'Comedy ... is a representation of inferior people, not indeed in the full sense of the word bad, but the laughable is a species of the base or ugly. It consists in some blunder or ugliness that does not cause pain or disaster, an obvious example being the comic mask which is ugly and distorted but not painful' (ibid.: 19–21, 1449a). Among the many summary descriptions of tragedy in the *Poetics* the following brings out its difference from comedy: 'The change must be ... from good to bad fortune, and it must not be due to villainy but to some great flaw in such a man as we have described, or of one who is better rather than worse' (ibid.: 47, 1449a). In another passage it is said of the comic plot that the characters, even if they are bitter enemies in the story, Orestes and Aegisthus, for instance, go off as friends at the end (ibid.: 95, 1453a). So far the distinction seems clear, and it has been, and is, extremely important in the understanding of literature and in literary scholarship. Indeed, Byron claims that

> All tragedies are finish'd by a death,
> All comedies are ended by a marriage
> The future states of both are left to faith
> ...
> They say no more of Death or of the Lady
> (*Don Juan*, III, 9, 65–72)

In our time Northrop Frye, for instance, has used this distinction. He sees comedy as a basic story about the crystallization of a new society around the comic hero, or rather the comic couple. It typically ends with a feast celebrating marriage, a feast to which everybody, or almost everybody, is invited. Tragedy, by contrast, is, according to Frye, the basic story about the alienation of the hero from society, ending in his death (Frye 1957, 1966).

There is no denying that Frye (or Byron) points to basic, existential themes with which literature has always been preoccupied. What is denied is that the traditional *differentiae specificae* of tragedy and comedy are, in fact, sufficient to classify all dramas as one or the other. Complications start in the *Poetics* itself because, in discussing the merits of different relationships between recognition and action and their ability to arouse pity and fear, Aristotle distinguishes four different ways of committing/not-committing the tragic act: (1) to do it knowingly and wittingly (Euripides' *Medea*); (2) to refrain from doing it because of already existing knowledge; (3) to perform the fearful act, but unwittingly (Sophocles' *Oedipus*); and (4) to intend to commit the fearful act, but, discovering the truth before doing it, to refrain from committing the tragic act because of the acquired knowledge (Euripides' *Iphigenia in Tauris*, for this see *Poetics*, 51–3, 1453b–1454a). Aristotle prefers the fourth solution: the act is to be committed, but the revelation of an important piece of information, such as for example about the close blood kin of enemies, changes the mind of the agent, and disaster is avoided. This variant of the tragic plot makes it very difficult to distinguish between tragedy and comedy on the grounds of the opposite reversal of fortune. In fact, in Euripides' *Ion*, Ion and Creusa walk reconciled out of the temple, and nobody kills anybody. Other reasons, principally those relating to the social status of the protagonists and the seriousness of the perils, may be considered convincing evidence for classifying *Ion* as a tragedy, and not as a comedy. This example makes it evident, however, that even what has often been seen as the basic forms of drama are defined and delimited from each other by multiple and fallible criteria that are given more or less weight as the case may be. No wonder, then, that history has been rather rough on Aristotle's claim that comedy and tragedy had developed into their final form. Polonius's understanding of this question seems more to the point: 'The best actors in the world, either for tragedy, comedy, history, pastoral, pastoral-comical, historical-pastoral, tragical-historical, tragical-comical-historical-pastoral, scene individable, or poem unlimited; Seneca cannot be too heavy, nor Plautus too light. For the law of writ, and the liberty: these are the only men' (*Hamlet* [Arden 1981], II, 2, 392–8). First, in Shakespeare's time, some of the more sensible of the genre labels Polonius mentions were in fact officially used when a company of actors was licensed to act in public. Furthermore, other at least equally important mediating genres can be added to the list. The category tragicomedy is attested to in antiquity. And the very Plautus mentioned by Polonius lets Mercury ponder this question in *Amphitrion*. After Mercury has himself confusingly called it both a tragedy and a comedy, he solves the question thus: 'I will bring a mixture: Let it be a tragicomedy. For I do not think it proper to make it wholly comedy, since there are kings and gods. What then? Since there is also a slave, it will be just as I said, a tragicomedy' (Plautus 1916: 9–11). Plautus, or Mercury, clearly uses the social status of the characters in distinguishing tragedy from comedy. And it seems that Aristotle also, in the *Poetics*, is counting this criterion as decisive. Since Plautus, tragicomedy and its relation to tragedy and comedy proper have been discussed by playwrights (e.g., in prefaces) and scholars. However, already before Plautus Euripides had in fact brought tragedy and comedy together. Not only because the tragic disaster is avoided in several of his plays, a fact that Aristotle approved of, but also because in *Alcestis* he has indissolubly amalgamated comedy and tragedy.

As regards literary genres, the classificatory practice may be different from the classical idea of categorizing on the basis of *differentiae specificae*, that is, on features univocally deciding the category to which an object belongs. The work of the psychologist Eleanor Rosch broke new ground by showing empirically that even within a given category people distinguish between central and peripheral members. Some are felt to be exemplars or prototypes, while others are seen as bad representatives of their class. Thus, gradation is an important feature in our understanding of the objects of our lifeworld, including artefacts and works of art. The English linguist Jean Aitchison (1987: 54) humorously sums up the thrust of Rosch's work by making a diagram (see p. 10) of Rosch's study (1975) of how Californians rank individual species of birds according to their value as representatives of the genus. Americans in general see the robin as the prototypical bird, whereas the ostrich and penguin are represented as even leaving the periphery of the radially structured diagram, because they are considered such poor examples of birds. These distinctions of aptness of example within a fixed category, like that of birds, become even more important as regards genera whose boundaries are not drawn with much precision. The examples from epic and dramatic genres show that literary texts do not easily lend themselves to traditional classification. Not only do individual texts mix features mentioned in different genre definitions, but the criteria for categorization into different genres mentioned by authors and theorists vary throughout time and in space. Thus, not only is it the case that the tokens, the texts, do not comply with the type, the genre norm, it is even the case that there is no agreement about how to define the types. But before drawing conclusions from these undeni-

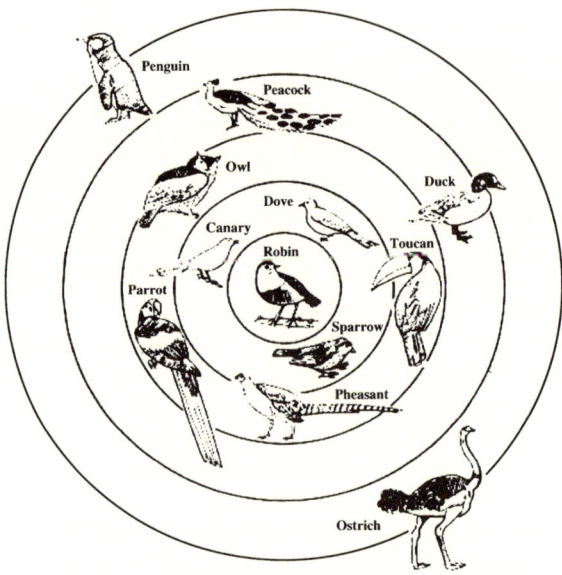

able facts, it might be wise to see whether the external frontiers of the province of literature are clearly drawn and secured.

2. The Todorov Hypothesis

Probably only a literary scholar will question the demarcation and independent status of the group of texts called literature. Indeed, it might not even occur to others that there is a problem. For many literary scholars, however, the very notion of literature is beset with the same problems as the genre concepts mentioned above. Roman Jakobson once remarked that '[t]he borderline dividing what is a work of poetry from what is not is less stable than the frontiers of the Chinese empire's territories' and 'the concept of poetry is unstable and temporally conditioned' (Jakobson 1987: 369, 378). It is to Tzvetan Todorov, however, that we owe an excellent short study of the problems connected with the distinction between literature and non-literature. Todorov deplores the lack of comparative studies concerning the use of the term *literature* and its congeners in different languages (Todorov 1990: 1), then goes on to distinguish two ways of defining and delimiting literature, the functional and the structural. And in this connection he poses the following problem:

An entity called 'literature' functions at the level of intersubjective and social relations; this much seems beyond question. Fine. But what have we proved? That in the broader system of a given society or culture, an identifiable element exists that is known by the label literature. Have we thereby demonstrated that all the particular products that take on the function of literature possess common characteristics, which we can identify with legitimacy? Not at all. (Ibid.: 2)

Todorov does not go into the possibilities offered by a functional definition of literature; instead he investigates the problems haunting the structural definition of literature. From antiquity to the mid-eighteenth century, Todorov claims, implicitly or explicitly the same definition recurs, but this recurring definition consists of two distinct elements. First, literature is representation of that which is itself not real, but fictional; consequently, literature is fiction. Second, its beauty or elaborate structure defines literature formally. However, the definition of literature as fiction runs into severe difficulties, because it may be argued that the fictional and the literary do not coincide. Indeed, on this view, poetry itself is not covered, because it does not relate events, but impressions, meditations, and emotions; and thus the term fiction is not applicable (this position in itself is indeed debatable, and will be questioned in chapter 3).

Faced with such difficulties, seventeenth- and eighteenth-century aestheticians argued that imitation must be artistic and that the imitated itself must be beautiful, *la belle nature*. According to Todorov, at the verge of romanticism a new conception of literature based on the concept of beauty emerges. Todorov cites Karl Philipp Moritz: 'True beauty requires that a thing signify nothing but itself, that it be a unity complete in itself.' He also mentions Novalis's idea that literature is 'an expression for the sake of expression.' Todorov points to the historical relationship between eighteenth- and nineteenth-century concepts of beauty and later concepts of form and structure. Literature, then, is defined by the highly elaborate and beautiful patterning of its language.

However, accepting the formal definition of literature, we are immediately confronted with the following question: Are literary texts the only ones that display an elaborate patterning? Not at all. In many non-literary kinds of texts we find very careful patterning and embellishment. Todorov himself points to classical oratory, and to rhetoric as the sister discipline of poetics (which was already Plato's point in *Gorgias*,

502a–e). Oratory and literature use the same linguistic patterns and devices. Consequently, it is possible neither to delimit a set of formal properties, linguistic features, that are exclusively used in texts we call literary, nor to point to features that a given text must necessarily possess in order to count as literature.

The conclusion to Todorov's brief investigation is that we have two main criteria of literature: fictionality, which, according to Todorov, is a specific mode of reference, and poeticity, which is a fuzzy set of devices and structural features characterizing many literary texts. Both definitions cover vast masses of texts and they seem to have certain affinity, but they certainly do not imply each other. For Todorov, it is a main problem that they are huddled together and used interchangeably. This causes confusion and is detrimental to literary scholarship.

To remedy this situation Todorov introduces the concept of discourse. Within contemporary philosophy, linguistics, and literary theory discourse is understood in many ways. On Todorov's definition, however, discourse is the structural correlative to the functional concept of 'use.' It is made up of the rules, other than linguistic, that govern the production of texts relating to a specific subject within, it should be stressed, a certain institutional context; among concrete discourses we would find medical, scientific, juridical, religious, and philosophical discourses. Discourse, then, is made up of rules that pattern texts in a certain way by constraining the freedom of individual speakers and writers.

Finally, Todorov asks the inevitable question, Is it possible to point to a set of discursive rules that plays a formative role in the production of all the texts we are wont to call literary? He, again inevitably, answers with a 'no.' He suggests therefore that we turn away from the grand category of literature to its subcategories, and points out that the definition of literature as fiction applies particularly well to narrative, whereas literature as form or structure applies particularly well to poetry. It is in this connection, however, that he formulates what I have dubbed the Todorov Hypothesis:

> I shall thus propose the following hypothesis: If one opts for a structural viewpoint, each type of discourse usually labeled literary has nonliterary 'relatives' that are closer to it more than are any other types of 'literary' discourse. For example, certain instances of lyric poetry and prayer have more rules in common than that same poetry and the historical novel of the War and Peace variety. Thus the opposition between literature and nonliterature gives way to a typology of discourses. (Todorov 1990: 11)

Introduction: Literature? 13

It might seem sensible to subscribe to the Todorov Hypothesis, but looking back at the trouble with genres described earlier, one should not be too sanguine as to the success of the program. And what follows from accepting Todorov's fundamental premises without necessarily choosing his solution? Of several possible options, let me indicate three.

Faced with the confusion caused by the fuzzy boundaries within the province of literature and the distressing fact that even its borders with other provinces of discourse are both unmarked and changeable, the scholar may attempt to apply a permanent set of criteria to every text. And in imposing such criteria, he or she may ignore or disregard the problems and inconsistencies that will follow from this procedure. Such criteria may be applied to what the scholar believes constitutes literature in general, or other more specific criteria may be applied to different genres. We saw earlier, however, that eternal genre criteria do not work, so Todorov's optimism concerning finding the rules of specific subcategories needs some qualification. And Todorov himself has indicated that a purely structural definition of literature is not possible. Creating a kind of systematic typology of literature based on essential definitions that is insensitive to changes may be useful for some specific purpose, but as a general way of conceiving literature it will not do, because it will miss a central feature: literature's historicity.

Another possibility is the scholar's attempt to follow the classificatory praxis of the time and literary tradition of the text. He or she may also try to figure out the broader set of distinctions that governed the classificatory practice of the period and culture in question. If he chooses the latter alternative, he may provide very valuable information about the way in which genres are conceived within a specific literary institution. Rarely, if ever, however, will the scholar be able to reveal a uniform and consistent classificatory practice. This, of course, is not a big surprise, considering that contemporary genre categories are not that consistent either.

A third possibility is to explore the explicatory potential of the other way to define literature mentioned by Todorov, the functional one. Todorov is, however, not eloquent concerning this possibility. Nevertheless, by placing literature within the wider context of society and culture, and thus inquiring into literature's functions as a kind of public discourse, the scholar adds a pragmatic aspect. Furthermore, in this approach the classificatory practice, that is, genres and literary conventions, is seen as historical, and thus relative, rather than logical and absolute. 'Relative,' however, means that criteria are changing over time, not that they are negligible, and without force, while they last. That texts comply with or contest aesthetic norms testify to their reality. The inquiry into literature's functions seems a promising road to take, but before we set off in that direction, it might be interesting to ask whether there is a reason for the protean nature of literature and its subcategories.

3. Exemplars and Contests

In his book *Philosophy and Historical Understanding* (1964), W.B. Gallie claims that concepts belonging to such fields as aesthetics, political and social philosophy, and philosophy of religion are, in his terms, essentially contested. Such concepts are essentially contested because groups of people always disagree about their proper use. For the outsider it is clear that these concepts are used in a variety of different ways and that they serve distinct, although not unrelated, functions and purposes. According to Gallie, the dispute concerning the right definition of these concepts cannot be reduced to a conflict about interests, tastes, and attitudes because 'there are disputes, centered on the concepts ... which are perfectly genuine: which although not resolvable by arguments of any kind, are nevertheless sustained by perfectly respectable arguments and evidence. This is what I mean by saying that there are concepts which are essentially contested, concepts the proper use of which inevitably involves endless disputes about their proper uses on the part of their users' (Gallie 1964: 158). Gallie exemplifies his ideas by imagining teams that, having all developed distinctive methods, strategies, and styles of playing, are competing for the championship in a specific kind of game with the following special rules: (1) the championship is awarded on the level of style, for the 'best way of playing the game'; (2) there are neither a system of points nor officially appointed judges; instead (3) the championship is awarded continuously; and (4) it is decided by the number of supporters. The effective champions are the team that has most supporters at a given time. Gallie points out, however, that although this way of deciding the championship leaves no doubt as to who are the effective champions, it does allow supporters of the other teams to think of their teams as being the 'true,' 'moral,' or 'destined' champions.

On the basis of Gallie's analysis of this imaginary game, he attempts to generalize his ideas. According to Gallie, essentially contested concepts have seven characteristics. (1) They have an axiological aspect, or, as he says, they are appraisive. (2) They are internally complex, and their value is owed to the effect of their interacting parts. (3) They are appraised with reference to some parts of their total structure or performance, but the importance allotted to these parts may differ between different groups of people. (4) They are appraised according to their sensitivity to context, their ability to change with the change of circumstances; and their modifications can neither be prescribed nor predicted in advance. (5) Each group using the concept knows very well that other groups contest its specific use of the concept on grounds that are more or less familiar to all the groups. Thus, the use of an essentially contested concept is explicitly or implicitly maintained against other uses, that is, it is used aggressively and defensively. (6) In an effort to distinguish between an essentially contested concept and a concept that is just confused, Gallie adds that an essentially contested concept is derived from an exemplar whose authority is generally acknowledged by all the contesting users of the concept. (7) Finally, the 'continuous competition for acknowledgment as between the contestant users of the concept enables the original exemplar's achievement to be sustained or developed in optimum fashion' (ibid.: 168).

Gallie gives a brief but interesting analysis of art as an essentially contested concept. His example is painting, but the level of description makes his points applicable to literature as well. Art, and literature, we may add, is seen as a complex activity that admits of very different, but equally interesting, relevant, and illuminating descriptions. (1) Writing literature means the concatenation of words into a text that, among other things, takes into account their material and formal properties. (2) It is also a piece of craftsmanship, an artefact produced in relation to – whether in accordance with or in opposition to – the techniques and standards of the traditions of the craft. (3) The literary text is the outcome and expression of the way its author sees things, whether in his or her imagination or in the lifeworld shared with others. (4) The author's expression of what he sees is always potentially communicative. This, of course, is even truer of the material of literature, words, than of the painter's pigments. (5) Every successful work of literature is a source of aesthetic enjoyment to an audience or readership. Theories of aesthetics, and more specifically of literature, may be focused on one of these five ways of describing the aesthetic object.

The study of the way in which signs are concatenated and patterned in literary texts leads to formal and structural theories of the distinctive features of literature in comparison to other ways of using language, to its 'literariness,' as the Russian formalists would say. Considering it a craft means studying traditions and developments of poetic diction, dramatic convention, and narrative techniques. Although the two perspectives certainly have much in common, they do not coalesce; they are related to each other in a way similar to that of synchronic linguistics and philology.

Theories about the ways authors conceive and represent the world come in many varieties: from ideas about the privileged insight of the creative genius into the hidden unity and secret forces of nature, dear to European romanticism, to the author as the conscious, or unconscious, spokesperson for his or her class and its world view.

While theories of the creative act tend to celebrate the author as creator, such views easily lead to another conception of the writing of literature: seeing it not as the gratuitous gesture of individual expression, but as a communicative act that mediates understanding of the human condition. Such theories tend to see the main role of literature as that of representing models of the lifeworld as it is conceived within a given society, or within certain classes or groups.

Finally, theories privileging the response of the reader are known from antiquity onwards. Although Plato's attack on literature covered most of the aspects mentioned above, he is especially worried about the impact of literature on the audience because, in addition to imparting false knowledge, literature is capable of stirring their emotions and thus impairing their ability to judge rationally (cf. *The Republic*, book X, and many other places). Aristotle made up for Plato's attack on literature. Like Plato's, his theory covers most aspects of (dramatic) literature, and, like his predecessor, he privileges the response of the audience: the role of tragedy is claimed to be the arousal and purging of the emotions of pity (eleos) and fear (phobos) in the audience. But Aristotle's evaluation of the cathartic effect on the audience is positive, and this is one of the main differences between his and Plato's theory.

For painting Gallie gives a historical synopsis of how the prevailing points of view have changed from the eighteenth century until the beginning of this century. Like Todorov, Gallie starts by mentioning that at the beginning of the eighteenth century traditional aesthetics combined two theses: works of art were representational and they imitated nature through their formal and beautiful properties and patterns. Gallie claims that the idea of art as imitation of nature was soon given up, because philosophical reflection made it evident that several of the arts were not imitative at all (e.g., music, but see chapter 5). However this may be, in literature, represented reality – that is, literature's reference to the lifeworld – sticks to its very material, words. Consequently, in literature ideas of representation and imitation are not easily dismissed; and for this reason alone, in order to draw such a sketch of ideas about literature one has to do it differently. Obviously, the purpose of giving such a brief sketch is only to exemplify the changing points of view in their opposition to one another.

Much eighteenth-century literary theory is subjective, in the sense that it focuses on the enjoyment of the reader, but the reader is certainly a social being. And thus literary criticism of the spectator kind is bent on educating the aesthetic judgment of its readership to raise it to the refinement of the privileged audience, the connoisseurs. It is the reader (turned connoisseur) who attributes the mark of excellence to a given work of literature. Thus his or her taste and judgments are decisive, and it is up to the literary work to live up to the readership's expectations. However, even if the aesthetic judgment is based on the feelings of the perceiver, and thus subjective, features of the aesthetic object will be instrumental in calling it forth. Consequently, the judgment concerning its beauty may lay claim to universality because it ought to be the same for everybody (see, for example, Kant's attempt to walk the fine line between a subjective and an objective stance on art).

Romanticism changes the emphasis radically because its aesthetics privileges literature as the expression of the creative genius. The poet, or author, is in open or latent conflict with the readership, among other things, because he or she is supposed to/supposes themselves to possess a privileged insight into the deeper nature of things and their, often organicistic, relationships. Together with this claim to insight often comes a critique of society, of its exploitation of the greater part of its members, and of the shortsightedness and philistine tastes of its ruling classes.

About the middle of the century, realism, which is not mentioned at all by Gallie, made an attempt to revitalize literature's claim to be a representation of inner and outer reality. The objective of realism, and later of naturalism, is to represent social and psychical reality objectively, that is, without admitting any false ideas of (as they see it) metaphysical and religious dimensions to human existence. Instead of revealing nature's profundity, realism and naturalism attempt to reveal the repressive power mechanisms of society. Indeed, realist and naturalist authors' principal critique of their romantic colleagues is that their cloudy idealism prevents them from effectively fighting the oppression of power and ideology. Whether this critique is fair is not our subject, but it was certainly launched (e.g., by the Danish critic Georg Brandes).

At the end of the century, a significant number of European poets and authors turned away from realism to a celebration of art for art's sake (*l'art pour l'art*, already prepared for by romanticism). In contradistinction to many of the romanticists, however, a significant number of these authors did not believe in a religious or otherwise transcendental reality.[5] Instead they turn to aestheticism. The art object, poem or narrative, as aesthetic form becomes an end in itself. Very often the subject of the literary text is literature, or art, itself, a celebration of perfection. And, in contradistinction to most realists, these authors not only deny art's subservience to other purposes, but claim that purposiveness is detrimental to it.

In this sketch literature as communication has not been exemplified by any literary school or movement (although Gallie exemplifies by mentioning a single author, Tolstoy). The reason is that literature, being a kind of public discourse, has always a communicative function, although its readership may be very small at a certain time.[6] The idea of communication varies, however, with the general attitude towards literature. There is, for instance, a notable difference between the conversational style of much eighteenth-century literature, the prophetic attitude of many romanticists, the concealment of the presence of the utterer attempted by realist authors, and the symbolist poet's turning his back on the general readership.

By pointing to differences of emphasis, and to confrontations and mutual critique among the literary movements, this sketch exemplifies literature as an essentially contested concept. Consequently, the five points Gallie makes about art seem valid for literature as well. These points, substituting literature for art, are that (1) literature is partly, but not exclusively, used as an appraisive term; (2) achievement accredited to literature is always internally complex; (3) the literary achievement can meaningfully be described in different ways, and different periods and movements have emphasized different aspects of artistic activity and of the literary work; (4) literary activity is always open-ended because (a) standards for literary excellence and representative relevance change and (b) it is not possible to predict the direction of such changes; and (5) the concept literature is used both aggressively and defensively (for this last point, see Gallie 1964: 177).

With some modification we can also add Gallie's last two general criteria for an essentially contested concept, namely, that it is derived 'from an original exemplar whose authority is acknowledged by all the contestant users of the concept' (ibid.: 168). Clearly this is not the case in literature and the arts, because neither a single work of art nor a single literary text possesses both indisputable authority and an always equally appealing relevance. Indeed, although the authority of the classics, and their imitation, lasted for centuries, still there were both Virgil and Ovid, and no single work is absolutely unique and beyond comparison and criticism (even Homer sleeps sometimes, and he was translated in very different ways).

If we relativize Gallie's point concerning an original exemplar and put it in the plural, however, it becomes valid: (6) Concepts of art and literature always point to exemplars in order to show that their ideas are of the noblest lineage and to make it plausible that their goal can be attained, since analogous achievements have been made in former times. Finally, Gallie's claim, that 'the continuous competition for acknowledgment between the contestant users of the concept enables the original exemplar's achievement to be sustained or developed in optimum fashion' (ibid.: 168), may also, reformulated, be valid for art and literature: (7) Only through development and change may the exemplars' achievements be paralleled. The sheer repetition of traditional ways of representation and of devices and techniques in a non-static world would be detrimental to their relevance and significance. And excellent and ambitious writers do believe that their works offer an artistic representation of contemporary ways of feeling, thinking, and acting that supersedes those of their predecessors. They think that their work is truer to the fundamental concerns of their fellow beings, and therefore, they claim, is of the utmost importance and relevance; indeed it is necessary.

Gallie's thesis that literature and its subcategories are essentially contested concepts offers an explanation of the changes over time of the distinctive features within the bundle of texts that are normally considered members of the same genre. The very act of adding a new text to a genre may – but does not always in fact do so – challenge the prior and contemporary notions of it (cf. Eliot's ideas about the dialectic between the canon and the individual text: 1932). It might be objected that even if the dominant way of writing at a given time is contested, it is not contested that the predecessors' writings are literature (just as the supporters of a team do not deny that another team whose play they don't like is playing, say, baseball). Nevertheless, the point is that the contesting trend or school within literature is changing the rules for writing contemporary and relevant literature, claiming that even if what the older generation is doing is writing literature, their way of doing it is obsolete. It is, in fact, not uncommon that even the predicate 'literature' is denied to new works. One of the important offices of literary history is to investigate the reception of texts. Let one example suffice.

When Ibsen published *Per Gynt* in November 1867 in Copenhagen, the Danish critic Clemens Petersen reviewed it negatively, even denying it the predicate of 'real poetry.' According to him it placed itself between art and reality, being neither. Instead Pedersen categorized it as 'polemical journalism.' Of course Ibsen was offended and wanted to beat up the critic, but his truly interesting reaction we find in a letter to Bjørnstjerne Bjørnson of 9 December 1867, where he says:

> My book is poetry; and if it is not, then it will be. The conception of poetry in our country, in Norway, shall be made to conform to the book. There is no stability in the world of ideas ... If it is to be war, then let it be war! If I am no poet, then I will have nothing to lose. I shall try my luck as a photographer. My contemporaries in the North I shall take in hand, one after the other, as I have already taken in the nationalist language reformers. I will not spare the child in the mother's womb, nor the thought or feeling that lies under the word of any living soul that deserves the honour of my notice. (Ibsen 1970: 145–6)

Today *Per Gynt* is counted among the masterpieces not only of Scandinavian but of world literature. So Ibsen was right that the Norwegian conception of poetry was made to conform to his ideas of it. The interesting point is, however, the agonistic and undecided character of the original situation, and the fact that the critic felt that the new text constituted a challenge that had to be fought. And it is seen that Ibsen takes it as a declaration of war, and that he sees it as one of the roles of literature to combat cultural and political ideas to which the author objects. This situation is not the exception, but the rule, as soon as a novel text transgresses the contemporary aesthetic norms. Such constant challenges and changing of the rules for good writing mean that any rich definition of literature on a low level of abstraction is made illusory, because not only a few individual texts, which we want to call literature, but whole schools will offend against such definitions.

It might be argued that even if it is true that authors constantly engage in fights and contests about right ways of writing, scholars ought to be objective and just keep records of the action. There is certainly no denying that studies in literary history ought faithfully to state, as best they can, what is known about claims, challenges, and disputes about literature and poetics at different times. In order to do this, however, the scholar is forced to recognize the appraisive nature of his subject. Indeed, it would be a misunderstanding to represent it as a dispassionate exchange with nothing at stake.

Furthermore, it is a moot question whether it is possible, and even preferable, for the scholar to remain absolutely neutral in relation to his subject. An investigation into literature, that is, into attempts at wrestling with language to represent human existence in meaningful, passionate, and existentially relevant ways, needs itself to recognize the importance and share the concerns of such enterprises. The obligations and commitments of scholars do not prevent their being partisan in the sense of preferring some ways of representing the human condition over others. (And such preferences are, at least partly, responsible for the choice of subjects; some scholars study realism, some romanticism, some narrative, some lyrical poetry.) Scholarly commitments should prevent them, however, from ignoring or distorting evidence, from concealing what they know to be certain or probable – scholars are not defence attorneys – and such obligations certainly should prevent them from shunning dialogue and closing their ears to the arguments of fellow scholars.

In spite of the, on my view, decisive differences between literary writing, on the one hand, and scholarly and critical writing, on the other, they may very well be animated by similar desires; namely, to understand, explain, and express what are, or seem to be, significant ways of discoursing on self, world, and others.

Part One

Sign, Dialogue, Discourse

One

From Sign to Dialogue

It appears to me that the essential function of a sign is to render inefficient relations efficient ... Knowledge in some way renders them efficient, and a sign is something by knowing which we know something more

(CP 8.332)

[N]o mind can take one step without the aid of other minds.

(CP 2.220)

All thinking is dialogic in form. Your self of one instant appeals to your deeper self for his assent.

(CP 6.338)

On the view presented in the introduction, literature is first and foremost a species of discourse. In addition to general linguistic rules and constraints, different kinds of discourse are characterized by sets of non-linguistic rules or conventions specific to each of them. Before we go into the vexing questions of the number and nature of discourses (the subject of chapter 2), one basic feature common to all of them should be mentioned: they are collections of conventions and patternings partly governing the production of concrete texts. Texts are utterances[1] made up of a number of signs, uttered about something by somebody to somebody. They are species of sign action, semiosis. Thus, one way of approaching the problems of discourse, and literary discourse in particular, is through semiotics, the study of signs in general. Semiotics is, however, a vast area of inquiry with different subjects and disciplines.[2] Thus, a brief outline of Peirce's idea of semiotics is in order here (for a much more detailed treatment see Johansen 1993a).

1.1 Representation

Peirce understands semiosis as productive and interpretive sign action. A sign action is conceived as a process through which three elements – an object, a sign, and an interpretant – are connected. This is why Peirce claims that a sign is dynamic and triadic. A third feature of his sign concept is its generality. In fact, according to Peirce signs processes are active everywhere, and every phenomenon is a potential sign: 'A word represents a thing to the conception in the mind of the hearer, a portrait represents the person for whom it is intended to the conception of recognition, a weathercock represents the direction of the wind to the conception of him who understands it, a barrister represents his client to the judge and jury whom he influences' (CP 1.553). All these cases have an identical representational structure: A represents B to C, or lets us, like Peirce, indicate blanks to be filled in: — represents — to —. A sign, then, is not characterized by any inherent properties: both a barrister and a weathercock are signs, but by its function, that is, representing something to something else, a sign mediates between an object and an interpretant. Consequently, every phenomenon that occupies the first blank of the above formula is a sign (as vehicle), whereas a sign proper is every relation of three elements that satisfy the formula. The basic Peircean notion of the sign may be diagrammed as shown in figure 1. Sign in lower-case letters, or sign(vehicle), is the sign as an entity that stands for an object and indicates an interpretant. However, because signhood implies the representational relationship between all three elements, it is their dynamic unity that is the sign proper, here placed within the triangle in capital letters. In this relational and dynamic sense, SIGN is the outcome of semiosis, sign action, and interpretive action, that is, the process by virtue of which its three elements are related.

1.2 Immediate and Dynamical Object

Peirce divided signs in a variety of ways according to different criteria (see Johansen 1993a). However, the criterion most relevant to this study is that of signs in relation to their dynamical objects, according to which

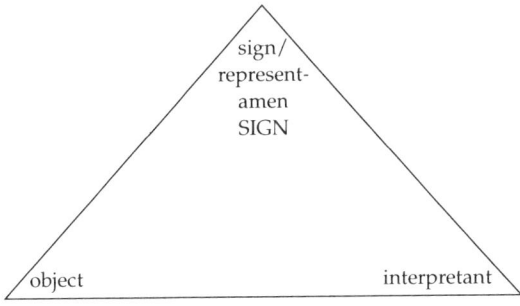

Figure 1

signs are divided into icons, indices, and symbols. However, before expounding this second trichotomy of signs, it is necessary to understand what Peirce means by object: it is 'anything that comes before thought or the mind in any usual sense' (SS 1977: 69).

Peirce distinguishes two kinds of objects: the immediate object within the sign and the dynamical object outside it. The immediate object is the object as it is represented in, and by virtue of, the sign, whereas the dynamical object is the object independently of any specific representation of it: the object as an outside force influencing semiosis. A portrait photo is a sign that represents, indeed contains, its immediate object within itself because its immediate object is the model as he or she is represented by the sign (the photo) itself. In this case, one might even ask what the difference is between sign and immediate object. However, when we ask who the person in the photo is, we do distinguish between the sign as a concrete, material (and two-dimensional) object, on the one hand, and the fact that it represents a (three-dimensional) object, that is, the immediate object, on the other hand.

The photographic subject is the dynamical object of the sign. The model's face and figure has influenced the way the light has hit the film in a concrete, physical manner; this relation is causal. The photographic subject certainly exists independently of the photo. Furthermore, its representation, the immediate object, is only like the model in certain respects and consequently does not give us any exhaustive information about it; indeed, it offers little knowledge. Nevertheless, if the model disappeared, her photo might be used to retrieve her. We only perceive the influence of the dynamical object in the creation of the immediate object, but never, strictly speaking, the dynamical object itself unmediated by the immediate object.

The relationship between the immediate and the dynamical object should not be understood as a difference between two distinct objects. Rather, it is a difference between what is perceived or known of, or believed to be known of, the object – that is, the immediate object – and that which is not (yet) known, although it influences the sign – that is, the dynamical object. Umberto Eco has called the immediate object a cultural unit. This is acceptable, if it is well understood that this cultural unit may be not only an idea in our minds (although it may be only that). It may also be something we perceive and interact with, something we would claim has a mind-independent existence, even if it is understood through the notions of a given culture.

No state of knowledge remains forever unchanged, and thus the relationship between the immediate and the dynamical object changes. Our understanding of, and interaction with, the object changes because of an increase, but also very often a decrease, in information. Thus, our idea of the object, that is, the immediate object, may grow, and in a perfect state of information there would be no distinction between immediate and dynamical object.

The fact that the dynamical object functions as a source (of energy and information) for the generation of immediate objects is important. In order to reach a decision concerning the true nature of an object, state of affairs, and so on, we try to make the object answer our questions, to provoke responses from it; that is, we attempt to predict and produce future immediate objects, future states of affairs.[3] Above, the relation between the immediate and the dynamical object was defined as interdependence, because we create objects and conditions that, although they are of our own making, confront us as mind-independent objects. On Peirce's definition, such objects are real. The year before he died, he explained reality in this way:

> I was many years ago led to define 'real' as meaning *being such as it is, no matter how you, or I, or any man or definite collection of men may think it to be*; where I use the long and awkward phrase in order to avoid all appearance of meaning *independently of human thought*. For obviously, nothing that I or anybody ever can mean can be independent of human thought. That is *real* which men *would* eventually and finally come to think to be absolutely necessary to be thought in order to understand the truth, supposing the existence and advance in knowledge of the human race to be continued

without any limitation; though I cannot pretend that I have as distinct an idea of exactly what that means as I could wish. (MS 681, 1913: 38–9)[4]

Peirce's concept of reality is broader than that of existence, since it includes laws, rules, and habits, that is, what Peirce calls 'would-be's, the certainty or probability that something will be the case in the future, because it is rule-governed.

Do signs exist, however, that do not represent that which exists or has reality? Such signs would necessarily have immediate objects, because in Peircean semiotics the representation function, the fact that a sign is something that stands for something else – *aliquid stat pro aliquo* – is a *conditio sine qua non* for signhood. But while signs need to have immediate objects, it is a fact that not all signs (texts) have dynamical objects, namely, signs that represent a fictional universe of discourse (this will be the subject of chapter 3).

1.3 Icons, Indices, and Symbols

According to Peirce his distinction between iconic, indexical, and symbolic signs is the most fundamental (cf. CP 2.275). By this division, he tries to answer the question that is central to any semiotics: how does a sign succeed in representing its object? His answer is that the relation between sign and object is one either of similarity, of contiguity, of convention, or of habit; or rather, in the concrete uses of signs, a combination of all four.

A scale model, say of the CN Tower in Toronto, is an example of a predominantly *iconic* sign. Such a model signifies its object by similarity: it resembles what it represents. Tears are most often an *indexical* sign of sadness or despair (or of peeling onions); that is, there is a real, causal relation between sign and object: the sadness, or the onion, causes the tears. A linguistic sign is most often a *symbol*. The relation of a symbol to its object is not based on either similarity or contiguity; it is arbitrary and conventional. The word cheese does not resemble its object nor is it connected to it by contiguity; it is connected to its object by use. However, within other linguistic communities other words for cheese are used ('ost' Danish, 'fromage' French, 'Käse' German, 'formaggio' Italian). Hence, in the symbol the relation between sign and object is said to be arbitrary.

However, to signify anything, signs have, or imply, iconic, indexical, and symbolic aspects. A photograph is iconic because it bears some resemblance to its object. It is indexical because it is produced by a real, physical connection between object and sign (the light waves hitting the film). And a black and white photo certainly uses, with regard to the object, an arbitrary code to articulate the sign.

1.3.1 Iconic Signs

The signhood of iconic signs is due to their own properties. Furthermore, according to Peirce they are signs of possibility, and thus they are possible signs of whatever possesses the same properties because they are related to their object by similarity, that is, by having properties in common with them.

The concept of similarity is, however, much debated (see Johansen 1993a: 93–106). Still, taking the preconditions of purpose and frame of description into account, we are justified in talking about similarity between sign and object. To the question 'To what is the photo of John similar?' one may answer both 'To John' and 'To another photo.' Both answers will most often be correct, and maybe relevant, but not in the same context. Furthermore, it makes sense to ask whether the photo is a representation of John rather than of Jane. And it may reasonably be argued that according to certain criteria, which can be made explicit, it is a sign of the former rather than of the latter. However, in order to advance further into the fascinating realm of iconic signs, let us consider Peirce's subdivision into images, diagrams, and metaphors.

1.3.1.1 Images

The semiotic concept of an image is more restricted than our common notion of it. An image, in the restricted sense, is a sign that has qualities in common with its object. A piece of red cardboard used to show what colour of paint one wants is a perfect example of an image, because its likeness with the desired paint consists in this simple quality. Images, in our ordinary understanding of the word, such as pictures and portraits, are also partly images in the technical sense. In painting, the painter may attempt to represent his model by representing the profusion of hair, its colour and fall, the hue of the skin, the form of the head, and the brilliance of the eyes and direction of the gaze, and so forth. In doing so he may attempt faithfully to represent the likeness of his model – as he conceives it. He may succeed, if we, knowing the model, can recognize the painting as a portrait of him or her, precisely because of the represented qualities and the relations between them.

Images, in the technical sense, are not confined to visual representations; they include representations of all the sense qualities. The actress who screams in terror is producing a sound image imitating real horror. An after-shave lotion is marketed as imitating the scent of human maleness. Imitation crab meat is artificially flavoured fish that is supposed to taste like real crab meat.

Images, in this technical sense, exist in pure form only in very special cases. Normally, predominantly iconic representations are a mixture of different modes of representations, where image, diagram, and metaphor amalgamate, and all three iconic modes are combined with indexical and symbolic ones:

> We say that the portrait of a person we have not seen is *convincing*. So far as, on the ground merely of what I have seen in it, I am led to form an idea of the person it presents, it is an icon. But, in fact, it is not a pure icon, because I am greatly influenced by knowing that it is an *effect*, through the artist, caused by the original's appearance, and is thus in a genuine Obsistent relation to that original. Besides, I know that portraits have but the slightest resemblance to their originals, except in certain conventional respects, and after a conventional scale of values. (CP 2.92)

This passage shows Peirce's awareness that not only are pure images rare, but so are pure icons. This is why I prefer to speak about (predominantly) iconic signs instead of icons. I will return to this topic in discussing the symbolic sign, but let us now turn to the second species of iconic signs.

1.3.1.2 Diagrams

While images have qualities in common with their objects, diagrams have relations in common with theirs. When we open a good tour guide of, for instance, Greece or Italy, we will see a photo of a temple, and next to it is placed a diagram showing its ground plan, that is, the relative sizes and relations of the different areas making up its base. Such a diagram is showing something that could most often not be perceived at a glance. So while the photo may convey an aesthetic impression, a feeling of the temple, by representing a range of qualities, the diagram conveys understanding of its design.

Compared to an image, a diagram is less bound to the object it represents because it may achieve a high degree of abstraction determined by a selection of properties and relations according to criteria of relevance. This is why sketches and paintings are diagrams as well as images, or even more so. Thus, a diagram is an intellectualized and generalized representation of its object.

A city map, which of course has strong indexical features, is an example of such a process of abstraction according to criteria of relevance. On the map, colours are conventionalized in order to distinguish between buildings, streets, squares, parks, lakes, and so on. The reason for this reduction of information lies in the purpose of the map. If it were made to guide strangers through a city, too many details would make it less useful. This is why maps exist on different levels of detail, some for the military, some for tourists, and so forth.

While city and country maps are still tied to individual objects (a map of Odense, Denmark, could not be used in Berkeley or Toronto), other diagrams do not represent individual objects but, for instance, properties of species. Gray's anatomy textbook does not represent the bones and muscles of Mr Gray, but a standardized version of *homo sapiens*, though differentiated in the female and male skeleton and specific organs.

Both the map and the anatomy textbook show that diagrams may represent through abstraction and generality, but they can do more. First, a diagram need not represent (an abstraction of) something that exists. It is not only a model of something, like the diagram of the temple in the guide, it is also a model for (the production of) something, like the architect's blueprint which is a set of building instructions. Second, a diagram need not represent relations between sensory and material properties; it may just as well represent intelligible relations: All M are P,/S is M,//S is P. This diagram represents logical relations. It is a formal inference (a syllogism) claiming universal validity.

Third, iconic signs, and especially diagrams, can be experimented upon, both in mind and on paper. From the architect at his drawing board and the mathematician or logician trying out arguments and proofs to the author of fiction experimenting with relationships between characters and the developments of action, diagrammatic creativity is blossoming.

Fourth, diagrams, including most paintings, are conventional in the sense that several different but equally valid ways of representing the same relation(s) exist. Peirce gives the following example of a diagrammatic representation of intelligible relations, namely, the relationship between the sign and its three subclasses according to the second trichotomy:

sign $\begin{cases} \text{icon} \\ \text{index} \\ \text{symbol} \end{cases}$

We may, however just as well draw the following diagram, *Sign (icon, index, symbol)*, and still preserve the relationship. We *cannot*, however, form this diagram as *Icon (symbol, sign, index)* and still claim to represent Peirce's idea. The latter diagram is simply wrong.

Thus, a diagram possesses the following features: (1) relative independence in relation to its concrete object; (2) abstraction according to criteria of relevance; (3) possibility of generalization; (4) representation of intelligible as well as sensible relations; (5) conventionalization; (6) creative potential; (7) usefulness as an outline of thought and action; and (8) indispensability in formal reasoning. These features make diagrams formidable instruments of understanding – and instruments that we unwittingly use all the time.[6]

1.3.1.3 Metaphors

Peirce offers this rather convoluted definition of metaphors: 'those [signs] which represent the representative character of a representamen by representing a parallelism in something else, are *metaphors*' (CP 2.277). A metaphor, according to Peirce, is a relation between two signs in which the representative character of the former sign is expressed through, and by virtue of, the latter. A thermometer is primarily an indexical sign (because it is influenced by temperature), but its indexical relationship is expressed in a metaphor, because heat, which can be felt, but not seen, is transformed and represented as height. The height or length to which the pillar of mercury extends corresponds to the intensity of bodily fever, and so the pillar of mercury represents body temperature as a parallelism in something else. An oscilloscope provides another example. A heartbeat is not a small luminous dot pacing across a screen, it is an effect of an organ pumping blood, a muscle contracting, but this action may be transformed into an electric signal and represented as a dot. And this representation of a process in something else is both true, reliable, and eminently useful for acquiring knowledge, although restricted in scope and informational power.

In chapter 4, linguistic and poetic metaphor will be discussed as a subcategory of analogy. Here let us just mention a single metaphor used by Aristotle, 'the evening of life,' to point out that, in spite of obvious differences, the same mechanism, namely analogy, is present both when heat is translated into height or length and when the cycle of day and night is projected onto the course of human life. Certainly, heat is not really height or length, just as old age is not really the end of a day, but in both cases what is thought to be relevant and important about temperature and old age is pointed out by the metaphor. In the former case, the metaphor offers something very important, namely, the possibility of creating a scale and a digitalization that make precise measurement possible. In the latter case, many of the connotations of the concept of evening are made available for characterizing old age; for instance, after daytime activity there follows a restful evening or, in a more sinister vein, after the distinct perception and comprehension of daytime follows the dimmed perception and unclear comprehension of drowsiness. Furthermore, it is always possible to reactivate such a traditional metaphor by exploring possible but unnoticed parallels.

It is certainly true, as pointed out by Lakoff and Johnson (1980) and Lakoff and Turner (1989), that metaphors play a much more important role in the categorization of our lifeworld than we normally recognize. One example of the almost all-pervasive influence of metaphor is our inclination to understand all kinds of phenomena in spatial categories. Indeed, speech itself is organized in relation to an I-here-now-point, that is, in relation to our body and the place it occupies in space. We experience something as being in front of or behind us, to the right or to the left. When we say, 'He was knocked down from behind,' no metaphor is involved, we are just indicating a spatial relationship between victim and agent. However, when we say 'He was taken aback by her rebuff,' then we are using a metaphor. Likewise, when we say that the prices are high, that the stocks are rising or going down, we are using metaphors, without even thinking about it. Relations of rank and power are often expressed spatially, the basic idea being that a person is on top (of something), whereas others are under, down, or below.

A final point about metaphors is that they may be intellectually productive. The metaphorical extension, or projection, of a concept, or a net of concepts, from one scientific or scholarly discipline to another may further research. When, for instance, neurologists begin to talk about the brain as a computer, of wetware and of programs and programming, specific points of view, a conceptual network, and a number of insights and problems are made available to them. In a certain phase of neurology, then, the metaphor 'the brain is a computer' is investigated, and its range and validity is inquired into. Some years later, computer scientists start to talk about the computer in terms of a brain –

for example, neural networks – and to explore the implications (insights and problems) of neurology for computer science.[6]

1.3.2 Indexical Signs

While iconic signs can be used as signs of every object to which they happen to be similar, an indexical sign is a sign of actual relationship. Joseph Ransdell has elegantly demonstrated the difference between an iconic and an indexical sign. Suppose that we look at a photo of one of two identical twins whose looks are in fact indistinguishable. In this case the photo could be an iconic sign of either twin – it happens to be similar to both – but it can only be an indexical sign of the twin who was actually photographed because only he has actually had a physical influence on the film (Ransdell 1979: 56).

1.3.2.1 Reagents
Peirce distinguishes between two kind of indexical signs, reagents and designations. As an indexical sign (it is iconic as well) the photo is an excellent example of a reagent, because, as the word itself indicates, a reagent is an object that becomes a sign by virtue of being really influenced by the object it represents. Reagents may be divided into traces and symptoms.

Traces constitute a broad class including, for example, the footprints of animals, the twigs broken by them, tufts of hair or feathers, smell, urine, and droppings. Traces are signs of their objects because they are actually caused by them, whether we recognize this causal relationship or not. Thus, traces are metonymically related to their objects as effect to cause. In fact, our world is full of unrecognized reagents because we all always leave behind an indefinite number of traces. Under certain circumstances we look for traces, and we actualize and scrutinize them as reagents that may furnish information about their objects. In order to validate a hypothesis about the history of a landscape, a geologist may look for specific traces, for instance, for fossils of certain animals. Likewise, in order to confirm a suspicion, a detective will start looking for traces of the sometime presence of the suspect at the site of a murder (for this see also Ginzburg in Eco and Sebeok 1983: 81–118).

While traces have been left behind by an object, and may eventually lead us to it, symptoms are co-present and a part of the object; they are synecdochical signs. Red spots of a certain kind are a symptom of measles. The red underside of the male three-spined stickleback during mating season is a symptom of its active sexuality. The coughing of some eminent semiotician is a symptom of the effects of excessive smoking. Reading symptoms is a part of medicine, and what we normally call symptomatology is still also called by its original name, semiotics. Indeed, in antiquity semiotics was a part of medicine.[7]

Most often both subjective symptoms, that is, those perceived by the patient ('My left arm hurts') and objective ones, those detected in a medical examination (for instance, by an electrocardiogram), are ambiguous, indicating a range of possibilities that have to be further examined rather than a specific illness. Symptoms may, however, form a characteristic combination, the so-called syndromes, which make up a complex sign that with a higher degree of probability indicates the presence of a specific disease. The parallel to a syndrome, as regards traces, is a set of circumstantial pieces of evidence pointing to the role of an object in a course of events (for instance, indicating the perpetrator of a crime).

Until now only unquestioned physical relationships between reagents and objects have been mentioned. There exist, however, symptomatic relationships that cross the borderline between psyche and soma. Certain facial signs, in fact symptoms, of elementary emotions, such as anger, fear, disgust, and sadness seem to be encoded and omnipresent in us. They even seem to have both their own distinctive patterns of autonomic nervous system signification and a universal, that is, transcultural, one (for this see the important work by Paul Ekman; e.g., 1994). Furthermore, mental illnesses, just as well as physical diseases, have more or less distinct and trustworthy symptoms, such as the persecution mania of paranoia, the ritualistic behaviour of obsessional neurosis, and the psychogenic paralysis and anaesthesia of hysteria. However, the borderline between what is understood as belonging to the realm of the psyche and what is judged to be somatic is, to recapitulate the phrase of Roman Jakobson, 'less stable than the frontiers of the Chinese Empire's territories.' Although, according to Peirce, reagents 'may be used to ascertain facts' (CP 8.368, n. 23), what symptoms are symptoms of, that is, what their dynamical objects are, is precisely the subject of inquiry. And progress within the natural sciences consists mainly in discovering and validating the links between reagents and objects and in establishing the exact nature of such relationships.

Peirce's reagents have an impressive ancestry. In Aristotle, such a sign is called a necessary sign (*tekmérion*). The presence of milk in the breasts of a woman, for instance, is, to him, a necessary sign of her having given birth (*Rhetoric* 1357b). In Quintilian the example of such a sign is pregnancy as a sign of sexual intercourse (*Institutio oratoria*, V, ix, 3). Such signs were called natural signs: *urina est signum sanitatis*, it was said in the Middle Ages. They signify, according to Eco, by virtue of implication: if milk, then childbirth, if pregnancy, then sexual intercourse (see also Eco 1984: 34–6). These two venerable examples, however, exemplify themselves the historical transition from a sign's being considered necessary to only being seen as possible, since they are no longer irrefutable evidence. Indeed, Aristotle's example is not well chosen, since in many traditional societies grandmothers suckle the infants of their daughters, and modern medical techniques of conceiving have made Quintilian's example obsolete. The lesson to be learned from these examples confirms Peirce's point that abductive reasoning does not lead to necessary truths. Indeed, it is most fallible.

1.3.2.2 Designations

As regards reagents, the direction is from object to sign because the former determines the latter. Concerning the other class of indices, the designations, the opposite is true, because designations function similar to the pointing finger (Latin *index*). A designation locates and identifies an object in time and space within a given universe: the physical universe or some possible world or fictional universe of discourse. Furthermore, the objects are located according to certain time-space coordinates that may either have the egocentric I-here-now point as their centre or some conventional and intersubjective systems of identification, such as the system of longitudes and latitudes of geography or the Gregorian calendar. According to a conventional system of identification, Odense is a city located at longitude 55°N and latitude 10°E. According to the Gregorian calendar, Peirce was born 10 September 1839 and died 19 April 1914.

For the individual, the I-here-now point is the natural and obvious system of coordinates in relation to which the surrounding world is structured. However, the coordinates, memory, and prospects of the individual are of short-termed validity, are incidental and unstable, while collective systems of coordinates are rooted in tradition, are stable and durable. Whenever we interact with others, we need to agree on a system of identification. And unless we can easily bring our interlocutor to share, or match, our egocentric time-space construction, we must have recourse to an intersubjective one, such as the Gregorian calendar and the system of longitudes and latitudes – or most often, rather, to less distinct ideas about time and the parts of the world.

Indexical signs, both reagents and designations, represent the object by contiguity. The object directly determines the reagents, both traces and symptoms, while designations indicate it. The relation between index and object implies their former co-presence. The symptom is the most conspicuous part of the disease, and even the trace is a sign of the former co-presence of object and sign; it is precisely what remains as a sign of the influence of the object. The label on the bottle of medicine and the street sign are designations placed in direct contiguity with the objects referred to. The direct relation of determination between sign and object, whether it goes from object to sign (reagents) or from sign to object (designations), and the possibility of their co-presence are the reasons why indices are the class of signs the child first learn to interpret. As we proceed from the indexical to the symbolic sign we have to remember, however, Peirce's claim that '[i]t would be difficult, if not impossible, to instance an absolutely pure index, or to find any sign absolutely devoid of the indexical quality. Psychologically, the action of indices depends upon association by contiguity, and not upon association by resemblance or upon intellectual operations' (CP 2.306).

1.3.3 The Symbolic Sign

> A chalk mark is like a line though nobody uses it as a sign; a weather-cock turns with the wind, whether anybody notices it or not. But the word 'man' has no particular relation to men unless it be recognized as being so related. That is not only what constitutes it a sign, but what gives it the peculiar relation to its object which makes it significant of that particular object. (MS L75, 1902: Cr 149)

Here Peirce sketches both the negative and the positive characteristics of symbolic signs. Negatively, they are related to the object neither through similarity nor through contiguity. It is neither the sign's own features nor a real relation between sign and object that make a symbol a sign. Symbolic signs are established by the fact that they are used to indicate given objects or states of affairs in the outer or inner world.

Natural languages display systematic features: that is, internal relationships exist between the elements on different levels. The number of distinctive features and phonemes, as well as their combination, are specific and different for natural languages. Each language has its own inventory of elements, on different levels, together with a set of combination rules. A simple example is the distinction between phonemes according to the distinctive features of which they are made:

	A	B			A	B
(a)	p	t	and	(a)	man	woman
(b)	b	d		(b)	boy	girl

Each phoneme is defined differentially and negatively in relation to the other phonemes in the paradigm, because they can be parsed into their constitutive elements (distinctive features), namely A, bilabial; B, labio-dental; (a), unvoiced; and (b), voiced.

Classical European structuralism (Saussure, Hjelmslev, and Greimas) claimed isomorphism between the expression and the content planes of language. Therefore it was believed that content could be analysed in the same way, that is, into constituent elements or semantic primitives. The following is one of structuralism's most cherished examples: 'According to structuralist analysis the above paradigm was broken down into A: masculinity; B: femininity; (a): adulthood; and (b): childhood. This analysis is, of course, valid. The problem is that whereas the phoneme (b) and its distinctive feature (voiced) are on different levels, /man/, /masculinity/, and /adulthood/ are all on the same level, since they are all signs. Nevertheless, Saussure was justified in claiming that in language the linguistic units are what the others are not, which is another way of pointing to the systematic nature of the relationship between linguistic signs (Saussure 1959: 6–20).

Natural languages are by far the most important symbolic system. It has sometimes been argued that their importance is due to their being pass-key languages, that is, languages into which all other sign systems can be translated (see, for instance, Hjelmslev 1973: 122). This, however, is not necessarily true. The mathematical sign systems used to represent theories of the universe, or other complex matters within the sciences, seem to defy translation, in the sense that a linguistic representation of the theories, if possible at all, will lack the rigour necessary to make them worth discussing for scientists. But even if translating propositions represented in specific sign systems into natural languages is not really possible, the precondition for learning such systems is to master a natural language. Languages are powerful sign systems developed to represent ourselves and our interaction with others in a world inhabited by us, other beings, and natural forces. They seem first and foremost good for representing what can be perceived and what can immediately be inferred on the basis thereof. Natural languages and our common conceptual schemata are very good for making distinctions and structuring basic levels of experience of a middle-sized world easily accessible to our senses and relevant to our actions – the level on which we, according to Mark Johnson, 'distinguish elephants from giraffes and walking from running' (Johnson 1987: 208).

Although man is the prime user and inventor of symbolic sign systems, the replication and interpretation of symbolic signs are known in most or all species. The mating colours of the peacock are an indexical, in fact synecdochical, sign because they are a (conspicuous) part of its sexuality. Another example is the male three-spined stickleback, whose underside turns red during mating season (cf. Tinbergen 1953). Of course, such signs are primarily indexical, that is, symptoms of the male sexuality of the species. However, if we ask whether they are motivated or arbitrary, it is clear that the specific colours and forms do not matter. During mating season the male ten-spined stickleback develops a pitch-black colour, in contradistinction to the red one of its three-spined cousin. The important thing, then, seems to be a marking of sexual maturity vs. non-maturity and of mating season vs. non-mating season. Accordingly, this aspect of the sign is symbolic in the sense of being differential and arbitrary.

1.4 The Uses of Iconic, Indexical, and Symbolic Signs

> The value of an icon consists in its exhibiting the features of a state of things regarded as if it were purely imaginary. The value of an index is that it assures us of positive fact. The value of a symbol is that it serves to make thought and conduct rational and enables us to predict the future. (CP 4.448)

These three modes of signification, representation by similarity, by continuity, and by differentiation and convention, are irreducible and indispensable; meaning is simply dependent on their interaction. These modes are not each attached to different kinds of signs. When we talk about iconic, indexical, on or symbolic signs, we mean signs whose predominant mode of signification is either iconic or symbolic. Meaning, however, is dependent on their cooperation, even if the non-predominant modes are presupposed rather than manifest.

Furthermore, Peirce's division has been supported by cognitive and developmental psychology (e.g., the works of Jean Piaget [with B. Inhelder, 1969] and Jerome S. Bruner [1966]). In empirical psychological studies these authors argue that the child learns such modes of representation in a certain sequential order. First, the child becomes conscious of the representational function of signs of continuity and influence. It recognizes its bottle, hidden behind a pillow, from the nipple sticking out from it. This is a sign by contiguity where something is recognized as a part of a whole. Second, it learns to recognize something as a sign of something else by the similarity between them. A small child using a tablecloth as a pillow in pretending to go to sleep has discovered and uses the similarities between them (their softness, pliability, warmth, etc.). Finally, the child learns the meaning of conventional symbols, first and foremost those of language.

However, even the simplest production and interpretation of signs necessarily includes indexical, iconic, and symbolic aspects. For the child to recognize a small part of its bottle, which is visible as a sign of the presence of the whole bottle hidden behind a pillow, the indexical relation of contiguity between the visible and the invisible parts of the bottle is presupposed. It also implies, however, the judgment that the present percept is a part of a bottle, or maybe rather *the* bottle. This means the recognition of similarity (matching with memory) is involved, and thus iconicity plays an important role. We must, however, take our reasoning one step further, because recognizing similarity or identity means being able to distinguish figure from ground and, consequently, recognizing difference and dissimilarity. Difference, however, is precisely what characterizes symbolic signs.

On this point of view, even the simplest semiosis will always contain all three aspects of the signifying process. They may differ, however, as to which aspect is the predominant one. The psychologist may very well be right in claiming that signs whose indexical aspect is predominant play a major role in the first stage of the acquisition of semiotic competence and that the next signs to follow, before the ability to recognize symbolic signs is finally acquired, are the predominantly iconic ones.

Learning to master the predominantly symbolic signs (e.g., language) does not mean that the two earlier stages are transitory and lose their importance. On the contrary, they remain necessary modes of signification, modes without which symbolic signs could not function at all. In mastering all three aspects of semiosis we are able to switch between the three significational modes without any effort and without being conscious of doing so. Answering the door means responding to a predominantly indexical sign, recognizing a person by means of a photograph means focusing on the iconic aspect, and following the argument of a treatise means being absorbed in language. Answering the door, however, also means identifying the sound as a conventional sign of contact, a phatic sign. In identifying somebody by means of a photograph we act on the assumption that a physical relation exists between the photographic subject and the picture. And following an argument most certainly implies diagrammatic reasoning. The necessity of this interaction did not escape Peirce: 'It is frequently desirable that a representamen should exercise one of the three functions [i.e., the iconic, indexical, and symbolic] to the exclusion of the other two ...; but the most perfect of signs are those in which the iconic, indicative, and symbolic characters are blended as equally as possible' (CP 4.448).

1.5 The Interpretants

The interpretant is the third indispensable element in semiosis. It is best understood as transformation rules that translate signs into something else; and interpretation of course takes place within nature just as well as within culture. For instance, the red underside of the male three-spined stickleback and the impressive tail of the peacock only function as signs of male sexuality because they are – as a rule – interpreted so by the female of the same species. The interpretant, then, as a rule-governed response to the influence of a given sign, is omnipresent wherever life exists. Indeed, it might plausibly be argued that semiosis and life are coextensive (cf. Short 1982: 285–310 and Sebeok in numerous places, e.g., 1994).

We constantly engage in interpretation as translation both within the same sign system (bachelor: never-married adult human male, or academic degree, or young male seal), and between sign systems, as when we draw a map to supplement or replace a verbal description, or when we point to a picture in order to explain a linguistic symbol. An interpretant that translates one sign into another sign is called a logical interpretant.

However, if there were nothing but logical interpretants, that is, translations of signs into other signs, then the process of interpretation would become infinite, since the interpretant, being itself a sign, would necessarily call forth another interpretant, and so on ad infinitum. There are three other kinds of interpretants, however: in addition to the translation into another sign, a sign may be translated into a feeling, into an effort, or into a habit.

1.5.1 Emotional, Energetic, and Logical Interpretants

Listening to a piece of music or a poem may call forth an instantaneous emotional state of consciousness that does not imply or lead to any kind of analysis, but has an immediate impact on the feelings of the recipient. Peirce calls such an interpretant the emotional interpretant. It consists in a general, unanalysed feeling that lasts for a while and then dies away without undergoing any further translation.

If a mosquito bites you and you hit it, this will most often be the end. The pain is a sign of the presence of the irritating insect and your hitting it stops its biting. The sign, then, is translated into a certain, adequate, physical action. And if there are no further complications, this effort will be the end of the sign action. This reaction is spontaneous; from a certain age, most of us would react in this way. According to Peirce, such an effort constitutes an energetic interpretant that is related to the category of will, effort, and action.

In approaching an intersection by car as the light turns red, we would normally put on the brakes. This, of course, is an effort, but in doing so we would respond to the sign by an action founded in a habit we have learned. Habit, in fact, is the fourth way in which we translate a sign into an interpretant. Instead of being translated into another sign, the sign is interpreted by the implementation of habitual action.

The above distinctions provoke immediately the question whether the four different interpretants are found in pure form in actual speech and action. The answer, I think, is no. Actual human sign interpretation will most often include emotional, energetic, logical, and habitual components. When stung by a mosquito a pain is felt, and body and brain react. The effort to hit the insect is triggered by this feeling. Furthermore, spontaneous as the action may seem, it is nevertheless an innate reflex: every human being reacts to painful stimuli from the outside by either trying to remove them or by fleeing from them.

Between the reflex action of hitting the insect and the learned action of putting on the brakes in stopping for a red light there is continuity. Peirce, following Darwin,[8] includes instinctive action under the more general concept of habitual action: 'Side by side, then, with the well established proposition that all knowledge is based on experience, and that science is only advanced by the experimental verifications of theories, we have to place this other equally important truth, that all human knowledge, up to the highest flights of science, is but the development of our inborn animal instincts' (CP 2.754). Peirce points out that the

'Rational Mind' may be seen as an 'Unmatured Instinctive Mind' that is capable of development because of the prolonged childhood of man. Furthermore, precisely because of its weakness, human instinct becomes 'infinitely plastic, and never reaches an ultimate state beyond which it cannot progress. Uncertain tendencies, unstable states of equilibrium are conditions *sine qua non* for the manifestation of Mind' (CP 7.381). On Peirce's view of evolution, it is important that instincts are not wholly fixed, neither in man nor in animals (cf. C.P. 6.498), but are capable of development. Instincts are innate habits, and habit formation is an ongoing process serving the survival of the species through adaptation. Peirce draws the obvious conclusion that 'all reasoning ultimately reposes on "instinct"' (ibid.). Thus, interpretant-formation is a semiotic competence we share with other species, but the species certainly differ in their capacity to create, emit, and interpret signs.

1.5.2 Immediate, Dynamical, and Final Interpretants

The division of interpretants into emotional, energetic, logical, and ultimate logical, or habitual, interpretants is a subdivision of Peirce's most well-known division of the interpretant, the division into immediate, dynamical, and final.

This distinction reflects the process of interpretation in the sense that the immediate interpretant is the interpretant indicated by the sign itself, before any actual interpretation takes place. It is the sign's potential meaning, its meaning potential. The dynamical interpretant is the interpretant resulting from an actual process of interpretation, that is, its actual translation into an emotion, effort, sign, habitual interpretation, or, more likely, a mixture of these. The final interpretant is the interpretant that would result from sufficient, perhaps endless, study by an unlimited community of researchers. It is '[t]he opinion which is fated to be ultimately agreed to by all who investigate, is what we mean by the truth, and the object represented in this opinion is the real. That is the way that I would explain reality' (CP 5.407). Needless to say, although we may very well already have reached the final interpretants of many phenomena, we can never, given the fallibility of man, be certain that interpretations that seem absolutely well founded will not be challenged in the future. In actual research the final interpretant is a regulative principle rather than something given. A final interpretant would be an actual, that is, dynamical, interpretant that would never again be contested.

Signs' potential significations, their immediate interpretants, are not existent either, because any manifest interpretation will necessarily be a dynamical interpretant, an actual translation of the signs' meaning potential. They are ranges of possible translations (in the wide sense) based on patterns and rules on different levels. With regard to linguistic phenomena, these rules will be phonological, morphological/syntactical, semantic, and pragmatic, together with their interrelations. In the case of visual iconic signs, there will be different rules of visual representation, some of which may be transcultural, whereas others will be cultural and historical, and some, from different perspectives, both.[9]

The dynamical interpretant is, in Peirce's words, 'the effect produced upon a given interpreter on a given occasion in a given stage of his consideration of the sign' (MS 339d: 546). It is also said to be a 'determination of a field of representation exterior to the sign (such a field is an interpreter's consciousness) which determination is affected by the sign' (MS 339c: 504). Since the dynamical interpretant is the outcome of a concrete process of interpretation, the concrete context of the sign and the agent of interpretation (the interpreter) are added to the sign's range of possibilities. The context means a specification of the sign/text[10] as a historically grounded utterance referring to objects, states of affairs, mental states, actions, and so on, within a given universe. Consequently, in addition to the constraints exercised by the different rules and structures of the immediate interpretant, the context furnishes additional evidence for choosing one interpretant over another, but rarely with absolute certainty. A simple example of this difference is offered by the problems of choosing in cases of lexical ambiguity. Out of context, the sentence 'They can fish' is ambiguous (at least when written). Changing the situational context into a cotextual specification does away with its ambiguity: 'In this cannery they can fish' vs. 'They can fish in Lake Tahoe.' However, Peirce's understanding of the dynamical interpretant also poses the problem of the relation of sign to utterer and interpreter. And since research, according to Peirce, is a communal and communicative enterprise, the dialogic dimension of semiosis is already indicated. To Peirce it was important, however, not to reduce semiosis to communication between persons: 'I define a Sign as anything which is so determined by something else, called its Object, and so determines an effect upon a person, which effect I call its interpretant, that the latter is thereby mediately determined by the former. My insertion of "upon a person" is a sop to Cerebus, because I despair of making my own broader conception understood' (SS 1977:

80–1). In this quotation it is, however, rather the concept of the individual person than that of utterer and interpreter that is repudiated. This scepticism concerning the individual is constant in Peirce's writings. Being a nineteenth-century scientist and philosopher of science, he considered individuality a source of error: 'There is nothing which distinguishes my personal identity except my faults and limitations' (CP 4.672).

1.6 Interpretant and Dialogue

However, as regards signs, Peirce never doubts that some units of sending and receiving must be present:

> Admitting that connected Signs must have a Quasi-mind, it may further be declared that there can be no isolated sign. Moreover, signs require at least two Quasi-minds; a *Quasi-utterer* and a *Quasi-interpreter*; although these two are at one (i.e., *are* one mind) in the sign itself, they must nevertheless be distinct. In the sign they are, so to say, *welded*. Accordingly, it is not merely a fact of human Psychology, but a necessity of Logic, that every logical evolution of thought should be dialogic. (CP 4.551)

In fact, Peirce did sketch a division of the interpretant based on communication between the parties of a dialogue. In a draft letter to Lady Welby of July 1905 we read:

> There is the *Intentional Interpretant*, which is the determination of the mind of the utterer, the *Effectual* Interpretant, which is the determination of the mind of the interpreter; and the *Communicational* Interpretant, or say the *Cominterpretant*, which is the determination of that mind into which the minds of utterer and interpreter have to be fused in order that any communication should take place. This mind may be called the *commens*. It consists of all that is, and must be, well understood between utterer and interpreter at the outset, in order that the sign in question should fulfill its function. (SS 1977: 196–7)

Compared to the division of the interpretant into immediate, dynamical, and final, this division seems to insert itself into the distinctions of the former. The intentional interpretant presupposes the immediate interpretant (which is also defined by Peirce as 'the interpretant a sign has before it gets an interpreter'). Thus, the immediate interpretant indicates a wide range of possible significations, only some of which the utterer intends to be conveyed (thus the utterer is also the interpreter of the sign he utters). The effectual interpretant is a specification of the dynamical interpretant as regards the actual reception of the sign by a mind or quasi-mind. The cointerpretant, however, cannot be identical to the final interpretant because what the parties of a dialogue agree upon need not be the last word concerning the issue in question.

Consequently, we get the following series: (1) immediate interpretant (the sedimented meaning of a sign); (2) intentional interpretant (the meaning intended by the utterer, whether this is common or innovative); (3) dynamical/effectual interpretant (the meaning actually conveyed to the interpreter (this may of course differ from the one intended by the utterer); (4) cointerpretant (utterer's and interpreter's common understanding of the sign); and (5) final interpretant (the interpretant that will remain unchanged by any further scrutiny (see also a more elaborate description of the sequences of interpretants in Johansen 1993a: 162–82).

Peirce's idea of a fusion of minds in communication, the cointerpretant and the commens, is not a kind of mysticism. It seems justified to talk about a fusion of minds of the parties in a dialogue, when dialogue (as Peirce does) is considered an inferential process. In this sense dialogue can be described as a development of an argumentation in order to reach a conclusion. Such a conclusion may be trivial, or it may constitute an effort to solve important existential, scientific, or philosophical problems. Whatever the nature of argument and conclusion, the parties may each supply premises that become integrated into the argument. Consequently, by participating in such a dialogic and inferential process, their minds are indeed fused into one, in the sense that they are both part of a communal thought process.

Peirce's concepts of the cointerpretant and commens point to the fact that we inescapably belong to an indefinite number of systems and processes of signification while we, at the same time, make up our own unique system. Our personal mind is, semiotically speaking, an individual and changing subsystem of significations, including small parts of coherent thought in a fabric of bits and pieces and threads of every imaginable colour woven into the most varied patterns, and with the loom constantly at work. Our mind changes by becoming hooked up with other minds to the effect that we either integrate reasoning already done or collaborate on producing chains of inferences, that is, discourse.

Obviously, nothing guarantees the attainment of the cominterpretant in dialogue (not to speak of the attainment of a final interpretant), although it would be strange to deny its possibility. Our daily dealings with others indicate that, at least concerning practical matters, we very often achieve this fusion. According to Peirce, this is not really surprising given that the normal preconditions of human communication obtain. On Peirce's analysis, every successful dialogue between two parties presupposes that both parties possesss six requirements: (1) knowledge of the specific language used; (2) knowledge of the rudiments of universal grammar; (3) the most important attributes of the genus *homo*; (4) a similar experience of life concerning elementary items of experience; (5) control of body and of thought; and (6) the knowledge that the second party takes this control for granted in the first party, and vice versa, together with the knowledge that both parties know that the parties presuppose such a taken for grantedness of each other (cf. MS 612, 1908: 2–3). These six requirements mean that the parties of dialogue must possess common, species-specific sensorimotoric and ratiocinative capacities, that is, the same, or almost the same, capacity for experiencing the surrounding world (you cannot talk to the blind of colours). Consequently, their elementary experiences of life (e.g., of bodily needs) will be close to identical. It furthermore follows that they have at least a certain semiotic competence in common, namely, the above-mentioned capacity for processing the sensory input both from the surrounding world and from the body. Let us call this kind of semiotic competence informational. In addition, every species has a communicational competence, that is, the capacity to emit and interpret signs among its members (and in relation to other species as well). In man both the informational and the communicational aspects of the semiotic competence are multiple, complex, and integrated. Communicative competence consists of several semiotic systems among which language is the most prominent. The semiotic link between language and the other informational and communicative semiotic systems is the iconic and indexical signs, because iconicity and indexicality are both prominent features of language and basic to other informational and communicational systems. The answer to the question of how arbitrary (unmotivated) and conventional symbols such as linguistic signs ever come to signify anything is that they are embedded in different significational structures that are related to their objects by similarity and contiguity.[11]

1.7 Utterer and Addresser, Addressee and Interpreter

To have meaning signs must be grounded in a situational and communicative context that to a certain extent must be known and shared. Certainly, texts differ widely in the extent of their immediate groundedness: conversation among family members or friends are often only half comprehensible to others because so much common background knowledge is presupposed that dialogue becomes elliptic; other texts, such as works of literature, usually pack as much information about context and presuppositions as possible into the text itself. The belief that any self-explanatory text exists is, however, an illusion. Texts remote in space or time demonstrate this fact, because present-day readers most often will lack the background knowledge tacitly presupposed by the text, and consequently they will only understand it partially and often incorrectly. This partial knowledge is due to lack of full access to the network of the text's immediate interpretants. Consequently, the reader will not be able to form any qualified opinion about the intentional interpretant either.

Furthermore, the utterer may willfully attempt to mislead the interpreter, that is, he may be lying. The mere possibility of lying makes it necessary to split the utterer's pole (and that of the interpreter as well) in communication. Just as in the case of object and interpretant we distinguish between the immediate and the dynamical, so we should distinguish between the immediate utterer within the sign and the dynamical utterer outside it.

In analogy to the immediate object and immediate interpretant, the immediate utterer is the utterer as he or she appears in and through the sign; let us call him or her the addresser, and keep utterer for the actual producer of the sign. The same split has to be made in the interpreter's case. The immediate interpreter is the interpreter as he or she appears in, or is indicated by, the structure and purpose of the sign itself; let us call this role, viewpoint, and set of values and norms pointed out by the text and ascribed to the intended receiver, the addressee. However the dynamical interpreter, that is, the actual interpreter receiving the text, may very well refuse to assume the role as addressee indicated by the text and may even respond angrily.

In the triadic concept of the sign, the sign-vehicle is conceived as a mediator between an object and an interpretant by virtue of which information is passed on. In human communication, this triangle has,

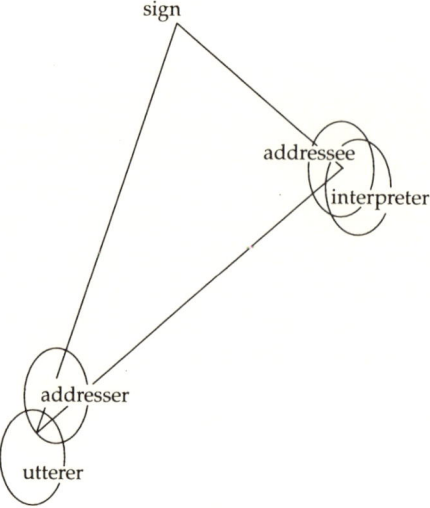

Figure 2

however, to be supplemented by another one, the one between utterer, sign, and interpreter, as shown in figure 2. The reason why the circles around utterer and addresser (and addressee and interpreter) only partly cover each other is that although they mutually influence each other, they are nevertheless distinct and often not in agreement with one another.

That the actual utterer influences the addresser is obvious since he or she produces the sign/text and thereby ascribes properties to the addresser. Very often the addresser reflects the utterer as he wants to appear to the addressee (that is, his idea of the actual interpreter). Thus, the addresser will be the persona the utterer wants to show, or it may contain features that reveal his true intentions in spite of his effort to conceal them.

It may be less obvious that the addresser influences the utterer; still, the addresser influences the utterer even before the fact. Whenever we communicate, we are offered, and most often use, models and styles of communication in which the properties and role of the addresser are de- and prescribed (cf. manuals of good letter writing, manuals of proper behaviour and etiquette, etc). In fact, the attributes of the addresser are a kind of dress fitting the occasion that is made available to the utterer. Certainly, the utterer may reject the customary dress, but his doing so may become eminently meaningful to his interlocutor(s), and it sets him apart from his social group.

That the addresser influences the utterer after the fact is basic to speech-act theory (see Austin 1962 and Searle 1969 and 1979), because utterances have an illocutionary aspect that commits the addresser in different ways. If I promise to pay back a friend from whom I borrow $10,000, but I, although making a $50,000 profit, spend it at the track, then, as an actual agent, I am certainly not complying with the rules for making promises. Instead I have effected a split between myself as the actual utterer and the commitments and obligations concomitant with an addresser's making a promise. It may also happen, however, that because I have made a promise, I conquer my desire to play the horses and do pay my friend back. In the latter case, the fact that, in order to borrow the money, I have dressed myself up as a reliable promise-maker does influence my later action.

The influence of the addressee on the actual interpreter is no surprise, because as a function of and position within the text the addressee is designed have such an influence. The addressee may be defined as the ideal interpreter, as conceived by utterer and text (such an ideal interpreter may, from the utterer's point of view, very well be somebody easily duped). Like the addresser, the addressee is, at least partly, stereotyped within different kinds of texts, most often as the sympathetic and intelligent interlocutor who understands and appreciates the argument and the emotional appeal of the text. And in many cases utterer and text do succeed in influencing the actual interpreter to assume their point of view and standards.

However, just as the addresser influences the utterer, so the interpreter may retroactively influence the addressee through resistance, refusal, and redefinition. Joking is a case in point. Joking is extremely vulnerable to the resistance and refusal of the interpreter. According to Freud, utterers of jokes need the laughter, and thereby the approval, of the interpreter in order to enjoy their own joke and to release their own laughter; especially if the joke is tendentious, obscene, or aggressive, directed against a third party (see Freud 1960). In such cases the interlocutor may easily destroy the joke simply by refusing to take upon him or her the role of the presupposed addressee. In doing so, he or she will, implicitly or explicitly, question the standards according to which the utterance is supposed to be witty with a 'Is this supposed to be funny?' Thus, addressee and addresser are redefined as despicable creatures without any sense of propriety. And since values and morals change rather dramatically in time and space, such redefinitions are going on all the time.

The utterer's attempt to influence the interpreter, by tailoring an addressee who will fit his own purposes, implies ideas about the nature of the interpreter to be influenced; and thus the utterer will become influenced by his own ideas about the interpreter and, indirectly, by the interpreter himself. When adults talk to children, the specific way they address them is governed by assumptions about the intellectual capacities and emotional responsiveness of children.[12]

The fact that the utterer often attempts to take into account the (presumed) perceptual and ratiocinative capabilities, the knowledge, and the aesthetic and ethical standards of the interpreter raises the question of how many 'interlocutors' are present or presupposed in actual dialogue, which by definition involves taking turns. In principle, six 'interlocutors' take part in dialogue. I: (a) utterer^1 in flesh and blood; (b) the addresser in the intention of utterer^1, i.e., addresser^1; (c) the interpreter (= utterer^2) in the intention of utterer^1, i.e., the addressee^1. II: (a') utterer^2 in flesh and blood; (b') the addresser^2 in the intention of utterer^2, i.e., addresser^2; (c') the interpreter^2 (= utterer^1) in the intention of utterer^2, i.e., addressee^2. The minds of the utterer-interpreters are not transparent, however, and this is why the utterers are addressing their own hypothetical constructions of one another:

> But the utterer has no ideas but his own ideas ... Let him try to specify a place on the interpreter's panorama [of life, JDJ], and he can only look over his own panorama, where he can find nothing but his own ideas. On that panorama he has, however, no difficulty in finding the interpreter's life, that is to say, his idea of it, and among the interpreter's ideas, that is his own idea of the interpreter's idea, he finds an idea of that part of panorama to which he conceives this scrap [of the utterer's ideas] should be attached and this he expresses in his sign for the interpreter's benefit. The latter has to go through a similar round-about process to find a place in his own life that seems to correspond with his idea of the utterer's idea of his life and with all these changes of costume there is such imminent danger of mistake ... (MS 318, 1907: 198–9)

It may well be asked whether Peirce holds two different and conflicting views on the possibilities of reaching a common understanding through dialogue. Above, the cominterpretant implying a fusion of minds into a commens was claimed to be a possible, and not infrequent, outcome of semiosis, while here the interlocutors seem locked inside their individual panoramas of life; and, even in dialogue, they seem to be communicating with figments of their own minds. However, it is only when seen from a static point of view that the two descriptions are opposed. When dialogue is seen as an evolving exchange of utterances, the seeming contradiction disappears because the way in which the parties construct addresser and addressee is influenced by the response of the other party to the first party's constructions and vice versa. This may happen because utterer^1 explicitly, or implicitly, presents utterer^2 both with an image of himself and of his interlocutor (utterer^2). And thus the text itself, either implicitly or explicitly, will reflect the utterer's understanding of the dialogue:

$$\text{UTTERER}^1 \text{ (addresser}^1 \to \text{text}^1 \to \text{addressee}^1) \to \text{TEXT}^1 \text{ (addresser}^{1a} \to \text{text}^1 \to \text{addressee}^{1a}) \to \ldots$$

The communication within the parentheses is the communication as it is imagined by utterer^1. The utterance in fact produced by utterer^1, that is, TEXT^1 is influenced by its utterer's calculation of its effect in relation to his or her purpose of communicating. Obviously, utterer^1 may choose to represent both him- or herself (i.e., the addresser) and the addressee differently from the way he or she imagines them to be, that is, he may create personae for both of them in the text (addresser^{1a} and addressee^{1a}). Utterer^2 responds not only to the locutionary part of the text, but to the represented images of addresser and addressee. He may contest the images and try to correct them according to his own understanding of their relationship:

$$\ldots \leftarrow \text{(addressee}^{2b} \leftarrow \text{text}^2 \leftarrow \text{addresser}^{2b}) \text{ TEXT}^2 \leftarrow \text{(addressee}^2 \leftarrow \text{text}^2 \leftarrow \text{addresser}^2) \text{ UTTERER}^2$$

In his next response to utterer^2's utterance, utterer^1 may incorporate his understanding of utterer^2's image of both himself (utterer^1) and the other party's self-representation. Consequently, his next utterance (TEXT^3) may contain an adjustment of both his representation of the other party and of his self-representation because he, most often unconsciously, has matched addresser^{1a} with addressee^{2b} and addressee^{1a} with addresser^{2b}. In his turn, utterer^2 may make a comparable adjustment, and so on and so forth as long as the dialogue is continued.

Certainly, nothing guarantees that such an adjustment will lead to mutual understanding and recognition. This happens very often, however, either because the roles of addresser and addressee are stereotypes with a, more or less, standard interpretation, or because dialogue makes the parties negotiate their different conceptions of themselves and the other. The two views, dialogue as fusion of minds and dialogue as based on auto-communication, do not contradict but supplement each other. They show the initial difficulties that dialogue always has to confront and indicate an inherent endeavour to overcome them (see below). It should be stressed, however, that such an understanding is always partial and brittle, and that it has to be renewed again and again

1.8 The Semiotic Pyramid

The two triadic relations – the triad object, sign, interpretant and that of utterer, sign, and interpreter – are always related and interacting in human communication. Their interaction may be represented in figure 3.

The pyramid represents a dialogue between two parties. The solid line represents semiosis seen from the utterer's point of view; the broken line the interpreter's point of view. In a dialogue, the verbal text will be instanced as a string of tokens, emitted by the utterer. To understand it, however, the interpreter must identify it as replicas of types, that is, as genuine instances of linguistic signs, and this involves interpretation connecting the sign string with object and interpretant. If understanding between the parties is perfect (with regard to the purpose of the dialogue), utterer and interpreter will identify the tokens as instances of the same signs; the immediate object or 'idea' referred to would be (for this purpose) sufficiently similar. Among the possibilities given by the network of immediate interpretants the interpreter will choose the one(s) intended by the utterer, and each will understand and recognize their respective roles within semiosis and recognize each other as persons. Moreover, explication can correct dialogical communication by metalinguistic activity, by reference to a common universe (e.g., ostensive identification), by statement of intentions and purposes, and by questioning.

Perfect dialogic understanding would not need the distinction between the utterer's and interpreter's points of view. Such understanding is, however, only common within stereotyped and constantly reiterated situational and communicative contexts and with topics that, within a given culture, are dealt with routinely (e.g., clearly defined cooperation in work situations, buying groceries, seeking information about facts of everyday life). It takes very little, however, to necessitate

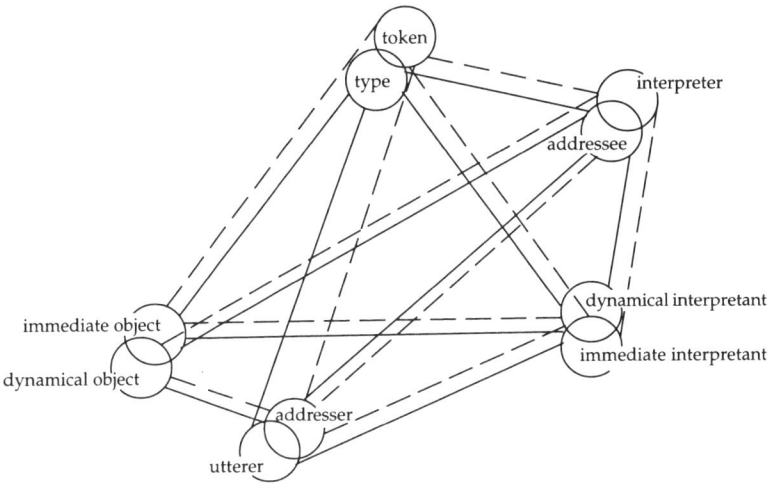

Figure 3

this distinction. What may seem perfectly simple – for instance, asking for directions to find a given street – may cause an intense exchange of questions and answers in order to reach agreement about simple coordinates in relation to the identical physical location of both parties. The semiotic pyramid can be used to scan, as it were, the point, or points, where a dialogue fails to establish a common ground of understanding.

Here face-to-face dialogue is given methodological and, in the history of the subject, also ontogenetic priority, because we learn to speak through dialogue. Indeed, we become subjects through dialogue and interaction with others; the humanization of the infant is bound up with the acquisition of our species-specific semiotic competence (language or other semiotics related to it, as for instance, ASL, American Sign Language). Thus, the acquisition of semiotic competence takes place through a process that is from the beginning necessarily asymmetrical, since it is a dialogue between 'learner and learnee.' Furthermore, since it is, at the same time, a process of socialization, learning the mother tongue (not really a metaphor, but a synechdoche) also means learning the beliefs, norms, and values of the community – learning about them and learning to conform. The reciprocity of dialogue between responsible adults that is directed towards understanding and communicative action (described by both Peirce and Habermas; see chapter 2), or to discourse without constraints and relations of power, is not, and could not be, at the entrance into dialogue. Between adults perfect dialogue is, simultaneously, something that is experienced every day and a distant goal to be realized in a changed society because symmetry in dialogue is counteracted by social asymmetries.

Each element of the semiotic pyramid has been characterized here one after another. However, just as the sign, according to Peirce, is an indissoluble triadic unit comprising sign(-vehicle), object, and interpretant, so the elements of the pyramid only exist by virtue of each other. Utterer and interpreter and addresser and addressee are correlative elements mutually keeping each other in place. Indeed, the act of uttering would make no sense without an interpreter, but, of course, this interpreter may be the utterer him- or herself. Indeed, in addition to others to whom the message is directed, the utterer is always his own interpreter (see above concerning the auto-communicative aspect of every dialogue).

Another important feature of the pyramid's communicative dimension is that all four references have a tripartite structure:

1. Sign—immediate object—dynamical object
2. Sign—addresser—utterer
3. Sign—addressee—interpreter
4. Sign—immediate interpretant—dynamical interpretant

In all cases we have a double reference, an internal and an external: the sign refers to, or even displays, an immediate object, addresser, addressee, and at least one immediate interpretant, but these four internal references are related to four others that are external to, but either determining or determined by, semiosis.

The immediate object, indicated by the sign, is supposed to represent the dynamical object under a certain description and according to a certain interpretation and, often, to be a phenomenal manifestation of it (e.g., a percept or mental image). Thus, the immediate object refers itself to something beyond its appearance in the individual semiosis. This beyond, the dynamical object, is, however, only accessible through other sign actions, other semioses; that is, as other phenomenal manifestations of the dynamical object.

In like manner, the addresser is determined by the utterer, the producer of the text, and is supposed to be a representation of him or her. As a representation, it refers back to the utterer, but it is an incomplete sign in need of completion and clarification, and it is often perceived as such by the interpreter. The addressee is not just a phenomenal representation of the interpreter; it is the utterer's representation of the interpreter. In the course of real dialogue, however, the interpreter in flesh and blood may influence this representation. Dialogue is also a negotiation of representations of self and other. Finally, the sign refers to, or indicates, the immediate interpretant(s), but as a field of possible significations. The dynamical interpretant, which is the result of an interpretive action, is a selective translation of the sign, it is to be hoped, on the basis of the possibilities offered by its immediate interpretants; that is, it is an actualization of parts of the sign's potential signification. In other words, the dynamical interpretant claims to be a realization of the meaning indicated by the sign. However, such an assertion may very well be contested, as, for instance, when an utterer rejects the interpreter's interpretation of his utterance by referring to his own intended interpretant as the true interpretation of the sign's meaning. From the above it should be evident that open-endedness is an inherent feature of dialogic semiosis, because the four immediate referents of the sign are themselves potential signs; signs that may be thematized in another semiosis.

However, the potential for infinite dialogue should not let us forget that most dialogues do end, namely, when both parties believe that they have reached sufficient and mutual understanding of the sign and of one another[13] – or when dialogue seems impossible. In order to get an idea of how people may understand one another, let us turn to the ground floor of the pyramid.

The ground floor of the pyramid is made up of two triangles, one between object, utterer (utterer 1), and interpretant, the other delimited by object, interpreter (utterer 2), and interpretant:

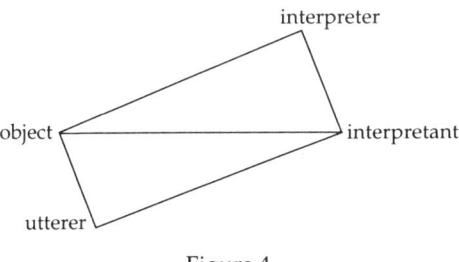

Figure 4

Each of the two triangles constitutes an informational semiosis through which the sensory input from the external and internal environment is processed; that is, it is interpreted according to codes and structures that are, to exploit the computer metaphor, partly common species-specific wetware and partly culture-specific software. The object's (phenomenal) representation is the result of the species-specific processing. Such processing mechanisms, the perceptual apparatus and our experiential and conceptual grids, which are related to our bodily orientations and actions within our lifeworld, make up important parts of the immediate interpretant.

Communicative semiosis is raised on the basis of the informational ground level. However, the informational and communicative semioses mutually presuppose each other. Indeed, perceiving and processing conventional signs is just as much a matter of being confronted with a sensory input as is one of being bit by a mosquito. Furthermore, although language is the most important, and the most conspicuous, human semiotic, it would be a mistake to reduce human communication to that. Posture, gesture, facial expression, touch, olfactory signs, and, of course, ostensive identification probably play a more significant role than language in a great variety of everyday situations.[14]

Nevertheless, we have to distinguish between different kinds of information: information that is the result of the constant bombardment of our senses from the inside and outside, that is, of our being assaulted by what to us are interpreted or uninterpreted indexical signs, and information through intentional communication exchanged between an – in principle – infinite number of interlocutors (we still read the *Iliad*). An important part of the latter kind of informational process is conducted by means of language, whose signs are said to be arbitrary, related to their objects neither by similarity nor by contiguity. The utterances made up of them, however, are both motivated by the purpose of the dialogue and related to its context by contiguity.

1.9 The Interrelations of the Immediate Interpretants

According to pragmatism, phenomenology, and some branches of cognitive science, intellectual predication, the use of concepts in describing and understanding self, other, and world, originates in perception, that is, in the processing of an input of indexical signs. For Peirce, both a pragmaticist and a phenomenologist, any universe imaginable by man is, in the last analysis, related to perception. 'The percepts force themselves upon us, they are independent of our minds in the sense that their characters do not depend on our will, although that it [i.e., the percept] is only known in its relation to my organs is obvious enough.' Peirce goes on to claim, however, that this fact in no way contradicts its independence, 'unless one was nominalist enough to deny that independent objects can be members of pairs of which pairs something is true' (MSL427, 1904: 21). Thus, this basic universe of perception is only given through experience, that is, through interpretation of the interaction between mind and object: 'Experience can only mean the total cognitive result of living, and includes interpretations quite as truly as it does the matter of sense. Even more truly, since this matter of sense is a hypothetical something which we never can seize as such, free from all interpretative working over' (CP 7.538). On this point an interesting agreement exists between Peircean semiotics and cognitive philosophy and semantics. In *The Body in the Mind*, Mark Johnson argues that '[a]lthough there may be uninterpreted perceptual inputs, it is only such inputs comprehended in acts of propositional judgment that can serve to ground knowledge claims – and *these* are theory-laden by virtue of the very fact that they are taken up into propositional judgment' (Johnson 1987: 199). Furthermore, according to Johnson (and Lakoff) our conceptual system reflects our bodily interaction with our lifeworld on two levels:

> (a) The *basic level*, at which we distinguish elephants from giraffes ... and at which we distinguish walking from running, and standing from sitting. This is the level of understanding that we have evolved to permit us to function passably well in our environment ... (b) The *image-schematic level*, which gives general form to our understanding in terms of structures such as CONTAINER, PATH, CYCLE, LINK, BALANCE, etc. This is the level that defines form itself, and allow us to make sense of the relation among diverse experiences. (Ibid.: 208)

The image-schematas have been intensely studied by Johnson, Lakoff, and their co-workers (see, e.g., Lakoff and Johnson 1980, Johnson 1987, and Lakoff 1987). To give an idea of the importance for semiotics of this field of research, let us look at Johnson's short exposition of the image-schema LINK. At first, links are physical and biological phenomena. We owe our very existence to being linked with our biological mother, or today at least birth mother, through the umbilical cord. This cord exemplifies the basic idea of the link as the linking of at least two entities: A•———————•B. In addition to spatial and physical links we experience temporal links between events that we do not necessarily perceive as physically related at one instance in time. The experience of temporal linkage allows us to understand our lifeworld in terms of causal connections. Johnson adds, '[W]ithout such causal conjunction we could never experience our world as a relatively comprehensible place' (1987: 118).

Linking and links need not be physical. As Johnson puts it: 'The severing of the umbilical cord launches us into an ongoing process of linking, bonding, and connecting that gives us our identity (ibid.: 117). Johnson does not say more about human bonding. However, physical connectedness is very important in the early stages of the infant's bonding (cf. the psychoanalytical concept of 'holding,' e.g., the mother's holding the infant, the importance of which has been stressed by, for instance, Winnicott 1971). Although contiguity and physical closeness continues to play a major part in human bonding throughout life, bonding soon transcends mere physical contiguity. It also involves caring, benevolence, emotional comfort, security, trust, respect, and love. Furthermore, bonding may be extended to persons with whom the individual has never had any physical contact; for instance, to charismatic leaders and to non-human entities, gods and demons, or to abstract ideas (the nation, progress, revolution, justice, etc.). In human bonding the emotional dimension is foregrounded, indeed the metaphor 'emotional ties' testifies to its importance. And this locution is at the same time an example of metaphorical extension of the image-schema of physical linking to mental states. Johnson points to another extension of the simple LINKschema in saying that it 'makes possible our perception of *similarity*. Two or more objects are similar because they share some feature or features. Those shared features are their cognitive links in our understanding. Here, obviously, we have a highly abstract notion of linkage, in which the 'third thing' that binds or relates two objects is a perceptual or logical feature' (1987: 118–19). What Johnson calls a metaphorical extension of the LINK schema from relations between physical entities is in Peircean semiotics the distinction between indexical (especially reagents) and iconic signs, namely, the linking of signs and objects, or signs and signs, by contiguity and by similarity. Furthermore, the LINK example offers an illustration of the fruitfulness of the distinction between emotional, energetic, and logical interpretant. It is used primarily with regard to material and energetic relationships between physical objects, but also metaphorically to cover psychical and ratiocinative relations, that is, feelings and thoughts

As to the extension of this schema, one may point to syntax because it is the system of rules for linking linguistic entities to each other, and, in an extended sense, we talk about syntax in relation to other semiotic systems (narrative grammar, architecture). Johnson himself mentions that logical predicates and propositions are related via 'logical connectives' ('and,' 'but,' 'or,' 'if-then') in an act that he calls 'intellectual linking' (1987: 119). What, however, is the force, or evidence, for such intellectual links? Why are we in cases of correct deductive reasoning compelled to acknowledge the soundness of the argument? According to Peirce the compelling nature of intellectual linking lies in the fact that it is iconic and, more specifically, diagrammatic:

> ... necessary reasoning makes its conclusion Evident. What is this 'Evidence?' It consists in the fact that the truth of the conclusion is *perceived*, in all its generality, and in generality the how and why of the truth is *perceived*. What sort of a sign can communicate this Evidence? ... It is true that ordinary icons, – the only class of signs that remains for necessary inference, – merely suggest the possibility of that which they represent, being percepts *minus* the insistency and percussivity of percepts ... It is, therefore, a very extraordinary feature of Diagrams that they *show*, – as literally *show* as a Percept shows the Perceptual Judgment to be true, – that a consequence does follow, and more marvelous yet, that it *would* follow under all varieties of circumstances accompanying the premises. (MS 293, c. 1906: 13–14)

Lakoff exemplifes the possible role of image-schemas in reasoning by another of the important structures, namely, the CONTAINERschema. He points to the traditional representation of classical logic by Venn diagrams (see Lakoff 1987: 456–9).[15]

However, representation by means of the CONTAINERschema seems to relate to basic ways of perceiving and interacting with the world. Our bodily and procreative functions tell us that, in a very fundamental way, we are ourselves containers that need to be filled, and containers that receive, store, transform, secrete, and discharge what is put in them. This is why Isak Dinesen somewhat ironically lets one of her characters in 'The Dreamers' suggest that basically man is nothing but a 'minutely set, ingenious machine for turning, with infinite artfulness, the red wine of Shiraz into urine' (Dinesen 1991: 275). Furthermore, in addition to filling our own and each other's containers, including our mental containers, our minds, we spend much time putting and taking things, again including our own bodies and minds, into and out of containers. We are born from, and we live in, containers, and when we die, we are put into containers; some in a well-wrought urn, others in a leaden coffin within an oak coffin within a marble sarcophagus in a mausoleum.

Peirce's icon, index, symbol distinction and Johnson and Lakoff's work on basic-level concepts and image-schemas are important because they offer penetrating, albeit partial, explanations of how meaning is possible. Both in Peirce and in cognitive semantics, a major objective is to mediate between perception and cognition (there is a common point of departure in Kant). Johnson, following Kant, explains that the role of schemas is to accomplish mediation between images, or objects of sensation, and concepts. Schemas are able to do this because they can be 'a rule-following or rule-*like activity* for creating figure or structure in spatial and temporal representations' (Johnson 1987: 155). Consequently, neither to Peirce nor to Johnson and Lakoff is meaning confined to propositions. In Johnson's words, meaning 'permeates our embodied, spatial, temporal, cultural, and value-laden understanding. The structures of imagination are part of what is shared when we understand one another and are able to communicate within a community' (ibid.: 172).

According to the view proposed above, the networks of immediate interpretants that make communication possible consist of codes, rules, and structuring devices on different levels and governing different areas of semiotic competence. If we follow the views of Johnson and Lakoff, image-schemas mediate between perceptions and concepts, making the former recognizable and furnishing evidence for the latter.[16] The schemas themselves have a double origin in our innate and learned sensorimotor activities made possible by wetware and upbringing. As structuring devices of the imagination, the schemas constitute a semiotic competence that makes categorization and concept formation (both logico-mathematical and linguistic) possible. The close relationship between actional and cognitive development, in Peirce between energetic and logical interpretants, is obvious (cf. also Piaget's description of the psychical development of the child: Piaget and Inhelder 1969).[17]

Furthermore, certain general hypotheses concerning sign processing are implied in the position sketched. First of all, it presupposes that outer reality exists, and that its representation in the mind is influenced by this reality as well as by neurophysiological make-up and cognitive processes specific to man. Furthermore, it strongly suggests a realistic position concerning our cognition of outer reality. It seems a well-founded hypothesis that the objects appearing before our minds may have the characters that we attribute to them. Our species-specific perceptual apparatus processes them in such a way that they have near-identical characters for all of us; and, hence, veridical perception is possible. We seem able to know parts of things as they are, although we will never know every aspect of them. And thus we are able to bring one another to have at least near-identical experiences of our common world. However, since sensorimotor and ratiocinative capabilities and emotional responses are formed not only by the possibilities offered by our body, but also by learning processes, it is no wonder that each of us understands and categorizes the world differently. The point is not that a common understanding of the surrounding world is a matter of fact – it is not – but that there seems to be no compelling reason why such understanding should not be possible.

1.10 Language

The structuring function of language parallels that of image-schemas. Certainly, language would not be able to signify at all without the indexical and iconic patterning of the lifeworld offered by the image-schemas (at least the strong version of the hypothesis that language structures perception seems now obsolete; see, for instance, the discussion on colour perception in Posner and Raichle 1996: 74–6). Nevertheless, the linguistic aspect of categorization, and in general the role played by language in our understanding of one another, our lifeworld, and ourselves must certainly be recognized.

The study of language as a system consisting of elements and combination rules has traditionally been divided into phonology, grammar (morphology and syntax), and semantics. This is not the place to sketch these traditional linguistic disciplines. It should mentioned, however, that although they presuppose each other, these disciplines govern different levels of the linguistic text, and that the constraints differ according to the levels in question:

> Thus, in the combination of linguistic units there is an ascending scale of freedom. In the combination of distinctive features into phonemes, the

freedom of the individual speaker is zero: the code has already established all the possibilities which may be utilized in a given language. Freedom to combine phonemes into words is circumscribed; it is limited to the marginal situation of word coinage. In forming sentences with words the speaker is less constrained. And finally, in the combination of sentences into utterances, the action of compulsory syntactical rules ceases, and the freedom of any individual speaker to create novel contexts increases substantially, although again the numerous stereotyped utterances are not to be overlooked. (Jakobson and Halle 1956: 74)

The rules governing the combination of distinctive features into phonemes, and these into syllables, are valid for any chain of sounds, long or short, within a given language. They govern, however, only this level of text generation and nothing else (of course other aspects of sound patterning may play roles on other levels, e.g., intonation in sentence formation). Likewise, the rules for combination of clauses into sentences do not govern the combination of sentences into paragraphs. Furthermore, as attested by Jakobson, traditional linguistics, from its point of view, has little or nothing to say about text generation above sentence level; except for stereotypes, the speaker decides. However, we should certainly not underestimate the role of stereotypes. Even curses are, according to Tristram Shandy, stereotypical: 'Now don't let us give ourselves a parcel of airs, and pretend that the oaths we make free with in this land of liberty of ours are our own; because we have the spirit to swear them, – imagine that we have had the wit to invent them too' (Sterne 1980: III, xii, 132). Concerning phonology, syntax, and semantics, Jakobson has pointed out and analysed the role played by global phonological and grammatical patterns within poetic texts (see chapter 4 below). And, with regard to the text generation above sentence level, he has pointed towards pragmatics.[18] Furthermore, within contemporary linguistics and philosophy of language much has been done to show that the alleged unrestrained freedom of text production above the sentence level is indeed relative. A host of conventions and principles of diverse nature regulate text production: poetic and rhetorical rules governing different types of speech acts, so-called pragmatic principles, and discursive and social constraints. This diversity is both the strength and weakness of pragmatics.

The problem with regard to pragmatics is its scope and delimitation, specifically in relation to other new disciplines such as discourse analysis and text theory, text grammar, and/or text linguistics (for a fine survey of these disciplines see Gorlée 1996). As a rule, pragmatics does not analyse sentences produced by the linguist him- or herself and claimed to be paradigmatic (a common and sensible practice when language is studied as a system); instead it studies actual texts produced in specific contexts.[19] Furthermore, pragmatics studies linguistic units above the level of the sentence, and it takes into account the roles, intentions, and purposes characterizing utterer and interpreter in the communicative situation. Without being too reductive, one could say that while phonology, grammar, and semantics strive to parse, analyse, and explain what is manifest in the linguistic text itself, contemporary pragmatics proceeds by interpolating the contextually given presuppositions. From the point of view of pragmatics, however, such interpolations are already implicit in the other linguistic disciplines because semantics, which is presupposed in phonology and grammar, is inextricably intertwined with pragmatics.

In one of the classics of this young discipline (Levison 1983) the point is made that it is essential to decide the logical ordering of components, or levels, within an integrated theory of linguistic competence. Further, just as Chomsky has demonstrated that syntax is autonomous in relation to phonology, whereas the opposite is not true, so it can be proved that syntax is not autonomous in relation to pragmatics since some syntactic components are dependent for their analysis on a pragmatic input. As regards the relationship between pragmatics and semantics, Levison argues that there are good reasons to claim that just as semantics may require a pragmatic input, so may pragmatic analysis require a semantic input (e.g., understanding an ironic utterance presupposes a(nother) semantic understanding of the sentence uttered). The conclusion that Levison draws is very clear: 'But if pragmatics is, on occasions, logically prior to semantics, a general linguistic theory simply must incorporate pragmatics as a component or level in the overall integrated theory' (Levison 1983: 35). In a later book on pragmatics, Jacob Mey has widened the scope and objective of linguistic pragmatics:

> Language is the chief means by which people communicate. The use of language, for various purposes, is governed by the conditions of society, inasmuch as these conditions determine the user's access to, and control of, their communicative means.
>
> Hence, *pragmatics is the study of the conditions of human language uses as these are determined by the context of society.* (Mey 1993: 42)

Thus, a closer look at language in use or, as Peirce said, the sign *in actu*, is necessary for the proper study of the subject of this book.

1.11 From Language to Text: The Three Levels of Linguistic Communication

According to Peirce's classification of signs, linguistic signs, which are mainly symbolic, refer to and signify objects and states of affairs because they are understood to do so by a community of utterers and interpreters. This reference to the community underscores that the meaning of signs is socially established and somewhat stable. Consequently, linguistic signs have, at any given point in time, a set of quasi-stable significations delimiting them from one another in a more or less systematic fashion. This is why Peirce's concept of the immediate interpretant presupposes that signs have significations prior to their use in the individual utterance and the individual act of interpretation.

Moreover, rules are operative in generating phonemes, syllables, signs (morphemes), and sentences – even if those rules are unknown to the speaker and unconsciously applied. Thus, to understand linguistic texts means to understand their inventories, both below and above the sign limit, and a complex set of combination rules of their language. This viewpoint favours the so-called code model of communication according to which a message is given a linguistic representation by being encoded by the utterer followed by a symmetrical but reversed process of decoding by the interpreter.[20] Thus understanding is possible because of code sharing.

Although there is some truth to this model because certain aspects of linguistic sign production and interpretation are plausibly explained by it, as a general explanation of text interpretation, it is much too narrow. One serious problem is its lack of dynamism. If understanding a text were nothing but decoding it according to a pre-existing code, that is, matching parts of the text with a grid of coded significations, then it would be hard to explain how changes of significations brought about by the text itself are understood. And not only literary texts, but also informal conversations, abound in sliding meanings and changes in the significations of vocabulary.

A less narrow understanding of linguistic communication is to see it as an intentional action on the part of the speaker. A text is a means of getting a message through, of doing something by making one's intentions clear; that is, you intend to produce a certain response in your interlocutor by the fact that he recognizes your intention. According to this model, the role of text interpretation is to uncover the meaning ascribed to the text by its utterer. Such an achievement is made possible because both utterer and interpreter know how to use and interpret a number of speech acts such as making an assertion, a question, a promise, a warning, and so forth.

It would be odd to deny that the purpose of linguistic messages includes communicating the position of the utterers concerning their respective themes. If my wife asks me to bring coffee from the store, it is certainly important that I understand her utterance as a request. I will also, unconsciously, hypothesize that this request complies with a number of more or less trivial preconditions: for instance, that the store carries coffee, that we usually drink coffee, that we are out of or soon expect to be out of coffee, that we have the money to buy coffee, etc., etc.

However, although recognition of intentions is a very important aspect of text interpretation – and consequently biographical information, contrary to the prevailing stance of literary theory, concerning the utterer may be important – understanding texts cannot be restricted to this element. One very important reason is that, contrary to the belief of Humpty-Dumpty (in Lewis Carroll's *Through the Looking Glass*), in several ways the utterer does not control his own text. First of all, utterers may not be aware of the meanings that are expressed. They may think that they are kindly asking their interlocutor a favour, while they are actually giving an order of command in a hostile way. The general point is that we are not transparent to ourselves, and so we transmit more and other information than we intend, and we are always making several speech acts in one utterance. Second, although in our own understanding our text ought to be received as a certain kind of speech act eliciting a predictable standard response, the actual effect on the interlocutor depends on factors over which we have only a very limited control. Such factors are some of the reasons why, for instance, Hans-Georg Gadamer has claimed that the meaning of a text, not only sometimes but always, transcends the *mens auctoris* – but, even if this is certainly true, we may nevertheless better understand an utterance by knowing more about its utterer.

What I have pointed to here is similar to what within speech-act theory has been formulated as the distinction between the locutionary, the illocutionary, and perlocutionary aspects of an utterance. However, although speech-act theory deserves much praise for systematizing the problems involved in 'how to do things with words,' the idea that several aspects of the text collaborate in order to make the text understandable – or that their apparent or real discord makes interpretation difficult – can be found elsewhere. Peirce, for instance, was well aware of this issue. About the word he says:

> A word has meaning for us in so far as we are able to make use of it in communicating our knowledge to others and in getting at the knowledge that these others seek to communicate to us. That is the lowest grade of meaning. The *meaning of* a word is more fully the sum total of all the conditional predictions which the person who uses it *intends* to make himself responsible for or intends to deny. That conscious or quasi-conscious *intention* in using the word is the second grade of meaning. But besides the consequences to which the person who accepts a word knowingly commits himself, there is a vast ocean of unforeseen consequences which the acceptance of the word is destined to bring about, not merely consequences of knowing, but perhaps revolutions of society. One cannot tell what power there may be in a word or phrase to change the face of the world; and the sum of these consequences make up the third grade of meaning. (CP 8.176)

What do the distinctions between different levels, or aspects, of the text and their separate complexities mean to text interpretation in general and to that of literary texts in particular? In the attempt to give a partial answer to this question, let us stick to the tripartite distinction between (a) the level of the locution, or propositional content, of a text; (b) its enunciative level, or its illocutionary aspect; and (c) its actually being uttered, its perlocutionary aspect including its situationality, the fact that it is an action located in time and space and directed to somebody.

On the first level, that of propositional content, or of sign inventories and their combination rules, we notice two disturbing phenomena. First, we cannot, most often, ascribe a single well-defined signification to the signs in question (although maybe one or more focal meaning[s]), that is, the elements of the inventories are polysemic. Second, the rules according to which they are combined are vague or ambiguous with regard to their significations, since it is not possible to infer some decisive features concerning sentence meaning from the syntactic rule according to which it is formed.

As regards illocution, speech-act theory,[21] by describing the conditions that have to be met in order for a given utterance to count as a certain kind of speech act, has shown the extent to which linguistic communication is conventional, rule-governed. I do not doubt the impact and tremendous usefulness of this approach to text understanding. One reason for its importance is that it points to the network of obligations and consequences in which our communicative acts are inscribed. It seems reasonable to suppose that a common knowledge as to the meaning of expressions such as 'I assert ...' 'I promise ...' 'I warn you ...,' etc. exists, and that such common knowledge commits the utterer in certain ways. Obviously, the force (Searle) that different speech acts carry obliges the utterer to different degrees; swearing and presuming certainly do not commit the utterer in the same way (the former may have legal consequences, the latter is only a weak commitment to a belief). In imagining that no speech acts have a reasonably stable range of meanings and no agreement exists concerning the approximate commitments and consequences tied to the uttering of such acts, the importance of this approach to utterances is made clear: institutions would not function, communication would break down, and communal action would become impossible; in fact, it would mean the dissolution of society.

However, although most of the time, at a certain level, speech acts are uttered and interpreted without difficulty according to explicit or implicit agreement on their significations and implications, it is not to be questioned that in innumerable cases no consensus can be achieved concerning their meaning and implications. The very existence of courts that try cases of civil law testifies to the fact that people do not always agree on the right interpretation of the commitments involved in agreements and contracts.

There are several reasons for this predicament. First of all, the speech act intended by the utterer may not have been expressed with sufficient clarity ('I never promised you to do it. I said I would think about it'). Such a lack of clarity may also be intentional: because of consideration and shyness, or because of guile, the utterer does not go clearly on record, but expresses him- or herself indirectly and/or ambiguously. For much the same reasons, the interpreter may be just as vague, one-sided, and blind to the wording of the text. Second, in a situational context a text may, indeed most often will, express several speech acts at one and the same time. Further, the speaker may be both unaware of this fact and under the illusion that he or she is expressing one kind of speech act, while he/she according to the interlocutor, and to an observer, is in fact expressing another one (e.g., he may think he warning someone, while he is in fact intimidating or threatening).

Thus, the autonomy of the level of illocution is both real and illusory. It is real because illocutionary acts do have social consequences; it is illusory because in real communication factors intervene that complicate, weaken or efface, and change the clear-cut significations of textbook cases of speech acts.

Illocution's lack of autonomy is due to the influence of the third level, that of perlocution, on which it becomes apparent that utterances are complex symbolic actions fulfilling an indefinite number of purposes and creating an indefinite number of effects, some of which are unpredicted and unpredictable. On the level of uttering, we encounter both the unpredictability of concrete individual action and the patterning of behaviour through habit-taking. The most salient feature on this level is the situationality of the utterance, the utterance as a concrete event inscribed in a historical context. From this perspective text production is an interactional venture always entering into an explicit or implicit dialogue, always purposeful, directed towards the achievement of some goal, and therefore always concerned with its own potential effect on the interpreter, that is, always considering itself as a kind of argument, and as a kind of persuasive action.

The importance of the situationality of the text has been recognized from almost every quarter of semiotics, linguistics, and text science.[22] The problem is how to transform situationality into explicit preconditions expressed in language. In many cases this is easily done. Using the example from above – 'They can fish here' – let us imagine the two parties of a dialogue standing (a) in front of a factory, and (b) looking at a lake; in both cases the sentence 'They can fish here' is uttered. Transforming the situational context into an explicit one is rather easy. In the former case, the sentence is taken to be about canning fish to preserve it as food, while the latter is taken to be about the possibility (for people with a licence) of catching fish in the lake in question. In both cases the transformation from situational to explicit context means the linguistic explication of the deictic sign 'here,' which is bound to the point of view of the utterer. In this example the polysemy of the sentence is transformed into two different univocal utterances: in this cannery versus in this lake. The role of the context is to delimit the range of possible meanings of a text, because knowledge of the context of utterance points out that some interpretations are more plausible than others.

Thus, it seems evident that a situational context may offer us the possibility of procuring additional knowledge through dialogue and an immediate opportunity for collateral experience. You may ask your interlocutor about the significations of the signs he uses and ask him to explicate and improve his argument. Indeed, often you may become directly acquainted with the object under discussion.

The importance of the situational context is due to the fact that elements whose meaning is not is clear from the linguistic text itself may be immediately explicable from this kind of context. Hamlet's 'a rat, a rat' becomes immediately understandable because we know that Hamlet believes Claudius is hidden behind the curtain (but how could the king have got there before Hamlet?). In order to understand a text we always have to interpolate a situational context that is not specified by the linguistic text itself and that indicates or stipulates factors needed to make sense of the text. But there is an element of chance in all uttering because suddenly, on the spur of the moment, the situation may change the direction of the dialogue and produce an unexpected text. Thus, such influences have to be witnessed, or they must be (re)constructed and made probable mainly through pointing to allegedly analogous cases.

From a purely methodological point of view, the importance of contextual specification for interpretation means that the full-fledged dialogue about what is present to both utterer and interpreter takes precedence over other modes of communication. What the situational context makes possible is intersemiotic cross-reference and translation; that is, symbolic signs refer to and are translated into iconic and indexical ones and vice versa.[24] However, intersemiotic, like intra- and interlinguistic translation, is always selective. There is no one-to-one correspondence between iconic, indexical, and symbolic signs.

Actual dialogue makes accessible that which is not recognized when communication is only considered as rule-governed behaviour. At the same time, it makes available to us tools of interpretation not at our disposal on the other levels. Such tools include, for instance, the possibility of reading other, non-linguistic features (facial expressions, gestures, tone and cadence, etc.) of the other party; that is, the possibility of using non-linguistic, cognitive models (of perception and interaction), models of social interaction such as frames and scripts, and loose sets of maxims of conduct believed to govern behaviour concerning well-defined sequences of actions within smaller or larger segments of society. Although such maxims are only nodal points in folk theories of psychology and action, they are nevertheless operative because they guide reciprocal expectations and, consequently, interaction itself.

The situational context, the elements of semiosis present at the moment of utterance, is a necessary and important part of the contexts, in the plural, of the text. However, the contexts necessary for understanding a text always exceed the situational context, because reference to non-explicit and general presuppositions will always be needed.

In the preceding all three levels of discourse have been described as partially rule-governed, because on each one it is possible to point to inventories and combination rules that are instrumental in generating sentences, speech acts, and utterances. From the point of view of interpretation, however, indeterminacy exists on each level, since in many cases the rules in question are not in themselves sufficient for one to decide between different interpretations, although they may be sufficient to rule out certain specific interpretations.

In the interaction between the three levels we rediscover the same doubleness. On the one hand, deciding that an utterance represents this or that kind of speech act may solve problems about the semantic interpretation of a given syntactic structure. Likewise, facial expression and tone of voice may solve questions concerning what kind of speech act is represented, for instance, whether or not it is ironic. On the other hand, however, going from one level to the other may evoke open questions of interpretation that are not, and cannot be, asked on the other level, although the text certainly allows, indeed may call for, such questioning.

There are two main reasons for the complexity of text interpretation, an intra- and an intersemiotic one. First, there is an intricate balance between relative autonomy and interdependence among the levels of discourse. If you intend to convey a message influencing your interlocutor in a certain way, you are bound to express yourself according to a certain usage. Conversely, you are not (normally) forced to use one and only one way of expressing yourself. Second, although language consists mainly of symbolic or conventional signs, text interpretation is not possible by using only conventional knowledge of the meaning of words and referring to language as a system.

Language in use, speech or texts, unites two different semiotic principles, two different ways of understanding. In order to know the meaning of a text, one needs to recognize the symbolic signs of which it is made as tokens, or replicas, of types whose meaning you have previously learned. In your memory you have a kind of dormant semantic network allowing you to recognize a very large number of such signs and to endow them with signification in given contexts. Thus, one precondition for text interpretation is matching: the sign calls forth our prior knowledge of it.

However, this precondition is not sufficient because text production is (symbolic) action. Certainly, recognition of action is in many ways similar to recognition of symbolic signs. Actions are also partly rule-governed behaviour within certain frames and according to certain scripts. At the same time, however, text production is a process originating in one or more utterer(s) at a certain point and place in time, and it is directed to one or more interpreter(s). This directedness calls for another kind of knowledge, which we have met in connection with genuine indexical signs (reagents), namely, inferential knowledge.

Thus, we are close to Peirce's description of the process of inquiry in which the manipulation of iconic and indexical signs is of great importance. We infer that our interlocutor is angry because we take facial expression and tone of voice as indexical signs that this is so. In other words, we infer a determination from object to sign, the sign being a trace or symptom of and cue to the object. Even in the case where an actor mimes the wrath of a character, either we will understand tone of voice and facial expression either as indexical signs, because we forget that he is play-acting, or we see them as mimicry, as iconic signs similar to their indexical originals. Thus, text interpretation means the collaboration between different kinds of knowledge and different ways of knowing that simultaneously let the text appear as a, more or less coherent, network of significations and a set of cues, clues, and traces.

To the literary scholar such an approach to linguistic texts is meaningful, since literature is a species of linguistic communication, of speech. This approach also stresses another important point, namely, the eminently social character of text production. Since literature functions within the context of society, pragmatics' stress on the framing, institutionalization, and power involved in speech also points to preconditions for the production of literature.

Two

Discourse and Text

> [T]he analysis of discourse, is necessarily, the analysis of language in use. As such it cannot be restricted to the description of linguistic forms independent of the purposes or functions which these forms are designed to serve in human affairs.
>
> *(Brown and Yule 1983: 1)*

Pragmatics, text linguistics, and linguistic discourse analysis are all productive fields of research. It is not easy, however, to tell them apart, especially because there seems to be no stable terminology: what some scholars call discourse is called text by others, and vice versa (see Vitacolonna 1988: 421–39). Furthermore, there is, in my view, a point in textual analysis where the formal study of linguistic properties has to give way to the historical study of human interaction. It is, of course, both legitimate and fruitful to investigate how far it is possible to advance into specifying linguistic or linguistic-like rules for text production. In the context of the semiotics of literature, however, two other non-linguistic approaches seem more promising because they unite the study of speech, history, and lifeworld, namely, the two different concepts of discourse of Foucault and Habermas. These two approaches are important in the present context because they discuss the presence of regularities, rules, and forces other than the linguistic in the production of discourse in general, and because, although very different, both are of immediate relevance for literature.

2.1 Two Concepts of Discourse: Foucault and Habermas

The Foucault – Habermas debate, which has been characterized as a debate between a postmodernist and a modernist approach to a critique of society (see Mumby 1992: 81–106),[1] is interesting because there is both a common ground and a vast difference between the two approaches. Furthermore, there is both a direct relationship and a debate between them because Habermas has criticized Foucault (see Habermas 1987b). Michael Kelly has cogently stated the common ground and the most important difference as follows:

> In Foucault's words, modernity is more of an attitude than a historical period, an attitude 'described as a permanent critique of our historical era' in the pursuit of enlightenment. For Habermas 'Modernity can and will no longer borrow the criteria by which it takes orientation from the models supplied by another epoch; *it has to create its normativity out of itself* (19876: 7). If Foucault and Habermas's characterizations of modernity are conjoined the result is that 'the permanent activation of a critical attitude' inaugurates modernity's task of 'creating its own normativity.' That modernity is critical toward its own present and that it must perpetually create its own normativity are thus the points in which Foucault and Habermas agree. Yet they do not agree on how this normativity is justified, or on whether this normativity is as local as the historical context out of which it emerges and toward which its critical eye is vigilantly turned. (Kelly 1994: 383)

This quotation suggests that the stakes are high in this debate, but, nevertheless, here there will be no analysis of these very different conceptions of modernity and of the role of discourse in contemporary society. This would be a subject for a book, and there exists already a rich literature on these two important thinkers. My aim is much more modest, namely, to attempt a juxtaposition and confrontation of their opposed and conflicting understandings of discourse.

Dealing with Foucault's concept of discourse is not easy, however, because he uses discourse in different senses, a fact that he is well aware of and points out to the reader: 'Lastly, instead of gradually reducing the rather fluctuating meaning of the word "discourse," I believe that I have in fact added to its meanings: treating it sometimes as the general domain of all statements, sometimes as an individualizable group of statements, sometimes as a regulated practice that accounts for a certain number of statements' (Foucault 1972: 80). Nevertheless, Foucault's approach to discourse seems valuable because he firmly situates discourse within history and society. He sees discursive practice as one practice among other social practices. His idea of discourse is also related to main themes in his thinking such as the disappearance of the subject, the denial of the *œuvre* as a privileged object of analysis (I am sceptical as to his analysis of these two points), the heterogeneity within and among different realms of knowledge, and the eminent role of power (and desire) in discourse. In the *Archaeology of Knowledge* (1971, French orig. 1969) Foucault mentions discourses such as clinical discourse, economic discourse, the discourse of natural history, and psychiatric discourse (subjects he has treated in his other books), and he defines discourse as follows: '[A] group of statements in so far as they belong to the same discursive formation; it does not form rhetorical or formal unity, endlessly repeatable, ... [I]t is, from beginning to end, historical – fragment of history, a unity and discontinuity in history itself, posing the problems of its own limits, its divisions, its transformations, the specific modes of its temporality' (Foucault 1972: 117). At least prima facie, the end of a discursive formation, and of the texts it makes possible, is to produce knowledge, not necessarily science, but also discursive formation outside of, and even hostile to, scientific discourse. In this connection Foucault speaks of setting free subjugated knowledge. Literature too is, in his view, a way of producing knowledge (it is doubtful, however, that this is the primary concern of literature; see pp. 296–8 and 312). The formation of objects, of subjective positions, of concepts, and of strategic choices effectuate this knowledge production. The two main points are, first, that the production of knowledge is only possible within a complex and heterogeneous field where many practices, institutions, and social and ideological forces are at play and often at war with each other. Second, objects, subjective positions, concepts, and strategic choices do not precede the discursive formation; they are formed by it. The discursive formation is the precondition for their appearance. Within medical discourse, for instance, the objects analysed, for instance, the diseases, are specified, studied, and treated by virtue of the discursive, experimental, and social practices. The same analysis is applied to the position of the doctor (and his gaze), to the medical concepts, and to the strategic choices made, for instance, to avoid apparent inconsistencies in the discourse, or in order to make possible certain lines of research.

Here an important point in Foucault's analysis of discourse is already implicit: discourses are intellectual instruments of exclusion just as much as of formation; or, rather, formation and exclusion are two sides of the same coin. This point is made very explicit in his inaugural lecture at the Collège de France, 'The Discourse on Language' (1970, in Foucault 1972),[2] in which the mechanisms of discursive control are enumerated. In any society, Foucault says, 'the production of discourse is at once controlled, selected, organized and redistributed according to certain numbers of procedures, whose role is to avert its powers and its dangers, to cope with chance events', (Foucault 1972: 216). Discourse, then, practises several rules of exclusion. In addition to stark prohibition (e.g., taboo and censorship), which attempts to prevent themes, viewpoints, and lines of reasoning from appearing within given discourses, Foucault mentions division and rejection, as for instance in the distinction between sanity and folly and between true and false. He also speaks of the will to truth as a regulatory force constraining discourse, and further points out that truth 'moved over from the ritualized act – potent and just – of enunciation to settle on what was enunciated itself: its meaning, its form, its object and its relation to what it referred to' (ibid.: 218). This will to truth has its history that includes, among other things, the different modes of inquiry and scientific practices. It also rests on institutional support, on systems of diffusion and exploration of knowledge – and on systems of exclusion. Knowledge exercises a pressure upon other forms of discourse. Foucault mentions that literature has attempted to comply with the demands of plausibility, sincerity, and science (the poetics of Zola would be a prime example). Although true discourse is a discourse liberated from desire and power, it is established, Foucault holds, on a 'prodigious machinery of the will to truth, with its vocation of exclusion.' Indeed, the relation between knowledge and power is the governing idea of his work. Already in *Discipline and Punish* (1975) he claims that 'there is no power relation without the correlative constitution of a field of knowledge, nor any knowledge that does not presuppose and constitute at the same time power relations' (1977: 27).

In addition to the rules of discourse related to power and desire, Foucault mentions internal control systems such as commentary. In Foucault's view, commentary is designed to keep the authoritative, not to say authoritarian, texts (e.g., religious and legal texts, but also literary classics), alive, to explain them, but also to institute and defend the rightness of the exegetes' own interpretations. Commentary allows us to infinitely produce new texts that pretend to speak about the same text, the text commented on, and reveal its meaning while adapting the discourse to a changed world (the eternal problem of theological and juridical exegesis). In this connection the idea of the author functions as a principle of unity, especially in literary discourse, and assures its link with reality. It offers a point of reference that seems both to explain its individuality and to function as a norm for statements about the texts: has the critic grasped the intentions, conscious or unconscious, of the author?

Opposed to both commentary and author is the formation of disciplines defined by their 'groups of objects, methods, their corpus of propositions considered to be true, the interplay of rules and definitions, of techniques and tools' (1972: 222). Contrary to commentary, the objective of a discipline is to formulate an infinity of fresh propositions (believed to be true). Disciplines, however, do not consist only of truth; they contain errors as well. Nor do they contain all that is true about given objects, only what, at a given time, can appear within their framework. Their propositions must refer to a specific range of objects and comply with the theoretical field in question. This is why certain contributions to a discipline are rejected, even if they speak the truth (Foucault's example is Mendel's work on heredity). He sums up his position in this way: 'We tend to see in an author's fertility, in the multiplicity of commentaries, and in the development of a discipline so many infinite resources available for the creation of discourse. Perhaps so, but they are nonetheless principles of constraint, and it is probably impossible to appreciate their positive, multiplicatory role without first taking into consideration their restrictive, constraining role' (ibid.: 224). Exclusion, rarification, discontinuity, and specificity characterize discourse, according to Foucault. It cannot be reduced to a prior system of signification, and it is a specific 'violence that we do to things, or, at all events, as a practice we impose upon them.'

As a fourth principle of analysis of discourse, Foucault claims its exteriority. Instead of looking for its hidden meanings, we should analyse its external conditions of existence, including its materiality and its event and chance character – even if discourses certainly also exhibit regularities. The analysis of discourse that Foucault proposes studies critically its inner systematicity, but also its gaps, omissions, and exclusions, and it is supplemented by a genealogical analysis that studies its effective formation and the power inherent in this process. Later he points out that archeology is the appropriate methodology of the analysis of 'local discursivities, and genealogy would be the tactics whereby, on the basis of the descriptions of these local discursivities, the subjected which were thus released would be brought into play' (Foucault in Kelly 1994: 24). This interest in local struggles concerning knowledge, and the exclusion of subjugated knowledge, comes from distrust in global and universalizing theories (whereas universalization is a key concept in Habermas). The critical potential of his own work Foucault sees as the laying bare of 'this insurrection of knowledges against the institutions and against the knowledge and power that invests scientific discourse' (ibid.: 26).

In Foucault's view, the unfolding of discourse, like the formation of knowledge, takes place through a chance-ridden, discontinuous process, and certainly not only as an successive unfolding of consequences and corollaries of a basic theoretical position (although this also plays a role). It is a complex activity that is governed by different, opposing, and partly contradictory internal and external factors. Discursive practice (a body of anonymous, historical rules of a given geographical and economic area – see 1972: 117) is one among others constantly influenced by other practices affiliated with it (e.g., clinical and experimental practices, legal procedures and court decisions, responses and judgments of critics, connoisseurs, and audiences). It is further influenced by other discourses and their practices. At a given time, a hierarchy of discourses exists. The hegemony of a discourse is related to the structure of society and to social and economic movements. Thus, discourse is inextricably bound up with power and desire, and it is jealous and anxious, aggressive and competitive, attempting to hold its ground against various attacks, of which scholarly, or scientific, objections and remonstrances are only one kind and often not the decisive one.

In the context of his theory of discourse, Foucault does not deny the distinction between true and false statements (although Mendel's theory was rejected by his contemporaries, what he claimed was true). He also concedes that knowledge formations may develop and even progress: today more is known within the sciences than earlier. Foucault's point is, rather, that (1) in knowledge formation there is no uniform development governed by an internal logic; (2) all thought processes are somehow related to power and desire, even if the disinterested search for truth is claimed to be their only objective, and (3) the fate of a given theoretical position is decided by factors external to it. He makes the further important point that these conditions are not foreign to discourse formation; although they may seem to impose irrelevant criteria and demands from the outside, they are the always present and inescapable preconditions for its existence. Moreover, claims that, although power and truth are certainly not identical, there is an inner relation between them. 'Power never ceases its interrogation, its inquisit in, its registration of truth: it institutionalizes, professionalizes, and rewards its pursuit' (Foucault in Kelly 1994: 32).

80   Part One: Sign, Dialogue, Discourse

Habermas is highly critical of Foucault, whom he sees as entangled in contradictions. Among other things, he very much doubts that Foucault has succeeded in replacing hermeneutic understanding by non-hermeneutic analysis of structures, validity claims by power relations, and value-free historical explanation by a consistent justification of his own critical enterprise. Thus, in Habermas's view, Foucault's genealogical historiography emerges as 'precisely the presentistic, relativistic, cryptonormative illusory science that it does not want to be' (ibid.: 87-8). One important reason why Habermas takes this stern view of Foucault's project is that it is almost exclusively concerned with relations of power (in Foucault, for instance, the self is also an effect of power), whereas the dialogic dimension, with its symmetry and reciprocity, is absent.

Precisely concerning dialogue Habermas differs from Foucault. For Habermas, there are two main modes of action among the members of a society: communicative action and strategic action. By using any expedient means (sometimes force and/or guile, and certainly persuasion), strategic action is concerned with realizing the objectives and interests of an individual or group through goal-rational behaviour. Communicative action, by contrast, is directed towards the establishment of communal understanding and, on the basis of this understanding, towards agreement on which action to choose. Understanding is defined as follows:

> The goal of coming to an understanding [*Verständigung*] is to bring about an agreement [*Einverständnis*] that terminates in intersubjective mutuality of reciprocal understanding, shared knowledge, mutual trust, and accord with one another. Agreement is based on recognition of the corresponding validity claims of comprehensibility, truth, truthfulness, and rightness. We can see that the word understanding is ambiguous. In its minimal meaning it indicates that the two subjects understand a linguistic expression in the same way; its maximal meaning is that between the two there exists an accord concerning the rightness of an utterance in relation to a mutually recognized normative background. In addition two participants in communication can come to an understanding about something in the world, and they can make their intentions understandable to one another. (Habermas 1979: 3)

Thus, the four validity claims (of universal pragmatics), mentioned in the quotation, are (1) *comprehensibility* of the linguistic expression, (2) *truth* of the state of affairs referred to, (3) *truthfulness* on the part of the utterer, and (4) *rightness* in relation to a given norm. In order to fulfil the preconditions for participating in a dialogue directed towards understanding, the utterer must further posses an adequate *communicative competence*:

> By 'communicative competence' I understand the ability of the speaker oriented to mutual understanding to embed a well-formed sentence in relation to reality, that is:
>
> 1. To choose the propositional sentence in such a way that either the truth conditions of the proposition stated or the existential presupposition of the propositional content mentioned are supposedly fulfilled (so that the hearer can share the knowledge of the speaker);
>
> 2. To express his intentions in such a way that the linguistic expression represents what is intended (so that the hearer can trust the speaker);
>
> 3. To perform the speech act in such a way that it conforms to recognized norms or to accepted self-images (so that the hearer can be in accord with the speaker in shared value orientations). (Habermas 1979: 29)

The four validity claims of universal pragmatics can easily be mapped onto the semiotic pyramid because these claims concern the sign's (in Habermas, proposition's) relation to object and interpretant and to utterer and interpreter (see Figure 5). Truth is the most important characteristic of the relation between sign and object. We need to know whether the sign offers a true representation of its object. In dialogue truthfulness applies equally to utterer and interpreter. Both comprehensibility and rightness involve the relationship between sign and interpretant, because although both parties will separately assert that they comply with the two claims, they will also hold that their interpretation of the claims is in accordance with a general norm and thus is related to the interpretant. As regards comprehensibility this claim is evident, because in order for a sign to be understandable it must lend itself to translation. Nonsense words, for instance, are language-like entities that cannot be translated. Rightness is also related to the interpretants, because sign interpretation certainly has a normative aspect (although language as a system has not). We not only translate signs, we judge them according to ethical and aesthetic standards, and such standards are important parts of the immediate interpretants (cf. Habermas's point that understanding has a minimal and a maximal meaning).

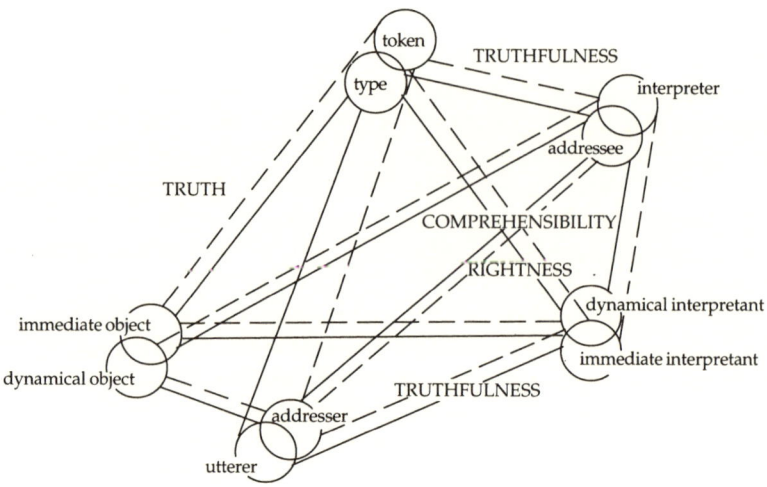

Figure 5

Validity claims and their mapping on the semiotic pyramid are related to different speech functions. According to Habermas, speech is the medium that represents and mediates three worlds: (1) external reality, (2) the social world consisting of normatively regulated and legitimate interpersonal relations within a given community, and (3) the internal worlds of utterer and interpreter. Speech and language make it possible to communicate about these worlds; and, sometimes, to direct the other party to having experiences near-identical to those of the utterer and to reach understanding about them.

Obviously, Habermas knows that what he is describing is an 'ideal speech situation' (his own expression) – something that is not often fully realized, and that is certainly very often intentionally flouted. Furthermore, even if the interlocutors are sincere and honest, they may disagree concerning both the nature of the external world and the legitimacy of a given action. Indeed, disagreement may arise even about the inner nature of the two interlocutors, in spite of their privileged access to their own inner world. Such disagreement is often the case in the therapeutic dialogue between therapist's understanding of the patient and patient (the patient is deluded about the workings of his own psyche – or the therapist is wrong). To the first objection Habermas answers: 'The ideal speech situation is neither an empirical phenomenon nor a mere construct, but rather an unavoidable supposition reciprocally made in discourse. This supposition can, but need not be, counterfactual; but even if it is made counterfactually, it is a fiction that is operatively effective in the process of communication' (Habermas 1979: 258). It must be admitted that most often we do make this supposition in communicating with others because, in the ordinary matters of daily life, the ideal speech situation is realized constantly. Furthermore, if in most cases we did not subconsciously assume this to be the case, communication would break down; we could not trust any information, we would be constantly afraid of being deceived. To Habermas, the ideal speech situation and its compliance with validity claims and communicative action are bound up with rationality. Indeed, rationality is explicitly linked with validity claims:

> Rationality is understood to be a disposition of speaking and acting subjects that is expressed in modes of behavior for which there are good reasons or grounds. This means that rational expressions admit of objective evaluation. This is true of all symbolic expressions that are, at least implicitly, connected with validity claims ... Any explicit examination of controversial validity claims requires an exacting form of communication satisfying the conditions of argumentation. (Habermas 1984: I, 22)

However, it is a fact that people act strategically and this is one of the main reasons (along with misunderstandings and lack of knowledge) why the validity claims of universal pragmatics are constantly flouted. Although empirically, reliable communication directed towards understanding is most likely when nothing is at stake for the parties of the dialogue, when the discussion is about matters vitally important to the parties, and their interests are opposed, it takes a great effort not to act strategically. The fact that flouting of validity claims is a common experience is, however, not an argument against the necessity of supposing that as a rule they will be observed if there are no indications to the contrary – suspicion presupposes trust. Hence, even the flouting of the rules governing communication directed towards understanding presupposes the expectation, by the other party, that they are being fulfilled: for no liar keeps faith in the matter about which he lies. He wishes, of course, that the man to whom he lies should place confidence in him; and yet he betrays his confidence by lying to him (St Augustine 1952a: 635).

To introduce Habermas's answer to the second objection, the actual

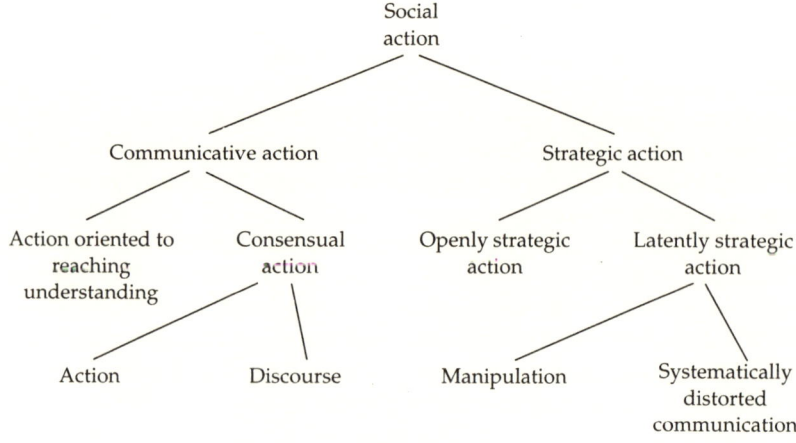

Figure 6

flouting of the validity claims, and thus his concept of discourse, it might be fruitful to represent his own schematization (Habermas 1979: 209) of the relationship between the different kinds of social action. Discourse, as seen in figure 6, is in Habermas a technical term with a restricted meaning. It is a form of communication that may be resorted to the moment it becomes clear that the parties do not agree on a state of affairs or on the legitimacy of norms (or values and significations, see below). Habermas defines discourse as

> that form of communication which is liberated from experience and relieved from the pressure to act. By its structure it is guaranteed that only virtualized validity claims for assertions or recommendations and warnings are discussed. It is further guaranteed that there will be no restrictions as to the participant, subjects, and contributions except maybe with regard to the examination of problematized validity claims, that no force except that of the better argument is exercised, and that, as a result, all motives except that of the cooperative search for truth are excluded. If under these conditions a consensus about the recommendation to accept a norm arises argumentatively, that is, on the basis of hypothetically proposed, alternative justifications, then this consensus expresses a 'rational will.' Since all those affected have, in principle, at least the chance to participate in the practical deliberation, the 'rationality' of the discursively formed will

consist in the fact that the reciprocal behavioral expectations raised to normative status afford validity to a common interest ascertained without deception. The interest is common because the constraint-free consensus permits only what all can want, it is free of deception because even the interpretations of needs in which each individual must be able to recognize what he wants become the object of discursive will-formation. The discursively formed will may be called 'rational' because the formal properties of discourse and of the deliberative situation sufficiently guarantee that a consensus can arise only through appropriately interpreted, generalizable interests, by which I mean needs that can be communicatively shared. (Habermas 1975: 107–8)

This long quotation contains the most important elements of Habermas's concept of discourse. In contradistinction to Foucault, discourse here is a form of communication characterized by virtualization, that is, a discussion of criteria for truth and for the validity of norms, and so on, liberated from the need to act and from the power hierarchy involved in decision making. There is a direct relation back to the Enlightenment and to Kant; for instance, to his pamphlet 'What Is Enlightenment?' in which unswayed dialogue is claimed to be that which brings about the liberation of mankind from minority (*Unmündigkeit*, that is, tutelage to authority). Not surprisingly, Habermas links the different discourses to scholarly and scientific fora, first and foremost to theoretical and practical reflection, to law, and to political institutions within the democratic state. Again, there is a clear difference from Foucault, for whom institutions are first and foremost instruments of constraint and power; Habermas, in certain conditions, sees them as helpful in ensuring the possibility of unswayed discourse.

At first sight, it is as if Foucault and Habermas are describing different worlds, but they are, of course, only analysing different features, and identical features in different ways, of the same historical universe. These features, although opposed to one another, are all found within contemporary Western societies. Nevertheless, in my opinion, it will be very difficult, nay impossible, to reconcile their points of view, because their perspectives are radically different. Even though Habermas is well aware of the constant flouting of the preconditions for communicative action and of its breakdown, he maintains that the presupposition of validity claims is a necessary condition for belonging to and existing within a community. Indeed, he holds that the understanding of the individual self, as a person and as a member of a community, is based on the members' reciprocal recognition that in turn presupposes communicative action and moral argumentation (see Habermas 1993: 48). Conversely, he maintains that an absolute sceptic would not only exclude himself from society, he would grow insane or commit suicide.

This is not the place to get into a long discussion of the relative merits of the two approaches to discourse, let alone of Foucault's and Habermas's thinking in general. In relation to the semiotics of literature, both afford precious insights. Foucault's description of discourse as a 'field of dispersion' is well suited for understanding literature (for instance, the variety and development of genres), as are his ideas of the discontinuous and fragmentary nature of discourse. Furthermore, the relation of discourse to desire is nowhere more conspicuous than in literature, and its constant determination by relations of power, and by the intervention of other discourses, is what the literary historian has always known.

Nevertheless, I will instead follow Habermas's understanding of discourse as a special kind of communication liberated from the pressure to act, whose role it is to debate questions of truth, ethics, and so forth. In the tradition of critical philosophy, Habermas distinguishes theoretical and practical discourse, but he has done little within the realm of Kant's third critique. He does, however, distinguish between norms whose validity is supposed to be capable of rational justification in moral discourse and values that are entrenched in the lifeworld. Values may thus be adhered to whether they can be justified or not from the point of view of rationality – he says that such values are candidates for becoming norms. In this connection he talks about the 'softer' discourses of aesthetics and therapy, that is, discourses that cannot totally be loosened from their relation to the culture-specific, historical lifeworld, and to the emotions, the body, and the emotional colouring of the environment. Thus the place of literature and the arts is indicated in Habermas's conception of discourses. However, that place is not elaborated, with regard either to aesthetics in general or literature in particular, beyond defining the communicative mode or, as he says, the characteristic speech act of literature (and the arts) as expressive (in contradistinction to other kinds of speech acts: constative, regulative, and imperative).

One main difference between Foucault's and Habermas's conception of discourse is the level of specificity. Foucault speaks about medical discourse (and even about the clinical and psychiatric discourses), about juridical, economical, philosophical, religious discourses, and so on. Thus, he situates the concept of discourse on a level close to that of disciplines and genres – or, as he himself admits (see p. 75), he speaks about discourse on different levels. Furthermore, he explicitly questions the familiar divisions of the discursive field:

> Can we accept, as such, the distinction between the major type of discourse, or that between such forms or genres as science, literature, philosophy, religion, history, fiction, etc., and which tend to create certain great historical individualities ...: after all, 'literature' and 'politics' are recent categories, which can be applied to medieval culture, or even to classical culture, only by a retrospective hypothesis, and by an interplay of formal analogies or semantic resemblances; but neither literature, nor politics, nor philosophy and the sciences articulated the field of discourse, in the seventeenth or eighteenth centuries, as they did in the nineteenth. (Foucault 1972: 22)

Habermas speaks of discourse in relation to his idea of universal pragmatics and discursive ethics, and consequently his concept is situated on an another level and within another dimension, because it is systematic rather than historical. His idea of discourse is linked with certain questions concerning conditions for comprehensibility, truth, rightness, and truthfulness, and consequently there will only be a limited number of discourses (to my knowledge he has, however, not specified the number). His idea of discourse is valuable because it allows both a systematic study of the presuppositions and conditions that discussions of truth and ethics should respect and a historical and comparative study of the actual traditions as regards these subjects.

2.2 Discourse and Text

From the points of view of both Foucault and Habermas – and in general – it is essential to distinguish between discourse and text. Whether discourse is defined as a specific form of dialogue governed by certain procedures or as a heterogeneous group of constraints and rules, practices, institutions, and power relations, it exists on a different level from that of the individual text, and also on a different level from that of the genres. The relationship between discourse and text is analogous to that between language, as a system, and the individual utterance/text. However, discourse and language do not belong to the same dimension. While language makes speaking and writing possible, discourse attends to the communicative situation and its procedures, to the relation between utterer and interpreter, to the purpose and object of speaking and writing. According to the Danish linguist Louis Hjelmslev:

> [A] language is a semiotic into which all other semiotics may be translated – both all other languages and all other conceivable semiotic structures. This translatability rests on the fact that languages, and they alone, are in a position to form any purport whatsoever; in language and only in language we 'can work over the inexpressible until it is expressed.' ... It is an all but obvious conclusion that the basis lies in the unlimited possibility of forming signs and the very free rules for forming units of greater extension (sentences and the like) which are true of any language and which, on the other hand, make it possible for a language to allow false, inconsistent, imprecise, ugly, and unethical formulations as well as true, consistent, precise, beautiful, and ethical formulations. The grammatical rules of a language are independent of any scale of values, logical, aesthetic, or ethical; and, in general, a language is independent of any specific purpose. (Hjelmslev 1953: 70)

It might, of course, be asked whether language, even as a system, is immune to speech, that is, communication and dialogue, and whether it may be possible, maybe even easy, to find vestiges of speech use within the system itself. Nevertheless, Hjelmslev is certainly right that languages possesses neutrality as regards true and false and right and wrong; and in neither Foucault's nor Habermas's view is this the case for discourse.[3]

Discourse, then, is a set of procedures and regulatory devices that are bound up with the purposes and objects of text production, and thus it governs (parts of) the individual text. Furthermore, according to Habermas, discourse is a specific communicative situation within which the pressure to act is suspended in order to undertake a principled discussion of the validity of given positions. Discourse, in this sense, means resorting to a meta-level to inquire into the presuppositions of knowledge, techniques and capabilities, ethics, and how to reconstruct the past. The outcome of such discussion and reflection will typically be texts, but also, for instance, common rules of conduct and other practices. Thus, just like language, discourses are manifested in texts and are especially visible in their self-exegesis.

Moreover, just as discourse may contain several semiotic systems, so texts may certainly contain several discourses. The eminent literary scholar Northrop Frye distinguishes a certain kind of literary texts that he calls encyclopedic. According to Frye, the Bible is a prime example. In principle it is a sacred narrative of the creation and fall of man, through the redemption of mankind by Christ, to apocalypse, doom, and eternity. But evidently it is much more complex and rich than that. Frye describes the origin and development of sacred texts in this way:

> The pull of ritual is toward pure narrative, which, if there could be such a thing, would be automatic and unconscious repetition. We should notice too the regular tendency of ritual to become encyclopedic. All the important recurrences in nature, the day, the phases of the moon, the seasons and solstices of the year, the crises of existence from birth to death, get rituals attached to them, and most of the higher religions are equipped with a definitive total body of rituals suggestive, if we may put it so, of the entire range of potentially significant actions in human life. (Frye 1966: 93)

Such texts cover, even from Foucault's point of view, almost any imaginable kind of discourse, and although most texts are less encyclopedic, only absolutely specialized ones will be confined to one discourse.

The relationship between text and discourses is dialectic, otherwise discourses would not change. Discourses – that is, complex dialogic procedures with their rules and conventions for representation and argumentation – may be flouted by the individual text, among other things by bringing in modes of description and reasoning from foreign discourses.

2.3 The Four Discourses

What is, however, the number of discourses? Following Habermas's line of thought, I will argue for a limited number. In fact, in his early work Habermas analyses what he calls cognitive interests that are bound up with the actual life, survival, and development of communities, with labour, social interaction, and communication; and these interests constitute different and specific kinds of knowledge formations. He distinguishes the technical interest that constitutes the empirical-analytic sciences, primarily the natural sciences, but also certain aspects of the social sciences. Sciences of understanding, or hermeneutic sciences, are related to practical interest, to the extent they serve the understanding of the development of social formations. Finally, the emancipatory interest is at the basis of critical sciences directed towards the unravelling of societal repression and distortion of interaction and communication (his examples are psychoanalysis and the critique of ideology by emancipatory social sciences; see Habermas 1971)

Here a slightly different approach will be attempted, an approach, however, that agrees with that of Habermas in the important supposition that knowledge is bound up with the basic interests of communities and their members. In order to argue for a rather limited number of discourses, let us imagine a traditional, non-secular, oral culture; not any specific society, but an ideal type. What would be the minimal number of discourses necessarily operative within such a relatively simple community? Let us suppose a hierarchy of orally transmitted texts to exist that constitutes the collective memory of such a society (and according to Lotman, culture may be defined as the collective non-hereditary memory of a community; see Lotman and Uspensky 1978: 210–32). At the top of this hierarchy is mythical, religious discourse and the texts related to it; the texts representing other types of discourse will be forced to conform to the teaching of these religious texts. In such a case a certain uniformity of thought will prevail, not only imposing limits on what can be said and transmitted, but also forming an interpretive pattern according to which structures of social relations, incidents, events, and changes may be understood.

Although what we will have in such a society will actually be religious texts, I would not term the type of discourse that these texts chiefly belong to religious or mythical (cf. Northrop Frye p. 89). I would prefer to call it theoretical in order to underscore that its subject, purpose, and function are to explain existence, including the universe, the world, and the place of man within them. My reason is that mythology and religion are not necessarily the only candidates to fulfil this purpose and function. What has sometimes been called the Platonic revolution was one of philosophy's attempts to substitute itself as the source of true knowledge. In the Western societies of today, moreover, many people think that science constitutes true theoretical knowledge and should be the arbiter in questions concerning universe, world, and man. The point is that one discourse may house different, and often contradictory, ideas, hypotheses, and belief systems because there are competing explanations attempting to answer identical or similar questions. In addition to theoretical discourse, at least three other types of discourse will exist: technical, practical, and historical discourse.

Technical discourse will regulate and is influenced by the texts concerned with the maintenance and improvement of the material reproduction of society; for instance, the handing down of knowledge about hunting and/or agricultural skills, the preparation of food, the manufacturing of clothing, and so on. Technical discourse is concerned with material production at large. Its most important questions are how do we manage to procure or produce this and that, and which is the most expedient and least costly way of doing it. Thus, technical discourse is concerned with feasibility and means, with how to obtain the results wished for by mastering outer nature.

Practical discourse influences texts explaining and regulating the social structure and interaction of society, the relationship between groups and individuals, between men and women and adults and children, in short, the explicit and implicit laws, rules, conventions, and moral standards of interaction. Offending against what is thus laid down will be followed by sanctions, by punishment, or by disapproval.

Historical discourse regulates texts concerning tribes, clans, families, and individuals, and texts about events and places in the surrounding world. The texts belonging to historical discourse include chronologies, genealogies, topographical descriptions, and chronicles relating the past of the community. Historical discourse offers a partial explanation of the present as a consequence of the past (however, always at least implicitly in cooperation with theoretical discourse). Further, again in collaboration with theoretical discourse, historical discourse may also reveal the destiny of the community and thus teach about future action. Indeed, in traditional societies, theoretical discourse exists as a kind of historical discourse, namely, in myths narrating the origins of the cosmos, the gods, and man. In modern societies, however, there is a difference between historical accounts and systematic accounts of the nature of things (see, e.g., Bruner 1986). This difference makes the distinction between these two discourses necessary, although they both are supposed to comply with the validity claim of truth.

I have not yet mentioned a fifth type of discourse, mimetic – in our case literary – because in this ideal description it has not yet been separated from the other types and institutionalized as an independent form of discourse. For instance, texts that from our point of view would count as primordial forms of literature – such as myths, hunting songs, women' songs, songs connected with rituals, spells, traditions, and so on – would exist, but they would belong to the other four forms of discourse. However, in reality some forms of mimetic discourse are present in all traditional societies (see below).

Furthermore, the four different types of discourse interpenetrate and support each other. Theoretical, here mythical, discourse lends authority to practical discourse (the gods will it so). The different material practices transmitted by technical discourse may likewise be given a ritualistic explanation. Moreover, mythical and historical discourse may constitute a continuum, so that accounts of the recent past are linked with myths of origins; for instance, stating that the gods are the ancestors of the present society. This connection and interpenetration between the four types of discourse will strengthen the order and unity in such a society's daily life, and it will facilitate the preservation and transmission of collective memory, making up for the lack of efficient semiotic systems such as writing.

I also presume that the four types of discourse have, in the opinion of the members of such a culture, the same ontological status; that is, the objects of the different discourses are thought to refer to basically the same reality. This does not mean, of course, that no divisions and distinctions are allowed within such a universe or between the beings that inhabit it. On the contrary, the realms of heaven and underworld may be separated from the earth, and the gods may be immortal and infinitely more powerful than humans. The point is, however, that they are thought to inhabit the same universe, and even if such a universe is divided by borderlines and characterized by different levels of power and perfection, it is conceived as a unified whole.

As mentioned above, the sacred texts of higher religions show a strong tendency to become encyclopedic. Thus, theoretical, in this context religious, discourse may subsume the other forms of discourse by making them part of an overall imaginative and narrative pattern. All four types of discourse can be found, for instance, in the Old Testament, but they are certainly not on equal footing. As regards the mythical and historical discourses this collection contains both a cosmogony and the relation of the history of the tribes of Israel, that is, a kind of historical discourse telling us about events supposed to have really taken place in the way they are related. Scholars warn us, however, not to miss the point that, in this era, historical discourse does not exist as an independent type. Taking the Book of Judges as an example, Frye put this warning as follows:

> This book, a collection of stories about heroes who were originally tribal leaders, has been edited to present the appearance of a history of a united Israel going through a series of crises, all of much the same shape. Israel, in

whom the spirit of apostasy appears to be remarkably consistent, deserts its God, gets enslaved, cries to its God for deliverance, and a 'judge' is sent to deliver it. Here there is a series of different contents, along with a repeating mythical or narrative form which contains them. The heavy emphasis on the structure, where because of the moral interest we are in effect being told the same kind of story over and over again, indicates that the individual stories are being made to fit that pattern. They are as distantly related to historical events as an abstract painting is to realistic representation, and related in a similar way. The priority is given to the mythical structure or outline of the story, not to the historical content. (Frye 1982: 40–1)

As regards what here is called practical discourse, the Book of Deuteronomy contains the Ten Commandments, and these certainly function as laws regulating social interaction between the members of the society in question. They prescribe, however, the relation between Israel and God as well, and social regulation is thought out within the religious context. In the same book of the Old Testament we find similar regulations concerning many subjects, some of which are included under technical discourse; for instance, the list of permitted and forbidden food (14: 1–21), and even the following rule for food preparation: 'Thou shalt not seethe a kid in his mother's milk' (14: 21). Obviously, such regulations, which seem arbitrary from the point of view of a technical discourse (why not cook meat in milk?), are ritualistic: understandable only as taboos connected with the rules for worship in general.

Further, practical discourse, such as texts arguing for the right political order, very often seeks support and authority from historical and, in the last analysis, theoretical discourse. In James I's pamphlet *Trew law of Free Monarchies* (1598), a forerunner of the doctrine of the divine rights of kings, we read:

> Now then, since the erection of this Kingdome and Monarchie among the Iewes, and the law therof may, and ought to bee a paterne to all Christian and well founded Monarchies, as beeing founded by God himselfe, who by his Oracle, and out of his owne mouth gaue the law thereof: what liberty can broiling spirits, and rebellious minds claime iustly to against any Christian Monarchie; since they can claime to no greater libertie on their part, nor the people of God might haue done, and no greater tyranny was euer executed by any Prince or tyrant, whom they can obiect, nor was

here fore-warned to the people of God, (and yet all rebellion countermanded into them). (James I 1965: 55)

James proceeds from founding his argument on history to arguing from ontology: the nature of the world is guaranteed by God. Thus, in non-theoretical texts theoretical discourse may assume supremacy in relation to the other discourses.

Another question is whether it is always necessary to distinguish four types of discourse whose texts make up the collective memory of a culture. Wouldn't it be possible for a culture to survive with only two types of discourse, technical and practical? First of all, even if we are here considering a simplified model, not a specific culture, it is nevertheless an empirical fact that theoretical and historical discourses are integrated in all known traditional cultures. One might still wonder, however, whether a culture really needs these two types of discourse to survive. As to historical discourse I do not doubt that it is absolutely necessary. Skills and norms, that is, technical and practical discourse, are not sufficient for the survival of a given culture, because even if they might make production and interaction possible, they could not ensure cultural identity. Identity requires a sense of belonging to a past that is supposed to be common to the members of a community, and historical discourse offers such a common horizon.

Whether any specific form of theoretical discourse (e.g., mythological and religious discourses) is a necessary part of collective memory is quite another question – a loaded and controversial one at that. Traditional religious discourse normally fulfils several functions. It relates the cause and origins of cosmos and of man; it informs about forces operating in the universe and within man, and it teaches about what is right and wrong, to a greater or lesser extent prescribing the actual behaviour of believers. Because religious discourse exists primarily as narratives, it may also enlighten us as to the ultimate fate of cosmos, mankind, including ourselves.

In our culture religious discourse has lost its monopoly. It exists together with, or has been replaced by, a plurality of other subtypes of theoretical discourse, such as philosophical ontologies and theories of knowledge, the different sciences, which attempt to give different answers to questions about origins, causes, and relationships within the universe and human cultures. In most of these subtypes of theoretical discourse, a narrative element still exists (you can tell, or attempt to tell, the 'story' of the universe from the *Big Bang* to the present whimper).

However, compared to full-fledged religious discourse these discourses are characterized by de-anthropomorphization and demythologization, and their scope is more limited. They offer more elaborate answers to more narrow questions. It must be remembered, however, that the importance of religious discourse varies enormously within different regions of the world and within different groups within the same society. Nevertheless, even if the future survival of religious discourse as a publicly recognized form of theoretical discourse is uncertain, it is certain that some form of theoretical discourse will always subsist.

First, hypotheses about relationships, about the almost infinite and bewilderingly complex ways in which matter is organized and functions, are necessary to develop technical discourse, because doing, the objective of technical discourse, is dependent on, at least, a partial theoretical understanding of the nature of the field in question. Second, practical discourse has been, and will always be, dependent on theoretical discourse. When pro-lifers are killing pro-choicers in order to stop the implementation of free abortion, questions belonging to theoretical discourse are at the bottom of the matter. The justification of abortion and murder respectively is based upon different hypotheses about the nature of man (and about the eventual existence of a Supreme Being). This example also shows the curious, but very real and important, relationship between theories and emotions. Consequently, theoretical discourse will subsist because it answers an indestructible, presumably specifically human, desire for explanations concerning almost everything imaginable: cosmos, society, interpersonal relationships, the environment, the body, the working of the brain/mind, and so on.[4]

The four discourses are interrelated, always influencing one another. Nevertheless, as to their subject, purpose, and objective they are distinguishable. The purpose of theoretical discourse is to explain the nature of things regardless of the exploration, or even exploitation, of its knowledge. It is concerned with true descriptions and the conditions for obtaining them. Technical discourse is concerned with doing, with discussing the means of bringing about changes in the physical world through material production. The link between these two discourses is very strong: both because they influence each other and because theoretical discourse offers another perspective on the object of technical discourse, the material world.

The purpose of practical discourse is to debate, and arrive at decisions about, the right regulation of human interaction. Such a debate is related to theoretical discourse because, among other things, it borrows ideas of human nature from it. It is, however, also closely related to historical discourse, because regulation of interaction presupposes an analysis of the interconnectedness and sequentiality of events. The relationship between technical and practical discourse is potentially agonistic. Technical discourse is here defined as applying to outer nature, as being the discourse that discusses how to master and transform the environment to serve the purposes of human needs. Already at this point technical and practical discourse may become agonistic (e.g., concerning the defence of animals' rights). A second, more serious, source of conflict between them is the application of result-oriented techniques to human interaction, that is, using strategic measures (e.g., manipulation, concealment, force) in order to make others serve the particular interests of individuals or groups. When used in human interaction, technical discourse is identified as instrumental rationality.

The object of historical discourse is the narration of the changes over time concerning persons, groups, peoples and nations, regions and continents, but also institutions, disciplines, concepts, and so forth. Its purpose is to create links between different objects, events, and states of affairs in time and space. A specific purpose is to connect the present with the past in order to discover the historical basis of present identity. Historical discourse investigates the concatenation of events at different levels and the structures based on and determining mental and actional habits and their interaction. It also inquires into whatever may reverse and break up sections of a society or society at large, including the element of chance always present in human action.

Obviously, historical discourse also treats the history of the other discourses. Over the course of time the relation between theoretical and historical discourse has changed. In premodern cultures theoretical discourse most often was embedded within a historical narrative, that is, within sacred history. In modern times the function of historical discourse as a form of theoretical discourse has receded. It seems impossible, however, that it should disappear, because emergence, change, decay, and disappearance constitute life.

These four discourses are committed to describe, truly and truthfully, the nature of things and man; to discover how humans should interact with nature; to describe forms and norms of human interaction in the past and present; to debate the right norms and forms of interaction in future communities; and, finally, to discover and explain the interconnections between different objects, events, and states of affairs of the past, that is, reliably to narrate what has, or is supposed to have, happened.

These discourses are, in Habermas's words, 'liberated from experience and relieved from the pressure to act'; they are only governed by the four validity claims postulated by universal pragmatics – the claims that have just been rehearsed in the preceding paragraph. It seems, however, that, in addition to the four discourses treated above, another kind of discourse is needed, one that is also, to some extent, liberated from these claims themselves, namely, mimetic discourse, or to narrow the field down to the present investigation, literary discourse.

2.4 Literary Discourse

Literature is simultaneously closely allied to and radically different from theoretical, and especially from practical and historical, discourse. Indeed, Habermas opposes the levelling of the distinction between philosophy and literature, and the distinction between logic and rhetoric (see Habermas 1987: 185–210). Literature resembles philosophy and rhetoric by relating the actions and passions of human beings situated within a certain universe imagined to exist. Literature is certainly anthropomorphic and mythical, and it is concrete and specific, telling about named persons and places. Indeed, in certain cases it might be difficult to tell whether a given text is mythical or fictional or historical or fictional because we do not have infallible criteria to distinguish between them.[5] On the other hand, literary texts seem to be radically different from both theoretical and historical texts, and although it is risky business to attempt a definition of literature (cf. Todorov 1990: 1–12), I will nevertheless point out some useful, if not infallible, criteria. My point of departure will be the model of dialogic semiosis expounded in the preceding chapter, including the four validity claims of universal pragmatics discussed above (cf. figure 5).The features that in my view characterize literature are (1) fictionality, (2) poeticity, (3) inquisitoriality, (4) licence, and (5) contemplation.

These five features distinguish in most, but not all, cases a literary from a non-literary text. In non-literary language use the text refers, normally, to a common universe, most often a lifeworld, that exists, has existed, or is supposed to exist in the future, while in a literary text the reference is most often to a fictional universe of discourse. Consequently, one of the most salient features of a literary text is its fictionality, understood as (the production of) a hypothetical state of affairs or mind that is ontologically different from the experiential universe within which we live. The fictionality of the universes of literary texts very often furthers their representative force; they become exemplary. Thus, (1) fictionality and exemplariness will most often characterize literature as regards its universe. Whereas the plane of expression and the content plane in non-literary texts are used instrumentally, in the sense that they serve specific communicative purposes and tasks, the structuring of both expression and content planes achieves a certain relative autonomy in literary texts. This means an additional, or surplus, coding of the elements of speech compared to non-literary text, (2) its poeticity (metre, rhyme, euphony, different compositional principles, thematic symmetry, etc.). As to rightness, texts functioning in everyday interaction most often imply accepted norms and values. In the rarer cases in which they question and break up consensus, they become part of practical discourse, that is, overtly argumentative – or of power play.

Literary texts, however, very often contain full-fledged ethical argumentation and reflections. In rhetoric there is a distinction between general and specific questions; for example, whether 'a man should marry' and 'Cato should marry.' However, according to Quintilian, 'in every special question the general question is implicit, since the *genus* is logically prior to the *species*' (Quintilian III, v; 1920: I.401). Thus, in order to decide whether Cato should marry, it should be decided whether marriage is desirable. In literature the debate concerning the general question will often be covert because the story told, or the situation and mood represented, becomes an example (one of the proofs of rhetoric) and thus an individualized, narrativized, and specifically situated argument. Therefore, literature combines inquisition (in several of its meanings) and example, so that adherence to common standards of rightness is often replaced by its (3) inquisitoriality. The roles of the utterer and addresser in literary and non-literary texts are different in many respects. One very important difference lies in the commitments faced by the utterer. Whereas the commitments of the utterer in non-fictional, serious discourse are to tell the truth, to be sincere, and to follow the rules and norms of social interaction, these commitments have no, or only a weakened, force in literary texts. The author is not tied down to the particularities of the actual; he or she is, more or less, free to assume the point of view of different narrators that may be reliable or unreliable (see Booth 1961).[6] He may cast doubt on or reject the values and norms of his society – although often to his own peril (see chapter 6). These features constitute what could be called the (4) licence (*licentia poetica*) of the literary text. Correspondingly, the reader of literature is not given any possibility of intervening in what is narrated, and, consequently, what is told her in the text does not oblige her in any way, although it may strongly recommend or reject a given position and behaviour. This means that, in the reading of literature, (5) a contemplative attitude is furthered. This preference for contemplation is classical (e.g., Aristotle). The testimony of Quintilian has a certain relation to our subject, when he says that an orator who stops pleading does not cease to be an orator. He continues: 'Perhaps the highest of all pleasures is that which we derive from private study, and the only circumstances under which the delights of literature are unalloyed are when it withdraws from action, that is to say from toil, and can enjoy the pleasure of self-contemplation' (Quintilian II, xviii, 1920: I.347).

Obviously other types of discourse share one or more of the five features mentioned above. A text belonging to theoretical discourse, such as a philosophical tract, is, most often, non-instrumental; a moral exhortation very often uses examples; a joke is insincere; a ceremonial speech often has strong rhetorical and poetic qualities; and a daydream has, indeed, many fictional elements.

These five features of literature – (1) the fictionality of its universe, (2) the poeticity of its language, (3) its inquiry into norms and values by assuming an exemplary function, (4) the non-committal expressiveness of its utterer, and (5) the non-committal contemplation of its interpreter – seem to characterize it as an institution and set it apart from other types of discourse. In this way literature has achieved a relative autonomy. It goes without saying, however, that even if literature is mediately, not immediately, related to our lifeworld and to our actions, it is not valuable because it bears no relation to our world, but because of the specific way it *is* related to it.

Most often the mimetic nature of literature is understood as its representation of reality. I certainly subscribe to this understanding of literature (cf. chapter 3), but in literature from antiquity on, mimesis has also been understood in another way, as the imitation of other texts, of the classics. Sometimes the classical poet's work is identified with nature itself,[7] but even if this is not the case the importance of the classics as exemplars, models to imitate, is evident throughout literary history. The imitation of the classics, however, only has to do with the internal structure of literary mimesis. There is, in addition, the external influence on literature, namely, the fact that literary discourse imitates other discourses: less often technical discourse, although examples can be found,[8] but certain kinds of theoretical discourse, for instance, mythical discourse. Furthermore a good deal of literature contains, or is even conceived as, ethical debate or legal proceedings. Finally, the imitation of historical discourse by literary discourse is obvious. Indeed, where decisive information has been lacking, agreement has sometimes been hard to reach as to which discourse a given text belongs to.

But why do we need a kind of discourse that imitates the other discourses and one that is only indirectly bound to the validity claims that make communicative action possible? An attempt to answer this question should follow an exposition of the different dimensions of literary discourse, not precede it (see the Conclusion).

2.5 Literature Becoming Literature

Although it does not invalidate the distinctions between the five discourses, Foucault's claim that literature is a modern concept that retroactively is projected onto the texts of earlier times has to be taken seriously. What follows are some points concerning the historical changes in the distinctions between different kinds of texts.

There are two main reasons why it is difficult to point to the moment when literature is separated from, for example, religious texts, songs related to ritual or work, and historical narrative. First, on the view presented here, texts are most often plurifunctional, that is, they fulfil more than one function and belong to more than one type of discourse. Every time we classify a text as literature, history writing, a tract on morality, and so forth, we do it according to its predominant function and its predominant structural features related to this function. For the most part we classify it for very good reasons, because texts serving specific purposes are influenced by the role they fulfil and by the logic of the institution to which they belong. This is why it would be hard, indeed almost impossible and certainly boring, to read the *Code Napoléon* as a work of literature. It clearly belongs to a specific part of practical discourse; it was designed to play a decisive role in the functioning of the French legal system, as a set of guidelines for and constraints on juridical argumentation and for passing judgment and sentence.

The recording of every trial, however, contains a narrative: something extraordinary is supposed to have happened, but it remains to be decided which kind of action occurred, whether it was accidental or premeditated, whether legal or illegal, whether punishable or not, and if so what the punishment should be. And such narratives easily travel from the annals of legal history to literature or are imitated by it (trials have always been great shows, even before O.J. Simpson; see below).

2.5.1 After Dark

The difficulty of pointing to the roots of separation between literary discourse and the other discourses is due, in addition to the plurifunctionality of texts, to the fact that somehow such a distinction has always been operative. The anthropologist William Bascom investigated the classification systems of a number of tribal societies, and found that, in all but one, there was a designated distinction between two kinds of texts: texts relating the (mythical) origins of the universe, the gods, and the tribe itself and its further history, that is, what we would call myths and legends (or sagas); and texts that told about humorous, exaggerated, excessive, and inordinate events, that is folk tales or tall tales (and, according to Bascom, this distinction was operative even in the tribal society that had no name for it). While the mythical stories were told or recited at any time, but very often related to some kind of ritual, the folk tales were often restricted to being told after dark. They functioned as entertainment while people sat around the fire (see Bascom 1965/84).

Further, it is interesting that the classical scholar Walter Burkert, taking Propp's *Morphology of the Folktale* as his point of departure, impudently reduces the thirty-one Proppian functions, or sequence of motifemes, to one verb, *to get*, or rather to the imperative *get*. Burkert continues:

> And this three-letter word does imply quite a complicated program of actions. To 'get' something means: to realize some deficiency, or receive some order to start; to have, or to attain, some knowledge or information about the thing wanted; to decide to begin a search; to go out, to meet partners, in a changing environment, who may prove to be helpful or antagonistic; to discover the object, and to appropriate it by force or guile, or, in more civilized circumstances, by negotiation; then, to bring back the object, while it still may be taken away by force, stolen, or lost. Only after all that, with success established, has the action of 'getting' come to its end. (Burkert 1979: 15)

Burkert goes on to claim that, in fact, this *program of actions*, as he calls it, covers Propp's functions from number 8 to 31, and says further:

> In fact if we ask where such structure of sense, such a program of actions, is derived from, the answer must evidently be: from the reality of life, nay, from biology. Every rat in search of food will incessantly run through all these 'functions,' including the peak of agitation at the moment of success: then the rat has to run fastest to find a safe place before its fellow rats take its prey away. In the Propp series there is the motifeme sequence called the 'magical flight,' which often constitutes the most thrilling part of a fairy-tale, when the magical object, or the bride, has been gained and the previous owner starts a pursuit. This probably is just a transformation of the action pattern described. (Ibid.)

Burkert is, of course, well aware that he might be accused of a *reductio ad absurdum*, but this truly audacious correlation of narrative structure with biological needs and biocybernetics is worth considering. What Burkert offers is nothing less than a hypothesis about the biological foundation of fictional narrative. And, although it is audacious, it is also a reformulation of a well-known idea about the function of fiction, namely, the psychoanalytical one. According to psychoanalysis, such tales formulate deep-rooted conflicts between the individual and the community, but (in case of the folk tale) offer a solution that is a wish fulfilment. Burkert's hypothesis does not put the emphasis on the didactic elements in the tales, but he describes the audience's response to such tales as highly drive-cathected:

> The deepest deep structure of a tale would, then, be a series of imperatives: 'get,' that is: 'go out, ask, find out, fight for it, take and run.' And the reaction of an audience to a tale is in perfect accordance with this: under the spell of a thrilling tale, we will ourselves perform one by one the actions described – in idle motion, of course. Thus communication in the form of action sequences, in the form of a tale, is so basic and elementary that it cannot be traced to 'deeper' levels; we may note, in passing, the parallel with dreaming, which also involves action patterns in idle motion. (Ibid.: 16).

Thus, it may well be that the folk tale, like its older unruly cousins, dream and daydream, has been there from the beginnings of human communication. Such tales have been recognized as fictional narratives that do not tell what happened according to probability and necessity but, in spite of these, according to our hearts' content. By this hypothesis, literature as fiction is an anthropological constant.

2.5.2 Literature and the Other Discourses

Nevertheless, even if fiction is omnipresent, there is still a changing relationship between literature and religious and historical discourse. Historical discourse is one of the four basic discourses; in some way most non-literary texts belong to it (although most often in combination with the other discourses). Indeed, most texts tell about states of affairs and of mind, about decisions, actions, events, and so on. History, however, exists on many levels and is of many kinds: micro- and macrohistory, histories of events and of mentality, to mention a few kinds and trends within professional history writing, historiography. Professional history writing itself rests on testimonies, interviews, documents, monuments – in principle, on every scrap of recorded life, thought, and action.

However, history writing, theoretical writing, and literature are not necessarily manifested in separate kinds of texts; and their overlapping or distinctness cannot even be described as the result of a linear development, although, within modern high cultures, they are distinguished and each is assigned to one or more institutions.

This tendency towards distinctness is part of a growing division of labour in societies based on agriculture and its related technical innovations (e.g., irrigation) that necessitated large-scale cooperation; example, in the digging of canals and in the building of cities. Instrumental in this development was the exteriorization of memory through the fixation of the system of numerals and the basic arithmetic operations – and through writing (on writing see Gelb 1952).

Nevertheless, it is, for example, very difficult to date the moment, indeed even the century, in which the Homeric epics became literature, that is, came to be considered fictions by an audience and readership at large. It is certain, however, that for some time they functioned in a different way because they were supposed to contain the truth about the gods and the history of the Achaeans. One answer to the question about their transition from religio-historical narratives to fictional ones is that it happened from the sixth to the fourth century BC. Already in the sixth we find the allegorical reading of Greek mythology, for instance, the adventures of Hercules by Hecaetaeus. In the fifth century BC there followed the moral criticism of the amorality of the Homeric gods by Xenophanes, who also claimed that the gods of lions would look like lions. This denial of anthropomorphized gods constitutes a step towards monotheism. In the fourth century we find both the critique of poetry, Homer not excepted, by Plato, and the outspoken skepticism of Euripides about the very myths he was staging in the theatre; as in the following passage from *Iphigenia in Aulis*. The chorus is talking about the misey caused by Helen and concludes: '[It is] all because of you, child of the long-necked swan, if the story they tell is true, that Zeus changed his form to a winged bird. Or are these things just stories, without point or truth, brought to mankind from the pages of the poets?' (Euripides 1966: 333). Concomitant with the sharper distinction between fact and fiction, philosophers and historians began to propagate the view that fiction is deceptive and harmful. In the first century AD Plutarch, for instance, narrates the following anecdote about Thespis and Solon (who was himself a poet):

> Solon ... went to see Thespis himself ... act: and after the play was done, he addressed him, and asked him if he was not ashamed to tell so many lies before such a number of people; and Thespis replying that it was no harm to say or do so in play, Solon vehemently struck his staff against the ground: 'Ah,' said he, 'If we honour and commend such play as this, we shall find it some day in our business. (Plutarch 1864: 115)

Whether or not Solon did confront Thespis in this way, the anecdote reveals one major attitude towards fictional literature in antiquity, an attitude most forcefully argued by Plato (also an author and poet): namely, that literature and the arts are harmful for two principal reasons. First, since the imitators, poets and painters et al. possess no real insight into the essence of things, their works are trice removed from truth; the carpenter's knowledge of beds is superior to that of the painter and closer to their idea (see *The Republic*, book X). This lack of insight means that poetry and the arts are objectively spreading false knowledge harmful to a credulous audience. Second, since the extreme is easier to imitate, and the sensational arouses more curiosity than the normal, poets present and celebrate strong and, very often, immoral passions and disturbed states of mind instead of praising the serene and the moral. Thus, the passions of the audience are roused. The influence of literature on the tender minds of youth, therefore, is definitely thought to be malign.

The other major tradition, that of Aristotle, counters these accusations by arguing, first, that the instinct for imitation is innate and that much can be learned from contemplating literature and art. They may both embody the general features of objects and of human behaviour. Further, the one-sided perspective through which the object may be seen (e.g., either tragedy or comedy) may be edifying or relaxing. Second, it is precisely the role of tragedy to stir and relieve the audience's passions of pity and fear (or lamentation and terror) through catharsis. In the later short anonymous tract on comedy, *The Coislinian Tractate*, it is said that the mother of tragedy is grief, while that of comedy is laughter, and that comedy 'through pleasure and laughter' effects 'the purgation of the like emotions' (in *Readers' Encyclpedia* 1969: 950). Both the Platonic and the Aristotelian traditions presuppose, however, that literature, whether regarded favourably or unfavourably, is understood as a kind of discourse in its own right: it is different from, but closely related to, historical and theoretical discourse.

Nonetheless, the different reactions of intellectuals to the fictionality and emotive nature of literature is one thing; the status of, for instance, the Homeric epics within society at large is another. In spite of the fact that the truth of some parts of the poems was questioned, they still held their ground as a common reference point for the educated; indeed, for centuries they used the poems to learn to read, in spite of the attacks of Plato and others.

One important reason for the status of these epics is a concept of history different from ours. Fiction and history are correlative concepts, and in antiquity and the Middle Ages the concept of history was much more inclusive than today's. Still, the issue is complicated. Already Thucydides thought that the distinctive feature of history writing, in contradistinction to literature, is its truth and trustworthiness:

> However, I do not think that one will be far wrong in accepting the conclusions I have reached from the evidence which I have put forward. It is better evidence than that of the poets, who exaggerate the importance of their themes, or of the prose chroniclers, who are less interested in telling the truth than in catching the attention of their public, whose subject-matter, owing to the passage of time, is mostly lost in unreliable streams of mythology. (Thucydides 1972: I, 47)

Although Aristotle followed this way of distinguishing between history and literature ('The real difference is this, that one tells what happened and the other what might happen' [*Poetics*, 1451b]), a strict distinction between myth and the actual past did not exist. Individual authors often worried about the myths, however, and hence the rationalistic and allegorical interpretations of mythology. There were two reasons for fuzzy boundaries between history and fiction: first, only a small minority had mastered writing and reading, and thus, in spite of writing, the oral element in culture still prevailed. Further, also for those who had mastered writing, what was written had per se a claim to authority (one wonders whether this is not true even today). This awe for the written was strengthened by a respect for tradition and authority at large. Consequently, the response to conflicting historical information would very often be an attempt at conciliation. Second, history writing itself was allowed to employ imagination in order to dramatize the story and bring out its political and ethical significance. Even if the strict Thucydides disliked the fact that Herodotus brought tall tales into his history, he continued his practice of writing the speeches of the main actors of history. Indeed, about one-quarter of the *Pelopennesian War* is made up of speeches of his own making, and the Mytelinean debate has even a dramatic, dialogical structure (see Thucydides 1972: III, 212–23).[9]

With the advent of Christianity, according to H.-R. Jauss, something interesting happens regarding the distinction between reality and fiction, namely, 'a sense of reality that, in contrast to the classical notion of reality derived from the immediate evidence of human knowledge, might best be characterized as an indifference to the probable in comparison with the contrafactual truth of Christian religious conviction' (Jauss 1989: 6). Thus, a distinction was made between the true stories of the Gospels, the histories of the martyrs, the miracles of the saints, and the false and superstitious tales of the ancient gods and heroes. Nevertheless, there was also a constant conciliatory attempt to harmonize Greek and Roman thinking with the teachings of Christianity, but under the supremacy of the latter. Furthermore, in spite of this distinction, both historiography and epic poetry mix the historical and the legendary without worrying about it. The great Catholic poet, Dante, in order to exemplify the sins punished in Hell, uses not only figures from the history of Christianity, from classical antiquity, and from his own time but also figures from the legends of chivalry (Tristan in *Inferno*, V, 67). Even a minor character from Virgil's *Aeneid*, Rhipeus, is one of the good princes in Canto XX of *Paradiso* (although the eagle itself declares his presence incredible). Even if the *Divine Comedy* is a work of art, this example shows that Dante's encyclopedic work, although in one sense it is supposed to represent truth, does not concern itself much with the ontological status of its figures (see Jauss 1989: 7).

The church most often frowned upon literary fiction, professing that man should spend his tears on his Saviour's sufferings, not on the secular and carnal loves of knights and damsels. Nevertheless, the church recognized the uses of imagination, both in the description of the creation and of God (and God could only be conceived by means of analogy, *analogia entis*) and as a means to bring home an edifying message. Hence, the use of *exempla*, collections of which were made for the clergy, who used them in sermons (e.g., the late-thirteenth-century *Gesta romanorum*). *Exempla* are stories followed by a *moralisatio* or *reduccio*, that is, an allegorical interpretation identifying the historical or fictional (it did not matter) characters as representing either the ethical or unethical actions of mankind in general or the actions of the Devil, Christ, and God.

What makes the reception and experience of literary, religious, and historical texts in the Middle Ages special, and different from ours, is a constant referral, a constant analogization from one kind of text to another under the supremacy of the religious and ethical interpretation. It is not only a question of fiction paying lip service to the authorities to stay out of trouble (although this certainly was an important motive); there is also a metaphysical assumption that each part of the universe, and every action on earth, can be related to and comment on one another because they are all part of a grand design.

Consequently, when the self-conscious twelfth-century writers of the Arthurian romances (e.g., Chrétien de Troyes) protest that their stories are valuable because they are instructive and have a moral, their protest is not only ironic and defensive, it can also be seen to have some truth to it. Even with the Arthurian matter (*la matière de Bretagne*), which is most fairy-tale-like, there is a give and take between entertainment and morality. Indeed, some of these stories, by writers such as Chrétien de Troyes and Wolfram von Eschenbach, are used to represent the superiority of the religious quest over that of chivalry (both have a *Parcival*). Further, the Arthurian matter is rewritten to serve explicit religious purposes (e.g., the huge, anonymous *Lancelot Prose*, around 1225).

One important feature of the thinking and the aesthetic principles of the High Middle Ages is the preference for similarity, not a similarity with social and physical reality (as in nineteenth-century realism), but similarity understood as a principle of allegorical interpretation. Therefore, with few changes, the same stories could be used again and again and be made to testify to the general and moral order of things, an order within which there was room for the carnal and the grotesque as well.

However, not only in the Middle Ages was the state of fiction precarious; in the Renaissance the same misgivings about the invented flourished. William Nelson sums up the situation as follows:

> Freedom to invent whole stories is limited to the genres of allegory and beast fable, dramatic comedy, dialogue, and such tales as Lucian and Apuleius told – Milesian tales ... For the rest, while the author is required to observe, more or less respectfully, whatever is known or generally accepted about the past, the less substantial the knowledge the greater the admissible admixture of invention. The way opens, therefore, for fiction set in the far away or long ago to take the form of history without pretending to be history, to present itself as a work of the imagination. When such stories are documented (as *Utopia* and *Garguntua* are), the documentation becomes a jest. (Nelson 1973: 48)

The lines of defence, according to Nelson, were much the same as those used in the Middle Ages, namely, that fiction, 'like ancient myth and Biblical parable, was a rhetorical device for expressing moral, religious, or historical truths, useful because it was delightful and memorable' (ibid.: 49). References were also made to Aristotle's definition of poetry as valuable because it represents the typical, or the world as it should be; as a result, literature is instructive. Nevertheless the malaise concerning fiction was not overcome. Even if Spenser's apologetic attitude about his 'continued Allegory, or darke conceit,' *The Faerie Queene*, should be taken with a grain of salt, nevertheless, his preface stresses the instructional purpose of the work:

> The generall end therefore of all the booke is to fashion a gentleman or noble person in vertuous and gentle discipline: Which for that I conceived shoulde be most plausible and pleising, being coloured with an historicall fiction, the which the most part of men delight to read, rather for variety of matter, then for profite of the ensample ...
>
> To some I know this Methode [i.e., the allegorical method] will seeme displeasaunt, which have rather have good discipline delivered plainly in way of precepts, or sermoned at large, as they use, then thus clowdily enwrapped in Allegoricall devises. But such, me seeme, should be satisfide

with the use of these dayes, seeing all thins accounted by their showes, and nothing esteemed of, that is not delightfull and pleasing to comune sense. (Spenser 1966 [1589] 41)

At least on the face of it, literature is still defined as an indirect and, as it were, secondary way of imparting moral knowledge, and its fictionality is – ostensibly – regarded as a dubious means of doing something else: literary discourse as a guise for practical discourse.

Indeed, as late as the eighteenth century Richardson is reluctant to use Bishop Warburton's preface to *Clarissa*, because the bishop treats the novel explicitly as fiction (Nelson 1973: 111). Richardson's worry may have been unwarranted, however, because in the course of this century the audience seems to have come not only to accept fiction in its own right but also to admit and defend its position.[10]

These few and fragmentary remarks concerning the intricacies of the relations of various discourses to one another from antiquity onwards certainly suggest that one should be careful about assuming that the concept, and practice, of writing literature has remained unchanged. This brief sketch does show, however, that distinctions have been operative from the beginning concerning the relation of what is recognized as physical reality, what is recognized and firmly believed to be metaphysical reality, and what is supposed to belong to the fictional world. It also shows that these distinctions constantly have caused frictions and problems, although in ways different from today.

Part Two

The Four Dimensions of the Literary Text

Three

Mimesis: Literature as Imitation and Model

> It is clear, then, ... that the poet must be a 'maker' not of verses but of stories, since he is a poet in virtue of his 'representation,' and what he represents is action.
>
> (Aristotle, Poetics, IX, 1451b)

> Finally, the thousands of fables and fictions, in whose lie men take delight, are human devices, and nothing is to be considered more peculiarly man's own and derived from himself than anything that is false and lying.
>
> (St Augustine [397–426] 1952a: 649)

> 'He [Cid Hamete Benengeli] makes a great point of insisting that everything in the book really happened in the world.'
> 'Exactly. Because the book after all is an attack on the dangers of the make-believe. He couldn't very well offer a work of the imagination to do that, could he? He had to claim that it was real.'
>
> (Auster 1990: 117)

> '... Then I might take a page of your writing, and line it up with what I already have, and do the same thing all over again.'
> Suddenly indignant, Beckett asked, 'You're using other writers' words?'
> 'Words don't have brands on them the way cattle do,' Burroughs said. 'Ever heard of a word rustler?'
> 'You can't do that!' Beckett said. 'You can't take my writing and mix it up with newspapers.'
> 'Well, I've done it,' Burroughs said.
> 'That is not writing,' Beckett snorted, 'it is plumbing.'
>
> (reported in Morgan 1988: 323)

In semiotics, or at least in what Thomas Sebeok calls its major tradition from Hippocrates to Peirce and onwards (see Sebeok 1976: 181 and 1979: 63–4), the sign is first and foremost characterized by its representative function. Peirce takes up the sign definition of the schoolmen: *Aliquid stat pro aliquo*, that is, something [the sign] stands for something (else) [the object].

Likewise, the major conception of literature, from Plato and Aristotle to contemporary works on mimesis such as those of Prendergast (1986) and Gebauer and Wulf (1992), understands literature as representation, although the nature of literary representation is a controversial issue. Experience also seems to corroborate this understanding. Most teachers likely find that young students' understanding of literature – and their primary interest in it – is substantive, that is, they see it as representational, and what it is taken to represent are states of minds and states of affairs. Students are touched, or appalled, by the representation of thoughts and emotions and excited, or bored, by the stories. They claim that literature teaches them about the world and themselves. It represents recognizable and important emotions, thoughts, conditions, conflicts, choices, developments, changes, and solutions, or dissolutions that are existentially relevant to them. Their teachers may, of course, point out that literature need not be representational in the sense of creating a fictional state of mind or a world. However, even though it is a basic tendency of the human mind to engage in, and utterly enjoy, the formation of jingles, rhymes, and nonsense verse, it may well be argued, in an important sense, that non-representational literature is marginal, maybe even non-existent (see chapter 5). The basic reason for this is that one of the main functions of the medium of literature, language, is to represent: to represent states of affairs in the world, certainly, but also to represent the parties of a dialogue to one another, to communicate and explicate meanings. Thus, reality and human interaction stick to words and phrases even before they are used in any concrete, individual speech act. Literature, as well as the other kinds of discourse, necessarily inherits these features.

3.1 Literature as Representation and Fiction

In what follows, the mimetic dimension of literature – literature as representation and imitation – will be analysed by using Peirce's second trichotomy of signs: that is, the distinction between the indexical, the iconic, and the symbolic, applied to literary texts conceived as complex signs. In the previous chapter, the first mentioned of the preliminary criteria of literary discourse was the fictionality of its universe. In the same breath, however, it was said that this criterion is not infallible, and it was pointed out that a daydream, for instance, creates an imaginary universe that shares many features with a fictional one. The same is true of certain kinds of children's play. Further, fictions are created in other media than language, such as paintings, sculptures, comics, and ballet. The distinction between fiction and non-fiction may, however, be dependent on speech, since names and naming play a crucial role in deciding about the fictionality or non-fictionality of a non-linguistic phenomenon. Still, we often classify texts as literature although they clearly refer to former or present states of affairs in the world. Thus, we should not too hastily equate literature and fiction.

Furthermore, although, a novel most often, but not always, 'contains signs whose function is to remind readers that the tale they are being told is imaginary' (Rifattere 1990: 1), such signs are not certain indicators,[1] and thus it is not easy to distinguish between a non-fictional and a fictional universe. Indeed, Peirce may well be right in claiming that

> [t]he real world cannot be distinguished from a fictitious world by any description. It has often been disputed whether Hamlet was mad or not. This exemplifies the necessity of indicating that the real world is meant, if it be meant. Now reality is altogether dynamic, not qualitative. It consists in forcefulness. Nothing but a dynamic sign can distinguish it from fiction. It is true that no language (so far as I know) has any particular form of speech to show that the real world is spoken of. But that is not necessary, since tones and looks are sufficient to show when the speaker is in earnest. These tones and looks act dynamically upon the listener, and cause him to attend to realities. They are, therefore, the indices of the real world. (CP 2.337)

Thus, identifying the reference to ontologically different universes implies not only textual features, but a complex communicative context transcending what can be established by the text in itself; deciding about the status of the universe necessitates background knowledge.

Certain features of indexical signs and their use in fiction will be treated below. Here, however, the distinction between fiction and non-fiction will just be taken for granted, because today our default concept of literature is, de facto, bound up with fiction. A proof of this is that even in reading lyrical poetry in the first person, which according to some scholars[2] (in my opinion wrongly) is taken not to represent a fictional universe, we, nevertheless, think of the poet as assuming a persona. Thus, we have been taught not to identify the voice represented in the text with the voice of the empirical author, although we do not doubt at all that the text was written by him or her – and, consequently, in some sense it must be his or her voice. In poetry, he or she may speak in the first person, but it is a poet speaking, and what is said is not necessarily directly related to empirical reality (for further ways of distinguishing between author and narrator/lyrical I see chapter 5).

3.2 Signs and Universes

Let us approach the question of fictional universes from the viewpoint of indexicality and return to the object of the sign. Are we, from the point of view of Peircean semiotics, justified in talking about signs if they do not represent that which exists? The question may seem facetious, but let us for a moment reflect on what Peirce has to say on this matter. First of all, it should be pointed out that such signs would necessarily have immediate objects because the representation function, the fact that a sign is something that stands for something else, is a *conditio sine qua non* for signhood. But while signs must have immediate objects, it is a fact that not all signs (texts) have dynamical objects, for example, signs that represent a fictional universe of discourse. Peirce seems a little hesitant to recognize such signs, but he grudgingly acknowledges them as follows:

> In order that a thing may be a true sign its proper significate mental effect [i.e., its interpretant] must be *conveyed* from another object which the sign is concerned in indicating and which is by this conveyance the ultimate cause of the mental effect. In order to be the cause of an effect, or *efficient cause*, as the old phrase was, it must either be an existing thing or an actual event. Now such things are only known by observation. It cannot be any part of the mental effect, and therefore can only be known by the collateral observation of the context or circumstances of utterance, or putting forth. But the sign may describe the kind of observation that is appropriate and even indicate how the right object is to be recognized. The meaning of the sign is not conveyed until not merely the interpretant but also this object is recognized. But although the full realization of the meaning requires the actual observation, direct or indirect, of the object, yet a close approach to this may be made by imagining the observation. If the sign is not a *true*, but only a *fictitious* sign, it is the mere semblance of a sign. If, however, it

be so far true as to profess to be in certain respects fictitious, the conditions of a true sign hold in slackened force. (MS 318, 1907: 33–5)

Of course we may shrug at these hesitations of a nineteenth-century philosopher of science, but the interesting point is that Peirce mentions four different ways in which signs may be related to their dynamical objects.

(a) In the first case, the ideal one for Peirce the scientist, the sign uttered by the speaker indicates an object to the hearer and leads to his perceiving it through collateral observation. In other words, the sign has both indicated the (alleged) nature of the object and been instrumental in acquainting the hearer with it to the effect that it may prove a source of an indefinite number of percepts, that is, indexical signs, adding to his knowledge of it. These are favourable conditions of dialogue and inquiry, because description and acquaintance (cf. Russell 1948) are co-present.

(b) In the second case, the sign uttered by the speaker does not immediately lead to an acquaintance with the object. However, it indicates a procedure that may eventually lead to its recognition and it allows hypotheses about it. For instance, through the indication of clues, the hearer may be able to construct the object in his imagination. Without actually having a sensory experience of it, he forms a hypothesis about its nature, a hypothesis that may be falsified when he eventually experiences the object. The scientist, the physician, and the detective construct such objects (cf. below).

(c) In the third case, the sign is uttered with the pretension of indicating an object or a state of affairs, and so forth. It fails, however, to do so, either because it is intentionally put forth to mislead, or because the utterer is mistaken; that is, we are dealing with lies or errors.

(d) The fourth case is interestingly similar to the second. In both cases the sign offers indications of how to make a hypothetical construction of the object. In the second case, however, it is presupposed that such a construction may later be matched against sensory experiences of the object, that is, signs whose source is the dynamical object and not an utterer. In the case of fictitious signs,[3] such a double access to the object is not – and will not be – possible. The fictional object's source is only in the signs uttered by the utterer: 'For the *fictive is* that whose characters depend upon what characters anybody attributes to it' (CP 5.152).

In principle, however, as Peirce points out, we cannot know what kind of universe a text refers to by virtue of the text itself: 'In every proposition the circumstances of its enunciation show that it refers to some collection of individuals or of possibilities, which cannot be adequately described, but can only be indicated as something familiar to both speaker and auditor. At one time it may be the physical universe, at another it may be the imaginary 'world' of some play or novel, at another a range of possibilities' (CP 2.536). This brief description of a universe of discourse makes an important point, namely, that it is not possible to assign a given kind of universe to a text on criteria internal to the text itself (cf. above, p. 115). This means that symbolic signs may indiscriminately refer to universes that are ontologically different (cf. Hjelmslev's remark that language does not care about truth and rightness; see p. 88). Such a universe may be actual, potential, or virtual (a 'virtual X (where X is a common noun) is something, not an X, which has the efficiency (*virtus*) of an X' (CP 6.372). The fictional is a species of the virtual, because a fictional universe is something that in relevant respects has the *virtus* of the actual universe without being part of it. As regards linguistic texts, however, we cannot even tell which kind of universe they refer to without bringing in additional knowledge. Look at these four propositions

   Alexander loves Roxanne
   Charles loves Camilla
   Léon loves Emma
   Donald loves Daisy

Within our contemporary culture most people interested in literature and history would probably associate the two first with historical figures, the third with a French literary masterpiece, and the fourth with the fictional world of Disney, Inc. In the first two cases, we would presume that the persons referred to all belonged to the (same) historical universe of discourse, the first couple to days bygone, while the second one is very much alive, at least according to British newspapers. The third couple are famous adulterers, never met apart from the pages of Flaubert's wonder of a novel. The last couple inhabits the cartoon world – another separate, fictional universe. We notice that while it obviously makes sense to say that the first and second couples belong to the same universe, although they certainly do not inhabit it simultaneously, it makes no sense to say that Léon and Emma and Donald and Daisy Duck belong to the same universe. While there is only one existing historical universe, an infinite number of fictional universes exist, because virtual worlds may be produced at will, by a creative fiat.

Two points should be made, however. First, without further indexical specification our classifications are, in fact, unwarranted. Charles and Camilla may be fictional figures (indeed some would claim that they have crossed the borderline into fiction, although strictly speaking this is not true) and, conversely, Léon and Emma and Donald and Daisy may be somebody's neighbours. These examples do show, however, that fictionality depends on which universe the indices of the text (are taken to) refer to (or which predicates are ascribed to them; cf. below). To know this we either need information from other sources or we must rely on the indirect probability offered by conventions. Second, even if no universally valid indicator of fiction exists, there is a large number of signs that within a given tradition will make a well-informed reader quite confident that the text is fictional. In favourable cases, however, the direct way of reaching a decision concerning the status of the universe will be to investigate the indices. As regards the indices of fictional entities, their references stop short: the proper names Don Quixote, Mr Micawber, or Emma Rouault are not entered into any parish register (or, if they were, the data there would not fit the data of the texts). So we must, at least at first, return to the work of fiction for any information concerning these beings. Thus, because of its peculiar indexicality, the literary text seems to be the privileged, indeed the only, primary source of information concerning its universe of discourse.

On the one hand, parish registers have not been kept from the times we began to produce fiction, and even when existing, they are not always reliable. On the other hand, some literary texts simulate non-fictional discourse so well that people disagree as to whether or not they should be classified as fiction. For instance, at present there is general agreement that the famous *Lettres portugaises* (published 1669 in Paris) is a work of fiction written by Vicomte de Guilleragues. This has, however, not always been the case. In fact, until the middle of this century some scholars argued that they were genuine love letters written by a Portuguese nun to her unfaithful lover (an opinion defended by scholarly arguments as late as 1944). In this case, then, even if the letters were suspected to be fictional and Guilleragues was thought to be their author soon after their publication, the convincing evidence, mostly philological comparison with other texts, was only established after almost three hundred years.

One very interesting feature of a fictional universe is that it is a universe concerning which we lack additional relevant sources of information as regards certain important indexical signs; and thus certain important questions of interpretation cannot be given a definitive answer. Within literary scholarship, there is of course a vast, ever-increasing number of references to the book *Madame Bovary* and to the character Emma Bovary. However, these references are all secondary to the Flaubert's novel. As Peirce formulates the problem: 'When the universe of discourse relates to a common experience, but this experience is of something imaginary, as when we discuss the world of Shakespeare's creation in the play of Hamlet, we find individual distinction existing so far as the work of imagination has carried it, while beyond that point there is vagueness and generality' (CP 3.172). Thus, an indefinite number of questions concerning such a universe cannot be answered. Poking fun at the meticulousness of German scholarship gone astray, Peirce gives the following, imagined, example of such a situation:

> When we busy ourselves to find the answer to a question, we are going upon the hope that there is an answer, which can be called the answer. It may be there is none. If any profound and learned member of the German Shakespeare Society were to start the inquiry how long since Polonius had his hair cut at the time of his death, perhaps the only reply that could be made would be that Polonius was nothing but a creature of Shakespeare's mind, and that Shakespeare never thought of the point raised. (CP 3.61)

Well, Polonius's haircut before his rather sudden death does not worry very many scholars. Moreover, though his haircut on the day of his death is not of much concern to Shakespeare scholars, for every director staging *Hamlet* it is a question that has to be decided. Thus, a creative realization, such as a staging, necessarily has to provide iconic signs to supplement the symbolic ones of the text (and, it is hoped, at one and the same time, be true to and add to the meaning of it). Readers, however, may disregard this particular point, although they will iconize other parts of the text (cf. chapter 6).

However, in order to understand the text as a sense-making totality, or to understand why it is not coherent, everybody has to presuppose what is not explicitly stated, but implied, or supposed to be implied, in the text. We project onto the fictional universe the interpretive habits that we have developed through living and interacting within others in the surrounding world. The specific features of the fictional universe, however, also govern what can be mapped from our experience onto the fictional universe of discourse in question. If seven-league boots are part of the props of a fairy-tale universe, we must willingly suspend our disbelief in the existence of such a means of transportation as far as that universe is concerned.[4]

A further peculiarity of a fictional universe is that more than one version of it may exist; moreover, two such versions may be radically different. A well-known example is the end of *Great Expectations*. In the first written version, Pip and Estella are not united, and the narrative ends on a note of resignation. In the published version they seem to become united, and thus the end becomes conciliatory. Dickens was persuaded to suppress the first version, because Bulver-Lytton told him that his readership would object to it. Another case is one of the most celebrated erotic/pornographic novels of the last century, Pauline Réage's *Histoire d'O* (*The Story of O*), which ends as follows:

> In a final chapter, which has been suppressed, O returned to Roissy where Sir Stephen abandoned her.
> A second end exists to the *Story of O*. Seeing that Sir Stephen is at the point of leaving her, she prefers to die. He consents. (Réage 1954: 245; my trans.)

It is even more interesting that Pauline Réage, on the first page of the sequel she wrote to *Histoire d'O*, makes the following statement: 'The following pages are a sequel to *The Story of O*. They are deliberately cast as a vulgarized continuation, and they will never become a part of it' (Réage 1975 [1969]: 29; my trans.).

This case is different. Dickens suppresses one, already written, version in favour of another, that is, he changes the end but sustains the pretence that this first-person narrative is the true narrative of a boy becoming a man.[5] Pauline Réage, on the contrary, breaks up the pretence that the narrative is a representation of what has happened, and this rupture with reality is strengthened by the prefatory note to the sequel – which is both announced and disclaimed as a sequel! Nevertheless, the sequel does choose between the two endings sketched at the end of the first novel by letting O return to Roissy (in fact it is Sir Stephen who dies in the sequel). The point is, however, that neither would be possible in narratives that claimed to be historical accounts. Here Pip would either be united with Estella or not, and O would either return to Roissy, or she would commit suicide. Furthermore, Pauline Réage disclaims the sequel as a sequel for stylistic reasons and in spite of the fact that – as to its universe, persons, and action – is contiguous with its predecessor. If a detective declared that two of his reports concerning the same person and reporting about a time-space continuum should remain unrelated because of stylistic diversity, one would hardly accept the argument that, owing to a difference in writing, they were not about a contiguous series of events and actions.

Obviously, we also have contradictory accounts of human actions in our experiential, non-fictional universe. They are not, however, both accepted as true, even if lack of evidence makes it impossible to choose one over the other. Both fictional cases show how different fiction and non-fiction are. In fiction, we are able to entertain two contradictory possibilities, precisely because of their hypothetical nature. The infinite games that can be played in fiction are not allowed in non-fiction. Indeed, they are even forbidden in realism and certainly in the so-called non-fiction novel (see below); and Dickens only published one version of *Great Expectations* himself.

On the other hand, fiction may also offer a certainty not often matched by the attempts to establish the facts of the matter within our lifeworld. In A.S. Byatt's novel *Babeltower* (1996), Frederica takes Nigel to court to get a divorce. Had the divorce case been a real one, it would, on the basis of the testimonies, have remained undecided whether he really did throw an axe at her. In this fictional case, however, it makes no sense to doubt the authority of the omniscient and reliable narrator giving a scenic description of the axe-throwing.

3.3 Ten Features of a Fictional Universe

In the preceding discussion an attempt has been made to describe some critical features of a fictional universe of discourse. Let us relate these features to other features of the production, communication, and reception of a fictional universe of discourse.[6]

1. A fictional universe is the product of a speech act through which the utterer asserts that something is the case without being held responsible for asserting that this state of affairs can be pointed out and identified neither within a common experiential world nor within a common historical past – even if he or she does assert the reality of what is related, which is most often the case.

2. Because the fictional text creates its own universe, its claims concerning elements and relations within its universe must be accepted unless they are contradicted by other claims in the same text. Thus, the

validity of its propositions is decided on the basis of coherence within this particular discursive universe, not by any correspondence with other universes (e.g., the experiential universe). Consequently, the relations of causation and interaction are established autonomously by virtue of specific textual conventions.

3. Since relations of causation and interaction are only valid within the fictional universe, their validity outside this particular universe is – in principle, but not in fact – accidental. Thus, propositions valid within a fictional universe of discourse have no immediate bearing on other universes of discourse.

4. A fictional universe of discourse is communicable and intersubjectively understandable in so far as the fictional text is conveyed by means of an intersubjectively interpreted semiotic system (e.g., a natural language) or through a text that can be interpreted by being related to such a system.[7]

5. By being related to an intersubjectively interpreted semiotic system, the fictional universe of discourse is, at the same time, related to common experiences, world views, and kinds of social interactions, all of which can immediately or mediately be experienced in other ways.

6. Nevertheless, there is a radical limitation of information concerning a fictional universe of discourse compared to the abundant wealth of information available concerning a historical and experiential universe of discourse.

7. The limitation in the amount of information concerning elements and relations within the fictional universe means that its realization in the imagination through intersemiotic translation (i.e., transformation of symbolic signs into iconic and indexical ones) allows individual variations that are all valid in so far as they do not contradict what is indicated by the text's syntactic-semantic and pragmatics features.

8. Point 7 implies that very many propositions about a fictional universe of discourse can be neither validated nor falsified. They may, however, be made probable or improbable in relation to a given context.

9. Since a fictional universe is only accessible through the imagination, it allows the recipient no possibility of interacting and interfering with states of affairs inside it.[8]

10. The limitation mentioned in point 9 is responsible for the strange relation between a fictional universe of discourse and its reader(s). On the one hand, a fictional universe is autonomous and separated from his or her world of experience; on the other, its concrete realization is

dependent on the self-same experiential world as it is represented in the reading subject (for the last four points see chapters 5 and 6).

These ten points indicate tensions and ambiguities in the status of a fictional universe that are linked both with features of the fictional texts (e.g., the specific use of indices) and with the way in which the fictional, and literary, text is approached. Seen as the outcome of an individual enunciative act, that is, as an utterance, the fictional text is the result of a creative fiat, an expression of the imagination of an individual or collective mind. Seen as a communicative phenomenon, it is a symbolic action inscribed in a specific historical context. And when actually realized as a fictional universe in the imagination of the reader, the text is linked with, and dependent on, the experience of the recipient. Thus, besides the elements that set it apart from a given experiential universe, other features of the fictional text indicate important relationships with the historical universe of discourse and with the experience of readers.

3.4 The Relation of Fictional and Historical Universes

A fictional universe is related to the experiential universe of our lifeworld in four ways: (a) by contiguity – for instance, fictional indices function within a universe indicated by non-fictional indices; (b) by similarity – that is, the fictional text imitates both the course of events and the ways in which we are talking/writing about such events and describing the surrounding world and each other – hence, literary mimesis is primarily a representation of ways of using language in discoursing on the world rather than world imitation; (c) by conventionality – that is, laws, habits, and norms valid in a non-fictional world, which is thought to be continuous with or homologous to the fictional universe, are transferred to it, provided that they are not suspended by the fictional text itself (e.g., fairy tales, fantastic literature); and, finally, (d) by figurative intensification and distortion including metaphorical mappings – that is, elements and relations within the fictional universe are interpreted as figurative and intensified expressions of elements and relations within our world or psyche.

3.4.1 *Contiguity: The Magic Map*

To the semiotician map-making in itself is a fascinating discipline, because it combines iconic, indexical, and symbolic, that is, conventional signs. Ideally, cartography should reflect our growing knowledge of world and universe by making maps that are both more specific

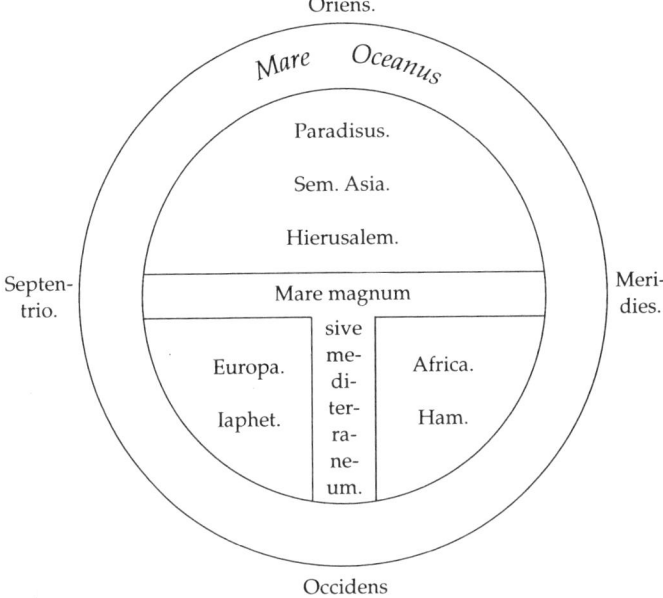

Figure 7
(Source: *Encyclopaedia Britannica*, 9th ed., 1883: XV, 518)

(showing different aspects of the regions in question – geological, political, climatological, etc.) and more detailed and trustworthy. The development of cartography, however, has been dependent not only on the gathering of information by explorers and the developments within mathematics, technology, and so on, but also on changing ideologies. The reproduction in figure 7 shows one prototype of a medieval map, a so-called wheel map, or a T-O map, since it represents the world as a disc divided in three parts by a T that also symbolizes the Cross. Christian faith is certainly responsible for its very design, for placing Jerusalem at its centre and the earthly paradise at the top, which is in fact the Far East. Such features make the author of the *Encyclopaedia Britannica* article (9th ed., 1883: XV, 514–24) begin his section on medieval maps by stating that scholasticism made cartography fall back into a second childhood. He also assumes that medieval geography conceived the earth as a disc, not as a sphere, but this point is disputed (see Harley and Woodward 1987: I, 318–23).

This almost moralistic denunciation is understandable from the point of view of today's scientific criteria for map-making – wheel maps, it must be admitted, do not help us very much in moving within physical space. A literary scholar will, however, look more favourably upon such maps. He or she will forgive their distortions in representations of the planet earth and value them as an interesting iconization of a system of beliefs. To the literary scholar, as to the historian, their location of Jerusalem and mapping of Paradise are precious testimonies to the shaping force of mythical and religious imagination on the contemporary conception of geography. Bevan and Phillott also stress this point concerning medieval maps in their book on medieval geography: 'A map was an "estoire" ... i.e., an illustrated record, and its office was more to delineate objects of popular interest than objects of scientific value. The taste of the age ran in favour of the marvellous, and the mappa mundi was to a considerable extent addressed to the illustration of this department of literature' (Bevan and Phillott 1873/1969, § 10). To the student of literature such mapping is indeed familiar because literature also combines what is represented in the universe, as it is otherwise known, with the shaping of an imaginary space that is congenial to the themes of the text. Furthermore, locations in literature are very often described in accordance with rhetoric and tradition rather than by observation (e.g., the *locus amoenus*, a beautiful place described according to literary tradition).

Nevertheless, in most literary texts the fictional locations are solidly embedded within historical space and time. We have, of course, formulaic expressions in fairy tales, such as 'once upon a time' and 'east of the sun and west of the moon' that only very vaguely connect the fictional time-space to our world, and we have as well the non-specificity of much fiction concerning its spatio-temporal coordinates. We may understand, for instance, that an action takes place in our time in rural Denmark, but it may be very difficult, even impossible, to localize and date it exactly. Most often, however, the text will contain a mixture of indices of fictional and historical objects that nicely locate the fictional within the historical universe.

In the utopian and dystopian novels travels to strange locations traditionally play an important role, and often it seems essential to the narrators to indicate the time of visiting and the location of these strange countries. Indeed, maps are often drawn to inform the reader of their precise locations; for example, the maps of *Gulliver's Travels*, in one of which Lilliput and Blefuscu are located within the known world across from Sumatra. However, in many such cases the precise location does not matter much. Had Swift placed the two islands across from the east coast of Africa nothing essential would have changed. For different and conflicting reasons, what matters is that such imaginary places of the distortion and figurative intensification of society (see below) are claimed to be part of real geography. On the one hand, the authors often poke fun at the credulity of natural histories and travel descriptions, contemporary or ancient. On the other, the location within the known world is seriously meant in the sense that the features of the strange societies described in the texts are all too familiar within the society of the author and contemporary reader. Thus, location is at the service of comparison between an embodied hypothesis – a model society – and actual society as conceived by the narrator (see section 3.7).

Location may matter in more elaborate ways, however. Thomas Hardy is an example of a writer who followed another practice, namely, to rename the world of his childhood, Dorset and its neighbouring counties, to which he gave the old name of Wessex. In spite of this renaming, his representation of the landscape, cities, and towns is so precise that it has been used as a topographical description of the actual landscapes, and several Wessex guidebooks have been published. Furthermore, Hardy himself drew a number of maps of this landscape, especially one for the Wessex edition of his works (1912–13) that was placed in each volume. He saw to it that the fictional and non-fictional names on the map were printed in different letter styles; and he suggested corrections and improvements to his publisher several times. He further wrote a personal key to the non-fictional equivalents of the fictional region that he lent to people and publishers.[9] But why this renaming when the topography is so precise? Hardy talks of his Wessex as 'landscapes of a partly real, partly-dream-country (Hardy 1967: 9). And he further explains the amalgamation in this way:

> Thus, though the people in most of the novels (and in much of the shorter verse) are dwellers in a province bounded on the north by the Thames, on the south by the English Channel, on the east by a line running from Hayling Island to Windsor Forest, and on the west by the Cornish coast, they were all meant to be typically and essentially those of any and every place where
>
> Thought's the slave of life, and life time's fool,
>
> – beings in whose hearts and minds that which is apparently local should be really universal. (Ibid.: 46)

In his essay *The Profitable Reading of Fiction*, Hardy sees the necessity of inventing plots and fictional characters in the fact that the accidental, the monstrous, and the inexplicable play an important role in our existence, and thus the artist must regard 'accident, hindrances to clearness of presentation, and, hence, weakeners of the effect' (ibid.: 117). As regards fictional characters, he says that 'what is called the idealization of characters is, in truth, the making of them too real to be possible' (118).

Another example of the importance of the link with actual geographical location we find in Flaubert. As the subtitle of *Madame Bovary*, *Moeurs de province* (provincial manners) indicates, in this novel it matters very much that the protagonist belongs to the poor provincial bourgeoisie of the France of her time, because her daydreams and actions are shaped by this fact. The introduction to the second part of the novel reads as follows:

> Yonville-L'Abbay (named after an old Capuchin abbey of which not even the ruins remain), is a market-town some twenty miles from Rouen, between the Abbeville and Beauvais roads. It lies at the foot of a valley watered by the Rieule, a little river that runs into the Andelle after turning three water-mills near its mouth; it contains a few trouts and, on Sundays, the village boys entertain themselves by fishing.
>
> Leaving the main road at la Boissière, one reaches the height of Les Leux from where the valley comes into view. The river that runs through it has divided the area into two very distinct regions: on the left are pastures, while the right consists of tilled land. (Flaubert 1965: 49)

This geographical description is very precise. It indicates a town in Normandy and its distance to the capital of this province of France, Rouen. Further, several coordinates containing names of actual French towns (for instance, Abbeville and Beauvais, and the road between them, certainly existed and exist) and an existing river (the Andelle exists, the Rieule does not) are mentioned. Everything is accurate, except that if you use a pair of compasses and draw a circle whose centre is Rouen, you will find no Yonvillle on the circle line at the distance indicated. Such precise indications, and such a precise description of this market town (elsewhere in the book), and no town – this must not be! Consequently, within Flaubert scholarship there were, at one time, warring factions trying to show that Yonville should be understood as a fictionalization of a given Norman town. Unfortunately, the scholars could not agree on which town was the model. There were three parties – the Ry-ists, identifying Yonville-L'Abbay with the town Ry, Neufchâtel-en-Bray-ists, favouring another town, and Forges-les-Eaux-ists, a third existing town – each claiming their town to be the model on the grounds of elaborate and sophisticated arguments involving excursions to the sites, studies of maps, and topographical descriptions. Yet, in spite of Flaubert's claim that he had no specific Norman model for his novel and that he, like Hardy, wanted to create types not to portray existing people (letter to M. Cailteaux, *Correspondance*, II [1980]: 728), the warring scholars nevertheless searched his huge correspondence and the works of his friends for casual remarks or clues to substantiate their views (see Herval 1957). It is easy to regard this scholarly battle as a mild expression of human folly. But even if the ardour and meticulousness of this research might have been worthy of a better cause, they bespeak a human passion for truth and reality, for finding the, supposed, facts behind the fiction. It also shows how literature insidiously maps the imaginary onto the historical. The Normandy of *Madame Bovary*, like Hardy's Wessex, becomes a magic space of interchange and transference between the physical space of writer and reader and the created fictional space. Riding in the stagecoach with Emma from Rouen to Yonville, we cross this borderline without being able to indicate the precise point of transition.

However, is there really a crossing, is it really the case that two ontologically different spaces coexist within a work of literature? In my view, the right, but perhaps not the most enlightening, answer is yes and no. Certainly, an imaginary space is created that is claimed to be located within historical space, and postulated to be itself historical. Furthermore, the Flaubert scholars attempting to identify the model of Yonville were well aware that they would never find Yonville proper, because, for ontological reasons, it is not possible to travel physically to this place. However, fictional characters do travel. Before her suicide Emma Bovary travelled once a week to Rouen to meet and make love to Léon. But even if their lovemaking is represented as taking place within an existing locality, their hours of dalliance are certainly fictional, imagined and written by Flaubert, and revived in the readings of the novel. Thus, within the deictic system of the novel, there is no difference in the use of indexical expressions whether a fictional or a historical entity is mentioned.

Part Two: The Four Dimensions of the Literary Text

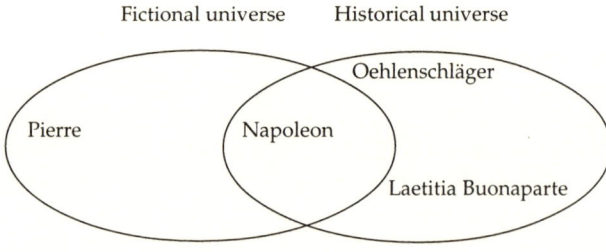

Figure 8

Literature favours, indeed encourages, this practice because of its hybrid universes. Emma Bovary is a fictional character, but the cathedral of Rouen, and the city itself, are certainly firmly located within our own historical universe. And so is Napoleon within Tolstoy's *War and Peace*, whereas you cannot look up Pierre and Natasha in Russian parish registers. Consequently, the statement 'Pierre did not see Napoleon when he was a French prisoner' is a true proposition about the fictional universe of the novel, but it would be false if predicated of the historical universe, simply because this universe does not contain Tolstoy's Pierre. But what about Napoleon? These complications are illustrated in figure 8, which represents two intersecting universes: the historical universe that, besides Napoleon, contains Napoleon's mother and Adam Oehlenschläger (a great Danish poet from the time of the Napoleonic wars), who are not present in the fictional universe, and that of the novel which, besides Napoleon, includes Pierre, who is not present in the historical universe. Thus, Napoleon is a member of both universes and, more importantly, is a member of the universe of *War and Peace* in his capacity of historical figure. Indeed, even the title of the novel refers to his presence as an agent on the scene of Russian history, since the war is caused by the invasion of the French army led by the emperor.

Obviously, in reading the novel, we are not supposed to distinguish between Napoleon as a fictional character and Napoleon as a historical figure. On the contrary, it is presupposed that the index 'Napoleon,' the proper name, should be taken to refer to the historical figure Napoleon, just as the index 'Pierre' should be taken to refer to a being with the same ontological status as the being referred to by the proper name 'Napoleon.' Instead of Pierre making Napoleon into a fictional entity, it is rather the other way around: the presence of Napoleon seems to vouch for the reality of Pierre. However, in fictions following other conventions, the play of indexical signs may function the other way around.

The reason for including both Adam Oehlenschläger and Napoleon's mother in the diagram is that although neither of them is mentioned in the novel, one might say that Napoleon's mother is presupposed by the text, because it is implied that he had in fact a mother. Oehlenschläger, however, is in no way presupposed; as a historical figure he is totally foreign to the novel. Still, even if the existence in the past of Napoleon's mother is implied, there needs to be a reason for activating this presupposition in reading the novel. For all interpretive purposes, Laetitita Buonaparte may be just as irrelevant to the reading of *War and Peace* as is Adam Oehlenschläeger, although the chances that she may be relevant are higher than those of the Danish poet. This reasoning seems sensible, but generally the problems concerning what is implied and not implied in a fictional text are intricate. For instance, is mentioning or non-mentioning a valid criterion? Hardly: in one of the last paragraphs of Flaubert's *Salammbô* we find the following sentence: 'Carthage was, as it were, convulsed by a spasm of titanic joy and a hope without limits' (Flaubert 1961: 352; my trans.). In this novel we leave Carthage in its finest hour, celebrating the hard-won victory over its revolting mercenaries and former allies (in 238 BC). However, at least to my mind, it is absolutely impossible to read the last paragraphs of the novel without bearing in mind that Carthage was completely destroyed by the Romans in the third Punic war about a hundred years later (146 BC). It may well be argued that it would be a serious misreading of the novel not to take into account the future fate of Carthage, because it underscores the narrative's *sic transit gloria mundi* theme and adds the final touch to its ferocious feast of destruction. Thus, how much of the historical universe within which a fictional universe is inserted should be presupposed in reading and interpreting the text will need separate scrutiny in each case. It will depend on explicit references, implications, reading conventions, and the presupposed historical knowledge of the readership.

In daily life, the reality testing of the individual person plays an important role because ascribing reality to one's individual figments of imagination may be dangerous to oneself and may lead to exclusion from the community. In reading fictional texts, we use a double strategy. On the one hand, we practise the willing suspense of disbelief (otherwise we could not really relate to their fictional universe). On the other, from a certain age (because reality-testing has to be learned), even while reading we are subconsciously aware of the texts' fictionality, and we do not use them a sources of reliable information concerning the historical universe (although they may be shrewdly reliable).

Nevertheless, when historical figures or settings are introduced into a fictional universe, a specific comparison is invited. Does the representation of the historical figure in the fictional narrative agree with ...? Indeed with what? The answer must be, with the way in which he or she is represented in the historical recordings and monographs. After all, historical figures survive only through the historical records and the narratives of historians. They possess, however, a double status and function in relation to the texts about them. On the one hand, they determine, at least to a certain extent, the signs relating to them. On the other hand, they are also the final outcome of the process of interpretation. Peirce imagines a discussion of Richard III, and he distinguishes two objects in the following way: 'Thus if a person ... remarks that Richard III appears to have been an able ruler, it is a hundred to one that he never read any first hand testimony concerning Richard ... He refers merely to the current notional Richard. The real object ... is that figure of Richard which we should ultimately have in our minds as the result of sufficient information and reflection' (MS 318, 1907: 342–3). Here the distinction between the dynamical and immediate object is used to distinguish our actual, but partial and deficient, and probably in many respects false notion of the historical figure, the current notional Richard. The dynamical object is the sometime Richard III in flesh and blood who left an indefinite trail of indexical signs (the testimony of others, etc.), some of which are not yet discovered, while the real Richard would be the flawless reconstruction that resulted from sufficient (and perhaps endless) study. Thus, the real Richard would be a true and, in the relevant respects, complete account of the dynamical object Richard III. Consequently, compared to the author of fiction the historian is handicapped by the fact that he writes of what is independent of his own mind. He must take into account traces, testimonies, documents, and so forth, and he is constantly confronted with other historians' interpretations and arguments; arguments that refer to the same signs as his do.

But attempts to solve the riddle of the fictional character Richard III's ruthless and evil behaviour in Shakespeare's *Richard III* must be confined to this play and, in certain respects, to Shakespeare's other plays; that is, one cannot study the character apart from these plays, primarily

Mimesis: Literature as Imitation and Model 133

the histories. Furthermore, historical documents introducing light and shadow into the characterization of the historical Richard III would carry no weight as regards Shakespeare's play character.

Hence, there is an important difference between (the representation of) historical and fictional universes concerning the question of co-referentiality. There are two aspects of this problem: the one mentioned above, the fact that historians are using the same, publicly accessible, material in writing their accounts; and, second, the fact that their accounts are supposed to link up with one another. Paul Ricoeur has expressed the ethos of history writing as follows:

> We can expect that the facts dealt with in historical works, when they are taken one at a time, interlock with one another in the manner of geographical maps, if the same rules of projection and scale are respected, or, yet again, like the different facets of the same precious stone. Whereas there is no sense in placing stories, novels, and plays side by side, it is a legitimate and unavoidable question how the history of a given period interlocks with that of some other period, the history of France with that of England, for example, or how the political or military history of a given country at a given time dovetails with its economic history, with its social history, and its cultural history. A secret dream of emulating the cartographer or the diamond cutter animates the historical enterprise. Even if the idea of universal history must forever remain an idea in Kant's sense of this term, ... the work of approximation that brings the concrete results attained by individual or collective inquiry is neither useless nor meaningless. To this desire to tie things together on the side of historical facts corresponds the hope that the results reached by different investigators can be combined, due to their complementarity, and that they can mutually correct one another. The credo of objectivity is nothing other than this twofold conviction that facts related by different histories can be linked together and that the results of these histories can complete one another. (Ricoeur 1984: I, 176)

Obviously, Ricoeur is right that fictional universes created by different authors normally do not tie in with one another (cf. the lack of relation between Léon and Emma and the Disney ducks). The same is true of those universes of individual authors; indeed, those of two different versions of the same text may even exclude one another.[10] This difference may be due to a difference in priority of perspectives. Whereas in history writing, the universe – the complex network of states of affairs and actions – takes precedence over the individual figure (even in case of writing a historical biography), in literature the universe may be changed in order to fit character, plot, and theme. An important privilege of literature is this possibility of adjusting the universe to the needs of what is thought to be necessary features of important elements within it.

Thus, while the actions and attitudes of fictional characters are only bound by the conventions laid down by the text itself, and by literary tradition of course, the representation of historical characters is bound by what is known to be, or thought to be, true of them. In contradistinction to the historian, the author of fiction can disregard historical scholarship and choose to represent characters otherwise to suit his or her own purposes. He may even produce a counterfactual fictional narrative: for instance, everyday life and a crime mystery in Berlin at the time of Hitler's seventy-fifth birthday, 1964, after Nazi Germany had won the Second World War, as in Robert Harris's novel *Fatherland*.[11] However, an important part of the effect of the novel is due to the presupposition that the reader knows it to be counterfactual. The novel is secondary in relation to the historical representation. Such a novel flouts knowingly what binds the historian, namely, the restrictions posed by the co-reference of other texts to his subject.

The theoretical interest of such novels lies in the fact that what is a true proposition about their fictional universe – for example, that Poland and European Russia have become parts of Nazi Germany after the termination of the Second World War – is manifestly false when applied to the historical universe. Such novels meticulously work out and present a hypothesis, as for instance: If Hitler had won the war,/ then large parts of Eastern Europe would have become a part of Germany,// but Hitler won the war;/// so large parts of Eastern Europe are a part of Germany. However, such a literary universe is not represented as a (counterfactual) hypothesis, but as a matter of fact. In Harris's novel, Hitler *has won* the war. Moreover, in literature in general, we are not presented with something in the conditional mode, but with assertions about what is claimed to be an actual state of affairs.

Precisely this interchange of the conditional and the indicative characterizes, according to John Searle, the logic of fiction. Thus, statements made by the lyrical I, or a narrator, about fictional universes are, although they have the form of assertions, the outcome of an act of pretence by the author that is accepted by the reader. Searle's point is that a social convention exists that undercuts the pragmatic rule that normally, in the proper context, makes indices refer to social-historical reality. In most literature, however, they do not, despite the fact that the text clearly tells us that they do. This specific convention also prevents literature from being seen as misinformation, as a form of lying (see Searle 1979: 58–75).

In my view, this is a felicitous way of stating a fundamental presupposition for the production and reception of literature. It is important, however, that this understanding is tacit; that is, the hypothetical nature of fiction is presupposed, but it does not interfere with either writing or reading. If it does, we have a special kind of literature, metafiction, which is an articulation and exploration of what most often is suppressed, but in no way repressed, in the willing suspension of disbelief.

A fundamental ambiguity is bound up with the use of indices in fiction. They certainly function in the same way that indices in speech refer to our physical and social environment, despite the fact that their reference stops short of, and they do not commit their utterer to, truthfulness (nobody will accuse Harris of being a madman or a liar). And it is precisely because texts are taken as narrations about fictional beings that they are understood as asserting something important about the human condition. However, it is also precisely because they do not refer to beings that are otherwise known (or because, if they do, they are not worried about respecting the limitations imposed by co-referentiality) that they are able to produce an exemplary narrative. The mythic love of Shakespeare's Antony and Cleopatra may well have been a political alliance including sex as a part of the deal.

3.4.2 Conventions of Embedding and Representation

An attempt was made above to present the principal features of the relations between fictional and non-fictional reference and to point out some major ambiguities. However, in addition to these intricacies, there are also the questions of aesthetic conventions: a realist text, for instance, should – at one level – be read as a narrative about what took place within the historical universe. Other reading conventions may work in the opposite direction, so that such texts – again at one level – should be read as a kind of text-world: not, or only indirectly, referring to the historical world, but either self-contained or related to other texts. And in such texts historical characters will be taken as textual entities, having only a faint relationship with the historical figures whose names they bear. Consider the following examples.

136   Part Two: The Four Dimensions of the Literary Text

A Step, noose, mask; but before the mask was adjusted, the prisoner spat his chewing gum into the chaplain's outstretched palm. Dewey shut his eyes; he kept them shut until he heard the thudsnap that announces a rope-broken neck. Like the majority of American law-enforcement officials, Dewey is certain that capital punishment is a deterrent to violent crime, and he felt that if ever the penalty had been earned, the present instance was it ... He remembered his first meeting with Perry in the interrogation room at the Police Headquarters in Las Vegas – the dwarfish boy-man seated in the metal chair, his small booted feet not quite brushing the floor. And when Dewey now opened his eyes, that is what he saw: the same childish feet, tilted, dangling. (Capote 1965: 340–1)

B Let me tell you now the measures I have ordered taken to deal with Denmark and the reasons for my decision: (Picks up his pointer and turns to a map of Scandinavia)

First: despite the treacherous manner in which the Pro-Pornography government in Copenhagen has moved against the United States, I have responded swiftly and effectively to gain the military initiative. (Roth 1973: 87)

C 'But did you really see and speak to Napoleon, as we have been told?' asked Princess Maria.

Pierre laughed.

'No not once ever! To hear people, one might imagine that to be a prisoner is synonymous with being on visit to Napoleon. Not only did I never see him – I never even heard him mentioned. I was in much lower company!'

Supper was over and Pierre, who had at first declined to talk about his captivity, was gradually led on to do so. 'But it's true, isn't it, that you stayed behind in Moscow to kill Napoleon?' Natasha asked him with a slight smile. 'I guessed so much when we met you at the Suharev tower – remember?'

Pierre acknowledged that this was true and, thus started, allowed himself to be drawn by Princess Maria's questions, and still more by Natasha's, into giving them a detailed account of his adventures. (Tolstoy 1978: book 4, part 2, chap. 17, 1323)

D March had seen a score of young men like Jost in the past year. There were more of them every day. Rebelling against their parents. Questioning the state. Listening to American radio stations. Circulating their crudely printed copies of proscribed books – Günter Grass and Graham Green, George Orwell and J.D. Salinger. Chiefly they protested against the war – the seemingly endless struggle against the American-backed Soviet guerillas, which had been grinding on the east of the Urals for twenty years. (Harris 19932: 17)

E 'I shall leave with you.'
'To go where?'
'Anywhere!' Tintin exclaimed, his being flooded with a surge of images. 'To Brazil, perhaps. To the moist green nights of Rio or Bahia, where I have never been. To hot sheets, and hotels, to sexlove and sexkiss and sexsigh and sexbreath to sex longings and sex spendings, and more.'
'Oh! Tintin, your words compensate for your inexperience. But leave words now, and let us swim longer in the flowing wet of love.'
'Clavdia, yes, but let's pause awhile to look at the moon' (Tuten 1993: 57)

F The final protection ... was based on the fact that Melquiades had not put events in the order of man's conventional time, but had concentrated a century of daily episodes in such a way that they coexisted in one instant ...
Aureliano skipped eleven pages so as not to lose time with facts he knew only too well, and he began to decipher the instant that he was living, deciphering it as he lived it, prophesying himself in the act of deciphering the last page of the parchment, as if he were looking into a speaking mirror. Then he skipped again to anticipate the predictions and ascertain the date and circumstances of his death. Before reaching the final line, however, he had already understood that he would never leave that room, for it was foreseen that the cities of mirrors (or mirages) would be wiped out by the wind and exiled from the memory of men at the precise moment when Areliano Babilonia would finish deciphering the parchment, and that everything written on them was unrepeatable since time immemorial and forever more, because races condemned to one hundred years of solitude did not have a second opportunity on earth. (García Márquez 1971: 382–3)

G Attorney General For Fear announced yesterday the discovery that cries of nepotism might 'form a new mineral damaging to the President' Insidious form of high density silica as extremely small particles got into politics with Lyndon B. Johnson, wife of two Negro secret service men – Another Mineral American formed by meteorite impact – 'And it would make a splendid good talker,' he said –

At these tables there is virtually jostling diplomats – Some displacement of a sedate and celebrated rose garden but ideal for the processes of a quiet riverview – Police juice and the law are no cure for widespread public petting in chow lines the Soviet Union said yesterday – Anti-American promptly denounced Kennedy's moribund position of insistence:

'Washington know-how to deal with this sort demonstration in Venezuela of irresponsible propaganda – Outside Caracas I am deeply distressed at the Soviet Union's attempt to drag us back just when we was stoned in violation of the administration's twenty billion dollar solemn word –' (Burroughs 1968: 80–1)

These seven quotations represent very different ways in which universes of fiction are related to the historical universe, to reality. The first quotation is from the last pages of Truman Capote's *In Cold Blood*. Even the subtitle of this book, *A True Account of a Multiple Murder and Its Consequences*, signals that the text is placed on the borderline between a historical narrative and fiction. On its own premises, it should be read as a trustworthy journalistic report about a real, and horrible, crime, the so-called Clutter murders. However, at the same time, it is an ambitious literary enterprise. This is made clear from the beginning, because the first chapter is written with the traditional art of the novelist using zooming: landscape, village, individual persons, mentioning of the event bringing short fame to the forlorn village, and then the victims. These few lines testify to the literariness of the text: 'Like the waters of the river, like the motorists on the highway, and like the yellow trains streaking the Santa Fe tracks, drama, in the shape of exceptional happenings, had never stopped there' (1965: 5). Thus, *In Cold Blood* exemplifies the necessity of distinguishing between literature and fiction, even if fictionality is most often an important feature of literature. Indeed, Capote himself created a new genre label, the non-fiction novel, and this kind of writing is blooming both within narrative and in TV docudramas.

There are two related reasons why such narratives are seen in the double context of history writing and literature: they belong to the first in so far as they are committed to historical truth and their indices refer to historical beings, times, and places. Thus, the novel's departure from well-established facts about the course of events would ruin Capote's own purpose in writing it. The novel belongs to the second, however, because it uses devices that, in our time – Thucydides would probably have approved of Capote's technique – are most often used in fictional literature. In the quoted passage about the execution of one of the killers, Capote is using an omniscient narrator, because even if he and police officer Dewey were both present at the hangings, Capote could not have been placed inside the head of Dewey at the moment of the second execution.

Thus, this kind of literature is basically ambiguous. On the one hand, it certainly cannot, in any important sense, be characterized by the act of pretending (Searle's criterion for fictionality), because – in principle – the statements contained in the text (lay) claim to be true to facts. The indexical signs are intended to be taken to refer to real persons, and what is predicated of them is claimed to be true. On the other hand, such texts aspire to be something else, and more, than historical narratives. And, even though such books are often the result of thorough research, this ambition makes them less trustworthy as history writing. The reason is that although the narrator, and author, claims not to imagine, but to relate, what in fact has happened, that is, to write non-fictional narrative, they use devices from the discursive register of literature. In addition to the use of the omniscient narrator in the passage quoted, there is also the representation of the murderer's small feet dangling in the air, both in the memory of the police officer and in front of him when he opens his eyes. Such a unifying repetition certainly belongs to the imagination, and trade, of the skilful writer of fiction.

Concerning *In Cold Blood* in particular, there is another problem: Capote was fiercely attacked for interfering with the trial of the killers by writing their story. It was even implied (by Kenneth Tynan) that Capote made no effort to get the two murderers a reprieve because their execution would serve as an impressive finale to his book. Justified or not (Capote was reported to be very satisfied, even happy, when he heard of the death sentence), this accusation shows that an author of this kind of writing may be held accountable, not only for the truth claims of his narrative, but even for moral obligations concomitant with being a part of its events.

Whereas Capote crosses the borderline between historical narrative and fiction from the side of history, Philip Roth crosses it from the side of fiction. *Our Gang* is a *roman à clef* intended (successfully) as a biting satire on the political immorality of President Richard Nixon, in the novel named Trick E. Dixon, and his staff. The whole raison d'être of the text is that its character, the president, shall be acknowledged as a fitting representation of the (at that time) actual president of the United

States. In Trick's address to the nation, he takes the credit for a military operation in Denmark, including the liberation by the Marines of Hamlet's castle in Elsinore (an operation never noticed by the Danes), that is, an event manifestly both fictitious and ridiculous. Thus, the fictional setting and events constitute a device allowing the author to give a witty but disturbing fictional exemplification of the mercenary political thinking and low moral standards of which he is accusing the Nixon administration. In fact, he could have been sued for libel, and probably convicted, if the administration had so desired.[12]

In Cold Blood and *Our Gang* both owe their existence and significance to the borderline between fact and imagination and to the concomitant relationship and dialectic between historical narrative and fiction. They have a double perspective on their respective universe that is expressed in the attitude of the narrator to what he narrates. Often, however, the interplay of the historical and the fictional is not thematized in the attitude of the narrator; it is just presupposed, as in quotation c from *War and Peace*. The fictional aspect of Capote's text is an effect of the co-presence of enunciative conventions that point in different directions, and that of Roth, an effect of traditional devices of satire. In Tolstoy, however, we find the standard presupposition of realistic literature, namely, that what is narrated and represented has happened or is happening. The master device of such literature is the indiscriminate mixing of non-fictional and fictional indices (cf. above, pp. 128–31).

Now, if Pierre in Tolstoy's *War and Peace* had not only dreamt of killing Napoleon, but had in fact done it, we would have had the kind of counterfactual narrative that is represented by the quotation from *Fatherland*. Such a narrative is just as dependent on the putative illusion that it is a historical narrative as is realistic fiction. From the point of view of the phenomenology of reading, both co-factual (e.g., realistic texts such as *War and Peace* and *Madame Bovary*) and counterfactual fiction (e.g., *Fatherland*) presuppose a double perception, that is, however, that in the case of counterfactual fiction, part of the excitement stems from the fact that such texts are not satisfied with locating a fictional world within the factual; they change what is supposed to be unchangeable. Here history is not the backdrop of fiction. Rather it is itself intentionally changed into fiction.

Two contrary movements have been operative in the production and reception of these four textual universes: the inscription of fiction into reality and the fictionalization of reality. However, only superficially are these movements contrary; they are rather oscillations within universes that are all explicitly dependent on a specific relationship with the historical universe. All texts must be faithful to it in certain respects relevant to their purpose and manner of writing. Roth, for instance, must be faithful to certain features of the argumentative style of the Nixon administration in much the same way as a caricature must have recognizable features in common with its model.

The passage quoted from Tuten shows that just as historical figures may become literary characters, so literary characters may travel from one fictional universe (here a universe of comic strips) to another. Just as knowledge about a historical figure is somehow transferred to the fictional universe (cf. the Napoleon of *War and Peace*), so our knowledge of the doings and character of Tintin is transferred from the strips of Hergé. Tuten is, if not counterfactually in the sense of Robert Harris describing the days before the celebration of der Führer's seventy-fifth birthday, at least untrue to the 'innocent' behaviour and character of Tintin (although it is an improvement to provide him with an adult love life). The tricky point here is, of course, the parenthesis, because it reveals the *tertium comparationis*, that is, expectations concerning grown-ups issuing from lifeworld experience. Obviously, not all grown-ups have a love life; but reasoning from prototypes we project expectations concerning such instincts and behaviour onto comic-strip protagonists.[13] At the same time, however, knowing Hergé's Tintin, we see that such expectations are not fulfilled. Consequently, we realize that Tuten is drastically remodelling the protagonist. We are put between cognitive models relating to three, not two, universes; in addition to our lifeworld-based expectations, there is Tuten's fictional universe. This universe, however, is created by blending, and of course developing, two pre-existing fictional universes, namely, Hergé's comic strips and Thomas Mann's *Magic Mountain*. In fact, the woman taking Tintin's virginity is Clavdia Chauchat, who, together with other key characters from Mann's novel, has been placed in Tuten's. Nevertheless, the intertextual play still has an implicit comparison with the lifeworld.

In an important sense, this *tertium comparationis* (expectations based on lifeworld experiences) will always remain with the interpreter. The text, however, may play all kind of tricks with the text–world relationship. In the passage from *One Hundred Years of Solitude*, the story, or myth, is incorporating history and lifeworld. Thus, all its characters are, certainly without knowing it, acting according to a script. This script is at once revelation and prophecy, and it subsumes the chain of events and actions in the novel and parts of the history of Latin America as well. Indeed, even the attack by Sir Francis Drake on Riochacha is said to take place in order to make possible the love of Amaranta Ursula and Aureliano (p. 382). Thus, *One Hundred Years of Solitude* is, at the end, revealed to be a kind of secular scripture.

The quotation from *Nova Express* is an example of William Burroughs's so-called cut-up technique.[14] Dada and surrealism are ancestors of this technique that Burroughs recognizes. He mentions, for instance, that Tristan Tzara once challenged an audience by promising to produce poems by drawing words written on pieces of paper out of a hat. In the quotation above Burroughs combines texts by folding and juxtaposing them. At the same time, however, he is very active as an editor: although the texts are clearly referential, sown together they create a kind of weird, autonomous text world. According to Robin Lydenberg, the cut-ups are closely related to Burroughs's theory about 'the parasitic invasion of the word virus.' He continues: 'The cut-up describes how this linguistic invasion instills fear in the victim and reduces all affective animal life to a fossilized and controllable organism, Another mineral America' (Lydenberg 1987: 105). Burroughs's technique is radical because it displays the textuality, not only the literariness, of the text. The text, though obviously still an artefact produced by an author in flesh and blood, is decentred and fragmented. Here the fictional universe is transformed into scraps of citations with no apparent utterers. At least at certain points (there is a story as well), the text displays a heterogeneous and anonymous intertextuality.

The examples above show a remarkable variety of text – world relationships. It is, however, a question of emphasis rather than of categorical difference. Roth, for instance, is certainly dependent on, and obliquely but unmistakably referring to, American politics at the time of his novel. However, even if he is not using cut-ups in the form of direct citations, he is miming and caricaturing the style of Nixon's speeches (and his ideas about Nixon's way of calculating effects). Furthermore, the world in *Our Gang* is obviously very much a spoken world, not only because it consists of dialogues, but also because it is about the lack of relationship between words and world. In creating a text world that has little to do with social reality, except for the attempt to manipulate it, Trick E. Dixon is spreading a contagious and harmful word virus. Capote, writing non-fiction, is expertly using well-known nineteenth-century novelists' tricks of the trade, while Márquez is exploring the potentials of the combination of anecdote, family saga, history writing, and myth.

In asking, 'What is any writing but a cut-up?' Burroughs claims the generality and formative force of intertextuality, with all its different kinds of miming, allusions, and citations (quoted in Lyderberg 1967: 45). We too should recognize the importance of the imitation of other texts, and Burroughs's cut-up technique is a special kind of imitation. However, recognizing that writing literature is a craft in which the development of existing literary forms and the invention of new ones play a major role should not blur the differences between different works and epochs. An account of the Clutter murders written by means of a cut-up technique would be a very different book from Capote's. It would represent a nightmarish text universe whose references to actions and events would be opaque, whereas the precise anchoring of the text in an independent historical universe is a hallmark of Capote's book. Such differences in ways of writing reflect differences in conceiving the world and the role of literature. There are always, from the beginning of the process leading to tragedy and comedy, different viewpoints available, views that are plausible as partial perspectives on the lifeworld.

3.4.3 Improving the Universe

The examples in the preceding section, show different kinds of relations between historical and fictional universes. Tolstoy exemplifies the realistic convention, the mapping of the fictional universe onto the historical, while Roth, Harris, Márquez, and Burroughs are, in their different ways, playing with the borderlines dividing the historical and the fictional. Tuten plays with the interrelation of fictional universes, whereas Capote fuses two kinds of writing, the journalistic and the literary. There is, however, an even more radical way of playing with this relationship, as when a work of literature maps the world, as it is known, within a much larger universe of metaphysical spaces. This is, in fact, what Dante does in the *Commedia Divina*. Here the common world of the living is left already in the third canto, and a journey through the three otherworldly provinces of the universe begins. Thus, Dante fills in the blanks of the universe as it is believed to be shaped according to his times and faith.

He is, however, not only summarizing and fleshing out what were common assumptions about the nature of the other worlds. According to the French medievalist Jacques le Goffe (1981), Dante's representation of Purgatory was an especially creative feat. Purgatory, of course, has a long and well-known history within Christianity. Four particular biblical passages are evoked as testimonies to its existence, namely, 2 Macc. 12: 41–6,[15] Matt. 12: 31–2, and Luke 16: 19–26. One passage from Paul's First Epistle to the Corinthians, however, turns up again and again:

> For other foundation can no man lay than that is laid, which is Jesus Christ. Now if any man build upon this foundation gold, silver, precious stones, wood, hay, stubble; every man's work shall be made manifest: for the day shall declare it, because it shall be revealed by fire; and the fire shall try every man's work of what sort it is. If any man's work abide which he hath built thereupon, he shall receive a reward. If any man's work shall be burned, he shall suffer loss, but he himself shall be saved, yet so as by fire. (1 Cor. 3: 11–5)

No wonder that discussions of the nature of otherworldly purification were evoked by these enigmatic verses; but it is still more curious that, according to le Goffe, centuries passed without any urgent need for specifications concerning this kind of atonement.[16] Thus, Dante's description of Purgatory is related to the contemporary history of dogma. Purgatory was not officially recognized by the Catholic church until the synod in Lyon in 1274 (i.e., not long before Dante started to write the Comedy), owing, among other things, to pressure from the laity and lower clergy (pressed in turn by their parishioners). Thus, one important reason for the eventual acceptance of Purgatory was the demand for imaginative specificity on the part of the laity. Since most of them could count on spending a good time in this place, they wanted, reasonably enough, to know more about it. Equally reasonably, however, the church was rather hesitant to be too specific about its nature and location. This cautious attitude was also necessary because different heretic movements and the Greek Orthodox church denied the existence of Purgatory as a located time-space entity.[17]

Obviously, there is an enormous difference between the abstract character of the official doctrine and dogmas of the Roman Catholic church, on the one hand, and the popular and literary imagination, on the other. In literature, the conceptual generality and vagueness concerning the other world must somehow materialize into scenic description, and this was precisely what Dante offered. In fact, his description took part in the shaping of popular ideas about this place. While other descriptions of Purgatory existed before Dante's *Comedy*, no description whatsoever is comparable to Dante's in scope and detail. In the *Comedy* we are informed of the date of creation of Purgatory, the way it was formed by the mounting of the earth caused by the fall of Lucifer into Hell, its precise geographical location as an island in the Southern Hemisphere exactly opposite Jerusalem on the Northern, and, of course, its topography.

It might be objected that Dante's universe is not fictional, because it is consistent with contemporary Catholic doctrine, and therefore a true description of a metaphysical space as it was believed to exist by the faithful. However, this is not the case. Dante was venerated by the Catholic church, but his description of the other-worldly provinces was the product not only of doctrine, but of imagination, learning, folklore, and doctrine amalgamated by his creative power. It was, moreover, venerated as a vision and an allegory, not as a literal and true description. In fact, these places could only be imagined through analogy, and thus any detailed description had to be an imperfect human attempt at expressing what could not be accurately imagined.

Although Dante's work is the most magnificent undertaking in metaphysical geography and topography, adding to the universe, or describing regions believed to exist, is quite common. The books of Jules Verne, Rider Haggard, and H.G. Wells, all exploring – that is, imagining – depths or heights unknown to man, have fascinated many. A whole subgenre, science fiction, is blooming and, at high speed, producing 'new parts' of the universe or new details about distant galaxies for its eager readership.

I firmly hold that imaginary and fictional universes are secondary to the experiential and historical universe to which they owe their being and within which they are imagined being (for a somewhat different point of view see the excellent book by Pavel, 1986). There is no denying, however, that once created, they may retroactively influence the experimental universe. In the case of mythological and religious universes, this influence may certainly become a shaping force of and within communities. Literature, however, is related to the world of experience in an ambiguous way. Whether the fictional universe is a circumscribed, but invisible, part of the geographical maps or inscribes the experiential universe within its own wider spaces, their contiguity is, simultaneously, accepted and denied. It is accepted because, in order to make sense of what is represented, we have to accept the presuppositions laid down by the text. Accepting the fictional universe as a fact of historical reality would, however, lead us into serious difficulties. While we accept that the real universe is used as a part of a fictional universe, we do not accept a fictional universe as a part of our real world without a label attached to it saying 'fiction'; or we rely on its fictional character being common knowledge.

But why, it might be asked, is this difference between the experiential-historical and the fictional universe so important? Are not the borderlines between reality and fiction dissolved, or in the process of dissolving, anyway? Not quite. The difference matters, because the two kinds of universes allow different kinds of action, including interpretive action.[18] When some part of the surrounding world functions as an indicated or presupposed universe of discourse, it allows – in principle – the parties of the dialogue other ways of experiencing the topic of the dialogue, namely, through what Peirce calls collateral experience. If the objects of the text exist independently, then assertions contained in the text may turn out to be false. The same is, in principle, true of texts referring to a historical past, for although the state of affairs referred to is irrevocably gone, the possibility remains that evidence may be found that will either strengthen or weaken what is supposed to have been the case. Thus, the belief that propositions about the past are true rests not only on the assumption that known evidence supports what is claimed, but also on the belief that any future additional evidence will corroborate it: 'The truth of the proposition that Caesar crossed the Rubicon consists in the fact that the further we push our archaeological and other studies, the more strongly will that conclusion force itself on our minds forever – or would do so, if study were to go on forever' (CP 5. 565). Precisely at this point there are serious constraints on our possibilities of acquiring further reliable information as concerns fiction (as argued above; see pp. 119–21).

The amalgamation of the fictional and the historical is made possible because language indifferently and equally well represents that which is and that which is not. Indeed, without background knowledge and/or specific labelling we are not able to decide which is which. The deictic system – that is, indices, tenses, adverbs, and so forth – creates points and coordinates that make up universes (most often with fuzzy boundaries) that transcend our basic ontological categorizations to better suit our desires.

3.5 Similarity

Contiguity is, however, only one of the master devices of literary representation. The two others are relations by similarity and by conventionality. In talking about similarity and literature we have, however, to distinguish between three kinds of similarity: (1) similarity between sign and object, that is, the way sign (qualities and/or structure) and world (qualities and/or structure) resemble one another; (2) similarity between a given sign and other signs, that is, the similarity between a work of literature and other texts (literary or non-literary); and, finally, (3) the internal similarity between the different parts of the sign, that is, the similarity of patterning on different textual levels. While the last kind of similarity will be treated in the next chapter, the first and the second belong to this one.

3.5.1 Iconic Relationship between Sign and Object

Relation by similarity is characterized by resemblance or contrast, most often conceived as structural homology or significant deviation. According to Peirce, three grades of iconicity exist. First, the sign (text) may be an image of the object (i.e., having qualities in common with it). Certain kinds of poetic texts exist that attempt to imitate the external, spatial form of the object. They describe it by breaking up the linearity of written language. These pattern poems (*carmina figurata*, *Bildgedichte*) are more or less like drawings. They exist, for instance, in Old Persian poetry, in the Renaissance and the baroque period, in modernist writings (e.g., by Guillaume Apollinaire), and in concrete poetry.

Such poems are interesting because they attempt to make iconic and linguistic patterning interact. I will concentrate, however, on iconic effects that are inherent possibilities of linguistic patterning, that is, on the literary text's ability to exhibit the relations of the object (the diagrammatic [structural] relationship between word and world), and on its metaphorical potential.

According to the second sense of iconicity, a text describing a fictional universe of discourse is similar to a text describing a historical universe if they have syntactical and semantic properties in common, because then they will be as alike as diagrams. In order to judge their similarity, one may erase their indices. See the examples used at the beginning of this chapter:

Alexander loves Roxanne
Charles loves Camilla
Léon loves Emma
Donald loves Daisy

When these lines were first presented, what mattered were the indices, and their reference to different universes (or to different times and locations within the same universe). However, it was not mentioned, only presupposed, that the basic structure of the proposition (here a sentence) is the same whether or not the reference is to a historical or fictional universe. Consequently, regardless of the ontological status of the universe referred to, we will understand the propositions in the same way because of their identical predicative structure:

X loves Y,   or simply,   – loves –

Obviously, each of the propositions (provided that their references are specified) raises serious questions. As regards the first proposition, the conception of love and politics in antiquity may be inquired into. The second may be the subject of contemporary biographical research. Whether Léon loves Emma may be discussed from the evidence offered by *Madame Bovary*, measured by an implicit or explicit standard of how love between a man and a woman is to be recognized. In the case of Donald and Daisy Duck, it may be seriously questioned whether the proposition makes any sense at all. Not because of the metaphorical mapping of human emotions onto hybrid beings such as the Disney cartoon figures (Andersen's Little Mermaid certainly loves), but because *love* in any real sense of the word seems absent from the fictional universe of these ducks.

In order to even raise such questions, however, the propositions must initially have been understood in the same way. The questions all concern the possible meanings of the verb 'love' and its applicability or non-applicability to the relation between certain beings. However, even disregarding the specific meanings of the verb, the fact that the sentence structure in each case is the same is decisive. According to Roman Jakobson it is iconic, because, in a basic sense, the iconicity of literary and, generally, linguistic texts may consist in the correspondence between the order of words and the order of the world.

Roman Jakobson, following Joseph Greenberg (see Jakobson 1965), claims that it is a near universal feature of natural languages that the doer, the subject, precedes the object. Obviously, in English (as in Danish) word order is material to sentence meaning. There is an all-important difference between saying 'Catullus loves Lesbia' and 'Lesbia loves Catullus.' According to Jakobson, however, although in a language such as Latin you may equally well say 'Catullus amat Lesbiam' and

'Lesbiam amat Catullus,' even here the common word order would be 'Catullus amat Lesbiam,' that is, with subject preceding object.

Another feature of speech that, according to Jakobson, is also near universal is the metaphorical use of word order to imitate relations of rank and power. To a Dane, 'The Prime Minister and the Queen were both present' would sound a little odd compared to 'The Queen and the Prime Minister ...' Accordingly, we have to be careful not to count any kind of iconicity in language as literary (on linguistic iconicity, see the fine article by Nöth, 1990: 191–209). Or, more to the point, we should recognize that literariness (as the Formalists called it) is not something completely new added to everyday speech, but an exploration of what is already familiar within it (see further chapter 4, pp. 176–81).

3.5.2 The Text-mediated Relation between Literature and the Historical Universe

In the general introduction of the icon, index, and symbol distinction (pp. 29–30), it was pointed out that there are two equally valid answers to the question of whether a portrait photo is 'similar,' namely, to the model or to another photo. As regards texts made up by symbolic signs, such as literary texts, it is only on an abstract level, as diagrams, that a likeness between text and object is relevant (with the exception of pattern poems). As regards the iconic relationship between text and text, however, there are plenty of examples.

Because Aristotle's *Poetics* deals primarily with tragedy, his basic sense of mimesis is the imitation of men in action (*Poetics*, VI, 12, 1450a). Hence, mimesis refers to the similarity between speech and action as it is conceived in the dramatic text in comparison to non-fictional dialogues and physical actions. The narration of the dialogues and deeds of men in action is diegesis, not mimesis, since mimesis involves direct, unmediated representation of them (unmediated by an explicit narrator); still, in Aristotle, mimesis may well be refined and elevated, set apart from ordinary speech (see below). Debate, in addition to informal dialogue, is also imitated in drama. Indeed, at certain points drama tends to crystallize into almost quasi-juridical forms of argumentation (in many cases from the *Oresteia* onwards, dramatic texts represent 'real' trials).

The history of drama is also the history of the changing conceptions of how to imitate the speech of men in action – evident, for example, in the choice of a great playwright to cross over from romanticism to realism. On 15 January 1874, Ibsen wrote to Edmund Gosse, responding, among other things, to Gosse's criticism of *Emperor and Galilean*. Gosse had wished that the play had been written in verse, not prose. Ibsen retorted:

> You are of the opinion that the drama ought to have been written in verse ... Here I must differ from you. The play is ... conceived in the most realistic style; the illusion I wished to produce was that of reality. I wished to produce in the reader that what he was reading was something that had really happened. If I had employed verse, I should have counteracted my own intention and prevented the accomplishment of the task I had set myself ... Speaking generally, the style must conform to the degree of ideality which pervades the representation. My new drama is no tragedy in the ancient acceptation; what I desired to depict were human beings, and therefore I would not let them talk the 'language of the Gods.' (Ibsen 1970: 269)

However, while Ibsen defended his choice of prose and explicitly declared that realism was his objective, he recognized (a) that theatrical representation is not necessarily an imitation of what may happen, at any time, outside the theatre and (b) that an internal logic exists of the relation between theme, plot, and style.

Since theatrical dialogue concerns the spoken, realism in dialogue should mean imitation of the way people actually talk to one another (giving different characters different speech habits or using dialects are ways of giving an impression of realism). However, the theatre semiotician Keir Elam, quoting Erwin Goffman, remarks: 'What passes for the representation of interpersonal communication on stage, in practice, departs radically and systematically from an imaginable original' (Elam 1980: 91). Goffman is right, of course. If one sits in a café or in a train compartment and is able to hear every word of a conversation between friends or family members, one is forced to admit that it is at best half comprehensible because references, idiolects, and attitudes are opaque to the outsider. Elam mentions four principal ways in which theatrical differs from everyday dialogue, namely, in (1) its syntactic orderliness, (2) its informational intensity, (3) its illocutionary purity, and (4) its floor-apportionment control (its neat way of regulating taking turns at talking') (ibid.: 180–1). The problem is that a theatre audience *is* a collection of outsiders who must be let in on what a play is all about, something our elliptical everyday dialogues do not do. The models of theatrical dialogue, conversation and debate, are fluid, changing colours and levels of formality all the time; and they disappear – *verba volent, scripta manent*. In writing, the face-to-face dialogue with its possibility of adding information asked for on the spot is broken, and consequently more information must be included in written dialogues (see Ricoeur 1991: 43–64).[19]

The imitation of written discourse is easier to accomplish and potentially more faithful than the imitation of speech. Furthermore, imitating written works either involves an imitation of forms of communication that the author already engages in non-fictionally (e.g., writing letters or a diary) or it allows for consulting at any time the works to be imitated.

Narrative especially uses the resources of other kinds of writing, to such an extent that it seems more accurate to say that fictional narrative represents the way we write about the world rather than the unmediated experience of it (whatever we are to understand by that). Literature is the kind of discourse that may iconically represent, that is, imitate, all other discourses (see pp. 97, 99–100). This is the case with regard to many subgenera: an epistolary novel is made up of fictional letters, while a fictional autobiography presents itself as memoirs or confessions. Furthermore, in a nineteenth-century novel we may find fragments of different styles of writing: legal, religious, technical, and historical; and we may be confronted with anything from recipes to legal procedures and prayers. This is not surprising, since literature is concerned with man's perception of his lifeworld and with his emotional, practical, and intellectual involvement with it.

Human beings *do* spend most of their time talking (or writing) about themselves and their interaction with their fellow beings, and about their social and physical environment, either in the informal ways of dialogue or e-mail or in a multitude of professional and formalized form. The time it takes a murderer to commit a murder and the time it takes society to retaliate by executing him are both infinitesimally short compared to the time spent in court attempting to establish facts, motives, and reasons in dialogues that eventually are put to an end by a monologue: his conviction and sentence pronounced by jury and judge. Indeed, this is certainly the way it should be – although the execution should not be. It illustrates, however, that man spends most of his time in discourse, not in action.

Literature's imitation of other kinds of texts constitutes a rich field of research. We only have access to the past through documents and monuments. Consequently, the scholarly understanding of a work of literature presupposes a comparison with non-literary texts from the same period, especially those having formal properties and a problematic in common with the literary texts (cf. also Todorov's hypothesis, pp. 10–14). Moreover, by imitating other kinds of discourse and other kinds of texts – such as interjections, prayers, conversations, telling of anecdotes and tales, correspondence, diaries, confessions, memoirs and autobiographies, travelogues, police reports, trial records, annals, chronicles of families, provinces, and cities, and even (short!) versions of world history – the work of fiction also indicates which perspectives and conventions should be used in reading it. Literature may certainly transgress and poke fun at such conventions, but again, to enjoy the wit of rule-breaking, the rules must be known.

On that account, Plato's accusation in the *Republic* that literature is an imitation of an imitation (in our terms, an imitation of a linguistic representation of a state of affairs) is often warranted. Literature certainly appropriates other discourses and uses them for its own purposes – but the difference in use and objective is decisive. That is, even if literature, in a certain, non-pejorative sense is second to non-literature, it is by no means second-rate, and that which it imitates could not be substituted for it. For instance, it is interesting to compare the letters of Abelard and Heloise with Pope's poem 'Eloisa to Abelard' (1717), but it may be even more interesting to know the translation (Hughes, 1714) that served as the source of the poem, and to be aware of the unfaithfulness of this particular edition to the authentic letters. However, it would be curious to claim that having now a critical edition (and good translations) of the letters themselves, we should substitute these for the poem. For certain purposes the letters may serve much better than the poem, but such a substitution would be void of meaning in contexts relevant to literature.

To this point the iconic relationship of representation between the literary text and the universe represented has been conceived as a structural homology between sign and universe, as when the order of the signs 'veni, vidi, vici' is taken to mirror what they represent: Caesar's arrival, surveying, and victory; or as the identical way that fictional and non-fictional texts may represent the universe: 'Charles loves Camilla' and 'Léon loves Emma.' On a basic level, the linguistic representation, at least in English, is identical regardless of whether the universe referred to is fictional or historical (e.g., verb tense is no certain indicator).

On the level of discourse, however, literature seems to borrow extensively from non-fictional discourses and non-fictional kinds of texts (see the important modification of this claim in the next chapter). In both cases, however, the similarity concerns structural properties. As regards the borrowing from other discourses, what is borrowed are ways of modelling experience (see below).

3.5.3 Figurative Representation in Literature

The vexing questions concerning metaphor (both in general and in literature) will be discussed both in this section and in the next chapter. While the next chapter will focus on the structural properties of metaphor as a species of analogy, here metaphor will be analysed as a disturbing feature in the representation of the fictional universe. See this paragraph from Kafka's *The Trial*:

> 'What is this?' he asked the painter. 'What are you surprised at?' returned the painter, surprised in his turn. 'These are the Law Court offices. Didn't you know that there were Law Court offices here? There are Law Court offices in almost every attic, why should this be an exception?' (Kafka 1956: 205)

This passage beautifully exemplifies how easily our reading is disturbed by the dilemmas that literary texts force us to react to. On the one hand, as readers we must respect the fact that courts are situated in almost every attic in the city, because Titorelli's statement is confirmed by the rest of the text. On the other, taken literally, the statement makes the fictional universe strikingly dissimilar to the lifeworld of both utterer, Kafka, and interpreter, the actual reader. The statement would certainly be false of the big cities of central Europe in the second decade of the twentieth century, and neither is it true today. Obviously, we can leave it at that, since we can easily enjoy a text by just accepting the weirdness of its universe as the rules of the game. While watching football, we rarely discuss the arbitrariness of the rules; they are simply taken for granted, even if they are often hotly debated in other contexts and sometimes even changed.

However, every species needs to interpret its environment, and humans seem to feel a need, not only to interpret their actual environment, but also to both make sense of the virtual realities of their own making and refer them back to and compare them with their experiential universe. Consequently, very often in practice, and always in principle, we do not leave it at that. We embark on a quest for a meaning applicable to our lifeworld. We start practising a double reading: a literal one respecting the uniqueness of the fictional universe as a world distinguished and separated from our own; and another that takes the propositions about the fictional universe to be figurative expressions whose interpretation says something about the lifeworld in which the text is produced – and about our own.

Read figuratively, the passage from Kafka may be related both to psychical and social conditions characteristic of Kafka and his age. There are, in fact, two fairly standard readings of this passage. One treats it as a metaphor for a lethal state of mind caused by unconscious guilt in relation to father figures. According to this reading, the placement of the court in attics make sense because the process is going on in the head of the protagonist, which is at the top of the body, as is an attic to a house (a house as the body is a common metaphor based on the container-schema). The other reading stresses that, within the novel's universe, there are courts in almost every attic in the city and then interprets this as a hyperbolic expression of real dictatorship, a kind of police state where everybody is watched (and surveillance is easier from above).

The passage from Kafka proves that, in interpreting literature, the literal sense, based on contiguity and similarity with the lifeworld of author and reader, is only one level of signification and not necessarily the most important. Indeed, if we look at the history of literature, it appears that, most of the time, readers and critics have favoured literature's figurative, or allegorical, representation of reality. Dante, for instance, defined the literal meaning of literature as a 'beautiful falsehood' that hides the truth, which is supposed to be the allegorical meaning (see also Spenser, quoted on pp. 108–9):

> Writings may be understood and ought to be expounded chiefly in four senses. The first is called literal (and this is that sense which does not go beyond that enunciated by the fictitious word, as in the fables [*favole*] of poets). The next is called allegorical, and this is that which hides beneath the mantle (*manto*) of such fables, and is a truth hidden beneath a beautiful falsehood: such as when Ovid says that Orpheus tamed wild beasts with his lyre and made trees and stones move towards him, which shows how the wise man makes cruel hearts grow tame and humble with the instrument of his voice, and how he makes those who have no feeling (*vita*) for

science and art moving according to his will; and those who have no rational life at all are little better than stones. (Dante in Minnis, Scott, and Wallace 1988: 396)

Although we might be bored or amused by many traditional allegorical interpretations (e.g., that the breasts of the Virgin Mary signifying the Old and the New Testaments), nevertheless all of us allegorize when reading fiction. Sometimes we do so because, on the literal level, the text is strange, defying our attempt to make sense of it, but even if it seems fully comprehensible on this level, we are looking for the *sensus plenior*, the more complete meaning, as the biblical exegetes of the Middle Ages said (see Grant 1965 and Smalley 1986).

In doing so, we should, however, take very seriously the warning of St Augustine. In the *City of God* Augustine relates that some interpreters allegorize everything concerning Paradise, and he goes on to say:

> No one, then, denies that Paradise may signify the life of the blessed; its four rivers, the four virtues, prudence, fortitude, temperance, and justice; its trees all useful knowledge; its fruits the customs of the godly ... These things can also and more profitably be understood of the Church, as it is called in the Canticles, so that they become prophetic foreshadowings of things to come. Thus Paradise is the Church, as it is called in the Canticles; the four rivers of Paradise are the four Gospels; the fruit-trees the saints, and the fruit their work; the tree of life is the holy of holies, Christ; the tree of knowledge of good and evil, the will's free choice ... These and similar allegorical interpretations may be suitably put upon Paradise without giving offense to any one, while yet we believe the strict truth of the history, confirmed by its circumstantial narrative of fact. (Augustine 1952b: XIII, chap. 21, 371)

Although I must confess that I have grave doubts concerning the 'strict truth' of the story of Genesis, Augustine does point to something that is of the utmost importance to literature's universe of discourse: the fact that we should accept its pretension that literature's universe – at a certain level – has the same ontological status as our experiential world and that we should relate to it in the same way as to texts about the experiential and historical universe (but see his view of fiction in the epigraph to this chapter).

Part of literature's power to fascinate us is due to its basic ambiguity, to a tension between its almost frightening concreteness and its point-

156   Part Two: The Four Dimensions of the Literary Text

ing beyond the individuality of the narrated towards some general principle according to which the universe functions (thus, at the same time, becoming a principle of interpretation). Here is the conclusion to the *Trial*:

> But the hands of one of the partners were already at K.'s throat, while the other thrust the knife deep into his heart and turned it there twice. With failing eyes K. could still see the two of them immediately before him, cheek leaning against cheek, watching the final act. 'Like a dog!' he said; it was as if the shame of it must outlive him. (Ibid.: 286)

Reading this passage we do not transcend the concreteness of the scene and the horror of K.'s fate. Nevertheless, in the next moment, we will ask for the signification and significance of this, as it seems, unwarranted execution, and ask about the law according to which K. may be guilty and his penalty justified. The unreality of the fictional universe slyly promotes the quest for meaning, but at the same time its individuality captures our attention and arrests this quest. In literary representation two opposite forces seem at work alternately, indeed almost simultaneously. A centrifugal force hurls us away from the sign and immerses us in the represented universe. At a certain point, however, the fictional universe cannot be investigated further because the reference of the indexical signs stops short, blocking the road to other sources of information (whereas, to extract more information, an archaeologist may return to his excavation and the detective to the site of the crime). At this point a centripetal force brings us back to the sign, since it is only through rereading the text that novel aspects of the fictional universe may be inferred.[20] Thus, we are forced to penetrate more profoundly into its potential meanings.

At the same time, however, through the process of continued interpretation, we become more and more aware that the text is itself shaping our conception of its universe and, by analogy, the experiential universe as well. When we, for instance, say that this or that society is Kafkaesque or talk about the Bovarism of suburban life, we are discovering features and patterns in our lifeworld that are represented in masterly fashion in these novels. It was pointed out above (p. 120) that a fictional universe of discourse feeds on the experiential universe simply because presuppositions necessary to make sense of the fictional universe have to be transferred from the lifeworld (this will be treated in greater detail in chapter 7). There is and will remain an asymmetry between the historical, experiential universe and the infinite number of fictional universes. However, it is certainly true that fiction influences history: Oscar Wilde was right in saying that life imitates art; but not, on the view presented here (and in spite of postmodernism and the media), to the same extent that art imitates life (see chapter 6 on ideology).

From the point of view of communication and discourse there is another important difference between fictional and non-fictional texts. Normally the meaning potential of texts that serve strategic or communicative action is actualized in a given situational interpretation; and this selective interpretation is their death, as it were. They disappear after having fulfilled their purposes. Sometimes lawyers or historians go on interpreting and disputing the meaning of certain texts, but luckily most texts pass away unheeded. Of course, literary texts will also fall into oblivion, as all texts finally do. However, the interference of the literal and the figurative and the tension between their centripetal and centrifugal aspects make literary texts seem to suspend actualization, or at least they hold back a full realization of their potential meaning. They point towards collateral experiences that we can never have, and for that reason they continue to elude our attempts to exhaust their meaning.

3.6 Literature and the Claim to Truth

According to universal pragmatics, the validity claim with respect to the relation between sign and object is truth. But is this also the case with regard to literature? Before discussing this question, however, a short preamble might be in order, because to mention the concept of truth is certain to invite argument immediately. At present we have a rather paradoxical situation: it is very often claimed that there is no truth, at least not in the singular, but people nevertheless vehemently defend and ingenuously argue in favour of general positions and argue about the (true) nature of specific issues.

Furthermore, as regards matters of personal life, most people find it rather important to distinguish true from false in an everyday pre-philosophical sense: whether or not your partner is cheating on you, whether some fraud has been committed, or whether a tumour is benign or malign. The physicians analysing the tumour are also interested in establishing whether it is cancerous, and they are generally eager to discover the not yet fully known interplay between a not yet fully known set of factors that cause (different kinds of) cancer.

Obviously, it may very often be that it is either not possible to establish what the truth is, or it is not possible to point to a specific set of causes, not to speak of reasons, that are responsible for the present state of affairs. Or, perhaps there is a very real danger that something has been declared to be the case for reasons external to the search for truth and by neglecting evidence to the contrary. Furthermore, knowledge is fallible; in principle, it is not possible to immunize interpretations from being wrong. Indeed, it is certain that a number of well-established interpretations of the universe, societies, the individual, the body, and so on are wrong – we just do not know which ones until their refutation. Finally, it should be noticed that the myriad hypotheses that constitute the different fields of research are constantly being revised. Some of these revisions are minor and leave the general hypotheses in question untouched, but others may call for dramatic general revisions.

Some of the disagreement about the concept of truth may be explained by understanding truth as a radial concept. This is what Lakoff does. According to him we have central and non-central truths. Central truths are 'characterized in terms of directly understood concepts, concepts that fit the preconceptual structure of experience' (Lakoff 1987: 296), that is, basic-level concepts and general schemas tied up with experience. The fact that 'the telephone is to the left of me on the desk,' to use one of Lakoff's examples, is a central truth that nobody would deny because it is true 'by virtue of the directness of the fit between the preconceptual structure of experience and the conceptual structure in terms of which the sentence is understood' (ibid.: 297). As Lakoff also points out, there is nothing exciting about central truths. Only non-central ones that are not directly related to preconceptual experience are interesting: 'But most cases of truth involve indirectness. That is, they make use of indirect understanding: higher-level categories, metaphoric and metonymic understanding, abstractions, etc.' (ibid.).

However, in spite of these well-known complications regarding the concept of truth, (1) the search for it, in the everyday sense, is operative in most of our activities, the trivial as well as those breaking new ground; (2) criteria for and ways of validating or, especially, falsifying interpretations are constantly discussed and refined; (3) truth, most of the time, means material truth and signifies the applicability or non-applicability of propositions to state of affairs, that is, some minimal version of the correspondence criterion of truth (also a part both of Habermas's universal pragmatics and of Peirce's consensus-correspondence theory of truth); and finally (4), as Peirce observed, 'The essence of Truth lies in its resistance to being ignored' (CP 2.139). Both in our daily inquiries and in research, phenomena repeatedly present themselves to us whether we like it or not.

Literary discourse differs from theoretical and historical discourse in this respect. Not only is it liberated from the constraint attending the need to act and from the authority exercising power (for some important modifications of this statement see chapter 7), it is also liberated from complying with a correspondence criterion of truth. This is no new discovery, for was pointed out in the first real tract on the theory of literature in Western culture, Aristotle's *Poetics*: '[A] poet's object is not to tell what actually happened but what could and would happen either probably or inevitably ... The real difference is this, that one tells what happened and the other what might happen. For this reason poetry is something more scientific and serious than history, because poetry tends to give general truths while history gives particular facts' (Aristotle 1927: 35, *Poetics* 1451a-51b). The universe of literature has a virtual reality. It is like a hypothesis exemplified as if it were something actual. Nevertheless, according to Aristotle, it constitutes a genuine means of knowing about human existence; and to fulfil its explanatory role, it must be related to the experiential universe of its audience in relevant ways.

According to Roman Jakobson, the poetic function of language involves the projection of the principle of equivalence from the axis of selection onto the axis of combination; that is, similarity is made into a formation rule for the string of signs in literature (see the next chapter). It seems that fictionality promotes a similar process as regards fictional narrative, in the sense that contiguity is put at the service of similarity. The probability of fictional texts is enhanced by their feigning that what has happened within their universes of discourse is a part of what has happened within the historical universe, because the probable is that which is similar to how things usually are. By postulating that a frame of reference is the known and familiar world, we are more likely to think it credible. This is why many writers have eagerly professed to the truth of what they represent. In the first chapter of *Le Père Goriot* the narrator, who is very much like the Balzac of the prefaces, says: 'After having read the secret misfortunes of Father Goriot, you will eat dinner with appetite while blaming your insensitivity on the author, taxing him with exaggeration accusing him of telling tales [*de poésie*]. O, know: this drama is neither fiction nor novel. All is true [English in the original], it is so real [*véritable*] that everyone will recognize its elements within himself, maybe in his heart' (Balzac 1989: 32, my trans.).

In addition to similarities of universes and of linguistic structures that exist between fiction and non-fiction, fictional discourse also imitates the other four discourses. Thus, in these respects, we are well within the aesthetics of similarity. However, the third kind of iconic relationship between sign and object, the metaphorical – or considering the different devices of rhetoric, it might be better to say the figurative or allegorical – flies in the face of such aesthetics.[21] The aesthetics of Kafka's work, for instance, seems to be one of difference; that is, what happens in the fictional universe is inexplicable from the point of view of similarity. To understand such a universe, we have to suspend our ideas about causes and reasons operative in our lifeworld. Only after having accepted a universe governed by strange and perhaps, in the last analysis, inexplicable principles, in a second move (logically speaking), we relate it to our world by interpreting it figuratively; that is, similarity is only recognized mediately.

The functions of indexicality and iconicity in the relation between text, fictional universe, and experiential universe are basically ambiguous, indeed paradoxical. As regards continuity (or contiguity), there is, in literature, a double message saying 'part of' and 'separate from' the experiential universe; and as regards similarity, it is saying 'just like' and 'different from.'

The ambiguous and paradoxical nature of literature also affects its relation to the truth claim of universal pragmatics. Aristotle distinguishes between general truth and particular facts, which rules out truth as correspondence because correspondence is concerned with facts. The particular facts of literary texts are true by definition (if not contradicted by internal evidence). Heydrich does live in 1964 within the fictional universe of *Fatherland*, but such a fact is not transportable; it cannot be moved from the virtual universe of the novel to the historical universe without becoming false, because he was, in fact, killed by Czech partisans in 1942. Of course, a good many propositions within a literary text may well be transported from the fictional to the experiential universe while still conserving their truth value. But on the view presented here, this transportability is logically contingent, although as regards the text's probability it may be very important.

In Aristotle, probability and necessity are connected with human action and the disposition of the characters. Furthermore, adding the propositional attitude of the lyrical I and narrator(s) in diegetic texts only confirms that literary texts are primarily concerned with emotions, cognitions, attitudes, and actions. This may explain why within the fictional universe very strange settings and weird laws, habits, and events are as a rule accepted, provided that the attitudes and actions of narrators and characters, especially those of the protagonist(s), make sense. However, to make sense does not necessarily mean to act according to standards for reasonable behaviour within a given community. Aristotle further explains that the characters of literature are different from historical characters, either better (tragedy) or worse (comedy). What is more, people may behave both irrationally and inconsistently. In this case the art of the poet represents inconsistent behaviour consistently (1927: 55, 1454a). Thus, probability is itself divided: on the one hand, it is related to the accord between fictional and experiential universes and especially to the behaviour of the protagonist(s). On the other, even if the behaviour of the protagonist(s) may flout social standards of behaviour, such behaviour is probable according to conventions internal to the fictional universe.[22]

The probability of the behaviour of fictional characters is a special, and important, case within the general question concerning similarity between the fictional and experiential universes at large, including its ambiguities and paradoxes. It might be tempting to cut the Gordian knot by claiming that the fictional universe is ultimately separate from the lifeworld and that what happens in the former is a question of conventions anyway. Thus, closing the case by espousing, as it were, an extreme version of Russian Formalism: in literature words and meanings are material to be formed by art, and the universe of literature is made up of a collection of devices (see Shklovsky 1965: 3–24 and Erlich 1965). But there is a price to extreme formalism which is much too high to pay, namely, the disappearance of the interface between literature and lifeworld.[23] The representational dimension of literature feeds and thrives on this paradoxical relation, on the fact that the same literary text may, in certain respects, be exactly like, different from but probable, and strange and not-possible compared to an experiential universe.

Although statements about a fictional universe of discourse cannot (other than contingently) be true of other universes, they may be true to them. This 'being true to' does not imply that they represent a universe qualitatively similar to (non-fictional descriptions of) a historical one, although such statements may do that. It does imply, however, that the fictional universe can be related to the historical universe in an existentially relevant way. The fictional universe must represent perceptions, cognitions, attitudes, reflections, actions, and events that, interpreted literally and/or figuratively, by similarity and contrast, are examples of what matters to members of a given community. It must be understood as an iconic exemplification of a relevant interpretation of what matters to the community.

To this point only indexical and iconic relationships between text and universe, and between text and text, have been analysed, while the inquiry into the symbolic relationship between word and world has been postponed. Further, there have been no direct references, let alone discussion, of the interpretant, although it is an indispensable element of the sign. These postponements are justified by the necessity to isolate relationships for the purpose of analysis. However, fictional universes are not only representations of virtual realities, they are also exemplifications of ways of conceiving the human condition. Indeed they offer suggestions or prescriptions for behaviour and action.

3.7 Fiction, Model, and Lifeworld

Symbolic signs are related to their objects by habits, by the fact that they are interpreted as representing it. Every time a sign is instanced, it may add to, or change, its prior significations, but most often its instantiation does not make such changes, and even if it does, its prior significations are still important to understanding it. It is only by knowing how a sign has been used in a number of previous (stereotypical) occasions that it is possible to understand, and appreciate or object to, its new nuances or radical changes of meaning. Literary texts, too, rely on habitual relationships between signs and objects – even if they create these relationships themselves; and even if they change the meanings of signs, prior significations matter to them.

The idea that literature should be understood as an exemplification of habitual interpretations of given lifeworlds may seem strange, even galling to some, because literature is thought of as unique, the outcome of singular and individual creative acts. This idolization of literature may be justified from a certain perspective, but if this were the only approach to literature, not only would the scholarly study of literature be impossible, but, worse, reading and enjoying it would also lack important dimensions. Further, to claim that literature is *not* an exemplification of habits of interpretation related to the author's lifeworld would in fact be much more strange, whereas the approach suggested here may lead to understanding further dimensions of the literary text. This is, moreover, an approach already found in Aristotle. In his view, the delight we take in literature is caused by two innate instincts, for representation and for tune and rhythm. About the former he says in the *Poetics*:

> From childhood men have an instinct for representation, and in this respect man differs from the other animals in that he is far more imitative and learns his first lessons by representing things. And then there is the enjoyment people always get from representations. What happens in actual experience proves this, for we enjoy looking at accurate likenesses of things which are themselves painful to see, obscene beasts, for instance, and corpses. The reason is this. Learning things gives great pleasure ... to ... men ... The reason why we enjoy seeing likenesses is that, as we look, we learn and infer what each is, for instance, 'that is so and so.' (Aristotle 1927: 13–15, 1448b)

To some, Aristotle's position may seem biologically biased and much too intellectual, foreign to the pleasures of the literary text. In my view, however, it views literature from an important perspective, namely, literature as a knowledge-acquiring device or, in the words of I.A. Richards, literature as a speculative instrument (Richards 1955: 151–2).

However, to make credible the claim that literature exemplifies common habits of interpreting the lifeworld, we should look upon the issue from the opposite perspective, namely, from that of interpreting literature. The most salient feature of literature's indexicality is the limited amount of information offered by the text because its references stop short. In order to understand literature, then, it is necessary to interpolate common knowledge of how 'things are,' how people react and interact, and so forth. Although in its scholarly study literature's historical context is scrutinized for contemporary habits of interpretation, it also remains dependent on the interpreter's habits of interpreting his or her own lifeworld. There is a fundamental question that interpreters cannot avoid asking in some form or another, namely, 'If you imagined a given fictional text to be a non-fictional report about a state of mind or a course of events that had actually happened, would you then believe it?' We all reason in this way because we must compare and measure everything in light of our previous experiences (including, of course, our reading of fiction and our professional training). There are several ways of mending and clarifying this way of reasoning; for instance, we might not compare a piece of fiction with our own individual beliefs, but with what is, or was, collectively thought to be credible (cf. the notion of doxa). Nevertheless, it may seem a little contradictory and somewhat absurd to have a whole institution cultivating a discourse that is not committed to being true to facts, when the first thing we do is to compare literature to what, in our opinion, might be true.

Another way of putting this matter is to say that we match the information offered by the text with our general understanding of our own world, and so we supplement the missing information from our general understanding of the functioning of the world. Maybe this description solves the problem. We do *not* compare fictional thoughts and feelings, or a fictional plot, to what is going on in the world; rather, we compare these elements to our interpretation of the forces, desires, and reasons governing man and his relation to his lifeworld. In effect, we compare the fiction to a model of the world, a model that, at least in most cases, is both inconsistent and fragmentary.

But literature itself offers a model of human emotions, thought, and action, and we interpret this model by comparing it with our own model. Basically a model is a simplified representation of an object that it resembles in certain respects relevant to its purpose. This is why Aristotle is justified in stressing the intellectual and didactic aspect of literature. The acquisition of knowledge through contemplation of likenesses involves making inferences about the nature of a given phenomenon by using a model, that is, an iconic representation, of it.

There is a benign polysemy in the word 'model.' It may signify several things, among which the following are interesting from our point of view: (1) It may mean the construction and representation of a phenomenon as an object of knowledge by means of signs – for instance, the mapping of relations between objects in the external world as relations between elements of pictures, maps, verbal descriptions, and mathematical relations; (2) a model may be a prototype (for instance, a new model of a car is a prototype); (3) another signification of model is related to prototype, but nevertheless different, namely, that of an ideal or exemplar: somebody may be a model of virtue or beauty;[24] and finally (4), to confuse things, 'model' may also be used of an object that is imitated, for instance, a person sitting for a painter.

According to Yuri Lotman (1967), literature, as a model, is an iconic representation, or an analogue, of the object it represents. The individual model belongs to a modelling system, and literature is a so-called secondary modelling system, that is, a system built upon language as the primary modelling system. A modelling system consists of an inventory of elements and their combination rules, and it holds an analogical relation to its object. The literary work of art is, at the same time, both a representation of the object by means of the system's elements and relations and its analogue. In other words, a literary text is always, at once, conventional and the likeness of a given object. For that reason, the literary text is different from the linguistic sign because not only does it serve as a substitute for the object (a sign represents its denotatum by convention), but since it is also an icon of it, scrutinizing the text will teach us about the object (the parallel to Aristotle is obvious).

However, what are literary texts models of? According to Max Black, standard models are miniatures, three-dimensional models of 'some existing or imagined material object' (Black 1962: 219). Such objects he calls *originals* of the models, and the models themselves he terms *scale models*. Representational paintings may in certain respects be fruitfully considered and treated as two-dimensional scale models, and representational sculpture as three-dimensional scale models. Literature, however, is no such model because a scale model's conventions of interpretation rest on 'partial identity of properties coupled with invariance of proportionality' (ibid.: 220), and obviously literature consists of strings of symbolic signs that do not share the properties of what they represent or depict. Flaubert's description of the vapours of Emma's kitchen does not itself have a smell. The only way in which literature may bear qualitative resemblance to its object is in the representation of speech or of written texts, but in such cases scale is irrelevant. Qualitative, literal similarity, then, is negligible in literature (cf. p. 147).

Black mentions three other kinds of models: analogues, and mathematical and theoretical models. The latter two have little relevance to literary mimesis (although there is an affinity between metaphors and theoretical models; see chapter 4). It seems fruitful, however, to consider literary texts as analogues of an existing or imagined universe. Like Peirce and Lotman, Black also sees such a model as iconic, but in a more abstract sense than with the scale model. Instead of having partial identities of properties, an analogue is isomorphic with its original; it displays the same 'structure or patterns of relationships' (ibid.: 223), that is, an identity of structure, not of qualities (cf. also Peirce's distinction between qualitative and diagrammatic, or analogical, similarity). According to such a view, states of affairs and states of mind represented in a literary text are analogous to such states within a given lifeworld or are, rather, analogous to interpretations of such phenomena. The reason why representations of fictional universes may, and do indeed, serve as models of human existence is that they are construed and understood according to the conventions used in interpreting lifeworlds.

The reason for the usefulness of models, as mentioned before, is that they are purposeful simplifications of the object represented. However, they are also related to a specific theory or a set of hypotheses, and as world-making, they create new worlds by using and transforming the elements and patterns of other worlds. Philosophers differ on the question whether there is one basic world, or basic world-version, from which all others are built. A radical relativist like Nelson Goodman denies both the defensibility and usefulness of this idea, yet points out that '[f]or the man-in-the-street, most versions from science, art, and perception depart in some ways from the familiar serviceable world he has jerry-built from fragments of scientific and artistic tradition and from his own struggle for survival. This world, indeed, is the one most often taken as real; for reality in a world, like realism in a picture, is largely a matter of habit' (Goodman 1978: 20). Even if one disagrees with his philosophical position (and wonders about the exact meaning of 'largely' in this quotation), Goodman is right in claiming that our interpretation of the lifeworld is sketchy, fragmented, and incoherent. It seem to me, however, that there is one very good reason for ascribing to this interpretation a privileged position and taking it as point of departure in interpreting other worlds or universes: namely, we are bodily present in this experiential world – we perceive, act, and suffer and die within it. And poets, artists, scientists, and, although it sometimes seems doubtful, even philosophers are also men-in-the-street.

Departing from the habitual elements in our experience of the world, Goodman points out that artists' visions will most often differ from most viewers' perceptual and interpretive habits:

> Many of the differences among portrayals by Daumier, Ingres, Michaelangelo, and Rouault are differences in aspects accentuated. What counts as emphasis, of course, is departure from the relative prominence accorded the several features in the current world of our everyday seeing. With changing interests and new insights, the visual weighting of features of bulk or line or stance or light alters, and yesterday's level world seems strangely perverted – yesterday's realistic calendar landscape becomes a repulsive caricature. (Ibid: 11)

Goodman sees world-making as an activity by which, taking from some already existing world version as the point of departure, one creates a new world by the following five procedures: (1) *composition and decomposition*, that is, making distinctions and identifying and naming elements, and thus seeing their interrelations and repetitions according to the organization of the particular world; (2) *weighting* or *emphasis* (see the quotation above); (3) *ordering*, that is, making systems of divisions such as the different calendars; (4) *deletion and supplementation* (according to Goodman, 'our capacity for overlooking is virtually unlimited, and what we do take in usually consists of significant fragments and clues that need massive supplementation'), two structuring devices whose relevance to literature is obvious; and finally (5) *deformation*, as in, for instance, a given representational habit such as a caricaturist deforming the face of his victim.

At first glance, what has been said above leaves us with conflicting points of view. On the one hand, it seems that the idea of literature as a model of the lifeworld presupposes both that there is a basic world to be represented, and that there are true and false ways of representing it, that is, true or false models. On the other hand, it seems that the world itself only exists in different representations, and that consequently there is no standard according to which the models can be judged. The view that all models of the world are ultimately to be measured against our understanding of our lifeworld may certainly be defended. However, even if it is denied that different world descriptions can be related to one basic world, it may nevertheless be plausibly argued that, at a given level, world versions may be tested as to their truth and relevance. Thus, although final proof is thought to be unavailable, good reasons for preferring one version to another may be given.

As regards literature there is a specific difficulty because the world version relevant to it is the historical world of human interaction, which of course is the most complicated version of all. Its complexity is due to its double dependence on human minds. It is not only dependent in the sense of being given to, and only accessible through, the mind (such are all world versions), but also because a good part of it is made up of ideas and beliefs, wishes, passions, and norms and actions. In other words, it is inherently endowed with meaning and interpreted in multiple and conflicting ways before it ever functions as an original to become represented in a model. And since no commonly accepted version of the historical and experiential universe exists, there will also be multiple ways of making models of it. A further consequence of the mind-perfused nature of the historical-experiential world is that a model of it may legitimately reflect norms and ideals in the very way it is structured. Max Black suggests that we disregard the senses 'in which a model is a type of design – or, on the other hand, something worthy of imitation' (Black 1962: 219), but precisely this disregard is impossible when dealing with literature. This is why, to Aristotle, the question of worth lies at the very heart of poetic representation: 'Since living persons are the objects of representation, these must necessarily be either good men or inferior ... that is to say either better than ourselves or worse or much what we are ... For instance Homer's people are 'better,' Cleophon's are 'like,' while ... in Nicochares, the author of the *Poltrooniad*, they are 'worse' (Aristotle 1927: 11, 1448a).

The precondition for Aristotle's division is that we know what we are like, but do we? The enlightening answer to this question may be that we do, and we don't. We hold reasonably well-founded beliefs and opinions concerning the general motivations of people and their patterns of interaction – in a given period within a given culture. We also know the (most often conflicting), norms and ideals according to which people are supposed to act, and we know of the general ways in which compromises are made between such norms of conduct and personal strivings for survival or for one's interests and advantages. The point is, however, that individual, singular action cannot be predicted with certainty, although afterwards it may be explained – at least beyond reasonable doubt. Furthermore, both heroic and ridiculous actions do happen in real life; and thus the range of ethical greatness, average behaviour, and baseness is well known within our lifeworld.

There are, however, two further problems with seeing a given text as a model of individual and social life. First of all, what, and where, is the original of which the text is supposed to be a model? A model of the CN Tower has its original in the tower standing in Toronto, and a model of the human female skeleton has a kind of standardized diagram of innumerable human female skeletons as its original. Now, characters in an individual literary text may well have, probably most often do have, individual persons as originals. Indeed, it would be preposterous to deny the use of originals because imagination without memory is unthinkable. There are, however, two main reasons why the use of originals in literature is very complicated. First, fictional characters are very often blendings of several originals, along with much that is unidentifiable.[25] Second, even if it is possible to point to individual originals for a fictional character, the fictional universe in toto – that is, the fictional space with its different backdrops, sets, and props, and characters moving within it during fictional time – is structured in a way that will not precisely match any non-fictional universe.

In addition, and more importantly, the literary text also has features in common with the scale model of parts of species and kinds, such as the model of the human female skeleton, because literature deals with what is considered typical. Indeed, the idea that literature is a concrete and particular embodiment of what is (supposed to be) universal has been claimed of and for it since Aristotle (see *Poetics*, ix, 1451a–b), through Hegel, until today. And one has to agree. It is probably the combination of following the actions and passions of fictional characters (or individual mental events of imagination, ratiocination, and emotion in lyrical poetry) and their concomitant interpretation as exemplars of the human condition that make the reading of literature so intellectually and emotionally rewarding.

Literature, as a model, functions much in the same way as when we say that somebody is a model of something, for instance, of courage, beauty, or evil. In saying so we abstract from other features of such a person. The paragon of courage is, at the same time, a number of other things, but we use him or her to exemplify this quality. Literature, of course, may, to use E.M. Forster's term (1927), represent 'round characters,' that is, characters endowed with multiple features, but still characters and society in a literary text (even in George Eliot or Proust) are composed of a limited set of features. There is yet another aspect to this, which is brought to the fore when genre conventions are prominent, namely, that features are selected according to certain conventions. Aristotle's ethical distinction between tragedy and comedy is an example. Thus, literature offers several conflicting models of our lifeworld, each structured according to different sets of internal conventions (cf. Lotman). One of the enjoyments literature offers is precisely a certain purity, or one-sidedness, of representation; that is, we enjoy it for being different from and not true to life.

In view of these reservations, it may well be asked why we should be interested in seeing literature as a model of life. The answer is, first, that many of the difficulties mentioned are linked with representation in general, and not specifically with literature. Furthermore, among other ways of reading, we also read literature as a representation of a universe supposed to exist independently of the text, and it is, in most cases, meant to be read in that manner. What is more, only by reading in this way are we able to make sense of the text, because only so may we supplement what is not mentioned but necessarily presupposed. Consequently, one of the most important dimensions of literature would disappear from literary scholarship if we, mistakenly, considered ourselves too refined to pay it attention.

3.7.1 Literary Representation: Model and Exemplification

A model is a purposive and reductive representation of important features of its object, that is, it generalizes and standardizes.[26] These features are obtained through selection by conventions (the limited number of colours used in making maps ensures generality and uniformity). There are no literary texts that do not use conventions, although through history they have used different ones.

In modelling the world, the representational conventions used are not considered arbitrary; they are thought to be motivated, justified, even necessary, in order to achieve a true and/or proper representation of it. Truth and propriety, however, are most often at war with one another because they are, to speak with Foucault, both 'mechanisms of exclusion,' although they exclude different, most often opposed, properties of the lifeworld. For example, in French literature of the seventeenth and eighteenth centuries there is a constant clash between *le vraisemblable* (the truth-like, the probable) and *les bienséances* (propriety, the proper social behaviour). At one point, the nature to be imitated was restricted to *la belle nature* (beautiful nature, which is rather nature beautified), and there are parallel discussions in English literature, indeed in literatures all over Europe. To get an inkling of what is a stake in the constant clashes between these two claims on literature, one only needs to think of Leopold Bloom's visit to the outhouse in the fourth chapter of *Ulysses*. Although a natural ever-returning event, Joyce's representation of it is still offensive to many.

Some think that propriety demands that phenomena whose existence nobody would dream of denying – but would like to ignore – should be excluded from literary representation because they are not discussed publicly among the cultured. However, those who, in their own understanding, stand up for truth show no pity when it comes to the ruling social and literary stereotypes. Since they are fighting for other ways of representation, they easily and erroneously equate the conventional with falsity. They cannot see that in our species there is continuity between instincts and habits; that is, habit formation and habit change are ineradicable parts of human nature.

However, even if it is beyond doubt that models rest on representa-

Mimesis: Literature as Imitation and Model 171

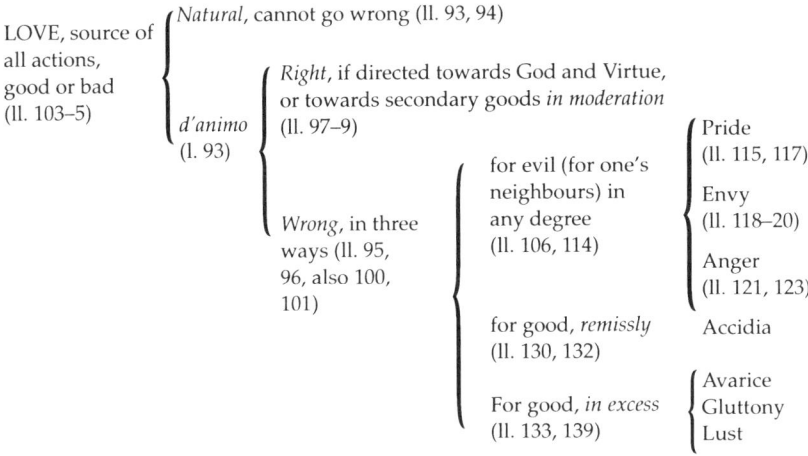

Figure 9

tional conventions that are motivated (and may be contested and defended) and that literature, among other things, is a model of changing, if only partly, socially constructed worlds, the individual literary text does not appear as a generalizing model. On the contrary, it appears as a representation of a specific, and individualized and personal, state of mind and/or state of affairs (cf. the role of indices in literature, pp. 118–20). How, then, can it be reasonably claimed that a literary text is an exemplification of habits of interpretation? This claim is justified because a dialogic relationship exists between a given text and a selection of interpretive habits of the community to which it belong. And such interpretive habits involve evaluation, related to ideas of the good life and the right way of acting and thinking. In order to exemplify this point, let us return to Dante's Purgatory.

In 3.3.3 certain historical facts and structural features of Purgatory itself were presented, but one important aspect was saved for now, namely, the self-exegetic nature of Dante's texts as regards the structure of this part of the otherworldly universe. In Cantos XVII and XVIII Virgil discourses on love. He explains that it is the supreme power moving man and universe. He further explains its nature, and stresses the fact that love need not lead to virtue. It may go wrong in three ways: by being either perverted, or defective, or excessive, it may lead to deadly sin. At the same time, however, he is describing the topography of Purgatory. Figure 9 shows the intelligible relations between Virgil's

172 Part Two: The Four Dimensions of the Literary Text

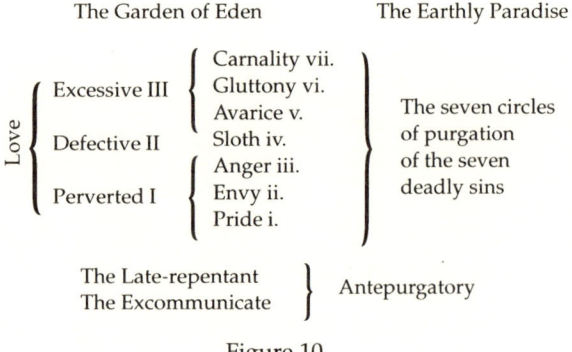

Figure 10

varieties of love going astray. This diagram is a faithful representation of the intellectual skeleton of Dante's version of the Catholic explanation of the seven deadly sins. The diagram itself is of the usual dendrogrammatic type, catching the procedure of defining by distinguishing. To make it a diagrammatic representation of the location imagined by Dante, however, we have to turn it upside down: see figure 10. This diagram, obviously, agrees with parts of the first one. It does not show the more general levels of the dendrogram, but it adds other elements, with the effect that it become a more faithful reprresentation of the actual topography of Purgatory. In fact, it agrees admirably with the attempt to pictorially represent this part of the other world displayed in figure 11. This drawing attempts to make visual Dante's and Virgil's route from the shore of the island of Purgatory to the Earthly Paradise. Obviously it lacks many details, but as a visual representation of the general outline of Purgatory, that is, as a pictorial translation of Dante's linguistic description, it is fairly accurate.

There is no doubt that much of the force of Dante's Purgatory is due to its scope and detail and to its brutal concreteness. Nevertheless, a part of the compelling strength of his vision is certainly also due to its being a diagram of intelligible relations, which he, in fact, inherited (his classification of the seven deadly sins differs only in one point from that of St Thomas Aquinas).

From a semiotic point of view, Dante has achieved a total equivalence between the universe referred to and the meaning signified. And he has also exemplified an interpretive habit, or rather a complex set of habits, namely, the Catholic faith of his time. Purgatory is, of course, a landscape of the mind. The text does not function as an iconic representa-

Mimesis: Literature as Imitation and Model   173

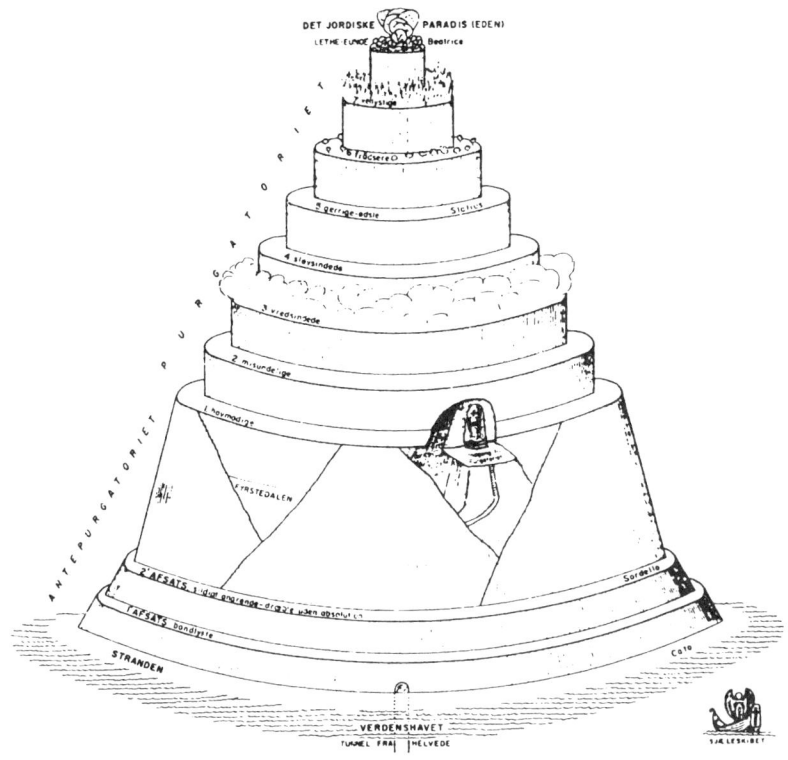

Figure 11
Dante's and Virgil's route from Purgatory to the Earthly Paradise (from the Danish translation of Dante's Divine Comedy by Knud Hee Anderson, vol. 2; reproduced by permission of G.E.C. Gad Publishing House, Copenhagen)

tion of a part of the world; instead, it creates, as far as language is able, an iconic exemplification of a conceptual and moral order. Consequently, in talking about the representative and iconic nature of literature, we should be aware that it is just as much a symbolically mediated icon of a mindscape as it is one of a landscape; indeed, even more so. And the force and attraction of literature is due to the intimate and intricate relationship between two varieties of iconicity, the interpenetration of structure and quality and of design and image.

Four

Self-representation and Analogy in Literature

[W]e all live, and speak, only through our eye for resemblances. Without it we should perish early

(I.A. Richards 1936: 89)

[W]e are obsessed with correspondences. Similarities between this and that, between apparently unconnected things, make us clap our hands delightedly when we find them out. It is a sort of national longing for form – or perhaps simply an expression of our deep belief that forms lie hidden within reality; that meaning reveals itself only in flashes.

(Rushdie 1982: 300)

Analogies are never perfect, for an analogy that should be made perfect is more than an analogy.

(CP 6.325)

The preceding chapter has dealt with literary representation as the representation of something else, as other-representation. Even if a universe of fiction is in fact created by an enunciative act, we nevertheless perceive the text as referring to something apart from itself. At one level, we treat fiction as we do a newspaper article, that is, we suppose it is about something that has happened irrespectively of whether it is reported. Obviously, as regards literary fiction, we know that this is not so, but in some phases of our reading, listening to, or watching literature we respond as if this were the case; and if we did not, we would lose an important dimension in our experience of literature. Readers imprisoned on the meta-level of reading should be pitied, not envied.

However, in addition to its capacity for other-representation, literature also has a capacity for self-representation: its self-reflexive capacity with specific ways of mirroring itself. As classical rhetoric has shown, such ways are common to literature and other kinds of artful speech and writing. In explaining what a figure is, Quintilian defines the nature of speech from the point of view of rhetoric:

> The first point for consideration is, therefore, what is meant by a *figure*. For the term is used in two senses. In the first it is applied to any form in which thought is expressed, just as it is to bodies which, whatever their composition, must have some shape. In the second a special sense, in which it is called a schema, it means a rational change in meaning or language from the ordinary and simple form, that is to say, a change analogous to that involved by sitting, lying down on something or looking back. (Quintilian 1921: III, 353, IX, i, 10–11)

He also compares rhetorical speech to use of certain attitudes and gestures, and he sums up his own understanding of figure by saying it is 'a form of expression to which a new aspect is given by art' (ibid.: IX, i, 14).

Quintilian is well aware of the difficulties of distinguishing figure in the first sense from that of the second. It may be argued, of course, that speech is always formed according to certain schemata that are traditional within given linguistic communities and linked with specific communicative purposes. Using his own analogy, we may point out that a human body will always be standing, sitting, or lying down, or have some kind of intermediary form, and it will always be at rest or moving. An example of this kind of objection to the classical view is today made by cognitive science insisting that the metaphor is not an ornament of language but a universal and inescapable form of cognition. However, even outstanding proponents of cognitive science, such as Lakoff and Mark Turner, hold that differences in degree exist between the number and complexity of figures used in literature and in non-linguistic discourses. Although metaphorical mappings are at the core of our thinking, poetic metaphors are often distinguished from basic ones by their ability to (1) extend and manipulate conventional metaphors; (2) compress several basic metaphors into a few sentences; and (3) complexify the text by combining metaphors with other tropes and figures (see Lakoff and Turner 1989: 53–6).

Thus, the study of the self-representing capacity of literature has a long history within Western culture from classical rhetoric onwards. And there is little doubt that contemporary literary studies profit from the insights of rhetoric. With regard to figures, classical rhetoric (see Bullinger 1968 and Lausberg 1960) distinguished between figures of omission (*figurae per detractionem*, elliptical figures, e.g., ellipsis itself), figures of addition (*figurae per adiectionem*, pleonastical figures, e.g., repetition and parallelism), and figures of change (*figurae per transmutationem*, or *immutationem*, the change of the usage, order, or application of words, e.g., anastrophe, metonomy, and metaphor). It is not the objective of this book to expound on rhetorical criticism or to treat the figures at large. Here the goal is much more modest, namely, to illustrate the self-representing capacity of literature by some reflections on repetition and similarity. These phenomena cover both what seem simple reiterations of sound patterns and tropes based on analogy, such as simile and metaphor. Indeed, it may turn out that analogy is the common mechanism of these apparently diverse phenomena and that analogy, as proportion and inference, is the prime device of the self-reflexivity of literature.

4.1 Repetition as a Proto-aesthetic Phenomenon

In relation to literature, analogy may mean different things and function in different ways. This diversity of meanings and functions is interesting and important because the formal structure(s) of analogy, as a relation and as a form of inference, binds together different dimensions of the literary text.

Let us first look at the following proto-aesthetic example of analogy. How does a clock sound or, rather, how is its sound transcribed? Well, at least in Bulgarian, Czech, Danish, Dutch, Finnish, French, German, Italian, Norwegian, Spanish, and Swedish it is transcribed tick-tack (with different spellings, of course), while the English-speaking nations are more liberal, since they allow both tick-tack and tick-tock. I would like to claim, however, that a clock does not at all makes such a sound, although it seems to us that we hear it that way. On the contrary, I will claim that a clock really sounds:

tick, tick, tick, tick, ...

that is, endlessly repeating the same sound (in this I agree with Frank Kermode, who has used the tick-tock example to illustrate beginning, tick, and end, tock; see Kermode 1966: 44–6). However, when we are imitating the sound of the clock, we are deforming it by a double dichotomization: We parse the string of continuous but discrete sounds into pairs:

tick-tick, tick-tick, tick-tick, ...

and we ascribe contrasting vowels (light and dark) to each member of the pair:

tick-tack, tick-tack, tick-tack, ...

This double dichotomization has two aspects: one has to do with other-representation, the other with self-representation. As regards other-representation, the Dutch semiotician Barend van Heusden has pointed out to me that although the i-a-alternation certainly has nothing to do with the sound of the clock,[1] it may represent the movement itself. Just as zigzag represents a going forward while moving from side to side, and ding-dong (a and o seem to be interchangeable with i-a in this respect) represents the sound made by a bell moving up and down. Thus, the i-a-alternation would not only represent two separate points in time and space, but the very movement from one to the other and back again, that is, tick-tack, on this view, is a minimal version of mimesis, of other-representation through sound patterning (see also the end of this chapter and Nöth 1990: 191–209).

Looking at this phenomenon as a case of linguistic self-representation, a display of systematic relations involving similarities and contrasts, we perceive already the formal structure of an analogy, namely:

tick : tack : : tick : tack,

or in a generalized form:

a : b : : a : b, which can also be written $\frac{a}{b} : : \frac{a}{b}$

4.2 Repetition, Analogy, and Poeticity

Obviously, tick-tack is not (yet) literature; it is an elementary and universal way of structuring the phonological stratum that has an oblique, but perceptible, iconic relationship to what is represented. To explore these aspects a little further, let us return to Jakobson's ideas about the general iconicity of language and especially to his using the words carried before Caesar in his triumphal march – *veni, vide, vici* – as an example. Jakobson comments on Caesar's dictum as follows: 'The chain of verbs – *Veni, vidi, vici* – informs us about the order of Caesar's deeds because the sequence of co-ordinate preterits is used to reproduce the succession of reported occurrences. The temporal order of speech events tends to mirror the order of narrated events in time or in rank' (Jakobson 1965: II, 350). However, in spite of this utterance's 'naturalness,' it is certainly not the only way in which Caesar's arrival, inspection, and victory may be expressed. Even using the same words, the sign might have read:

vici ut vidi cum venissem
vici veniendo postquam vidi
vici veniens postquam vidi

These three examples are different from the actual dictum because they are analytical. They use relational words (ut, postquam) and verb tenses to explain the relationship between Caesar's three deeds, whereas the chain *veni, vidi, vici* displays or mimes the temporal and causal order. Interesting also is the option to use another vocabulary. Caesar might have said:

perrexi, circumspexi, superavi

For informational purposes it is equivalent to what was written on the sign board in his triumphal march; and what is more, it is not only semantically, but also morphologically and syntactically equivalent. In fact, it has exactly the same degree of iconicity as *veni, vidi, vici* with respect to the relationship between sign and object. In both the above cases a diagrammatic resemblance exists between order of events and word order. What is different is the internal organization of the sound pattern. The chain *veni, vidi, vici* is built on internal similarities that have nothing to do with the relationship between signs and objects. Obviously, we may have internal sound patterning similar to *veni, vidi, vici* without any relationship to an object: *vilix, velix, valix* is a series that explores parallel patterning of the expression just as thoroughly as Caesar's words. The difference, however, is that it doesn't mean anything, because although it resembles a string of Latin words, it is not Latin.

The comparison between these two strings highlights what is going on in *veni, vidi, vici*, because compared to the non-signifying *vilix, velix, valix*, what we witness is the transition from patterned nonsense to surplus meaning. As to the effect of such patterning, Jakobson points out that '[t]he symmetry of three disyllabic verbs with an identical initial consonant and identical final vowel added splendor to the laconic victory message of Caesar: "Veni, vidi, vici"' (in Sebeok ed. 1960: 358). Here Jakobson makes the point that the representational iconicity that holds between text and object is intrasystematically redoubled in the repetitive sound pattern. As regards its other-representational capacity, Irmengard Rauch has pointed out (personal communication) that its iconicity is further enhanced by the consonantism, which loses sonority in this sequence. According to Otto Jespersen's scale of sonority whereby [n] is most sonorous, [d] is less so, and [k] is least sonorous, the sequence produces an effective meaning suggestive of hastened progression with a final punch in victory.

According to Peirce, the iconic aspect of a sign is bound up with its relation to its object, because sign and object have common properties. Caesar's *veni, vidi, vici* is, to Jakobson, iconic because the word order mimes the (alleged) course of events. Let us term this syntactic parallelism between order of event and order of signs first-degree iconicity. Propp's functions and Burkert's programs of actions are, like Caesar's *mot d'esprit*, examples of first-degree iconicity because the order of functions is identical to the (supposed) chronological order of events. First-degree iconicity, however, is only one aspect of the complex phenomenon of poetic repetition. In comparing *veni, vidi, vici* and *perrexi, circumspexi, superavi*, it is seen that both have the same first-degree iconicity, whereas only the former phrase combines this kind of iconicity with intrasystemic similarity. This kind of similarity between phonemes and syllables has nothing to do with the relationship between sign and object: it is an intralingual not an intersemiotic phenomenon. Even if every linguistic expression is structured by differences and similarities (from the distinctive features onwards), the interplay between such differences and (especially) similarities is not necessarily displayed in speech in a systematic way. According to Jakobson, however, the poetic function means precisely an elaborate patterning of the linguistic texture that brings about this effect. Some other kind of iconicity is at work here: not a similarity between sign and object but one between the material and formal qualities of the signs themselves.

For that reason we must distinguish two kinds of iconicity, namely,

```
                  horizontal        b   d        v   r
                  rotation          p   q        e   o
                                                 r   t
                                                 t   a
                                                 i   t
                                                 c   i
                                                 a   o
                                                 l   n
```

Figure 12

first-degree iconicity, which holds between the linguistic text and the represented universe (cf. chapter 3, p. 147–9), and second-degree iconicity, which holds between the elements of the linguistic text itself. Second-degree iconicity may be illustrated by simple graphematic forms, as displayed in figure 12. In this writing system p, q, d, and b are four different ways of placing the same figure, by horizontal and vertical rotation, on the same sheet.

I claimed that the information contained in *veni, vidi, vici* and *perrexi, circumspexi, superavi* is identical. This, of course, is only true from a certain perspective, because whereas the first expression seems to imply the predetermined and destined nature of Caesar's victory, this aspect is less marked in the second and almost absent in the analytical ways of expressing the message. As in tick-tack, the parallelism (the interplay between repetition of identical elements and systematic differentiations) in Caesar's words seems to lend itself to semantization (cf. Irmengard Rauch's observation above). From a formal point of view, however, parallelism is a minimal exemplification of the poetic function of language. Jakobson (following, among others, Bishop Lowth and Gerald Manley Hopkins) expressed his firm conviction that parallelism is the most basic poetic device (see also Fox 1977: 59–89) in the following celebrated passage from the seminal 'Linguistics and Poetics':

> The poetic function projects the principle of equivalence from the axis of selection into the axis of combination. Equivalence is promoted to the constitutive device of the sequence. In poetry one syllable is equalized with any other syllable of the same sequence; word stress is assumed to equal word stress, as unstress equals unstress; prosodic long is matched with long, and short with short; word boundary equals word boundary,

no boundary equals no boundary; syntactic pause equals syntactic pause, no pause equals no pause. Syllables are converted into units of measure, and so are morae or stresses. (Jakobson 1960)

What Jakobson describes here is, in fact, an application of the formal structure of proportion, or analogy. On this simple basis it is possible to invent an – in principle – infinite number of metrically different stanza forms by a procedure that from an analytical point of view consists of four steps: (1) through a combination of instantiations of the elementary opposition feet such as the iambus, trochee, anapest, dactyl, and others are formed; (2) feet then are combined into different kinds of verse such as hexameter, iambic pentameter, or others; (3) verses are combined into stanza forms such as the octave, the sestet, and others; finally (4) such stanzas may be combined according to certain rules to form specific kinds of poems such as the sonnet, the ballad, and others. The above would certainly make up a very unsophisticated and poor analysis of poetic metre *in actu*, but the point is that such a combinatory system is operative even if the sound shape of individual poems includes other important features as well.

The minimal unit, tick-tack, is already repetitive on the levels both of expression and of content, since it is a (mis)representation of the identical repetitions of one sound that go on and on infinitely. What has been sketchly exemplified for metre as repetition on the expression plane, and for reiteration as a simple form of semantic (and morpho-syntactic) repetition, is equally true of other levels of the literary text (see King Henry's soliloquy below). Within the phenomenological study of literature and the Prague School's structuralism, a division of the literary text into layers, or strata, was common. Roman Ingarden, for instance, distinguishes between the layers of (1) word-sounds and the higher sound formations built thereon; (2) different units of significations (words and sentences); (3) represented states of affairs; and (4) schematized aspects (our phenomenal constructions of the represented objects according to schemata of experience evoked by the text; see Ingarden 1965 [1931]). In the important book *Theory of Literature* (1942), co-authored with Austin Warren, René Wellek follows Ingarden, distinguishing between the sound-stratum, the stratum of meaning, and that of the represented world. I am neither going to discuss the phenomenological reasons for such layering nor compare their merits. Looking at the issue from the point of view of semiotics, however,

Ingarden's view agrees well with the semiotic pyramid. The layer of sound corresponds to the structure of the sign-vehicle, the layer of signification to that of the interpretant, the represented world to that of the object, and the layer of schematized aspects to the way in which the representation, as a unified collection of schemata, influences the apprehending subjects, author and reader; that is, the immediate object as it is constituted through interpretation.

It seems possible, however, to make a more complete list of the layers, or aspects, of the linguistic text on which such analogical combinations are operative. Let me just suggest the following: (1) sound (different phonological features); (2) metre; (3) rhythm; (4) graphematic patterning; (5) morphological patterning; (6) syntactical patterning; (7) narrative patterning; (8) semantic patterning; (9) rhetorical patterning: figures and tropes; (10) logical (argumentative) structure; (11) the structure of the represented universe; and (12) the pragmatic and communicative structures. It is the interplay between all these partial structures of the text that makes up its global effect. Poeticity from a convergence point of view, favoured by formalist and structural poetics, consists in (a) the structuration of each stratum according to the patterned opposition and recurrence of recognizable elements and (b) the coupling (cf. Levin 1962) between a plurality of layers, two being the minimum.

Obviously, there need not be any correlation, or coupling, between the different strata of the text. Its formal patterning, according to rhetorical rules, may contribute little or nothing to the text's semantic structure. Let me borrow an example of this patterning by Alexander Pope from E.L. Epstein (in Fowler 1975: 40–78):

> Adieu ye Vales, ye Montains, Streams and Groves,
> Adieu ye Shepherd's rural Lays and Loves,
> Adieu my Flocks, farewell ye Sylvan Crew,
> Daphne farewell, and all the World adieu!

Epstein points out the rhetorical patterning of the lines:

> There is a double chiasmus expressed in the third and fourth lines syntactically, and a (related) grade of phonological chiasmus.
>
> 1. The *Adieu* clauses are in chiasmus:
> *Exclamation–Nominal : Nominal–Exclamation*
> Adieu   my flocks   :   all the world   Adieu

2. The farewell clauses are in chiasmus:
Exclamation–Nominal : Nominal–Exclamation
farewell ye sylvan   Crew Daphne farewell

3. The repetition of sounds is chiastic:
Adieu farewell   farewell Adieu

He concludes his analysis with the following comment:

> Thus a double syntactic chiasmus is enclosed within a phonological chiasmus. This elegance of patterning, however, mimes no aspect of the situation expressed. It seems to be motivated rather by the formal aspect of the *Pastorals* themselves; Pope seems to feel the need for a 'decorative' ending to provide a formal climax to his structure. (ibid.: 45)

There is certainly no criticism of Pope implied here. Pope is a wonderful poet, but he wrote in a tradition within which the display of sheer craftsmanship is honoured. However, the fact that its coupling devices do not serve to unify structures of expression, content, represented universe, and communicative situation represented in the text makes such lines seem a kind of gratuitous showing off to many modern readers. Let me give an example of some lines, just as rhetorically well formed as those of Pope, in which the just mentioned aspects of the text are integrated:

> Would I were dead, if God's good will were so!
> For what is in this world but grief and woe?
> O God! methinks it were a happy life
> To be no better than a homely swain;
> To sit upon a hill, as I do now,
> To carve out dials quaintly, point by point,
> Thereby to see the minutes how they run –
> How many makes the hour full complete,
> How many days will finish up the year,
> How many years a mortal man may live.
> When this is known, then to divide the times –
> So many hours must I tend my flock;
> So many hours must I take my rest;
> So many hours must I contemplate;
> So many hours must I sport myself;

> So many days my ewes have been with young;
> So many weeks ere the poor fools will earn;
> So many years ere I shall shear the fleece;
> So minutes, hours, days, weeks, months, and years,
> Pass'd over to the end they were created,
> Would bring white hairs unto a quiet grave.
> Ah, what a life were this! How sweet! How lovely!
> (Henry VI, Part 3, V, vv. 19–41)

The beauty of this fine example of early Shakespearean eloquence is an effect of its rhetorical clarity. Here the compositional principles of identical repetition and parallelism are literally on display. As regards its themes as well, the speech is exemplary for several reasons. First, it is repetitive in another sense, namely, intertextually. The comparison of the evil and turbulent life of the high and mighty with the good and peaceful life of peasants and shepherds constitutes a literary topos repeated again and again from antiquity and throughout European literature. Further, both theme and composition are indebted to the Bible, and especially to Ecclesiastes, where we find not only one of the most forceful expositions of the *vanitas mundi* topos, but also (as pointed out in many commentaries on the above soliloquy) such specific phrases as 'The sleep of a labouring man is sweet, whether he eat little or much: but the abundance of the rich will not suffer him to sleep' (Eccles. 4: 13). There is another reason Ecclesiastes comes to mind, namely, its idea of calculation and division of man's life to form a pattern: 'To every thing there is a season, and a time to every purpose under the heaven: A time to be born, and a time to die, a time to plant, and a time to pluck up that which is planted' (Eccles. 3: 1–2). Intertextuality, then, turns out to be a form of iconicity because a relation of similarity is established, not within, but between, texts.

In King Henry's speech two different, but intertwined, conceptions of human existence can be discerned, a cyclical and a linear, the former constituting a repetitive pattern, the second a progression towards fated death. The repetitive pattern is built on two dichotomies: labour versus rest and sporting/bodily exercise versus studious/spiritual exercise; whereas the linear pattern is built on a single dichotomy, that of birth versus death. The speech expresses a time-honoured attempt to conceptualize human existence by means of a strictly limited set of generalizations reducing life to a universal repetitive natural order (in contradistinction to the unnatural course of events represented in the play). It is significant that, within the rhetorical patterning of the soliloquy, the dichotomies are, so to speak, framed within identical or slightly varied repetitions, to the effect that the quantitative aspect, the division of time, tends to level the actual and conceptual distinctions between different human activities.

In this example we have a threefold repetition: intrasystemic, mimetic, and intertextual. The text achieves a double imitation, both of nature (as it is conceived) and of tradition. This imitation is made effective by its rhetorical devices (its intrasystemic structure), which reflects both the nature of the object and the topoi, the figures of thought and speech, traditionally attached to its literary representation. It might perhaps be objected that the preceding is just a roundabout way of saying that the soliloquy is a traditional and rhetorically effective way of expressing a cliché. However, such an objection misses the point that these different kinds of repetition support each other: the text represents the repetitive character of nature by repeating a topos in a repetitive way. It is precisely because these kinds of repetition reflect each other, in and by virtue of the text, that the soliloguy has, or at least seems to have, a claim to validity. As mentioned above, this use of repetition on the surface level of the text explores the iconic potential of language.

Thus, the underpinning of language's self-reflexivity means that the same formal principle is operative on the phonological, the syntactic, and the semantic levels. This structural device is called parallelism by Jakobson. However, I prefer to call these mechanisms analogical, and thus to speak of analogy instead of parallelism. My reason is that analogy has a double meaning. On the one hand, like parallelism, it signifies a proportion, a static relationship among different kind of elements. On the other, it is a type of inference, that is, it is a cognitive process by virtue of which we learn to know what we did not know before because we draw conclusions from the similarities we perceive between phenomena belonging to different kinds or realms of experience.

4.3 Analogy as a Cognitive and Textual Structural Principle

Before going further into the structuration of literary texts through analogy, I would like to point out other ways in which analogy is operative in formal and informal reasoning and in the structuring of texts.

In mathematics the concept of analogy, as mathematical proportion, was used very early. In ancient Greece a distinction was made between three, or rather four, forms of mathematical analogy:

1. Arithmetic analogy involves similarities and differences and is founded on subtraction:

$$a - b = b - c \text{ (e.g., } 8 - 6 = 6 - 4 \rightarrow 2 = 2)$$

2. Geometric analogy concerns proportion of division. There are two forms: continuous analogy comprising three elements,

$$a : b = b : c \text{ (e.g., } 8 : 4 = 4 : 2 \rightarrow 2 = 2)$$

and the so-called discontinuous analogy comprising four elements,

$$a : b = c : d \text{ (e.g., } 8 : 4 = 6 : 3 \rightarrow 2 = 2)$$

3. Harmonic analogy combines the arithmetic (subtraction) and the geometric (division):

$$a - b : b - c :: a : c \text{ (e.g., } 6 - 4 : 4 - 3 = 6 : 3 \rightarrow 2 = 2)$$

In our context subtraction and/or division are not important, only the terms and the relationship between them.

Furthermore, analogy is an instrument of practical and theoretical reasoning, as noticed by Aristotle, who says:

> The examination of likeness is useful with a view both to inductive arguments and to hypothetical reasonings, ... because it is a general opinion that among similars what is true of one is true also of the rest. If then, with regard to any of them, we are well supplied with matter for discussion, we shall secure a preliminary admission that however it is in these cases, so it is also in the case before us: then when we have shown the former we shall have shown, on the strength of the hypothesis, the matter before us as well. (Aristotle 1941b: 205, *Top.*, I, xviii, 108b)

Here Aristotle links hypothesis and analogy, since knowledge of other cases lends strength to the hypothesis that the case under discussion is like the others in the relevant respect because it is similar to them in other respects. In this analysis he was followed by Peirce who, in accordance with tradition, distinguished between three kinds of inferences, deduction, induction, and abduction, or hypothesis. He too mentions a fourth form, namely, analogy. And although analogy is constructed by using the three other inferential forms, the eminent role it plays in our daily life earns it special mention. Informally Peirce characterizes analogy as 'the inference that a not very large collection of objects which agree in various respects may very likely agree in another respect. For instance, the earth and Mars agree in so many respects that it seems not unlikely they may agree in being inhabited' (CP 1.69). Peirce links analogy with the iconic sign that 'exhibits a similarity or analogy to the subject of discourse' (CP 1.369). Further, he sees analogy as a combination of an inductive and a hypothetical inference. The formal structure is as follows:

1.

S', S'', S''' are taken as being P', P'', P''',

S', S'', S''' are q;

(By induction) P', P'', P''' is q,

t is P', P'', P''';

(Deductively) t is q.

2.

S', S'', S''' are, for instance, P', P'', P'''

t is P', P'', P''';

(By hypothesis) t has the common characters of S', S'', S'''

S', S'', S''' are q;

(Deductively) t is q.

(CP 2.513)

In addition to analogy as a form of logical inference, we should consider three other, but related, uses of analogy.

Analogy, whose formal properties are studied by logic and mathematics, is also used in informal reasoning, whether theoretical or everyday reasoning. Like its formal counterpart it is founded on patterned repetition of identical or similar elements (similarity or proportion). Aristotle says:

Likeness should be studied, first in the case of things belonging to different genera, the formula being 'A : B = C : D' (e.g., as knowledge stands to the object of knowledge, so is sensation related to the object of sensation), and 'As A is in B, so is C in D' (as sight is in the eye, so is reason in the soul, and as is a calm in the sea, so is windlessness in the air), ... We should also look at things which belong to the same genus, to see if any identical attribute belong to them all, e.g., to a man and a horse and a dog; for in so far as they have any identical attribute, in so far they are alike. (Aristotle 1941b: 204, *Top.*, I, 17, 108a)

In this passage Aristotle gives us both his understanding of likeness as the sharing of common attributes (see also *Metaphysics*, V, 9, 1018a) and the formula of analogy. And he makes constant use of analogical reasoning; for instance, in his zoological studies.[2] Selection by analogy may bring to the fore what is qualitatively, structurally, and/or functionally similar between different species: 'We cannot find a common name to give to a squid's pounce, a fish's spine, and an animal's bone, although these too possess common properties as if there were a single osseous structure' (*Post. An.*, II, 14, 97b).

Analogies used in scientific and informal reasoning may, according to Mary Hesse (1966), be further divided into four types. First, analogy may be founded on common properties: the earth and the moon are both 'large, solid, opaque, spherical bodies receiving heat and light from the sun, revolving on their axes, and gravitating towards other bodies' (Hesse 1966: 58). The common properties constitute, in Hesse's words, their positive analogy. That the moon is smaller than the earth and that it has no atmosphere and water are part of their negative analogy. In addition to the positive and negative analogies between two objects, Hesse also talks about a neutral analogy, that is, the juxtaposition of properties from either object about which it is not yet known whether they are positive or negative. The inquiry into this question is precisely what may add to our knowledge.

In a second type of analogy similarity of properties constitutes the positive analogy, in contradistinction to the identity of properties of the first type. As an example Hesse mentions the properties of sound and light, such as echoes and reflection, loudness and brightness, pitch and colour, and so on; properties between which there is similarity, but not identity. Both types of analogy have the same structure, namely, a set of horizontal and vertical relations like this:

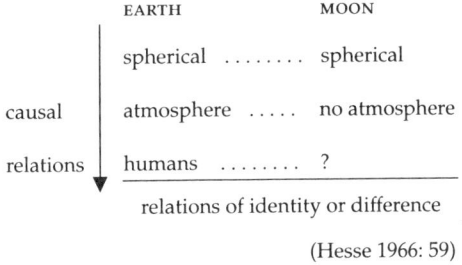

(Hesse 1966: 59)

In the second type, the horizontal relations are similarity and dissimilarity, while the vertical are causal. The third type is an Aristotelian, zoological classification: wings, lungs, and feathers in birds are analogous to fins, gills, and scales in fish. Here the horizontal relationship may be 'one or more similarities of structure or of function,' and the vertical ones may be either causal relations, as in the two previous cases, or they may be no more than relations of a whole to its parts. Hesse's fourth analogy is the political analogy used by Plato:

father : children : : state : citizens

In explaining such an analogy it is claimed, for instance, that the father is responsible for the maintenance, welfare, and defence of the child as the state is for citizens. And as the child owes obedience and respect to its father, so does the citizen to the state. According to Hesse, however, there are several important differences between this analogy and the other three, namely: (1) there is a difference in purpose: such an analogy, says Hesse, is persuasive rather than predictive; (2) it does not, like the other three, involve reasoning from three known terms to one unknown: it rather points to norms and to a moral, that is, it is normative rather than descriptive; (3) the vertical relations are not specifically causal: instead, several relations are put together in a persuasive manner (e.g., you should be obedient to your provider); and (4) there are no horizontal relations independent of the vertical relations: that is, it is only because, for instance, obedience is predicated of both the father–child relationship and that of state–citizen that father and state are conceived as analogous. Like most scientists and philosophers of science, Hesse sees analogy as a useful tool when information is missing. At a later stage of inquiry, it should, however, be replaced by other forms of inferences, specifically by inductive arguments, just as whole–

part relationships should be replaced by causal ones. It goes without saying that analogies and metaphors in literature are more akin to the fourth kind of analogy than to the other three.

In addition to its use in mathematics and scientific and practical reasoning, analogy plays an eminent role within rhetoric. In rhetoric analogy and metaphor are closely related. According to Aristotle metaphor by analogy is only one of four different types (*Poet.*, XXI, 7–14, 1457b), but it is the best and most popular. It can be argued, however, that metaphor, in the modern sense, is a subset of analogy. This understanding of metaphor also agrees with Aristotle's point of view that simile and metaphor are very close:

> The simile also is a metaphor; for there is very little difference. When the poet says of Achilles,
>
> he rushed on like a lion,
>
> it is a simile; if he says, 'a lion, he rushed on,' it is a metaphor; for because both are courageous, he transfers the sense and calls Achilles a lion. (Aristotle 1926: 367, *Rhet.*, I ii, 4, 1406b)

The quoted passage is the first formulation of the so-called similarity-comparison view of metaphor, a view that, although it has been heavily under attack in the last century, is still the most commonly accepted. According to this view, we have a small series of rhetorical figures based on comparison. This series is summarized in figure 13.

On this view, simile, parable, metaphor, hypokatastasis, and allegory are all different species of analogy. From a structural and cognitive point of view, the differences between them are minor and have mainly to do with the force of the utterance. In American movies, the heroine will often call the hero an animal because he either drinks, fights, or wants sex. This, of course, is absolutely unfair to animals, since they don't drink alcohol, fight as little as possible, and only have sex during mating season. However, in this case, the heroine may either spell out her disgust by comparison: 'You are like an animal: filthy, smelly, aggressive, inarticulate, brainless, and horny,' or she may scream 'Animal!' at him. She will not, however, start an elaborate parable or allegory. But this is precisely what a teacher, religious or profane, will do in order to guide the behaviour of pupils or disciples by showing them a parallelism in something else.

	short version	long version
r	you are like an animal ⟶	PARABLE = continuing simile
e	SIMILE by comparison: similarity	(e.g., Matt. 25: 1–18, on the ten virgins)
d		
u	you are an animal	
c	METAPHOR by representation: identity --->	ALLEGORY = continuing metaphor
t		(e.g., Matt. 3: 12, on the wheat
i		and the chaff)
o	animal!	
n	HYPOKATASTASIS by implication	

Figure 13

We have sketched three uses of analogy: (1) analogy as mathematical proportion, (2) analogy as a formal type of inference and a tool in scientific and practical reasoning, and (3) analogy as a rhetorical device. In all three cases, analogy is based on a comparison of identity or similarity of elements or relations, that is, on shared properties or identical relations. As a form of relation the structure of analogy is either a relationship comprising three elements,

a : b : : b : c

indicating that b has the same signification and/or value in relation to a and c (see below); or a four-term relationship,

a : b : : c : d

saying that the relation between a and b is the same, or homologous, to that between c and d. In the first case, identical or similar properties, b, are attributed to a and c; in the second case, it is the relations that are homologous.

4.4 Analogy and Metaphor

Dedre Gentner (the psychologist who perhaps has contributed most to the study of similarity, analogy, and metaphor) has attempted both to define analogy and to distinguish it from metaphor. Gentner's point of departure is the so-called structure mapping, which is defined as the projection of knowledge from a base to a target. According to this definition, literal comparisons, just like analogies, are structure mappings. Gentner defines a literal similarity as follows:

> A *literal similarity* statement is a comparison in which a large number of predicates are mapped from base to target, relative to the number of unmarked predicates ... The mapped predicates include *both* object-attributes and relational predicates. (Gentner 1983: 159)

Gentner's example of literal-similarity comparison is that a star system in another galaxy is like our solar system. Her point is that in literal comparisons inferences cover both object characteristics (both the sun and the X12 star are yellow and medium-sized) and relational characteristics (in both cases the planets revolve around the sun/X12 star). Thus, a literal comparison implies a rich mapping from base to target. An analogy, by contrast, is defined as follows: 'An analogy is a comparison in which relational predicates, but few or no object attributes, can be mapped from base to target' (ibid.). Her example is Rutherford's analogy: 'The hydrogen atom is like our solar system.' She points out that here the intended inferences concern relations such as 'The electron REVOLVES AROUND the nucleus, just as the planets REVOLVE AROUND the sun,' but not 'The nucleus is YELLOW, MASSIVE, etc., like the sun' (ibid.).

Gentner has devoted quite a few articles (see Bibliography) to questions relating to structure mapping, analogy, and metaphor. One point of departure is the seeming contradictory evidence: on the one hand, very young children can use metaphors (in fact Gentner mentions that a fifteen-month-old girl used the word 'moon' to refer to half a grapefruit and a hangnail). On the other hand, she tells us that not until they are fourteen years of age will an expression like 'the prison guard was a hard rock' make sense to children (Gentner 1988: 47). In order to explain this phenomenon she distinguishes between four different kinds of metaphors: (a) attributional metaphors, such as 'The sun is like an orange,' 'Her arms were like twin swans,' and 'Hair is like spaghetti;' (b) relational metaphors such as 'A roof is like a hat,' 'Cigarettes are time bombs,' and Virginia Woolf's 'She allowed life to waste like a tap left running;' (c) double metaphors: for instance, 'Plant stems are drinking straws for thirsty trees' 'This metaphor,' says Gentner, 'conveys both the common attributes "long, thin, tubular" and the common relational structure "raises fluids from a lower to a higher place in order to benefit some creature"'; ibid.: 48); and, finally, (d) complex metaphors, such as Dylan Thomas's 'On a star of faith pure as the drifting bread,/ As the food and flames of snow' and e.e. cummings's 'the voice of your eyes is deeper than all roses.'

First of all, her examples show that Gentner finds a distinction between simile and metaphor superfluous or at least of minor importance (a point of a view that I share). She understands metaphors generally as 'nonliteral similarity comparisons' (Gentner, Falkenhainer, and Skorstad 1988: 171), a view on metaphor that is controversial within analytical philosophy (Goodman and Searle) and in cognitive studies (Lakoff, Gibbs, etc.). I, however, side with Gentner on this point (see, on similarity and iconicity, pp. 33–4 and 178–80). The reason metaphors only constitute a subset of analogy is that in order for an expression to be metaphoric, there need to be a categorical clash or a form of transfer from one field or level to another. The reason 'Spartacus is a lion' is discovered to be a metaphor is that it clashes with another proposition 'Spartacus is a man': since men and lions belong to two different species, being a member of one excludes being a member of the other. However, as regards metaphor, the incompatibility of the two predicates, '—is a lion' and '—is a man,' does not mean that one of them is deemed false when applied to the subject in question. Instead, the unorthodox categorization is given an interpretation that is compatible with the one that is considered irrefutable. But not only that: the metaphorical proposition is thought to be a valuable way of characterizing the subject in question. If the proposition 'Spartacus is a lion' is deemed false, it will not be because of the objection that he is a man, but because it is thought that he is a coward.

Further, I do not think it is by accident that Gentner's examples of complex metaphors are literary. Since she is an experimental psychologist, it would be unfair to blame her for establishing a group of metaphors that are not easily computable. She herself points out the reason why these metaphors are more difficult to handle: 'they resist analysis as one-one mappings,' that is, they cannot be analysed as a single projection from one base to a target.

The contradictory evidence concerning children's capacity for understanding and producing metaphors can, according to her investigations, be explained by the distinction between two kinds of metaphors: attributional metaphors, that is, metaphors of appearance, of surface similarity, that very young children will understand, and relational metaphors that are learned later and, when learned, preferred by adults, indicating an age-conditioned shift in the structuration of knowledge.

Gentner's work on similarity, analogy, and metaphor is rewarding reading. In my context, however, it is her answer to the question whether all metaphors are analogies that matters. According to her, this is not the case, inasmuch as she claims that there are two kinds of similarity, attributional and relational; and while she understands relational metaphors as analogies, she sees attributional metaphors as non-analogical.

On what, however, is the distinction between attributional and relational similarity based? It should first be pointed out that what Gentner calls relational metaphors are perfect examples of a discontinuous analogy comprising four elements: 'A hat is like a roof' is analysable as hat : head : : roof : house.[3] Her example, 'Hair is like spaghetti,' seems a better instance to back up her distinction between relational metaphors (i.e., analogies) and attributional metaphors that, on her view, are non-analogical. We may, however, construct this comparison as a continuous analogy, hair : long, thin, greasy, cordlike, twisted : : long, thin, greasy, cordlike, twisted : spaghetti. I would claim that it is possible to construct all the so-called attributional metaphors in this way. This is why all metaphors are probably based on and may be construed as analogies, either continuous or discontinuous.[4]

Three-term and four-term analogies make up the formal basis of metaphor. This point can be further exemplified by the following two metaphors: 'Achilles is a lion' and 'The Lord is my shepherd.' The first may, following Aristotle, be construed as an analogy as follows: Achilles : courage : : courage : lion. However, if we allow the courage applied to Achilles and to a lion to differ in some unspecified way (cf. 'Connexions requiring proof which are identical by analogy have middles also analogous,' Aristotle 1941a: 182, *Post. An.*, II, 17, 99a), we would rather write: Achilles : courage : : COURAGE : lion, to mark the difference: that is, a : b : : B : c. The second metaphor may be construed as an analogy in this way: 'The Lord : me : : shepherd : (flock)'; that is, a : b : : c : d. This means that although we should keep the distinction between three-term and four-term analogies, they come closer to one another because the two instantiations of the middle term in a three-term analogy are semantically non-identical when related to the first term and when related to the fourth (the courage of a man and a lion differs; see also Lakoff and Turner 1989: 195–8 concerning this point).

The non-identity of the middle term in a metaphor, when it is construed as a three-term analogy, is one source of the indeterminacy of metaphors. Another is the indeterminacy of the attributes, in this case the semantic content of the middle term, that link source domain and target domain. Aristotle tells us that Homer compares Achilles to a lion because both are courageous. However, couldn't it have been for other reasons, for instance, because they share the attribute strength, or ferocity, or deadliness, or majesty, or magnanimity? The point is that source and target will always share an indefinite number of attributes. The formula for the construction of metaphor as an analogy must take this fact into account. Thus, it would be more correct to represent the formula as

$a : b_1 ... b_n :: B_1 ... B_n : C$

because this representation makes visible its double indefiniteness.

With Gentner, we most often think of metaphors as the linking of two semantic domains through the mapping of one realm, the so-called source (or base) domain, onto the other, the so-called target domain, by the projection of elements and structures from source onto target, with the effect that the concept of the latter is structured by the former (very often the source domain will be physical or at least concrete and well known, while the target domain tends to be mental, abstract, or little understood). Let one of Turner's many examples suffice, namely, LIFE is a PLAY (1991: 159):

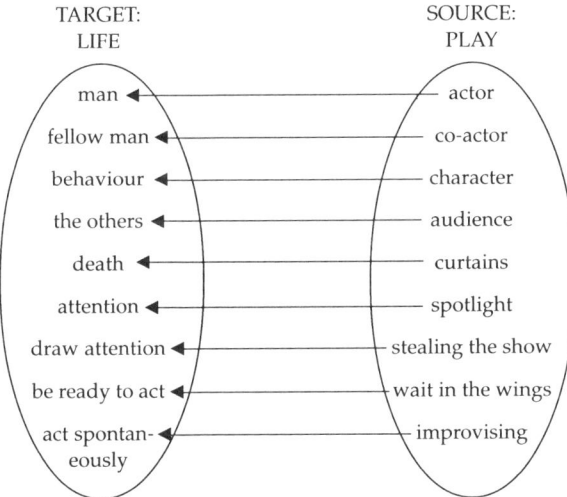

The point is that because such a metaphor is established by the projection of a whole conceptual structure, it is potentially eternally productive; there is no end to the continuous addition of novel variants to the metaphor LIFE IS A PLAY and no predictability as to the forms these may take.[5]

But what about Gentner's so-called complex metaphors that do not allow a one–one projection, such as, for instance, 'the voice of your eyes is deeper than all roses'? In such a case, the analysis may proceed by disentangling the different semantic relations within the expression. First, there is the comparison between look and voice, as in the commonplace 'an eloquent look,' that is, look : eloquence : : eloquence : voice; 'deeper' may, of course, be predicated of voice, for instance, 'a deep voice.' However, 'deep' has already other, also metaphorical, significations, such as 'serious,' 'grave,' 'difficult,' and 'unfathomable,' that may be predicated of 'voice' (and equally well of 'look'). The other comparison is that between the voice ('of your eyes') and what it is deeper than, 'all roses.' This is a four-term analogy in which the fourth term is missing, namely, eloquence : eyes : : roses : ?. This '?' may be replaced through interpretation; 'love,' for instance, may be a likely candidate (because 'love' may be inferred from 'roses'). This would give us, then, eloquence : eyes : : roses : love. However, this comparison, by using the comparative degree, explicitly says that the other person's look is far more (cf. 'all roses') eloquent of love than all traditional tokens ('roses') of it. Thus, this complex metaphor can be analysed as the combination of a three-term and a four-term analogy. Obviously, the accomplished poetry-reader grasps this in a split second.

This is one way of handling complex metaphors. Within cognitive studies the source-target model (used by Lakoff) has been developed. Although the larger theoretical framework and the perspective of the older model (cf. the diagram of the LIFE IS A PLAY metaphor above) were, and are, profoundly interesting and important (and in concrete analyses often brilliant), many scholars have rejected this model of metaphor as unacceptable for two reasons: (1) its unidirectionality – the mapping, it is claimed, is only from source to target; and (2) the denial that similarity plays any important role in the discovery of or invention of metaphors. In the revised model by Fauconnier and Turner these obstacles seem to have been be removed, or at least the model may be used whether one agrees or disagrees on these issues. Metaphor is now treated as a case of blending, and is defined not as a projection from one domain into another (from source domain to target domain) but as a projection of two or more input spaces (sources) into a common blended space (the indefinite number of input spaces makes it easier to handle complex metaphors). Thus, the revised model allows multiple influences from different directions in the blended space. It is also stressed rightly that the blended space possesses emergent qualities, that is, features that cannot be ascribed to any of the input spaces but result from the blending itself. Furthermore, in addition to an indefinite number of input spaces and the blended space, which is the actual online text, the revised model also has a so-called generic space, of which Turner says: '[T]he cross-space mapping between the inputs is the content of the generic space. The generic space typically contains an abstract structure viewed as applying to both inputs' (1997: 36).

Here a five-space version of the model is filled in with a (partial) representation of the proverb/metaphor 'When the cat's away, the mice will play.' Cats, mice, and the relation between them constitute one input space that, like most proverbs, is projected into a blended space. The other input space, which is implied rather than mentioned online, will be the concrete situation to which the proverb is applied; stories from school, from the office, or from marital life. Let us here stipulate a conversational context giving the second input space, such as, for instance: 'Mabel and Hank have been doing it the entire week. Poor Jack! Well, when the cat is away ...' Notice that the status of the proverb as a metaphor comes from its use, the fact that it is not used about cats and mice, but about people. Notice, further, that we need three input spaces to indicate that, in this case, it is about marital unfaithfulness, not about taking the day off when the boss is away. According to the analysis by Lakoff and Turner (1989), the application of the proverb to a concrete case is an instance of the mechanism called 'generic is specific,' that is, a concrete input contains an abstract structure, located in the generic space, that can be applied to an indefinite number of inputs in the blended space because they share this abstract pattern; and, consequently, the input spaces will have counterparts that allow their blending (the absent husband will be the cat, the unfaithful wife and the lover the mice). It may also be possible to express the content of the generic space differently from that of the input space, as in, for example, 'lack of control breeds transgression.'[6]

It is further important to remember that the concept of metaphor is not confined to the blending of conceptual spaces, that is, different realms of connected concepts and lexical units. It will be remembered that in Peirce iconic signs are subdivided into images, diagrams, and metaphors, and the latter are said to 'represent the representative character of a representamen by representing a parallelism in something else' (CP 2.277). Consequently, a broad conception of metaphor is in order. In my opinion we should count both *veni, vidi, vici*, and Rimbaud's famous statement in a letter from 1871, *Je est un autre*, as metaphors.

198   Part Two: The Four Dimensions of the Literary Text

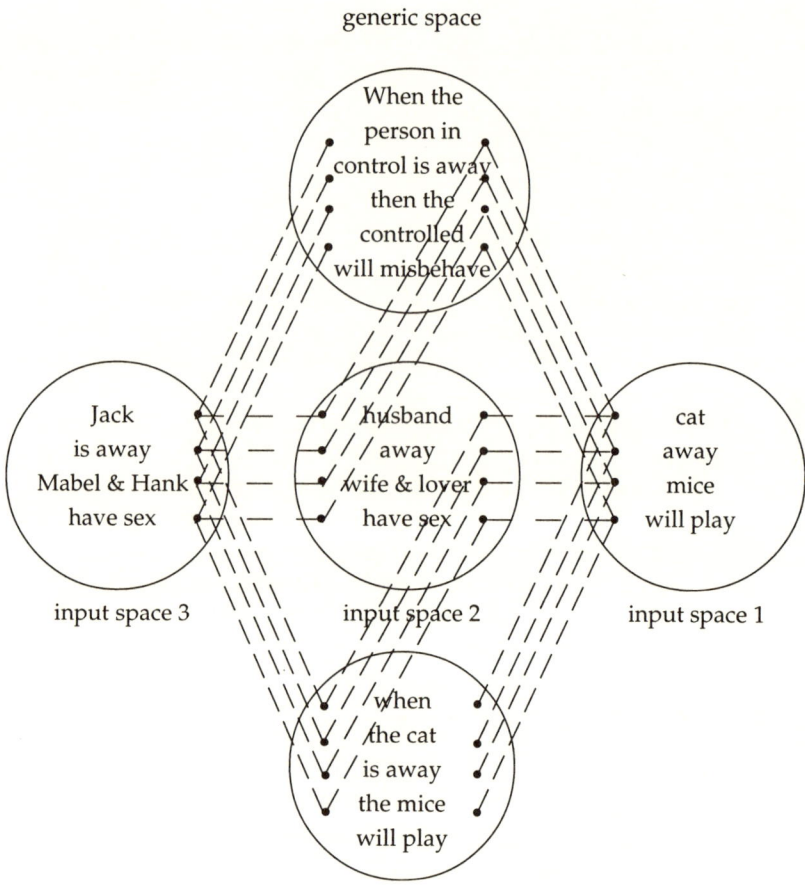

Figure 14

Unless you doubt his command of French, the grammatical 'error' he commits is eminently significant. And it is a metaphor. In fact, it constitutes a flawless analogy: [moi] : je : : je : est because linking the first-person singular personal pronoun with the third-person singular indicative present of *être* creates an (a)grammatical construction that mirrors the alienated state of mind referred to.

The same effect is achieved a little differently in *veni, vidi, vici*. Here the material and formal parallelisms are added to the first-degree iconicity of the phrase, which is itself diagrammatic. It may seem strange to talk about metaphor in this context, because metaphor is tied up with semantics, and here only formal and material properties of the expression have been discussed. I would certainly not claim that any formal arrangement of expression that works with similarities (such as rhythm, metre, rhyme, euphony, etc.) per se is metaphorical, since metaphor necessarily involves elements of reference and meaning. In Caesar's dictum, however, these preconditions are fulfilled, because in *veni, vidi, vici* the first-degree iconicity is supplemented by the intralinguistic play between similarity and dissimilarity. The two kinds of iconicity are quite independent of each other, but here, as in Rimbaud, they are fused, with the result that the representational (referential) and the self-reflective (poetic) aspects of the text mirror one another (see further on this in the next chapter).

4.5 From Repetition to Metaphor

Species of analogy such as parallelisms, similes, and metaphors are all rhetorical or poetic devices that produce or discover similarities. They are specifically elaborated forms of general ways in which phenomena are related to one another in the mind (already Aristotle distinguished between association by similarity, by contrast, and by continuity in time or space (*De memoria et reminiscentia*, [1942]: 451b). They serve a double purpose, to make us perceive the unity of the text both as a material texture and as an argument, and to make the subject intelligible and probable by showing how it is related to what is otherwise known or considered probable. Metaphors and similes are absolutely important to literature. Nevertheless, they are just one form of analogy, semantic analogy, the two other major forms being analogy of sound, or sound parallelism, such as alliteration – 'Down dropt the breeze, the sails dropt down,/ Twas sad as sad could be' (cf. also tick-tack) – and syntactic analogy (cf. the chain *veni, vidi, vici*, which of course is also phonological and semantic).

The power of metaphor is founded on its ability to perform two operations simultaneously: it connects different semantic or cognitive domains, and thus it brings different spheres of experience into relation with one another; and it uses this linking in the production of knowledge, whether trivial or innovative. Max Black has pointed out that metaphor can be regarded as a species of model. Indeed, he says that 'every metaphor is the tip of a submerged model' (in Ortony 1993: 30) because a metaphor's secondary subject offers an perspective through which its primary subject is seen (Achilles, or Spartacus, is seen in a lion-perspective).

The study of analogy may serve as a meeting place for classical rhetoric and contemporary studies in poetics and semantics. There is, it seems to me, in spite of some disagreement, a profound similarity between, for instance, Aristotle's view on the role of comparison and fable, the structural study of poeticity in structuralism (Jakobson, Mukarovsky, and Lotman and, for narrative, Propp, Lévi-Strauss, Holbek, etc.), and the study of literature within cognitive semantics (e.g., the work of Lakoff, Johnson, and Turner).

The precondition for comparison, parallelism, and analogy is repetition, whether identical or varied. Identity or difference is, however, a question of level of abstraction: for most purposes, two genuine ten-dollar bills are identical and lawful replicas of the same type, but obviously under a minute physical examination they are different. The tic-tac, tic-tac phenomenon exemplifies a minimal but systematic use of the interplay between identity and non-identity in repetition. Being an onomatopoeticon, it further exemplifies a basic mechanism, the combination of iconicity and conventionality in the production of signification. In this case, the sign's referential fit is motivated by a certain likeness that in some respects, however, is a highly arbitrary (mis)representation of the object that is (mis)conceived as a self-delimiting time-segment. Minimal as it is, it nevertheless unites first- and second-degree iconicity because its referential function is mirrored by its internal similarities. Thus, meaning grows out of the interplay between similarity (identity), difference, and the indexical function of the sign. In this context, however, what is most interesting is the role played by repetition. Obviously, on an abstract level repetition is always a precondition for the emergence of meaning, because without something being recognized as similar to something else, and without a discernable pattern in the sign itself, meaning is not possible – the absolutely unique would not signify anything. It is important to repetition in literature, however, that signification and aesthetic effect are merged, and that repetition takes place simultaneously on more levels and is more prominent than in texts belonging mainly to other discourses.

If the thesis is accepted that all metaphors are, or at least may be construed as, analogies, and that analogy is a kind of comparison, it will follow that metaphor is a specific kind of semantic, or, to be more precise, a semantic-pragmatic analogy. If one says, for instance, 'Why keep a dog and bark yourself,' there is a double metaphorization, semantic and pragmatic. To describe the warning/scolding of a person as barking is a semantic projection from the animal kingdom to the human, but to this must be added the proverb's use, which is metaphorical, since it is used of servants not of dogs (master : dog : : employer : employee). However, non-metaphorical semantic-pragmatic parallelisms also abound in literature. The Psalms and Proverbs, for instance, are full of them:

20 My son, keep thy father's commandment,
and forsake not the law of your mother:
21 Bind them eternally upon thy heart,
and tie them around thy neck. (Proverbs 6: 20–1)

Verse 20 is an example of a semantic parallelism. Verse 21, however, is a metaphor, since one cannot bind laws and commandments upon the heart, or tie them around the neck (you can do it in ritual of course, but such a ritual already constitutes a metaphorical action).

The syntactic and semantic parallelisms of verse 20 combine simple repetition with antithetical parallelism: The verbs 'keep' and 'forsake + negation' are syntactically parallel, and both are in the imperative mood; 'commandment' and 'law' are semantic parallelisms, while 'father' and 'mother' are parallel, that is, both signify 'parent,' and antithetical.

Verse 21 is a syntactic and semantic parallel to verse 20, because the two sentences of this verse are both parallel to each other and to the two sentences of verse 20. Thus, the four sentences are variants of the same message, the request or summons to remember to be always faithful to the teachings and moral laws of one's parents. The metaphors, however, consist in the projection of physical relationships onto mental and moral matters, namely, a bag or purse bound around the chest or hanging from the neck on the chest close to the heart. This relationship may be constructed as an analogy with four elements: the memorable : memory : : treasure : purse. Also the simple semantic parallelism may be constructed as an analogy: father : commandment : : mother : law. The difference between ordinary semantic parallelism and metaphor is that while the former combines semantically homogeneous elements, the metaphor, according to Peirce, manifests a parallelism in something else; or as Aristotle would have explained it, this metaphor transcends the limits of one genus. Both the ordinary semantic parallelism and the metaphor are analogies, but while the former is isotopic, the latter is heterotopic (trans-categorical).

Repetition is the reiteration of elements or relations that are fully or partially identical. Thus, the precondition of repetition is similarity (and similarity is only recognizable by virtue of repetition). And the rhetorical figures of addition are different ways of handling similarity and repetition. Repetition may be identical or show variation. The varied repetition is called parallelism. Parallelism also involves the relationship between elements of expression and of content, and it exists on several linguistic levels, phonological, syntactical, and semantic (in literature often at the same time). It reigns from alliteration such as 'O wild West Wind, thou breath of Autumn's being' to hermeneia, that is, the rhetorical figure adding and explicating the self-exegesis of the text: 'For I will pour water upon him that is thirsty, and floods upon the dry ground: I will pour the spirit upon thy seed, and my blessing upon thy offspring' (Isa. 44: 3). Parallelism may be represented in the form of continuous or discontinuous analogies. Semantic analogies may be either homo- or heterotopic. Homotopic analogies are constructed by the linking of semantic elements from the same semantic domain, whereas heterotopic analogies relate significations whose parallelizations unite what is categorically different, such as, for instance, material and immaterial, inorganic and organic, body and mind. The heterotopic semantic-pragmatic parallelisms make up parts of the figures that classical rhetoric called tropes, but similes evidently belong to this group as well, although they were placed with the figures rather than with the tropes.

Even if there are solid indications and arguments for holding that all metaphors may be construed as one or more analogies with three or four elements, one should be cautious because this thesis needs further scrutiny. It is beyond doubt, however, that a very great number of metaphors allow such a transformation and analysis. Thus, there is a continuity from parallelisms of expression to a semantic-pragmatic figure like metaphor. The same interplay between similarity and dissimilarity in the chain of signs that, according to Jakobson, characterizes poetic language is active on and between all textual levels.

4.6 The Self-representation of Narrative

To this point the examples illustrating the self-representational capacity of literature have been taken from poetry (or from poetry-like soliloquy and proverbs). The reason for this is obvious: poetry cares for, patterns, and displays the materiality of language. 'For the ear trieth words, as the mouth tasteth meat,' as É-li-bú told the wise men (Job 34: 3). What is more, reading and writing poetry means being involved in an activity that is often felt to be somatic as well as mental because syllables, words, and verses become, as Jakobson says, something palpable and cause a joy that is felt to be sensuous and bodily.

Sometimes poetry is simultaneously seen as an unmediated expression of the poet's mind and as self-reflexive, preoccupied with its own patterning. This view, however, is self-contradictory. If meditation on, and display of, a rich patterning play an important role, and indeed it does, then poetry's expressivity is certainly mediated. Furthermore, poems are, as drama and narrative, most often representational (some think that, for instance, dadaistic poems like the one cited on p. 266 are exceptions). They represent states of affairs, situations, events, dialogues, and actions as reflected in the mind of the lyrical I and his or her emotional attitude towards them. I would venture to claim that poems are truncated narratives. Before crying sacrilege, however, it should be well understood that poems are not second-rate narratives. They are the peak moment, as it were, of a narrative made autonomous – or rather relatively autonomous. However, in order to understand, and to enjoy, the poem, the reader must, at least subconsciously, reconstruct a minimal dialogical context; and through such contextualization it also becomes inscribed in a minimal narrative. Marvell's 'To His Coy Mistress' depends on our understanding that it represents a critical moment in the wooing of the woman addressed; that is, it should be read as an act of persuasion pointing out for the hesitant maiden a powerful exhortation to seize the day. If one disregards its place within *Songs of Experience* (and *Songs of Innocence*), Blake's 'The Tyger' demands at least a minimal contextualization, namely, the confrontation of the lyrical I with metaphysical evil and his meditation thereon; furthermore, the poem even contains a truncated narrative of the revolt of the angels. Eliot's 'Sweeney Among the Nightingales' contains a murder in a sleazy brothel and, into the bargain, a reference to the murder of Agamemnon.

Even a poem devoted to meditation such as Wordsworth's 'Tintern Abbey Re-visited' tells about a process of mental transformation. These examples strongly indicate that poetry is both representational and narrative.

The reason why the narrative element in poetry is often ignored is that the perspective of poetry is mostly that of communicating the impact and significance of states of affairs, situations, events, and so forth upon the perceiving and reflecting subject. In this sense, the primary concern of lyrical poetry is most often the representation of present states of mind rather than worlds: for instance, the fervour and eagerness of Marvell's lover, the wonder and horror of Blake's protagonist, the musement of Wordsworth's lyrical I, and the fascination, attempted aloofness, and disgust of Eliot's narrator. However, both self-experience and emotion are mediated by an object (in Peirce's sense). For that reason, even if it may be true that the primary subject of representation in poetry is states of mind, such states are the arrangement of trains of emotionally charged thought, of experiences of confrontations with objects. And both the objects and the confrontations with them have a story, if most often only intimated, left for the reader to complete.

It is not the case, either, as it has been amply proved from Aristotle's *Poetics* to Todorov's *Poetics of Prose* (1977), that self-representation is absent from narrative and drama. First of all, a lot of poetic devices (metre, verse, etc.) are shared by narrative and poetry, and there are the prose poems. This is why it is so difficult to distinguish poetry from other forms of literature. Eliot despaired because he thought that he lacked a concept: he only had the distinction between verse and prose, but could not find the opposite of poetry (often, in the Middle Ages and the Renaissance, verse was, in spite of Aristotle's warning, the criterion used to distinguish poetry from eloquence). He further points out that while verse versus prose is a descriptive distinction, the term poetry also introduces a distinction between good and bad verse, whereas the concept of prose is neutral (Eliot 1949: 11). Eliot's own attempted solutions, for there are at least two, are to stress the role of musicality in poetry (which of course is the classical *differentia specifica* of lyrical poetry), that is, the so-called auditory imagination and the indirect, even subconscious, communication of meaning effectuated by the sound patterning of poems (see Eliot 1957: 238). The problem is that rhythm and verse, so important for this definition, do not play a role in prose poems, for prose has it own kind of rhythm, different from that of verse. Consequently, Eliot also uses the image as a criterion to define poetry and to distinguish it from both verse and prose. Poetry, according to

Eliot, is typified by a 'cumulative succession of images each fusing with the next; or by the rapid and unexpected combination of images apparently unrelated, which have their relationship forced upon them by the mind of the author' (Eliot 1921: 9). Eliot is not, however, really satisfied with his own reflections that will lead to associating imagination with poetry and prose with reason. Hence, he points out that 'it does not follow that there are two distinct faculties, one of imagination and one of reason, one of poetry and one of prose, or that "feeling" in a work of art is any less an intellectual product than is "thought"' (ibid.). Consequently, he ends up by recommending a technical distinction between verse and prose rhythm (again a classical criterion). Later, in his 1958 preface to the English translation of Valéry's *Art of Poetry*, Eliot confessed: 'I do not believe that any distinction between prose and poetry is meaningful' (quoted from Ricks in MacMaster 1972: 505). Even so, Eliot's reflections are valuable and also instructive as an example of the vainness of attempts to make traditional categorical distinctions work, for the distinction between verse and prose is clearly a distinction by scale, not by cut. One could also say that poetry is a very good example of a radial concept.

On the view presented here, it is unhelpful to distinguish sharply between narrative (including drama) and lyrical poetry. Nobody will deny the difference between *Pilgrim's Progress* and 'To His Coy Mistress.' But this difference is not due to the lack of a narrative core in the poem but to the way in which narration, description, reflection, exclamation, and evocation are balanced against each other – and, of course, to the role of musicality and verse rhythm in the poem. It is its elliptical nature and concentration that characterizes most lyrical poetry, not the absence of narrative features. As pointed out before, nowhere does the idea of the radiality of concepts seem more apropos than in the study of literature. The soundest approach to the problems of genre is after all a historical one. Within a literature at a given time certain literary works are felt to exemplify, even to embody, the conception of that genre at that age, but since literature changes, at another time other works may be considered exemplars.

However, in order to point out the ubiquitous role of analogy in literature's self-representation, we will exemplify by structures that are analogical but not metaphorical, and that are most explicitly represented in narrative. As regards narrative Northrop Frye has observed that 'in reading fiction there are two kinds of recognition. One is the continuous recognition of credibility, fidelity to experience, and of what is not so much lifelikeness as livelyness. The other is the recognition of

206   Part Two: The Four Dimensions of the Literary Text

the identity of the total design, into which we are initiated by the technical recognition of the plot' (Frye 1963: 29). This double perspective (which we have already met in the preceding chapter) is unavoidable and constitutes an important dimension in the dialectic of reading literature. As regards the internal perspective, Frye talks of the recognition of the identity of the total design and, specifically, about plot recognition.[7] Here the internal, self-representational nature of narrative (and of drama) will be exemplified by a discussion of two common ways of plotting specific types of action and conflict: the plotting of the crisis of adolescence in the fairy tale and the plotting of family history in myth and tragedy. It goes without saying that these ways of plotting are here presented and treated only as examples of narrative designs.

4.6.1 The Crisis of Adolescence in Fairy Tales

Considering the enormous field of twentieth-century study of narrative structure in general, and of fairy tales in particular (Olrik, Propp, Lüthi, Greimas, Dundes, and Meletinskij, to mention just a few prominent scholars), the warning that the following accounts of narrative structures serve only as examples is certainly justified. As regards the fairy-tale structure, I will stick to the analysis of my compatriot, Bengt Holbek, in his huge dissertation *Interpretation of Fairy Tales* (1986) and the subsequent book in Danish *Tolkning af trylleeventyr* (1989, also meaning *Interpretation of Fairy Tales*). The reason for this choice is not chauvinism, I hope, but the fact that Holbek offers a new perspective on the tales by stressing that they have not one but two protagonists, a hero and a heroine, and that the distinction between masculine and feminine tales does not alter this fact. It only marks who is active and who is passive in the different sections of the tales. Another fresh perspective on the tales is a corollary of this understanding, namely, that it is possible to discover a general narrative structure to the tales that consists in five moves; or, as Holbek later says, the generic fairy tale has five acts.

The point of departure for Holbek's analysis is Köngäs Maranda's analysis of the European fairy tale into three thematic oppositions (Köngäs Maranda and Maranda 1971) involving (social) status: the opposition between high (H) and low (L); as regards age, that between young (Y) and old (O); and finally the opposition between male (M) and female (F). These oppositions are combined to form a set of eight tale roles that subsume what characterizes individual fairy-tale figures. Köngäs Maranda (1971: 23) presents the relationship between the roles in a diagram (see figure 15).

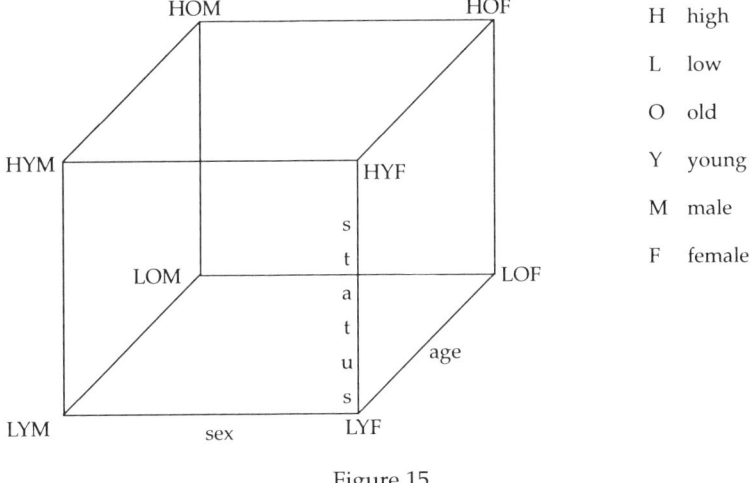

Figure 15

In the fairy tales the oppositions between high and low status, between old – or in Holbek' preference – adult and young, and between male and female are transformed into conflictual action in a characteristic way that remains constant in all the tales (although the order in which the acts are narrated may change, and acts may be left out in individual tales). The first act consists in the following:

ACT I: INTRODUCTORY SEQUENCE
Stimulus: Testing (the maturity of) the Young Hero(ine)
1' a) an interdiction is announced
    b) reconnaissance by villain to get information
    c) trickery (by villain)
1" *Response: Failure to Pass the Test*
    a) interdiction violated
    b) information given to villain
    c) complicity
1''' *Result*:
    villainy/lack/immobilization

Act I ends with the helplessness of one of the two protagonists. In Act II the other protagonist prepares for the rescue that follows in Act III by acquiring the necessary qualifications:

ACT II: DONOR SEQUENCE
Stimulus: Testing (the maturity of) the Young Hero(ine)
2'   hero(ine) is challenged by donor
Response: Passing the Test
2"   the hero(ine) does the right thing
Result:
2''' provision or receipt of a magical agent

Propp has seen these tests as preliminary tests, but in a later study (Russ. 1946, Ger. 1987: 60ff.) he understands them as maturity tests (and links them with ancient initiation rituals). It is significant that while the young high-status hero(ine) fails to pass the test in Act I, the young low-status hero(ine) passes it in Act II. Holbek sees Acts I and II primarily as the articulation of the conflict between generations: the fight for, and success or failure of the young in seeking, independence, that is, the liberation from the authority of, emotional attachment to, and control by the adults (the parents). The failure of the young high-status person (whether male or female) and the success of the young person with low status (again either male or female) are explained by the fact that these stories were primarily told in rural communities and rather among the peasants than among the lords. The order of Act I and II is variable in the individual tales. For Holbek, the important point is that the fairy tale has a double beginning – two, not one, initial situations – even if the extent to which the beginnings are elaborated, or even left out, varies from tale to tale. The result is, however, that at the end of Act II, the young high-status hero(ine) is immobilized, literally or symbolically, unable to liberate him- or herself. Thus, on the high-status level alone, the conflict between the generations cannot be solved.

Maturity, whether the concrete test is passed or not, includes sexual maturity. Hence, in Act III hero and heroine will meet, and thus all three basic oppositions, and conflicts, are activated. Holbek describes the situation at the opening of Act III in this way:

> When the move [Act III] begins we have, on the one hand, a hero(ine) who has been recognized by his/her elders, who is adult, mature, independent, mobile, and capable (equipped with 'magic' gifts); on the other, a future spouse who is transformed into an animal, petrified, imprisoned, under a spell, in a deathlike sleep, abducted, or on the verge of being given to a dragon. These two, the future marriage partners, are as distant from each other with regard to the three dimensions of the paradigmatic model – age

group, status, and sex – as can be imagined. The overcoming of this distance is often described in the tales as a long and dangerous journey ... As may be seen, the initiative always comes from the character on the LA [low, adult] axis. (Holbek 1986: 423)

The general pattern of Act III is as follows:

ACT III: CONTACT AND RESCUE
  3′   confrontation with the evil, immobilizing force (troll, dragon, etc.)
  3″   the evil force is defeated by the active hero(ine)
  3‴ contact with and rescue of passive hero(ine)

In Propp, who only analyses the tales from the point of view of the active hero(ine), this sequence is primarily seen as containing the main test (the fight, for instance, and victory over the immobilizing force). In Holbek the matter is more complicated, since he points out the importance of the sexual encounter between the future couple. Whereas the second sequence is somehow related to ancient initiation rites, Holbek assumes that this third is related to the custom of bundling in rural communities of the past (ibid.: 424). This encounter and alliance between hero and heroine, is, however, a misalliance that has to be kept secret, and this misalliance, and the secrecy it entails, makes the two last acts necessary.

Act IV contains either the attempted revenge of the defeated or the resistance of the parents against recognizing the relationship of their son or daughter. Very often both conflicts are present and integrated:

ACT IV: THE EXCLUSION OF THE ACTIVE HERO(INE)
  4′   the, until now, active hero(ine) becomes passive (e.g., sleeps exhausted after the fight)
  4″   the passive and the active hero(ine) are separated by guile or violence
  4‴ the till now active hero(ine) is excluded from the community

Act V has three main variants:

ACT V: RECOGNITION, INTEGRATION AND MARRIAGE
  5′   a) the, until now, passive hero(ine) becomes active and finds or sends for his/her rescuer
       b) the hero(ine) who has been active all the time is challenged

and tested once more by the parents of his or her (future) spouse
c) the rival/false hero(ine) takes credit for the rescue
5″ a) the resistance of the older generation is overcome
b) the final test is passed
c) the active hero(ine) reveals the fraud of the rival/false hero(ine)
5‴ a) the secret misalliance is made public and legal, and the young couple assume their rightful position in the hierarchy and order of succession
b) the hero(ine) passes the test
c) the hero(ine) assumes his/her rightful position, while the false hero(ine) is executed

The common features of the three variants are recognition and integration by virtue of the young couple's last successful effort (sometimes called the glorifying test), which finally secures their rights. The normal ending of a fairy tale is marriage, which celebrates the merging of personal maturation, the sexual union of male and female, and the exceptional, it should be stressed, social mobility transforming low status into high status. After the marriage, the young couple, according to the formula, 'live happily ever after.' This formula stresses that the fairy tale is about the crisis of adolescence and its being overcome by the individual attributes and maturity of the low-status hero(ine) and by the fidelity of the young couple after Act III.

From the perspective of this chapter it can be seen that analogy plays a major role in the narrative structure in different ways. Looking from the outside at a great number of different tales, it is evident that they are analogues of each other: they all share a generic fairy-tale structure, despite their different surface structures. Internally each of the five acts shares the same generic structure: (1) task, (2) success/failure, (3) result. Furthermore, the following analogical structure is valid for the first two acts:

low status : positive individual attributes : maturity : success
high status : negative individual attributes : immaturity : failure

Furthermore, Act I is to Act IV as Act II is to Act V, because in the first act the failing hero(ine) is immobilized, and in Act IV the same happens to the successful hero(ine); and in both the second act and fifth act the active hero(ine) successfully completes a task and is recognized by the elders. From another perspective, however, Act I and Act V are correlated in the same way as Acts III and IV: Act V is a reversal of Act I in that in the latter the passive hero(ine) fails to complete a task or violates an interdiction and is therefore not recognized, whereas Act V brings the recognition. For the successful hero(ine) this is different: in Act III the active hero(ine) completes the main task and makes contact, whereas in Act IV he or she is immobilized and loses contact. Again, from another perspective, namely, that of the relationship between sexuality and community, Act V is the reversal of Act III, since the sexual relationship between the young couple is secret and illicit in Act III, but public and sanctioned by the community in Act V. As Propp and Greimas, among others, have shown, it is quite possible to further dissolve the plot structure into smaller semantic units, and in that process a host of additional analogical relationships will present themselves. However, the point should be clear that narrative structure is a kind of syntax that promotes similarity to a constitutive device just as does the use of parallelisms in lyrical poetry, and that what Hjelmslev would call the content form of the fairy tale is analogical at its very core. However, the fairy tale is a specific genre. In order to demonstrate that analogy is all-pervasive in narrative, let us also look at a mythic family saga.

4.6.2 Family Business: The Fateful Square

The fairy tale illustrates how the story pattern is built up by replication and reversal of sequences (e.g., tests), and thus fairy-tale plotting is an elementary example of variant or analogical repetition that constantly rearticulates a small number of oppositions and conflicts. There is, of course, another kind of analogous repetition, namely, in the production of an almost infinite number of tales using the same generic plot structure. Another form of repetition becomes apparent when the focus is changed from adolescent crisis to a full-fledged family saga. In the *Poetics* we read:

> We must now decide what incidents seem dreadful or rather pitiable ... [W]hen these calamities happen among friends, when for instance brother kills brother, or son father, or mother son, or son mother – either kills or intends to kill, or does something of the kind, that is what we must look for ... So this is the reason ... why tragedies are about a few families. For in their experiments it was from no technical knowledge but purely by chance that they found out how to produce such an effect in their stories.

So they are obliged to have recourse to those families in which such calamities befell. (Aristotle 1927: 51–5, *Poetics*, 1453b)

The basic pattern of the family tragedy, according to psychoanalysis, is Oedipal. I think that this claim is essentially correct both for tragedy and for the fairy tale (at least as an important partial analysis), and it seems to be convincingly substantiated by the stories themselves. It is, however, not reducible to the triangle hero–mother–father or heroine–father–mother; it is rather a square and a fateful one (figure 16). The plots of such family tragedies are engendered by the feelings and actions of the family members towards each other and by the power linked with their position within the square and within society. Since the subject of this part of the chapter is the repetitive and analogous nature of narrative, I will not offer an interpretation of a specific text, but will attempt to reconstruct the story of how the potentially fateful relations of the square is multiplied within one family for six generations. This family is the Tantalids or, as they are more often called, the Pelopids (maybe the name of Tantalus was too odious). Parts of this family saga have been told and retold in antiquity from Homer to Hyginus and recycled in European literature. It does not exist in one authorized version, but has to be gathered from different sources.[8] The story does not start as a full-fledged version of the square but as a double father–son relationship:

Tantalus is the son of Zeus, dearly loved by him and allowed to his table. He commits, however, two terrible crimes: he steals nectar and ambrosia from the gods and gives them to men; and, to try the omniscience of the gods, he kills Pelops, his own son by Dione, and serves him as a dish for the gods. Everybody, except the sorrowful Demeter who eats some of one shoulder, discovers the crime. Pelops is restored in a magic cauldron and given an ivory shoulder. Tantalus is eternally punished in Tartarus.

Here the conflict and transgression is double: between man and god and between man and man: Tantalus's filicide and cannibalistic act is a horrible crime both against family bonds and human law and as a revolt against the father god. It is interesting that this first part of the saga is occupied with defining what is, and especially what is *not*, the proper food for man (cf. Vernant's studies in this aspect of Greek mythology, in Détienne and Vernant 1989: 21–86). From our perspective, however, Tantalus as a son attempts to bridge the distance to the

Self-representation and Analogy in Literature   213

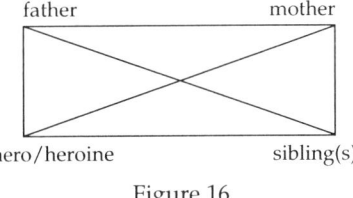

Figure 16

father-god; and as a father Tantalus is too distant from, or alien to, his own son Pelops.

Pelops woes Hippodamia, daughter of King Oenemaus and Sterope. Oenomaus, not eager to part with his daughter, challenges every suitor to a run. Since his chariot is run by a team of winged horses (a gift from Ares), he easily overtakes the suitor and kills him with his spear. Before Pelops's arrival, fifteen young men have already been killed. Apollodorus (1921, vol. II, 157–9) gives two reasons for Oenomaus's unwillingness to part with Hippodamia: (1) he is himself in love with her, and (2) it has been prophesied that he would die at her wedding. Pelops, however, is the lover of Poseidon, and receives another and swifter team of winged horses. Furthermore, he, or Hippodamia, bribes Oenemaus's charioteer, Myrtilus, to loosen one of the chariot's wheels, with the result that Oenemaus is killed and Pelops succeeds him. The bribe offered by Pelops is variously given as half of the kingdom or the favours of Hippodamia. Pelops kills Myrtilus (in some accounts because the latter tries to rape Hippodamia). Myrtilus, however, is a son of Hermes and curses the family of Pelops before he dies.

This part of the saga sets the stage for the full-fledged family drama: the father-daughter incest is intimated and the father-son rivalry of the first generations is repeated, but displaced in the deadly hostility between father-in-law and son-in-law. Furthermore, in some variants, Myrtilus is the rival of Pelops, and Hippodamia herself causes her father's death by bribing Myrtilus. Thus, to the fight between two generations for the sexually desirable object and for power is added the fight within one and the same generation; at this point, however, not yet between brothers. Guile and treason are prominent: Myrtilus breaks his allegiance to his sovereign, who dying curses him and wishes for Pelops to treat him the same, and Pelops and Myrtilus mutually break their pact. The gods play some part in the action, especially because Pelops kills the son of a god and is cursed by him.

From the marital relationship between Pelops and Hippodamia spring two sons, the later infamous brothers Atreus and Thyestes. Pelops has, however, another son from an extramarital relationship with a slave or nymph (Damais or Axioche). This son, Chrysippus, he loves and favours. The jealous Hippodamia persuades the legitimate brothers to kill the bastard. After the murder, Pelops curses and banishes Hippodamia and her two sons.

Here we have the full-fledged fateful square: sons siding with their mother against their father and killing off their half-brother. In the conflict between the 2nd and 3rd generations, Oenomaus's illicit, incestuous love for Hippodamia was intimated. Within the 3rd generation, it has been replaced by another kind of illicit love: Pelops's extramarital relationship that, however, leads to a new conflict between generations. Myrtilus's curse on Pelops's family is duplicated by Pelops's curse on his sons.

Banished by Pelops, Atreus and Thyestes flee to Mycenae. When its king, Eurystheus, dies, Atreus and Thyestes dispute the succession. Atreus has sworn to sacrifice the finest sheep in his flock to Artemis. However, when he finds a golden lamb, he hides it. This golden lamb is given to Thyestes by Atreus' wife, Aerope, whom he has seduced. Thyestes, subsequently, suggests that he who possesses the golden lamb should become king, and Atreus willingly agrees. When Thyestes produces the lamb, Zeus, through Hermes, makes Atreus suggest that he should rule if Helius should journey backwards. Thyestes agrees, and the miraculous event happens. Atreus then exiles Thyestes; but learning of the unfaithfulness of his wife, he pretends to be reconciled and invites Thyestes for a banquet. He slaughters Thyestes' sons, Aglaus, Callileon, and Orchimemus, however, and serves them as a dish to their own father. When Thyestes learns that he has eaten his own sons, he wants, at any price, to get even with Atreus. An oracle tells him that only by conceiving a son with his own daughter, Pelopia, will he be revenged. The accounts of the details of the act differ, but he does conceive a son, Aeigistus, by his own daughter. Pelopia, however, becomes the mistress of Atreus, and consequently Aeigistus is brought up as a son of Atreus. Being exiled for the second time, Aeigistus brings with him Atreus's and Aerope's lawful son, Pleisthenes. Thyestes sends Pleisthenes to murder Atreus (his own father), but he is killed by Atreus who immediately afterwards learns that he has killed his own son. In his turn Atreus sends Aeigistus to murder Thyestes (his own father), but they recognize each other, and Pelopia recognizes that her own father is the father of her son and commits suicide. Consequently, Aeigistus returns and kills his unsuspicious foster father, Atreus, and restores his real father, Thyestes, to the throne of Mycenai. Later, Atreus's lawful sons, Agamemnon and Menelaus, exile Thyestes. Agamemnon marries Klytaimnestra, who was married to Tantalus II, a son of Thyestes. To do so he kills Tantalus II and his newborn son by her.

The brothers' fight is a breach of normal family relations, and it is paralleled by Atreus's 'unfaithfulness' towards the goddess (Antemis) and by Aerope's unfaithfulness towards Atreus. Thus, all three bonds, religious, social, and sexual, are broken. Furthermore, the relations between the brothers are, at one and the same time, too distant, because they are enemies, and too close, because they share the same woman. Through the guile of Atreus, Thyestes eats his male children, unwittingly treating them as belonging to another category of beings, that is, both too distant and too close. By raping his own daughter he certainly does not keep the proper sexual distance from his children. Pelopia plays havoc with the distinction between generations by being both the child of one brother and (in different ways) the mistress of both brothers, that is, her father and uncle. Furthermore, the brothers exchange sons and give them the mission to kill their own father, so that Atreus, unwittingly, commits filicide and is killed himself by his foster child who also exiles his foster brothers, while they, in their turn, exile him. Finally, Atreus's son, Agamemnon, kills his cousin Tantalus II and his newborn child and marries the mother of the child, Klytaimnestra.

In this part of the saga it seems as if the very fact of being related laterally or by lineage by itself engenders unnatural and horrible deeds that repeat, but intensify, the actions of the previous generations. And this state of affairs is carried on in the last and best known part of the saga:

Agamemnon is only prevented from sacrificing his own daughter Iphigenia (by Klytaimnestra) to Artemis by the goddess herself. And everybody, including himself, thinks he has done it. The sacrifice is necessitated by Agamemnon's claim that he is a greater hunter than Artemis. After the fall of Ilion, Agamemnon is allotted Cassandra, the daughter of Priam, who is cursed by Apollo for having rejected him. By her Agamemnon has two sons, Pelops II and Teledamas. Meanwhile Agamemnon's cousin and foster brother, Aeigistus, lives with Klytaimnestra and rules the country, treating Klytaimnestra's two children by Agamemnon, Electra and Orestes, badly. Klytaimnestra has a daughter by Aeigistus, Erigone. When Agamemnon returns from Troy, he is killed by

Aeigistus and Klytaimnestra, and so is Cassandra and her two sons by Agamemnon. Orestes, then, is faced with the terrible dilemma: to revenge his father he has to kill his mother. He finally kills both Klytaimnestra and Aeigistus. Haunted by the Erinyes, he comes to Tauris, where he is almost sacrificed by his own sister, Iphigenia, but recognizing each other, they flee back to Greece together. Orestes is acquitted of the murder of his mother by the Areopagos and Pallas Athene. His further destiny exists in two versions: Either he marries his cousin Hermione, to whom he was formerly betrothed, after infamously having slain her husband, Neotolemos, the son of Achilleus. Or he has a child by his half-sister Erigone, the daughter of Klytaimnestra and Aeigistus. She bears him a son, Penthilos, who goes as a colonizer to Lesbos. In other accounts Erigone charges him with matricide at the Areopagos and commits suicide when he is acquitted. This last phase certainly repeats the inverted and unnatural relations within the fateful square. At the same time, however, the acquittal of Orestes puts an end to the story.

Looking at the whole myth of the Pelopids from the perspective of repetition and analogy, it becomes evident that the individual narrative sequences articulate the same pattern: the transgression of the distinction between gods and men combined with the transgression of family bonds, whether lateral or by lineage. The basic motives are the acquisition of power and the gratification of lust. The fulfilling of these desires leads to crimes that have to be revenged. Revenge itself implies another crime because it necessitates a similar transgression of divine and human laws. Matricide, filicide, and fraticide, incest and rape constitute the fatal actions that carry on the story almost endlessly. And at the centre lie two horrible relationships between parents and children: cannibalism, the eating of the children, and incest. Both actions imply the denial, or transgression, of kinship and its rules. They are, moreover, opposed to each other as unnatural destruction to unnatural generation. One wonders whether the central mythical germ of the story is the terrible father figure filling his stomach with his sons and filling the 'stomach' of his daughters.

As anthropologists, such as Lévi-Strauss, have repeatedly pointed out, it is through narration that myths are effective, or rather as effective as possible, in interpreting and reconciling the basic oppositions that confront man, such as life–death, nature–culture, sacred–profane, man–woman, and parent–child. The narrative manipulation of such oppositions results in a narrative pattern that has a certain explanatory and conciliatory power due to the significations, and especially the order, of

Self-representation and Analogy in Literature 217

the individual actions that make up the narrative. The following schematic representation may bring out the systematic uses of analogical patterning:

	Subject	Action	Object
I	*father* Tantalus	slaughters (knowingly & voluntarily)	*son* Pelops
	son Tantalus	is executed for crime by (heavenly)	*father* Zeus
II	*future father-in-law* Oenemaus	attempts to kill	*future son-in-law* Pelops
	future son-in-law Pelops	kills	*future father-in-law* Oenemaus
III	*sons* Atreus & Thyestes	kill (knowingly & voluntarily)	*stepbrother* Chrysippus
	(instigated by their *mother*, who has been cheated by their *father*) Hippodamia		Pelops
IV	*father* Thyestes	eats (unknowingly & involuntarily)	*sons* Aglaus, Callileon, Orchimemus
	father Thyestes	rapes (knowingly & voluntarily)	*daughter* Pelopia
	father Atreus	kills (unknowingly & voluntarily)	*son* Pleisthenes
	(foster)son Aigisthos	kills (knowingly & voluntarily)	*(foster)father* Atreus
V	*father* Agamemnon	'slaughters'/sacrifices (knowingly, but forced)	*daughter* Iphigenia
	wife Klytaimnestra	kills (knowingly & voluntarily)	*husband* Agamemnon
VI	*son* Orestes	kills (knowingly, but forced)	*mother* Klytaimnestra

In this schema I have concentrated on the sequences of interactions between the family members, since the protagonists are all related and the most important conflicts are those within or across generations. There is the opposition between parents and children, and we have among the parents the opposition between husband and wife and among the children that between siblings, especially brothers, while daughters and sisters are victims; in other words, conflicts provoked by sexual transgressions and conflicts due to parental and/or filial loyalty or disloyalty. The myth begins with a father killing his son (and serving him as a dish for the gods), and it ends with a son killing his mother to revenge his father. Thus, we get the following structure, which is both analogical and sequential:

father : son : : son : mother

The reason for this analogy is that the relation between executioner and victim remains constant:

executioner : victim : : executioner : victim

However, another parameter changes, namely, that between guilt and innocence, and thus we get:

father	:	son	: :	son	:	*mother*
executioner		victim		executioner		victim
guilty		innocent		innocent		guilty

The explanatory force of the narrative structure is obvious: by giving opposite signs to the second executioner and victim (as compared to the first pair), the series of murders is terminated. Tantalus starts the sequence of crimes by transgressing the borderlines between humans and gods, and Zeus himself gives him a punishment fitting his crime. Klytaimnestra's transgression of the borderline between femininity and masculinity is also such an abominable crime that Apollo commands her son to execute her. Thus, Orestes is forced into solidarity with his own father and with the father-god and his son. The pattern evolves from the fight between the father-god, the father, and the son to their conciliation in the common fight against the vigorous, and therefore monstrous, woman.

These implications of the plot structure and its solution are further strengthened by the fact that after the establishment of a traditional family in the saga, each generation has its trouble-making and ominous woman. In the second generation Hippodamia is actively involved in killing her father to get a husband, and is perhaps sexually involved with Myrtilus. Later she revolts against Pelops's extramarital affair and is especially jealous on the bastard son, Chrisippus. She turns her sons against their own father, and they kill Chrysippus. Although, according to our standards, Hippodamia is the one who is insulted, these standards are not that of the myth. In the fourth generation, Atreus's wife, Aerope, becomes the mistress of her husband's brother, Thyestes, and she betrays him in other ways (in one version she is killed by the raging Atreus). In the fifth generation, this role is allotted to Klytaimnestra. And in spite of the fact that Agamemnon has killed both her first husband and her son by him, has sacrificed their own daughter, Iphigenia, to Artemis, and begotten sons with his concubine, Cassandra, Klytaimnestra's unfaithfulness and her blood vengeance on her husband are so abominable that the younger gods acquit Orestes of murdering her. Thus, if we look at the role of the women throughout the family history, we find that the non-sexually-active maidens are victimized, sacrificed, or raped (Pelopia, Iphigenia, Cassandra), while the sexually active are represented as perpetrators (Hippodamia, Aerope, and Klytaimnestra).[9]

In Aeschylus's *Oresteia*, however, we see how the narrative loses its self-explanatory power and becomes the subject matter of forensic deliberation. In Aeschylus's version, the monstrosity of matricide has tainted Orestes and caused his insanity and his persecution by the Furies. His liberation requires both purification and acquittal. In order to justify this case of matricide, many features of the specific circumstances are mentioned and argued. Instead of guarding the royal house while Agamemnon is at war, Klytaimnestra defiles his bed. Furthermore, she oversteps her own sex and challenges the distinction between male and female, while conversely Aegisthos is seen as effeminate by the chorus, as one who plots the vile murder of the legitimate king and warlord, but leaves it to his mistress to commit the crime. And afterwards they reign by usurping the crown by force and, having already exiled Orestes, force Electra into a vile marriage.

However, these extenuating circumstances are not in themselves enough to justify Orestes' deed. Consequently, a court is created to pass sentence, and in this formal setting for practical (here juridical) discourse further arguments are offered by Apollo and Athene: (1) marriage is sacred ('Marriage, that joins two persons in Fate's ordinance, / Guarded by justice, stands more sacred than an oath'); (2) Agamemnon is killed, not in battle, but treacherously by his wife; and (3) a father is closer to the child than the mother.[10] The votes are even, but Pallas Athene gives Orestes her vote because, except for marriage, she favours 'male supremacy in all things.'[11] Pushed to its logical conclusion, Aeschylus's play acquits Orestes for two reasons: (1) because a man is always more valuable than a woman, and (2) because Klytaimnestra on two decisive points has not respected the limits set for her sex: she has had an undomesticated sexuality, and she has acted like a man, that is, rationally, purposefully, ruthlessly, and in a criminal way. Whatever else the *Oresteia* may be, it is also a testimony to the transformation from opposition and struggle between the sacred and the profane, between divine and human, that is, male humanity, to an opposition and battle between the male and the female principle, that is, a transformation from a set of oppositions in which man inescapably was the loser to his position as a certain winner; hereafter any women's revolt has been denounced as unlawful and unnatural – and damned.

In this context, however, the point is that narration is no longer considered sufficient. What is narrated is not disputed as a set of facts, a sequence of actions; what is at stake is their signification and significance, that is, their moral and religious implications, all of which are debated and decided in and through practical (juridical) discourse. Drama, of course, is a genre eminently geared to represent the intersection of narration and (practical) discourse, and most often in drama, discourse – that is, reasoning, argumentation, and debate – completes the narrated through the self-exegesis of the text. It is the final word pronouncing an interpretation, and is very often, explicitly or implicitly, a rule of interpretation for what has happened.

In the case of the *Oresteia* there is a curious ambiguity. It might be argued that narration and discourse support each other since they are saying the same thing, namely, that active women have to be suppressed or expelled (killed). It may also be argued, however, that what, on the Areopagos, is established as a rule of interpretation, and as a general law regulating the respective worth and forms of interaction between the sexes, means a reduction of the significations of the narrative pattern; the entire myth represents oppositions and transformations that are forgotten or repressed in the trilogy and its trial: for instance, the difference between the gods and mankind, and especially the question of their diet. It is significant that the *Oresteia* only retells a part of the myth, namely, from the crimes of Atreus and Thyestes onwards and with special emphasis on the sacrifice of Iphigenia (in the trilogy Klytaimnestra's reason for hating Agamemnon) and the illicit sexuality of Klytaimnestra herself (and of Helen). Thus, there is a certain tension between the trilogy's self-exegesis through discursive thematization and the significations of the narrative pattern of the entire saga.

The reconstructed story of the Pelopids is mythic in the traditional sense, that is, it structures and transforms basic distinctions, especially the one between divine and human (which is present from Zeus's imprisonment of Tantalus in Tartarus to Athene's acquittal of Orestes). However, it also contains fairy-tale features inasmuch as the stress on marital and on sexual relations generally is much more prominent in tales than in myths. But the saga is certainly not a kind of extended fairy-tale. If anything, it is the opposite; it is a story of the impossibility of reconciliation both between the sexes and between the generations, because a resting point from which it would be possible to announce that 'they lived happily ever after' is never reached. The principal characters never survive to die a natural death. Nevertheless, as regards narrative structure, the same structural devices, repetition and analogy, are used whether the story concentrates on a transitional crisis or concerns the fate of a family through six generations.

4.7 Literature and the Existential Analogy

On the basis of the preceding analysis of both poetic and narrative structures, it seems justified to hold that analogy is a basic poetic principle. A further question maybe asked, however, namely, whether analogy and narrative are alike, not only structurally in binding different parts of the text together, but also functionally; that is, may they serve the same function from the point of view of oratory and literature? In this regard, it is interesting that Aristotle, with respect to juridical argumentation and deliberation, holds that comparison and narrative do serve the same purpose, that of making an argument convincing. He writes: 'Fables are suitable for public speaking, and they have this advantage that, while it is difficult to find similar things that have really happened in the past, it is easier to invent fables, for they must be invented, like comparisons' (Aristotle 1926: 277, *Rhet.* 1394a). In this remarkable passage fable and comparison are linked,

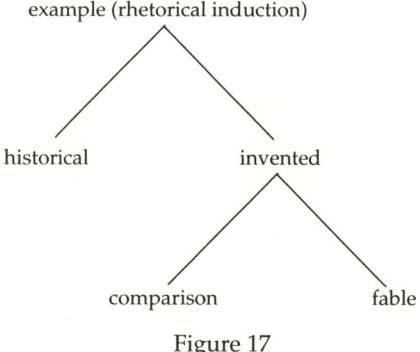

Figure 17

because in Aristotle's division of rhetorical devices fable and comparison are both species of the example. His classification is sketched in figure 17.

Aristotle explicitly mentions comparison and fable as the two species of the invented example (or rhetorical induction). The reason is that, in certain respects, they are equivalent because both are used as an argument to make probable that something was or will be the case. The point is to 'find similar things,' namely, similar to the case under discussion. With respect to comparison and fable, there is no reference to a historical past but an invention of a parallel case. Comparisons are examples constructed by changing the variables but preserving the relationship, as when Socrates says that magistrates should not be chosen by lot, because this 'would be the same as choosing representative athletes not those competent to contend, but those on whom the lot falls' (1393b). This parallelism can be constructed as a four-term analogy: magistrates : government : : athletes : sports. Comparisons indicate a parallelism between two realms of experience, but without creating an independent fictional universe.

In the fable a full-fledged alternative, that is, a fictional universe, is created (in Aristotle's case the reference is to animal fables). Rhetoric, however, is primarily concerned with juridical and political argumentation, and thus fictions have no independent status; they are persuasive devices whose value is instrumental. And even the third kind of speech, the epideictic, that of praise or blame, also has mainly practical purposes such as for obituary, official speeches, demonstration, and teaching. However, from a more general point of view, epideictic speech is very important because it serves to establish and confirm the values of the community (even humble speeches at private birthday parties still fulfil this function, and obituaries, which were the first epideictic speeches, in praising the achievements of the deceased, also still display and confirm the values of the community; see Perelman and Olbrechts-Tyteca 1969: 47–54).

Given that in rhetoric fiction is subordinated to whatever non-linguistic purpose the speech serves, how can this humble position function as an indication of the role of literature, which ostensibly serves no purpose but its own. It may be, however, that literature is never art for art's sake – not even within the movement named after this position – it may be that literature is always mediately related to the experiential world of its writers and listeners or readers. If this is the case – something that I think cannot be seriously disputed – then the comparison with the fable's use in oratory may be fruitful after all. Traditionally, the objective of oratory is to serve one, or more, of three purposes: (1) to establish what happened and why (forensic oratory); (2) to argue what is worthy of praise and what of blame (epideictic oratory); and (3) to deliberate about what to do in order to secure happiness or avoid unhappiness and disaster (political oratory).

It is hard not to see profound resemblances here to what literature is about. First of all, most often literature, poetry included, presents itself as an account of what is supposed to have happened and/or been experienced. Second, literature is often a commemoration either of those who are praiseworthy or a celebration of the enjoyable and the blissful; or it may be derogatory, attacking those who offend against the laws or the moral standards of society (cf. *Our Gang*, cited in the preceding chapter). Or, even more often, it may lament the conditions allotted to man, the brevity of his happiness, and the certainty of his fated end. Finally, precisely because it pretends to represent what has happened, or is happening, literature may contain a profound discussion of the standards and reasons for action. From ancient tragedy to serious modern drama, and in the development of the comic genres as well, the theatre has been a forum for the representation of the main interests, concerns, and conflicts of society's powerful classes; and narrative and poetry, in addition, have long fulfilled similar roles.

The difference between the uses of comparison and fable in oratory and in literature lies rather in the nature of the case. It is easy to point to the common features of literature, especially drama, and of legal reasoning and trials, because very often in literature the protagonist stands trial, literally or figuratively, for what he or she has done (from Orestes and Antigone to Borkman and Rubek in Ibsen's last plays and, in our century, Beckett's protagonists). It would be ridiculous, however, to reduce literature to jurisprudence, for the very basic reason, for instance, that in an infinite number of literary texts, from the point of view of law, there will be no case at all. In jurisprudence and other forms of oratory, comparison and fable serve as analogues that are supposed to strengthen the case of the orator. In literature, at least on the face of it, the comparison *is* the argument, and the fable *is* the case. The analogue has become all there is.

Even if the analogue is not present in literature, it is nevertheless presupposed. The point is, however, that in literature what the literary text is the analogue of is not some specific action and/or state of mind. If literature were tied up to particular cases (which it may be in the so-called *romans à clef*), it would reduce its scope and interest. Instead, literature is the analogue of whatever is like it, that is, it is in this respect an iconic sign. This is also the point of view in Aristotle's definition of the difference between the historian and the poet (the former tells what actually happened, while the latter tells 'what could and would happen either probably or inevitably'). Thus, the poet is concerned with 'general truth'; as Aristotle explains further, general truth means 'the sort of thing that a certain type of man will do or say either probably or necessarily' (Aristotle 1927: 35, 1451b). On this view, literature aims at being representative of human action and behaviour in general, and thus strives to be an analogue of the experiential and social universe, of the mental life, of the imagination, and of the desires of its audience. We relate to and understand the literary text by referring it to our own experience and *vision du monde*. Even if we are aware of decisive differences between the universe of the text and ours, the text will nevertheless gain significance only by becoming related to us by similarity or by contrast, that is, by analogy. This analogy I would like to dub the existential analogy. Literature is analogical because what is represented is different from but, at the same time, similar to what we have experienced in action or in conscious or unconscious thought. Thus, the text is an analogue of parts of our life. It is existential, because in making sense of the literary text we necessarily bring to it all the dimensions of our being: understanding, emotions, desires, and even bodily sensations and responses.

In an earlier section of this chapter, 'Analogy and metaphor,' I mentioned that Peirce defines analogy as a form of inference that makes use of the three others: hypothesis, deduction, and induction. Here, at the end, it should be pointed out that literature is both analogical and hypothetical.

Hypothesis, or abduction, means the attempt to explain a case by forming a provisional rule from which it would follow as a result:

RULE: if q then p,
CASE: but p,
RESULT: then q.

There are two ways in which the literary text may be called hypothetical. First, it is hypothetical in the fundamental sense that it does not tell 'what actually happened but what could and would happen either probably or inevitably.' It is hypothetical in nature by the very fact that it posits an alternative universe, that is, it presents something that is imagined as if it really were the case. The fundamental 'as if' of literature is beautifully exemplified in explicit counterfactual narratives (for instance, Robert Harris's thriller *Fatherland*; see chapter 3, p. 134).

There is, however, a second sense in which the literary text is hypothetical. It not only posits a hypothetical universe; very often the text is self-exegetic, that is, it indicates itself how it is best interpreted (by means of commentary by explicit narrators, or by the logic of processes and of events). Very often literature takes its self-exegetic endeavour further, claiming that it is exemplary, that is, that from the represented case a maxim, or a set of maxims, may be inferred; and these maxims are supposed to be generally valid. Accordingly, literature is also hypothetical in the sense that it offers both hypotheses about human nature and causes and reasons for social interaction.

This feature may be exemplified by a fable by John Gay, 'The turkey and the ant' (number XXXVIII), which begins as follows:

> In other men we faults can spy,
> And blame the mote that dims their eye,
> Each little speck and blemish find,
> To our own stronger errors blind.

The story itself starts with a turkey looking for ants and, at the same time, complaining to its children about the fate of turkeys: to be eaten by humans at Christmas. It concludes its complaint as follows:

> From the low peasant to the lord,
> The turkey smoaks on ev'ry board.
> Sure men for gluttony are curst,
> Of the sev'n deadly sins the worst.

At the same time, however, the turkey has been busy devouring ants. An ant that has escaped its fate comments on the turkey's speech:

> Ere you remark another's sin,
> Bid thy own conscience look within.
> Controul thy more voracious bill,
> Nor for a breakfast nations kill.

This fable is clearly argumentative. It states as the major premise a general observation, or rule, saying almost the same as Matthew 7: 3: 'And why beholdest thou the mote that is in thy brother's eye, but considerest not the beam that is in thy own eye?' The story itself and the two speeches it contains constitutes a case that may be subsumed under a rule that it allegedly illustrates and validates. The argumentative structure is not exterior to the fable as a genre; it is its very pith and marrow. Because of this feature, it might be objected that the fable is a very special case whose structure is due to its extra-literary function as a didactic instrument using logical-rhetorical devices. My point of view is the opposite, namely, that the fable is one of the most typical kinds of literature inasmuch as it lays bare the intrinsic relationship between representation and discourse that is found or presupposed in most literature.[12]

Furthermore, from the point of view of this chapter, Gay's fable is interesting as it uses analogy both internally and externally: internally, because it is built on the analogy man : turkey : : turkey : ant; externally, because the maxim – that although we easily spot the faults of others, we are blind to our own faults – is indicated as the rule that covers both cases. And this maxim, it is supposed, can be transferred from the fictional universe to our lifeworld. Further, the fact that an animal fable exemplifies this carrying-over from fiction to lifeworld ensures that such transference is independent of whether the surface characteristics of the fictional universe are 'realistic' or not.

On the one hand, then, in order to make sense of the literary text, we have to make analogical inferences from our experiential world to the fictional universe (by analogy because they are ontologically different).

On the other hand, literature itself claims that, by analogy, we should make inferences concerning our world from the states of affairs and minds within the universe of the text. On that account, analogy is the form of reasoning par excellence that ensures a bidirectional fit, a two way-traffic, between literature and lifeworld.

Analogy, then, seems to be an all-pervasive feature of literature. It operates on sound, syntax, and meaning, and among and between them, on both meaning and use, and between them, and on both fiction and non-fiction, and between them.

At this point, we should reflect on the epigraphs introducing this chapter. I.A. Richards stresses the necessity of having an 'eye for resemblances.' If we could not reason by analogy, we would not be able to cope with variety and change. In most cases repetitions are only partial. Every event or action within our lifeworld contains something novel and unexpected, although by focusing on what matches with what we have previously experienced, we deal with the new event or action as if it were identical to former experiences. As Richards points out as well, the same goes for speech. Indeed, it is likely that precisely by articulating experience in speech, we standardize it, so to speak, because what is unique easily disappears in being rendered in a linguistic utterance. Although likeness is not identity, it may function as if it were. Indeed, it may be expedient, even necessary, that it functions in this way. Peirce warns us, however, that analogy has its limits, that within it there is a difference that has not been levelled out by comparison and similarity. But the point is that analogy may be both reductive and illuminating. It may both make the strange familiar and the familiar strange.

Thus, on the one hand, reasoning by analogy may further automation of thought and action because it means disregarding what is particular in order to catch similarities. On the other hand, using analogies is a way of comprehending what might otherwise defy understanding. Literature, which uses analogy on different levels and with different functions and purposes, also has this double nature. On the one hand, it stabilizes meanings, norms, and values; on the other, it attempts to catch what is levelled out by ordinary speech and habitual thinking and to make what is different and novel accessible to us.

Five

Literature as Self-expression: Subjectivity and Imagination

> No man is an island, entire of itself; every man is a piece of the continent, a part of the main; ... any man's death diminishes me, because I am involved with mankind; and therefore never send to know for whom the bell tolls; it tolls for thee.
>
> *(Donne [1624] 1967: 101)*

> But it follows from our own existence (which is proved by the occurrence of ignorance and error) that everything which is present to us is a phenomenal manifestation of ourselves. This does not prevent it from being a phenomenon of something without us, just as a rainbow is at once manifestation of the sun and of the rain.
>
> *(CP 5.283)*

> Resemblances and signs have dissolved their former alliance; similitudes have become deceptive and verge upon the visionary and madness; things still remain stubbornly within their ironic identity they are no longer anything but what they are; words wander off on their own, without content, without resemblance to fill their emptiness; they are no longer the marks of things; they lie sleeping between the pages of books and covered in dust.
>
> *(Foucault 1970: 47–8)*

The sign–world relationship is basic: meaning presupposes reference to a universe and, I would claim, in the last analysis, to a lifeworld. However, this relationship is also precarious, always in danger of being severed. The sign–world, or word–world relationship is always at stake in literature because of the inherent distrust in the representational power of words, because of the pull towards the figurative in literature, and its bend towards self-representation, and, last but not least, because literature serves self-expression; it is thoroughly marked by subjectivity.

Self-expression in literature should not be confused with self-representation, which was the subject of the preceding chapter. Self-representation refers to the different ways in which the semiotic systems (language, cognitive structures) are displayed in the individual text by means of different patterns, first and foremost analogy. Self-expression is related to addresser and utterer, to their points of view, attitudes, and emotional impregnation of the text.

Consequently, self-expression, the positioning of the subject within the text, is another decisive reason why the relation of texts to the world is problematic. In the short preface to his *Essais*, Montaigne warns his readers, 'I am myself the matter of my book.' Montaigne is true to his word; he certainly talks a lot about himself. His point is, however, also another one, namely, that even when he is not talking about himself, but about an astonishing variety of other subjects, he is nevertheless very present: as a conversing voice, as a point of view, or as a director staging different, often opposing, points of view; that is, present as the text's dialectical principle. He is also present as attitudes and emotional colouring and as a moral point of view. He could, he says in another essay, have done a better job in a more intellectually stimulating climate. However, in that case 'the work would have been less my own, and its principal end and perfection is to be precisely my own' (Montaigne 1965: 667, III, 5). This act of self-expression is, it turns out, at the same time an act of self-preservation. He has written the essays in order that his family and friends may remember how he was, remember his character and attitudes. His writing is an attempt to overcome death – a death, he says, that will soon be coming. And it is exhibitionistic: he wants to be heard and seen. He wants to bear witness about himself as a subject, both as a frail and desiring corporeal being and as an inquisitive mind. And if propriety had allowed it, he would have shown himself 'full-length and stark naked.' I presume that Montaigne's attitude towards his own writing is generally valid for poets and writers. And precisely because it is not tied down to relating the factual, literature becomes a privileged medium of self-expression, an anthropomorphic representation of the world as self and of self as world.

To this should be added, as Bruner has pointed out, that in their world-making capacity, literary texts construct two landscapes simultaneously:

> One is the landscape of action, where the constituents are the arguments of action: agent, intention or goal, situation, instrument, something corresponding to a 'story grammar.' The other landscape is the landscape of consciousness: what those involved in the action think, or feel, or do not know, think, or feel. The two landscapes are essential and distinct: it is the difference between Oedipus sharing Jocaste's bed before and after he learns from the messenger that she is his mother. (Bruner 1986: 14)

5.1 Self-representation and Self-expression

But who can tell the dancer from the dance? Exhibiting oneself, creating a world, and displaying a semiotic's immanent patterns are obviously not mutually exclusive. On the contrary, self-expression (of the utterer), creation of a virtual world, and self-representation (of textual patterning) are most often fused and collaborate to heighten the expressiveness and aesthetic effect of the individual text. Nevertheless, from the point of view of analysis they may be distinguished:

> What is it men in women do require?–
> The lineaments of gratified desire.
> What is it women do in men require?–
> The lineaments of gratified desire.
> (Blake 1971: 167)

Blake's wonderful little poem is certainly a showcase of poetic devices: all three kinds of analogies – phonological, syntactic, and semantic and their interrelations – catch and please ear and mind. It is thus exemplary of the self-representative capacity of poetry, of the force of analogy. At the same time, it is a poem about human desires and emotions. In fact, it not only claims reciprocity of desire, it represents, even mimes it: men : women : : women : men. This miming is effected by means of a varied repetition (here by chiasmus) patterned by a consideration for rhythm and euphony (e.g., the positioning of *do* in lines one and three). Furthermore, the use of repetition is thematically significant because it stresses the universality and reciprocity of its propositional content. The interplay between the poetic devices clearly serves the purpose of conjuring up a certain belief and a certain emotional attitude. This becomes obvious when we use the test of paraphrase. In prose the propositional content may be rendered: both men and women require proof of their ability to gratify each other's desire. This general proposition might prove hard to substantiate, and it might call up objections. One might claim, for instance, that people do not care for the satisfaction of their partners but only for their own. Or it might be objected that, since men and women do not understand and react to sexual desire in the same way, to see their desire as identical and reciprocal is false. Obviously we might also respond in this way to the poem and come up with similar objections. The poem's rhetorical force, however, makes such a response less likely. This strength is achieved through correlation between the repetitions on different linguistic levels and the poem's repeated parallel framing in question and answer. Blake's poem is, like poems in general, a complex system that engenders emergent qualities because the material and formal aspects of the text enhance the plausibility and force of its propositional content. Further, Blake's poem seems to imitate a preliterary genre that makes specific use of the question/answer structure, namely, the riddle. To solve a riddle is precisely what this poem pretends to do.[1] Accordingly, what with regard to its propositional content seems to be an assertion of a general state of affairs is, as regards its propositional attitude, a magical act, a conjuration to the effect that men and women desire each other's desire – as if to state the answer as a fact would make it one. In this way, the poem forcefully expresses an emotional state and a belief, namely, the conviction that something whose reality would be vitally important to most people is in fact the case. Hence, the focus of the poem has changed from what has been said about a (supposed) state of affairs in the world, that is, from the represented to the text as an utterance to which the utterer is committed and of whose truth and significance he attempts to persuade his interlocutors.

Here we confront one of the perennial questions about literature that worried Plato and made the romanticists and the New Critics happy, namely, the question of which kind of knowledge literature embodies. Does literature offer a kind of knowledge *sui generis*, revealing states of affairs accessible only through it? Or is the cognitive content of literature related to doxa, to that which is commonly thought to be the case, or to that which ought to be the case? In my opinion literature involves the latter, not the former. Without necessarily agreeing with all the views of the late Louis Althusser, I do find his short delineation of the difference between literature and science valuable in some respects:

'The real difference between art and science lies in the *specific form* in which they give us the same object in quite different ways: art in the form of "seeing" and "perceiving" or "feeling," science in the form of *knowledge* (in the strict sense, by concepts)' (1971b: 223). Siding with Plato and Althusser in these matters does not make me comfortable, and thus it has to be stressed that this is certainly not the whole story. Most often literature neither creates nor is it instrumental in bringing about novel knowledge, be it theoretical, practical, historical, or technical. Literature, however, does something else that, in my opinion, is even more important: it creates or, in any case, articulates novel ways of experiencing, in the sense that it exemplifies ways in which the subjects do, could, or should relate to each other and to the lifeworld. Knowledge involves either knowing that something is, or is not, the case, or knowing how to do something, and in case of science, knowledge is, as Althusser points out, conceptual. It is oriented towards either objects, processes, or achievements. Experience involves counting in the subject, and consequently being emotionally involved with and responding to what confronts us. Further, experience is felt as being synthetic and intuitive (although unconsciously it is most probably interpretive and analytic). Obviously, it will often become an object of reflection and interpretation (as in our experience of Blake's poem), but, at the same time, it is an event that occurs and matters to somebody. This is why it is questionable whether Althusser is right in claiming that literature and science are two specific forms in which the same object is given. Maybe it is more correct and fruitful to say that only on a very high level of abstraction can literature and science be said to treat the same object. Each rather seems to focus on opposite poles of the subject–object relationship. Experience, in my view, is related to the subject pole and knowledge to the object pole. Thus, it seems to be true that what is accessed through literature could not be accessed through science, for it would disappear by the way in which science would approach it. However, what is expressed in literature is not unique. On the contrary, literature expresses everyday experience; except that it often concentrates on peak moments or crises and rites of passage, and it may put into language something that would otherwise remain unsaid. Indeed, the fact that it expresses common experiences is its strength.

According to Bruner there are two modes of cognitive functioning, 'each providing distinctive ways of ordering experience.' They are thought to be irreducible to one another and to be operating according their own, different criteria of well-formedness. There is the narrative mode that deals with human interaction, intentions, and emotions; and there is the logico-scientific or paradigmatic one that attempts to fulfil the ideals of the natural and formal sciences through categorization and conceptualization, and system formation, and by being consistent and non-contradictory. It deals with causes and attempts to verify and test for empirical truth (see Bruner 1986: 12–13). One might wish to qualify the claims of Bruner concerning certain points. For instance, literature, including narrative, is also different from the paradigmatic mode of thought through the double insistency, even obtrusiveness, of language within it. On the one hand, language's materiality becomes palpable; on the other, the polysemy of words and phrases is explored (in other places Bruner recognizes this difference). Furthermore, although literature certainly includes and makes use of quasi-formal ways of reasoning, it uses them primarily rhetorically: the text is not created for the sake of the argument; the argument is created to contribute to the total effect of the text. Finally, it should be stressed that Bruner's description of the modes are, as he says himself, 'platonic'; it describes what the paradigmatic and the narrative modes ideally, but also typically, do; and thus leaves room for their blending in concrete instances. Bruner's distinction has been corroborated and developed by Merlin Donald, who in the mental, and cerebral, development of man, that is, cognitive evolution, distinguishes between the mythic and the theoretic culture, claiming that the mind of contemporary man is of a hybrid and multi-layered nature, containing different ways of apprehending the world (see Donald 1991).

Blake's poem illustrates the narrative-poetical, or mythical, mode of thinking: like most literature, it does not procure new knowledge. On the contrary, most grown-ups know immediately what the matter is – and that it matters. And this is precisely the point. The relevance and importance of Blake's poem lie in its integration of common experience and subjective/emotional engagement (here conjuring is supposed to bring about a wish-fulfilment) through the poetic expression.[2]

5.2 Subject, Subjectivity, and Self-expression

Far from being opposed to one another, poeticity and the expression of subjectivity join forces to persuade the addressee. Furthermore, subjectivity means the expression of the personal involvement of the utterer in what is represented. However, the ideas about subject and subjectivity are many, and the questions raised by them notoriously difficult.

They have a long history within philosophy and the humanities, but the very wealth of their definitions and the different dimensions of these concepts are bewildering rather than helpful in making clear what is meant by them.

One important reason for this state of affairs is the polysemy, the different contexts and uses, of the term subject. In logic, the subject is that of which something may be predicated: '– is mortal' is a predicate, while 'Socrates,' 'man,' or 'being' are subjects. The subject is that part of a proposition that serves to identify and designate (cf. the indexical sign in semiotics) what is the theme or topic (or subject[!]) under discussion, the predicate is what defines and characterizes the subject.[3] (In Greek philosophy there is an ontological twist to this: the subject is thought of as the substance, the unchanging, and the predicates are the accidents that may be ascribed to it.)

There is another understanding and definition of subject, not unrelated to those of logic and grammar, namely, the subject as a doer – the idea of agency. The subject may be an agent of cognition, that is, the epistemological subject.[4] To the subject of knowledge is opposed the object of knowledge, that which, as regards the dynamical object (on Peirce's view), is independent of the individual subject, but not independent of mind, because what can be known is necessarily connected with human thought in general. The philosophical discussions of the subject of knowledge are perennial, and no agreement exists about how it should be characterized. Related to this distinction between subject and object are the adjectives, or adjectives used substantively, subjective and objective, which are used in three related but different ways. First, a property is called objective if it is believed that it belongs to a mind-independent object, whereas what is subjective is related to the operations of the psyche and called forth in the mind of the perceiver (cf. Locke's distinction between primary and secondary qualities). Second, one talks about the merely subjective, that is, illusory phenomena related to the individual mind and unrecognized by others (Macbeth's dagger; cf. below on *Don Quixote*).

Third, 'subjective' is related to axiological statements and preferences, mainly in matters of sensuous experience, taste and aesthetics, norms, and values, but also as regards beliefs, especially religious beliefs. Thus, the subjective is sometimes related to what is considered existentially relevant and authentic. This is the framework within which, for instance, it makes sense for Kierkegaard to maintain that 'subjectivity is truth' and give the following definition of this truth: '*An objective uncertainty, held fast through appropriation with the most passionate inwardness, is the truth*, the highest truth there is for an *existing* person. At the point where the road swings off (and where that is cannot be stated objectively, since it is precisely subjectivity), objective knowledge is suspended' (Kierkegaard [1846] 1992: 203). However, as a doer, and without the existential (i.e., religious) seriousness of Kierkegaard, the subject is also connected with intention, with power to act, and with responsibility. Obviously, the subject of knowledge and the subject of action are related, and this is brought out in the fourth and very important acceptation of subject, namely, the ethical and juridical. Within most juridical systems, knowledge, power to act, and responsibility are correlative, because if the defendant does not know, or cannot help doing, he or she is either not held responsible, or the lack of knowledge or power will be counted as an extenuating circumstance. A fifth definition of subject, closely related to the ethical-juridical, is the political-juridical: the distinction between sovereign and subject. According to this definition, the subject is one *subjected* to the will of the sovereign, or to a principle of sovereignty, the state, the laws, and so on. The subject is obliged to be loyal to the sovereign and execute whatever is demanded of him or her in the name of lawful authority (whether a given authority is lawful, and perhaps even legitimate, is of course a matter for dispute). However, as a juridical subject the individual person is precisely not an unconditioned, free agent, but is subject to the law and responsible for any transgression.

The psychoanalytic conception of the subject combines the epistemological, the ethical-juridical, and the juridical-political conceptions. From Freud to Lacan, the psychoanalytic conception of the subject has been debated, changed, and made more or less complicated. However, some important features seem to remain valid for different psychoanalytic schools. First of all, the subject is divided qualitatively into what is conscious and what is unconscious. Dynamically, it is divided into different and opposed agencies such as the ego, the id, and the super-ego. Concerning the subject of knowledge, psychoanalysis claims that the conscious mind does not know what is going on within the psyche in its totality. The most important mental processes are unconscious, a claim almost all branches of psychology subscribe to. Further, such processes are also governed by biological needs, but first and foremost by drives, that is, pulsations that mediate between the somatic and the psychical. Such pulsations, or drives, can be identified, and prominent among them are sexuality, the ego-instincts, and even the so-called death-drive. Much fewer branches of psychology would subscribe to these claims. According to psychoanalysis, the ontogenetic development of the psyche takes place through a dialectic between needs, memories and fantasies, and social constraints; that is, the ontogenesis of the subject is based on conflicts, compromises, repression, and sublimation.

As regards agency, psychoanalysis sees the idea of the subject as free agent and master of his or her own house as largely illusory. On the contrary, according to Freud, the role of the ego (which is only partly conscious) is to mediate between two mainly unconscious agencies, the id and the superego, and external reality. Further, our actions are, so to speak, determined by our personal mythology (i.e., the network of conscious and unconscious fantasies that, although they are fragmentary, inconsistent, and contradictory, to a large extent governs our emotions, thoughts, and actions). Hence, our conscious and intentional actions are thought to contain significations and motivations that are not immediately accessible to us. The subject may, however, obtain self-knowledge through therapeutic dialogue; in addition, literature and art are supposed to inform about the subject. The subject, however, will never become fully transparent to him- or herself. According to psychoanalysis, the subject is definitely gendered and endowed with a sexed body. However, bodily needs, including sexuality, are always mediated by interpretation. Thus, a semiotization of what is needed takes place, so that what is desired may not be needed, and what is needed may not be desired (see the section 'The subjective thematics of literature,' below), because fears and desires are inextricably amalgamated with fantasies. Furthermore, according to psychoanalysis, the subject is constituted through interaction and communication. It is an agency consisting of more or less drive-cathected networks of significations, intentions, and motivations that interact; but not in concord, since to a great extent they contradict each other. Such significations and their interrelations are interiorized. And thus, despite the individuality of its constitution, the subject is eminently a social construct.[5]

As regards semiotics, it will be remembered that Peirce does not give any primary importance to the utterer in sign production. To him the important point is that the sign is determined by the object, and in talking about persons in relation to signs, he feels that he is giving in to trivial opinions about the nature of signs; this is his sop to Cerebus (cf. chapter 1, p. 45). Further, 'natural Signs and symptoms have no utterer; and consequently have no Meaning, if Meaning be defined as the intention of the utterer' (SS 1977: 111). Peirce is right in pointing out that one part of the so-called indexical signs, the reagents, are determined by their objects without any intervention by an utterer (in photography, however, the photographer is a kind of utterer). This may also be helpful in pointing to what subject, and subjectivity, may mean from a semiotic point of view, namely, that which is related to the utterer and interpreter as agents in semiosis. Red spots on the skin may be a part of the disease known as measles, and being reagents they have no utterer. 'I see from her spots that your child suffers from measles,' however, is an utterance whose source is an utterer, just as the source of the spots is the disease in general. Thus, when the source of the sign is located with its utterer, we will talk about the subject of the sign and about the sign's subjective dimension. The human subject, according to this point of view, is subject precisely because he or she is able to interpret and emit signs and more specifically because he or she is capable of assuming the utterer's position, that is, capable of being an, at least minimal, active factor in semiosis. Thus, it is semiosis that is the precondition for the subject and not the other way around.[6]

The structure of the semiotic pyramid (see p. 55) shows the interrelation of the subject with the other elements of semiosis, the informational circuit including object, subject, and interpretant, and its dialogic relation to the other subject. By representing both utterer and interpreter's points of view, it indicates (as far as a static model can do) how the subject is constituted by its being utterer and interpreter by turns. The split between utterer and interpreter is built into the subject itself as an internal dialogue, and it is homologous to the split subject of psychoanalysis.[7] Thus, the subject is constituted by virtue of interpretation and dialogue and through the significations 'sedimented' through these processes.

This is why the subject-position is a place within semiosis dependent on and defined by the other elements and its relation to them. It responds to, and is influenced and formed by, its environment. It is brought up by, and interacts with, concrete others. The positions of utterer and interpreter are constantly changing, and taking turns; that is, being a part of a dialogue is a precondition for becoming a subject. Consequently, being a subject means possessing a semiotic competence in common with others, that is, sharing systems of immediate interpretants with the species, culture, community, and subcommunity in question. The systems of immediate interpretants contain innate dispositions to interpret and act, that is, the species-specific semiotic competence. On top of this competence is layered the culture-specific habits of interpretation that, of course, are variable and changeable, different according to time and place. Further, within the same culture, different communities and subcommunities have interpretive habits of their own, and among them there may well be disagreement about the validity of ways of interpretation.[8]

Thus, in principle, systems of interpretation (immediate interpretants) are not linked with any specific individual. They are habits that may be activated and used in individual interpretation by subjects: utterers and interpreters. Subjects are agents using such habits in specific contexts to achieve certain goals.[9] From a semiotic point of view, concrete action means the specific selection and combination of interpretations governed by conscious or unconscious habits in order to survive, to fulfil and satisfy desires, to abide by communal laws and values, or to establish knowledge and meaning. Thus, a subject is a historical and context-bound agent (individual or collective) inscribed in semiosis, that is, someone who responds to a situation or state of affairs by directly or indirectly interacting with others on the basis of available interpretive habits in order to achieve certain goals.

Subjectivity, then, is context-bound, perspectival, and heteronomous. It is context-bound because it is placed within the coordinates of time and space, and it is discernable as dispositions of individual historical agents to interpret and act. It is perspectival, that is, it is a response to a situation or state of affairs viewed from a specific position and with a view to what matters to the agents in question. Thus, subjectivity is bound up with interests and fears and desires. It is heteronomous because it is informed by the agent's total bodily and mental presence within the lifeworld. Hence, it is influenced by many concerns: from subsistence in a potentially hostile environment, over gratification of desires, to care for survival and development of what is deemed important even if it transcends the existence of the agents in question.

Although we will typically identify the subject with a person, the utterer need not be an individual person; it may be collective, even an institution. Furthermore, the analysis of the subjective dimension of a text is not dependent upon any specific knowledge about its utterer as a known, individual person – although such knowledge may be very helpful. Even when a text is anonymous, we will still be justified in talking about its subjectivity, because the addresser as a position within the text is intact and points to its subjective dimension. Jean-François Lyotard quotes from A.M. An's description of Cashinahua narrative.

Within this community, a storyteller 'always begins his narration with a fixed formula: "Here is the story of —, as I've always heard it told. I will tell it to you in my turn. Listen." And he brings it to a close with another, also invariable, formula: "Here ends the story of —. The man who has told it to you is — (Cashinahua name), or to the Whites — (Spanish or Portuguese name)"' (Lyotard 1984: 20). The point of such formulas, according to Lyotard, is to claim that the narrative is a faithful transmission of what has been told 'forever.' The point here is that the traditional and formulaic nature of the narrative does not at all detract from its subjectivity, because subjectivity is not bound up with individuality but with the articulation of experience. And even if we know the name and some other data concerning the utterer, as for instance in the case of Shakespeare, we ascribe most of our knowledge about him to our reading of his plays and to our knowledge of his times through other records.

In chapter 1 I suggested a distinction between the immediate and the dynamical utterer of the text. The immediate utterer is the utterer appearing within the text. Wayne Booth calls this complex communicative agency within the text the 'implied author.' It is the agency that 'chooses, consciously or unconsciously, what we read' and, Booth continues, 'we infer him as an ideal, literary, created version of the real man; he is the sum of his own choices' (Booth 1961: 74–5). It goes without saying that there is an implied author in all texts, not only in literature. Booth's important point, however, is that the immediate utterer is a construct, consciously and unconsciously produced by the utterer and inferred by the interpreter. The immediate utterer / implied author is designed to answer the question of how the agency who communicates such a message has to be (see also chapter 7).[10]

The dynamical utterer is the utterer who has in fact produced the text, the real agent. But here we must add the usual proviso (valid for the dynamical object as well) that we only know the dynamical utterer as represented in the immediate utterer of a series of signs. Thus, semiotics agrees with psychoanalysis that the subject is split and opaque, such that total transparency is not possible. Nevertheless, there is an important difference between the understanding we get from analysing the implied author of an individual text and the utterer we reconstruct, or construct[11] from all available texts, including texts by other utterers. Such a (re)construction is often claimed to be a true representation of the dynamical utterer, the producer of all the texts assigned to him or her. If such a representation is the fruit of full-scale scholarly research, and if no serious objections substantiated by convincing evidence are raised, then we will most often take to it be a plausible, maybe even the best available, portrait of what the dynamical utterer may have been like.

5.3 The Subject in Literature and Fiction

The subject of the text, then, is something that is inferred from the comparison between what is taken to be the implied author of the individual text and a hypothesis about its dynamical utterer. Booth points to Defoe's 'The Shortest Way with Dissenters' as an example of a text whose irony only becomes apparent when this text is compared to the ideological attitude revealed by Defoe's other writings (1961: 318–20). According to Booth, and to those in Defoe's time fooled by the text, the claim that 'The Shortest Way with Dissenters' was written by a High Church Tory extremist (the explicit narrator in fact impersonated by Defoe) could not have been rejected because the internal clues to establish its irony were insufficient. In fact, Defoe's other texts that state his religious faith and political observation were needed to ascertain the meaning of this particular text. Thus, to establish a text's subjectivity a comparison between the immediate utterer and the idea of the dynamical one is needed.[12] And this is why it is – in principle – impossible to reject the possibility that historical, including biographical, study may be helpful in establishing the meaning of a literary text. Consequently, the subjectivity of the text does not reside only within the text itself, but resides as well in its inscription of utterer and interpreter: both as internal positions and as two gestures pointing towards the utterer and interpreter in a communicative act supposed to be (at the point of) taking place. In literature, however, this communicative act seems to be diverted. Instead of the text reaching a putative addressee, it reaches an audience or readership to which it need not be explicitly addressed.

Although fictional characters certainly receive and respond to messages, the framing communicative act of a literary text is necessarily ambiguous, and in most or all cases it does not take place the way it is described in the text itself. It is addressed to an indefinite number of people whom the poet may equally favour but who are unknown. If it were discovered that the same love letter had been sent simultaneously to several addressees (cf. *The Merry Wives of Windsor*), it would probably be detrimental to the intentions and purpose of the utterer, because each beloved would most likely strongly object to receiving the same attention and expression of tender feeling as several others. But this is precisely what happens in literary communication because of its mixture of the public and the intimate (see chapter 6). Furthermore, in spite of the note of intimacy, since the text is not meant for somebody in particular, and is not intended as a specific intervention in somebody's life, it is, as it were, suspended; it is not exhausted by a single act of reception and thus, in principle, is infinitely repeatable.

However, if we heed this ambiguity, the communicative structure of the text together with knowledge of conventions governing speech acts and social interaction at the time of its utterance allow us to investigate the position of the utterer in relation to his or her own text and its (putative) interpreter. The parameters mentioned by Searle – such as differences in purpose, fit between words and world, expressed psychological states, force, interests of speaker and listener, institutional relation, explicitness of the speech act, and style of performance – can be used to describe the kind of enunciative act in which the utterer is involved (see Searle 1979: 1–29). Further, such parameters may also be useful in describing features of literary genres and techniques. Ostensibly making the words fit the world – but still the writer's world – is the objective of realism, while the opposite approach characterizes folk tales and utopian and dystopian texts. An elevated Asian style may be extremely forceful, while classicist texts may aim at understatement, and so forth.

While we are concerned, with respect to non-fictional texts, about the possible pretence of the utterer, we have in literature, as Searle (1979) has pointed out, another kind of pretence. Although the author pretends to refer to real states of affairs, in literature an agreement of sorts exists between writer and readership such that, in principle, nobody is either fooled or harmed, although people may certainly misclassify individual texts – making Ovid's paradox, to conceal art with art, true (Dr Johnson and Walter Scott considered Defoe's *Memoirs of Captain Carleton* [1728] genuine).

In literature there is, however, another side to, and another kind of duplicity in, the relationship between author/poet and narrator/lyrical I, because the abolishment, or at least attenuation, of sincerity and accountability makes possible an inquiry into dimensions of subjectivity that, in most cases, are inaccessible in non-fictional discourse. The apparent paradox is that the licence to create a number of personae (e.g., the pseudonyms, or heteronyms, of Kierkegaard and Passoa) that are definitely supposed to be non-identical with the utterer makes it possible to know more about his mind – and ours as well. Such pseudonyms are markers of literature as diagrammatic imagination and experimentation: a narrator, or a lyrical I, who relates a story, or describes a state of mind as it must look from his point of view, is imagined. Other imaginary narrators tell the same story, or a somehow comparable story from their (i.e., from another) point of view. The point of using this device need not be to signal the instability of the world and the relativity of truth, although it may be that. Such a device may also be part of a strategy for exposing what is considered false and/or morally bad (not all of Kierkegaard's narrators are equally reliable; nor do they possess equal insight from the point of view of the subjectivity expressed in his entire work). The liberty to create a fictional world told by several fictional narrators allows the possibility of denying any direct relation to and responsibility for what is narrated. What is told is presented as a kind of reported speech (for which the putative utterer is a medium, not the responsible originator). Thus, in a certain sense, literature is a kind of quoted speech without quotation marks (cf. Ohmann 1971: 1–19).

In poetry also the lyrical I quotes rather than makes a report about himself. Lyrical poetry is not only an emotion recollected in tranquillity, and contemplated, which then produces a spontaneous overflow of powerful feelings in the poet's mind. Emotion and feelings are produced by virtue of the poem itself, by its struggle with language. The past is the source rather than the template of the text. It is also true that in everyday conversation people may talk themselves into an emotional outburst, carried away by the very text they produce. The difference (as Wordsworth also indicated) is that a poem is always composed with a view to its aesthetic structure. And the lyrical I is a part of its structure, while the poet in flesh and blood is its originator.

Still, the originators also quote themselves: not only in the obvious sense that poets and writers describe the same states of mind or tell the same stories over and over again, but also in the less obvious sense that they become distanced from their own text by the very labour they have put into its artfulness. Aesthetic distance is not only valid for reader or spectator; the struggle with language establishes, as it were, an extra filter between poets and the outer and inner world of their text. They become distanced from their own texts by the fact that they confront them as an artefact in the making, that is, as something to be worked on. There is an invisible 'as I am saying' implied even in the poet's ravings – and this is why the relationship between self-representation and self-expression is not a superficial connection, but involves an amalgamation.

The cumulative effect of the double unreality of universe and enunciation suffices to bring into play figments of imagination that otherwise would hardly be communicated to an audience – or to the poet him- or herself. This is why literature constitutes, among other things, an attempt to write up against, if possible pass limits of self-exploration that are not often crossed. And this is why the Danish storyteller Isak Dinesen, in 'The Cardinal's First Tale,' let the cardinal answer the lady in black's question about his identity by telling her a story. After he has finished his tale, he concludes that the story alone can enlighten us about our identity: 'For within our whole universe the story only has authority to answer that cry of heart of its characters, the one cry of the heart of each of them: "Who am I?"' (Dinesen 1957: 26).

This, of course, is not valid only for modern literature. A tragedy such as *Oedipus Rex* stages questions of identity. One of the roles of literature in general is to make possible conversation and reflection on identity, even if it may involve what is both improper and dangerous. This is why the story's power to enlighten us about ourselves is due to the hypothetical nature both of its plot and world and of its narrators,[13] who as narrators of fictions become infected, as it were, with the unreality of their own stories.

The imagining mind, however, is split between its origin, the historical-experiential universe, within which it resides in the body of the utterer, and the fictional universe, in which it can function as the creative and structuring principle without the restrictions of our being confined to one body and one mind each. Literature makes it possible for you to speak as if you were another or, rather, others. At first glance, it seems a trivial fact that the author is neither the narrator nor the protagonist; this is, however, the precondition for a less trivial fact, namely, an amalgamation of self and other. It is this amalgamation of self-as-other and other-as-self that makes possible the emergence of what would otherwise never appear.

It might be objected that, in the final analysis, such texts are masquerades and that behind the masks there is nothing but one self, or several selves, the utterer(s). Such a position confounds bodily identity with conditions for sign production. Obviously, there is no denying that the physical source of a text is often an individual brain in an individual body. The point here, however, is another one, namely, that the creation of an *alter*, of something that, in spite of its being a creature of the same brain, is conceived as a non-I, will call forth significations impossible without this interplay.

Testimonies to the complex relationship between author and text include the following two passages that, although both exemplary, point in different directions. About his play, *The Father*, Strindberg writes to Axel Lundegård, on 12 November 1888 (letter 1460): 'It seems as if I were a sleepwalker, as if fiction and life merged. I don't know whether *The Father* is a play or whether my whole life is one.' (Strindberg 1958: vol. 6, 298; my trans.). According to T.S. Eliot, however, 'a good love poem, though it may be addressed to one person, is always meant to be overheard by other people. Surely the proper language of love – that is, of communication to the beloved and to no one else – is prose' (Eliot 1957: 90). On the one hand, writing literature involves the writer to such an extent that it is hardly possible to distinguish the non-fictional from the fictional. On the other hand, in writing authors are always, in some corner of their brains, performing in front of an audience, striving as it were to be able to quote themselves. The point is that both of these positions and attitudes are true of this relationship, and they are true at the same time. Literature both offers access to, and shields writer and reader from, their own subjectivity, by putting it into words instead of into the variety of other kinds of signs that it inhabits – from gut-reactions of nausea or flickers of bodily motions of desire to visions – and by ascribing these words to somebody else.

One aspect of this interplay is the possibility of what psychoanalysts call denial. This mechanism allows the patient the double operation of stating and denying: 'It was not my mother,' says the patient, simultaneously putting into words what occupies and troubles him and denying its truth and reality. As regards literature, it is its institutionalized framing that, even before the individual writer starts writing, implies – indeed guarantees – that what is written belongs to the realm of the non-I, narrates about the non-me, and obliges nobody.

It is this negative relationship between literature, subject, and lifeworld that makes it possible for fiction to probe into the core of the nature of subjectivity and its preconditions, that is, to explore how it is formed by social constraints and discursive practices. It is only by pretending not to be sincere that our main concern can be narrated and become a subject for scrutiny in a form less restricted by considerations of safety, personal advantage, propriety, common sense, and social and political power.

The above discussion leads to the basic question concerning the subjective dimension of literature, namely, what the purpose is of producing literary texts from the utterer's, the poets' and author's, point of view. This question is complicated by the fact that, first, literature is multifunctional; it serves different purposes at the same time. Furthermore, through history literature has served different purposes, or, at least, different functions and purposes have been dominant at different times. Second, producing literature, even from the utterer's point of view, serves an indefinite number of purposes, from earning a living to staying sane. These purposes are also dependent on which kind of literature the utterer produces. There is a difference between what motivates a writer who is a part of a team that produces mass literature by a division of labour modelled after industrial production (somebody writes the plot, someone else the dialogue or descriptions, etc.), and a poet who spends years to produce a collection of poems for a highbrow readership.[14]

The motives for producing literature may be discerned by looking at what poets and authors are essentially making. In Goodman's phrase, they are world-making – making alternative universes. Not that they are free to create whatever they want, because making literature is subject to constraints concerning taste and morality. It is also subject to the general constraint that literary texts will have to please at least a fraction, and preferably a substantial fraction, of the audience or readership (see chapter 6). Furthermore, the idea that writers make novel worlds has to be somewhat qualified, because most often they are giving new shapes to pre-existing matter, motives, forms, and genres. When, in Ovid, Calypso wants to keep Ulysses on her island, she asks him to tell about Troy once more: 'And o'er and o'er she'd ask of Troy's travail:/ In different words, he'd tell the same old tale' (Ovid, *Ars amatoria*, 1990: 111), or

> O! know, sweet love, I always write of you,
> And you and love are still my argument;
> So all my best is dressing old words new,
> Spending again what is already spent:
>   For as the sun is daily new and old,
>   So is my love still telling what is told.
>   (Shakespeare, Sonnet 76)

Such retelling is, indeed, the very pith and marrow of the production of literature. However, Ovid also points out that the words are different, and if 'words' are taken to cover all formal, semantic, and cognitive patterning of the text, then what is retold is never the same. Thus, writers are at least partially making novel and separate worlds because they are restructuring them even if they are not inventing them.

Despite the limitations set to the production of alternative worlds, the writer of fiction is nevertheless more at liberty than others who communicate in public to invent settings, thoughts, and actions. The tension between authors being at the mercy of their readership and being free to do as they want is charmingly illustrated by the narrator in *Tom Jones*. On the one hand, he allows that an author should not consider himself a gentleman hosting a private party, but as one who keeps a 'public Ordinary, at which all Persons are welcome for their Money' (Fielding 1973: 25). On the other hand, he conceives the act of creating a fictional world as follows:

> For all which I shall not look on myself as accountable to any Court of Critical Jurisdiction whatsoever: For as I am in reality, the Founder of a new Province of Writing, so I am at liberty what Laws I please therein. And these Laws, my Readers, whom I consider as my Subjects, are bound to believe in and to obey; with which they may readily and cheerfully comply, I do hereby assure them that I shall principally regard their Ease and Advantage in all such Institutions: For I do not, like a *jure divino* Tyrant, imagine that they are my Slaves or my Commodity. (Ibid.: 59)

This world-making serves different purposes, one of which, not foreign to Fielding, was described in chapter 3, namely, the Aristotelian view that by observing literature we may learn something about our life-world – a view that underscores literature's cognitive and didactic function and purpose.

Literature offers not only generalized, simplified, and aesthetically pleasing models of human desires and emotions; it offers a veritable *éducation sentimentale* as well, because literature and fiction are one of the important means of forming and socializing our sentiments. However, in addition to teaching about which emotions are proper at which occasions, literature also, by stirring our feelings, attempts to move and please us. Fielding's invention, as he claims, of a new province of writing is designed to please us by presenting a world in which poetic justice reigns. The world-making of literature often serves poetic justice less today as regards highbrow literature, but even if injustice holds sway in fictional worlds, they are at least not chaotic. More importantly, however, literature tailors states of affairs and states of mind in patterns that serve human drives and emotions not easily satisfied in other ways. In this respect literature is Janus-like: one side is turned outwards to represent, but of course also to question, the values and norms of interaction within a community, and so represents what should please and what should outrage us. The other side represents a turning inwards to our fantasies; to those that we would most often publicly deny that we have, and to those that we even do not know are active within us.

In the second epigraph to this chapter, Peirce makes the general point that, because man is involved in every semiosis as a sign processing and interpreting agent, what is experienced is also a manifestation of the subject itself, 'just as a rainbow is at once manifestation of the sun and of the rain.' However, he does stress that, directly or indirectly, the sign will be a manifestation of something else, that is, both self- and other-representational. And Peirce finds that it is possible to distinguish between these aspects and urges us to do so. In the third epigraph, Foucault speaks about a specific literary text, *Don Quixote* – a text in which, as he rightly points out, words are mostly used to create fictions: both those read by the Don and those he creates himself. Although these words are utterly inadequate and at odds with reality as it is represented in the novel, their very inadequacy adds another dimension to the positioning of the subject in literature: to create fictions and, in case of the Don, to fictionalize one's surroundings means, among other things, to turn topsy-turvy the world–word, or world–mind, relationship. Instead of being a model of the world as it is believed to be, literature becomes a means of producing alternative worlds that satisfy the subject. Don Quixote, however, forgets that such worlds belong at the campfire after dark; he literally mistakes his physical environment for his wish-world. In doing so, he crosses the line dividing illusion from delusion. But Sancho Panza, most of the time, and the narrators do not cross this line, and thus the novel is able to extract enjoyment from the representation of a hero who is admirable because he moulds the world to fit his ideas of how it should be. At the same time, however, we also pity and feel superior to the Don because, first, his ideas are not really his own; he has taken over a universe and an ideological construct that are hopelessly outdated and out of tune with his contemporary community. Thus, although his commitment to his wish-world moves us, his life lacks authenticity. Second, by confus-ing mind-dependent and mind-independent worlds he turns his worldly existence into a mess. Hence, as metafiction, the novel offers a reflection, in the form of a multilayered exemplification, on the disaster of breaking down reality-testing in the attempt to gratify desire. In thematizing desire *Don Quixote* is exemplary of literature in general. There are, however, other kinds of desire than the narcissistic eros displayed in Cervantes' novel.

5.4 The Subjective Thematics of Literature

The question of what a work of literature is about may elicit many different answers. The *Odyssey* is about the delayed return of a hero from the Trojan War. *The Divine Comedy* is about the narrator's travel through three other-worldly provinces of the universe. *The Trial* is about Joseph K. unsuccessfully trying to find out what he is accused of and about his final execution. 'Tintern Abbey' is about the reflections of the lyrical I on revisiting the banks of the Wye. Such answers, if they are elaborated, are of course essential, because they inform us about what kind of universe is represented and what is going on within it.

There is, however, a limit to how much such answers enlighten us as to what seems to be the main concerns of such texts; to what, for all we can say, constitutes their 'why' (as Paul Hernadi would say), their reasons for being told. We live in a world partly that is due to nature and partly the result of the collective actions of mankind through millennia. But although we have changed and moulded this world to become inhabitable and to serve our needs, and although laws and norms of interaction have been made, with more or less success, in order to make cooperative action and peaceful coexistence possible, this world does not in any way fulfil our wishes and fantasies. The best that can be said for some parts of it is that they offer tolerable, or maybe even acceptable, conditions for living. This world is, however, not able to ensure either happiness or meaning.

In representing a fictional universe, literature takes its point of departure from, and reacts to, the conditions in, the part of the world in which it is written, and that world will directly or indirectly be a part of the fictional universe. But literature also does something else: it articulates a diagram, as it were, or sketches another version, of the human condition. In describing the iconic sign, Peirce gives the following example of a diagram. A man is asking himself whether he really wants something: 'He makes in his imagination a sort of skeleton diagram, or outline sketch of himself, considers what modifications the hypothetical state of things would require to be made in that picture, and then examines it, that is, observes what he has imagined, to see whether the same ardent desire is there to be discerned' (CP 2.227). What Peirce describes is what we all do in examining our desires. Either we reject them and attempt to suppress or even repress them, or we recognize them and make plans to put them into effect. We may, however, also just keep them as cherished, often secret, fantasies in the recesses of our minds; close to where we most often dwell. In Peirce, imaginative experimentation is related to predicting a future state of affairs within the lifeworld of the experimentator. One of the main roles of literature, however, is to make diagrams of human fears and desires that are only mediately related to our actions. In the preceding chapter it was pointed out that literary texts are analogues, that is, iconic signs, of whatever states of affairs in the world they are like. They are, however, also diagrams of subjectivity, of the infinite vicissitudes of human desire. And even if, at least in principle, every utterance (but not every sentence or proposition) is unique, is produced as an individual action at a given time and place, utterances, and specifically literary texts, are recognizable diagrams and orchestrations of a limited number of fears, anxieties,[15] and desires.[16]

Desire is related equally to present, past, and future. At a certain point in time a desire becomes effective as a psychic reality and, consciously or unconsciously, is directed towards future fulfilment. At the same time, however, it is inextricably linked to the repetition of past, primarily unconscious, fantasies in an impossible attempt to revive former experiences of fulfilment that can in fact only be re-established as caricatures (and by paying a high price, mentally and socially). Like desire, fear and anxiety are also bound up with the repetition of past traumas and conflicts.

The paradoxical nature of desire is due to the unconscious mapping of past scenarios of fulfilment onto the future. This makes desire always non-contemporaneous with itself. In search for that which might earlier have brought fulfilment but cannot be identically repeated – and even if this were possible, would not bring fulfilment – desire's actualization becomes its death. This sets in motion what according to Lacan is characteristic of desire, its metonymic sliding from one object to another.

It goes without saying that desire is not only unconscious. We are certainly painfully aware that we desire, especially when the object of desire is unattainable. We are, furthermore, able to both stage and pronounce our conscious desires. Staging desire is what we do all the time in the inner movie theatre of daydreaming, while we transform desire to demand by asking the other to make her- or himself available as an object of desire. And we further demand that we ourselves become the object of the other's desire. Unconscious desire, however, is never fulfilled; it is, in essence, unfulfillable. In addition to all the psychic and interpersonal problems inextricably bound up with demand in its relation to conscious desire, there is the basic problem of the relationship between conscious and unconscious desires, because these two desires are displaced in relation to, and do not cover, each other. They are not only different; they are at variance.

Because the pleasurable activities of the subject meet with repression and reprisals, such clashes, contradictions, and conflicts are unavoidable, with the effect that unconscious desire becomes inextricably bound up with fear and anxiety. The repression of early desires and their replacement by other, less dangerous objects and goals mean that we may consciously desire what is, in effect, a defence, a reaction-formation, against our unconscious desire. On the one hand, what makes us anxious and fearful may well be what we desire unconsciously, and, on the other, what we consciously desire may unconsciously arouse anxiety. Thus, in a certain sense but only in a certain, albeit very important sense, we do not know what we desire. As a result, we are always chasing what we fancy may still our desire. But from what has been said above, it also follows that we will never find it and, therefore, will never stop hunting for it.

The outcome of our inner, personal conflicts, together with the extreme difficulty, indeed the impossibility, of two, or more, persons matching and fulfilling each other's conscious as well as unconscious desires, makes us vulnerable, bewildered, and potentially always on the verge of unhappiness. We are, however, supple and inclined to reach compromises with ourselves and others because this has been a precondition for our surviving the process of growing up – and for the species to survive. Yet the constant sliding of desire is not in itself disastrous. To chase fulfilment, even if it is never realized, and even if its simulacra give only momentary relief, means to be constantly engaged and directed. Finally, the ongoing replacement of desires opens up the wide field of sublimation. Even if Freud is probably right in pointing to the origin of sublimation in repression and suppression,[17] what is erected on this basis may become in themselves vitally important and pleasurable activities bringing their own kind of fulfilment. Sublimation's embellishments are not adequately understood when viewed only as cover-ups and protections. They also become marks of progression in semiotic competence, in the handling of the complex networks of personal and social significations.

Nevertheless, to the lack of concord between unconscious and conscious desires, and their ever-present relation to fears and anxieties, we must add the simple fact that neither unconscious nor conscious desire is whole and undivided. Desire, as well as fear and anxiety, is always divided among an indefinite number of objects. Even more importantly, desire never exists in the singular, but as a plurality of attempts at fulfilment linked with different, diverging, incompatible, and even warring objectives. The inventory below lists what seem to be the principal fears and desires of our species.[18] Other distinctions might have been drawn, but what is important is the indication of different, and often irreconcilable, kinds of fears and desires that, whether or not we are aware of them, are active in our minds.

Desire for		**Fear of**
1. sensuous and pleasurable satisfaction of bodily needs	vs.	frustration of bodily needs, pain
2. sexual gratification	vs.	sexual frustration
3. mastery and possession	vs.	social and mental deprivation
4. power	vs.	impotence
5. recognition	vs.	contempt
6. friendship and love	vs.	estrangement, enmity, hatred
7. knowledge and meaning	vs.	ignorance and lack of meaning
8. immortality	vs.	death

The opposition between satisfaction and frustration of bodily needs and the desires related to them may mean the contrast between physical pleasure and pain but also the less acute, but equally important, contrast between well-being and indisposition, between physical comfort and discomfort. According to psychoanalysis, the pleasure-pain principle is basic to individual development. Indeed, until the supremacy of the reality-principle is attained, the borderline between subject and world is felt to coincide with that between the pleasurable and the painful. Although we are forced to give up the idea of this merging of self with what is pleasurable, the opposition between bodily pleasure and pain remains fundamental and decisive for our quality of life. Along with the necessary satisfaction of bodily needs, the desire for experiencing bodily pleasures, and for avoiding what is painful, remains with the subject, constantly active in his or her memories and fantasies. The gratification of these desires involves the five senses, which are analysed and aestheticized as their potential for arousal and yielding pleasure is developed in arts such as gastronomy, perfumery, haute couture, dance, music, and the visual arts.

Despite common prejudice, pleasure, in psychoanalysis, is not synonymous with sexual pleasure. On the contrary, early psychosexual development is a complicated and fateful drama about the encounter between pleasure and sex. Certainly psychoanalysis speaks about oral and anal sexuality, but only because the vital needs linked with these orifices are sexualized *après coup*, as it were; not because ingestion and evacuation in themselves are sexual, although they are certainly pleasurable – and painful. On the one hand, this kind of pleasure/pain is inextricably bound up with the functioning of bodily organs, and especially with the genitals, but on the other, sexual pleasure is precisely psycho-sexual, and thus equally tightly linked with unconscious and conscious fantasies, fears, and wish-fulfilments.

This double, and unbreakable, connection with the body and with fantasies, that is, fictions, makes possible the astonishing, infinite variety of ways in which sexual gratification is achieved, from what is most common within a given culture, through what to many seems grotesque but harmless, to what is destructive and horrifying.[19]

A good deal of literature focuses on describing the crisis of adolescence and its rites of passage, and is thus especially preoccupied with the relations between men and women and their bonding. It should be pointed out, however, that sexual desire, and even love, is only a part of this drama. Sexual desire, because of its infantile entrenchment and history and, consequently, because of its idiolectic and idiosyncratic nature, hampers and inhibits adult bonding, while it is incited and prompted by it. Durable bonding between grown-ups is probably founded on the satisfaction of needs and interests more than on desire, on friendship no less than on sexual desire. Furthermore, desire is always on the road, fleeing from and towards what is, in a basic sense, unknown to it. Desire, and especially sexual desire, is bound up with vanity and vexation.

On the desire/fear list, the desire for mastery and possession (Freud's *Bemächtigungstrieb*) is distinguished from the desire for power. The former is more immediate and specific. It is a desire to achieve and master bodily and mental skills; a desire to take possession of much-coveted objects in the surroundings, but also to be able to monopolize others. The desire for mastery is bound up with the pragmatic attitude of the subject regarding his or her lifeworld. Alfred Schutz justly remarks that 'daily life is, above all, although not exclusively, concerned with the mastery of typical, recurrent situations' (Schutz and Luckmann 1973: 139). However, this desire goes further than that; indeed, ultimately we desire to master fate itself.

The desire for power is, in contradistinction to that for mastery, absolute. We may distinguish between the power over oneself – self-control – the subjugation and control of others, between the power to create and to destroy. Power, however, tends to reach out for omnipotence, the omnipotence that we believed we possessed in the narcissistic phase of our development and that we have never – unconsciously – given up. We hide a craving for absolute power within us, but it is a craving constantly held in check by our knowledge of the very real limits within which we are able to exercise power. While the craving for absolute power most often is warded off before reaching consciousness, and does its work unconsciously, the fear of impotence and submission is alive in our consciousness as a fear of indignity and of violation – imagined or justified – of our mental and physical integrity.

Whereas the opposition between power and impotence may be related to our physical survival, the opposition between recognition and contempt is related to our self-image and to how others let us know that they see us, that is, to our 'survival' within the community (in his description of the fight to death for recognition, Hegel combines these fears and desires; see Hegel 1977: 111–19, § 178–96). As in the case of the desire for power, we may distinguish between cravings for different forms of recognition. First of all, self-esteem, and its painful contrast self-contempt, are both dependent on the esteem of others. This is the reason for our thirst for recognition from our contemporaries, whose respect and admiration we wish so much to enjoy, while the contempt of others is unbearable. For psychoanalysis, the desire for recognition is related to early processes of identification and to the creation of the so-called ego-ideal. Thus, self-esteem is understood in relation to the introjection of parental figures. Sometimes the desire for recognition is directed not only towards one's contemporaries, but also towards posterity (indeed, there is also a megalomaniac desire to be recognized even by a Supreme Being).[20]

Although today we may be inclined to focus on love rather than on friendship, in historical perspective many features that we associate with love would earlier have been thought of as characteristics of friendship. We too, however, distinguish love both from pleasure and from sexuality, even if, in one of its main forms, love integrates them. Love adds, however, recognition, caring, and reciprocity (in antiquity features of friendship). However, particularly in a love-relationship, there is a tendency for the subject to place the beloved above him- or herself, while friendship, at least ideal friendship, is thought to exist between equals. The cool and clear-headed Freud spoke consistently about the lover's overrating of the sexual object. Nevertheless, the objective of falling in love and of love is reciprocity. In Hegelian-informed psychoanalysis the so-called desire for the other's desire is central, but desire does not imply reciprocity (we may well thirst for the other's desire, without ourselves desiring her or him). Unrequited, but persisting, love proves, however, that reciprocity is not a precondition for loving, only for loving happily (in friendship this is different). Thus, love may exist without any apparent gratification. Psychoanalysis claims, however, that libidinal gratification is present even in unrequited and unselfish love, since love for the other person, contrary to appearances, is intimately connected with self-love (self-love, it was formerly thought, is also a precondition for friendship). Narcissism and object-love not only function as communicating vessels, but the libidinal investment in the other person means the draining of the subject's narcissistic love, because love for the other both cathects the image of the other with libido and lets the subject indentify him- or herself with his or her love (for the other). This is one reason that the dissolution of a love-relationship is so painful; it affects self-image, consciously and unconsciously.

Love is, however, not confined to erotic love; affectionate and almost unbreakable may be the love of parents for their children and vice versa, and that between siblings may prove very strong as well. Nor is love only directed towards and sought from individual others. Actually, our craving for love – in contradistinction to our ability and inclination to give it – is infinite and unlimited. We have within us an excessive, unreasonable, and unrealistic demand for everybody's love, and sometimes even for the love of a Supreme Being ('So God created man in his *own* image, in the image of God he created him; male and female he created them. And God blessed them,' Gen. 1: 27–8).

The desire for knowledge and meaning is related to the desires for mastery and power, and the fear of ignorance and of lack of meaning is, correspondingly, a fear of mental impotence. Ontogenetically, psychoanalysis links the desire for knowledge with scopophilia and with the child's pleasure in investigating its surroundings in general, and its own sexuality and that of others in particular. It goes without saying, however, that desire for knowledge is just as much connected with the so-called ego-instincts as with sexuality. Knowledge is a precondition for the subject's survival; and in the human species learning processes play a more important role than do innate instincts. Nevertheless, the child's exploration of its own body, of those of others, and of its surroundings is also triggered as an investigation into the potentials for pleasure and for crossing the borders of that which is permitted. What is more, the drive-cathection of procuring knowledge continues in adult life.

The desired object of knowledge is, to begin with, basically the subject him- or herself, together with significant others. But self-interpretation need not consciously remain in focus; it may be replaced by the investigation of others, even by spying on others. Gossip is an elementary example of the attempt to satisfy a desire for knowledge directed towards others (but often in order to see how they match ourselves – and in order to gloat if they deviate in ways we consider unacceptable).

The desire for knowledge is unstable, going in many directions over time. It may also become attached to the process of procuring knowledge of almost any kind that seems remotely interesting. Thus, the very accumulation of knowledge and competence may become relatively autonomous sources of instinctual gratification, and thus an independent objective, although mediately related to sexual desire and the desire for mastery.

Self-knowledge, knowledge of others, and of the course of the world are sometimes clearly, sometimes indirectly, linked with the desire to know the future (after all, we are always calculating the consequences of future actions and events in order to survive and prosper). The desire for knowledge of the future is ultimately a desire to know the ways of destiny.

The excessive desire for knowledge is held in check by the fear of knowing – of knowing the truth about things, including the future. Although ignorance may easily cause a feeling of mental and social impotence, the fear of ignorance is not all-pervasive. The desire for knowledge finds its limit at the point where fear of the answer becomes the stronger, since powerlessness is already a fact.

Knowledge and meaning are not synonymous, since what is known may appear void of meaning (cf. the distinction between knowledge and experience, p. 232). Lack of meaning is, as it were, both an existential deficit and, in Habermas's words, a scarce resource in Western, post-industrial societies (Habermas 1979: 178–206). It is often held that this lack is an effect of the ongoing process of secularization that leaves mankind alone in the universe without the support of metaphysical powers. This complaint is especially related to the last oppositional pair, the fear of death and the desire for immortality.

There are two reasons for including this pair in this list of basic fears and desires, in spite of the fact that we live in a secular culture. First, we are dealing with subjectivity in a historical perspective, and it is self-evident that it has played an enormous role for millennia, and has a most impressive bibliography within all cultures. Second, the desire for immortality is deeply rooted in our psyche, since it is related to the early experiences of omnipotence during the narcissistic phase, as well as to the breakdown of this belief by virtue of unavoidable experiences of de facto impotence.

In its most extreme form, the desire for immortality gives rise to a belief in personal immortality, to the literal belief in the resurrection of the flesh together with ideas about Paradise, Elysium, Valhalla, and so on – places of bliss reserved for the pious, the just, and the brave. Also megalomanic, albeit to a lesser degree, is the belief in the immortality of one's personal deeds and achievements, even if poets, artists, thinkers, inventors, warlords, prophets, and magnates have had confidence that what they have done is immortal and will make them eternally remembered. However, even if this claim to immortality lacks the unfounded and inexplicable pretensions of that of personal immortality, it seems vain, because it presupposes that the human race will subsist eternally. Often, however, the desire for immortality is related not to the individual person but to the family or nation, or to a belief in the future victory and eternal reign of a movement or an idea. However, in these cases as well the continuation of history is presupposed.

Finally, the desire for immortality may be transferred to a metaphysical being who, or which, is conceived as being absolutely different from the material, and always changing, universe and its inhabitants. What man cannot hope for is imagined as realized in such a being. The indestructible, but irrational, desire for immortality is upheld by the fear of death. Because death is most often conceived as total deprivation, as a state of dissolution and non-being, this fear generally, but not always (cf. the idea of death as delivery from misery or of death as rest), provokes the most anxiety of all.

These eight oppositional pairs make up, I believe, the basic matrix of human fears and desires. The order in which they have been listed represents a progression from what is most tightly bound up with bodily sensations to drive-cathected, but incorporeal, hopes and fears of the unknown. Although they are all present from childhood on, they do not possess the same interest during different periods of the conscious psychical life of the individual. Thus, different pairs of fears and desires (for desires are always accompanied by corresponding fears) may be more or less dominant in different periods of the life cycle, although they cannot, on the view presented here, be reduced to each other. Moreover, if we suppose that the unconscious, in spite of its great rigidity, is also constantly influenced by new experiences, unconscious fantasies and wish-fulfilments will also change over time, even if it contains archaic layers of drive-cathected significations still active in patterning the current fantasies of the individual person.

To the individual variations related to sex and age in the fantasy life of the individual person should be added the fact that fears and desires are articulated differently at different times within different cultures and within different classes and subcultures of a given society. A given culture and society consist of systems of beliefs, norms, and values that are closely related to its material, political, and institutional aspects. These structures of signification regulate, more or less consistently, and more or less strictly, what can be expressed and what is interdicted; which physical and symbolic actions are allowed and which are punished. In regulating belief systems, norms, and values, a given society will also directly and indirectly mould the subjectivity of its members. As a result, the concrete articulation of fears and desires, how they are dressed up and how they appear to people in their dreams and daydreams – and in literature – depends on what is permitted and what is forbidden, on what is frowned upon and what encouraged, and on what the sanctions and prizes are.

On the one hand, I propose that this matrix of fears and desires is inextricably linked with our species's elementary experiences as physical beings who interact with others in the attempt to survive and live a good life, and who are endowed with a semiotic competence that makes possible the creation of alternative universes (and even a preference for these over our own lifeworld). On the other hand, these basic fears and desires are concretely articulated in an indefinite number of ways dependent on culture, society, subculture, and personal experiences.

There is no contradiction involved in claiming that some fears and desires are anthropological constants even though they are always encountered in concrete shapes that differ much from each other. On the contrary, if we were unable to discern abstract actional, emotional, and ratiocinative patterns in the concrete sign production of others, understanding and interaction would become impossible. If, however, no variations existed, feeling, acting, and thinking would become identical repetitions of invariant patterns leading to petrification of our mental and cultural life.

In relation to literature, the above matrix should prove useful in pointing out the building blocks and elementary relationships of which literature, in its capacity to diagram fears and desires, is made. Holbek's analysis of fairy-tale form, presented in the preceding chapter, is part of a larger analysis that also takes into account the telling of the tales and their function within rural society. It is immediately seen, however, that the narrative structure and transformations of the five-act fairy tale stage a drama of fears and desires involving every one listed here, except for the desire for immortality, whose corresponding fear of death is also played down (death and immortality, however, loom large in ancient myth, whereas marriage, which is immensely important in the fairy tale, is of secondary importance). Furthermore, in its stereotyped course of actions, the fairy tale also stages a traditional solution of conflicts that expresses a wish-fulfilment. Thus, fairy tales are not only fixed, or almost fixed, narrative structures; they are also stereotyped and infinitely revived diagrams of fears and desires.

In mentioning fairy tales as examples of the articulation of the subjective dimension in literature, one should avoid any confounding of subjective and personal, since there is nothing individual and personal in these tales. On the contrary, they stage fears and desires in forms that have been shared and appreciated by Indo-European rural societies for hundreds of years and that can appeal to children and adults even in societies with a different social structure. The reason they possess such general appeal is probably due to their staging of the perhaps most important transitional period in the life cycle of humans, namely, the passage from youth to adulthood with all its rites. But since the youth–adult conflict has precursors all the way through childhood, children are able to (re)interpret the tales according to their own fears, desires, and conflicts at different stages (see Bettelheim 1976), and thus to enjoy them.

Furthermore, fears and desires are always articulated according to the norms and values of the culture in question, and this is also valid at the unconscious level. Rather than just informing us about individual longings and about repression, traditional tales may enlighten us as well about the social unconscious of a society. Still, every society is confronted with the task of survival, and thus basic programs of actions are necessarily similar worldwide even if surface programs may differ widely. Thus, the description of their blueprints, the diagrams of desires, and narratology's objective – to found a basic grammar of action within generic fictional universes (e.g., Propp and Holbek) – support each other in the attempt to lay bare universal, or at least quasi-universal, patterns of thinking about instinctual gratification and deprivation.

From Anacreontic poetry celebrating the sensuous gratification of the senses to hymns praising the glory of God, and from collective forms (myths, fairy tales, hymns, etc.) to texts clearly carrying the seal of an individual author, subjective thematics has made up the pith and marrow of literature and its congeners. Literature not only imagines an alternative universe that may serve as a model for (aspects of) the lifeworld of the poet; it also imagines the course and states, and final fates, of desires and fears to which imagination has given concrete shape and a virtual environment:

> ... as imagination bodies forth
> The forms of things unknown, the poet's pen
> Turns them to shapes, and gives to airy nothing
> A local habitation and a name.
> Such tricks hath strong imagination,
> That if it would but apprehend some joy,
> It comprehends some bringer of that joy:
> Or, in the night, imagining some fear,
> How easy is a bush suppos'd a bear!
> (*A Midsummer Night's Dream*, V, i, 13–22)

5.5 Desire and Fiction: Persinna's Confession

The relationship between fiction and the basic fears and desires is reciprocal. Just as literature is informed by fears and desires, so are fears and desires unthinkable without the play of imagination, that is, without the creation of a rudimentary or full-fledged fiction.

About 40 BC the great, pleasant, and somewhat stolid Horace wrote his second satire. It exhorts young men not to become involved with married women; it is a diatribe against the lot of the fornicator. In arguing against being an accomplice in marital infidelity, Horace compares all the dangers, troubles, frustrations, and postponements the paramour of a married woman suffers to the safety, ease, and speed with which a man – since the addressees of the satire are certainly men – may gratify his sexual desire with lowborn women.

The satire is so coarse that it almost, but only almost, acquires a certain innocence. Nothing is hidden. To exemplify the dangers of the adulterous relationship and of satisfying sexual needs by possessing high-born women, Horace relates the story of Vilius, the lover of Fausta. She was noble indeed, the daughter of the dictator Sulla, and the poor Vilius had to bear beatings and suffer indignities. Horace imagines a dialogue between Vilius and his manhood:

> If, after witnessing that many miseries, Vilius' prick had
> Asked him the question: 'What *are* you about?! Have I ever demanded
> Cunt that was born and descended from blue-blooded consuls and which was
> Wrapped in a matronly stole, when my dander was up?,' what excuse could
> Vilius offer except that 'The girl has a high-ranking father?'
> (Horace 1983: 20, 64–72)[21]

In this debate between head and tail, Horace definitely sides with the latter. The fault of Vilius is that he is dazzled by wealth, status, power, attributes, which are all – this is the argument – foreign to lust and sexual gratification. Horace persists, and he generalizes the matter crudely as follows:

> No married woman in snowy-white pearls and emerald beads (though
> *You* may not think so, Ceríntkus) is softer of thigh or of leg more
> Shapely, and girls in the dark coloured togas are frequently better.
> Furthermore, *their* wares are free of disguises and dyes, what they have to
> Sell may be freely inspected, what physical charms they possess they
> Do not of touting and flouting while keeping their
>   blemishes hidden.
> Kings have the habit, when purchasing horses, of covering portions
> During inspection, lest excellent features ...
>   ... Should befuddle the buyer ...
>   ... Therefore you ought not to scrutinize physical merits
> Keen-eyed as Lynceus while being more blind than Hypsáea in seeing

> None of the shortcomings: 'Oh, what a leg! And what arms!,' when in
>   fact she's
> Flat in the buttocks, low-waisted, long-nosed, and her feet are
>   enormous.
> ...
> But with those others [freedwoman/prostitutes] no problem. In
>   gauzes from
>   Cos you can see them
> Practically naked: the leg is not bad and the foot is not ugly
> And you can measure a waist in a glance. Would you rather they
>   played you
> False and deceived you, collecting your money before there was any
> Showing of merchandise?
>
>   (Ibid.: 21, 80–105)

No doubt Horace is letting down his hair; some would say much too much. Satisfaction is the thing, satisfaction by means of one who is pretty and available; one who may be, or already is, bought, like one buys a horse. One should just do the right thing: exploit slaves and freedwomen. Is it, however, so simple? Is desire really satisfied by just mounting the defenceless victim. Horace feels forced to allow another opinion, and lends his voice to somebody expressing the hunter's unwillingness to kill the sitting game. This dissenting voice says that his love '[s]kips the already dished up to' and hunts 'quarry still running.' Horace, however, despises this kind of huntsman's pride; his own doctrine is preached in the following hard-boiled argument:

> Wouldn't you do a lot better to ascertain first what are Nature's
> Limits on appetite, which are the things she will tolerate, which are
> Those she would grieve at the loss of, and see what is substance and
>   what is Void. If you are dying of thirst, do you ask if the goblet is
>   golden?
> Or if you're famished and starving, refuse every food in the world save
> Peacock and turbot? Then why, if your groin is distended, and right at
> Hand is a slave girl or slave lad of yours you crave in the moment's
> Urgency, why would you choose to endure the discomfort of passion?
> *I* wouldn't. I'm for a love that's accessible, easy to come by.
>
>   (Ibid.: 111–19)

With this argument the case seems closed: immediate gratification of desire, when it visibly announces itself, is the thing. Longing and fantasy, passion and suffering are not on the program; indeed passion should be avoided.

Today, a couple of thousand years later, Horace's recipe, as presented till now, does not meet with sympathy. On the contrary, fantasies are now regarded as an important part of sexual interaction and eroticism. Collections of the erotic fantasies of men and women are published (e.g., Friday 1973, 1975, 1980, and 1991), and therapists urge couples to share their fantasies, to use them together when having sex. Before turning up one's nose at these practices, it should be remembered that, after all, such advice is based on the insight that we are such stuff as dreams are made of and that desire is always drenched in fantasies and memories.[22]

Erotic daydreams, or sadomasochistic rituals (see note 22), are not literature; they are, however, related to it. Like literature, they are articulations of instinctual currents, conscious as well as unconscious, of memories and sensations, and of their combinations in fantasy. The level of articulation in daydreams and rituals is, however, lower, and the rigidity much more pronounced because they are ephemeral, if recurring, images or role-playing directed towards individual, instinctual gratification. They have not been purified through the labour spent in modelling them in a stubborn material and in liberating them from the merely private. And, although narratives, they are cast as tableaux and fragments because they are geared towards an immediate gratification of desire or an immediate mastery of anxiety.

The close connection between fantasy, ritual, and erotic daydream may also be exemplified by the steady seller of all times, the Greek novel of love and adventure, Heliodorus's *Aethiopica* (2nd or 3rd century AD). This model of romance has everything: a girl, the heroine Charicleia, who is exposed as a newborn child and nurtured by foster parents; the virtuous, o so virtuous, love of the young couple, Charicleia and Theagenes; their forced separation and adventures; their reunion as prisoners bound to be sacrificed to the gods; a father who is on the verge of sacrificing his own daughter, Charicleia, because he does not recognize her. Through a late recognition, however, everything ends with one happy family. The fun and the entertainment are, it is revealed at the end, triggered by a daydream. The darkskinned king of Ethiopia, Hydaspes, has – and that seems fair enough – certain difficulties in recognizing the heroine, the fair-skinned Charicleia, as his daughter by his likewise dark-skinned queen, Persinna. The confession of Persinna, however, disentangles the knot.

Peculiar circumstances have been decisive at the conception, as Charicleia is told:

> Ten years had passed since Hydaspes made me his wife, and still no child had been born to us. But that day your father made love to me, swearing that he was commanded to do so by a dream, and I knew instantly that the act of love had left me pregnant.
> ... But you, the child I bore, had a skin of gleaming white, something quite foreign to Ethiopians. I knew the reason: during your father's intimacy with me the painting had presented me with the image of Andromeda, who was depicted stark naked, for Perseus was in the very act of releasing her from the rocks, and had unfortunately shaped the embryo to her exact likeness. I was convinced that your colour would lead to my being accused of adultery ... (*Collected Ancient Greek Novels*: 433)

Hence, the daydream and its consequences are the plot's motor: the conception and birth of the beautiful, fair-skinned girl who must be exposed, being alien and a putative proof of guilt.[23] However, the point is also that the disclosure of Persinna's guilt – her erotic reverie during the intercourse with her husband – brings about the dénouement. Something wonderful and strange happens in this novel – and in literature generally: the reverie materializes as a universe of action, albeit fictional, where that which is only thought becomes a consistent and fateful reality. Persinna gives herself to a reverie that in the novel is realized as the omnipotence of thought, and she becomes its victim. Within the story, image and fantasy are accepted as a sufficient explanation of reality, and as a pleasurable representation of an alternative world, a world that is an existentially important analogy to, and commentary on, our own inner and outer reality.

The universal nature of dream and daydream, the staging of desire through role playing, and our willing giving of ourselves to the pleasures of fiction and literature make us all confess to the guilt of Persinna. All of us? What about Horace? Isn't he totally present enjoying nothing but corporeal and dreamless pleasures offered by partners inspected like horses? Not quite; in truth not at all! I have just, as he does himself, deferred the point of the poem. We left him as he was calling the slave girl to satisfy his needs. He continues:

> Let her be comely and straight, and with just enough elegance so as
> Not to seem taller or whiter-complected than nature designed her:

> Once such a girl puts her left side up close to my right side, she then is
> Ilia to me, or Égéria – names I assign do not matter –
>
> (1983: 21, 123–6)

Ilia and Egeria are the noblest names: the first was mistress of Mars, the second a goddess. Contrary to what is stated earlier in the satire, here Horace makes clear that names, and fames and dreams, do matter very much. He turns out, more than anyone, to be the accomplice of Persinna. Literature constantly bears witness to the fictional core of our desires.

5.6 Language, Materiality, and Repetition in Literature

In addition to this experimentation on diagrams of desires and fears and its subjective thematics, there is another way in which the literary text becomes the carrier and arouser of drive-cathected excitement. While diagrammatic experimentation is occupied, as it were, with the grand design of the texts, their narrative and argumentative structures, texts also arrest the anticipation of the result, or as Peter Brooks would say, the desire for the ending. He points out that we desire the detour, desire to be arrested, to be held fast by the text (Brooks 1984: 103–8). One of the ways in which the anticipatory flight forwards is arrested is by virtue of the (erotic) appeal of language as patterned materiality that arouses the senses of poet and reader. This arousal is beautifully expressed by the awakening Helena's response to Faust's wooing. The language he is speaking, German, is unknown to her, but she is struck by the musical qualities and appeal of his words. She says:

> Ein Ton scheint sich den andern zu bequemen,
> Und hat ein Wort zum Ohre sich gesellt,
> Ein andres kommt, dem ersten liebzukosen.
> (*Faust* II, iii, 9369–71)

> Each sound seems to accommodate the other,
> And as one word repairs into the ear,
> There comes another to caress the first.
> (Goethe 1976: 237)

In fact, Helena is not so much attentive to the intentions of Faust, the meaning of which she does not understand; she is, rather, attentive to the interplay between the words themselves, that is, to their musical and erotic charm as strings of sound. The power of the music of words is also the subject of Eliot's reflections on what he calls auditory imagination,

> the feeling for syllable and rhythm, penetrating far below conscious levels of thought and feeling, invigorating every word; sinking to the most primitive and forgotten, returning to the origin and bringing something back, seeing the beginning and the end. It works through meanings, certainly, or not without meanings in the ordinary sense, and fuses the old and obliterated and the trite, the current, and the new and surprising, the most ancient and the most civilised mentality. (Eliot 1933: 118–19)

According to Eliot, this aspect of poetry (or of literature in general, since prose may have a rhythm of its own) should influence the reader's reception of the poem regardless of its meaning:

> The chief use of the meaning of a poem, in the ordinary sense, may be (for I am speaking of some kinds of poetry and not all) to satisfy one habit of the reader, to keep his mind diverted and quiet, while the poems do their work upon him: much as the imaginary burglar is always provided with a bit of nice meat for the house-dog. This is a normal situation of which I approve. (Ibid.: 119)

It is interesting that a very intellectual poet like Eliot points to the almost intoxicating qualities of literature and links them with a deeper layer of meaning than that related to its immediate world representation. In fairness to Eliot, it should be pointed out that he, very sensibly, finds that the greatest poetry unites mastery of both sound and sense. Very good poetry may, however, cultivate either one or the other to perfection. Further, as regards poetry especially concerned with sound, Eliot finds that there is 'a certain merit in melodious raving' (1957: 169). He even holds that such poetry may be a 'genuine contribution to literature' because it 'responds effectually to the permanent appetite of humanity for an occasional feast of drums and cymbals' (ibid.); or as Eliot does not hesitate to point out: we all need to get drunk sometimes.

Barthes also celebrates the pleasure stemming from the materiality of performing the text (rhetoric's *actio* and the not [yet] practiced *writing aloud*). In one of the last paragraphs of *The Pleasure of the Text* he writes:

> [W]hat [writing aloud] searches for (in a perspective of bliss) are the pulsional incidents, the language limned with flesh, a text where we can hear the grain of the throat, the patina of consonants, the voluptuousness,

a whole carnal stereophony; the articulation of the body, of the tongue, not that of meaning, of language ... [T]he anonymous body of the actor into my ear; it granulates, it crackles, it caresses, it grates, it cuts, it comes: that is bliss. (Barthes 1975: 66–7)

A wish to free the materiality of language from signification always exists; Dadaist poems written, as it were, in their own private language, exemplify this desire. See, for instance, the first stanza of 'Alma' by the Danish Dadaist Johannes Weltzer:

> Adakadejsan, simbira gastir,
> hamaradawan satinarundr.
> O, mala kirsej,
> O, serti mila,
> simbryligastur arkinarendr. –

Readers unfamiliar with Danish may believe that the poem is an inscription of a string of Danish words representing some state of affairs; but it is nothing of the sort. The inscription is formed in accordance with the Danish language system; but, prima facie, it represents nothing. At this point we should pause, however: is it really true that such a poem is non-representational? It might be argued that even if it does not represent a state of affairs, it may still represent a state of mind. One might object, however, that its representational character is based on nothing more than a (dubious) sound symbolism and possibly the connotations of the title, which is identical to a Latin word that is also used as a Danish first name for women.

However, this does not close the case. Even if the representational function of such a poem may remain vague as to which state of mind is represented, it may, nevertheless, portray a certain, perhaps ill-delimited, mood. It may arouse a range of feelings in the reader and may presumably have been created for that purpose. Obviously, this question is important, because in addition to such marginal phenomena like poems in self-invented 'languages,' there is the whole question concerning the representational nature of music.

In Aristotle's (and Plato's) reflections on politics and education music plays an important role. Music is understood as a means to arouse certain feelings, and then, through habituation, to form the character of the performer and listener:

Rhythm and melody supply imitations of anger and gentleness, and also of courage and temperance, and of all the qualities contrary to these, and of all the other qualities of character, which hardly fall short of the actual affections, as we know from our own experience, for in listening to such strains our souls undergo a change. The habit of feeling pleasure or pain at mere representations is not far removed from the same feelings about reality ... On the one hand, even in mere melodies there is an imitation of character ... Some of them make men sad and grave, like the so-called Mixolydian, others enfeeble the mind, like the relaxed modes, another, again, produces a moderate and settled temper, which appears to be the peculiar effect of the Dorian; the Phrygian inspires enthusiasm ... The same principles apply to rhythm, some have a character of rest, others of motion, and of these latter again, some have a more vulgar, others a nobler movement. Enough has been said to show that music has the power of forming character, and should therefore be introduced in the education of the young. (Aristotle 1941: 1311–12, *Pol.* 1340)

Concerning music, it should certainly be stressed that, whatever else music is, it is patterned sound and thus very much self-representational. Further, although it may in certain cases be easy to define the emotions that a certain piece of music provokes in listeners (within a given culture), in other cases opinions may vary very much as to the emotions expressed by a particular piece. However, with these provisos, some refined version of Aristotle's understanding of music (which was common in his time), seems by far the most helpful in explaining the unquestionable power of music. Briefly, music is other-representational as well as self-representational; it does not, however, represent external states of affairs (program music is an insignificant exception), but emotional states and emotional processes. Its lack of identifiable exteriority means a more direct link to the emotional make-up of listeners.[24] Emotional significance is matched with extreme semantic vagueness, such that music may represent and arouse general emotional attitudes connected with the individual experiences of each listener.

As regards literature, even the poetry of sound, there will be (absolutely idiolectic poems excepted) at least some specification concerning a universe and its interpretation. Outer reality is never totally absent. Nevertheless, with literature in general, and poetry of sound in particular, we are, once more, referred to similarity, repetition, and analogy.

Repetition is an inherent feature in language, in fact, in any form of cognition, because pattern recognition lies at the core of mental activity. Consequently, in literature, only repetition above and beyond what is always implied in language use is interesting. As regards this surplus coding of literature, however, the parallel in psychoanalysis may prove enlightening. Here repetition is operative on several levels: it plays an important role in our vital rhythms, heart beat and respiration, and in the biological conception of drive as founded on the cyclical nature of certain bodily processes (e.g., the alleged 90-minute cycle of sexuality). Repetition also plays the major role in such bold speculations as Freud's in *Beyond the Pleasure Principle* (1955).

From a semiotic point of view, Freud's, and other psychoanalysts', linking of representation (*Vorstellung*) and repetition (*Wiederholung*) is central. Representation is a keynote concept in Freud's description of the psychic apparatus. It is linked, on the one hand, to perception and memory trace and, on the other, to drive and affect. One might say that in Freud representation becomes the locus of exchange, articulation, and interaction between outer and inner reality. As regards the relation of representation to perceptional input from the outside, Freud distinguishes between memory trace, mnemic systems, and representation. The memory trace is conceived as the imprint of perception on the mind. In addition to the species-specific selection of stimuli, Freud conceives their further processing as articulations through different mnemic systems such as association by similarity and by continuity (including causation).[25] Consequently, conscious perception is the result of an unconscious elaboration of the input.

In relation to the perceptual aspect of representation, Freud's distinction between thing-presentation (*Dingvorstellung*) and word-presentation (*Wortvorstellung*) is important. Both have their origin in perception and both are complex, since they are syntheses of different kinds of sensory representations. They differ, however, from a topographical, a dynamical, and a developmental point of view. The nucleus of the unconscious is thought to consist of repressed thing-presentations that can never become conscious, and in general only thing-presentations are repressed, while word-presentations (in spite of Freud's famous Signorelli example) are almost always accessible. This means, however, that a chasm, or split, always exists between these two kinds of representation, because repressed memories and the unconscious fantasies connected with them cannot be represented verbally, at least not without some kind of therapy or, in rare cases, thorough self-analysis. Furthermore, from a developmental point of view, thing-presentations have priority because they constitute the earliest representational systems. The advent of language, according to Freud, involves a fundamental and decisive restructuration of the psyche. As a symbolic system partly detached from actual, perceptual experiences (because of its abstract, generalizing, and conceptual nature), language effectuates regroupings and reinterpretations of the iconic-indexical representation of the earlier systems. Furthermore, a part of the material of these earlier systems, says Freud, is not translated into speech and is consequently confined to the unconscious.[26]

In relation to the interior stimuli from bodily sensations and needs, which are the sources and pressures of the drives, the concept of representation takes on yet another meaning, namely, as one of the two ways in which a drive may be represented mentally. In this capacity it is called an ideational representative (*Vorstellungsrepräsentanz*) and is distinguished from the affect. Direct correlation between representation and affect is not mandatory, since the latter may be converted, displaced, or transformed.

The relationship between representation as cognition of reality by means of iconic, indexical, and symbolic signs, on the one hand, and representation as ideational representatives of the drives, on the other, is complex. It seems reasonable to assume that only a small part of the number of thing- and word-presentations are also ideational representatives, since a great deal of information may be instinctually neutral. At the same time, it seems obvious that every actual thought or speech event is governed by both conscious and preconscious purposes and by unconscious desires and fears. This is why Freud uses the concept of representation in still another compound, namely, in what in English is called the purposive idea (*Zielvorstellung*). According to Freud the stream of ideas is never without purpose, because when conscious and preconscious purposive ideas are absent, unconscious ideas take over (cf. Freud 1953–4: vol. 5, 528). Thus, to the activation of memory traces belonging to the preconscious are added those of unconscious representations and, consequently, of unconscious ideational representatives. Since these representatives are constituted by the fixation of the libido to early experiences, fantasies, and images, it follows that the part played by repetition in the general semiotic theory of interpretation (interpretation as translation) is supplemented by repetition as compulsion in the Freudian model.

At this point, the psychoanalytic conception of repetition becomes relevant once more. Most often repetition within psychoanalytic theory is described in relation to symptoms and to the sinister, so-called repetition compulsion (cf. below). It is important to realize, however, that from the beginning of Freud's writing, repetition was also allotted a brighter, more comforting function in the mental apparatus, namely, with regard to wishes and wish-fulfilment (e.g., the hallucinatory accomplished wish-fulfilment in dreams). The primitive goal of a wish, or desire, is to re-establish what Freud calls a 'perceptual identity' – a repetition of a perception linked with the satisfaction of a need (Freud (ibid.: 566). Wish-fulfilment, then, is inextricably linked with memory and repetition. Obviously, fantasizing cannot be reduced to a search for such perceptual identity. On the contrary, fantasizing is overdetermined by so many intervening variables that the primitive mechanism stipulated by Freud is overlaid and distorted (cf. Freud's own account of the dream work). Nevertheless both dreams, daydreams, and what is to a certain extent public and communal dreaming – literature – are, among other things, repetitions not only of programs of actions (see Burkert here, p. 101), but also of the success wished for, albeit embellished and larger than life, or of the primordial fears of destruction and death.

We arrive now at the sinister kinds of repetition described by psychoanalysis. Repetition is also painful and regressive. It signals the insistence of something within the subject that resists interpretation and rationalization (note that, within psychoanalysis, rationalization denotes a mechanism of defence).[27] According to psychoanalysis, we cannot escape repetition. First, it is inherent in the drives and their biological sources. We are bound to repeat a cyclical pattern of instinctual pressures during our progress towards our destined end. In this respect rats and heroes are alike. Second, and unlike rats, because of the fixation of psychical energy on unconscious (and conscious) patterns of experience and fantasy, we are bound to represent and repeat identical or parallel versions of quest and fulfilment, or defeat, of instinctual gratification, destruction, and death (cf. the discussion on myth and fairy tales in chapter 4).

According to Freud, word-presentations normally belong to the preconscious and are governed by the secondary process. Word-presentations, like thing-pesentations, are founded on memory traces of perceptions, but according to Freud their role is to invest thought processes with qualities that make their becoming conscious possible. Freud claims that through language 'internal thought-processes are made into perceptions,' indeed, 'thoughts are actually perceived – as if they came from without – and are consequently held to be true (Freud

1961: 23). Hence, through language we hear ourselves think, says Freud, just as we, in Peirce's view, see our thinking when we use our diagrammatic imagination. According to Roman Jakobson, the poetic function of language focuses on the qualities of the message itself, or as he says, 'for its own sake,' and the poetic function 'promotes the palpability of signs' (in Sebeok ed. 1960: 356).

It seems that within literature we are faced with an intensification of what, according to Freud, is the general function of language. At the same time, what Jakobson describes as a projection of equivalence from the axis of selection onto the axis of combination, psychoanalysis describes as a topographical regression of language from the secondary to the primary process. In other words, to handle language poetically is to consciously manipulate it in ways characteristic of unconscious thought processes.[28] The question is, however, why is this kind of manipulation so full of pleasure and so important? One of Freud's answers is that condensed expressions of similarity save psychical energy, and this in itself is pleasurable. Ernst Kris (1952) thinks that the constant shifts between different levels of the mental apparatus, as manifested in literature, offer an independent source of pleasure. Without disregarding these answers, I must admit that I do not find them adequate. Another solution offered by Freud is that literary and artistic form offers a kind of forepleasure preparing us for the deeper pleasure offered by the text's staging of preconscious and unconscious fantasies (cf. Freud 1959). This answer seems interesting indeed, except for the fact that it tells us nothing about the nature of this kind of forepleasure or about why literary form evokes such pleasure. In what follows I will try to point to what seems a more adequate answer to this question, an answer also provided by Freud himself.

In order to get an idea of the more profound relationship between the psychoanalytic understanding of how the mind works and of literature, let us return to the modest example of Caesar's dictum and to Shakespeare's more elaborate use of poetic devices in King Henry's speech. It was pointed out that both contained a first-degree iconicity: word order mirrored world order (see above, pp. 178–81). First-degree iconicity is, however, only one aspect of the complex phenomenon of poetic repetition. In comparing *veni, vidi, vici* and *perrexi, circumspexi, superavi*, it was claimed that both have the same first-degree iconicity, whereas only the former phrase combines this kind of iconicity with intrasystemic similarity. This kind of similarity between phonemes and syllables has nothing to do with the relationship between sign and object: it is an intralingual, not an intersemiotic, phenomenon. Even if language and speech are structured by differences and similarities (from the distinctive features onwards), the interplay between such differences and similarities is not displayed in speech in a systematic way. The poetic function, however, brings about this effect through an elaborate patterning of the linguistic texture. Another kind of iconicity, namely, the similarity between the material and formal qualities of the signs themselves, is at work here. This intrasemiotic (here intralingual) exploration of similarity I have called second-degree iconicity. It is intrasystematically diagrammmatic, but it may function metaphorically. This is precisely what happens in *veni, vidi, vici*; the material and formal parallelisms are added to the first-degree iconicity of the phrase, which is itself diagrammatic.

The effect is almost magical, because this way of structuring the linguistic expressions seems to pretend that no split between words and world exists. In the last analysis it implies the omnipotence of thoughts and words. One of the main reasons this magic works is provided by Jakobson, namely, that the inherent arbitrariness of linguistic expression, the relation between what it refers to and what it means, is overcome. Or to put it differently: the expression's density of structure appears to vouch for the relevance, truth, and veracity of its message.

Different factors collaborate to this end. First, the surplus coding of the expression, the strengthening of the intrasystemic relations between phonemes, syllables, words, phrases, and so on, is communicated to the elements of signification and thus to the denoted universe. The palpable and reiterated qualities that make the parts of the text mirror each other, its self-reflecting capacity, are so pervasive that they envelop the semantic differentiation in a haze of similarity and sameness. This belief in the interconnectedness, and the interaction, of expression and content has been clearly expressed by Jakobson: in poetry, any conspicuous similarity in sound is evaluated in respect to similarity and/or dissimilarity in meaning (in Sebeok ed. 1960: 372). Writers and poets have, of course, always believed in the power of their words to discover nature's secret correspondences.

Similes and metaphors are ways of discovering, or inventing, the same in the other, that is, of constructing an analogy to the primary subject in something else. Such discovery/invention means a unification of the different realms of the experiential universe. Even if such unity is often illusory – in the sense that it involves, for all we know, an absolutely unwarranted personification of nature – the desire for unity seems to be deeply rooted in the human mind. Indeed, it seems that a certain amount of anthropocentrism is unavoidable and even desirable. The role of the tropes in general, and their purpose in poetry and literature in particular, is to make us more at home in the universe, and to make it more understandable. This may be why Aristotle places such a value on poetic metaphor: 'But the greatest thing by far is to have a command of metaphor. This alone cannot be imparted by another; it is the mark of genius, for to make good metaphors implies an eye for resemblances' (*Poetics*, 1927: 91, 1459a). Looking at the universe as a set of resemblances, or correspondences, as Baudelaire would have it, is also the pith and marrow of magical thought. In fact, magical thinking seems to be closely allied to, and at the origins of, the poetic function. Lévi-Strauss has a wonderful passage in chapter 9 of *Anthropologie structurale*. He finishes an analysis of magic by saying:

> [W]e must see magical behaviour as the response to a situation which is revealed to the mind through emotional manifestations, but whose essence is intellectual. For only the history of the symbolic function can allow us to understand the intellectual condition of man, in which the universe is never charged with sufficient meaning and in which the mind always has more to which to relate them. Torn between these two systems of reference – the signifying and the signified – man asks magical thinking to provide him with a new system of reference, within which the thus-far contradictory elements can be integrated. (1967: 178)

Aristotle's pointing to the discovery, or invention, of similarities and Lévi-Strauss's definition of the basis and origin of magical thinking as the fact that meanings and universe, imagination and reality, are out of all proportion to one another both point in the same direction: namely, that the role of literature, as a kind of magic, is to create a textual universe in which there is a fit between signifier and signified, or as I prefer, between signs, objects, and interpretants.

The poetic surplus coding of literary texts amalgamates two processes that are normally opposed: mastery and regression. Clearly, according to psychoanalytic theory, such coding means a formal regression, because similarity and continuity constitute a kind of proto-syntax characteristic of primary-process thinking. To superimpose such structures on linguistic structures calls for an uncommon mastery of language. This formal coincidence of opposites Freud connects with the specific function of literature and art: 'Art constitutes a region half-way between a reality which frustrates wishes and the wish-fulfilling world of the imagination – a region in which, as it were, primitive man's strivings for omnipotence are still in full force' (Freud 1953: vol. 13, 188). Ontogenetically, on this view, literature is related to narcissism, because the narcissist is characterized by a belief in the omnipotence of thought and by megalomania, an overestimation of the power of wishes. During this early period of life language is acquired; and by the child it is considered a drive-cathected mode of magic action bound up with pleasure and pain and instrumental in bringing forth gratification or frustration. Obviously, the rational core of this belief is that, as a means of communication, speech *is* instrumental in bringing about pleasant and unpleasant states. The child, however, is not yet able to distinguish fully between self and world, and so its own thought and speech seem to confirm its omnipotence. Even if the belief in the power of words is related to the phase during which language is learned, and even if the learning of language puts, in fact, an end to the rule of the imaginary and to narcissism, the latter is never given up in earnest. Again, the rational basis for this belief in words is that from the moment we know how to speak, we never cease trying to influence others by stating our cases as convincingly as possible. And although we know that other factors are probably more important in determining our successes and fiascos, we have no choice but to use speech as best we can in negotiating our needs and desires.

There is, however, a peculiar kind of speech act that, to the believer, is a shortcut to, and an insurance of, the fulfilment of wishes: the charm. Charms are magic ways of gaining control and thus of bringing about a wished-for state of affairs. They may be used to get rid of something, to ward off diseases, or to get hold of something or somebody; for instance, the spells used to make somebody love you. The general idea is that by knowing the formula, the right words, one gains supernatural powers. The linguistic structure of charms is described as follows by Northrop Frye:

> The rhetoric of charm is dissociative and incantory: it sets up a pattern of sound so complex and repetitive that the ordinary processes of response are short-circuited. Refrain, rhyme, alliteration, assonance, pun, antithesis: every repetitive device known to rhetoric is called into play. Such repetitive formulas break down and confuse the conscious will, hypnotize and compel to certain courses of action. Or they may simply put to sleep, which is one of the primary aims of hypnotism. (Frye 1976: 128)

Frye here makes an inextricable link between the specific linguistic structure of the charm and its purpose and effect. The structure he is describing, however, is valid for literary texts in general.

5.7 Naming and Enumeration

By the reiteration of the same phonological, syntactical, and, except for the nouns, semantic patterns, naming, enumerations, and recordings make for relatively simple forms of textual repetition, such as we find them, for instance, in genealogical tables or catalogues. Such genealogical tables record the succession of generations from the origins of man (e.g., the generations of Adam, Jesus, and others in the Bible). In the Greek epics we find similar phenomena; for instance, in the famous muster of the armies, the Achaean catalogue, which contains no less than 275 verses (and which many scholars think is an adaptation of an older poem into *The Iliad*). Such enumerative formulas owe their simplicity to their oral origin. Their persuasive powers are enhanced, however, because the filling in of new contents in a many-times-repeated formula makes syntax and rhythm a prominent means of asserting their propositional validity. Another example is the Oceanid catalogue of Hesiod's *Theogony*:

> Calypso and Eudore, Tyche, and
> Amphiro, and Okuroe and Styx,
> Who is the most important one of all
> These are the oldest daughters who were born
> To Oceanus and Tethys, but there are
> Many others beside them, Oceanids,
> Three thousand nymphs with shapely ankles, who
> Are scattered everywhere, over the earth
> And on deep water, glorious goddesses
> There are as many roaring rivers, too,
> Children of Ocean, lady Tethys' sons;
> It is hard for mortal man to name their names,
> But they are known to those who live nearby.
> (*Theogony*, trans. Wender 1973: 34–5)

The above-mentioned examples are connected with commemoration, with the preservation and transmission of genealogical knowledge, and their additive-repetitive structure goes well with their topic: questions of origins, kin, nations and fame.

Such knowledge is extremely valuable, because it is a means of ensuring the identity of communities. It offers a (partial) answer to the question, Who are we? The ambition of the catalogue parts of the Old Testament and the Greek epics seems to go even further; they want to provide us with exhaustive knowledge of what has been. Whereas Homer claims that the immortal Muses make the enumeration of the leaders of the Greek campaign possible, in the *Theogony* Hesiod, stressing his mortality, recognizes his lack of knowledge, but consoles himself that those who live near foreign oceans and rivers know the names of Tethys' offspring. Thus, exhaustive knowledge seems still to be possible, indeed existent.

Enumeration of the elements of the universe, or a part of it, is a primitive but basic magical kind of knowledge linked with, or playing on, our desire for omniscience. Such knowledge is really the privilege of the divine beings, maybe only of the supreme godhead, but knowing and preserving collective memory was earlier honoured as a divine gift, since it was the only way of warding off oblivion (see below). Consequently, within myth and literature the objectivity and neutral nature of enumeration is deceptive because naming and recording gratify our desire for knowledge, which is itself closely related to the desire for mastery. Recollecting, recording, and repeating are all intertwined elements of a process that constitutes an attempt, and an effort, both to build up and ensure our identity and to place us within the boundaries of a familiar universe. The exhaustiveness claimed for mythical records functions as a defence against the ominous threat of the unknown and the *horror vacui*.

Further, knowing the name of somebody may mean controlling him or her because the name was, and still is, thought to be an essential feature of a being. The awe of the name is justified because naming categorizes, and thus naming becomes an absolutely important means of linking perception and cognition. From the point of view of psychoanalysis, naming becomes a locus of interchange between thing-presentation and word-presentation, and between primary and secondary processes, and it becomes both a means of control, as in magical thinking, and a way of mastering absence because the object is vicariously present in its name. Further, as embodied objects of thought, names may serve the binding or unbinding of affects. In the case history of the Rat Man, Freud tells about his patient, who during early childhood received a beating from his father: 'The little boy had flown into a terrible rage and had hurled abuse at his father even while he was under his blows. But as he knew no bad language, he had called him all the names of common objects that he could think of, and had screamed: "You lamp! You towel! You plate!" and so on. His father shaken by such an outburst of elementary fury, had stopped beating him, and had declared: "The child will be either a great man or a criminal"' (Freud 1955a: 205). Letting out his fury against his father by giving him the names of what he knows, the Rat Man's purpose is not to make an inventory of the nameable elements of his world, but he is nevertheless identifying his father with all these objects, and he trying to harm and control him by naming them. And in a certain way he is successful. Thus, naming and enumeration may not only be an attempt to bind thought and perception, and present and past, together, it may be instrumental in giving (by projection) the surroundings an emotional coating that make them mirror the fears and desires of the subject. And establishing this concord is also the objective of literature.

Inventories of this simple additive-repetitive kind may also be expressions of mirth and laughter. And they are also often used to express bawdiness and aggression. Rabelais offers a prime example of the first use in another catalogue of his, that of Gargantua's experimentation with different swabs (cf. Bakhtin's analysis in Bakhtin 1968: 371–81), which also runs on and on and is concluded as follows: 'Afterwards I wiped my tail with a hen, with a cock, with a pullet, with a calf's skin, with a hare, with a pigeon, with a cormorant, with an attorney's bag, with a montero, with a coif, with a falconer's lure; but to conclude, I say and maintain, that of all torcheculs, arse-wisps, bum-fodders, tail-napkins, bung-hole-cleansers and wipe-breeches, there is none in the world comparable to the neck of a goose, that is well downed, if you hold her head between your legs' (ibid.: 32). The aggressive use of the enumerative mode of description, of which the Rat Man's fury offered a non-artistic example, is wonderfully exemplified in Lautréamont's *Poésies I*, which contains a true eruption of invectives in a catalogue of what he despises and opposes. Here is only a part of it:

> ... perfumed chancres, thighs covered with camellias, the culpability of the writer who rolls down the slope of the abyss, despising himself with cries of joy, remorse, hypocrisy, vague perspectives which crush you in their imperceptible works, spitting on sacred axioms, vermin and their insinuating titillations, extravagant prefaces, such as those to Cromwell, those by Mlle Dauphin and Dumas the younger, decay, impotence, blasphemy, asphyxia, suffocation, fits of rage – it is time to react to these repulsive

charnel-houses which I blush to name, to react against everything which is supremely shocking and oppressive. (Lautréamont 1978: 256)

The use of the additive-repetitive mode of description has been pointed to above in the naming of sacred origins, in the exaltation of chieftains and nations, in the plea for subversive laughter, in a scatological feast, and in a truly creative torrent of invectives. From this variety of uses it would be wrong, however, to conclude that enumeration and repetition are nothing but formal literary devices lending themselves to whatever the poet intends. Obviously, catalogues and other repetitive patterns are not bound to specific subjects. They imply, however, a stirring of emotional and instinctual energy; indeed, to amplify the metaphor, they function as conductors of fears and desires. A main reason why they function so is their ability to make speech materially present as rhythm, pulsation, and breath in combination with semantic parallelisms.

The relationship between repetition as a principle of order and aesthetic pleasure / instinctual gratification has often been noticed by psychoanalysts. Hanna Segal, who has made Kleinian points of view fruitful for the study of literature, endorses Ella Sharpe's distinction between the rhythmic and arrhythmic: 'For Ella Sharpe, "ugly" means destroyed, arrhythmic, and connected with painful tension; beauty she considers essentially as rhythm, and equates it with the experiences of goodness in rhythmic sucking, satisfactory defecation, and sexual intercourse. Rickman equates beautiful with the whole object and the ugly with the fragmented, destroyed one. And he says that we recoil from the ugly' (Segal 1991: 90). Segal's pointing to repetition, to the rhythmical, as the aesthetically satisfactory is important. And although the examples of the prototypical bodily processes may seem peculiar to psychoanalysis, a romanticist such as Wordsworth comes close to the same conception, even if he seems to have it the other way around. In *The Prelude* he talks about how as a child he

> ... held unconscious intercourse
> With the eternal Beauty, drinking in
> A pure organic pleasure from the lines
> Of curling mist, or from the level plain
> Of waters colour'd by the steady clouds.
> (1979, I, 562–6)

He thus stresses the bodily nature of the pleasure linked with aesthetic perception, here vision.

Furthermore, in the 1850 preface to the *Lyrical Ballads* he declares that the role of the poet is to produce immediate pleasure. He warns us further that this should not be considered a 'degradation of the poet's art,' because it is 'a homage paid to the native and naked dignity of man, to the great elementary principle of pleasure, by which he knows, and feels, and lives, and moves' (Wordsworth 1974: 140). He further comments specifically on metrical language, holding that the pleasure derived from verse is related to 'the pleasure which the mind derives from the perception of similitude in dissimilitude.' He continues: 'This principle is the great spring of the activity of our minds, and their chief feeder. From this principle the direction of the sexual appetite, and all the passions connected with it, take their origin' (ibid.: 149). It should be stressed, however, that neither Segal nor Wordsworth leave it at that. Segal continues the text quoted above as follows: 'However, these authors equate "beautiful" with aesthetically satisfying. This cannot be so. If that were the case nothing would be more beautiful than a circle or a rhythmical drumbeat. The aesthetic experience is in my view a particular combination of what has been called "ugly" and what could be called "beautiful"' (ibid.: 90). Wordsworth too sees the pleasure derived from the order of metre as a way of counteracting the representation of the painful.

5.8 Plenitude, Variety, Lack

In the catalogues mentioned so far, repetition provokes pleasure either because it assures us that the universe is familiar and knowable or because repetition is a sovereign act by which the subject, the poet, masters (parts of) the universe himself. In both cases an important part of this pleasure is linked with a sense of plenitude, either through a description of a replete and abundant universe or as a forever-pouring stream of denominations, an unstrained and pleasurable magical act of supremacy.

Often professed landscapes of the mind are catalogued in the same meticulous way as those supposed to be historical (whether sacred or profane). In one of the longest 'dreams' in Western literature, *Le roman de la rose*, we encounter the same will to completeness and plenitude in the description of the garden:

> Among the trees that I remember well
> There were pomegranates, grateful to the sick,
> And many fig trees, date palms, almond trees.

> The nut trees were most plentiful of all,
> Such as are in their seasons fully charged
> With nutmegs not insipid nor yet sharp.
> A man could find whatever tree he wished:
> ...
> Hornbeams, beeches, aspens, and the ash,
> Maple, and oak, and spruce. Why mention more?
> There were so many trees of divers sorts
> That should I try to name them all I'd find
> The task a tiresome one.
>
> (Lorris 1962: 27–8)

The naming of the individual trees shows the abundance of the garden. It simply contains every possible tree that is beautiful and nurturing. The naming is, however, extremely important, because it adds distinctness and individuality to a completeness that would otherwise be vague and abstract. The sense of superabundance and plenitude demands a tension between a claim to totality and the naming of a variety of individual entities. This is why repetition at the lexical level of literature most often takes the form of parallelisms instead of reiterations of identical lexical units, at least when fullness and repletion is the subject. In contradistinction, identical repetition is often connected with an uncanny sort of repetition in the form of compulsion and depletion (cf. below).

Variety, then, becomes the precondition for plenitude, and this experience is founded on what is almost a *contradicto in adjecto*: the request, on the one hand, that repetition shall be forever novel and, on the other, that every new experience shall repeat what has before been sensed as pleasurable. This demand for simultaneous repetition and variety, as Shakespeare has acutely perceived, is of the nature of desire.

> *Enob.* ...
> Age cannot wither her, nor custom stale
> Her infinite variety: other women cloy
> The appetites they feed, but she makes hungry,
> Where most she satifies. For vilest things
> Become themselves in her, that the holy priests
> Bless her, when she is riggish.
> *Maec.* If beauty, wisdom, modesty, can settle

> The heart of Antony, Octavia is
> A blessèd lottery to him.
>> (*Antony and Cleopatra*, II, ii, 233–43)

Octavia's beauty, wisdom, and modesty make her a prize that any sensible man should fight for. Except that Cleopatra's magic is unmatchable: in her, eternity ('Age cannot wither her') is combined with an infinite variety feeding desire; on top of that, she is presented as a goddess capable of mediating between the sacred and the profane because her sensuality elevates desire to cosmic proportions. Infinity and variety are essential parts of a desire that is not willing to recognize the impossibility of both keeping and spending at the same time. This is why desire is very often staged as fantasies of superabundance and inexhaustibility. See the following lines from Ben Jonson's *Volpone*:

> Thy baths shall be the juice of July-flowers,
> Spirit of roses, and of violets,
> The milk of unicorns, and panthers' breath
> Gathered in bags, and mixed with Cretan wines.
> Our drink shall be prepared gold and amber;
> Which we will take until my roof whirl round
> With the vertigo: and my dwarf shall dance,
> My eunuch sing, my fool make up the antic,
> Whilst we, in changed shapes, act Ovid's tales,
> Thou, like Europa now, and I like Jove,
> Then I like Mars, and thou like Erycine:
> So of the rest, till we have quite run through,
> And wearied all the fables of the gods.
> Then will I have thee in more modern forms,
> Attired like some sprightly dame of France,
> Brave Tuscan lady, or proud Spanish beauty;
> Sometimes unto the Persian sophy's wife;
> Or the grand signior's mistress; and for change,
> To one of our most artful courtesans
> To some quick Negro, or cold Russian;
> And I will meet thee in as many shapes:
> Where we may so transfuse our wandering souls
> Out at our lips, and score up sums of pleasures ...
>> (*Volpone*, III, vi, 211–35).

Here Volpone stages sensual fantasies of superabundance and boundlessness. However, the point is that the possession of Celia in itself is not sufficient to satiate his desire because it is more imaginative than corporeal. Whereas Shakespeare's lines about Cleopatra only stressed desire's infinite variety, this speech focuses on the opposition between insatiability and weariness ('and wearied all the fables of the gods'). Furthermore, the fantasies, and the wish to act them out, imply a patterning that, simultaneously, endows the action with signification borrowed from the universe of myth and allows the individuals to transgress their own identity through impersonation. Here Jonson is pointing to the coincidence of abundance and dissolution as the ultimate consequence of unrestrained desire.

In a sense these lines represent us with the components of an elementary grammar of desire. Let us start at the top with active desire for the object and the passive wish to be desired:

1. I desire you
   I want to be desired by you

This is the point of departure in Volpone's craving for Celia: a subject's desire for an object, and his desire to become an object of desire for the one he himself desires. What happens in his speech, however, is that Celia becomes a kind of tailor's dress form on which the dress is constantly changed. This means, in fact, that for him her identity is lost, exchanged for the infinite displacement of desire:

2. I desire —
   I want to be desired by —

However, this process doesn't stop with the dissolution of the object's identity. Volpone imagines himself to change as well, and so we get:

3. — desires —
   — wants to be desired by —

'To score up sums of pleasures' in this way means an infinite re-identification of both subject and object with the effect that their identity, their *souls*, are dissolved. We end up with the transitive verb *desire*, in the active and passive voices, and with two blanks that have to be filled in incessantly by new entities. However, the protean nature of desire, splendidly displayed in Volpone's speech, is both very real and deceptive because the displacement of desire is repetitive as well as infinite. Indeed, it seems that this fantasy of constant novelty functions as a defence against a threatening ennui: against the fact that 'All things/ have surfeit – even sleep, and love, and song,/ and noble dancing – things a man may wish/ to take his fill of' (*Iliad*, 1974: 646–9).

The predicament of desire is that its seemingly infinite variety may be revealed as a masquerade unable to cloak its insistent monotony. Consequently, desire is characterized by an unstable transitivity. It is necessarily directed towards an object but rather as a pressure to realize something indefinite and ephemeral that sometimes yields gratification, but which is constantly exchanged for something else just as indefinite. The paradoxical nature of desire – its inherent duplicity of attachment, repetition, indeed fixation on the one hand, and dissolution, boundlessness, and indefiniteness on the other – means that it exists as an oscillation between lack and plenitude. And worse: through surfeit plenitude itself engenders lack.

The moment, however, that the beneficial action of desire is exposed as illusory and deceptive, existence becomes repetitive in the grim and uncanny sense of a mere compulsion to repeat what is void of value and meaning:

> To-morrow, and to-morrow, and to-morrow,
> Creeps in this petty pace from day to day,
> To the last syllable of recorded time;
> And all our yesterdays have lighted fools
> The way to dusty death.
> (*Macbeth*, V, v, 19–23)

Keeping in mind that this soliloquy fulfils a specific dramatic function in the tragedy, it nevertheless admirably expresses repetition as death operating within life, as an earnest of final destruction.

According to psychoanalysis, Enobarbus's 'Age cannot wither her' and Macbeth's 'To-morrow, and to-morrow, and to-morrow' are co-present and operative in our minds as a craving for ever-novel fulfilment and a disillusion barely held in check. Literature, of course, has always known this; indeed one of its main roles is to make us aware of the incessantly ongoing dialectic between desire and fear. From the point of view of the individual person, however, there is an end to this dialectic; it is terminated in death, which ends the pageant of representations and the repetitions of desire. As a kind of profane magus, the poet has to confront this predicament as well.

5.9 *Non omnis moriar*

Repetition has first and foremost been exemplified above by verbal repetitions within the text, and this phenomenon has been linked with both wish-fulfilment and the compulsion to repeat. There is, however, another way in which the literary text is a sort of repetition, namely, to the extent that it is based on the memories of its author. In chapter 3, the role of models in literature was discussed, and probable models for Proust's duchess of Guermantes were mentioned (note 24). The point was that, on the one hand, fiction certainly is memory-based and works with models. On the other, however, it is not a trustworthy recorder of a past, because it is concerned about creating meaning rather than being accurate about facts.

Of course, this editing process is going on also in our own (re)constructions of our life histories – we want, if possible, to establish a version flattering to ourselves, or at least a version a defence attorney would choose. Literature, however, allows the subject to create whichever versions he chooses because it is generally agreed that the relation to the lifeworld is suspended or, rather, attenuated. Consequently, we are presented with fantasies related as memories. One of the paradoxes of literature is that, to a certain extent, it is a retelling of a past that never was, and a past linked with attitudes and emotional stances that were never exactly so but have been ascribed to the alleged states of affairs and mind *après coup* (through deferred action). The reason for having an institution to do this kind of work is triple.

First, what literature relates acquires 'reality' by being written – it never was before, although it appears as if it presents memories of events and states of mind. However, this amalgamation of experiencing and telling, of past and present, is not specific to literature; it is connected with the general function of narrating. People very often, maybe always, search for experiences in order to be able to impress themselves and others by telling what they have experienced. Hence, we often experience something in order to be able to tell about it. Furthermore, there is a paradox in the relationship between experience and narration: on the one hand, the telling is felt to be untrue to what happened by the very fact that it is rendered in language. On the other hand, people often feel that the past only acquires reality by being told and retold. The word may murder the thing (or, semiotically speaking, the translation of icons and indices into symbols is inherently reductive), but it not only endows it with a durable post mortem reality; it may also make experience whole: 'I make it real by putting it into words. It is by putting it into words that I make it whole: this wholeness means that it has lost its power to hurt me: it gives me, perhaps because by doing so I take away the pain, a great delight to put severed parts together. Perhaps this is the strongest pleasure known to me. It is the rapture I get when in writing I seem to be discovering what belongs to what, making a scene come right; making a character come together' (Woolf 1976: 72). Further, there is a narcissistic urge to master one's past through thoughts and words that is satisfied in editing and telling. There is an implicit 'this is how it should have been' in literature. Since the subjunctive mode is replaced by the indicative, in literature 'it has been so.'

Second, in literature, such a will to master supports the tendency to maximize both the poetic and expressive import of the linguistic expression of the text and the arrangement of what it refers to. Its world is arranged to impress and please because of its consistency and effectiveness in relation to principles governing the universe in question (see the discussion of fairy tale and myth in the preceding chapter). Both efforts are connected with a striving for perfection.

Third, literature is a durable artefact, something that is meant to last. Thus, even in confronting death, the narcissistic belief in the omnipotence of thoughts and words is still in force in the poet. Writing is imagined to be a magical act of destruction or reparation and preservation (cf. Kleinian psychoanalysis's distinction between destruction and reparation). Certainly poetry may be used invectively and as a curse. Theognis, for instance, prays to Zeus for revenge on his enemies and asks to 'drink the black blood from their veins.'

However, the other side here is the belief in writing as an act of rescuing something, or somebody, from decay; that is, representation and repetition as preservation. Western poetry from the Greek epitaphs to the present has always been conscious of the poet's role as preserver and of the act of writing as being basically a fight against time. Narration has served, and serves, historical recording. Furthermore, in societies preoccupied with fame and glory, the role of the singer was to fight against oblivion by serving as the community's collective memory in remembering and glorifying its deeds. Some of the catalogues mentioned earlier are examples of this function of poetry. The performative aspect of poetic discourse may, however, be extended, and the claim that writing is doing is often carried further by poets. In creating poetry, the poet claims to interfere with the order of things, since his or her poem is said to change the natural state of affairs:

> ... your name will be spoken again
> as the young singers, with the flutes clear piping beside them,
>   make you into a part of the winsome verses, and sing
> of you. And even after you pass to the gloom and the secret
>   chambers of sorrow, Death's house hidden under the ground,
> even in death your memory shall not pass, and it shall not
>   die, but always, a name and a song in the minds of men,
> Kyrnos, you shall outrange the land of Greece and the islands ...
> (Theognis 237–47; 1960: 29)

These verses by Theognis are among the first to stress the magic power of poetry to transfigure and immortalize the beloved, but throughout Western poetry this claim is repeated again and again. In Shakespeare many of the sonnets thematize this struggle; for instance, sonnets 64 and 65. The former begins by describing the many destructive actions of 'Time's fell hand,' and it ends with the following reflection:

> Ruin hath taught me thus to ruminate –
> That Time will come and take my love away.
>   This thought is as a death, which cannot choose
>   But weep to have that which it fears to lose.

Here, the grim action of time works not only as a natural process of decay and destruction of individual life. It works as well on the consciousness of the poet, so that the very knowledge of the inevitable human condition already operates 'as a death' within him[29] to bring about a process of mourning while he is still in possession of his love. Thus, Time and death are duplicated as destructive forces in the imagination of the subject.

Since decay and death are forces in the psyche, the mind itself must fight them; and the next sonnet (65) attempts an act of preservation, of anticipated reparation brought about by representation as recreation:

> Since Brass, nor stone, nor earth, nor boundless sea,
> But sad mortality o'ersways their power,
> How with this rage shall beauty hold a plea,

> Whose action is no stronger than a flower?
> Oh how shall summer's honey breath hold out
> Against the wrackful siege of battering days,
> When rocks impregnable are not so stout
> Nor gates of steel so strong but time decays?
> Oh fearful meditation! where, alack,
> Shall Time's best jewel from Time's chest lie hid?
> Or what strong hand can hold his swift foot back
> Or who his spoil of beauty can forbid?
>   Oh none, unless this miracle have might –
>   That in black ink my love may still shine bright.

The only defence is 'the miracle' of poetry. 'Miracle' is certainly well chosen here, since the poet is fighting against the natural order of things. Not in the sense, of course, of attempting literally to reverse this order, but by transforming his love into the durable language of representation. In literature, however, the language of representation is nothing like the represented object; and this is the reason for the last line's conceit: 'That in black ink my love may still shine bright.' The object is only preserved by being made into something radically different from itself, and this is expressed in the oxymoron of life in death (bright/black). The implication is that transforming something into poetry is a double act of destroying and preserving. These sonnets are also epitaphs for somebody who is still living (in Lacan this ties in with the, in his opinion, close relation between the symbolic order and the death drive).

There is, however, a further ambiguity in the two poems: who or what is preserved? The obvious answer is, the fair youth. And I would certainly not deny its validity; indeed some of the lines make sense only if the beloved is thought of. Nevertheless, the expression used is 'my love,' and this has the double meaning of (1) the object of love and (2) the feelings of the subject towards the object. What is certain, furthermore, is that it is only through the represented feelings and the desire to express them that the object is preserved. In fact, these sonnets barely represent their professed object; what they forcefully represent are the anxieties and the desire of the loving lyrical I at the thought of death.

The fashionable view that literature is, basically, about itself, that it is non-representational, is a harmful exaggeration because it minimizes the importance of the narrated, of the fictional universe, and of the pleasure it offers the reader. Nevertheless, the desire for immortality does not relate only to the object of the text, not even when this object is professed to be the beloved. It primarily relates to the text itself and, by virtue of its immortality, to the immortality of its author.

This is why Horace's famous *non omnis moriar* (I shall not altogether die, *Odes*, III, xxx) provides the heading for this section. The immortality claimed by Horace – and implicitly or explicitly by every poet of rank – is founded on the belief in the power of words, written in black ink or preserved by other means. Writing, however, though replicable and repeatable, is mute. It is potentiality, not actuality. The omnipotence of the poet's words is dependent on their reiterated actualization. The desire for immortality in literature is thus inextricably linked with repetition and re-presentation. The poet is at the mercy of his audience.

Six

The Interpreters

In The first prelude, *the mental recreation of the place is made ...*
The second prelude *consists of asking for an intimate apprehension of*
...
The first point *is to see with the imagination ...*
The second point: *To hear with the imagination ...*
Third: *Also with the imagination to smell ...*
Fourth: *In similar imaginative manner, to taste ...*
Fifth: *With the sense of touch to feel ...*
(St Ignatius [1548] 1997: 23–4)

Say what some poets will. Nature is not so much her own interpreter, as the mere supplier of that cunning alphabet, whereby selecting and combining as he pleases, each man reads his own particular lesson according to his own peculiar mind and mood.
(Melville [1852] 1971: 342)

>   *Her speech is nothing,*
> *Yet the unshaped use of it does move*
> *The hearers to collection. They aim at it,*
> *And botch the words up fit to their own thoughts,*
(Hamlet IV, v, 7–10)

In the preceding chapter, literature was conceived as self-expression. Literature as self-expression is so important and compelling to its authors because either it directly focuses on the utterer (cf. Montaigne declaring himself the matter of his own book), or it stages a world existentially important to the utterers. It represents states of affairs and minds bound up with pleasure and pain, with exuberance, and with lack and loss, and thus it evokes a certain understanding of the human condition. Furthermore, as self-expression it may be multidimensional: it may reach backwards to memories that have been forgotten but that are now (re)constructed in shapes in which they have never been recalled before. And it may touch and reshape recurring fantasies that bind and unbind the passions.

It is not always the case, however, that our memories and fantasies, even in the shape of linguistically patterned and refined fictions, meet the interest or approval of our interpreters. Being ignored by the majority of potential readers because of being unknown to them, or simply being overlooked, is, of course, today the most common fate of literature meant for reading. Because of the development of the media, other forms of fiction have taken the lead. It hardly needs pointing out, however, that drama, prominent in the media, is a form of literature. To the competition from other media comes the sheer bulk of literature itself, with the result that even professional readers can read but a fraction.

Nevertheless, the often strong, often negative, reaction of the readership to the literature they do manage to read may seem strange at first. Why should it matter, it might sensibly be argued, what somebody imagines? There are, however, certain features of the literary institution that may explain why literary texts may be met with spite or even disgust and hatred.[1] Indeed, the alleged permissiveness of modern Western societies and the seemingly blasé state of mind of readers may be deceptive. Readers and critics are quite frequently outraged by literary texts for different reasons, among which obscenity, violence, and derogatory attitudes towards what is held to be self-evident values and truths loom large. Moreover, to the individual sentiments of readers and critics should be added the interference of authorities, the confiscation of texts, and the persecution of their authors. Hence, the subject matter of this chapter is the interrelation between the institutional aspects of literature and the way in which readers respond to it.

6.1 Literature as an Institution

A minimal definition of an institution is that it is a complex social organism that consists of agents holding different, often hierarchically ranked, offices and acting intentionally and/or routinely according to a sets of rules in order to fulfil certain functions, achieve certain goals, and serve a number of (integrated) purposes. As agencies, institutions are invested with the greater or lesser power and authority that are necessary for them in order to fulfil their duties. It is not mandatory, however, that an institution be transparent to its officers and clients or users; neither must its different functions and purposes necessarily be consonant; indeed, it may be characterized by internal tensions, oppositions, even by contradictions. Furthermore, institutions change over time, and thus more complex institutions are in a constant state of transition. Hence, they often simultaneously contain practices that contradict each other.[2]

Most institutions have another characteristic in common: they address a public. Typically institutionalized public forms of address include (1) laws and proclamations announced by public authorities; (2) priests' interpretations of divine providence and the will of the godhead as revealed in scriptures or through omens and sacrifices, etc.; (3) the teachings of the educational system at different levels and degrees of profundity delivered to different age groups and to different social groups within a society; (4) the order of commands teaching the drill, techniques, and right spirit of subordination and obedience within the army and other institutions monopolizing public coercion and constraint and the protection of citizens; and (5) the passing of sentences by assemblies, juries, and judges.

Such forms of address are complex in themselves and different from each other. First of all, even if a legislative assembly passes a bill that becomes law by the very authority of that institution, the assembly consists of a number of individuals joined in factions that disagree with each other. Further, the bill's passing itself has a history: the majority may have been by only one vote. Indeed, a certain piece of legislation may even have been imposed against the will of the legislative body by somebody more powerful. Furthermore, legislation may not be directed to the community at large, but to certain groups within it, increasing or decreasing their privileges or burdens. Very often legislation and the passing of sentences will coincide, and they may even be directed against a single individual, as for instance in a case of ostracism.

Priests, prophets, and sibyls may claim, and may be believed, to be the mere mouthpieces of the godhead, and what they reveal may be directed towards society at large or may summon or denounce a person. To believers what is revealed is divine law, while infidels may be executed for not believing.

The handing down of knowledge within a society is apportioned in different ways to audiences and pupils, who in turn are selected by diverse and often unmentioned criteria that may well be related to the preservation of the community's structure and power relations. Arcane knowledge, only allowed to a few, will exist, and so will different sorts of knowledge so intellectually demanding that they will not be accessible to most people. Often the knowledge allowed for men and women will be different. On the other hand, some basic beliefs, some moral guidelines, some technical skills, and some notions of the history and identity of the community will be shared by most of its members. The degree to which knowledge is apportioned among the members of a community is also dependent, of course, on the amount and complexity of what is known (or thought to be known).

Courts will interpret statutes of different generality and scope and apply them to individual cases. In passing verdicts and sentences they will address themselves to, and judge, individual persons (also juridical persons). A court's sentence will be based on the peculiarities of the case, the prevailing conception of justice, the considerations concerning its accordance with and effect on juridical practice itself, and the actions of citizens dealing with such matters. However, it will also be based on what seems to be politically correct and expedient at the time of its passing. A sentence will also depend on the attitudes and dispositions of those who judge, on their moral and political convictions, and on their characters and present states of mind.

The purpose of this imperfect sketch is to ensure that the complexity of public, institutional communication is not forgotten; nor, moreover, that institutions are represented by persons, and that public decision-making, in every case, is determined by factors of diverse nature and weight. The examples mentioned above have, however, one feature in common: the group to which they are directed, sometimes the community at large, cannot avoid dealing with them because they are words sacked with power to support them and make them true. Furthermore, those speaking are magistrates, the spokesmen of an institution who are supported by its power and supposed to act according to its code.

Furthermore, institutions may be more or less heterogeneous. The military, for instance, is a rather homogeneous and hierarchical institution (although its relation to the political institution is complex). Its homogeneity is connected with the fact that all its members are enrolled within it, in the emphatic sense of being both sustained by it and subject to its jurisdiction. The literary institution and other art institutions, by contrast, are heterogeneous because their different relationships and dependencies are less formalized and binding.

Calling literature an institution is based on the fact that it is a public form of communication in which, at least in principle, the community at large is addressed. Thus literature, like other forms of public communication, is dependent both upon the means of production used for public communication and upon the existence of frames and settings allowing such communication to take place. Furthermore, those in power and in authority regulate any public activity, and an important part of the history of imaginative literature is the story of how it has been censured and suppressed.

Although we should not exaggerate the difference between institutions such as those mentioned above and the literary institution, there nevertheless seems to be, or perhaps rather to have developed, an important difference between literature as a public form of address and other forms of institutional utterance. In earlier times most literature was created for public recital. In ancient Greece, literature was, among other things, enacted, as were athletic competitions, as a part of religious festivals (which included readings of the Homeric poems and competitions in different literary genres, e.g., tragedy and comedy). Hence, the poet was dependent on the public and on the authorities. Indeed, poets have always been dependent for their living on the rulers, the Maecenases, or the public at large, often on more than one of them at a time. Thus, literature was, and is, a public matter, whether the poet is a member of the court of a prince, recites his own poems or those of others in the marketplace, or competes to find a publisher for his work or a theatre company willing to stage it. Trading poems for coins in the marketplace, or trying to get published, stresses only the economic aspect of the literary profession, which of course is vital. There is, however, another way, touched upon above, in which literature is a public matter, namely, its dependency on the reaction of public and authorities. Although it should not matter what we imagine, as long as we keep it to ourselves, it becomes an altogether different matter when we go public.

The poet's fantasies and visions, however, are not just anybody's; he or she is, or aspires to become, the most important part of the literary institution. This institution, like all others, varies throughout time and space. Its complexity grows with that of society, but a sketchy and idealized version of the literary institution in early times may resemble the following.

The poet is a part of a prince's household charged with the task of commemorating in song the glorious past of the family and region and with celebrating the deeds of the present lord and his family, including marriages, childbirths, deaths, and funerals. Thus, one of the main functions of literature is not only to embody, but also to create, the collective memory of a community. The poet must praise the valour, strength, honour, and magnanimity of the men and the beauty, charm, chastity, virtues, and fecundity of the women; the richness of the soil, the abundance and quality of what is grown or raised; and the beauty and majesty of the landscape. He must denounce cowardice, ignoble deeds, meanness, villainy, and (enemy) cruelty. Furthermore, as comic relief he is also allowed, within limits, to satirize the values of the community, especially when through exaggeration they are turned into vices, and to speak about the ludicrous and ridiculous, the creaturely and the obscene.

This commemoration, celebration, and denouncing have a double purpose: to entertain the audience and to remind them of (a version of) the past; thus, literature instals or strengthens the values of the community in the listeners. Its second role is to ensure that the glorification of the family, community, or region in question is passed on to posterity. The distinction between history writing and epic is historical; it is not given, but emerges, and it takes a long time before it becomes established. Even after the rise of professional history writing, there have always been the two parallel tracks of the commemoration of the past: literature and scholarly history writing. The literary versions of the past have, however, continued to be those that matter most to the general public.[3]

Within such an early society, other forms of literature exist (hymns, choral lyrics, etc.). Thus, in addition to functioning as a historian, the poet voices the religious beliefs of the community.[4] Indeed, although we seem to be at the margins of the modern concept of literature, even technical knowledge is put into poetic form (Hesiod, Virgil's *Georgics*),[5] and didactic poetry in general is important because, in late antiquity and in the Middle Ages, the distinction between poetry and oratory often was identical with the one between verse and prose. Finally, in such a society, lyrical poetry also exists, voicing the small history and experiences of private citizens and expressing their personal fears and desires, their joys and sorrows. Further, diatribes and satires are developed as art forms, along with their opposite, panegyric, which is also an element in heroic poetry.

Even in the above sketch there is the primary agent, the poet, among and competing with other poets (the newcomer with the consecrated poets, as Bourdieu would say). They produce in a constant dialogue with the traditions of their trade, as traditionalists or innovators, as the case may be (again, in Bourdieu's words: ortodoxy versus heresy). They may be employed by a prince or may travel from town to town. There are users: an audience, the employer and his retinue, or people in the marketplace. There is a tradition to be reckoned with: other version of the myths and stories. There are other institutions, religious, juridical, and pedagogical, that the poet must respect. And there is lore, doxa, public morality, and religious beliefs. Further, there is the ambition and effort to determine the right version of history and the will to be in control of the name one leaves behind (princes also say *non omnis moriar*). Later, moreover, we will get a more principled criticism of literature, for instance, the critique of Homer in the sixth century BC. Thus, very early, all the principal elements of the literary institution are already in place.

From the point where literature becomes separated from the religious institution, in itself a long and complex process, its magical, mythical, and instructive elements become even more dependent upon its ability to arouse the interests of its audience; that is, literature must also prove itself entertaining. One of the shortcomings of many contemporary theoretical reflections on literature is the eagerness only to see it as a (quasi-) philosophical inquiry into the nature of man and the universe. Literature certainly constitutes such an inquiry, but at the same time it must entertain us by appealing to our senses and to our imagination. One main reason for this demand on literature is, of course, that its audience and readership are not obliged to listen to it or read it (except within education; see below). This non-obligatory relationship between writer and readership is paralleled by that between writer and employers and writer and authorities. The employers, who in fact very often are the authorities themselves, are free to dispense with the services of the writer whenever they want, and in principle, but not often in practice, the reverse is true. The authorities have the juridical power (and the monopoly of violence) to decide about the limits to the liberty of speaking in public. (Obviously, liberty of speech will be limited in any society whatsoever; blasphemy and libel, for instance, will be prosecuted.) Consequently, what the poet expresses may not too blatantly offend the moral and political standards as they are understood and upheld by authority.[6] Nevertheless, literature has been very creative in dissociating itself from centres of power and in opposing them in ways that have made it difficult for the authorities to respond fully to the challenge. However, despite the very real subversive thrust of much literature, it is necessarily closely related to the other institutions within society.

In our time the literary institution is characterized by the complexity and diversity of the economic, political, and social order of the society within which it exists. In all cases it will be influenced by division of labour and professionalization, by segmentation and the existence of several circuits (highbrow and popular literature, literature for adults and for children, for men and for women), and by the strong interconnection and feedback between the literary institution and other institutions. Indeed, the fate of the individual text in the long run, after its initial success or fiasco, is mainly decided by the educational system, because being on the curricula and reading lists of schools and universities seems to be the only way of fulfilling Horace's dream. Hence, these different agencies, and the feedback they receive from users, pupils, and customers, will determine the fate of a given text.

In the above characterization of the literary institution, one feature is prominent: its pluri-functionality. The office of literature is to both instruct about the past and about proper attitudes and to move in order to persuade. It is therapeutic (cf. Aristotle's concept of catharsis). It is supposed to enhance social cohesion and identity. Literature belabours speech to stretch and widen its significational and expressive potential. In doing so it creates novel ways of communicating perception and so also, in fact, novel ways of perceiving, since perception is an interpretive activity. It is also instrumental in creating a language for the emotions, channeling and articulating that which may be overwhelming because inarticulate (cf., on the epideictic speech, p. 222). However, in addition to these predominantly historical, theoretical, moral, and political concerns, literature is also supposed to entertain and to display the possibility of patterning and perfecting the materiality and structural features of language.

Of these functions, the hardest to define is entertainment. Copulating, dancing, exchanging ideas or discussing with others, fighting a ferocious beast, boxing are all wonderful, rewarding, horrifying, thrilling, despicable, or pleasurable activities, as the case may be; but to those involved, they are most often not entertainment (of course, there are forms of entertainment that involve the spectators to a certain extent, e.g., the masque). All of them have, however, sometimes clandestinely, been turned into entertainment throughout history. On the other hand, watching executions or the torturing or humiliation of others, bullfights, the display of deformities, and so on have been treasured as entertainment. What is shown or voiced must relate to and rouse our desires and fears. But entertainment implies being impressed, as spectators, by the activity and achievements, or the suffering and failure, of others. Most often there is a double attitude, a basic ambiguity, involved in being entertained. Entertainment may offer a spectacle of extraordinary and liminal events experienced by others. However, it may also represent an experience familiar to the spectators since the entertainers do something similar to what the members of the audience do themselves at other times (feats attained by strength, by litheness, by inventive bodily action, etc.). In both cases, witnessing may offer a pleasurable vicarious experience, during which the horrors suffered by others may thrill, maybe even purge, the mind. If what is offered for entertainment is within the range of familiar experience, it is stylized, made complicated, and its performance is perfected to a degree unattainable by the ordinary spectator, thus provoking amazement, admiration, and envy.[7] But entertainment also includes what the spectator would never do, unless forced to, that which involves embarrassment, ridicule, humiliation, and suffering. There is a kind of cruel delight on the part of the spectators that is related to excitement, fear, and aggression, another kind of vicarious experience in which somebody is suffering for others (this is also an eminent feature of many rituals, e.g., of scapegoating). Even the worst of cases, public killing, may turn into a kind of entertainment. Unfortunately, in many countries, public executions still draw a big audience. In such a case the audience goes through a complex process of identification with and disassociation from the victim; after all, after the event they are still alive and safe.

These features, belonging to other forms of entertainment, are equally a part of literature. First of all, literature does what its audience or readership do themselves: it uses words to speak to others. However, it does it better than people usually do because of its artful and expressive combination of words. Further, the subject of literature is the mental experimentation on common experiences, attitudes, and emotional responses. In many texts the affective and emotive responses may be very pronounced, for example, in diatribes and satires, texts dealing with and minutely developing, for the laughter of others, our shortcomings and lack of mastery, or detailing sufferings, horror, decay, decrepitude, and death.

In spite of its complicity in the darker aspects of entertainment, as an institution literature specifically interacts with the educational institution. The role of literature and its congeners in the learning processes is considerable in any known culture. In addition to myth and fairy tales (mentioned in chapters 3, 4, and 5) there is the fable (on our view certainly cruel), which likewise seems to exist in all cultures. Such elementary, and probably universal, forms are used didactically. They are communicated in order to enlighten (and entertain) listeners about the nature of the community and universe within which they live. Even fairy tales, which end by letting a wish-fulfilment become reality, are eloquent concerning hierarchies pertaining to status, sex, and age. In addition to these elementary forms of literature should be added, for instance, those that pretend to represent historical matters, such as sagas and legends, and those that are baldly didactic but yet poetical, such as proverbs (see the classical study by Jolles [1930]).

It might be thought that, for educational purposes, literary texts suffer from the drawback of not relating to facts. Most literature, however, uses mixed references (cf. chapter 3), with the effect that, even concerning their particulars, they are half-rooted in the lifeworld of the audience. Furthermore, precisely their fictionality makes them malleable enough to clearly exemplify, for instance, moral issues. For education involves learning to accept the morality of a community just as much as learning facts and skills.

There is a didactic vein in most literature. It wants to educate its readers in many ways, from relating about foreign countries to teaching the way a Christian should behave in this world of sin. Much eighteenth-century literature, for instance, was occupied with educating the bourgeoisie, installing and refining its moral sentiment and imparting standards of taste. Today this is very prominent in popular literature, for instance, in series for television. In almost every part of such series moral issues are raised in connection with problems of interpersonal and sentimental relationships, career problems, and problems of politics, local or general.

From the point of view of universal pragmatics, it will be remembered that rightness is one of the universal validity claims (see chapter 2, pp. 80–1). Although literature cannot be reduced to a special case of practical discourse, one of its main concerns is the exemplification, and the implicit and/or explicit discussion, of rightness, whether it be on the trivial level found in the products of the culture industry, mentioned above, or in a thorough critique of the morality of a given community and culture. This preoccupation with questions of ethics also explains one of the reasons people react strongly to literature: it challenges their conception of rightness. Readers have sought all kinds of knowledge in literature, from technical information to insight into the ultimate mysteries of the self or those of the universe. Central, however, is knowledge about the middle-sized world that we perceive and inhabit, the social constraints on our behaviour and interactions with others, and knowledge of norms and values, of good and evil.[8]

In chapter 3 the representational nature of literature was specified as being that of a model, an iconic representation and analogue of parts of the lifeworld and its boundaries. But what are the uses of such models? Lotman's examples of useful models are maps, play and games, military drill, and exercise. Maps, play, and games are alike in helping us to act in our lifeworld. In fact, a map will often be the only means by which we will be able to comprehend the structure of a foreign city and thus to find our way. Play and games both imitate patterns of behaviour and interaction and are clearly conventionalized and rule-governed activities. Playing and games are helpful models of interaction because they allow us to interrupt the action and to repeat and correct it. Like playing, military drill and other forms of training are preparations for acting adequately under very straining conditions. Furthermore, situations in actual life (which are unpredictable, seemingly amorphous, because bewilderingly filled with details, and irreparable) are simplified and made manageable according to a finite set of rules. In short, these model-processes serve preparatory and adaptive purposes, while maps furnish a surveyable model of that which cannot be perceived in toto. Obviously, literature has similar functions.

Furthermore, literature offers what Alfred Schutz calls the reciprocity of perspectives, that is, it allows people to understand and partly identify themselves with the perspective of others. This ability, the so-called congruence of relevance, includes understanding others' hierarchies of relevance and their plans at different levels, although the knowledge of others' perspective will remain imperfect.

Most serious conversation is about the nature of objectives and goals and the viability of plans, and parts of psychology and practical philosophy attempt to describe this field under headings such as the human condition, human happiness, the good life, morality and decency, personality studies, and so forth. Literature, however, does two things simultaneously: first, it transcends the limits of conversation and makes public the descriptions and discussions of hierarchies of relevance and the clash between plans at different levels. In this sense literature is, and has always been, an important instrument for revealing the interests, norms, and values that characterize a community. Second, in contradistinction to psychology and practical philosophy, literature proves, as it were, by means of rhetorical induction, that is, by example. The strength of literature consists, among other things, in that it stays very close to the level of lived experience – even if this experience is imagined.

Hence, literature offers indirectly what Clifford Geertz calls a thick description of our lifeworld. The description is thick because it includes a large number of phenomena, larger than the number of variables normally included in psychological and moral reasoning. Thus, literature is able to represent human thought and action as the outcome of a complex interactive process between factors that belong to different realms of experience, and as overdetermined by forces of different origins. This is possible because literature, even in representing the particular, the concrete thoughts and actions of individual, albeit fictional, persons, implicitly claims that it offers a model of human behaviour, at a given time and place, that possesses a certain generality and relevance. In pretending to represent the singular literature shows the complexity and heterogeneity of what determines individual man's inner and outer action. However, because it aspires to become a model, and because it is fiction, it simultaneously makes the course of thought, feeling, and action conform to general patterns of interpretation. Literature is interpretation by means of exemplification, and because the examples are fictive they are pliable; they may serve as premises in an argument (in fact, classical rhetoric defined the argument by example as the rhetorical equivalent of an inductive argument).

Literature, or rather one important aspect of literature, serves the same preparatory and adaptive purpose. In his fine short introduction to Aristotle's *Poetics*, Jostein Børtness tells the following anecdote that illustrates the model function of literature:

> In the Summer of 1970 I participated in *The Second International Ibsen Seminar* in Cambridge. As a part of the program I watched Ingmar Bergman's staging of *Hedda Gabler* together with other Ibsen scholars, among them the English psychiatrist Derek Russell Davies. After the performance he told me that every year he made his students read *Hedda Gabler*. 'Because,' he said, 'reality is much too complicated for a beginner. In *Hedda Gabler*, however, the students will find a model of reality in which all the relevant features are combined into a unified whole.' (Børtness 1980: 27; my trans.)

Despite the fact that most of us will probably still be beginners when we leave this world, the instructive value of literature is important. Furthermore, because of its affinity with imagination, literature, is related to the core of our mental activity, to planning and to daydreaming:

> Day-dreams are often spoken of as mere idleness; and so they would be, but for the remarkable fact that they do go on to form habits, by virtue of which when a similar real conjuncture arises we really behave in the manner we had dreamed of doing ...
>
> People who build castles in the air do not, for the most part, accomplish much, it is true; but every man who does accomplish great things is given to building elaborate castles in the air and then painfully copying them on solid ground. Indeed the whole business of ratiocination, all that makes us intellectual beings, is performed in imagination. (CP 6.286)

Thus by refining modes of thought already operative within us and vitally important to our existence, literature offers a model of (aspects of) the lifeworld to be scrutinized, and it informs us about what should be fought for and what should be avoided, what should be held in esteem and what should be despised. No wonder, then, that it is closely related to the educational institution (pedagogy certainly also is, or should be, about developing the pupils' imagination).

However, even if this close relationship with the educational institution is beneficial to literature as regards its survival, it may aggravate the ideological demands on it. Precisely because of this relationship (together with literature's ability to rouse the interests, fears, and desires of its audience) literature may easily get in trouble, if it goes against common prejudices. It has been, and still often is, extremely dangerous to defy doxa, that is, what is commonly believed. Generally, defying doxa constitutes different forms of heresy – and heresy is punished. Using the four basic discourses described in chapter 2, we may distinguish heresy in theoretical matters. It may be considered sacrilege and incur the death penalty, or it may stamp the challenger as ignorant, or deluded, to be despised, pitied, and not heard. Defying doxa in matters technical, arguing for the use of other techniques and strategies in the production of nutrients and in reshaping the material world, may provoke spite, refusal of cooporation, and even Luddism. Going against the professed morality of a community in the fight for a novel conception of how people should interact may stigmatize the challenger for life and lead to his or her exclusion from society, if not to worse. And toying with the community's conception of its history and identity may provoke rage because it means sabotaging its self-understanding.

The 'mays' in the above paragraph should be noticed, because few communities are for long periods so ideologically monolitic that absolute agreement on theoretical, technical, practical, and historical matters exists (or is demanded). Many modern societies have different and competing ideologies, philosophical doctrines, and religious beliefs. Often one ideology or religious belief will be in power and attempt to suppress the others, and history shows an almost infinite number of victims of such hegemony, but pockets of resistance will survive and perhaps in time get the upper hand. In these matters tolerance and (in most cases) the non-intervention of the authorities has, since the eighteenth century, led to multi-ideological societies in some parts of the world, but certainly not to mutual respect and idyllic coexistence. Ideologies, as more or less systematic aggregates of beliefs and values, are all-pervasive, agonistic, and hard to change because they make up an important part of the identity and self-understanding of their holders. At any given time, literature, as mimesis of the other discourses, inherits all their biases, visions, prejudices, and provocative and agonistic potential.

Speaking ex officio, magistrates are invested with the power of their institution; in principle they are representing and expressing its will – and prejudices. But even if we would want to speculate about the high office of the poet as a seer in mythical times, already in fifth-century Athens, the tragic poet staged as one of the competitors during the Great Dionysia, is nevertheless competing and speaking as a private citizen. Poets may be protected by the high and mighty, but the literary institution itself, together with other cultural institutions, has, in the short run, most often too little stamina to resist the pressure from institutions closer to the centre(s) of power: the juridical, theological, the pedagogical, and so forth.

Even when poets were invited by princes to celebrate the birth, history, and explorations of families and nations, their version had to agree with the prevailing ideology to keep them out of trouble. Furthermore, as private citizens, poets, novelists, and playwrights are very vulnerable, precisely because it is one of their roles, without speaking ex officio, to represent the traditions and self-understanding of their community or of a subcommunity within it. At the same time, however, they will necessarily offer a subjective (in the sense defined in the preceding chapter) reinterpretation that attempts to make sense of the scattered fragments of understanding of which doxa consists. There is, then, a reconstructive-deconstructive dialectic between the poet's work and the beliefs of his community that may be upsetting. To reconstruct ideological problems as images, narratives, and arguments may mean revealing conflicts, incompatibilities, and contradictions, and thus de facto deconstruct that which was thought unproblematic and consistent. Even if the poet does not, on my view, possess a special insight into the nature of things denied to others, he or she does spend a lot of time imagining, plotting, and arguing. Poets and authors may thus discover lacks of interconnection, incompatibilities, and contradictions between beliefs and moral precepts equally cherished within the fictional universe of his or her own invention. Such states of affairs may be projected onto the lifeworld of the audience by the audience itself – indeed, this is how literature should work. As the discoverer/constructor of lack and misery, dilemmas, dead ends, and forced and destructive solutions, the poet runs the risk (despite the saying) of being killed as the messenger. Precisely because they could have invented their worlds otherwise, they may be blamed for having constructed them as they have; poets do not even have the messenger's excuse.

However, although the literary institution does not give the words of the writer any power, it does – sometimes – protect him or her in one respect. Because the poet deals either with events and actions in a separate universe, or with mythical and historical material, he is allowed to structure it according to the needs of his art (cf. Thucydides' remark on the untrustworthiness of the poets, quoted p. 105). He is not held accountable for its being absolutely true to the facts, or to what are believed to be the facts. This licence allows him or her not only to change elements of the story as previously told, but also to change what is thought to be the correct use of language and to a certain extent, but at his own peril, to challenge some of the received wisdom concerning theoretical and practical matters. But even granted that this licence sometimes does protect the poet, he or she will still be at the mercy of the audience for recognition, and for staying in business.

6.2 The Interpellation: *Plaudite*

From what has been said until now, it is clear that literature is not only an act of omnipotence in the staging of fantasies; it is also communicative and thus heir to all the restrictions and dangers concomitant with speaking publicly. It addresses somebody, offers itself as a source of pleasure and knowledge, and in return demands attention and asks for sympathy and applause. In comedy, this demand was often directly expressed in the traditional *plaudite*, which Shakespeare's Rosalind handles as follows:

> My way is to conjure you, and I'll begin with the women. I charge you, O women, for the love you bear to men, to like as much of this play as please you. And I charge you, O men, for the love you bear to women – as I perceive by your simpering none of you hates them – that between you and the women the play may please. If I were a woman, I would kiss as many of you as had beards that pleased me, complexions that liked me, and breaths that I defied not. And I am sure, as many as have good beards, or good faces, or sweet breaths will for my kind offer, when I make curtsy, bid me farewell. *Exit*.
> (*As You Like It*, V, iv, 208–20)

Here it is asked that the play (literature) please both men and women and that it should be loved for the love that the sexes bear to one another. Furthermore, Rosalind's 'if I were a woman' expresses literature's tricks with identity and its ambiguous relation to reality. In the communication between author and audience, the literary text is offered as a libidinal object, as a gift, and appeals to be desired. From this point of view, literature's claim to our interest lies in its representing human desire, and, through its fictional repetition, desire is inflected and reflected, both through as mimesis and in the self-reflexivity of poetic speech. Further, Rosalind's speech, although jesting, uses the language of intimacy. She is speaking a person to a group of persons that she does not conceive collectively, but rather as particularized individuals ('I would kiss as many of you as had beards that pleased me, complexions that liked me, and breaths that I defied not'). And Rosalind is right in using the language of intimacy, of flirtation, because this is how we already know her from the play, flirting and jesting.

However, how is this intimacy in keeping with, as it was said above, the role of the poet as representing the traditions and self-understandings of his or her community. Here the point is not that there are different kinds of literature, each catering to the specific spheres of interaction, situations, desires, moods, beliefs, and attitudes of the readership. There certainly are, and it is very important that different genres formalize typical modes of experience. The point is, rather, that even solemn narratives of historical events, as for instance *The Iliad*, which for was centuries considered to be history rather than literature, speak the language of intimacy; not necessarily a flirtatious and jesting language, but intimate because it lets us in on the emotions and reactions of the characters. *The Iliad* is certainly a poem on the ideals of a warrior caste, but it is this by being first a poem about the wrath and despair of Achilles, the pettiness of Agamemnon, the magnanimity of Hector, and so forth.

In literature, intimacy and what is collectively shared, the self-understanding of a community, are not mutually exclusive. Indeed, literature may be one of the most important mediators between private and public. Thus, in spite of its non-binding character (cf. below), literature is instrumental not only in educating the members of a community but also in pointing out to them that what they believe to be signs of their particular psychical make-up are in fact features of a subjectivity that is common to most members of the community. Subjectivity itself is fostered by communicative and interactional structures prevailing within it.

Rosalind's epilogue also exemplifies the attempt to directly engage the audience in the play. As in the parabasis of the old comedy, the borderline between the fictional universe and the social one is crossed, and this moment reveals that what binds them together is the fact that they are parallel universes of desire, mirroring and elucidating each other.

But the epilogue also expresses the fragility of the voice of literature. The priest professes to declare the divine will, the legislative body decides about the legality of actions, and the judge passes sentence, forever changing the fate of the accused. Literature, however, invites, appeals, and solicits. Very often, as in Shakespeare, it explicitly points to its universe as a mere figment of the imagination, as something invented and separate from the audience's reality. Most often, literature will contain clues that point to its fictionality.

Literature can lay no claims to the necessity of paying attention to it because (except perhaps being considered an uncultured boor), nothing happens, at least not immediately and externally, if one does not bother to watch or read. And thus literature must survive on the goodwill and favour of the readership (and, in the long run, on the educational system). This apparent lack of necessity, may, however, become a strength because it places conversing with literature amid the realm of pleasures, not among the duties (except again within the educational institution). The work of literature, that is, its author through it, calls for applause, because it needs such expressions of pleasure and recognition to survive – Horace's proud *non omnis moriar* is only true as long as he is read – and because such expressions of satisfaction and pleasure are congenial to a part of its telos.

In the view of French philosopher Louis Althusser, Rosalind's appeal is that of literature's in general, namely, what he calls an interpellation. It addresses the subject, pretending to know him or her, and offers its reader(s) a place within the text and a perspective from which it may be viewed; a place that appears to have been reserved for this reader, in fact for any reader. There is, however, another side to this inviting gesture. Precisely because the reader is a precious and honoured guest, he is expected to follow the domestic discipline, that is, to see this part of the (fictional) universe to which he is not only admitted, but asked to enter, as his host does. Literature offers a way of viewing the world, but it most often also insists that this is the right and sensible way to see it.

Althusser's concept of interpellation is not construed with regard to literature but to elucidate the way ideology functions. According to him, the power of the state rests on two kinds of apparatuses, in fact on two kinds of institutions, the repressive and the ideological. The repressive institutions, which are built on power and attempt to monopolize violence, consist of government, administration, armed forces, police, courts, prisons, and so on. These are not the concern of this book. The ideological state apparatuses are, among others, the religious, political, and juridical institutions. Further there are institutions occupied with production and commerce (e.g., labour unions and employers' federations). The family and the educational system are, however, in Althusser's view, the central ideological state apparatuses. These core institutions are closely related to and feed on the institutions of information (press, radio, TV, etc.) and culture (sports, the arts, theatre, music, and literature). Such institutions are ideological rather than repressive, although discipline and the power to suppress or further the formation of public opinion certainly are central to them.

Ideologies are defined as systems of ideas, concepts, and images that dominate the mental life of a person or group. Their role is to give their holders an apparent identity and a world view that seems general and consistent. Ideologies disguise, however, the interests of classes and subcommunities and represent such interests as objective, as belonging to the nature of things. Ideologies may, of course, contain understandings and insights for which very good reasons may be given and attitudes and moral points of view that are defensible. The point is, however, that they place assertions and attitudes beyond discussion, because they found them in an authority that to their holders is unquestionable. By their seeming universality and naturalness, ideologies block the road of inquiry to further insight and any dialogue with others, with the effect that they become examples of systematically distorted communication. Obviously, ideologies are historical; they have both an internal and an external history. However, as forms of consciousness, of mental life, they seem, like the Freudian unconscious, to be eternal (as long as they are efficacious). Althusser's core definition of ideology is that ideology is an imaginary representation of the relations between individuals and their real conditions of existence. As regards ideology, what is decisive is what is believed, is imagined, to be conditions of reality, whether they are so or not:

> [I]t is not their real conditions of existence, their real world, that 'men represent to themselves' in ideology, but above all it is their relation to those conditions of existence which is represented to them there. It is this relation which is at the centre of every ideological, i.e. imaginary, representation of the real world ... [I]t is the *imaginary nature of this relation* which underlies all the imaginary distortion that we can observe (if we do not live in its truth) in all ideology. (Althusser 1971a: 164)

Ideology functions through interpellation. Interpellation generally means addressing, asking, and holding somebody accountable for something (a member of a legislative body may interpellate a minister, and the latter is forced to answer). In this context, connotations such as appealing to, stressing the importance of, and asking for are important. What interpellation does, according to Althusser, is nothing less than constitute the individual person as a subject. Ideology becomes invisible to the individual person precisely because it has constituted him or her as a subject. Thus people constituted as subjects by virtue of it, and recognizing themselves in it, will deny that (their) ideology is ideology. Further, since they are within it, and its boundaries are unknown, there seems to exist nothing outside it, although it itself is removed from science and from reality.

The interpellation of the subjects presupposes the existence of another, central and unique subject (such as for instance a godhead) so that there is a doubling of the subject: subject – Subject. Ideology thus implies a double mirroring (Subject mirrors subject and vice versa). The structure and functioning of ideology comprises four steps: (1) the interpellation (a prototype is the naming and addressing of the infant within the family); (2) the submission of the subject to the Subject (the child's submission to the parents, especially the father, the believer's submission to the godhead); (3) mutual recognition between subject and Subject (e.g., baptism), recognition among the subjects (they are all citizens, God's children, etc.), and self-recognition (I am, and I understand myself as being this or that); and, finally, (4) ideology's 'absolute' guarantee that it really is so (not only do I recognize myself as this or that, my fellow beings do the same, and superhuman, or at least superindividual, authorities vouch for the truth of this understanding) (see Althusser 1971a: 180-1).

What, however, has Althusser's conception of ideology to do with Rosalind's wonderful epilogue? A great deal, because seeing ideology as interpellation underscores the fact that addressing will almost invariably become not only an act of pointing out and identifying, but also one of definition and classification. Rosalind not only addresses the onlookers as audience, she (whose sexual identity is highly ambiguous both in the play and in the theatre in Shakespeare's time) addresses them as sexual and gendered beings; and it is on this act of recognition that she builds her argument.

Literature's act of interpellation is certainly not confined to parabases and to pro- and epilogues. Any literary text is directed and addressed to the individual spectator or reader, and it appeals for sympathy while, at the same time, it attempts to define him or her, that is, make him or her into a subject on the text's condition. Thus, the text models its immediate interpreter, that is, the interpreter as he appears in, or is indicated by, the sign itself, the implicit reader who is a function of the purpose and structure of the text. The split between implicit reader and interpreter is that between a textual construct and an actual person. Just like the implied author, the implicit reader is a kind of persona, a mask, that the actual reader is offered, indeed often tricked or bullied into assuming. Fielding's profession of sovereignty (quoted here on p. 246) is emblematic in this respect. His explicit narrator points himself to the gentle force exercised by fiction as ever deciding the rule of the game.

6.3 Mistrusting the Author

A reader may, however, refuse the rules and reject the work of fiction for many reasons, some of which will be discussed below. To exemplify this rejection, let us return to Rosalind's epilogue. If we were ill disposed – something almost unthinkable in connection with *As You Like It* – we might well be offended by Rosalind's insistence on talking about our love for the other sex, as if it were her business. We might also, and maybe even more, object to her soliciting. For is this not precisely what she is doing? She offers, or s/he would have offered, us men her lips if her sex had been right, in change for the favour that we applaud her and the world to which she belongs. She herself calls her soliciting conjuring, implying that she would like to rob us of our will by magic; a magic, as the co-text makes clear, that is founded in her erotic appeal. She is attempting to seduce us, and although most men, and women for that matter, would say 'Please go on,' some might object to the reckless arousing of the passions, to the immorality of her offer, and to the festive celebration of erotic love in the play itself. From Plato to this day there have always been proponents of this ascetic rejection of fiction as seduction.

But why this concern, this fear and mistrust of the utterer, whether fictional or non-fictional? Although there are important differences between the role of the utterer in the two kinds of texts, I will briefly inquire into our mistrust of the non-fictional utterer. This mistrust is based on the fear of being fooled and misled to believe and do something by trusting the false pretences of the artful utterer. In classical rhetoric, persuasion was seen as an art or craft, and according to Aristotle, the means of persuasion are three: the moral character of the speaker, the act of putting the audience into a certain frame of mind, and the real or putative proofs of the speech itself (Aristotle 1926: 17, 1355b–56a). Since rhetoric deals with the probable, not with certain knowledge, the trustworthiness and the moral character of the speaker become important. We tend to believe the testimony and advice of those we think we know to be honest and virtuous. Accordingly, the task of the orator is to ensure the attention and sympathy of the audience and to persuade them of his credibility, reliability, and high moral standards. The second kind of proof is, according to Aristotle, the rousing of a certain emotional state in the hearers: 'for the judgements we deliver are not the same when we are influenced by joy and sorrow, love or hate' (ibid.). Thus, benevolence becomes an essential ingredient in the construction of the image of the addresser in the sign because the audience ought to be persuaded that what is advised and prescribed is in its own interest, since the recommended decision will further their happiness or pleasure.

In spite of Quintillian's claim that in order to be a good orator you must be morally good (1922: IV, 355–6), orators do attempt to control their listeners by pretending, not for the good of the audience, but in order to secure personal advantages; or even for the good of the audience, but an audience they lie to for its own good, with the so-called 'noble lie' or 'convenient fiction' of Plato (*Republic* III, 10, 414–15). In such cases the split between utterer and addresser, which makes pretence possible, has been exploited. Thus, our efforts to bridge the split between utterer and addresser are well explained by our obvious interest in not becoming victims of the pretence of others. This is the reason we are morally and legally responsible for the personae we create, because of the consequences and obligations bound up with them.

In addition to the important question of accountability, there is another reason for the obsession with the origins of texts, with the question of their source; namely, their expressivity, the fact that they are symptoms. In treating texts as symptoms, we change focus from the object they represent to the state of mind of their utterer whom they are supposed to reveal. It seems that we can hardly bear the uncertainty that the split between utterer and addresser creates. We try to overcome it, as if it were a wound that should be healed (this is one of the main reasons for the indestructible appeal of biographies).

It might seem as if the effort to hold people responsible for the signs they utter and the search for other, non-obvious, meanings of the same signs are at odds. This apparent contradiction is explained by the fact that in holding people accountable, we refer to generally recognized standard meanings of words, phrases, and utterances. In inquiring into the expressivity and symptomatic value of a text, by contrast, we search the specific co-text and context of utterance for indices of individual attitudes. Thus, there is no contradiction involved in simultaneously holding somebody responsible for not keeping a promise and interpreting the uttering of it and its phrasing as a symptom of vanity.

Thus, there are good reasons for the resistance of the actual interpreter to texts pertaining to our lifeworld. Texts are the means used to negotiate not only what is supposed to be an adequate description of the world, what is good and what is bad, but also the place and position of the interlocutors within it, their duties and privileges. Consequently, texts and dialogues are used to establish a consensus or to realize that differences are irreconcilable.

But why is there just as much resistance to texts representing a world categorically different from the world within which writers and readers live and interact? Obviously, part of the answer, already indicated above, has to do with the fact that literary texts underscore questions and problems of value and of the validity of accepted interpretations of the human condition. Literary texts function as a means to test conditions and consequences of a given morality within an imaginary world. And in taking a stand, literary texts assume and suggest attitudes. Further, disagreement about attitudes often means a total rejection of the text.[9] In dictator-ruled countries, the very possession of certain texts doomed subversive is often sufficient reason to incur punishment because the owners automatically, and maybe unjustly, are identified as the addressees of these texts, as their consenting readers.

But since we are held accountable for telling a sleazy or politically incorrect joke that we haven't even made up ourselves, it is no wonder that the inventor of 'bad' or 'evil' texts, who has not the messenger's excuse, will be the target of anger, indignation, and resentment; and the poet especially so because he or she will somehow be protected by the *licentia poetarum* mentioned above. There is, however, another side to this licence, since it is often supposed not only to turn the poet into a dreamer but is also often supposed to incur, as it were, a moral flaw that turns him into an irresponsible maker of paradoxes and a gratuitous critic of shared values and vested interests that he should not be allowed to turn against without suffering the consequences. The very immunity of the poet – as far as it goes – gives rise to anger.

In the case of non-literary texts, a (sometimes unremitting) effort to tie the signs to the person exists for the very good reason that there is an important contractual aspect to most utterances. However, even as regards literary texts, which in principle – at least this is the current understanding – are supposed to be separated from their authors, this effort is prominent. In spite of all protestations from writers to the contrary, in spite of all the (faulty) theoretical reasons for not mixing up the production of fiction with the personal life of the writer, there is a deep-rooted desire in readers to tie the narrators, and the text in general, to their author, both to make him or her accountable for it and to peek further into the alleged facts and motives that are supposed to be the real creative forces behind the texts. Ultimately, neither biographers nor censors have ever respected the borderline between fictional and non-fictional texts. Poets and writers of fiction have been, and still are, both idolized as culture hero(ine)s and prosecuted as writers of pamphlets.

An important reason for the resistance to and rejection of individual literary works is simply that literature is rarely totally in agreement with and subsumable under a given ideology. Literature is simultaneously related to ideologies and a critical investigation of them. According to Althusser, 'ideology slides into all human activity, [and] is identical with the "lived" experience of human existence itself' (1971b: 223). But how then to distinguish literature from ideology?[10] Doesn't literature precisely represent the 'lived experience' of man? Althusser points to a time-honoured, but basic, definition of literature and art (in this book also held to be one of literature's fundamental functions); namely, that 'the peculiarity of art is to "make us see" (*nous donner à voir*), "make us perceive," "make us feel" something which *alludes* to reality' (ibid.: 222). According to Althusser, what literature and art make us see is precisely ideology in the sense of the lived experience. Literature 'make[s] us "perceive" (but not know) in some sense *from the inside*, by an *internal distance*, the very ideology' that dominates the readers (223). Although this potential double nature of 'real' literature, as simultaneously ideological and a critique of ideology, has to be scrutinized in each and every case, it may also be helpful in understanding the ambivalent reactions of readers.

Through this revealing of and display of ideological positions, literature often offends against some of the core beliefs and attitudes of ideology, even if it may in the main be sympathetic to it. This is why, according to those in power, writers and intellectuals in general are notorious as unstable, indeed traitorous, allies. Furthermore, in multi-ideological societies it seems rather difficult not to question at least some positions cherished by one or more subcommunities (e.g., the conflicts engendered by the existence of religious communities within a secular and profane society). But even when the literary text is in the main in accordance with the ruling ideology of a given society, in which other ideologies are suppressed or held in check, there is very often a latent, or patent, conflict with the authorities.

This conflict is engendered by the very fact that as literary texts exemplify, create, individual icons of meanings, norms, and values, a critique is almost bound to emerge. As Adorno has insisted in many places (e.g., 1970 and 1973), in stating – here inventing – the individual case, the writer turns, maybe even against his or her own will, into defending the particular against the universal, the subjective against the social dynamics of society. Representing a given state of mind and telling a concrete story often ends up in exemplifying the encroachments of those in power on the (legitimate) claim to freedom and independence of individual persons. There is, as it were, an unsubsumable concrete residual of lived life that, by the very way in which literary discourse operates, becomes valuable. This is why literature, in addition to being always used by the authorities, is, at the same time, profoundly mistrusted by them.

To this point there have been collected rather strong reasons for not succumbing to the temptations of reading literature: it has no authority; to know it is not necessary (except within the educational system); it claims to have reasons for unsettling cherished beliefs but proves by images and stories rather than by argument (and according to Plato's *Ion*, the poet is no expert anyway); its utterers are supposed to benefit from a certain licence accorded them because they deal in fiction or treat history after the fashion of fiction, and create a separate universe most often distinguishable from the one within which we do our business. Indeed, why bother with the non-existing imagined by people who, within certain limits, are licensed to be insincere. And why have one's desires aroused by airy nothing? Because literature is about vitally important subjects.

6.4 Vitally Important Subjects

Like many forms of public address, literature functions both collectively and individually in relation to the public. It addresses an audience or readership at large, and it addresses every single spectator or reader separately. This is one important reason why readers feel a certain intimacy in regard to the authors they care about, for they have been, so they rightfully think, interpellated (see above, pp. 307). But in contradistinction to most other forms of public address (interestingly enough with the exception of sermons, but sermons bear authority), what the interpellation is opening up is an imaginary space (see below).

One important aspect of reading literature as a collective activity is that an indefinite number of imaginary spaces, one for each reader, is nurtured by the same text. However, although the personal and private experience of the text is indispensable and of the highest value, the process does not stop at the solitary reading; it is most often continued by something just as valuable: the conversations about and the discussions of the text with others.

During such discussions, the validity and relevance of the different readings are tested, and in this process the points, issues, merits and faults of the text are scrutinized. It is by no means easy to formulate the 'abouts,' the 'whats,' and the 'whys' of the text: which kind of universe is it, what is really happening, which mood(s) does it mime, what are its themes, which devices are used and to what effect. But more important than these questions, at least to the general readership, are the more existentially relevant ones: what is the issue of the text, what is it pleading for and/or condemning, what is its vision of the present lifeworld and of the conditions of men and women.

The principal reason why these existential questions may be asked and answered – although there is no agreement about the answers – is that literature, on a certain level of abstraction, is about the human condition in the sense of discoursing on problems that are particular to us as a species. In the last chapter, human fears and desires were described because of their importance as the fuel that ignites the writing process of individual writers. But these fears and desires are, of course, the common property of man, although their peculiarities and mix are different in every person.

If we want to push the inquiry one step further, the question will be, Why does pondering on these relationships, and on the questions to which they give rise interest and bother us? A reflection on what is specific of man as a species, as *Homo sapiens*, is needed to answer such a question. This, of course, is to a great extent the field of biologists, psychologists, and sociologists. I would, however, venture to point out the consequences of a few characteristics of man as a species, since they seem to play an important role in the way we confront and interpret existence. In fact, only man ponders on, and rejoices or despairs over, the problems raised by them. This, I presume, is mainly due to five characteristics of our species:

(1) a huge neural capacity; (2) a long childhood; (3) no mating seasons; (4) the ability to engage in complex and hierarchically organized co-operation; (5) longevity

Of these five characteristics the first, the unparalleled brain capacity of man, is the most decisive since it makes possible (1.1) the invention of an unlimited number of representational systems, that is, semiotics, first and foremost language. Further, it makes possible (1.2) the creation of complex mental models of the surrounding world and of alternative worlds. Thus, the mental activity of man is not restricted to what is present in the surroundings, but is able to recall, reflect, construct, and project. Finally, (1.3) this capacity makes self-inspection and self-reflection possible.

Man's long childhood implies (2.1) a long and stable dependence on nursing and upbringing by others, which, for better or worse, (2.2)

leads to strong emotional ties between generations. The prolonged learning processes means (2.3) that instinctual behaviour is overlaid by the cultural.

The absence of specific seasons for mating, making sexual union possible at almost all times, furthers (3.1) durable relationships between men and women, which may lead to (3.2) intimacy and emotional bonding between sexual partners. Such ties makes possible (3.3) dependence on the specific other for the satisfaction of needs and desires (including the desire to be desired).

Man's ability to be a part of complex and hierarchically organized cooperation (made possible by the preceding characteristics) means the possibility of (4.1) grand-scale transformations of the environment, impossible for both individuals and for gregarious animals, (4.2) specialization, and (4.3) elaborate systems of social differences.

Longevity means (5.1) experiencing the historization of conditions of living and (5.2) the experience of changes of priorities within the subject and within the community during the life span of a person. It also means experiencing (5.3) aging, personal mental and physical decay, and knowing that death is the inescapable end – and waiting for it.

The experiences made possible by man's five characteristics are not univocal as to their meaning and significance; in fact, they elicit contrary interpretations, especially contrary as regards evaluation and emotional response. The subject may experience the multiple possibilities of representing self and world (the many different semiotics) as an invaluable epistemic treasure and as the precondition of progress. Conversely, the multiplicity of representations may, however, be experienced as a stumbling block for unambiguous and true knowledge. The ability to represent alternative mental universes may be conceived as a necessary tool in the fight for making the good life possible. But this ability may also be interpreted as a symptom of man's alienated state within the universe; and the establishment of alternative universes can be taken as proof that the actual world is inadequate. Self-inspection and self-reflection are considered necessary instruments for bringing man to perfection (cf. the enlightenment belief in man as a perfectible being). They may, however, also be taken to imply that the human subject is never a unity but is split in its very being. This split is then seen as an unavoidable and negative condition of existence.

Long dependency on nursing and nurturing persons makes possible, it may be claimed, a process of individuation, acculturation, and education that creates a harmonious and autonomous subject. Others may, argue, however, that this long dependency means that the subject will bear the mark of parental restraint and coercion that maims the individuality and the authentic self-realization of the subject. Strong emotional ties between generations are regarded as the precondition for the richness of human emotional life and its potential for development. Again, however, others argue that these ties chain the emotional life of the subject to the past and to infantile patterns of articulating feelings. The fact that prolonged learning processes mean that instinctual behaviour is overlaid by the cultural is seen as offering a precious possibility of changing anti-social to social behaviour through upbringing and the possibility of transforming, and sublimating, a good part of instinctual energy for other purposes. Others regret this overlay that brings about a split in the very being of the subject. It becomes a victim not only of clashing drives but also of an interiorized conflict between nature and culture.

Long-time coupling, some claim, enriches the subject by the fact that it creates emotional stability and peace of mind (and is often thought to be an ideal frame for raising children). From another point of view, it limits the subject's possibilities of multiple and gratifying experiences (and it also, some think, impedes an evolutionarily beneficial spreading of genes). Intimacy and emotional bonding between sexual partners enriches sexuality, so it is claimed, by integrating it in a wider interpersonal relationship. On the other hand, it is objected that such ties limit the subject's liberty and restrain sexual gratification by linking it with considerations and concerns irrelevant to it. Dependence on a specific other for the satisfaction of needs and desires (including the desire to be desired) means that sexual partnership will be based on reciprocity and mutual recognition and appreciation. But, say others, such dependency will lead to an eternal compromising that will corrupt the fulfilment of the needs and desires of both parties.

The grand-scale transformations of the environment effectuated by man's ability to be a part of complex and hierarchically organized cooperation make the world more inhabitable and more tuned to the needs of man. No, others argue, these grand-scale transformations have already shown themselves to upset nature's balance, and they may mean the extinction of our species. Specialization and division of labour are the precondition for development and progress, and the perfection of specific gifts and talents brings joy and satisfaction not only to those who perfect themselves but to the community at large. No, division of labour and specialization break up a community's unity and destroy the harmonious mental and corporeal versatility of man. They become the main cause of his alienation. Elaborate systems of social differences are grounded in differentiations within nature itself, and they are the precondition of survival and progress. Conversely, it is claimed that social distinctions and differences in privileges and obligations are not only unjust; they are detrimental to progress and the cause of conflicts that may even prove fatal.

To experience the historicization of conditions of living gives insight into the dynamics of individual and societal developments and makes intervention in or adaptation to changed conditions possible. No, say others, such changes destabilize the understanding of self and lifeworld and lead to a relativism ending in despair, because constant change is experienced as a loss of meaning. However, changes of priorities within the subject and within the community during the life span of a person are, say some, experienced as plenitude, since every period of life offers different but equally valuable possibilities of fulfilment. No, say others, through life's different stages such possibilities are constantly reduced, and the subject is left to regret time's passage. Aging, personal mental and physical decay, and finitude as man's inescapable end are accepted as a precondition for the value of the different periods of life, because such value is founded in the fact that they are transitory. No, knowing about aging, decrepitude, and ultimate death weakens or robs the different periods of their value, because the certain expectation of an end is in itself destructive.

The positions are presented here without any argumentation because, in this context, their respective validity is of no interest. The point is that people do hold these positions, and they are even well able to hold contradictory positions at the same time because ambiguity and ambivalence are outstanding features of these matters. Furthermore, it is possible to give elaborate arguments in favour of all these contrary positions; as a matter of fact, different answers have been offered for more than two millennia, and novel answers are still attempted. These questions and answers have implications for all four discourses, but their theoretical and practical import is underscored. However, although questions of ontology and epistemology will also raise questions of ethics, the implications of theoretical positions for ethics are not determined in advance. Parties may well agree on questions of epistemology and draw very different ethical consequences from the same position. These questions are constantly debated because they are the unavoidable concerns of everybody and are always present in the background of any reflections on self and lifeworld. Although perennial, the questions are asked against the background of widely different states of knowledge and are related to different ideological traditions. Thus, they are seldom given exactly the same answers, and if they were, an identical answer would function in different ways depending upon the general cultural and ideological background at the time of utterance.

The debates take place within different fora and institutions, among theologians, philosophers, scientists, scholars, and so forth. In literature, these species-particular concerns are staged as existential analogues in the form of musements or narratives comprising five motifs related to the subject. These motifs are the relation of the subject (1) to its own body, (2) to its own mind, (3) to the significant other and to others, (4) to its community, and (5) to outer nature.

1. The relation of the subject to its own body (to its functions and malfunctions)

This motif is important because we are never in full control of our bodies; we are even most often not at home in them. The body seems always to let us down; it seems never to be able to do and perform as we would like. As children we envy the strength and prowess of adults and older children. As grown-ups we feel insecure about our looks, about our physical, not least sexual, performances, and we fear or lament our physical decline. The subject's relation to its body seems unhappily suspended between 'not yet' and 'no more.' And then there are diseases, old age, and death.

And yet there are the moments of astonishing achievement, the feeling of growing mastery, of exquisite bodily beauty, and of erotic bliss and fecundity. There is, further, laughter at our physical shortcomings, at clumsiness and accidents, at the creaturely and the obscene.

2. The relation of the subject to its own mind: its feelings, reactions, actions, and thoughts, including memories, fantasies, and intentions and projects

The mind, too, is most often utterly beyond our control. We are reminded of this whenever it plays tricks with us, in our dreams, in our obsessions, and in our delusions. The mind is led astray by our fears and desires, and the conflicts between them, conflicts that may be painful and even mentally and emotionally crippling. Our mind, in the end, is always inadequate. Although it may function very well, we find that it/we should do better, better than we do, and better than others do. There is always a deficit of understanding: however much we attempt to comprehend, something will always remain beyond our reach, and we will always be uncertain that we have really understood the issues and problems that we seem to grasp. Moreover, we fear mental decline just as much as physical decline. After all, death is first and foremost conceived as the irretrievable loss of consciousness.

But again, there are the moments of discovery, of insight, and of invention, and the feeling of emotional and intellectual growth. There is laughter at stupidity and at the strange obsessions (of others).

3. The relation of the subject to the significant other and others

Although our desires, fears, and fantasies are, in an important sense, our own, they are fostered by our interaction with others and most often are dependent on others for their realization; we also to a great extent share them with others. Thus, our interaction with other persons, our divided attractions and loyalties, those people we desire and those we fear, the ones we admire and the ones we despise, make up the pith and marrow of our existence – and of most literature.

Even if the realized and possible combinations of this motif defy any effort of exhaustive enumeration, there are typical patterns of interaction that have been studied, among others, by narratology (cf. the presentation of fairy-tale structure in chapter 4). As in the subject's relation to his or her own body and mind, the central problem – and literary device – here is conflict. Lack of interest, other preferences, and resistance of the object may obstruct the realization of desire. Others who have the object in their power may prevent our attaining it. We may decline it because it has to be bought too dearly, because getting or keeping it may mean the loss of something else which is valued just as much. It may be prevented by a change of mind in the subject itself, a loss of desire, etc., etc. [11]

4. The relationship between the subject and the community

In contradistinction to the preceding, this relationship is not between one person and particular others; it involves the subject's relation to the collective as a hierarchical power structure and to its different institutions. Of course, in concrete texts and genres, (3) and (4) may merge.[12] Nevertheless, it is for several reasons important to distinguish between others as private individuals (cf. the etymology of 'private: separated, without public office) and as the embodiment of societal authority. The relationship between individuals is best described as the accordance or conflict of personal interests. In the relation between the subject and the community at large, however, the interests of the individual is matched either with the common interests of the community, that is, the political issues, or with its laws, i.e., juridical issues. In both cases, if there is a conflict, a moral issue will arise (is the subject a common criminal or a heroic fighter for freedom?). Furthermore, the wishes of the individual invested with the power of the community may be contrary to his or her duty as its representative, and this conflict may prove fatal to the subject (a variation dear to classicist tragedy). In addition, the subject may be up against anonymous powers whose servants may seem petty but are formidable and deadly adversaries (Kafka is a master of describing such cases).

5. The relation of the subject to outer nature, whether physical or metaphysical

The relation of the subject to the extra-human comprises very different forms of interaction and communication depending on the subject's ontological stance: whether he or she holds outer reality to be only biophysical or to be of a metaphysical nature. In the first case, outer reality is understood as basically non-anthropomorphic; as, at the same time, categorically different from man, but nevertheless forming the substratum that upholds or destroys what exists, including man. Most often, on this view, nature is conceived as subhuman, as a power that, although in the final analysis it will have the upper hand, should be controlled as far as possible. Thus, the interaction of mankind with nature is an effort to understand it (profane theoretical investigation) through asking questions of it in a kind of quasi-dialogue, where the 'answers' are due to the ingenuity of the asker. The goal is, however, not only theoretical; it is to control it as far as possible (technical knowledge).[13]

The other position is to hold that beyond or within physical nature there is another reality that may generally be described as mental but that is differently described in the different religions and metaphysical systems. On this view, there may be ulterior purposes for human existence, and for that of the universe, beyond what can be scrutinized by humans. Moreover, in some, but not all, versions of metaphysical systems, humans will even be able to enter into a dialogue with the superhuman, although on conditions different from those of human communication.

Both positions may describe the relation between the subject and outer nature as either harmonious or discordant (or both). Metaphysical thinking, however, may make distinctions between levels of outer reality, exceeding those between different levels of material complexity characteristic of the first position, with the effect that the physical and the metaphysical may be seen as opposed to each other.

Finally, both positions claim contiguity between outer and inner nature. The first position holds that man is the most complex natural (biological) being, but made of nature's stuff, and that the bodily and mental processes internal to man are of the same kind, albeit more complex, as those of outer nature. The second position sees part of man as different from outer, material nature, but this part is then related to non-material, metaphysical nature.

Furthermore, because of the temporality and finitude of existence, people are forced to make plans. Phenomenology sees planning as an effect of the meeting, even clash, between the stream of consciousness and world time. Even if subjects, during sleep, withdraw from the everyday lifeworld, waking up the next morning they will find that the world has grown older; world time has passed. Knowledge of one's own finitude compared to (the belief in) the duration of the world means that, from the perspective of the subject, time is a scarce resource. This leads to what has become a literary topos, to Horace's and Marvell's problem: Had we but World enough, and Time. Since, however, there is not time enough, humans are the victims of present exigencies that force them to carry out daily plans in the attempt to master the lifeworld and, simultaneously, to aim at realizing a life plan, or plans. Life plans contain that which we are aiming at doing and achieving before time runs out. Indeed, the knowledge that one becomes older and that something has to be achieved by a certain age or it will forever be outside one's reach, and the certainty that one must die, influences decisively our sense of relevance. Furthermore, most often an opposition will exist between the daily plans, on the one hand, and higher-order plans, maybe a life plan, on the other.

The constitutive elements of relevance, the desires and fears and the norms and values that determine our attitudes, are, however, not related only to the individual person's sense of finitude. They are also the outcome of the clash between the exigencies of the body, the cravings of the mind, and the demands of the community to which the subject belongs. To the hazards, oppositions, conflict, and clashes within and between the five motifs discussed above is added the question of timing: there is a time for doing, and for being able to do, things before it is too late. Furthermore, according to nature and the culture in question, there is also a time at which it is natural and/or appropriate to do certain things and be in a certain way – the right time.

Such a discussion illustrates the centrality of the five motifs and the question of timing because these motifs raise different claims about the understanding of the human condition in an individual text. The reason that most, if not all, literature is concerned with these motifs is that they are central in our effort to interpret ourselves and our place within the lifeworld and within the universe. However, in offering concrete imaginative, that is, iconic, exemplifications of the interplay of these motifs and their timing, literature becomes valuable to the community and its members because it, at least momentarily, stills a desire by providing the reader with a model, a complex diagram for imagining.

These five motifs are all parts of the riddle that literature attempts not so much to solve, as to stage, namely, our quest for self-knowledge:

> A being darkly wise, and rudely great:
> ...
> In doubt to deem himself a God, or Beast;
> In doubt his Mind or Body to prefer,
> Born but to die, and reas'ning but to err;
> ...
> Chaos of Thought and Passion, all confus'd;
> Still by himself abus'd, or disabus'd;
> Created half to rise, and half to fall;
> Great lord of all things, yet a prey to all;
> Sole judge of Truth, in endless Error hurl'd:
> The glory, jest, and riddle of the world!
>   (Pope [1733] 1969: II, 4–17)

6.5 Such stuff as dreams are made of

In reading, the reader makes room within his mind for a high-powered and highly structured mental model sketched by somebody else but left to him to finish as best he can. This is why the mechanisms of introjection, projection, and identification are necessary means in the reader's construction of the imaginary universe. This situation is of an extreme intimacy because it involves the intertwining of subjectivities. However, the intimacy is attenuated since, owing to the curious temporality of literary communication in a certain sense, there is no direct relationship with a speaker:

> 'Oh, I've had such a curious dream!' said Alice. And she told her sister, as well as she could remember them, all these strange adventures of hers that you have just been reading about; ...
>
> But her sister sat still just as she left her, leaning her head on her hand, watching the setting sun, and thinking of little Alice herself and all her wonderful Adventures, till she too began dreaming after a fashion, and this was her dream: –
>
> First, she dreamed about little Alice herself: ... and still as she listened, or seemed to listen, the whole place around her became alive with the strange creatures of her little sister's dream.
>
> The long grass rustled as the White Rabbit hurried by ... (Carroll [1865] 1971: 98)

Before we reach this point at the end of *Alice in Wonderland*, we have already been reading the adventures that Alice presumably dreamed; so we are told by the explicit narrator. But why, then, this episode with Alice's sister? First, it should be noticed that Alice's retelling of her dream to her sister seems to be not identical with what we, the readers, have read: 'And she told her sister, *as well as she could remember them*, all these strange adventures of hers' (italics added), because it seems that we have had the privilege of being let in on her dreaming the dream. However, Alice's sister starts re-dreaming a report of a dream with the effect that the surroundings come alive once more with the creatures of Alice's narrative.

Carroll seems to imply hereby that the experience of reading may be conceived both as simultaneity and as repetition. The sister's function in the text seems to be to point out the external sequentiality of literary communication: the result of the labour of the author, the text, is presented as a kind of script for the reader to translate and stage. And restaging the narrative is precisely what the sister does, so that her experience of it becomes a repetition. However, in reading (dreaming), readers are not aware of repeating anything, they are simultaneous with the progress of the text, and this is what we are told ourselves as readers of the *Adventures*. In the last analysis, Carroll is, of course, making the sister's re-dreaming a part of the fiction itself, and in this way he is indicating that reading/dreaming is an infinite cyclic process.

Obviously, as a description of the relationship between writer, text, and reader, Carroll's presentation is not accurate, at least not if it is meant to suggest that the reader identically repeats a writer's (dreamer's) previous experience. But although Carroll seems to imply such a kind of repetition, he contradicts it by marking the presence of a narrator of Alice's narrative. The 'original' experience, then, is related by somebody who is not supposed to have had it. In this case, however, the reader cannot repeat an experience, that of Alice, identically, because he cannot know what to repeat.

What he can do, and does, is supplement the significations of the text from a knowledge of language and from his own experiences. This does not imply, however, that the ideas of intimacy, the sharing of experiences and the intertwining of subjectivities – indeed, not even the curious interplay of simultaneity and repetition – are chimeras. The only chimera is the idea of reading as identical repetition. The idea of simultaneity makes sense, since to the reader what is happening is happening while he reads it, although he is well aware of reading, say, a fiction that imagines what happened in Carthage centuries ago. This consciousness of a re-staging of what is long gone makes the idea of repetition acceptable. However, in knowing that what is read is not a report, but a fantasy, what the reader may re-experience is the imaginings of the writer because, prima facie, it seems likely that the experiences of writing and reading should have something in common, but, without further information, we do not know what. Still, the reader knows that he has invested imaginary powers to reach to the recesses of his mind, and by analogy he presumes that both the writer and other readers have used similar resources. There is, however, little possibility of deciding about the similarity of the process and its contents in the writing and in the different readings except through concurrent statements about the nature of the mental acts involved and agreement about the interpretation of the text. Nevertheless, reading what poets and authors write about the process of writing, one finds evidence that in certain respects the mental processes of production and reception are similar. Thus, subjectivities are in fact intertwined through what seems an intimate process. Carroll beautifully stages these processes as collective dreaming by means of the narrative. And one of the roles of literature is precisely that it makes dream-sharing possible.

As the product of the imaginative and linguistic labour of another subject, the text is novel and strange to the reader. It is not only a question of making sense of the text by drawing on previous existing knowledge and experiences; the literary text also adds to the reader's stock of experiences, albeit imaginary ones. The supplementation of personal experiences by imaginative ones is necessary because the range of personal experience is absolutely inadequate to the capacity of our mind. The limitations to experience are others: our bodies, the community, and we ourselves.

Our bodies move within a time-space continuum that is foreign to the mind. Our bodies are frail and their capacity limited, while in imagination every hardship may be overcome. Further, a body has only one life to live, and even if the individual mind dies with the body, it contains, while alive, blueprints for a number of alternative lives; some worked out in some details, others barely sketched. Such blueprints are the homemade fictions of the subject. Thus, to what was said above about the inadequacy of the body should be added the fact that it lets us down because it does not multiply to suit our desires; hence, only flights of imagination are possible (this may be the reason for a persistent topos from Plato throughout Western literature: the body as the prison of the soul).

Communities distinguish between actions that are allowed and actions that are prohibited and between actions that are prescribed and those that are voluntary. Then there are the actions that are not prohibited, but frowned upon, and those that are not prescribed, but much encouraged. In most communities, however, there is a bigger or lesser gap between what it is forbidden or prescribed to do and what it is forbidden or prescribed to share with others in the form of fictions.

To these two limitations to what can or may be experienced in person can be added a third, which is also rooted in cultural norms but that is, so to speak, interiorized; namely, experiences that would be horrifying or revolting if we were confronted with them in reality, but that are thrilling when represented as fictions. Thus, we are able to enjoy even misfortunes, disasters, and death. As Aristotle remarks, 'we enjoy looking at accurate likenesses of things which are themselves painful to see, obscene beasts, for instance, and corpses' (1927: 13–15, 1448b). The enjoyment is further grounded in the fact that reading literature makes it possible to safely experience vicariously what is forbidden and punished, including what would go against the reader's conscience to witness were it really taking place.

Thus, the licence granted the poet is paralleled by the fact that the constraints and restrictions enforced by the community on the actions of its members are, more or less as the case may be, attenuated with regard to what they are allowed to read. In addition to this more indulgent attitude of those in power, there is an equally important symmetry between poet and reader. Concerning the utterer, it was claimed that the creation of one or more fictional voices who narrate what has never happened means access to and the expression of what would otherwise remain unsaid (see p. 244). These reports about the non-existing told by non-existent I's are directed to a readership that they attempt to engage and seduce by their existential relevance and poetical and rhetorical qualities. If this enterprise is successful, an internal dialogue between self and other begins, unconsciously as well as consciously. Because this dialogue is fuelled by the readers' own desires, the readers may react in a much more passionate way than would be expected from a purely practical point of view. At the same time, however, the literary text does not offer any direct possibility of action because the only access to its universe is through imagination. Because of the impossibility of influencing the text's universe, the reading has – in principle – no practical import, and the ensuing attenuation of responsibility and obligations may make the interpenetration of self and other more thorough than is possible in daily business. This means an enlargement of our minds, and an enlargement we are ourselves instrumental in bringing about.

6.6 Reading as Iconizing

Although literature does question common norms and ideas, I do not find this sufficient reason for the often violent reactions to it. However, literature also mimes or stages, as it were, desires and passions, that is, it invites not only intellectual understanding, but empathy. Furthermore, the mental processes active in reading fiction predispose the reader to react emotionally, because in order to make sense of a fictional universe of discourse the reader has (as pointed out by Ingarden [1931] and Iser [1978]) to supplement what is not mentioned, but is presupposed. In this sense literature, even the theatre performance, serves as a script:

> ... let us, ciphers to this great accompt,
> On your imaginary forces work,
> ...
> Piece out our imperfections with your
> Thoughts;
> Into a thousand parts divide one man,
> And make imaginary puissance;

> Think when we talk of horses, that you see them
> Printing their proud hoofs i' the receiving earth;
> For 'tis your thoughts that now must deck our kings,
> Carry them here and there, jumping o'er times,
> Turning the accomplishments of many years
> Into an hour-glass ...
> (*Henry V*, prologue)

There is, however, an indefinite number of equally valid ways of realizing what is indicated but not specified in the text, especially in the translation of the symbolic signs of the text into iconic ones. Intersemiotic translation always uses the stock of knowledge of the translator in question, and there is a 'private component' to every stock of knowledge (see Schutz and Luckmann 1973: 112). Thus, when a character or scene is imagined, there will be widely different solutions determined by the experiences and imaginary force of the individual reader, but solutions that may still be within the possibilities delimited by the significations of the linguistic text. Such intersemiotic translation is effectuated in public by the director, the scene painter, and the stage master, and by the actors, of course, who together transform the symbolic signs of the drama into iconic and indexical signs to fill the empty stage for an audience – and everybody knows the power of a staging to spoil or realize the wonders of a text. Such realizations of the text, 'its transmutation' as Jakobson calls this form of translation, are active in furthering the emotional engagement of the reader, because to iconize literary texts most often means to call up images related to memories and fantasies that are drive-cathected because they are related to the intimate and emotional life of the recipient.

6.6.1 *Three Ways of Iconizing the Literary Text*

Since there are three types of iconic signs, images, diagrams, and metaphors, there should also be three ways to iconize the text during reading. And indeed there are. The three ways are, first, the production of mental images triggered by what is represented in the literary text, that is, imaginative iconization, or imaginization; second, the structuring of what is represented as a network of relationships, i.e., diagrammatization; and third, the relating of elements and relationships of the universe represented in the text to other conceptual structures, i.e., allegorization.

6.6.1.1 Imaginization

Imaginization has to do with the use of imagination in linking the symbolic signs of the text with iconic ones. In fact some readers claim to experience reading, say a novel, like going to the cinema, since the text becomes realized as a movie on their internal screen. It must be stressed, however, that although vision is very powerful, imaginative iconization covers the different modes of perception. With regard to literature, this is especially important because the realization of both sound images and rhythm and the linking of these with emotions play an important role in reading poetry.

Furthermore, when the iconized text deals with representations of lifeworld and human interaction, enjoyment and suffering, it becomes invested with fragments of the readers' personal knowledge. This is why there is a double, and prima facie self-contradictory, reason for people's often passionate reaction to literature. On the one hand, readers are thrilled by visions or stories that are definitely coming to them from the outside and bringing something novel that enlarges their minds. On the other hand, in relating to the fictional universe they necessarily bring in memories and fantasies, and consequently also the love and hate, and the triumphs and humiliations they have gone through. Hence, reading literature means unconsciously, and sometimes consciously as well, working with two sets of references, one referring to the universe of the text, the other one to the lifeworld and the memories of the reader. The constant intertwining of these two sets of references ends in identification. That this is the case is also borne out by our sensory-motor reactions to exciting moments in literary texts.

Today every student of literature knows that this personal iconization makes for a bad reading because it brings to the literary text something foreign that will probably distort and trivialize it. Thus, so the story goes, the reader turns his back on the intricate fabric of significations and aesthetic devices and effects and reduces the text to a pretext for enjoying private reverie. I agree that bad readings, irresponsible and self-indulgent readings that go against the significations of the text, will often be the outcome of this practice. I must admit, however, that I don't see how we can put an end to it.[14] I am also confident that expert readers do the same thing. Indeed, they should read in this way because if they don't, they will miss an important way of experiencing the text and be blind to one of literature's main functions. They are just better at following the text's instructions.

To view the literary text as a set of instructions for different ways of iconization may be useful. And despite the fact that iconization is not restricted to vision, let us inquire a little further into the pictorial mode of imaginative iconization. First of all, it should be pointed out that literature favours imaginazation because attention is not directed outwards from text to lifeworld of the readers but inwards. The verbal representation is not compared and matched with perception; rather its instructions are matched with the imagined iconic representation it calls forth. As to instructions, literary texts differ widely both in the number and wealth of details and in the selection criteria of such clues for iconization. The study of literary descriptive techniques, of imagery and clichés, shows that different literary periods and movements each favour certain sets of rhetorical devices and have stock characterizations of scenery and characters. Some movements offer rich instructions for the imaginative iconization of the readers (as for instance both romanticism and realism, but in different ways); others are less generous (classicism).

A difficult question is the level of consciousness of imaginative iconization. Obviously, this process may be fully conscious; the reader, using partly the text's instructions, partly his memories and fantasy, actually sees with the mind's eye a character, a scene, a piece of action. However, most schools of psychology do agree that most mental processes are unconscious. Consequently, it seems likely that what calls forth conscious and emotionally charged images that, in addition to the text's instructions, are based on memory and fantasy also has an impact on similar unconscious processes.

Since these processes are more or less opaque even to the imagining subject, they seem little accessible for scholarly study. However, even if the precise nature of the images of individual readers is largely inaccessible, or at least only accessible through interviews (perhaps supported by tests), it may be possible to investigate types of images related to verbal descriptions of scenes and actions.

First of all, the text itself to a certain extent delimits what can and cannot count as valid imaginative transmutations, or an iconic exemplification, of it. A famous scene from *Madame Bovary* may illustrate this point:

> They gradually began to talk more frequently of matters outside their love, and in the letters that Emma wrote him she spoke of flowers, poetry, the moon and the stars, naïve resources of a waning passion striving to keep itself alive by all external aids. She was constantly promising herself a profound happiness on her next trip; then she confessed to herself that

> she had felt nothing extraordinary. This disappointment quickly gave way to a new hope, and Emma returned to him more avid and enflamed that before. She undressed brutally, ripping off the thin laces of her corset so violently that they would whistle round her hips like a gliding snake. She went on tiptoe, barefooted, to see once more that the door was locked, then with one movement, she would let her clothes fall at once to the ground; – then, pale and serious, without a word, she would throw herself against his breast with a long shudder.
>   Yet there was upon that brow covered with cold drops, on those stammering lips, in those wild eyes, in the grip of those arms, something strange, vague and sinister that seemed to Léon to be subtly gliding between them to force them apart. (Flaubert 1965: 205)

When *Madame Bovary* was charged with offending against public morals, this scene was cited by the prosecutor as admirable from the point of view of art but execrable from the point of view of morality. Indeed, today it may be considered outspoken, even graphic. Here it may exemplify that there is, first, a certain order of events that has to be respected. For instance, she drops her clothes after she has assured herself that the door is locked; it is the last act described before she throws herself at Léon's breast. Second, certain details are highlighted in the verbal description, for instance, the synaesthetic description of her ripping the thin laces of her corset. Third, a representation, which may count as an iconic exemplification of a linguistic text, has not only to be true to the order of events and significant details, it must also conform to the mood and emotional tenor of the text. In this case, any iconic representation staging Emma as an unworried person happily and carelessly enjoying sensual pleasures will be invalid. Fourth, however, there is very much indeed that is not specified at all: what dress is Emma wearing, how does she look in the nude? It would be a fair guess, indeed, that Léon is already in bed when Emma throws herself 'against his breast with a long shudder,' but in fact the text does not say so; he may just as well be standing.

Second, analysis of imaginization will use the knowledge that many objects, scenes, and actions have a limited set of typical realizations to fill in what is presupposed but not mentioned. There is a certain number of ways things are usually done and conceived, because within a given culture the members share a cultural competence. Within cognitive philosophy and semantics, especially in the work of Lakoff and Johnson, the integration of perception and conceptual knowledge is taken for granted, that is, our images are structured both by image-schemata and by stereotypes on the basic level (see chapter 1, p. 59). In this view, it is possible to describe typical mental imagery, or at least pertinent features of it, because it is linked both with common species-particular experiences and with conceptual structures within a culture. Furthermore, a stock of clichés, for instance pictorial, will exist that iconological studies may show to be common to the members of a culture, or to communities within it.

Imaginization is certainly subjective and personal, and it is precisely the fact that it uses personal and private experiences that gives it its emotional force. However, one should not confuse subjectivity, and not even the personal, with uniqueness. On the contrary, subjectivity is based on properties that we share as a species, properties related to age and sex, cultural properties, and properties characteristic of the communities to which we belong. This is true of mental imagery and fantasies as well. Although two readers will only rarely exemplify a symbolic representation with identical images, they may well be similar. Discussions of book illustrations and movies based on works of literature show that many people have vague, but nevertheless resistant, mental images of scenes and characters that allow them to launch an articulate criticism at other iconic exemplifications.

There is, however, a limit to the efficaciousness of imaginization, because in spite of claims made by some readers, it is hard to believe that anyone can experience a whole novel, say *War and Peace*, as a movie – if this claim is meant literally, not hyperbolically. As the example from *Madame Bovary* shows, the amount of work demanded for consciously filling in what is not mentioned in the text itself would be stunning (although, of course, there are different levels of perceiving and imaginizing). Anyway, other readers only experience fragments of the text, tableaux and scenes with the mind's eye – and texts only give instructions for the imaginization of parts of a scene, for imaginizing certain details while leaving it to readers to create pictorial unity (or unity within other perceptual modes). Hence, even if image-processing is constantly going on at an unconscious level, only fragments thereof need to become conscious. The dominant way of experiencing a literary text is for many readers not as a continuous flow of images, the inner movie theatre; it is diagrammatic. This bring us to the second way of iconizing the text.

6.6.1.2 Diagrammatization

Diagrammatization is abstractive, systematic, and concerned with the totality of the text, not with focusing on details. Concretely, some readers are less concerned with realizing images than with keeping track of the semantic attributes of the text elements, and see transformations and reversals as something abstract that affects the relations between the different parts of the text. They somehow look at the text as an algebraic structure, albeit a very peculiar kind of algebra.

It is a dogma of Peircean semiotics that signification presupposes the dynamic interaction between the iconic, indexical, and symbolic dimensions of signs, and to this dogma I myself subscribe. However, even if signification, in the last analysis, presupposes the possibility of intersemiotic translation, the different sign systems of human communication, and especially language, possess a relative autonomy, in the sense that understanding is possible without any conscious translation into other sign systems. During conversation or reading, we simply do not translate all parts of the text into still or moving pictures, and nevertheless we understand it. Hence, we need not consciously activate all semiotic connections in the mind to make sense of a text.

We do need, however, to keep track of relations and transformations on the given semiotic level. For instance, in reading the earlier quoted poem by Blake (see p. 230), we may remember the expression of gratified desire of one or several partners at one or several occasions, that is, it may trigger a number of individual memories and mental images. In many readers, however, this will not happen at all, or it may at least not be the first and principal effect of reading the poem. Instead, the reader may first notice its parallelism, that is, the almost identical wording of the two parts, the repetition of the rhyme, and its repeated question/answer structure. Second, as pointed out earlier, the poem may be interpreted as stating two universal affirmative propositions: (1) every man wants to make certain that he gratifies the desire of his female partner, and (2) every woman wants to make certain that she gratifies the desire of her male partner. It is a piece of gnomic poetry, a riddle, that attempts to establish what is universally – or perhaps we should say, desired to be universally – true. Instead of provoking mental images, the poem is preoccupied with sound because its sound shape supports its meaning and significance. Its formal and material properties are designed to convince or persuade the readers about its truth. And to understand it we only need to know the meaning of the words and recognize their concatenation. Such a reading is concerned with proportion and reciprocity, in the particular respect treated by the poem: man is to woman as woman is to man. The point of the poem is not at all to give instructions that may trigger vivid images. In fact, it seems to be about an image-schema rather than about basic-level images. Among the image-schemata mentioned by Mark Johnson is one called *matching* (Johnson 1987: 126), and because the two relationships mentioned in the poem are reciprocal and symmetrical, it seems to me that this poem offers an example of matching.

Texts call for, at least unconsciously, diagrammatization of relations and transformations at different levels. Such activities are systematized within the study of literature, especially within the semiotic tradition from Russian formalism to cognitive semantics. This effort is really an effort of discovering text properties, not of inventing them and adding to the text. In contradistinction to imaginative iconization, which clearly adds an iconic exemplification to the text (like a director who embeds the written text within an iconic exemplification), the diagrammatization of the text claims to lay bare what is already there. It is not a claim that a given particular diagram of the text is the only possible one at the level in question, but a claim that it is a valid representation of textual relations that may be pointed out in the text. For instance, the two great folklorists Vladimir Propp and Bengt Holbek, who builds on Köngas Maranda (see here p. 207), each made thorough studies of the folk tale, but they ended up with very different diagrams of its narrative structure. In my opinion, both diagrammatizations are valid because they structure the tales according to well-defined criteria.[15]

Concerning the relationship between images and words in literature, diagrammatization seems to favour words and to work with lexical meanings without calling forth rich imagery. It may be, however, that this is not the proper way to describe what is going on. Perhaps diagrammatization works with relations on both the level of language and that of image-schemata, with syntax, in an extended sense, within the verbal system (comparable to relations between objects within the non-verbal system). Furthermore, there is an important advantage in relying only on the linguistic level of meaning formation, namely, that it speeds up the process of understanding. While reading Blake's poem, we may consciously disregard any image on the basic level, only attending to the isomorphic nature of the semantico-syntactic structures. Thus, whether or not we are aware of it, we are dealing with (significant) form itself, as Mark Johnson would say.

Hence, diagrammatization is a process whose contribution to text

334   Part Two: The Four Dimensions of the Literary Text

understanding consists in the progressive linking of parts in the unfolding of the text. Novel meanings are created, not by virtue of modification of the semantic content of words or of basic-level mental images, but through the novel juxtaposition and combination of ready-made concepts. For instance, Holbek is not redefining either the conception of the young male or the young female or that of the meaning of active versus passive. He is offering a novel interpretation by noticing how these traditionally defined entities are combined differently in the course of the tale.

6.6.1.3 Allegorization

The metaphoric reading, finally, means to allegorize the text continuously. To allegorize means speaking otherwise than one seems to speak, and thus allegorical interpretation means looking for a second meaning.[16] In addition to the *sensus litteralis*, the common signification of words and the reference to historical facts, the interpreter is searching for a *sensus plenior*, a more profound meaning that is not apparent. Allegorical reading is a kind of abstractive and applicative enterprise that attempts to attune the text to what were, or are currently considered important aesthetic, moral, or epistemological issues. Thus, Paul writes to the Galatians:

> For it is written that Abraham had two sons, the one by a bondmaid, the other by a freewoman.
> But he *who was* of the bondwoman was born after the flesh; but he of the freewoman *was* by promise.
> Which things are an allegory: for these are the two covenants; the one from the mount Sinai, which gendereth to bondage, which is Agar.
> For this Agar is mount Sinai in Arabia, and answereth to Jerusalem which now is, and is in bondage with her children.
> But Jerusalem which is above is free, which is the mother of us all.
> (4: 22–6)

The underlying structural device of this little passage is analogy (see chapter 4), and it is already rather complex. It uses oppositions and identifications: Isaac is opposed to Ishmael as Sarah is to Hagar, and as Isaac is identified with the New Covenant, Ishmael is identified with the Old. Furthermore, Hagar is identified with Mount Sinai, which is identified with the Jerusalem of this world, and the latter is opposed to the Jerusalem above. Thus, there are transcateogrical linkings of different domains, persons (i.e., mothers and sons), locations, landscape and city, and contractual relationships between man and a Supreme Being. But this is not the whole point. The current interest of this allegory is, according to Paul, that the Galatian brothers are, like Isaac, the children of promise, and that they should stand fast in their Christian freedom and not 'entangle again with the yoke of bondage.' Thus, an application is added that itself adds another analogy to the semantic tissue, namely, as Ishmael is to Isaac so are the gentiles to the Galatians.[17]

In the attempt of making the following Old Testament text conform to a Christian interpretation – 'Thy teeth are like a flock of sheep that are shorn which came up from the washing, whereof every one bears twins, and none is barren among them' (Song of Solomon 4: 2) – Augustine expounds the principles that, on his view, ought to guide Christian allegorizing:

> For why is it, I ask, that if any one says that there are holy and just men whose life and conversation the Church of Christ uses as a means of redeeming those who come to it from all kinds of superstitions, and making them through their imitation of good men members of its own body; men who, as good and true servants of God, have come to the baptismal font laying down the burdens of the world, and who rising thence do, through the implanting of the Holy Spirit, yield the fruit of a two-fold love, a love, that is, of God and their neighbor; – how is it, I say, that if a man says this, he does not please his hearer so much as when he draws the same meaning from that passage in Canticles, where it is said of the Church, when it is being praised under the figure of a beautiful woman, 'Thy teeth are like a flock of sheep that are shorn which came up from the washing, whereof every one bears twins, and none is barren among them?' Does the hearer learn anything more than when he listens to the same thought expressed in the plainest language, without the help of this figure? And yet, I don't know why, I feel greater pleasure in contemplating holy men, when I view them as the teeth of the Church, tearing men away from their errors, and bringing them into the Church's body, with all their harshness softened down, just as if they had been torn off and masticated by the teeth. It is with the greatest pleasure, too, that I recognize them under the figure of sheep that have been shorn, laying down the burthens of the world like fleeces, and coming up from the washing, i.e., from baptism, and all bearing twins, i.e., the twin commandments of love, and none among them barren in that holy fruit. (Augustine 1952a: 638 [II, 7])

As to the question of figurative language in general, Augustine makes two points. First the alternation of literal and figurative language in the Bible is due to God's wish, on the one hand, to give clear directions concerning faith and morals, but, on the other, to humble the proud by making its interpretation difficult (ibid.). Second, he gives a more psychological explanation: the plain passages stills the readers' spiritual thirst for guidance in matters of faith, while the figurative passages prevent the readers from becoming satiated and stimulates their appetite for understanding.

From our point of view, Augustine's principle of interpretation may seem obscure. However, the principle is clearly to align the biblical passage to the Christian faith (as laid down by the church). He is quite explicit concerning this principle:

> Whoever, then, thinks that he understands the Holy Scriptures, or any part of them, but puts such an intepretation upon them as does not tend to build up this twofold love of God and our neighbor, does not yet understand them as he ought. If, on the other hand, a man draws a meaning from them that may be used for the building up of love, even though he does not happen upon the precise meaning which the author whom he reads intended to express in that place, his error is not pernicious, and he is wholly clear from the charge of deception. (1952a: 634 [I, 40])

In accordance with this general principle, Augustine derives the following rule for dealing with figurative language:

> Whatever there is in the word of God that cannot, when taken literally, be referred either to purity of life or soundness of doctrine, you may set down as figurative. Purity of life has reference to the love of God and one's neighbor; soundness of doctrine to the knowledge of God and one's neighbor. (1952a: 661 [III, 14])

Since allegory is species of metaphor, it is no wonder that allegorizing is a process that starts in the text itself. In fact, there seems to be an allegorical side to most, maybe all, literary texts, and some genres, such as the fable, make it a main feature. But that allegories need not be didactic is evident from Anacreon's very short, but complete, albeit implicit, allegory: 'Pray, why do you look askance at me, my Thracian filly, and shun me so resolutely as though I knew nothing of my art? I would have you to know I could bridle you right well and take rein and ride you about the turning-post of the course. But instead you graze in the meadows and frisk and frolic to your heart's content; for you have no clever breaker to ride you' (84 in *Lyra graeca* 1944: 181). What is this little poem about? Interestingly, it contains no clues whatsoever as to its allegorical nature. Why is it also about nubile maidens (a fact already stressed by the appended commentary in the *Lyra Graeca*), not only about fillies? The answer may be that the poem's basic analogy, that rider is to horse as man is to woman (very far from Blake's non-allegorical proportion woman : man : : man : woman), already explores pre-existing cultural stereotypes: sexual intercourse is like riding and to make a newly-wed woman obedient is like domesticating and breaking in a precious animal (Alcman has a direct comparison of maidens and horses). Furthermore, without the allegory, although it is objectionable, it would become, not void of meaning, but less interesting.

The thirst for metaphorical iconization, that is, allegorization, is part of our general quest for meaning. In case the reader believes that the second meaning is (thought to be) guaranteed by some kind of absolute authority, its importance is obvious. However, even when knowledge is considered fallible,[18] transcateogrical linking is often seen as something precious, despite the fact that it is well known that a difference persists between the elements belonging to the different categories (see below). There are, it seems to me, two reasons for this appreciation of the second meaning. First, the linking of two or more domains means that the principal domain is understood in the light of the other(s). The objectionable metaphor in Anacreon's poem, by giving a glimpse of how very many Greek men then looked at women, offers valid, albeit grim, information about sexual and marital relationships at that time. Precisely because it is highly charged, ideologically and emotionally, it tells us something significant about their attitudes. Hence, metaphorically created meaning is valuable both from a cognitive and an emotional point of view.

Second, even if second meanings do not reveal inappealable truths, they are felt to enrich the text in question simply by creating connections. The indication that what is represented is not only itself, but simultaneously a sign of something else, endows texts, lifeworlds, and human beings with a complexity that is most often conceived of as a profundity, because it is felt that new dimensions are added to the phenomena. Kafka's *The Trial* is not only about Joseph K.'s falling victim to the weird courts operating in the attics of the city. It is also about a person succumbing to his cruel superego, or about the mechanisms of dictatorship.

Finally, in allegorization there is most often, or always, a quest for the generic. The bondwoman Hagar and her son Ishmael are individual beings, but they are taken to represent the Old Covenant. Joseph K. too is an individual person, but allegorized he may, among other things, represent the son unsuccessfully trying to break away from the law of the father. When we allegorize the text, we are not trying to connect it with personal memories or fantasies; we rather attempt to tie it up with culturally shared patterns of interpretation. Paul's reading of Genesis 16–21 is an attempt to project a Christian reading onto an Old Testament text, and in doing so he applies the most general, and the most important, interpretive principle he knows. Hence, allegorization embodies general relationships or principles in a concrete case, and thereby, in addition to being a phenomenon, state of affairs, or action in its own right, what is represented becomes an example of what is generally believed to be the case.

6.6.2 Reading as Iconization

Even if, in different readers, one mode of iconizing the text may become predominant, the concrete reading process will switch between these levels. Sometimes the reading provokes a vivid image, or a series of images, whether visual, auditory, even olfactory, or of taste or touch, or weak feelings of pleasure or pain. Sometimes the text is experienced as a diagram, an equation, or a parallelogram of forces; and sometimes it is taken to exemplify conceptual structures contemporary with that of the text or with that of the reader. All three ways of reading are not only valuable, they are necessary for reading literature; otherwise the text will remain black marks on the paper.

The interplay between the three kinds of iconization will determine the nature and pace of the reading process. To actualize the rhythm and sound pattern of the text or to produce visual imagery from description and dialogue means dwelling on smaller segments of the text and thus breaking up the journey to look at self-created sights (or to listen to sounds). Reading diagrammatically means an effort to knit together the different parts of what is represented in the chain of signs. In this case the meaning of any segment of the text will depend upon its role and place in the text's process of transformation. Such a reading will tend to have a certain drive that urges on the reader to solve its riddles by knowing the end and, from this position, surveying it as a network of spatial relations, a kind of semantic skeleton. The allegorical reading, like the imaginative, also slows down the reading process because it is an attempt to relate textual patterns of meaning to another text that seems to belong to its immediate interpretants but which, nevertheless, has to be produced by the reader. In spite of the difficulties just mentioned, the ability, and necessity, to switch between the three readings will guarantee a good deal of common ground between the readings of members within the same culture.

Depending on genre, period, and movement, literary texts differ in whether they give priority to imaginization, diagrammatization, or allegorization. Some texts, like for instance gnomic poetry, favour the diagrammatic and allegoric, while realistic narrative favours imaginative iconization and pretends that allegorization, as a species of metaphor, does not matter at all – an illusion of course. However, although such differences are important, the efficiency and value of literature is to a large extent dependent on its simultaneous cultivation of all three modes of iconization. This makes it possible to dwell on the imaginative possibilities offered by the text, to experience it as representing a nearly, but not totally, coherent universe within which developments and transformations almost have a logic of their own, and finally it may point to an almost perfect matching between elements and structures of the text and a second pattern of signification.

In all three cases, however, there are openings, alternative ways of patterning, and partial mismatches. With regard to imaginative iconization, the translation of symbolic into iconic sign, only something, but certainly not everything, is prescribed (cf. a director's staging of a play). Diagrammatization clearly offers alternatives on different levels: one can choose between different systems of representation (e.g., geometric or arithmic representation and between curves and columns). Furthermore, diagrams are based on interpretations, and thus alternative interpretations (i.e., alternative linkings of elements) will produce different diagrams. Allegorization – metaphoric iconization – is, by the very nature of its process, bound to reveal mismatches, differences, incompatibilities.

Ricoeur's definition of a metaphor as a calculated category mistake (see Ricoeur 1978) points to the interplay between similarity and difference in any species of metaphor: Achilles is NOT a lion, old age is NOT the end of a day, the beloved's voice is NOT 'deeper than all roses,' two adulterous lovers are NOT 'mice playing when the cat is away,' and the evening is NOT 'spread out against the sky like a patient etherized upon the table.' All these metaphors contain the 'like' of Eliot's simile. And with reference to the examples used in this chapter it is equally evident that Peter, the Apostle, is NOT a rock, that sexual intercourse is NOT riding, and that patriarchal abuse of women is NOT breaking in an animal. There is an inherent split in metaphors, an imperfect match between the domains they align that simultaneously creates a surplus and a deficit of meaning, a 'too little' and a 'too much.' If we look at the mismatch in terms, on the one hand, from the perspective of propositional content and, on the other, in terms of basic-level images, one might say that the acceptance of metaphors seem to call just as much for suppression as for integration. Understanding and accepting the proposition 'Achilles is a lion' means disregarding many aspects of basic-level images that might be called forth by it. For instance, it means suppressing or disregarding the furriness and the beige or yellow colour of the lion's skin, its quadrupedity, its ways of hunting down animals, and so forth. The raison d'être of 'Achilles is a lion' is given by Aristotle as the fact that both are courageous. 'Courage,' however, is a dispositional term that indicates the habitual behaviour of the subject. It cannot be represented by one mental image because it is redeemed by repeated action, that is, narratively. Understanding the metaphor 'Achilles is a lion' means, I surmise, interpreting it as saying: 'It is in the nature of Achilles to act courageously' because, so the story goes, 'lions by nature act courageously.' One point that has often been made is, of course, that at present almost everybody knows that it is void of sense to claim that lions are courageous. Another point is, however, that, in making sense of the metaphor, we are consciously disregarding the elements that would make it absurd, that is, the furry yellow-skinned Achilles fighting his enemies on all fours. Indeed, bearing in mind that dispositional terms cannot be represented pictorially, one might say that linguistic metaphors in general, not only dead metaphors, seem to suppress very many basic-level images because such images would reveal the inherent incompatibility of the elements of metaphor.

The marked strangeness of visual metaphor may be proof of the suppressive function of its linguistic cousin. Figure 18 is a very simple example: Ferdinand Khnopp's symbolist painting *L'art, les caresses ou le sphinx* (Art, the caresses or the sphinx, 1896). The meaning of 'she is a leopard' will probably be interpreted as 'she is beautiful, graceful, lithe, attractive, but extremely dangerous and without mercy,' and no mental

Figure 18

(visual) image at all needs to accompany this interpretation. Looking at the painting, however, the strangeness of its motive is striking. We are not allowed to disregard its impossibility.

Earlier I proposed that staying at the level of linguistic semantics allows us to get and share a quick and uncontroversial understanding of the text in question. Now, at least according to the argument made above, it seems that linguistic metaphor acts similarly. Instead of calling forth a rich imagery, it seems to focus our attention on compatibility rather than on divergence because mental imagery is disregarded. Hence, the deal that language offers us is that we get access to semantic markers that are summative and part of a collective learning process. We need not necessarily turn to images, whether these are cultural cliches or more closely related to the autobiography of the interpreter. The treat is, however, that we can always choose the other alternative. For instance, we can insist on realizing the imaginative potential of a linguistic impression, and, at any time, we may summarize and translate perception into propositions, as when we say: 'Khnopp represents a woman as a leopard.' We may even, in language, approach the pictorial representation by saying: 'In this painting Khnopp represents a leopard-woman.'

6.7 A Space of One's Own

There is, however, still another aspect to reading literature. To host a literary text means to make room for another mind, including signs of unconscious significations and pulsations; and thus there is a dialectic of self-representation and other-representation at work in reading. [19] Moods, actions, events, thoughts, and attitudes of the text call forth corresponding (or contrasting) ones in the reader. The text functions partially like a screen on which are projected the fears, desires, moods, memories, and fantasies of the reader. This is the projective movement in the reading of fiction during which the text becomes coloured with conscious and unconscious material brought to it by the reader. But there is an introjective movement as well. The text, or rather some of its features and relations, becomes part of the reader's conscious or unconscious memory. We do remember (parts of) what we read, we may recall it at will, or we are indirectly brought to recognize that it plays an important role in our fantasies, even in those that we did not know that we had. There is, however, a third way of responding to poems and narratives: by identification. This process is publicly displayed in the play of children by their eagerness to impersonate the hero(ine) and by their attempts to avoid the role of the villain or to change the script if the lot falls on them. In reading, identification is silent but need not be less forceful; the tears that are spent on the tragic fate of the hero(ine) are not only those of pity, they are certainly those of self-pity as well.

Convincing evidence of the strong identificatory element in the reading of fiction is given by mass literature's catering to the ideals and fantasies of specific readerships. It offers role models ready-made for identification. They also flatter the self-image of the readers by using a language of desire that readers find daring but nevertheless acceptable to their norms and fantasies; compare the difference between romances addressed to a female readership and the hard-boiled, sexually outspoken series created for men.

Identification is also partly responsible for the fact that although we certainly know that what we read is fiction, we forget that while we read. On one level we do believe in the reality of the fictional characters, however implausibly they are described. Both we and the author are touched, as Andersen declared he was, by the fate of the Little Mermaid, as if she were one of us, although there is no doubt about her non-human status; indeed, in addition to being fictional, she is also a fabulous being: half-human, half-animal. And, more importantly, we are touched by her fate, despite the fact that if asked whether we believe that the indexical expression 'the Little Mermaid' refers to a being capable of suffering, we would answer that she is in fact made up of the words of Andersen's text and, consequently, incapable of any emotions at all. But this is not strange at all, since we in our own dreams are certainly capable of being touched by the fate of creatures that we, on waking up, know to be creatures of our own imagination.

These projective, introjective, and identificatory processes are illuminatingly united in D.C. Winnicott's description of the transitional object. The transitional object should be distinguished from the internal object, which is mental, and from the external object as well. In childhood, it is most often a concrete object such as a teddy bear. This object is characterized by its ambiguous status. Separated from the child and recognized as belonging to the outside, it is also called the 'first not-me possession.' Furthermore, it is, according to Winnicott, 'never under magical control like the internal object, nor is it outside control as the real mother is' (Winnicott 1971: 10). It has a very special status: it is highly drive-cathected, and it has to be present whenever the child asks for it. It must remain unchangeable, and its loss provokes anxiety and anger. Nor can a similar item, at first, be substituted for it, although the child may recognize that the substitute in itself is the more attractive. With this object at the centre, a half-way region, to use Freud's term, is created, in which the psychic reality of the child merges with outside reality. In the psychical development of the child, this is an early state that is succeeded by the full-fledged distinction between inner and outer. This, as Winnicott calls it, 'intermediary area' or 'potential space' between self and non-self (originally between infant and mother) is *'allowed to the infant between primary creativity and objective perception based on reality-testing'* (ibid.: 11; italics in orig.). This transitional phenomenon is further said to represent an early stage in the use of illusion which allows the infant to believe that what it creates really exists. At first, this area is the necessary precondition for the establishment of the relation between infant and reality. But it remains with us because we need a place where we can meet that which is foreign as if it belonged to ourselves, and we need to meet ourselves as if we were others. Even privileged moments of love and friendship, encounters in which self and other seem to merge, although extremely valuable (indeed, probably more so than interacting with transitional objects), are not quite the same. According to Winnicott, the possibility of psychotherapy is related to the transitional area, since it takes place 'in the overlap of two areas of playing' (ibid.: 38). Indeed, therapy is 'two people playing together' (the model being the mother and child playing).

From a semiotic perspective, the value of the transitional object lies in its being both an icon of desire and something lying outside of the subject. It functions as an extension of the subject, sufficiently malleable to become a sign of his or her inner world, but is also independent and structured enough to represent another world as well. It resists becoming entirely absorbed in the inner world of the subject because even iconic signs are perceived, and thus they demand an attenuated form of reality testing.

That language functions as a transitional phenomenon seems accurate because young children handle language as a material and signifying object and as an instrument suited both to express their desires through auto-communication and to satisfy them by communicating with others. Furthermore, even if the child indulges in fantasies of reigning over its little world by the omnipotence of its words, speech (like its teddy bear) comes to it from the outside. Indeed, in order to accommodate language to its own desires and fears, the child attempts to expropriate something that is common property and that it is allowed to share by learning it. But speech and language resist the child's efforts to mould them entirely to its imagination. On the contrary, they become one of the most important moulds that shapes the further development of the individual person. Nevertheless, language as a transitional object is never really given up; it survives in the personalized and poetic uses of language, primarily in literature.

Literature is eminently fit to function as a transitional object because it invites, indeed necessitates, the cooperation of its reader. Thus, reading means escaping into the making of a transitional space, the potential space of illusion, and while furnishing and populating it, the reader is not disturbed by interventions and demands from others. However, another subject is already inside the mind of the reader. But its silent, non-obtrusive, but nevertheless insistent, otherness (the text is also an interpellation) becomes an advantage in the construction of the fictional universe, because it relieves the reader of some of the responsibility for actualizing the text's significations and the images they provoke. Although reading draws on the reader's libidinal and fantasmatic resources, the subject may reassure him- or herself about calling on them since the realization of the text demands it. This, of course, is a way of fooling the internal censor. What one does not allow oneself to imagine one is much more innocent in reading because one cannot help it (cf. literature as seduction, pp. 304–8). But reading literature transcends the mere lifting of censorship. It may lead to recognition, not only of what one would rather forget or of what one has in fact repressed, but of what was previously foreign but now seems to have become a part of ourselves. This perspective parallels Winnicott's conception of the transitional object, because such objects are said to belong to the space of illusion. Further, as regards the infant, the mother's art is allowing the infant the illusion, or rather double illusion, that it creates what is really given (a toy) and that what it creates really exists, that is, the teddy bear as this unique drive-cathected and signifying transitional object. Similarly, even if the literary text is an artefact endowed with meanings irrespectively of any individual reading in reading it is the reader who allows the transitional object to exist momentarily undisturbed by reality testing. In reading and while reading, the subject is in an emphatic sense creating what is given. At the same time, the reader is half tricked to believe, half allowing him or herself to believe, that what is a potential space of illusion really exists. Reading literature means allowing oneself not only to understand the points, angle, and purpose of the other party of the dialogue but also to assimilate another's vision or narrative, view and perspective and to make them one's own. As pointed out above, what is taken over is a high-powered and highly structured piece of mind, probably more powerful and clear-sighted than the mind that hosts it.

In his study of children's play and intellectual growth, Piaget (1962) distinguishes between accommodation and assimilation. These are two different ways in which the subject interacts adaptively with the environment. Accommodation is the process through which mental structures and schemas are changed in the subject through influences from the outside. The subject accommodates him- or herself in order to achieve an adequate understanding of, and interaction with, the environment. Assimilation designates the process through which the child incorporates outside stimuli into its mental structures without changing the latter, whereas accommodation means mental restructuration. Obviously the two processes are connected, and to Piaget their equilibrium is ideal for psychological development. According to him, accommodation is linked with imitation because by imitating models, the child develops its mental capacities and interacts more easily with the environment. Assimilation, on the other hand, is related to play. At a later stage, accommodation will develop into reflective imitation and assimilation into constructional games.

Whereas psychoanalysis (Freud and Winnicott) is occupied with the affective dimension as related to the figurative, and thus is geared to handle products of the imagination, Piaget is mostly concerned with mental operations (for him the bond with the figurative characterizes early stages of mental development). However, the interaction between accommodation and assimilation catches an important aspect of what is going on in reading fiction. The assimilative aspect of reading literature is obvious: sets, props, narrative, and themes are matched with the memory and fantasy life of the reader through imaginization; and the text's overall structure, its tensions and conflicts, are interpreted to express his or her concerns. In this way the literary text is, consciously and unconsciously, used to recall and vitalize what is already in place. Further, literary texts are split up by the reader, and their elements are stored in different places in the mind, and thus they become set pieces and fragment of scripts used in the personal bricolage of the reader. On the other hand, being also an accommodative process, the reading of literature changes the reader's mental structures. Such changes are plausible because, among other things, literary texts are also iconic exemplifications of cognitive models, especially of complicated scripts for personal and social interaction and for typical and/or proper attitudes in stereotypical situations.[20] This aspect of the reading process is different from the assimilative because it respects the literary text's integrity as a model (i.e., diagrammatization). The metaphorical reading will relate both to the assimilative and to the accommodative mode.

By reading literature, readers are offered models of what they may not (yet) have thought or experienced, and thus their minds may be restructured and enlarged. Such enlargement takes place not only through playing, as in Winnicott and Piaget, but through contemplation. Contemplation is also study, as we are reminded by the epigraph to this chapter taken from St Ignatius. To him contemplation implies a (re)creating – in the mind's eye – of what is narrated, and thus it combines thought and sensuous representation, inquiry and imagination. This complex process in the solitary encounter with the text may lead to self-discovery: not necessarily as conversion or as dramatic new insight, but perhaps only as an inconspicuous growth of understanding that comprises both self and other and their inextricable connection – self-as-other and other-as-self.

6.8 Complexity and Ambiguity in the Communication of Literature

An objective of this presentation of literary communication so far has been to maintain and insist upon its complexity and ambiguity owing to the fact that it is a form of public communication. Literature has, however, an ambiguous place among the other institutions. As closely related to the educational institution, it seems to be at the core of the shaping of the self-understanding and social consciousness of the members of the community. It is, for instance, linked even with the teaching of the mother tongue. Since, however, it simultaneously belongs to entertainment, it is often deemed a luxury that should prosper or perish according to its ability to make an audience or readership pay for it as they do (or do not) for any other commodity.

The tension between being part of the communal treasure and a commodity is but one of the several ambiguities that haunts the communication of literature. Another, closely allied with this one, is the tension between ascribing extraordinary, indeed visionary, powers to the poet (the poet as *vates*) and seeing him or her as an irresponsible and immoral creature caught up in personal and perhaps even sick delusions.

It should be stressed that the ambivalence of public and rulers about literature corresponds to stances assumed by the poets themselves. Poets have always sought to please those in power, or the marketplace, to survive and to get staged or published. There is, however, a further motive: the fact that such an alliance gives them a chance to speak from the centre, as it were, to feel that they are in fact expressing a, maybe *the*, valid version of the understanding and sentiment of the community. Further, in expressing a communal understanding, they often choose the language of the current poetic idiom because it makes them easier to understand, and thus more easily heard. Other poets, however, have sought what to them were authentic modes of experience and honest perspectives on current affairs, irrespective of public opinion and sentiment. Often such a stance is combined with a search for a novel, and in their understanding, authentic poetic expression to succeed the outworn and stale. Thus, poets or writers will see their mission as educating people by changing their mode of perceiving and judging the world (and by changing their literary taste). Or, poets will turn their backs on their audience; they will write for each other and for posterity and count their fiasco with the public as their success (a stance called 'the game of loser wins' by Pierre Bourdieu; see 1993: 39).

The last two attitudes are often met with resistance from the public, from the authorities, and from well-established, 'consecrated' colleagues, because they challenge the habitual way of conceiving literary beauty. Although matters of taste are proverbially beyond dispute, people get really offended if their aesthetic preferences are questioned, because such preferences are intimately connected with their psychical make-up (literature as a transitional space), their upbringing, and their social status and aspirations. Furthermore, the aesthetic plays an import part in people's self-expression, including their tone of voice and manner of talking, the arrangement of their looks, their apparel, their gestures, postures, and gait, and the decoration of their homes. To challenge aesthetic preferences is a serious matter, because the aesthetic is not only amalgamated with cultural and personal values but is related to peoples' self-perception.

This role of the aesthetic in our identity and self-understanding explains why changes of aesthetic forms may cause passionate reactions. Further, the aesthetic is also closely related to, albeit not identical with, epistemological, moral, and political issues; and literature especially is about something. It indicates a model state of affairs or mind that it judges publicly but without authority. Writing literature is by necessity a narcissistic activity, because the writer is both drawing on his or her inner, highly drive-cathected world and celebrating the omnipotence of the act of writing. The same is, albeit to a lesser extent, also true of reading. Readers invest parts of themselves in the reading process. Consequently, if the text contradicts or disappoints them, they may easily feel betrayed, and this betrayal leads to a kind of narcissistic mortification that is turned towards the writer: 'Who are they to judge; what do they know; what moral and/or political views are these to propagate.' Such criticism is not launched only at contemporary literature; in fact, literature never becomes immune to this kind of criticism. From the philosophers' criticism of Homer onwards, the canons are always under some kind of revision. Texts that are criticized do not necessarily lose their place within the canon; they may, however, receive a label, a mark of warning.

The ambiguity of the communicative aspect of literature is another reason it is criticized. Literature has been defined here as mimetic discourse that imitates the four other discourses. However, literature also imitates different communicative situations: the solemnity of public address and official relation and recording; the conversation of private citizens, private letters, intimate talk within the family and among adults; and monologues such as confessions, diatribes and curses, and prayers. Yet whatever communicative situation, or combinations of these, is chosen, the communication of the literary text itself is public (here the private circulation of manuscripts is disregarded). Literature publicizes texts that are at the same time imitations of different forms of private communication and forms of verbal art. There is a voyeuristic enjoyment of disclosure, of revealing what is most often kept secret, even if the texts are make-believes, because the secrets revealed in literature are supposed to be analogous to those of life.

Most often being let in on secrets delights the audience or readership; one of the great pleasures of literature is certainly voyeuristic. Another thrill, related to the voyeuristic dimension, is that of comparing notes. In this respect, literature is certainly a mirror to nature. Indiscretion is one of the hallmarks of literature, but precisely this dimension of the text serves an important social function. Through literature readers get an idea of intellectual, and especially of emotional, features and processes as displayed in fictional minds (including the narrators' and the implied author's). Even if the existence of seven or eight basic emotions, which today are often taken for anthropologic universals, is not questioned,[21] the development and specific forms of emotions and sensibility are mainly a cultural and historical matter. To a great extent we learn to feel and express feelings in ways thought proper in the community and social circle within which we live; and literature is instrumental in describing, and even in shaping, these ways of feeling. It is also instrumental, however, in showing that we may feel and act otherwise than we like to think. This is why people often do not like what they read. When this is the case, authors will be accused of trespassing, of illegally revealing what should have remained private matters, or at least of bad taste. Prima facie, such an accusation seems odd in light of the fact that the doings, thoughts, and feelings are those of fictional characters.[22] However, the point is not indiscretion towards living or deceased persons. The complaint and resentment concern indiscretion as a revealing of features and dimensions of the psyche and social character of different types and circles of individuals; of forms of interaction; and of exploitation and abuse of power (i.e., literature as a critique of ideology).

There is still another structural feature to this often ongoing quarrel concerning literature's indiscretion, namely, the double form of addressing the readership (mentioned on p. 241). In reading literature, the reader is at the same time addressed and interpellated by a foreign and thus, in a certain sense, impersonal voice that is authorized to speak publicly (or is printed in Holland). This voice obviously assumes that what it says should concern the community at large, and assuming a questionable authority he or she informs, warns, exhorts, advises, and teaches the readership. At the same time, however, he or she will appear in the guise of somebody close to the individual reader, even pretend to be intimate with him, and, like Rosalind, attempt to seduce and appeal for applause. In short, the author behaves exactly like a private citizen, like we all do when we judge or abuse a third party, and even our interlocutor, even as we claim sympathy and applause. However, if the poet, or author, is just one of us, how dare he intimidate us? He appears to us like a defrocked minister who does not stop preaching although he has been removed from his pulpit. This reaction is, of course, unjust and unreasonable. It is precisely because of the vital importance of its topics, the complexity of its voices, and its lack of coercion that literature is so valuable.

Part Three

On Interpretation

Seven

Interpreting Literature

Stay, you imperfect speakers, tell me more
                      (Macbeth *I, iii, 70*)

Sign against sign, then.
      (Ibsen, Emperor and Galilean, *Part I, Act 3 [1986: 182]*)

The interpretation itself is experience ... [E]xperience is the entire cognitive result of living, and illusion is, for its purposes, just as much experience as is real perception.
                                                                (CP 7.527)

In the preceding chapter, literature was seen from the point of view of interpreters as readers. It was argued that there are two principal uses of literature. First, there is a social use of literature as an integrative, or subversive, agency that teaches audience and readership about the beliefs, values, and norms of society at large, or of groups within it. Literature is seen as a parallel to epideictic speech, but includes close parallels to the two other genres, the forensic and the deliberative. According to this view, literature is, through its virtualization of what it represents, able to speak more openly about what is existentially relevant to the community or to groups within it. Second, literature not only establishes a universe common to audience or readership, but allows every spectator or reader to relate to it individually, to create a transitional space where the text's universe neither quite belongs to the subject nor is just external to it. Both uses of literature, it was argued, fulfil important ratiocinative and emotive functions.

There is, however, another aspect to the reception of literature, to our interpretive effort to understand the meaning of the literary text. Its impact upon us and the use we make of it depend on our conscious and unconscious interpretations. In the preceding chapters, problems of literary interpretation have been touched upon on many occasions, but obliquely and in passing; the objective of this chapter is to inquire more fully and systematically into the problems of interpretation.

7.1 Interpretation as Semiosis

According to Peirce, interpretation is a translation of a sign into a feeling, an effort, or another sign, or into habitual action (see chapter 1). Obviously, a very important part of the aesthetic response lies in feeling and effort, including the corporeal reaction to the literary work (we may jump in our seat or be paralysed by horror, cry or burst out in laughter, etc.). Emotional stirring and gratification are very strong motivations for dealing with literature (cf. chapters 5 and 6). However, these aspects are not our concern here, nor is some kind of automated response triggered by the evocation of a habit. What is of interest here is the not (yet) automated response that makes us wonder about the meaning of the text, that is, the attempt to understand the text by finding a frame of interpretation and a context that fit it and make sense to us, to make us understand.

According to Habermas (quoted on p. 80), 'coming to an understanding,' that is, dialogical understanding, involves the validity claims of comprehensibility, truth, truthfulness, and rightness and concerns 'shared knowledge, mutual trust, and accord with one another' (Habermas 1979: 3). Furthermore, the parties may agree on states of affairs in the world and make their intentions explicit to each other. Understanding, however, says Habermas, has both a minimal and a maximal sense. Minimally it signifies an agreement between the parties to a dialogue about the meaning of a linguistic expression. Maximally it means that between the parties to a dialogue 'there exists an accord concerning the rightness of an utterance in relation to a recognized normative background' (ibid.). Hence, on Habermas's view, maximally understanding is more than intellectual insight, it is a precondition for mutual recognition and communal action. Thus, Habermas sees understanding as multidimensional and dynamic; it is both a point of departure and an end to be obtained. Indeed, although understanding may well be reached with regard to specific issues, the fact that new states of affairs and novel perspectives constantly develop means that reaching understanding is an ongoing activity. Understanding, however, is the outcome of interpretation, and hence, interpretation is an activity that goes on all the time, consciously and unconsciously. Furthermore, interpretation begins before and includes much more than the understanding of linguistic utterances. The way in which a hunter analyses the track of an animal or a citizen of today's metropolis reads the traffic are examples of important acts of interpretation that, although related to speech through learning processes, are inherently more behavioural than linguistic.

Speech is embedded in sensorimotor activity and human interaction, and both include the interpretation of non-linguistic signs, and thus linguistic competence is embedded in a wider semiotic competence: a species-particular capability to produce, emit, receive, interpret, respond to, and store signs. The interpretation of linguistic texts, of utterances, depends itself upon their relation to this wider semiotic context. According to Peircean semiotics, this relationship comprises four references. The utterance is related to its object, that which it is about; it is related to its interpretant, the meaning potential it signifies; it is related to its utterer and to what it is intended to achieve; and, finally, it is related to its interpreter, whom the sign impresses and who attempts to make sense of it (see the semiotic pyramid, p. 55).

A linguistic text represents and refers to a universe of discourse by means of linguistic rules, cognitive models, and discursive conventions (cf. chapter 1). Thus, one basic dimension of a text consists in the triadic relationship between sign, object, and interpretant (i.e., the rules, models, and conventions that make the text understandable). However, this simple triadic relationship between a sign(vehicle), the object referred to, and the signification indicated is, it will be remembered, complicated in Peircean semiotics because of his distinction between the immediate and the dynamical.

The immediate object is what is represented or indicated by the sign itself: the object as it is represented by the sign (for instance, a person as he or she is represented by a specific photograph). The dynamical object is an entity outside of the sign, influencing how the sign represents the object (the dynamical object of a photograph is the model that has causally influenced the photo but is absent from it).

The immediate interpretant is the interpretation, indicated by the sign. The immediate interpretant is the sign's range of potential meanings related to the rules, models, and interpretive conventions that the sign evokes. While the immediate interpretant is the sign's potential meanings, that is, an indefinite range of possible translations indicated by the sign, the dynamical interpretant is the actual translation of the sign into a feeling, an effort, another sign, or a disposition to act. Thus, it consists in a selection, in a conscious or unconscious choice between the possible translations of the text in question. The dynamical interpretant is the actual, individual interpretation of the sign, whether standard or innovative, plausible or implausible. If not invalid, a dynamical interpretant will have selected, actualized, and explicated a part of the text's meaning potential. This is why no single interpretation can exhaust a sign's meaning potential, and why we can never tell if all the potential meanings have been actualized. Furthermore, since the actual interpretation also depends on factors external to the sign or text, it may be extraneous to it and thus invalid.

The discursive universes represented by the text and its interpretants are intimately connected. On the one hand, what may be represented depends on the models and conventions at hand, but on the other, the fact that a text represents a given discursive universe determines the relevance of models and conventions. For example, the representation of a given state of mind, say melancholy, depends upon the theoretical models of mind in general, and there is quite a difference between conceiving melancholy as a state caused by an excess of black bile and seeing it as related to the manic-depressive psychosis. However, the very fact that the object represented is a certain illness of the mind narrows down the number of relevant cognitive models. Today, to conceive melancholy as caused by an excess of black bile would be deemed beside the point. Instead, a case of melancholy would evoke a discussion of whether it is better understood according to contemporary psychological or neurological models, involving a discussion of the relationship between mind and brain.

Let us finally, as regards linguistic utterances, add the distinction between the type as a set of rules for the production of the sign, and the token, the actual spoken or written sign.

In addition to being part of the triadic relationship constituted by object, sign, and interpretant, as an utterance a sign is a part of another triadic relation, namely, that of sign, utterer, and interpreter (see chapter 1). Often the dynamical object may be the source of the sign, such as the footprint made and left by an animal, and its dynamical interpretant is the hunter's recognition that it is an imprint caused by that particular species of animal. As regards linguistic texts, however, the dynamical object is not the source of the sign, or rather only indirectly so. The sign's source is an utterer. If a hunter says, 'Look, this is the track of a deer,' he will be the source of the linguistic sign, even if his statement is caused by the appearance of what he interprets as an imprint of the hoofs of a deer. Linguistic utterances are characterized by the separation of the source from the object.

As argued in chapter 1, just as a distinction is made between immediate and dynamical object and interpretant, we should also distinguish between an immediate and a dynamical utterer. The immediate utterer is the utterer as he, or she, appears in and by virtue of the sign, the image of the utterer as it is formed by it (e.g., the rhetorical self-representation of the addresser in a letter). The dynamical utterer is the actual producer of the text (perhaps a deceitful letter writer). The use of dissimulation in order to form and control the audience and the fact of lying have taught us that these two elements of communication need not be identical.

Symmetrically, we should also distinguish between the immediate and the dynamical interpreter. The immediate interpreter is the interpreter as he or she appears in and by virtue of the sign, the implied audience or reader. He or she may be conceived as a subject full of good sense and in agreement with the point of view expressed in the sign, or as a sceptic in need of persuasion. The dynamical interpreter is the actual audience, or reader, who may certainly reject the ideas and measures suggested in the sign (as when one says, 'Do you think I am stupid?').

If the triangle linking sign, object, and interpretant is combined with the one connecting sign, utterer, and interpreter, we will have the semiotic pyramid presented earlier (see figure 3, p. 55). Interpretation, from this point of view, means the attempt to ascertain the significations of the internal elements of semiosis and the agreement between the immediate and dynamic aspects of the sign. The practical import of being able to ascertain such agreement is obvious. We want for very solid reasons to ascertain whether we are experiencing a perception or a hallucination and whether a string of signs make sense according to grammar and usage. Further, an utterer wants to make certain that his message gets through and influences the interpreter according to his purpose – just as an interpreter wants to be sure that he understands the utterer and is not fooled by him or her.

We only have access to the dynamical, however, through the immediate; and thus our knowledge about what is outside semiosis must remain hypothetical, even if for good reasons we may be practically certain that something is the case. Our interpretations are, as Peirce claims, fallible. We only know the object through its representation in the sign, or most often a series of signs of what we, for good reasons, take to be the same object. The inherent polysemy of language and speech makes the choice between, and delimitation of, sign meanings doubtful. We only know an utterer through the signs he produces, whether intentionally or unintentionally, that is, as the addresser of the sign; and as utterers we address ourselves to interpreters that we know more or less, but always only partially. Thus the relates of the sign: immediate object, immediate interpretant, addresser, and addressee are themselves signs and always potentially in need of further interpretation.

This fallibility should not, however, make us despair, and neither should it lead to the claim that all interpretations are equally warranted. Even if we can never guarantee that an interpretation cannot be contested, and even eventually proved wrong, we most often have strong reasons for preferring one to another, reasons that may be successfully defended by arguments better than those of an opponent.

However, interpretation is a process that goes on infinitely, either as infinite repetition, as when organisms respond habitually to signs in the environment (the female birds responding to the mating colours of the male birds), or as an infinitely ongoing discussion through generations as scientific and philosophical discussions, such as those about the nature of matter and dualism versus monism. Thus, texts are conceived as inherently incomplete and fragmented, in need of supplementation, as questions and replies in an ongoing dialogue. Such supplementation is offered by contextualization.

But contextualization is itself in need of justification. One way of justifying a given contextualization is by arguing that it only makes explicit what is already implied in the sign itself. On this view, an important role of interpretation is to translate the sign into 'an equivalent sign, or perhaps a more developed sign' (CP 2.228). Concerning the apparent completeness of the sign, Peirce distinguishes three kinds of signs in relation to their interpretants, namely, rheme, dicent, and argument.

Rheme (Gr. verb form, 'the said') is today called a propositional function. It is an incomplete proposition consisting, for instance, of a predicate; '– is a man' is an example of a rheme. It is related to firstness and represents a possibility.

Dicent is what is now called a proposition. It is related to secondness and actuality and is used to assert that something is a fact. 'Socrates is a man' is a proposition.

Argument is an inference joining premises and, in case it is valid, drawing the warranted or even necessary conclusion. Consequently, the argument is related to thirdness, to what must necessarily be thought. 'Men are mortal/ Socrates is a man// Socrates is mortal' is an example of an argument.

A rheme is an incomplete dicent sign, and a dicent is a truncated argument. To interpret signs means to transform rhemes into propositions (dicent signs) by supplementation and to bind these, as premises, into arguments. Thus, to make signs understandable, they must be added to by being placed in larger contexts. At this moment, however, a circular movement and adjustment between sign and context starts. Thus, to interpret signs means not only to insert them into a context, but also to produce arguments that prove, or seem to prove, that the context in question is the right one; and that given this context, the text has to be as it is and must be translated in the manner suggested by the interpreter. Further, arguments, let us hope consistent themselves, will be designed to explain ellipses, ambiguities, and contradictions in the text.

For Peirce, arguments, in the sense of small and simple and, as it were, self-sufficient inferences, are not the end point. Arguments point to what he calls discourse:

> [D]iscourse consists of arguments, composed of propositions, and they of general terms, relative and nonrelative, of singular names, and of something that may be called copulas, or relative pronouns, etc. according to the family of speech that one compares the discourse to. (MS 939, 1905: 27)

Discourse is thus the higher unity of which arguments are only the building blocks. But Peirce does not stop here, because individual discourses are themselves connected with one another. He claims the following theorem for the science of semiotics:

> There is a science of semiotics whose results no more afford room for differences of opinion than do those of mathematics, and one of its theorems increases the aptness of that simile. It is that if any signs are connected, no matter how, the resulting system constitutes one sign; so that most connections resulting from successive pairings, a sign frequently interprets a second in so far as this is 'married' to a third.
>
> Thus, the conclusion of a syllogism is the interpretation of either premise as married to the other, and of this sort are all the principal translation-processes of thought. In the light of the above theorem, we see that the

entire thought-life of any person is a sign; and a considerable part of its interpretation will result from marriages with the thought of other persons. So the thought-life of a social group is a sign; and the entire body of all thoughts is a sign, supposing all thought to be more or less connected. (MS 1476, ca. 1904: 38)

At first, this perspective may make us dizzy! But supposing that the autonomy of texts is deceptive, it seems to be a consistent, if radical way of conceiving the interconnectedness of (all) texts. Peirce's concept of discourse is related to an infinitely ongoing dialogue that from a logical point of view consists of strings of arguments collaborating or contradicting each other. Consequently, on Peirce's view, the role of interpretation in general is to make the text understandable, and probable, by establishing it as part of an argument that is part of a discourse. Such a point of view highlights the explicit or implicit dialogical nature of texts. Texts are simultaneously attempted (explicit or implicit) answers to questions, questions for which the individual text itself has no answer or an answer that will be questioned or rejected in other texts (cf. also Gadamer 1960).

To establish the sign as a part of an argument implies three steps: (a) making explicit the meaning supposed to be obliquely expressed by the text; (b) supplementing and interpolating what is not there, but what, according to the argument of the interpreter, has to be presupposed in order for the text to become meaningful; and finally (c) the argument itself will borrow its authority from being a part of a certain discourse.

Interpretation, then, is an effort to make (the meaning of) a sign understandable, and probable, by establishing it as a part of an argument that itself forms part of a discourse that is supposed to lend the interpretation authority.

If the reader spots a certain circularity in the preceding paragraphs, it is not accidental, because what has been presented is a version of the famous hermeneutic circle. However, Peircean semiotics claims that interpretation cannot start from scratch. On the contrary, in his ongoing critique of Descartes and his, as Peirce terms it, paper-doubt, Peirce claims that the only possible beginning of an investigation is a doubt raised on the background of what is, at the moment, believed and unquestioned. Obviously, investigation may result in questioning what has previously been thought indubitable; that is, in order to overcome one doubt another one is raised. And we will never arrive at a state in which every belief has been thoroughly examined. An indefinite number of vague, and at the moment unconscious, presuppositions will subsist. Further, as regards linguistic texts, utterances, they are actions taking place at a given moment and within a specific communicative context that is always complex, not fully transparent, and irrevocably passing as a lived experience (see below).

In order to arrive at the most plausible interpretation, we use a set of procedures and tools. As regards the object, we use, if possible, what Peirce calls collateral observation. We may look at it once more and from another angle. We may call on the testimony of a variety of perceptual modes (sight, touch, hearing, etc.). And we may also call on encyclopedic and/or expert knowledge in order to identify and describe it. Concerning linguistic signs, we use dictionaries, grammars, and philological commentaries and knowledge of the culture of origin in order to understand their possible meanings. With regard to utterer and interpreter, we use our knowledge of him or her, or it or them, our knowledge of rules and conventions and our psychological insight.

7.2 Interpretation as Prediction and Reconstruction

Our interpretive endeavour is mainly either reconstructive or predictive, and one or the other perspective may dominate our interpretations. The townsman reading the traffic and the hunter shooting at a moving target will make inferences concerning the immediate future. The detective investigating a crime site will be concerned with reconstructing the past. However, the detective who is attempting to prevent a serial killer from committing new crimes will be very concerned about the future, just as a physician may, at the same time, be occupied with diagnosis, etiology, prognosis, and prophylactics.

As regards reconstruction, we will take a closer look to verify our first percept of an object. We presume that our second percept is of the same object as our first, and we try to reconstruct in our minds what to us is the real object. In attempting to understand an utterance, we try to reconstruct the meaning of words and expressions at the time of their uttering; that is, we are all naive intentionalists to start with. When entering into a dialogue we try to reconstruct the possible intentions of the other party, and in addressing somebody we try to reconstruct an image of the addressee from our present impressions and prior knowledge of the person, type, or institution in question. Because we suppose that the relates of the sign have influenced its meaning, we attempt to reconstruct a context that is prior to, or contemporaneous with, the production of the sign.

The reason for making this reconstructive effort is that, although most utterances are to a certain extent self-exegetic, no utterance is totally self-explicatory. Thus, reconstruction becomes a question of furnishing the missing information that will make the sign understandable within the semiosis in question. But why call this interpretive endeavour reconstructive, why not just constructive? Even Freud, to whom one of the objectives of psychoanalysis was to make conscious the hidden and repressed childhood experiences and fantasies, talks about constructions rather than about reconstructions (in fact, the title of one of his seminal papers is 'Konstruktionen in der Analyse,' 1937). In principle the difference seems clear: one may interpret a sign by placing it in a context without claiming that this context is identical, or similar, to the one actually influencing the production of the sign. But the question is (1) whether this is all we presume to do when we interpret signs, and (2) whether placing the sign within any seemingly coherent and meaning-giving context is sufficient for practical purposes. At least sometimes, it might be important that our interpretation agree with what is presupposed in the context of utterance (e.g., the intentions of the utterer).

In conversation we assume that both intentions and purposes determine the utterances of the other party, as do the constraints put on a conversation by a variable set of norms and conventions (e.g., 'he couldn't say that in public, but he intended us to understand'). When we are at a loss to construct, or rather in our understanding to reconstruct, the reasons for somebody saying something, we typically ask, 'What do you mean?' 'I don't follow you,' 'Why do you say so?' In listening we are not only preoccupied by understanding what is said but also want to make certain that we share this understanding with the other party.

The reason for this interest is double. First, for cooperation to take place a certain amount of common understanding is needed. Second, we often want to make sure that our way of per- and conceiving the world, and the judgments we pass on it, are shared by others. We want to ensure ourselves that we are normal and in agreement with the standards of the community. In understanding the other party's utterances, we also presuppose that we understand how they are related to the situational context and to (part of) what has determined them. We thus presuppose that we ourselves are able to give reasons for uttering them, reasons that we suppose have been operative in the mind of the other party.

Although I will continue to defend the position that basic acts of interpretation are mainly intended as reconstructive or predictive, I will qualify this position somewhat. It may be that interpretations of utterances and actions are successful because we share interpretive habits, not because we reconstruct the mind of the other party. It may be rightly objected, however, that such habits are part of the way of thinking of individuals, and that consequently, in presupposing such habits to be operative, we are reconstructing part of what has determined the utterance. However, any reconstruction in depth, that is, one that goes beyond determining what can commonly be recognized as good reasons for saying or doing something, is difficult; witness the task of historians, psychotherapists, detectives, and judges. To the unfortunate fact that people lie about the reasons for their actions is added the fact that they very often do not know what determined them, or know only part of it. Just as words are polysemous, so are actions overdetermined.

However, not only individual persons believe in reconstructive understanding; institutions do as well. Above, therapists and detectives and judges were mentioned because to establish the cause, reason, or motive for a certain behaviour is important within both the medical and the juridical systems, whether in order to cure an illness or to decide on a sentence. It goes without saying, however, that in the attempt to reconstruct a course of action or thought and its determinations, agreement quickly gives way to opposition between competing attempts at reconstruction.

Habermas points to the apparent paradox that we, on the one hand, seem to tacitly agree on many interpretations of states of affairs, of text meanings, and of intentions, expectations, and purposes. When, on the other hand, we start to make explicit our reasons for believing this or that, agreement often disappears. His explanation is that explication itself breaks up the agreement because making explicit the net of presuppositions underlying each person's understanding will reveal minor or major differences as to their validity (Habermas 1984: II, 119–52). This point of view agrees well with Peirce's seeing such presuppositions as vague, and with the fact that the very effort to make them determinate may break up a tacit consensus.

7.3 Reconstruction and/vs. Recontextualization

The above points to another obstacle to seeing interpretation exclusively as reconstructive. In interpreting the signs of others, we very often plainly reject their effort of self-exegesis, or rather this effort is relativized by being supplemented by other determining forces that undermine its authority. If, for instance, a believer in astrology explains his behaviour by the influence of the planets, incredulous psychologists and jurists may perhaps admit that his beliefs have to a certain extent determined his behaviour. They will, however, still answer with Cassius: 'The fault, dear Brutus, is not in our stars,/ But in ourselves' *Julius Caesar* I, ii, 140–1). And when Octavius, in the same tragedy, says of Brutus, 'His life was gentle, and the elements/ So mix'd in him that Nature might stand up/ And say to all the world, "This was a man"' (V, v, 72–4), we may endorse the character sketch, but we will reject the doctrine of elements and humours in which it is couched. In such cases we undertake a recontextualization because, for scholarly reasons, the original contextualization must be rejected.

Such recontextualization does not necessarily mean abandoning the idea of reconstruction. On the contrary, it is often claimed, or implied, that what is established in the new, recontextualized interpretation constitutes a, or even *the*, genuine reconstruction. The text's self-exegesis, so goes the argument, has obscured the true cause, motive, or reason because of personal prejudices, party interests, or unconscious motives or because of false notions of the workings of nature, man, and society. Interpretation is a dialectic of discovery, integration, and rejection. If we did not believe that we had good reasons for abandoning one way of looking at texts in favour of another, and consequently for recontextualizing texts and reframing our questions, then the process of interpretation would stop short (cf. below).

In assessing the validity of different approaches to text interpretation there are, however, certain general questions that are explicitly or implicitly answered in any interpretation of utterances. According to the Peircean model of semiosis, the sign is connected to four poles at the base of the pyramid and each of these are split in two: in an immediate, or intrinsic, aspect and in a dynamical, or extrinsic, one. Thus, there are eight basic questions to ask about texts:

1a. What is characteristic of the discursive universe represented by the text; which elements and relationships does it contain?

1b. How is the discursive universe related to what is otherwise known about the social-experiential universe it is supposed, directly or indirectly, to represent?
2a. Which linguistic rules, cognitive models, and discursive conventions are indicated by the text itself?
2b. How are these rules, models, and conventions related to the interpretive habits of the society that the text is supposed to represent?
3a. How is the utterer represented in and by the text?
3b. What is the relationship between the immediate and the dynamical utterer?
4a. How is the interpreter represented in the text; what is presupposed of him, and how is he expected to act?
4b. How is the text in fact received; how is the interpreter interpreting and reacting to it (at the time of its production and/or in later times)?

Each of these eight questions may give rise to different and even incompatible interpretations. However, in all cases, agreement or disagreement about an interpretation will involve at least one of the following four issues:

1. Concerning the relation of the sign to its object questions may arise as regards the identification, location, and description of the object. Furthermore, the parties to the dialogue may disagree about all three questions.
2. Concerning the relation of a sign to the interpretant, the parties may disagree about which codes, models, and conventions it indicates, and even if they agree about which codes, models, and conventions are relevant, they may still disagree about a sign's place and value in relation to them.
3. Concerning the relation of sign and utterer, there are questions of self-representations, intentions, and purposes. The parties may disagree about the identity of the utterer, about the kind of speech acts that are performed, and about the intentions and motivations of the utterer.
4. Concerning the relation between sign and interpreter, questions may arise about background knowledge, expectations, and norms and values. The parties may disagree about the identification of the addressee, about the qualifications attributed to the addressee in the utterance, about the kind of response appropriate to the sign, and so forth.

These are common sources of misunderstanding and disagreement.

Others could undoubtedly be added. Any interpretative difficulty that may arise will, however, either fall within one of the categories here mentioned or, what is more likely, will involve two or more of them.

7.4 Interpretation as Abduction and Rational Reconstruction

Before going into the specific intricacies of literary interpretation, I would like to expound briefly Habermas's idea of interpretation as rational reconstruction and outline Peirce's general understanding of the process of inquiry, because they agree on important points and supplement each other.

In chapter 2, Habermas's concept of discourse and his idea of a universal and necessary set of preconditions for communicative interaction were outlined. According to him, the four so-called validity claims are implicit every time we talk to each other in order to reach understanding. In one place Habermas states that the speaker in communicating claims to be:

> a) Uttering something understandably;
> b) Giving the hearer something to understand;
> c) Making himself thereby understandable; and
> d) Coming to an understanding with another person.

The speaker must choose a comprehensible [*verständlich*] expression so that speaker and hearer can understand one another. The speaker must have the intention of communicating a true [*wahr*] proposition (or a propositional content, the existential presuppositions of which are satisfied) so that the hearer can share the knowledge of the speaker. The speaker must want to express his intentions truthfully [*wahrhaftig*] so that the hearer can believe the utterance of the speaker (can trust him). Finally, the speaker must choose an utterance that is right [*richtig*] so that the hearer can accept the utterance with respect to a recognized normative background. Moreover, communicative action can continue undisturbed only as long as participants suppose that the validity claims they reciprocally raise are justified. (Habermas 1979: 2–3)

These ideas about the obligations of the utterer also have a bearing on his idea of interpretation. In an article entitled 'Interpretative Social Sciences vs. Hermeneuticism' (1983: 29–52), Habermas explicitly links the validity claims of universal pragmatics with the interpretation of texts, and he describes the task of the interpreter as follows:

Thus, the interpreters understand the meaning of the text only to the extent that they see why the author felt entitled to put forward (as true) certain assertions, to recognize (as right) certain values and norms, and to express (as sincere) certain experiences. The interpreters have to clarify the context, which the author must have presupposed to be common knowledge of the contemporaneous public, if the difficulties which the text presents did not arise when it was written. This is explained by the immanent rationality which the interpreters must impute to all utterances insofar as they ascribe to them accountability that they have no reason to doubt. The interpreters cannot understand the semantic content of a text if they are not in a position to present to themselves the reasons that the author might have adduced in the initial conditions. (29)

To contend that the four validity claims are presupposed in communication directed towards understanding is, of course, not to deny the fact that people often talk a lot of gibberish, are misinformed about the real nature of things, lie, and break rules and norms. The point is rather that incomprehensibility, false statements, untrustworthiness, and unethical action can only be recognized as such if the validity claims are indeed presupposed. In coupling the reconstruction of the text's context with the idea of its immanent rationality (founded in the validity claims), Habermas presents an interesting attempt to at least clarify, if not to solve, some major hermeneutic problems.

In older hermeneutics the double task of the interpreter was to acquire linguistic competence and to achieve a sort of psychological empathy: the reader was to put himself in the author's place, or rather in his mind. Gadamer argued that such an idea of entering into the spirit of another person was rather mysterious, and instead he pointed to the common ground of language, tradition, and lifeworld as sources of understanding. At the same time, however, he denied the possibility of a hermeneutics of reconstruction for two reasons: (1) the horizons and the prejudices of author and interpreter will always differ, however slightly, and (2) no set of universal rules and claims exists that possesses transhistorical validity. Consequently, for Gadamer an interpretation will always be a fusion or an integration of two horizons (*Horizontverschmelzung*), and it will always reflect the interest and the understanding of the interpreter himself.

Habermas, in contradistinction to Gadamer, proposes communicationally founded validity claims that might serve as heuristic principles of interpretation. If we choose to follow Habermas, we are offered general criteria for reconstructing the text as an argument by explication of its immanent rationality. One should not minimize this approach to text interpretation for two reasons. First, it is an empirical fact that we often approach texts in this way since we attempt to make sense of what people say by trying to figure out the rational purport of their utterances (cf. above about interpretation as reconstruction). Second, it might be argued that this way of interpreting a text, as a principle of charity, always ought to be tried before other approaches are used. Such a way of reconstructing the text means to see it as an incomplete argument (cf. above on the distinction between rheme, dicent, argument, and discourse), and its interpretation will consist in making implicit premises explicit. Instead of holding that a reconstruction of the utterer's psychological state is necessary and possible, that is, realist intentionalism, this approach attempts to reconstruct a chain of inferences, inferences given which the text would follow as the conclusion. This stance involves a kind of hypothetical intentionalism, saying that text interpretation presupposes hypotheses concerning the attitudes, beliefs, and purposes in uttering the text; that is, according to the view presented here, a reconstruction of the text's subjectivity.

Peirce's reflections on the process of inquiry are bound up with his categorical analysis according to which he distinguishes three kinds of arguments: abduction, induction, and deduction. According to Peirce, the interpretative process is founded on hypothetical (or abductive) reasoning, the only type of reasoning by which we acquire new knowledge, but also a kind of reasoning that offers little certainty. Peirce explains simple abduction as follows:

> The surprising fact, C, is observed;
> But if A were true, C would be a matter of course
> Hence, there is reason to suspect that A is true. (CP 5.189)

(a) Thus, inquiry begins with a moment of wonder or bewilderment and doubt called forth by the observation of a phenomenon that challenges our beliefs. Peirce gives the following simple illustration of an abductive argument:

> Fossils are found; say, remains like those of fishes, but far in the interior of the county. To explain this phenomenon, we suppose the sea once washed over this land. (CP 2.625)

(b) Since the beliefs of an individual researcher, or a community of researchers, are called into doubt, an explanation of this phenomenon is sought by forming a hypothesis that, if true, would make the bewildering phenomenon a matter of course. In Peirce's own example the following hypothesis is formed:

> If the sea once washed over this landscape
> *then the presence of fossils would be explained.*
> Therefore, we hypothesize the sometime presence of water in this part of the land.

(c) The third step is the deduction of necessary, or probable, consequences of adopting such a hypothesis, that is, what would necessarily, or probably, have followed from the sometimes presence of water (in addition to the fossils). Let us presume that salt ought to have been sedimented in the rocks if the water had covered the landscape. We can then deduct:

> Presence of fossils of fishes implies presence of salt.
> *Fossils of fishes are present.*
> Therefore, salt must be present.

(d) The fourth and last stage is the inductive one, during which it is ascertained whether the deduced consequence is in fact present. Perhaps taking samples will eventually confirm the presence of salt. If this is the case, then the explanatory hypothesis may be accepted as highly probable and further inquiry will be based on this premise.

If, after samples have been taken, no salt has been found, then parts of the argument will be scrutinized. For instance, it may be hypothesized that the fossils are not of seawater fish but freshwater fish or of some kinds of mammals.

Clearly the fossils are understood as indexical signs, more specifically as reagents both pointing to and determined by their object, the fish, and the preconditions for their sometime existence, the sea. Fish, that is, seawater fish, are related to the sea in such a way that they may represent it synecdochically.

Thus, there is a profound affinity between Peirce's idea of abduction and Habermas's idea about the reconstruction of the text's immanent rationality, except that instead of talking about 'the surprising fact, C,' we should talk about 'the problem of understanding C.' Habermas's criterion for the selection of contexts may be rephrased like this: Choose among the given possible contexts of a text the one that makes the text most meaningful. This is very close to Peirce's indication of the role of hypothesizing. The surprising fact, C, is observed; but if A were true, C would be a matter of course; thus A is the fact that would overcome the difficulty in explaining C.

As a starting point for text interpretation Habermas's maxim seems very helpful, but for several reasons it does not ensure any easy solutions to the problems of hermeneutics. The following four reasons show some principal difficulties that confront us when we read a text:

1. The text is ambiguous; it does not contain sufficient information for us to choose between two alternative contextualizations; i.e., the problem of scarcity of information.
2. The reconstruction of the text as an argument is only partial; it leaves elements that have to be interpreted by adding premises of a different kind; i.e., the problems of the incompleteness and heterogeneity of interpretation, and of the residual meaning potentials of the text.
3. The text has several layers of signification that make it possible to reconstruct different arguments that may even, if not necessarily, contradict each other; i.e., the problem of polysemy and indeterminacy of the semantic structures of texts.
4. The text is incoherent and resists the attempt to reconstruct it as an argument; i.e., the problem of structural deficiency and opaqueness of meaning.

Habermas's article is about the social sciences, not about the interpretation of literature, and below I will show the extra difficulties that arise in literary studies. For the moment I would like to point to ways of handling these difficulties as regards texts referring to a historical and social universe, such as newspaper articles, letters, contracts, memoranda, conversations about what has happened in the neighbourhood, and therapeutic dialogues. These kinds of texts may present all the difficulties mentioned above, and it may be impossible to reach any clear and well-founded understanding of what they signify. However, in order to ensure understanding of such texts, we would seek information from related but independent sources. To know whether a newspaper article is well informed and reliable as to events or states of affairs, we could start an independent investigation. To get a fuller knowledge of the obligations and rights prescribed in a contract we may seek legal advice. And to judge the sincerity of a personal letter or of a patient in a therapeutic dialogue we could compare the attitude in question to the person's other actions, physical and symbolic. This means to engage in a process of inquiry comprising the deductive and inductive modes of reasoning (in addition to abductive reasoning), as has already been exemplified above. This search for supplementary information takes place, however, within the same universe as that referred to by the text in question. In principle, there is no end to the amount of information that may be added, and thus, in interpreting experiential universes and actual minds, as they are represented in texts, we may endlessly add and drop collateral information. In fact, in most stages of such an inquiry, the text is put within parentheses, while other sources of information are investigated. Thus, although the question raised by the text may be answered, the text may remain just as enigmatic, ambiguous, contradictory, etc. as before. A problem has been solved by comparing the text with other available information, not by disentangling its polysemies, ambiguities, and contradictions by a more profound analysis, but by decisions made from collateral observations.

7.5 The Practice and Predicaments of the Literary Interpretation

Until now we have been talking about text interpretation in real-world situations, for instance, the interpretations of the physician and the detective so brilliantly described by Carlo Ginzburg (see Ginzburg in Eco and Sebeok 1983: 81–118), but what about the interpretation of literature? In chapter 2, literature was given a preliminary definition combining five features: (1) fictionality, (2) poeticity, (3) inquisitionality, (4) licence, and (5) contemplation; and chapters 3 to 6 inquired into the soundness and relevance of such a definition. It is evident that not all texts usually classified as literary possess all five features. Further, different readerships may even sometimes change the category to which texts are considered to belong to (e.g., texts once considered mainly historical or religious are later considered literary). Nevertheless, this definition of literature seems (1) to catch the most salient features of today's default concept of literature, (2) to include most of the texts traditionally termed literary, and (3) (taking into account that literary texts are radially organized) to indicate some, admittedly fuzzy, boundaries between literary texts and texts in the main belonging to other discourses. These features seem also, explicitly or implicitly, to play an

372   Part Three: On Interpretation

important role in the professional interpretation of literary texts, since they govern the scholar's or critic's investigation of the text, that is, what he or she quasi-automatically will be looking for.

According to the semiotic view represented here, theories, or (less demanding) strategies, of interpretation may be grouped as being mainly hypotheses and analytic procedures involving (1) sign–sign relationship, that is, the internal organization of signs within and among texts, (2) the relation of fictional universes to lifeworlds, (3) relations of the texts to their utterers, and (4) the relation of texts to their interpreters.

7.5.1 The Sensitivity of Listening: The Reader and the Dialogical Principle

There are good reasons for beginning the discussion of the predicament of literary scholarship with the text–interpreter relationship, because this is the immediate reality of interpretation. In the preceding chapter, the uses of literature by interpreters were described. The interpreter is, however, also a necessary factor in the establishment of text meaning. In this chapter we are not so much concerned about the why of reading as about the how of understanding. Very often the literary text's utterer is inaccessible; the world (represented by analogy) is itself only known through documents and monuments; and the reconstructions of historians and the linguistic rules and conventions are known only through philological commentary. No wonder that hermeneutics and recent theories of literature have stressed the role of the reader in establishing the meaning of the text.[1]

The semiotic and pragmatic approach embraced in this book also stresses the importance of the interpreter on different levels. First, the interpreter as a formative factor in the mind of the utterer. Second, the interpreter as the agent who produces the dynamical (effectual) interpretant, that is, the effect that the sign creates in a single semiosis, in contradistinction to both the intentional interpretant, the one intended by the utterer, and the immediate interpretant, the text's meaning potential. Third, and finally, for Peirce it is the unlimited community of researchers that decide about the final interpretant, that is, a dynamical interpretant that will be never abandoned. Obviously, we will never know whether actual interpretations will be final; we may, however, according to Peirce, reach practical certainty, that is, we may for good reasons believe the interpretation of a given phenomenon to be valid without being able to furnish a final proof.

Pushed to its extremes, this is the discussion of Alice and Humpty-

Dumpty over again: who is the master? But both extremes are self-defeating. The position that disregards the otherness of the text – for instance, treating a medieval text as if it were contemporary with its twenty-first-century interpreter – runs the risk of reducing the text to a pretext for indulging in individual fantasies, just adding some historical spice. Further, claiming that a text's meaning is created in an interpretive gesture, as it has been called, by an interpreter not accountable to anybody except perhaps to the subcommunity of interpreters to which he or she belongs, makes it hard to grasp how proponents of a certain interpretation can count on being understood themselves – unless they after all count on a certain stability of significations that makes communication possible. The other extreme, the position that texts have absolute, determinate meanings that are laid down in their uttering and that leave no room for different interpretations is, with regard to linguistic texts in general and literature in particular, indefensible as well. Peirce observes that 'every symbol is a living thing, in a very strict sense that is no mere figure of speech. The body of a symbol changes slowly, but its meaning inevitably grows, incorporates new elements and throws off old ones' (CP 2.222).

Confronted with these changes in the range of possible meanings, in different contexts and over time, there are two possible stances. According to the first, the role of the interpreter should be the attempt to establish the plausible meanings of a text in its historical context, that is, to make an attempt at reconstruction. According to the other stance, the interpreter should take an applicative approach to the text, that is, should interpret the text with a view to its present relevance. Choosing between these two interpretive principles is by no means easy, for several reasons.

First, there is the epistemological question of the possibility of reconstruction. In principle, and in practice, there is a limit to reconstruction. Even if the scholar has good reasons for believing that the perspective chosen was deemed important within the culture of origin, he or she will have no guarantee that some points would not have been perceived differently and maybe radically so. Furthermore, what for us becomes a part of a text's meaning has probably had a wider context of which the text only indicates a part; although we may suppose an important part, since traces of it have survived in the text in question, or in other texts (e.g., the poetic correlation between maidens and horses is indicated in Alcman but only presupposed in Anacreon). However, although there are limits to what we can reconstruct, and we can never be certain that the reconstructive work is finished, or ensure our interpretations against mistakes, this should not stop us from trying to do this work as meticulously as possible.

Yet even if such work is without doubt necessary and valuable, to take into account what seems important from a perspective contemporary with the interpreter, not only with that of the text, need not compromise the interpretation. The eminent danger is, of course, that of unwarranted identifications, that is, an uncritical staying in the position of minimal departure (cf. the next section). A lot of historical and cultural knowledge about literary texts is necessary not only to understand 'strange' passages and to become aware of dimensions not accessible through present standard knowledge, but also to enjoy the fact that the text represents other ways of experiencing, other perspectives, and other norms and values. However, if the otherness and strangeness revealed by such scholarship make no resonance at all, they only serve to make the text more distant. Obviously, it might be valuable to point out, at least from the perspective of today's Western readers, that something is completely obsolete and without relevance. Still, it may be more interesting to find the points of intersection and divergence between text and interpreter.

As regards the hermeneutic relationship between text and interpreter, contextualization should grow out of a dialectic of other and self rather than begin by framing the text in a certain way. The awareness of this dialectic is extremely important, because it is the only way to hold one's prejudices at bay. The best advice about interpretation, I believe, remains Freud's to physicians practising psychoanalysis. The technique consists in

> not directing one's notice to anything in particular and in maintaining the same 'evenly-suspended (as I have called it) attention' in the face of all that one hears ... For as soon as one deliberately concentrates his attention to a certain degree, he begins to select from the material before him; one point will be fixed in his mind with particular clearness, and some other will be correspondingly disregarded, and in making this selection he will be following his expectations and inclinations. This, however, is precisely what must not be done. In making the selection, if he follows his expectations he is in danger of never finding anything but what he already knows; and if he follows his inclinations he will certainly falsify what he may perceive. It must not be forgotten that the things one hears are for the most part things whose meaning is only recognized later on. (Freud 1958: vol. 12, 111–12)[2]

The last sentence of the quotation is important. It is a fact that we often suddenly realize something about ourselves and about the relationship to our interlocutor of which we were unaware at the moment of uttering. It is also a fact that we sometimes say things whose signification is pointed out to us by our interlocutors after they have overcome our initial response: 'I didn't say that.' Thus, there is a time before and a time after uttering during which meaning develops, and in order to grasp the implications of what is said or written, an unprejudiced sensitivity is required.

It might be objected that Freud's plea for the evenly suspended attention is utopian, because the interpreter cannot give up his or her professional training, including hypotheses and prejudices with regard to the working of the psyche or the text. Likewise, the utterer (in therapy the patient) will have his or her own agenda. However, as pointed out in chapter 1 (p. 53), there is, or rather there may be, a mobility and adjustability to dialogue that sometimes may result in interpretations that are in agreement with, not necessarily what the utterer intended,[3] or not only what was intended, but with parts of the indeterminate, but not infinite, field of significations laid out by the dialogue. Indeed, in my view, the attempt of maintaining an evenly suspended attention is the inescapable precondition for learning something from the text and for enjoying it. Thus, it should be the regulative idea of literary interpretation. The excellent interpretation, however, is achieved in the combination of this sensitivity with scholarly knowledge.

The principle of evenly suspended attention is a demand on the attitude of the interpreter in conversing with the text. The interpretive principles (the hypotheses about the nature of texts that guide interpretation) related to the other poles of the semiotic pyramid are concerned with elements, structures, and forces specific to them. To begin with, there are, however, two general definitions of and ways of looking at texts that are decisive for the study of literature:

1. A text is conceived as a structured whole that makes up a highly, but never totally, coherent unity, that is, the elements of the text establish relations to one another on and between different levels, whether such relationships are rule-governed and conventional, or innovative. The principles according to which they are related are describable even if an exhaustive description is impossible and even if texts, often in interesting ways, will violate and contradict patterns that seem well established within them (an aspect of literary texts studied in chapter 4).

2. A text is an artefact, a product of the action of one or more subjects, and as such it is intentional and motivated. It is the outcome of a complex and overdetermined process during which different and conflicting forces have been responsible for its production and final form. Texts are interactive in the sense that they carry out dialogues with tradition and with the historical conditions under which they have been produced. Thus, to understand texts means making hypotheses concerning what has influenced their production (cf. chapters 5 and 6).

7.5.2. The Text as Dynamical Structure

From the first general definition some more specific hypotheses and interpretive principles follow:

1a. *The paradigmatic structuration of the text.* Humans seem most often to think in similarities and dissimilarities, in oppositions and syncretisms, in homonyms and antonyms. Literature's tendency to a close and compact structuration and its use and piling up of the wealth of oppositions that exist ready-made in language make this feature even more prominent:

> The fear of the Lord prolongeth days:
> but the years of the wicked shall be shortened.
> The hope of the righteous shall be gladness:
> But the expectation of the wicked shall perish.
>   (Proverbs 10: 27–8)

In these verses simple parallelisms (syntactical and semantic) and oppositions (righteousness vs. wickedness, prolongation vs. abridgment, fulfilment vs. deception) abound. Even if the example is chosen to demonstrate the hypothesis, and even if the Book of Proverbs in general fulfils the criterion to perfection, it is always necessary to search literary texts for such patterns (see also chapter 4).

1b. *Textual invariance.* The structuration of literary texts by similarity and dissimilarity means that the similarities, on a higher level of abstraction, may be considered manifestations of an invariant structure. This hypothesis has already been demonstrated in the analysis of the semantics of the family saga of the Tantalids and by Holbek's analysis of the invariant narrative schema of the fairy tale. In poetry such invariance is prominent as well:

> Make haste, O god, to deliver me:
> Make haste to help me, O lord.
> Let them be ashamed and confounded that seek after my soul:
> Let them be turned backward, and put to confusion, that desire my hurt.
> Let them be turned back for a reward of their shame that say, Aha, aha.
> Let all those that seek thee rejoice and be glad in thee:
> And let such as love thy salvation say continually, Let God be magnified.
> But I am poor and needy: make haste unto me, O God:
> Thou art me help and my deliverer: O Lord make no tarrying.
>
> (Psalm 70)

It is obvious that this psalm, being a prayer, has an invariant structure (which it shares with many of the other psalms) both as regards locution and illocution: (1) the subject's urgent appeal to be delivered from his enemies, (2) an entreaty to punish the subject's enemies who are also the enemies of God, (3) a wish that the just may praise the Lord continually and thus be saved, and (4) a repetition of (1). Like fairy tales, psalms and prayers are highly formalized genres that manifest a specific pattern.

The relationship between variants and invariants is basic to literature, since its ambition to express the human condition may be successful only if it can make a case for its own generality; for instance, by pointing out man's common predicaments and fate, however these may be defined. Furthermore, the subsumption of variants under invariants is a precondition for understanding linguistic texts in general, a fact to which the redundancy of language testifies. However, as regards literature the interplay between invariance and variation takes on an aesthetic dimension that makes it attractive.

1c. *The correlation of elements.* This hypothesis involves the investigation of the existence of stable relationships between elements from different semantic realms and fields of experience. Is, for instance, a climatic phenomenon such as a draught co-present with the human experience of sexual frustration, and is sexual fulfilment preceded or accompanied by rain (correlations already stereotyped in *Gilgamesh*)? Or is rule-following behaviour linked with reward, and transgression with punishment (as in the fairy tale)?

The above are just examples of a few general questions that may be asked of any literary text. Is there an agreement between features in the text's representation of physical space, conditions within the social world, and the mental features of the characters or of the reflecting mind (literature as healing the split between man and world), is there a notable disagreement, or do these relations seem to be random? The answer to these questions is, in any case, of great importance to the interpretation of the text.

1d. *Transformation and co-variation.* While the preceding hypothesis looked at correlation from a static point of view, this hypothesis points to transformations and to co-transformations, that is, the possibility that transformation of one element, or clusters of elements, will provoke transformations of related elements in the course of the text. A core example of such a transformation is the change of an initial state of affairs to the opposite final state, or a mental transformation such as the transition from rejection to acceptance, or vice versa. In literature transformations are most often thought of in connection with plots (drama and story; cf. Aristotle's idea of peripeteia), but this is clearly much too narrow; lyrical poetry is equally built on transformation – of perspective, attitudes, and evaluation:

> ...
> O benefit of ill! Now I find true
> That better is by evil still made better:
> And ruin'd love, when it is built anew,
> Grows fairer that at first, more strong, far greater.
>   So I return rebuk'd to my content,
>   And gain by ill thrice more than I have spent.
>   (Shakespeare, Sonnet 119)

This fact may be connected with the other general hypothesis: texts are the product of actions. They are supposed to be intentional and, most often, to fulfil several purposes at once. Speaking, or writing, involves an attempt to bring about a certain state of affairs by influencing others (cf. rhetoric) or oneself. Consequently, a text will often contain a description of and/or an argument in favour of a transformation (cf. Psalm 70 above). According to the dialogical view on semiosis, this is the case whether the state of affairs, or of mind, is virtual or actual, and whether the subject is talking to another or to his or her, in Peirce's words, 'own critical future self.'

1e. *The necessity of approximate translation.* This principle has already been implied specifically in (1b) and (1c), because to interpret the relationship between variants and invariants means looking at, that is, translating, the variants according to a common denominator, in order to create a homogeneous network of significations.

Consequently, in my view, to make a distinction between literary analysis and literary interpretation is misconceived. It is sometimes held that, on the one hand, we have analysis that is objectively, or at least intersubjectively, verifiable and that is concerned with what is in the text itself. On the other, so it is thought, we have interpretation looking at the text from a specific perspective that is not necessarily that of the text itself. However, even approaches that for good reasons seem congenial to the text are reductive translations (not in a negative sense; all interpretation necessitates choices and thus reduction). This is clearly seen, for instance, in the valuable, but clearly different, interpretations of the folk tale by Propp and Holbek (see chapter 4). Both their analyses seem well founded, indeed, and they are not contradicting one another. Still, they are based on interpretive moves that, even if in these cases certainly warranted by the texts, add a perspective that makes their respective translations into general, and partial, structures very different.

In addition, comparisons across semantic fields necessitate translation, and the same is true of figures and tropes. The goal is not necessarily to translate metaphors into literal expressions (a trope-free language is an illusion), but to elucidate difficult phrases and passages, tropical as well as literal, for they must be translated for the text to be understood. Generally, homogenization and reduction (and literary interpretation certainly builds on these procedures) necessarily imply (intralinguistic) translation, because without discovering the common semantic features (from agreement between subject and verb to elaborate allegories) that bind the text together, understanding is not possible.

A natural language, however, in contradistinction to the system of numerals, for instance, does not translate very well. Within literature a paraphrase cannot be substituted for the literary text because literature involves just as much enunciation and enactment as statements, attitudes just as much as assertions. However, translation, and thus paraphrase, is unavoidable, and paraphrase is not only reductive but may also, in Peirce's words, mean a translation of the sign 'into an equivalent or a more developed sign.' With respect to natural languages, however, total equivalence between two different expressions is a limiting case; every translation is an approximation that seems to say, at the same time, too little and too much when compared with the original expression.

Furthermore, interpretation at large is itself translation; the text's dynamical interpretant purports to say the same as the text says, or, in a more realistic fashion, to say something purported to be in agreement with the text's supposed meaning and meant to elucidate it. Interpretation is necessary because texts are only partially self-exegetic; and of course the self-exegesis may itself be in need of interpretation. Thus, the moment interpretation is defined as translation, supplementation becomes necessary. The text offers only some indications as to its translation, but even such indications, the immediate interpretants, may point in different directions.

Supplementing the information contained in the text's representation of its universe is only one dimension of this reconstructive work. With regard to the other dimensions of the text, the interpreter has to interpolate interpretive principles in addition to those indicated by the text itself. The subjectivity of the text has to be reconstructed, as well as what is presupposed of audience and readership. The linguistic utterance, in an individual semiosis, does represent object, interpretant, utterer, and interpreter, but it represents them in the immediacy of a single sign action in need of interpretation by an interpreter. Consequently, the immediately given object, interpretant, utterer, and interpreter become, in the further process of inquiry, signs pointing towards the forces outside semiosis, that is, object, interpretant, utterer, and interpreter in their dynamical aspect.

7.5.3 *The Text as a Set of Traces and Clues*

Looking for sources of supplementation involves reflecting on the relevance of different contexts within which to insert the text. In the study of literature, contextualization is the result of a scholarly work that has to be tailor-made, as it were, to the individual texts. Further, there is no way either of deciding beforehand the number of relevant contexts or of knowing whether all relevant contexts have been investigated. Nevertheless, scholarly tradition has established certain contexts as worth scanning for supplementary information, such as:

2a. *The institutional character of literature: interpretation by genre and type.* This approach combines definitions (1) and (2) since it is a question of comparing texts to ascertain similarities and differences, but this principle of selection is related to the history of literature as an institution. Thus, chronology is an external ordering principle that is added to the comparative study of text properties. According to this approach, texts may be completely or partially interpreted in the light of the genre or type to which they belong (see also the quotation from Frye, chapter 4, pp. 205–6). What within individual texts may seem to defy, indeed insult, all standards of probability may be explained and become acceptable because of its adherence to genre conventions, as, we can see, for instance, in the conciliation and festive integration in the last act of a comedy or fairy tale.

To write within a certain genre at a certain time means to borrow a complex set of conventions that may comprise themes, motives, attitudes, linguistic expressions and level(s) of style, poetic and rhetorical devices, transformational and/or narrative structures, and points of view. Such features of genre and type may also be useful in conjectures about parts missing from the individual text. Sometimes large lacunae in the text force us to infer what has happened from only the parts preserved and our knowledge of the genre in question. Thus, such comparative studies may supply information needed to understand the individual text.

The study of genres and types (such as didactic literature, panegyric, religious literature, etc.), is further important to the understanding of literature as an articulation of experience, of how it functions within society and becomes a complex expression of its self-understanding, that is, its institutional nature (cf. chapter 6). The internal history of literature may be described as the interrelation of different clusters of conventions, viewpoints, and attitudes and their development. This view of literature also highlights the dialogical relationship between individual texts: their borrowing of themes and conventions from each other, how they are developed or transformed by imitation or parody, how they object to and correct each other.

Even if this dialogic relationship may be clearly discernible in the texts, it is a trivial, but sometimes overlooked fact that they do not write themselves. They are, as claimed in the second general hypothesis, artefacts, products of actions. Thus, from being a comparison between texts, the study of literature as an institution will transcend the analysis of text–text relationship and become related to the approaches based on the view of literature as a product of human action – and dialogue is a kind of interaction. Consequently, knowledge of the utterers has, even if the issue is sometimes hotly contested, always been thought useful for the understanding of the product, the texts. Therefore, authorship constitutes a common interpretive approach to text meaning.

2b. *Intertextuality and reciprocal interpretation based on authorship.* This approach is also on the borderline between the two general hypotheses about the nature of the text, since it combines text–text relationship with using the utterer(s) as a criterion of delimitation. A given text is often, and often for good reasons, understood in the light of other fictional texts by the same author(s), describing the same or similar fictional universes. It seems reasonable to understand Hardy's Wessex novels in the light of one another and to see Shakespeare's romances in the light of each other and of his comedies and tragedies, although each play describes a universe of discourse unrelated to those of the others. To compare, for instance, *Much Ado About Nothing*, *Othello*, and *The Winter's Tale* may be fruitful, as may a comparison of crises of world views in *Hamlet* and *King Lear*. Both the overall interpretation of a text and the interpretation of certain passages within it may profit greatly from the discovery of their similarity with other part of the oeuvre. In Andersen's 'The Snow Queen,' for instance, we read the following passage, when little Gerda starts out searching for Kai. She says to the river:

> 'Is it true that you have taken my playmate? I will give you my new red shoes if you will give him back to me.'
>
> She thought that the little waves nodded strangely; so she took her treasure, her new red shoes, and threw them out into the river. They struck the water not far from shore, and the waves carried them back to her. It was as if the river did not want her little shoes since it had not taken Kai ... [S]he thought she just hadn't thrown them far enough out; therefore, she climbed into a rowing boat ... and threw the shoes out over the water again. The boat had not been moored and ... started to drift. (Andersen 1974: 241)

Gerda's repeated action seems to be a kind of sacrifice, but what does it signify? The tale itself gives certain indications; the decisive clue to understanding this passage, however, is given in two other Andersen tales, 'The Girl Who Tread on Bread' and, especially, the scary 'The Red Shoes,' in which the red shoes become a metaphor for vanity, selfishness, and illicit sexuality. In this tale these forces dominate the girl to the extent that she is unable to take off the incessantly dancing shoes, and she has to ask the executioner to chop off her feet to be saved. In the light of this other tale it becomes evident that Gerda's throwing her red shoes in the river means that she renounces sexuality and selfishness, which is what allows her to save Kay.

Our knowledge that poems, novels, tales, and plays have an individual author, or authors, prompts us to investigate their intertextual relationship. Further, familiarity with an author's way of writing may be used in conjectures about authorship, for instance, in adding to or subtracting works from the canon.[4] And even if other kinds of intertextuality than common authorship may be just as, or in many cases much more, rewarding, there is no reason whatsoever to deny the usefulness of such an approach. As discussed until now, authorship has only functioned as a principle of selection, that is, as a way of establishing a corpus. But why restrict such a corpus to the literary work? It seems artificial to limit study to a comparison of the fictional part of an author's work to the exclusion of other sources. Thus, the study is widened to:

2c. *Reciprocal interpretation by intrasubjective reference*. The difference to (2b) is obvious, because the present hypothesis includes much more than (2b). It says that information about the producer may be helpful, whether or not it concerns the fictional work or non-literary texts dealing with the political opinions and activities, family matters, religious beliefs, mental health, love life, and so on, of the author in question. Thus, we have here full-fledged biographical study, which is a branch of historical research (combined with literary interpretation as the case may be). The wish to tie together lived life and the literary oeuvre is perennial. Moreover, the autobiographical works of and biographical works on scores of writers testify to the fact that this is not only the whim of lay readers but rather a passion shared by scholars – and by the writers themselves. In spite of the fact that New Criticism, structuralism, and poststructuralism seem to have agreed that the author is either irrelevant or dead (cf. Barthes 1986), it seems to me that no one has advanced a single convincing argument either for giving up studying individual authors or for restricting the study of an author to one kind of text. What has been argued is that we should concentrate either on the text or on ourselves, or enjoy the free floating of signifiers. These claims, however, are recommendations to read in a certain way, not arguments invalidating the author–text relationship. As regards the first issue, it should be recognized that the works of an author most often have a unity that can justifiably be singled out for specific scrutiny. Obviously, authorship is not the only way in which corpora may be established; it may not even be the most interesting object of research. To deny, however, that it is possible and potentially fruitful to study the production of an author and that such a study may contribute to several fields of knowledge such as literary history and history of culture and mentality seems odd – and to see such study as repressive study per se seems even stranger. Second, the reason such a study is possible and perhaps fruitful is that an internal dialogue transcending the divide between the fictional and the non-fictional writings of an author will exist. For one thing, because authors are often self-exegetic, for instance, in letters, speeches, and other non-fictional documents. In the preface to the chronological edition of his collected works (1898), Ibsen, for instance, claims that the fact that a new generation of readers only know his recent work, not his older plays, is the reason for many partial and faulty readings of individual texts. He continues:

> Only by conceiving and making his own my entire production as one continuous and connected whole, will the reader receive the intended, appropriate impression of its parts.
>
> In short, my friendly recommendation to the readers is, then, that you do not put away or pass over any play, but that you get to know the works – reading and living them through – in the same order in which I have written them. (Ibsen 1928–34: XV, 381–2; my trans.)

One may of course object to Ibsen's idea that the reader should necessarily follow the order of production in order to be able to interpret the texts adequately. For instance, it might be pointed out that each play takes part in several dialogues and may consequently be studied from different perspectives. Nevertheless, it seems to be agreed upon among literary scholars that the interpretation of literary texts proposed by Ibsen is one approach among others, and one that some scholars should pursue because scholars with other interests in an author's work may profit from a thorough chronological-biographical study. If this interpretive track is then followed, widening the scope of the investigation to include all writings and all documents relating to the author is reasonable because the emotional life, norms, values, and interpretive habits of individuals (their subjectivity) will, to a certain extent, remain relatively stable regardless of the kind of texts that express them. Consequently, the interpreter may profit from entering into a dialogue with all the texts produced by or about the author in question. However, the scholar needs further to assess the original communicative situation, purpose, and nature of the texts with which he is dealing. On this basis, he or she will attempt to reconstruct a plausible answer to the difficulties and enigmas that he or she sees in the oeuvre (for a fuller discussion of this issue see 7.7 below).[5]

Indeed, the refusal to admit biographical interpretation is most often quite illogical because scholars, refusing this approach may endorse many other kinds of historical interpretation. However, if literary texts are seen from, say, the perspective of the history of ideas, then it does seem mysterious to refuse to look into and use what may be known about authors' de facto reception of what was discussed and influential at the time they wrote their works. Such an attitude means neglecting the evidence and specificity of a dialectic between different kinds of discourse just because empirical authors happen to be the loci of exchange.

Biographical explanation, and the biographical study it necessitates, is inextricably bound up with much wider issues. Just as the relation to genre implied placing the text within the entire collection of literary texts, so the relation to the producer(s) implies its inscription in human action at large. There are two ways of conceiving such action, or two aspects to human action: it may be conceived as transindividual and transhistorical and as transindividual and historical.

2d. *The transindividual and transhistorical nature of literature.* According to this hypothesis, literature is the representation of an anthropological constant, a transindividual subjectivity (not just that of the utterer). Literature, on this view, represents existential situations and problems that are constant in our species and hence of continuing interest and relevance, or, to put it in an old-fashioned way, are concerned with the universally human. In such a perspective, Andersen's 'The Snow Queen' might be read as a universal 'myth' of self-perdition caused by male intellectual pride and sexuality and of a successful search and rescue because of the heroine's faith, piety, and self-renunciation. Such an analysis might be pushed further through, for instance, a Jungian approach. Furthermore, certain forms of psychoanalysis, viewing the Oedipus complex as a transhistorical, anthropological constant, would see the tale as the representation of the problems of, and regression beyond, this universal phase in the psycho-sexual development of both the male and the female child.

This hypothesis of the transhistorical signification of literature is justified by two arguments that are supposed to strengthen each other. It is claimed that mankind possesses a number of species-particular features that, on a certain level, are supposed to be replicated identically across historical and social changes. It is further argued that precisely because literature, as an institution, is to certain extent liberated from the immediate concerns of social life and the constraints that regulate social interaction, it will tend to stage and express the universal worries and joys of man. This conception of the role of literature has always been denied and attacked by the opposite hypothesis:

2e. *The transindividual and historical nature of literature.* According to this hypothesis, and in contradistinction to (2d), man is above all seen as a historical and changeable being. Consequently, literature is contextualized with a view to showing how specific historical and social conditions and circumstances have been instrumental in shaping the text(s). For this reason, literature is eminently relevant to the community within which it is created.

From this perspective, the interpretation of literature should associate itself with theories stressing the specificity of mentality (both within different classes and groups and in different historical epochs) and the role of and reasons for change in history. Mentalities, norms, values, and world views, it is argued, are closely related to differences in the organization and functioning of individual societies, in the available material resources and their distribution, in the way of living, and in official doctrines and the ideological pressure exercised by authorities and peer groups. Tension and strife between classes and subcommunities, the role allotted to the individual person in the community, and his or her obligations and opportunities are also decisive. As an institution, it is argued, literature is one of the privileged fora for representing and discussing not what at all time concerns and troubles us but what is currently troublesome and provokes anxiety, or what creates confidence and satisfaction.

On this view, literature represents and reacts to the social conditions of its time. It is, among other things, a kind of pleading; it is very often a protest against the present conditions and a plea for change, for bringing about the good life, and it may contain a sketchy blueprint of a new kind of community. This view is not only valid for literature that is deemed progressive and fighting for, as it were, a humanization of society. On its own premises, even a literature that advocates a return to authoritarian ways of organizing the community, and by being in favour of restricting personal freedom, is also fighting against the, on its view, deplorable moral decay and apostasy of the times and for the true interpretation and mode of life; that is, it understands itself as a humanizing force, even if others can in no way share its self-understanding. Literature is not immune to battles of ideology; on the contrary, they are all the time fought within it. An argument in favour of this way of understanding literature was given in the preceding chapter, namely, that literature has always been controlled by those in power and/or by the market. Censorship is the most obvious and heavy-handed means of control, but favours, rewards, and opportunities are, in the long run, more efficacious in shaping literature to serve different causes and interests.

From this point of view, the principal context of literature is the historical lifeworld as it is perceived and evaluated by its producers and receivers, that is, their conscious and unconscious reactions to the problems posed by society as a discordant totality of economical, social, political, cultural, and mental factors. Descriptions of states of affairs, of actions, of reflections, considerations, and attempts at integration and conciliation between positions and interests, of decisions and clashes, of discussions and fights, of compromises, of interpretations and reinterpretations, across discourses and different kinds of texts are called upon as testimonies in the reconstruction of the lifeworld in order to shed light on what seems to be the matter and the concern of the literature of a given time.

This understanding of literature will often stress its rhetorical dimension in that it sees its role as argumentative and persuasive. Andersen's 'The Snow Queen,' rather than being a timeless tale about individuation or the (putative) overcoming of the Oedipal predicament, is, on this view, primarily a manifestation of the provincial proletarian's encounter with the well-educated bourgeoisie of the metropolis. The tale is, further, clearly argumentative, in that it tries to persuade the reader by staging, as it were, a gentleman of nature's protest against the demands for intellectual achievement and breeding, which are traded for childlike piety.

The two general definitions of the literary text as structure and as a product of action, and the interpretive principles derived from them, are continually used in analysing works of literature. Different theories of literature argue for their individual dispensability or indispensability, their weight, and the way in which they are related to one another (for a comparison of the different contextualization see 7.8 below). The first set of principles specify aspects of the text as a network of significations, while the second sees the text as a collection of traces in need of contextualization. As has been argued, however, it is an illusion that the first set may function independently of the second, for two reasons. First, the structural, seemingly intrinsic, analysis of significations, their correlations and transformations, presupposes a general knowledge of language use springing from the communicative practice of the lifeworld. Second, even if self-representation is prominent in literary texts, they basically represent something other than themselves. Thus, the texts themselves point to contextualizations within realms of experience that presuppose knowledge of the relations, forces, motives, and so on, that exercise an influence on human interaction and attitudes; that is, a general semiotic and interactional competence is presupposed. To this knowledge must be added that of *realia*, encyclopedic knowledge as Eco calls it (Eco 1984: 46–86), that is, knowledge of items referred to by the text.

The interdependence of the two sets of interpretive strategies becomes apparent, for instance, in connection with (1b) concerning invariance that presupposes (1e), the possibility of approximate translation because the text alone does not contain sufficient information to subsume variants under invariants or translations of difficult passages such as metaphorical phrases. Such operations are made possible by knowledge about textual relationships that are unmentioned but presupposed by the text. Thus, contextualization is a precondition for structuration. Conversely, (2a) and (2b) are merely suggestions for extending the corpus of texts under consideration. The reason for this extension is, however, extrinsic, namely, the idea that forces that have been material in the production of the text – the author, the genre, the literary institution – are also important to understanding its meaning.

7.6 Interpretation by Analogy

To understand fictional literature necessitates cross-universe transfer of knowledge; for instance, of hypotheses about the cognitive and emotional life of man and about maxims of conduct and action. The reason our lifeworld may offer us the needed information is that it is the most richly semioticized of all the universes with which we are acquainted. Because we have multiple access to it, it is the primary locus of intersemiotic translation, and thus the understanding of other kinds of universes has to rely on experiences made within it.

In furnishing the missing but necessary information needed to understand the literary text, we most often act according to the 'maxim of minimal departure' (coined by Marie-Laure Ryan; see Ryan 1991); that is, we project interpretive habits from our lifeworld onto the fictional universe. Needless to say, such a projection is extremely risky, for nothing guarantees that our interpretive habits are valid within the universe in question. Indeed, projecting our habits onto a state of affairs within other cultures or our own historical past may prove disastrous.

The following passage near the end of the *Song of Roland* describes the single combat between Charlemagne and the Emir:

> In their bare byrnies now breast to breast they fight,
> The glittering sparks flash from the helmets bright.
> Nothing at all can ever end their strife
> Till one confess he's wrong, the other right.
> (*Song of Roland*, 1937: 187)[6]

According to our present conception of justice, this passage seems rather strange, since we are brought up to distinguish might from right. Thus, projecting our interpretive habits onto this passage would not work very well. However, projecting from the community contemporary with the epic would make sense, since this combat, originating from a compromise between Germanic law and Christianity, is a judicial combat, known at the time. Such a combat is supposed to evoke a *judicium dei*, that is, God gives the victory to the righteous party (as he in fact does right after this passage by sending Gabriel to encourage Charlemagne). Thus, the moment Charlemagne prevails, his enemy is supposed to become aware that not only is he defeated, but he serves an unjust cause and a false god (Josque li uns sun tort i reconnuisset).

This interpolation of information and interpretive principles is based on inference by analogy. In chapter 4 analogy was pointed to, both as a general principle of reasoning and as an absolutely important rhetorical device responsible for a good part of the structuration of literary texts. It was further singled out as the kind of inference that makes possible the application of the interpretations of fictional universes to our lifeworld; that is, analogy allows crossing over from one universe to the other. In the interpretation of literature, we infer by analogy from one type of universe to another. For instance, in analysing the fictional character Hamlet, the British psychoanalyst Ernest Jones endows him with a childhood (not mentioned in the play), and concludes his arguments as follows: 'This is at all events the mechanism that is actually found in the real Hamlets who are investigated psychologically' (1949: 70).

Jones's interpretation of *Hamlet*, or rather of Hamlet, is controversial (cf., for instance, Weitz 1964: 19–26), but it is certainly not only psychoanalysts who hold that mechanisms that are supposed to work in real people also work in fictional characters. We all do. The kind of argument used by Jones can be restated in this way:

The surprising fact, H's reluctance to revenge his father, is observed; but if H suffered from an Oedipal conflict, his reluctance would be a matter of course.

Hence, there is reason to suspect that H suffers from an Oedipal conflict.

This is an ordinary hypothetical, or abductive, inference. It is, however, founded on the following two arguments that together make up an argument from analogy:

1
The real people S', S", S''' have the characters P', P", P'''.
S', S", S''' suffer from Oedipal conflicts.
(By induction) P', P", P''' are signs of an Oedipal conflict.
The fictional character H has the characters P', P", P'''.
(Deductively) H has an Oedipal conflict.

2
The real people S', S", S''' have the characters P', P", P'''.
The fictional character H has the characters P', P", P'''.
(By hypothesis) H has the common characters of S', S", S'''.
S', S", S''' have an Oedipal conflict.
(Deductively) H has an Oedipal conflict.

By analysing the argument from analogy as a combination of two separate arguments, an inductive and a hypothetical, the possible twofold objection to any text interpretation is also made clear:

1. An interpretation may be rejected because the validity of the frame of reference is in itself denied, that is, by a refutation of the inductive argument, or

2. It may be rejected because the validity of the second, hypothetical, argument is denied. This denial may be founded either on the claim that lifeworld interpretations are not applicable to the universe in question, or on the refusal to interpolate semantic features that are not explicitly mentioned in the text.

These two objections can be raised to an argument about a state of affairs within one single universe as well. Even if psychoanalysis in general is accepted, it may well be denied that a given diagnosis applies to a certain patient. In literary interpretation, however, we are confronted with the additional problem that no direct connection can be established between the inductive and the hypothetical argument, because they are about two different universes. In other words, the imputed characters of a fictional universe will remain hypothetical. Further, it may always be objected that even if P', P", and P'" are the common characters both of the real people S', S", and S'" and of the fictional character H, and even if S', S", and S'" do suffer from an Oedipus complex, this does not allow us to infer that the fictional character H suffers from an Oedipal conflict.

One reason why the ascription of psychological states not explicitly mentioned in a fictional text is rejected is that characters are supposed to be nothing but the words they are made of, and we do not ascribe psychological states to words. Perhaps not, but this position is hopeless and indefensible because we do take utterances and actions as indexical signs representing psychological states. Look at this mini-story:

Pete entered the room, Jill blushed, and Jack's mouth turned into narrow slit.

For most of us, it would be hard, indeed almost impossible, to refrain from immediately turning this into a story of jealousy. Why do we do that? First of all, these three statements together seem metonymically to evoke a scenario that is well known from life, literature, and folklore: the confrontation, in a woman's presence, between two men who love her. Second, folk psychology endorses the reactions minimally described in the sequence as common and proper reactions fitting a scenario of the mentioned kind. Thus, we are prepared, almost programmed, to supply the missing information by specifying the encounter as one of erotic jealousy.

It goes without saying, however, that from the information contained in the statements, we are not allowed to infer very much. In fact, even if it seems natural to infer, from Jill's blushing, that she is embarrassed, from Jack's mouth turning into a narrow slit that he is angry, and from the concatenation of the statements that Pete's appearance is the cause of both reactions, we are not really justified in making these inferences. First of all, Jill's blushing and Jack's anger need not be at all related to the appearance of Pete. At the very moment he appears in the doorway, she may blushingly have rejected a proposal from Jack and thus caused his anger. Or Jack may for other reasons hate Pete, and Jill's reaction may be caused by the fact that she knows this. Pete may be Jack's brother, unknowingly interrupting a tender moment between Jack and

Jill, etc. etc. etc. The fact is that this series of events is so indeterminate that it may fit innumerable scenarios.

We create the story about erotic jealousy because of a small number of narrative principles and presuppositions about what a good story should be like. We use, for instance, a principle of maximal unification according to which there should be not only a temporal, but also causal or motivational, relationship between the sequences in a story. According to another principle, differentiations and oppositions should be made useful in plot creation. Thus the fact that both sexes are present should be taken as an indication of erotic tension or conflict, and the mentioning of two male characters together with a female character would indicate competition and enmity between them because of their relation to the woman. Thus, we fit, or at least we are strongly inclined to fit, narrative fragments into stereotypes and prototypical plots.

Prototypical plots are stories that within a given culture, but often also across cultures, are relevant and interesting to a large number of people. Such stories are about predicaments and jeopardy related to common fears and desires. They tell about liminal experiences linked with decisive passages and transformations in the life of the individual.

Our interpretive supplementations of texts are entrenched in and made possible by cultural stereotypes, and pattern recognition and the making of inferences are inextricably welded together. On the one hand, we interpolate from what is said to what is not in using the cultural stereotype most likely pointed out by and/or most likely fitting the said. On the other, in order to do so, we interpret the actions, emotions, and events represented in the texts as indexical signs having a motivated relationship to their objects. Further, prototypical stories are in themselves accounts of such relationships (another version of the hermeneutic circle).

7.7 Interpreting the Text as Enunciation and Utterance

One serious objection to infer by using lifeworld analogies, for instance, to the ascription of an Oedipus complex to Hamlet, is that plot and characters only constitute one level of the literary text. And since plot and characters are fictional, or fictionalized, the text should be studied as an utterance made by an utterer expressing what he or she has imagined.

To see the literary text as an utterance is, however, not less problematic than just to analyse it as a representation of a state of affairs or a state of mind. Although the categorical difference between author and fictional narrator, or lyrical I, seems sacred within contemporary literary scholarship, it seems impossible not to refer to the utterer, that is, to the real producer of the text, however obliquely. Peirce states the problem as follows:

> It is true that when the Arabian romancer tells us that there was a lady named Scheherazade, he does not mean to be understood as speaking of the world of outward realities, and there is a great deal of fiction in what he is talking about. For the fictive is that whose characters depend upon what characters somebody attributes to it; and the story is, of course, the mere creation of the poet's thought. Nevertheless, once he has imagined Scheherazade and made her young, beautiful, and endowed with a gift of spinning stories, it becomes a real fact that so he has imagined her, which fact he cannot destroy by pretending or thinking that he imagined her to be otherwise. What he wishes us to understand is what he might have expressed in plain prose by saying, 'I have imagined a lady, Scheherazade by name, young, beautiful and a tireless teller of tales, and I am going on to imagine what tales she told.' This would have been a plain expression of professed fact relating to the sum total of realities. (CP 5.152)

Here Peirce points (1) to the conventionality of fiction's claim to reality, a convention shared by author and readership; (2) to the responsibility of the author for his or her own creation; and (3) to the textual reality of what has been created. Thus, the agreement of author and readership about the fictionality of the universe, in spite of its pretended reality, does not affect the textual reality and the public nature of what has been represented, and thus the author cannot undo it. He may, however, very well explore possibilities offered by ambiguities and vagueness in the text to retroactively change the course of events (cf. Conan Doyle's revival of Sherlock Holmes).

The scholar's refusal to identify narrator and author is well advised when we are dealing with specific voices and explicit narrators; also, in the case of the first-person novel, it would obviously be wrong to identify Defoe and Moll, Pip and Dickens, and so on. As regards the implied narrator, understood as the subjectivity of the text, the case is different. Obviously, from a legal point of view, the author(s) is/are, and will be held, responsible for the text; who else could be? The same is true for morality. The author is held responsible for what he or she has written; the text's imaginative and fictional nature exempts neither it nor its author from moral criticism and accusations.

Obviously nobody has accused Brett Easton Ellis of the crimes committed by Patrick Bateman, the protagonist of *American Psycho*. But he has been accused of imagining a certain frame of mind within which such horror is reduced to pastime. The question, asked by people scandalized by the novel's fictional universe and its manner of narration, is double, namely, (1) what kind of mind is capable of imagining such a book, and (2) should its publication be allowed, or is it too offensive and potentially too harmful. The first question certainly does not respect the divide between author and narrator; it sticks to the fact that the text is a product produced by somebody and asks how this production is possible. This question, then, is reconstructive, concerned with discovering reasons, motives, and purposes determining the process of production. In this context, the second question is mainly interesting because of the way it is often linked with the first. A line of defence against accusations directed towards the author is the claim that one should not accuse him; one should rather accuse the mental and spiritual climate that is accurately, albeit hyperbolically, described in the novel. Again, such an argument is both analogical and reconstructive. Analogical because the fictional universe is compared with what is taken to be certain features of upper-middle-class mentality within specific circles in New York City. Reconstructive because it is supposed that features in the social environment of the author have been instrumental in shaping a part of the fictional universe.

The legal and moral point of view is one thing, but is the case different from the perspective of the theory of interpretation? If all the complex significations due to the interplay between narrators, explicit and implicit, personalized and impersonal, have been taking into account, that is, the implied narrator has been thoroughly described, then the identification of implied narrator with author seems justified to the same extent that it is thought justified in kinds of non-fictional texts.

The argument for a waterproof separation of implied narrator and author seems flawed, not because of too robust ideas about literature but because of what is implied in other kinds of communication. To which kinds of non-literary communicative acts is literature similar? Considering that it has been argued that literature is the kind of discourse that may imitate any other discourse, this question is not easily answered. As regards the position of the utterer towards the text, however, literature seems close to two non-literary forms of communication, conversation and letter writing.

Conversation is a very fluid kind of communication. It is composed of, and constantly switches between, narratives about states of affairs, and about the doings of others and of the parties themselves (gossip is an essential part of conversation); commentaries on these, including moral and aesthetic evaluation; and reflections on the alternative, 'right thing' to do. It often contains speculations about the road not taken, leading to hypotheses about alternative actions and states of affairs and alternative, counterfactual courses of events (hypothetical scenarios are an essential part of conversation). Conversation reports the present states of the parties, states of body and health, fears and desires, emotions and attitudes, beliefs and opinions (confession is an essential part of conversation). It generates general reflections on the way of the world, including comparisons with other states in the past, in other parts of society, in other cultures, and comparisons with how things ought to be, that is, between the actual and the ideal. Such themes often lead to general reflections on the nature of things, on forces of nature and society, motives and reasons for action and evaluation of these, sometimes amounting to general statements and maxims of conduct (display of worldly knowledge and wisdom are an essential part of conversation). In conversation we find negotiations over the relationship between the parties to the conversation, attempts at making the other party share beliefs, opinions, judgments, and reasons for actions done or planned. Moreover, it will contain attempts at enlisting and obliging the other party to further one's cause and objectives, attempts to endear oneself to the other(s), protestations of support for others and offers of cooperation, or denouncements of the conduct and plans of the other party (promotion and self-promotion are an essential part of conversation). Finally, conversation often stages self-reflexivity as regards visions, narratives, and wordings, leading to reflections on speech itself and on its rhetorical power, attempts at being witty and joking, experiments with words, visions, and narratives by changing phrases, sequences, and perspectives (displaying the medium itself is an essential part of conversation).

Conversation is a collective enterprise in which the contributions of individual interlocutors will be dependent not only on their own states, characters, and objectives but on the directions, turns, and twists brought about by collective action. Conversation is a kind of game during which topics and conventions suddenly turn up, are followed, and then abandoned in favour of others. In spite of this fluidity, we often feel justified in drawing a character sketch of interlocutors that we know well; and we do not distinguish between them as participants in a game and as persons, although we may think that, for instance, they were animated by the company and conversation.

Letter writing may come even closer to literature because of the isolation during the process of writing and because of the possibility of reflection and changes in the texts caused by second thoughts. Private letters may exhibit all of the features and topics listed for conversation, the difference being that private letters first and foremost represent a less spontaneous and a more considered, well-ordered, and deliberate text. Letters may have one or more addressees (cf. correspondence within the aristocracy and bourgeoisie of the eighteenth and nineteenth centuries, and today's American Christmas letters photocopied to relatives and friends). In addition to informing the receiver about the addresser's doings, situation, and frame of mind, and making inquiries about those of the addressee, letters often have one or more specific purposes: a message to the addressee such as a piece of information thought important, a request, a promise, a warning, and so forth. Most often, letters purport to strengthen the ties between addresser and addressee and renegotiate their relationship. In a different way, letters are just as dependent on the other party/parties as is conversation, since letters are addressed to specific receivers and concerned with achieving multiple purposes.

In interpreting letters, we would probably recognize the influence of the addressee on the mind of the letter writer (cf. chapter 1) in the letters themselves. We would spot the different personae that a given person would assume in letters written to different addressees, along with the different topics, attitudes, and stylistic differences dependent on the relationship of addresser and addressee. Certainly, making claims about the personality of the letter writer on the basis of a few letters, and without knowing the conventions of letter writing prevalent in the period and circle in question, would be risky business, to say the least. However, after having analysed a huge correspondence, say that of Mme de Sévigné (about 1500 letters), scholars may rightly claim that they know a lot about her, including much about her personality, beliefs, feelings, attitudes, likes and dislikes, fears and desires. Again, her letters are tuned to the receivers (she writes differently to her daughter and to friends), but one may argue that together, the letters, by recurrent themes, attitudes, and preoccupations, will make possible the reconstruction of at least parts of the subjectivity of the text.

By Dickens we have fifteen novels, Christmas stories, other stories, sketches, etc. To the fictive oeuvre could be added journalism, editorials, travel books, public letters, and even *A Child's History of England* and *A Life of Our Lord* (for children). If we stay within the fictive oeuvre – but why should we? – we would certainly miss most references to the empirical person, Charles John Huffham Dickens. However, on the basis of careful analysis of the fictional texts alone, we would learn a great deal, enabling us to reconstruct parts of what is here called the subjectivity of the texts, that is, the network of skills (semiotic, linguistic, and literary competencies) and knowledge, beliefs, attitudes, intentions, feelings, fears, desires, and fantasies (including visions and narrative patterns) that can be discerned by studying the corpus in question. Now, whether this subjectivity is called the implied narrator (of all the texts) or the author seems a minor point.

In any case, the question leading to the reconstruction of the texts' subjectivity is, What kind of subjectivity would make the existence of such a corpus a matter of course? Since the texts are often problematic and enigmatic, the interpreters must, as Habermas says, be able to imagine and argue for the reasons that the author might originally have had for writing them (see here p. 367). Some important reasons may, however, hardly be accessible to the author him- or herself, at least not immediately because rational reconstruction may, nay, will most often, necessitate recourse to that which is most irrational.

This reconstruction of the subjectivity of the text is independent of whether the author is individual or collective, known or anonymous. For instance, the author of *The Song of Roland* is anonymous, but that does not prevent the reconstruction of the subjectivity of the text with respect to such important issues as religious faith, aristocratic and warrior ideals, ethical norms, the relationship between lords and vassals, the relation of men and women, and so on.

But to reconstruct the subjectivity of the text by asking how it has to be in order to fit the text is certainly not the same as endorsing the view that the text is self-sufficient as a basis for interpretation. Contextualization is necessary since the significations of a text can never be plausibly established by relying only on the 'knowledge of words'; texts, and words, are related to wider historical and cultural contexts. The sometimes apparent absence of contextualization means either that it is presupposed as common knowledge or, unfortunately more likely, that the interpreter remains at the unavoidable initial step of 'minimal departure' that should be supplemented by further investigation.

For two reasons it has been argued that the second general definition of text as (a result of) an action must be applied to literature as well, in spite of its institutional peculiarities. First, any text, because of its unmentioned presuppositions, needs to be inserted in a, at least, minimally communicative context. Moreover, such a context of utterance points necessarily to the utterer as the locus and agency of exchange between text-world and lifeworld. With respect to both non-literary and literary texts, there are an indefinite number of specific kinds of speech acts (asserting, testifying, joking, confessing, warning, promising, etc., etc.) and of contexts of uttering (unofficial/official, voluntary/forced, strategic/communicative, etc., etc.) that must be taken into account in interpreting texts. There are, however, no specific reasons that prevent us from making inferences from a corpus of literary texts about their utterers. Even if writers of literature may be allowed to play with personae and identity in a more systematic fashion than others, they will leave imprints in the texts that may be read symptomatically. We will proceed in a similar way as we do in abstracting a subjectivity from our conversations with others, and from the collections of letters or the memoirs we read. Whereas, in principle, albeit not in practice, a fictional universe is radically separated from the experiential universe, the act of representing such a universe is an act of uttering that takes place, not within the fictional universe, but within the experiential universe itself. Obviously, fictional characters, which may be discernible only as voices, belong to the fictional universe, but uttering the text in its entirety does not. Thus, there is, as it were, a referral outwards, from the enounced to the enunciation, and from the illocutionary to the perlocutionary. In interpreting literature, just as in interpreting other texts, the utterer becomes the nexus of exchange between lifeworld and text-world. The subjectivity ascribed to the text, through rational reconstruction and abductive reasoning, may with the same right be ascribed to its author as that which is ascribed to a letter writer or the writer of an autobiography.

Such reconstructive work will be complex because it involves following an indefinite number of clues through the texts. It will involve intentionalism, since it will claim that authors intend their texts to mean something. Such intentionalism may, however, often remain hypothetical because it may be impossible to demonstrate evidence that an author was in fact aware of, or motivated by, this or that at the time of composition. As mentioned earlier, the reconstruction of the text's subjectivity is rather akin to rational reconstruction and abductive reasoning; that is, it is an attempt to answer the question, What intentions would make this text a matter of course? Why then bother about authorial intentions and motivations? Because the opposite view, that texts are non-intentional, seems very difficult to sustain. Since uttering is an important kind of action, and a text is an utterance, it seems hard to deny that, among other thing, a text is intended. 'Please hand me the salt,' it seems to me, is an utterance not only intended as a request but also intended to be recognized as intended as a request (for this see the seminal work by Grice, in Searle, ed. 1971: 54–70). Even taking into account literature's special form of communication does not make it unintended and unintentional.

Authorial intentions, whether conceived as rational reconstructions or related to the empirical author by means of evidence thought convincing, only constitute a part of the text's meaning-giving context. Furthermore, since Schleiermacher, it has been claimed that the role of the exegete is to understand authors better than they understand themselves. But to this must be added that such understanding may mean understanding otherwise or something else. (As Gadamer has strongly insisted, 'It is sufficient to say that when one understands at all, one understands otherwise'; 1960: 280, my trans.). Thus, we will often understand something different from what was originally meant and possibly something of which the author was not aware. Gadamer's claim that we understand something differently from how it was understood in the original communication is true in the obvious sense that the mental states of utterer and interpreter will always differ. And this is, of course, true even as regards utterer and interpreter in the original communication, since we are not able to enter into the minds of others. However, as pointed out in chapter 1 (pp. 50–5), in real dialogue it is possible to reach a common understanding as to the main purpose of the utterances. Thus, as a generalization about the main import of simple face-to-face dialogues, Gadamer's position is unwarranted.

What Gadamer has in mind is, rather, a reading of classical texts, that is, a situation in which (1) the utterer is not accessible, (2) the text is complex, and (3) utterer and interpreter belong to different cultures. In this case, dialogue is turned into a quasi-dialogue. Furthermore, the cultural difference means that questions asked and (attempted) answered by utterer and interpreter cannot be identical because interpretive habits and background knowledge will necessarily be different. There is no denying that difficulties confront the interpreter or that absolute certainty as to the truth of the reconstruction cannot be reached. What is denied is that it is possible to interpret a text without, at least implicitly, some ideas about its subjectivity (already deciding whether a text is naive or ironic implies such ideas). This being the case, it seems sensible to study other texts by the same author in order to look for similar utterances and attitudes. Further, it also seems sensible to ask how the author's texts were understood by contemporary interpreters; and, in a broader perspective, to inquire into how subjectivity was conceived within the culture of origin.

Schleiermacher's and Gadamer's idea that the interpreter should transcend the self-understanding of the author is put into practice – e.g., by criticism of ideology and psychological criticism (psychoanalysis) – every time the text is taken to mean something of which the author has probably not been aware. Such forms of interpretation are systematic explorations of the common experience that dialogue partners may utter something that reveals something they are not aware of or are unwilling to admit.

Consequently, although it is true that the reconstruction of subjectivity will always be partial and never finally proven, there seem no further reasons to refrain from such enterprises. On the contrary, we not only always do it, whether we admit it or not, we are even forced to do it to make sense of what is told us, because speech is basically intentional.

It should also be pointed out that in speech, to a great extent, conventionalized intentions are already attached to different speech acts and other stereotypical expressions. So the point of departure for establishing the text's subjectivity is not some arcane insight into another psyche. It is, rather, the comparing of the signs pointing to the implied communicative situation of the text with our general understanding of such types of communication.

7.8 Contextualization: Exclusivity or Integration?

Within the well-interpreted literatures (e.g., the Greek and Roman, the English and American, and the French and German literatures), most of the so-called canonical texts have already received from a few to an overwhelming number of interpretations. Consequently, in many cases one can talk about this or that, or a third or a fourth, approach to a given text. The most important reason for this plethora of interpretations is differences in contextualization. Since contextualization is unavoidable, the question of which contexts should guide the interpretation of given texts is decisive. Indeed, most debates between different theoretical trends or schools are debates about the necessity versus contingency and relevance versus irrelevance of specific contextualizations. In the previous section, different contexts were sketched: genre, institution, biography, general psychology, and theories of subjectivity (whether anthropological or historical). The question is, however, whether such contexts are mutually exclusive, interdependent, or freely combinable.

Of the approaches mentioned above, only (2d) (claiming the transhistorical nature of literature) and (2e) (claiming its historical nature) seem, prima facie, to be mutually exclusive; and without qualifications they are opposed to one another much as nature is to culture – a perennial opposition and battlefield. Unqualified, however, both positions are untenable. On the one hand, to claim total immutability for any species, let alone man, goes against the idea of evolution, that is, against the most well-argued paradigm for the study of life; and, in fact, 'transhistorical' most often only indicates that species-particular features are believed to change slowly. On the other hand, to deny that people have some important features in common, even if they belong to different historical epochs and cultures, seems hasty. People seem to be endowed with identical, or near-identical, physical and psychical make-up (their wetware), and cross-cultural communication in space and in time seems possible, at least to a certain extent.

It may also be that the two approaches do not clash in practice because they deal with different aspects of literary texts. In fact, individual theories have attempted a precarious combination of both positions (as, for instance, in Frye's *Anatomy of Criticism*, 1957). However, the difference between focusing on the alleged permanence of the dimensions of literary representation versus focusing on literature as an indicator and mediator of changing social conditions, of ways of human interaction, and of mentality is a major difference that deeply influences concrete interpretations. Nevertheless, the two positions have somehow to be reconciled. The position favoured here is also an attempt at a precarious balance that claims that the themes and motives of literature are closely related to species-particular needs, fears, and desires as they become articulated by virtue of man's semiotic competence, primarily his astonishing ratiocinative capacity. However, such themes and motives are represented differently under different social conditions, and since, from a semiotic point of view, representation and experience cannot be distinguished, their concrete – conscious and unconscious – articulations are obviously not identical. They may, however, be recognized as representations and attempted solutions to similar problems.

The mutual exclusiveness of contexts most often becomes prominent within single, not among different, approaches. Within single categories of contexts, for instance, two psychological theories and concomitant analytic procedures may be mutually exclusive. Analyses of literary texts from the point of view of Jungian archetypes and of the stages of psychosexual development according to Freudian psychoanalysis are not compatible, and an approach to the historical development of literature from the point of view of historical materialism and from that of positivistic sociology will clash. It is logical and unavoidable that incompatibility arises between theories treating the same field of research from different points of view, using different methods, and having different criteria and ways of assessing validity. Indeed, most often different linguistic and semiotic, psychological, and sociological theories respectively have had their origins in a dissatisfaction with other theories within the same field. Furthermore, since there is a plethora of theories and variants of theories, at least within the humanities and the social sciences, there is necessarily much disagreement concerning basic questions as well as the details of concrete interpretations.

Of course, competing theories are not opposed to each other on every question. Peircean and Saussurean semiotics, for instance, share some very important insights into the nature of signs, and this is also true of, say, a Freudian and a cognitivist approach to the psyche. However, even if in most cases such a common ground between theories of the same field exists, the choice of contextualization implies the adoption of a specific point of view that rules out others dealing with the same field, on the same level, from an incompatible perspective.

The combination of points of view dealing with separate approaches to the literary text is a different matter. Combinations are necessary because no super theory of text interpretation exists that is able to describe and explain all features and aspects deemed relevant – nor is it likely to materialize. As regards the attempts to generalize theories from a specific area of research to cover other fields, *vestigia terrent*. It has often proved disastrous to explain social processes by psychological theories or mental phenomena by sociological ones without mediation and without taking into consideration that moving from one level to another means the intervention of factors not accounted for in the original theory. Consequently, theories dealing with phenomena of another order will often treat them as phenomena of the same order as the ones these theories originally were constructed to describe. Linguistic semantics, for instance, is not sufficient to handle text meaning because at the level of utterance, factors unaccounted for by linguistics – for example, intentional and unintentional action – intervene.

A further complication in interpreting literary texts is the necessity to fuse different sets of interpretive principles. We are using a model of the text's discursive universe in which (1) some elements come from the individual fictional text, (2) some from the genre and other literary conventions contemporary with the text, (3) some (principles of interpretation) from the lifeworld contemporary with the text, and (4) some from the lifeworld of the interpreter.

Departure from principles of interpretation valid within our lifeworld, which is obvious as regards, for instance, fairy tales because of the peculiar nature of their physical universes, may always take place in literature. Different kinds of literature are based not only on cognitive models valid within their culture of origin but also on models that are specific to them (the hero of tragedy is 'better than ourselves'; in comedy he is inferior to us).

Thus, we are confronted with a fourfold task in interpreting literature. Using our own interpretive habits as a point of departure, we must (1) identify the properties and relationships within the text (what is included and what is absent from it); (2) compare it with other texts, especially with those belonging to the same genre and period; (3) compare it with what is known about the social and experiential universe within which the text is produced (or within which it is received) in order to establish similarities and differences; and (4) explain the differences between text universe and lifeworld.[7]

Interpreting text meaning is like explaining the weather: the actual weather is not the outcome of a single factor, but is due to sea currents, the height of mountains, the rotation of the earth, the influence of the sun, and so on. Nevertheless, there may be an explanation for the existence of the present weather that is not only convincing but may also explain in a satisfactory fashion why it was not predicted. Meteorology and text interpretation are heterogeneous enterprises. Rather than adding up to uniform theories, they function as sets of hypotheses that explain the outcome of the interaction of connected factors without having theoretically integrated the different parts. Furthermore, the theories, they are borrowing from are, like all theories, provisional.

The necessity of interpreting by a provisional integration of perspectives borrowed from different traditions does not, unfortunately, guarantee any agreement in practice. On the contrary, to the discussion on the choice of theoretical position on each level, which of course continues, will be added the discussion of whether theoretical points of view, even if they belong to different fields, are compatible. Is any theory of the sign combinable with any theory of the psyche, and may any theory of the latter kind be connected with any theory of social interaction? In addition to this discussion, there is the important one about the analytical implications of this heterogeneity, first and foremost about the weight that should be attributed to individual factors. Is text production the result of the interaction of factors that contribute equally to the outcome, or do some factors carry more weight than others? And is the weight of the different factors the same in all cases (something that seems quite implausible) or is it rather specific to each text, or to certain groups of texts? Furthermore, regardless of the process of production, it may be asked whether all dimensions of the text are equally relevant? The answers to these questions and the priority given to them are, of course, decisive for the analytical practice of the individual interpreter.

The American scholar of literature and of law Stanley Fish once made the claim (1980) that because literary texts lack, or have lost, a situational context, text meaning and context are created simultaneously in one interpretive gesture by the interpreter. He further claimed that there is no way to determine the validity and relevance of the different, or even opposing and mutually exclusive, interpretations that result from the different contextualizations favoured by different subcommunities of interpreters. According to Fish, which interpretations will prevail is decided by the institutional power of the respective interpretive subcommunities.

It is valuable to point out the power of institutions to further their own interpretations and to suppress others, and generally to point to the agonistic element in the practice of literary interpretation. Nevertheless it seems that, over time, institutions are not successful in suppressing interpretations even if they are opposed to the one favoured by the institution in question.[8] Consequently, even if it may be true that a given subcommunity can freely create contexts of their own – who is going to prevent this in a democratic society – they may still be considered invalid by other scholars concerned with the subject and not be rehabilitated by later research.

The reason most often given for rejecting an interpretation is that it is considered invalid because of some flaw in its argument. Such a reason is, in a broad sense, logical, whether the rejection is based on the presuppositions and basic premises of the rejected argument or on the actual manner of making inferences concerning a specific text. Further, to change interpretive habits, that is, to change theoretical position and analytical practice, is not (only) a question of following a trend in order to remain/become fashionable; there is always an attempt to give reasons for such changes, and these reasons fall mainly into three categories. A given approach to literary texts is abandoned

(1) when it becomes considered incoherent and self-contradictory beyond reparation, that is, when adjustments to objections considered sound fail;

(2) when it becomes considered worn out, that is, uninterestingly predictable because it is always yields the same analytic results and is thus incapable of innovation;

(3) when it is considered insufficient for discovering and analysing dimensions and features of the texts that are deemed relevant and important by the interpreter.

Thus, inconsistency and lack of innovative potential and relevance are the factors most often considered as reasons for abandoning a given approach. Conversely, consistency, innovative potential, and relevance are the reasons usually given for adhering to a theory or embracing a new one. It goes without saying that no agreement exists as to which theories are inconsistent and/or obsolete. Nevertheless, such confrontations are valuable because, in the long run, they will change the interpretive practice; parts of theories (and sometimes whole theories) will become obsolete. Cases in point are the formalistic and structural theories from Russian Formalism to cognitive literary theory, which have in fact changed the analytic approach to literature, although many of their claims about the nature of texts and about the consistency and analytic powers of these schools have been shown to be false or exaggerated.

However, collaboration between different approaches is just as common and important as confrontation. Since texts are necessarily overdetermined, it is not possible to establish a simple and homogeneous principle according to which they are (supposed to be) generated or interpreted. Consequently, contexts may modify each other without being mutually exclusive; and thus analytic practice will most often consist in a more or less, but never totally, unified cluster of approaches. According to the present approach, in interpreting a text, all four dimensions – the mimetic, the self-reflexive, the symptomatic, and the communicative – should be taken into consideration.

In the analysis of individual literary texts, however, there will always remain some aspects of the text that cannot be understood and explained by means of general theories because significations are also local. They may come into being as effects of specific intertextual relations that cannot be inferred from general hypotheses concerning the production of certain types of texts but are only known by grasping the interplay between specific texts. Literary texts talk with, allude to, quote, steal from, and criticize each other. With which other texts a given text engages in dialogue and for what purpose is individual. Although it may be possible to make sense of a text without being aware of such a dialogue, the explicit or implicit confrontation with other texts adds to the meaning of the text in question, and thus a fuller understanding will have to take it into account.

That the complexities described above most often do not surface in the individual analyses is something for which we should be grateful. But the presuppositional network on which they rest is certainly not simple, even if its complexity is hidden. And the question may be asked whether interpretations are not, at first, founded more on common sense and folk theories (of language, consciousness, human interaction, etc.) than on elaborate theoretical reflections.

Standard knowledge of psychological and social matters necessarily exists as a part of the semiotic competence of the members of a given community. This set of interpretive habits is, of course, consulted first when we are confronted with signs. First, however, the semiotic competence immediately available is often insufficient, and thus the interpreter is forced to call in points of view directly related to more elaborate theories. Second, where do folk theories and common sense come from? Unless one is prepared to claim the existence of a kind of transhistorical common sense, these must be related to doxa, the set of beliefs and opinions commonly hold by the members of a community at any given time. To earnestly request that somebody use his or her common sense most often means a summons to reason like everybody else, that is, in accordance with doxa. The common beliefs themselves are most often the appropriation for common use of truncated versions of more elaborate arguments. Thus, there is no reason to isolate common sense and folk theories. They are already parts of arguments, not ultimate and immediately given truths. Moreover, literary texts often challenge our interpretive habits.

A further complaint against this description of text properties and structures and of different contextualizations might be that, when one uses such analytic instruments, what is essentially literary disappears. This complaint is, however, founded on an illusion. It presupposes that literature possesses an essence in addition to the way in which it articulates in language a universe representing what, at any given time, concerns, worries, and gives pleasure to man. Literature is a specific form of communication linked with a specific institution that makes possible saying what would otherwise be suppressed. It constitutes a reserve, or protected area, within which it is possible to experiment not only with language, but also with emotions, with the interaction of people, with social reality, and with the alleged order of the world. Through its very medium, language, literature is inextricably bound up with the historical universe, because reality always sticks to words, despite the never completely successful attempts of poets to rarefy it and 'donner un sens plus pur aux mots de la tribu.' The clash, however, between speech's link to muddy reality, with its propensity for stereotypes, and literature's fight for structure and expressivity suffices to light its fire:

> Verse has a middle nature: heaven keepes souls,
> The Grave keepes bodies, Verse the Fame enroules.
>   (Donne 1933: 221)

Literature's middle nature should not be forgotten. It mediates between the universalizing abstraction of reflection and the embodied worldliness of individual experience, between other-representation and self-representation. Thus, literature's nature is not to have an unchangeable essence but to constantly adapt itself to, and differentiate itself from, other discourses and other kinds of texts.

7.9 Infinite (Re)interpretation?

Peircean semiotics is famous for its alleged stress on infinite semiosis, understood as ongoing and never-ending interpretation. Strong reservations have been made to this understanding of Peirce in this book. After all, the so-called ultimate logical interpretant, which is not a sign in need of another interpretant but a disposition to act in a certain way (in addition to feeling and effort, which are not signs either), is supposed to put an end to interpretation. And if experience could not terminate in habit-taking, life would be destroyed. Infinite interpretation, as an ongoing translation of texts into other texts, is certainly only one way of exercising semiotic competence. With respect to literature, however, the case is more complicated.

As regards communication and discourse there is an important difference between literary and non-literary texts. Normally the meaning potential of texts that serve strategic or communicative action is actualized and exhausted in a given situational interpretation; and this selective interpretation is their death. Of course literary texts will also fall into oblivion; all texts finally do. Some of them, however, older than the invention of the writing system of their language, have been handed down through millennia, and they still survive, although their way of functioning within the community has changed.

From a communicative and institutional point of view, the following facts seem to have been instrumental in securing their longevity. They have been separated from the instrumental actions connected with the daily business of the community. The public nature of their being, by contrast, means that they have been repeated again and again in connection with rituals and/or as entertainment (e.g., the public readings of the Homeric poems and the re-staging of tragedies in Athens from the fourth century BC onwards). Furthermore, they have been on the curriculum in educational systems. Thus, they have served formative, contemplative, and diversionary purposes; and they have been objects of conversations, both social conversation and professional dialogues – pedagogical, critical, and scholarly.

Further, their blending of individual and general, of concrete and abstract, of literal and figurative, as well as the tension between their centripetal and centrifugal aspects (the fact that their references stop short and return the readers to the signs and their interpretants), mean that literary texts seem to suspend actualization, or at least that they hold back a full realization of their potential meaning. Literature points towards collateral experiences that we can never have and hence continues to elude our attempts to exhaust it. Consequently, as long as they are of current interest or remain a living heritage that engage us, literary works will be re-staged, reread, and thus reinterpreted by new actors, singers, etc. and received by new audiences, readerships, and critics. Moreover, because of the complexity and vagueness of their contexts, their polysemic edge, and the liberty of their utterers and interpreters they will be open for different interpretations.

Although its difficulties have not been brushed aside, reconstructive interpretation has here been advocated here. There is, however, a genuine tension between a reconstructive and an appropriative, or applicative, effort in the interpretation of literature. Since Gadamer, it has been usual to distinguish between reconstructive, integrative, and applicative hermeneutics. On his view, any interpretation means a fusion of two horizons of understanding, that of the text and that of the interpreter. Yet according to Gadamer, although the extremes cannot be realized, the interpretive effort may still be directed mainly either towards reconstructing an understanding that may with some plausibility be ascribed to its culture of origin (to the author's or to that of a contemporary audience and readership) or towards a frame of reference contemporary with the interpreter. The first effort is usually taken to be that of scholarship, the latter that of artistic revival; for instance, the difference between a Shakespeare scholar and a director staging a play by Shakespeare. However, can a scholarly approach be exclusively concerned with the context of origin? Bakhtin sees the following difficulty:

> We can say that neither Shakespeare himself nor his contemporaries knew that 'great Shakespeare' whom we know now. There is no possibility of squeezing our Shakespeare into the Elizabethan epoch ... Modernization and distortion, of course, have existed and will continue to exist. But that is not the reason why Shakespeare has grown. He has grown because of that which actually has been and continues to be found in his works, but which neither he himself nor his contemporaries could consciously perceive and evaluate in the context of the culture of their epoch.
>
> Semantic phenomena can exist in concealed form, potentially, and be revealed only in semantic cultural contexts of subsequent epochs that are favourable for such disciosure. The semantic treasures Shakespeare embedded in his works were created and collected through the centuries and even millennia: they lay hidden in the language, and not only in the literary language, but also in those strata of popular language that before Shakespeare's time had not entered literature. (Bakhtin 1986: 4–5)

A reconstructive perspective, and effort, is necessary and valuable in order to avoid reducing the meaning of texts distant in time, space, or mentality to what is immediately explicable from our own interpretive habits. If we do not respect the strangeness, as it were, of the text, we will always rediscover what we already know. Nevertheless, I do not believe that the work of the literary scholar can be exclusively preoccupied with the context of origin or that his or her role should be confined to that perspective. Gadamer and Bakhtin are right in stressing that to restrict the meaning of a literary text to what has probably been perceived by its producer and its original audience will be too narrow and will make it less relevant.

There is a certain tension, perhaps even a paradox, as regards the interpretation of literary texts: research may seem exclusively focused on the production of new knowledge. The reason for publication is, ideally, that what is written should contribute to a novel understanding of the given text. However, as regards the humanities in general and literary analysis in particular, this demand runs parallel to a demand related to another important task, namely, an exegesis of texts that, at the same time, (1) offers a plausible reconstruction of the text's original dialogic and historical context, (2) relates itself to the meaning ascribed to it by tradition, and (3) accommodates itself to the actual needs of the community, or subcommunity. Thus, the ideal interpretation would seem to be one that, through a dialogue with the scholarly tradition and on the basis of a reconstruction of its original dialogic context, convincingly argues for a novel interpretation that satisfies the present ideas about relevance and importance in the object of research. One need hardly point out that fulfiling such demands is not easy.

What is important, however, is not the individual scholarly contribution in isolation, but the ongoing dialectic between interpretations that explore the different dimensions and aspects of the literary text. Such investigations will also show in which respects the text is still relevant and in which it remains tied to interpretive patterns that are now considered invalid and obsolete. However, in specifying what is invalid and obsolete, one is implicitly pointing out what is important today. Thus, one of the reasons that we need literature, need the classics, is that the make us aware of our own identity. This happens not only because of our identifications with them, but just as much because they make us realize that in certain respects we either do not understand them or do not care for them. The changing social conditions and mentality/self-understanding of man seem to make continuous reinterpretation necessary. Nevertheless, the objective of text interpretation, at large, should be to resist the impending violence done to the alterity of the text by its undiscriminating subsumption under current paradigms of interpretation, while at the same time to clarify the extent to which a dialogue with it is possible and interesting. Even if this seems an almost impossible task, we should persist in attempting to accomplish it. Thus would we be heeding Socrates' point in *Meno*:

> Most of the points I have made in support of my argument are not such as

I can confidently assert; but that the belief in the duty of inquiring after what we do not know will make us better and braver and less helpless than the notion that there is not even a possibility of discovering what we do not know, nor any duty of inquiring after it – this is a point for which I am determined to battle, so far I am able, both in word and deed. (Plato, *Meno*, 86; 1924: 323)

Conclusion

Conclusion: Literature!

Sir, more then kisses, letters mingle Soules,
For, thus friends absent speake ...
                      (Donne [1633] 1933: 159)

A few years ago, the act of concluding was suspected of displaying an unwarranted belief in the possibility of stopping the unpredictable and indomitable flow of signifiers. At the end of a book, it was then fashionable to point out that concluding would be an illusory act of authority, and instead it was trendy to recommend seeing the text as an attempt to further an ongoing dialogue by publishing a provisional contribution already outdated when it became available.

I absolutely agree that the idea of being able to close the discussion here is vain and harmful. There will always be dissenting or supplementary voices, arguments will always be contested or ameliorated, and new examples or counterexamples will be offered. Thus, every article and book, if they are read and discussed at all, will necessarily become a part of an ongoing dialogue. However, this knowledge should not prevent us from taking the responsibility for ending an investigation, and from looking back to see what has materialized. The author should also suggest to the reader an intended interpretant, as Peirce would say, even if we know that the effectual interpretant, the way the actual readers in fact interpret the text may differ from the author's interpretation. Nevertheless, to strive for the cominterpretant (see chapter 1, p. 47), the agreement on how to interpret, indeed, to strive for the fusion of minds as far as the interpretation in question is concerned ought certainly to be a regulative idea of scholarship. Moreover, to sum up what has been argued is at the same time a gesture of politeness and a final effort to state the recommended point of view before the author rests his case.

8.1 Literature's Heterogeneity

That scholarship has become more and more infected with competition, using techniques borrowed from the world of business, is a very important reason for the almost bewildering diversity of recent literary theory, or rather theories, and for the single-mindedness and tenacity of its different branches. Theories have become products that are marketed to make a profit.

Another reason may, however, be found in literature itself (and in its development in the nineteenth and twentieth centuries). First, literature serves a multiplicity of functions and purposes within the community, and its hierarchy of functions changes over time and place. Second, at a given time literature is divided into forms and genres that are structurally and functionally diverse and are used at occasions with different communicative purposes and catering to the diverse attitudes, moods, interests, fears, and desires of its audience or readership. Third, literature develops in an agonistic fashion because it is an essentially contested concept (cf. Gallie). Most often, one movement explicitly aims to replace other forms of literature, older or contemporary, because it is claimed the new movement better represents nature or, at least, is more adequate in relation to its community. Hence, literature is deeply involved with its contemporary society and lifeworld, observing it and criticizing.

The reaction of scholars and critics to such complexity is double. On the one hand, they often concentrate on features that to them are salient in and typical of literature. Priority is claimed for such features either because they are thought to embody the timeless essence of literature, or because they seem to capture the vigour of a specific kind of, most often contemporary, literature. On the other hand, they understand the office of criticism and scholarship in a way analogous to that of literature, that is, it should simultaneously be professional and political, it should fight oppression and point to better ways of living.

Marxists claim that the outstanding feature of literature is that it offers an intensive totality representing the dominant conflicts of society within its particular fictional universes. The objective of this kind of criticism is to critique ideology. The early Formalists held that the proper study of literature is not the texts in their totality, but the features distinguishing them from other kinds of texts, their literariness (*literaturnost*). Their goal, like that of literature, was to fight stereotypical ways of perceiving society and lifeworld. Psychoanalysts and psychoanalytically informed critics have underscored the kinship between writing literature and daydreaming and literature's intimate relation with desire. Psychoanalytical criticism wants to enlighten us about what forces, behind our back, co-determine our behaviour. Reception theorists stress the role of the reader in the creation of the text's meaning, and thus their stance is anti-authoritarian.

In my opinion, all these approaches highlight important features and functions of literary texts. The point, however, is that, due to its plurifunctionality and complex linguistic and rhetorical structure, the literary text wills always more or less fully manifest these four characteristics, and many more. *Hamlet*, for instance, may certainly be seen as embodying several conflicts and antagonisms central to its age (among other things, as epitomized in the four characters of Hamlet father and son, Claudius, and Fortinbras). Its combination of stylistic levels and its imagery and other rhetorical devices set it apart from the non-literary language of its day and create its specific idiom that makes it possible for the spectator to get another perspective on his or her lifeworld as well. Furthermore, in spite of alternative interpretations, and despite any necessary acknolwedgment of the Renaissance conception of incest, *Hamlet* seems also to remain a play about conscious and unconscious fears and desires related to incest in its modern conception. Finally, it is a prime example of how a literary text may endlessly engender markedly different receptions.

As for the Prince of Denmark himself, it has been remarked that in the nineteenth century he was conceived as the noble prince, whereas the twentieth century most often saw him as a problematic, unpleasant, and troubled character. These states of affairs (especially the issue of Hamlet's character) open up the whole question of the criteria for validity in interpretation. Although the different interpretations of the character must, of course, be recognized, one might nevertheless claim that they are not equally well argued. It might, for instance, be argued that Hamlet's nobility is mostly referred to by other characters (e.g., Ophelia and Horatio) as a thing of the past, while his present behaviour is more moody and troubled than noble.

The basic stance of this book is that it is not only impossible but also harmful to attempt to do away with the heterogeneity and complexity of literature. The approach of Peircean semiotics has been chosen because, within its own framework, it allows, indeed necessitates, a fourfold way of accessing and analysing literature.

8.2 Other-representation and Self-representation

The fourfold semiotic approach mentioned above is the result of combining two ways of sign processing always co-present in speech, namely, the object – sign – interpretant relationship and that of utterer – sign – interpreter. Both relationships may be seen as the combination of other-representation and self-representation. In Peirce's own definition of the sign, its other-representational character is essential; a sign stands for something, its object, and he quotes the medieval sign definition, *aliquid stat pro aliquo*, with approval (see chapter 1). Everyday experience corroborates this understanding of the sign: we communicate, among other things, to lingually represent states of affairs that are not linguistic. And literature, whether a meditative poem representing a state of mind or a narrative representing a fictional universe, is no exception; it stands for and refers to an object, and thus it is certainly other-representational.

However, both non-literary and literary texts will, at the same time as they represent a mind or a universe, necessarily manifest their own structural properties as a specific semiotic (Lotman would say a specific modelling system). Thus, a linguistic text is at the same time other- and self-representational. On the one hand, its universe is moulded by the semiotic through which it is represented, but, on the other, the nature of its universe will influence the selection of the means of representation. The meaning and effect of a text is the outcome of the dialectic between the concrete encounter and the interaction of other- and self-representation (cf. *veni, vidi, vici*).

Utterances, however, contain an additional dialectic between other- and self-representation. From a communicative point of view, an utterance will also necessarily become self-representational. The utterer, whether strongly present or barely traceable, will be a part of the utterance simply by the fact that a hypothesis about his or her propositional attitude is a precondition for understanding the utterance. However, such self-representation, involves other-representation since the response of the interpreter, before the fact, is a shaping force in the production of the utterance. Thus, the imagined dialogue with an interpreter in the mind of the utterer will be present in the text, either as an effort to reach understanding or as a tactic of persuasion (cf. chapter 1).

A text, then, is the outcome of a double dialectic: that between object and interpretant and that between utterer and interpreter; that is, the outcome of two intertwined and insoluble cases of other- and self-representation. In addition, however, the object-pole of semiosis, like the other poles of the semiotic pyramid, is precisely defined as a place, not as a specific kind of entity. Consequently, any of the other poles may be duplicated by becoming the object of the text, that is, that to which it refers. 'I am myself the subject of my book,' says Montaigne, pointing to literature as self-expression. By contrast, petitions, exhortations, commands, judgments, and sentences, and curses are not only addressed to somebody, they mention and refer to this fact and make it the theme of the text. Furthermore, a text may become self-referential, its own object, and point to its properties as a text; for instance, cases of self-exegesis, in which parts of the text take other parts as the object of interpretation.

In addition to this form of duplication through reference, which of course is also widely used in literature, the poles are represented in the textual properties and relations themselves. In addition to being about states of affairs in the world, the text may be filled with idiomatic expressions symptomatic of its utterer. Its rhetoric may clearly indicate that a specific audience is addressed, although it is nowhere mentioned. Furthermore, its properties and internal relations may certainly be on display without commentary; just as a conclusion may be implied without being mentioned. This is why texts about a certain object, by referring to it, will at the same time manifest or imply the other poles.

Duplication, indirect representation, and the creation of internal tensions or amplifications make possible literature's rhetorical and argumentative complexity. For instance, to relate or simply list atrocities in the simplest, most colourless way to create a tension between the text's other-representation, the universe referred to, and its manner of self-representation, its rhetoric. Humility to the point of self-effacement on the part of a commanding officer addressing a private creates an unexpected effect compared to a self-asserting and commanding tone, etc., etc. The variations and the complexity of the interplay between other- and self-representation and between reference and indirect representation are practically infinite. Literature, imitating other discourses and types of texts, explores these possibilities inherent in linguistic communication. This exploration serves the double purpose of representing the complexities of the dialectic between subject, others, and lifeworld and of making present and palpable the qualities and structures of the text itself.

This dialectic has also been the subject of this book. In Part One, the discussion of the general semiotic and discursive framework has shown that sign processes, semioses, are inherently complex since they presuppose the co-presence and interaction between causal relationships (some kinds of indexical signs and some aspects of perception and motor activity) and a multitude of culturally formed interpretive habits. Linked with the causal processes within the species and the individual is our diagrammatic (Peirce) or image-schematic (Johnson and Lakoff) activity, which is grounded in our bodily presence in the world. In Peirce (and in Darwin), the concept of habit strides the nature/culture distinction. Culturally sedimented grids of interpretation further overlay innate dispositions. Together with what is inherited through evolution, such grids make up the immense and enormously complex collection of immediate interpretants that, within a given culture, are accessible at a given moment. Even if, at any given time, some interpretive habits are revised, together they offer sufficient stability of meaning(s) to make possible communication within, and even between, communities. Furthermore, changes in interpretive habits take place at different paces; some are ephemeral, some are entrenched in our physical and mental make-up. The relationship between individual semiosis and the grids of interpretive habits is one of interdependence. On the one hand, production of meaning presupposes pre-existing interpretants – creation ex nihilo is not a human activity. On the other, only through novel interpretations (changing and adding to the stock of interpretive habits) is it possible to change the lifeworld and to adapt to those changes that confront us.

Processes of signification are divided here into informational and communicative (see chapter 1). The former has to do with the processing of environmental inputs through perception and motor activity, the latter with dialogues between utterers and interpreters. While the former primarily, but not exclusively, are experienced as indexical and iconic signs, the symbolic signs play an important role in the latter; although they certainly need the two other kinds in order to signify. However, both informational and communicative semioses are inferential, and they presuppose each other: learning processes, which are communicative, mould our finer categorizations and thus our reading of the environment. Further, internal interpretation is itself dialogic because it is directed at convincing the future critical self, as Peirce says (i.e., it implies a split of consciousness). In a wider sense, dialogism, as the interaction of agencies, is probably also a fruitful way of looking at unconscious mental processes, especially since such processes are purposeful, even though they are not intentional.

Communication is purposeful action. We may, however, with Habermas, distinguish between strategic action that is directed towards success and mastery and communicative action that is directed towards understanding. If the goal remains the creation of mutual understanding, the moment consensual action is questioned, a change of level takes place, and the participants engage in discourse in an attempt to establish (or re-establish) consensus. Discourse means a lifting of the pressure to act immediately and a virtualization of the validity claims under discussion in order to establish the truth of a theoretical position or the normative rightness of an action, custom, or positive law.

Both discourse and literature (and the other arts) share the liberation from experience and the pressure to act. From this perspective, literature, like discourse, becomes a means to open up the world in the sense of questioning agents, forces, and rules and routines. Thus, discourse and literature agree in offering alternative scenarios for interpretation and action. For Habermas, however, discourse is concerned with rationality, while literature and the arts are dramaturgical, concerned with the realm of the subjective.

Taking Habermas's concept of discourse as the point of departure, I find it useful to add two further kinds of discourse to theoretical and practical discourse, namely, technical discourse and historical discourse. Second, literature is added as a fifth discourse, but as a one that is able to imitate and concretize the other four discourses through exemplification, that is, by giving a local habitation and a name to the general concerns of the other discourses. Third, even if it is certainly true that subjectivity and expressiveness are hallmarks of literature, it is much too narrow to relegate it to this one world. Literature, I claim, by imitating the other discourses, also encompasses the worlds to which they apply: outer nature, the lifeworld of social interaction, and the medium itself, language, in addition to the inner world.

This conviction is responsible for the way the central part of this book has been conceived and structured, namely, in four chapters each dealing with one of the poles on the ground-plane of semiosis. The argument of these chapters should substantiate the plausibility of the initial hypothesis, brought to the study of literature from semiotics, namely, that meaning is only explainable as the outcome of the dynamic relationship between all the relates of semiosis. Concretely, the four chapters make up two pairs of other- and self-representation. Literature as mimesis (chapter 3) is concerned with literature's other-representational capacity, whereas the self-reflexive dimension (chapter 4) explores its self-representational capacity. Literature as self-expression (chapter 5) is devoted to literature's subjective dimension, that is, to its capacity to express the very complex position of the utterer, whereas chapter 6, 'The Interpreters,' inquires into the features of literature as an institution. This institution, it turns out, is torn between the role of affirming the culture and community to which it belongs and a subversive wish to plead for transcending their boundaries. Literature also cares for its readership by (among other things) creating a position ready-made within the literary text for the interpreter, that is, the addressee. Actual readers' fascination with literature is, however, not necessarily dependent on the role assigned to them by the text. It may rather stem from literature's sensuous riches together with the possibilities of identification it offers, identifications that may transcend those foreseen and laid out by the text itself.

The hypotheses that all four poles are intimately connected in the literary text and that they mutually presuppose each other are borne out by the present inquiry.

The seemingly simple question of the mimetic nature of the literary text, about what and how it imitates, turns out to demand a complex answer involving intricacies concerning relations of contiguity, similarity, and conventionality between text universe and lifeworld. On top of this, the universe of the literary text may, indeed most often will, contain a transfiguration and intensification compared to the historical universe. Thus, from intuitively understanding literature as other-representational, we are forced to take into account its self-representational dimension. From being seen as a mere reflection, it becomes a model for exemplifying ways of conceiving the world, not its mirror image. We become aware of the fact that what is represented in literature is dependent not only on the state of mind or action to be imitated, but also on the constraints due to the means of representation. We become aware of the shaping force of the semiotic and of the techniques and devices of the genre and forms in question.

However, this insight is reversible. The perhaps most prominent self-representational device of literature, namely, analogy, may be confined to a formal, 'syntactic,' relationship of properties of sound and sight. The moment, however, the text's (other-)representation of a universe endows it with a meaning, it becomes interpretable only because it directly or obliquely calls upon interpretive habits founded in lifeworld experience, that is, by bridging the two universes through analogical reasoning. On the one hand, literary mimesis implies that imitated minds and lifeworlds are moulded by patterns and rules belonging to the interpretive grids specific to different forms and genres. On the other hand, such structural principles and specific interpretive habits are both thought to interpret the experiential world (e.g., the worldly wisdom and moral precepts of the animal fable) and are, in the last analysis, dependent on knowledge from the very world of which they are supposed to be models. Thus, the dialectic of self- and other-representation within the text is duplicated in the text–world relationship.

The text, however, has its source in the utterer(s). Consequently, in addition to being about an object, a mind, or a universe, it is the self-expression of its utterer. At the same time, it is also an utterance addressed to somebody, and its addressee is both represented within it and is its target. Thus, as regards its communicative dimension the text is also both self- and other-representational. The self-expression of the utterer is influenced by the wish to position him- or herself in relation to the interpreter. This positioning, however, is dependent on the way in which the communicative target is envisaged. Thus, although the representation of the other depends upon the imagination of the utterer, the text as self-expression is influenced by what is certainly conceived of as not-self, as 'you.'

In literature this dialectic of the four relates of the text is further complicated because the text–world relationship is attenuated by all of the following: (1) the fictionality of the represented universe, (2) the playfulness of the poet's linguistic devices, (3) its experimentation with normative rightness, (4) the personae of the utterer, and (5) the indefinite number of interpreters and the fact that even if the text interpellates them, it does not commit them.

8.3 Eight Paradoxes of Literature

The last paragraph of the preceding section summarizes, in my view, important structural, rhetorical, and functional properties of literature. There are, however, certain consequences stemming from these features together with the way in which literature places itself – and is placed – as one discourse among others within the community. These consequences are of a paradoxical nature because, prima facie, ends and means seem at odds with each other.

1. True lies:
Literature's ambition is to reveal a state of mind or to tell a story that is truer than those of autobiographical reports and history writings. In order to do so, it tells about that which has never happened –

2. Difference in similarity:
The states of mind and affairs represented in literature are interesting and existentially relevant to the extent that they are recognizable as representations of general predicaments that confront man. However, they become only aesthetically relevant, relevant as art, to the extent they are markedly different from everyday experience of the lifeworld –

3. Self-reflecting view:
Literature's ambition to represent mind and world in an exemplary way means aiming at transparency of expression in order to view the object clearly. However, in literature language is constantly drawing attention to itself and thus pointing to the text as an artefact, something made with art –

4. Studied expressiveness:
Literature's ambition is to speak more expressively than any other kinds of speech. In order to do so it speaks with reserve, it always quotes itself, and even in torrents of words it is reticent –

5. Vicarious subjectivity:
It is the aim of literature to make the subject familiar with parts of him- or herself by provoking (and, in a certain sense, even stilling) his or her desires. However, in order to do, so it creates another desire that functions as a vicarious subjectivity left for the readers to imagine, but from which they are separated by an ontological split –

6. The allegorization of the particular:
Literature relates something very concrete about a particular state of mind and/or a specific universe of action. It is through the individuality and particularity of the case presented that it appeals to both our imaginary powers and to our emotional responses. Nevertheless, the

self-exegesis of the literary text invites, and the response of most readers favours, generalization and allegorization. Thus, the text is both understood as literal statements about the particular and as general statements about something abstract that is rather inferred from than mentioned in the text –

7. Effective ineffectiveness:
Literature's ambition is to influence the life and opinions of its audience. In order to do so, it interpellates its readers and appeals to them. However, neither interpellation nor appeal have any force at all; they do not obligate the audience in any binding way. But even if literature does not commit its readers, it is efficient enough (sometimes) to be accused of stirring in them something of which they may themselves disapprove –

8. Provisory licence:
Literature as an institution allows writers a certain freedom to question social interaction, communal values, metaphysical suppositions, and the use of language, and it somehow protects them against both authorities and audience. Nevertheless, the publication of every single work of literature may provoke a renegotiation of poetic licence and eventually its revocation. Poetic licence is a privilege that is never certain. Although it ought, in principle, to make up part of the preconditions for writing literature, it is really always granted *post festum*, as the absence of punitive measures –

The apparent paradox concerning the text–world relationship is attenuated by realizing that truth cannot mean correspondence with particular states of affairs. Rather, it means corresponding to what is deemed exemplary as regards subjectivity, interaction, and lifeworld at a given time. Thus, it is agreement with models accepted by an audience or readership that matters most. In Althusser's words, it is man's imaginary world relationship that is important, not necessarily the real conditions.

Even in literature, which is the privileged place of imagination, the text–world relationship is not altogether dissolved because of the tension between its affirmative and subversive aspects. By construing an alternative world, literature does sometimes attempt to break through what is commonly held to be true. In such cases, the idea of revealing the real state of affairs is regulative. Thus, fictionality is not an accidental property of literature; it is the very precondition for representing model cases not only of common beliefs but also of what is supposed to cut through prejudice and illusion in order to represent the human condition as it really is. To boot, fictionality makes possible the concrete representation of what ought to be.

Further, the invented states of mind and states of affairs are only interesting – as art – provided they contain a dialectic between what is supposed to be similar to experience and what is supposed to be different from it. Literature obeys rules of its own. Its world is stylized, either idealized or made grotesque, or both, and its hyperbolic or litotic nature, that is, the experience of difference, is in itself a source of enjoyment.

Whereas the first two paradoxes concern the intricacies of the relationship between text-world and lifeworld, the third is an effect of the relation between other- and self-representation in the text. Literature certainly highlights its status as artefact through the triple nature of literary imitation (of world, other texts, and the internal duplication of textual features). One might argue, however, that since the idea of unmediated world access is illusory (perception being itself a semiotic process), and since literature displays the properties of its medium, it is just honestly drawing attention to what is generally necessary for experiencing and attributing meaning to phenomena.

However, this is the easy way out. Literature is not mainly concerned with displaying the general semiotic precondition for signification and interpretation. This effect is a byproduct of two other concerns more important to it: feasting on the corporeality of language and momentarily bridging, or spectacularly pointing to, the split between mind, world, and language. However, using the enchantments of language's materiality to heal the universe cuts both ways, because literature will also reveal itself as an effect obtained by art. Thus, to experience literature becomes like looking at drawings and figures by Escher or Kanizsa. Just as we involuntarily (and voluntarily) switch between seeing such drawings as three-dimensional spaces and as surfaces, so we experience literature as world representation and as texture.

The fourth paradox is related both to the distance effectuated by the work with language and to the communicative function of literature. Emotions are always controlled in literature because the passion spent on heating up the text subtracts from the passion invested in the cause it promotes; and the emotive force is chanelled into the intricate network of textual relations.

This paradox is also related to literature's communicative function. Literature embodies the imaginary in figures and fables for the benefit of strangers. Thus, it must express not only the fears and desires of the utterer, but what is supposed to be a concern of others as well. Its producers are, therefore, in some corner of their minds, distanced from their own imaginations. Diderot's paradox of the actor is, I think, valid for literature in general.

The fifth paradox points to the fact that literature expresses what is thought to belong exclusively to the subject and what are sharable emotions and significations. Thus, to both writer and reader it offers a screen in the double sense of allowing projection and offering protection. Furthermore, it is already concerned with interpretation because it motivates such emotions and attitudes by stories, encounters, arguments, and visions. Even if the impetus of literature is, it seems to me, more magical than epistemological, it is concerned with offering explanations of the human condition, and consequently what is experienced is also, explicitly or implicitly, commented upon and made probable. Thus, literature underscores the fact that what seems to belong to the intimate parts of selfhood is produced socially. No wonder, then, that the reader's subjectivity can feed on and be formed by vicarious experiences.

The intertwining of the communal and the subjective is also related to the sixth paradox. Basically, I suppose this drift towards generalization and allegorization of the particular is grounded in our iconic imagination. Outside literature, these dispositions are eminently important to our survival. Pattern recognition, subsuming a case under a rule, ascribing a phenomenon to a category are all necessary – and pleasurable – operations of the mind. But literature itself prompts this drift, because imaginary visions and relations must be offered for a reason. Why, is the reader's implicit question, should I bother to read about that which is not? How can I profit from it? Part of an answer to this question relates to the first paradox, namely that, despite, indeed by virtue of, its irreality, literature is a surveyable analogue of that which is; and thus it satisfies our diagrammatic imagination. The allegorical dimension, the search for the surplus meaning, the *sensus plenior*, of the text, is also related to our passion for knowledge and order. Allegorization provide us with a universe united by analogical networks that link relations and meanings and the sensuous and the conceptual in ways that are only possible in literature. But it seems that the force of the allegory depends on the concreteness of the representation as if the worldliness of the text somehow proved the presence and importance of its conceptual structure. We are, after all, earthen beings.

The seventh paradox, literature's ambition to reach out and move its audience or readership to accept its lesson without any means to oblige it, is, at least prima facie, a striking case of the incongruity of ends and means. However, concerning this point, literature agrees with the general idea of discourse. The effort to reach consensus through discourse means precisely to abstain from using any forms of power and coercion. Thus, if literature had had the power to dictate the opinions and moral judgments of its readership, it would become authoritarian, or a part of strategic action. Its powerlessness, therefore, ensures that its ability to convince its readership is due to the force of the case it presents, not to coercion or guile (just as theoretical and practical discourse should result in the acceptance of the better argument).

The eighth paradox is the coexistence of recognition and non-recognition of poetic licence. The greater literature's challenge to the community is, and the more effective it is, the more imminent is the danger that there is no protection to be had from claiming this licence. The powerlessness of literature lies not only in its lack of authority to dictate beliefs and values but also in its inability to defend itself.

In relation to this vulnerability, there is another problem related to literature's status as discourse: literature is most often either used for strategic purposes or it is censored. Yet this problem is not specific to literature; contributions meant to further the other discourses are treated the same. This is not surprising, because to suggest and argue that something is or should be the case does influence, or potentially influence, the state of affairs to which the suggestions and arguments apply. Thus, those profiting from the acceptance of other viewpoints will defend them, and will do so most often not only through scholarly or scientific arguments, but also through the exercise of institutional power.

As regards literature, there are, however, two specific problems connected with this issue. On the one hand, literature's ability to afford pleasure seems enhanced by its fictionality and by the fact that it does not seem to oblige either utterer or interpreter. On the other, it is impossible for it to liberate itself from praxis and morality; these concerns are simply its matter. Furthermore literature, being a mimetic representation of the desires that such matters arouse within its universe, will, in its turn, arouse those of its audience or readership.

Literature, however, includes both reason and desire, for it not only arouses them but offers a meditation on and arguments about imagined desires and their effects. In exemplifying attempts at mediation between what is reasonable and what is desirable, literature easily becomes a victim of its own inclusiveness and ambivalence. It will be accused of calling forth even that of which it disapproves. Thus, instead of being prosecuted for coercion, it has (since Plato) been accused of seduction. However, its seductive powers are also the reason for its being idolized.

These eight paradoxes and incongruities are not independent of each other. The fictionality of the represented universe is the precondition for the possibility of representing adequately both that which is supposed generally to be the case, that which ought to be the case, and that which fulfils man's desires or agonizes him.

Literature's work with language is in itself pleasurable, because it means patterning its sensuous riches and exploring its meaning potential. It is, however, also the precondition for representing the fictional universe, for communicating the text's putative totality of feeling, attitude, and signification, and for sharing what otherwise would remain a dumb, uninterpreted insistence within each subject for itself. However, literary language necessarily expresses on its own conditions, and the putting into words will to a certain extent trade expressiveness for expressibility. Thus, a belabouring of language to make it translate and represent that which is not in itself linguistic is an ongoing enterprise that attempts to widen the realm of what is expressible in language without ever being assured of having reached its limits.

Even if fears and desires are responsible for a large part of the architecture of literary universes and what takes place within them, literary texts have their own attenuated version of a reality principle, and this is why not only communicability but also internal, and often even external plausibility set limits to what is represented. The fictionality of the represented and the indirect form of communication mean that both writers and interpreters are at a certain distance from what the text tells.

The fictionality and aesthetic distance of literary texts set them apart from everyday business and make possible their non-committal nature. This means that interpreters are at liberty to meditate and experiment upon them, to add what is not explicitly said and, in addition to allegorization, to play serious games of projection and identification. Yet in spite of such efforts to make the literary text one's own, it remains in some respects strange, and thus capable of widening the perspective and the understanding of its interpreters.

What is common to the eight paradoxes diagnosed here is that they all represent both oppositions and ambiguities and an arrested gesture of mediation: an effort to bridge the gap between, and somehow reconcile, fiction and lifeworld, self and other, desires and fears, imagination and reason, received morality and reasoned transgression, licence and oppression, and the gap between expressiveness, expressibility, and poeticity. However, much of the value of literature, in my opinion, resides in the fact that it does not claim to have arrived at a flawless conciliatory synthesis. It points towards such unification, but it most often shows both that this synthesis is made with art and belongs to the realm of art, and that even within its own universe the fractures are visible. It is a magic that, in an important sense, does not believe in itself, and this is perhaps why it may be both fascinating and wholesome.

8.4 Literature!

The title of the introduction ended with a question mark to indicate that the concept of literature is much questioned because it defies attempts at rigorous definition. There has been no attempt here to create a definition that may infallibly point out literary texts and distinguish them from the non-literary. Indeed, there has not even been a search for such a definition, because such a search would be contrary to the bundle of features (fictionality, poeticity, inquisitoriality, licence, and contemplation) that are here supposed to be common, but not necessarily always co-present, in all literary texts. It would also run contrary to the definition of literary discourse as the discourse that is able to imitate the other discourses.

To give the protean definition to literature as the discourse that may take the shape of one or several other discourses is not a move to find an easy way out. On the one hand, it is given in order to account for the peculiarities of a group of texts whose ontological status has been debated for centuries, namely, texts that have alternately been classified as fiction and as non-fiction (such as *Les lettres portugaises*). Obviously, this phenomenon is marginal, but in an interesting sense its marginality is contingent. The reason there are so few such cases is that the history of a text's publication and reception, the reigning reading conventions (including signs often considered trustworthy indicators of fictionality), and the process through which the text is institutionalized as literature prevent most mistakes. On the other hand, such a definition points to an, in my opinion, important function of literature. If we attempt to answer the question asked by Barend van Heusden and Paul Hernadi – Why literature? or Why is literature? – from a Peircean perspective, the answer may be that literary texts are iconic signs that do certainly not copy reality like scale models but are analogues of ways in which we categorize, model, and discourse on our lifeworld. Further, instead of being analogues of any particular states of mind or affairs, they are analogues of whatever is like them. But why do we need such analogues? Part of the answer is common to all iconic signs: they exhibit the relations they represent (e.g., a geometrical diagram), they allow a certain generality (e.g., the anatomic atlas), they offer intuitive and perceptible evidence for their proofs (e.g., Venn diagrams and algebraic formulae), they represent indifferently facts and fictions, and finally they allow experimentation (e.g., architects and artists changing their sketches).

Even if literary texts are made of symbolic signs, they explore the iconic possibilities of language, for instance, its diagrammatic and metaphorical potential. They are able to switch between showing and telling, they always lay claims to the representative force of their specific cases, they prove by imagining and displaying states of mind and affairs, they mix fictional and non-fictional, and they are certainly the result of experimentation. Indeed, literature is, perhaps even first and foremost, imaginary experiments with experience.

For several reasons such experimentation is valuable and important. First of all, to be able to make hypotheses about the nature of things and future states of affairs is a necessary precondition for the survival both of the individual person and of the species (by not predicting the future position of a truck, we will get run over, and by not predicting a future shortage of natural resources and taking measures to avoid it, we will become extinct). In both cases, however, we remain inside the same universe, and imagination and prediction, that is, hypothesis making, are means that make planned action possible.

Despite the ontological difference of its universe (yes, I still think the difference between the fictive and the real matters very much), literature functions in a similar way as the discourses it imitates. It affords vicarious experiences that, in addition to somewhat stilling our desire to be able to safely transgressing our bodily and social constraints, also enhance our understanding of others and our capacity for empathy. It offers exemplary representations of states of mind and narratives that transmit both cultural heritage – literature being an important reservoir of cultural memory – in concrete form and blueprints for what is claimed to be proper or deplorable reactions to the present condition. Its concrete nature, the fact that it represents the particular, that it is focused on its own universe, means that it is capable of comprehensively showing the interaction of needs, compulsions, emotions, values, norms, and reason in mental processes and in the interaction of individuals. And that it is not committed to any particular facts ensures both its experimental and its sometimes exemplary character. This is why literature may offer lifeworld models that are cognitive and emotive, both subjective and communal, grounded in individual experience and generalized. The value of such models is obvious: they allow their readers to assimilate the perspectives and understanding of the texts through identification, and thus a growth of cultural and social competence is furthered.

Literature, however, unites the iconic and the symbolic, and language is capable not only of asserting facts, including facts concerning fictional universes, but also of offering arguments that, in the case of literature, supplement the intuitive proofs of the iconic aspects of the texts. This is why literature is not only iconic, although it certainly is that; it is also doubly argumentative, owing partly to its rhetorical patterning of the text, partly to its questions and reflections on what it represents. Literature not only presents icons of the human condition, it offers arguments about them.

If this sounds familiar, it is no wonder, for that is what we are ordinarily doing when we relate and judge what is happening around us. And this is the point! Literature matters because it is capable both of simulating everyday experiences (obviously including fateful ones as well) and of transforming/transfiguring them.

Parts of everyday experience, however, change through the ages. Consequently, in addition to its internal development as a craft, literature's link with lifeworld experiences alone suffices to provoke constant changes. This is the main reason it is impossible to discover waterproof criteria that distinguish literature from non-literature. The tension between simulation and transfiguration creates an internal variety that makes it possible to say only what is most often, but not universally, true of it.

However, this state of affairs is no reason for disappointment. On the contrary, if literature were not protean, it would be incapable of fulfilling one of its main functions: that of offering models of and for experience. This is why I have ventured to change the initial question mark attached to literature to a mark of exclamation to indicate that, although literature may defy (too narrowly conceived) standards of classification, it is certainly there to enlighten us, both about experiences we desire and fear and about those we ought to have – and to make us take delight in them.

Notes

Introduction

1 According to convention, in references to *The Collected Papers of Charles Sanders Peirce* (CP), the number left of the decimal point designates the volume number, and that to the right the paragraph number.
2 Such a development may be illustrated in this way:

t: Text properties		A: a, b, c, d, e, f
t + 1:	"	B: c, d, e, f, g, h
t + 2:	"	C: e, f, g, h, i, j
...		
t + n:	"	Z: g, h, i, j, k, l

3 Goethe to Eckermann, 25 January 1827.
4 In fact, this position has been pointed out by Anthony Burgess (1984).
5 Cf. Hugo Friedrich's (1956) analysis of the roots of modernism in the nineteenth century.
6 The French symbolists for example, according to Bourdieu (1993), wrote for one another.

Chapter 1   From Sign to Dialogue

1 Text and utterance may be used interchangeably. A text is an utterance, because it is the outcome of the action of uttering; i.e., a text, as an artefact, has a history and a maker. Within natural languages, texts are made of linguistic signs, but signs have to be instanced as utterances/texts to

acquire definite meaning by being embedded in contexts of uttering and referring. When dealing with complex, written strings of linguistic signs, uttered at a given time, we most often speak of texts.

2 Such as visual semiotics and the semiotics of the other senses, zoosemiotics, anthroposemiotics, semiotics of culture, semiotics of law, of religion, etc. (see Eco 1979, Deely 1982 and 1990, and Sebeok 1994). It is also a field with different, and sometimes conflicting and competing, traditions and doctrines.

3 Such attempts are obviously the bone and marrow of the experimental sciences, because they try to make nature answer questions concerning its own structures and functions. However, humanistic disciplines, such as history, jurisprudence, and the study of literature, do something comparable. Their sources of information are the documents and monuments – the texts in the extended sense of this concept – and scholars also try to elicit probable answers from them; only prediction plays a lesser, but certainly not a negligible, role here.

4 In quoting from the unpublished manuscripts, the manuscript number and data are given according to the Robin catalogue (Robin 1967). With regard to the page number, I follow the pagination of scholars from the Institute in Pragmaticism (ISP), Texas Tech University, Lubbock, Texas.

5 It should be mentioned that there are important similarities between Peirce's understanding of iconic signs, and particularly of diagrams, and the way cognitive science studies the schematizing activity of the mind. Mark Johnson and George Lakoff, jointly as well as separately, have especially explored the role of image-schemata in the establishment of meaning. According to their view (inspired by Kant), image-schemata mediate between perception and concept formation, and such schemata are founded in our bodily presence, orientation, and functioning in our lifeworld. In Peirce's terminology such schemata would be diagrams mapping our place and movement in a time-space continuum (see Lakoff and Johnson 1980, Johnson 1987, and Lakoff 1987).

6 Another example is language. In this century language has been looked upon as an algebra (C.S. Peirce, Saussure, and Louis Hjelmslev), as a generator (N. Chomsky and others), and as action (analytical philosophy and linguistic pragmatics). This importation of perspectives, which are all only partly valid, has been beneficial to linguistics precisely because they point out and explore parallelisms with something else.

7 In the Hippocratic writings (5th and 4th centuries BC), and in those of Galen (c. Ad 139–99), we find the first systematic exposition of diagnosing on the basis of signs. Some symptoms are invaluable to the physician

because they almost unambiguously indicate a specific illness and thus, perhaps, a certain treatment.
8 'If we suppose any habitual action to become inherited ... then the resemblance between what originally was a habit and an instinct becomes so close as not to be distinguished' (Darwin [1859] 1968: 235).
9 The contested concept of perspective seems to be such a case. Even if its laws relate to human vision in general, perspective was introduced in European pictorial representation at a given time, and even from that time it has certainly not been applied universally. Some of the approaches within cognitive semantics and philosophy seem promising for the study of conceptual structures in general. They study the classificatory principles actually used by the members of a given culture (e.g., categories with a radial structure; see Lakoff 1987: 83–4), and they offer a prolegomena to a general theory of cognition. This theory, being representational and phenomenological (the schematizing activity of imagination) is also semiotic (see Johnson's analysis of the relation between object, perceived image, schema, and concept; Johnson 1987: xxxvii and 139–72).
10 Peirce does not distinguish between sign and text.
11 Peirce points to the necessary correlation of speech and experience: 'It is not the language alone, with its mere associations of similarity, but the language taken in connection with the auditor's own experiential associations of continuity, which determines for him what house is meant. It is requisite then, in order to show what we are talking or writing about, to put the hearer's or reader's mind into real, active connection with the concatenation of experience or of fiction with which we are dealing, and further, to draw his attention to, and identify, a certain number of particular points in such concatenation' (CP 3.419).
12 Such ideas may rest on experience and on systematic experimentation and gathering of data. Pedagogy is the discipline that studies and teaches the (presumably) best way of imparting knowledge and standards to children.
13 When discussing literature we will return to the questions of infinite semiosis.
14 Even in speech, the so-called paralinguistic features of speech – intonation, pitch, loudness of voice, etc. – are extremely important. People most often respond to oral, indeed to most linguistic, messages globally, i.e., they do not pay particular attention to lexicon and syntax (they most often cannot recall even brief messages verbatim). They are, however, extremely sensitive to tone and body language, because they indicate the personal relationship between the interlocutors.
15 According to Peirce, not only the CONTAINERschema as exemplified in

436 Notes to pages 62–5

the Venn diagrams, but also the other way of representing the syllogism (all M are P / all P are S // all M are S) are diagrammatic, because the position of the middle term in both premises is *shown* (see CP 3.363).

16 Near-identical wetware and shared networks of immediate interpretants make near-identical experience possible. Experience is related to perception (and motility) and to the formation of mental images. In 'the reduction of the manifold of sensation to the unity of perception,' to use a Kantian phrase, the role of image-schemas seem crucial. Indeed, Lakoff suggests that 'our perception and our mental images are structured by image schemas and that the schemas associated with lexical items are capable of fitting the schemas that structure our perceptions and images. On this hypothesis, we do not have pure unstructured perceptions and images. Perceptions and images are not merely pictorial. In perceiving and forming images, we impose a great deal of image-schematic structure. It is this image-schematic structure that allows us to fit language to our perceptions and rich images' (Lakoff 1987: 455). If this hypothesis is substantiated by further studies, it will bridge the gap between language and perception by pointing to the role played by image-schemas originated in the representation of the interaction of body and environment in both perception and language. It tallies with the idea that there is an order of acquiring semiotic competence in which understanding of iconic signs is a precondition for the learning of language (see pp. 40–1). And it furnishes further explanation of the important iconic features of language itself that have been pointed out by, among others, Peirce, to whom 'language is but a kind of algebra' (CP 3.419).

17 However, the role played by emotion must not be neglected. The relationship between the emotional and the ratiocinative is close. It is also plausible that the ultimate reasons for both action and thought are emotional (cf. also Peirce's idea that aesthetics concerns what is in no need of further justification; e.g., CP 1.615). Pascal may be right that *le coeur a ses raisons que la raison ne connaît pas.* However, despite their sometimes apparent irrationality, emotional reactions may be perfectly understandable when they are seen in relation to their survival value, to their history in the individual and in society, and to norms and ideals.

18 In fact, as a general framework for the study of literature, the structuralist Jakobson constructed a functional model of language communication, the celebrated model from 'Linguistics and Poetics' (Jakobson in Sebeok, ed., 1960: 350–77), in which he distinguishes six communicative functions: emotive, conative, referential, poetic, metalinguistic, and phatic.

19 Lyons calls such sentences 'system-sentences,' in contradistinction to

text-sentences, which are defined as being context-dependent utterance-signals; see Lyons 1977: II, 622.
20 For expounding speech according to a three-level model, I am indebted to the excellent exposition by Deborah Schiffrin (1994); the division, however, in the context of pragmatics, goes back to Austin.
21 E.g., the impressive work of Austin, Searle, and Grice.
22 See the following testimony from rather unexpected quarters. In *Prolegomena to a Theory of Language* Hjelmslev points to what to him is a mistake, namely, the idea that words have meanings independent of their co-text and context. He continues: [T]here exists no other perceivable meanings than contextual meanings; any entity, and thus any sign, is defined relatively, and only by its place in the context ... In absolute isolation no sign has any meaning; any sign-meaning arises in a context, by which we mean a situational context or an explicit context, it matters not which, since in an unlimited or productive text (a living language) we can always transform a situational context into an explicit context. Thus we must not imagine, for example, that a substantive is more meaningful than a preposition, or a word more meaningful than a derivational ending' (Hjelmslev 1953 [1943]: 28). Although Hjelmslev claims that a situational context can always be translated into an explicit one, he is silent about how to do so.
23 A person observing the weathercock (an indexical sign) may remark, 'The wind is easterly,' thus translating its silent indication into an utterance by means of symbolic signs. Conversely, a sign saying 'Watch your step' may initiate a careful observation of the ground looking for signs of its being slippery.

Chapter 2 Discourse and Text

1 Habermas prefers to distinguish between modernity and postmodernity.
2 The French title 'L'Ordre du discours' is more to the point.
3 Furthermore, is the medium of discourse confined to natural language? Even staying within the realm of semiotics concerned only with predominantly symbolic signs, the answer is negative. Science, which is a part of theoretical discourse, uses both numeral systems and so-called artificial languages, not as auxiliary systems or short hand, but as systems in their own right, systems that are absolutely essential to their scientific argumentation. Thus one discourse may contain several semiotics. It goes without saying that language may express (parts of) all discourses, but only parts because it seems that language is not able to translate the formal languages used in the sciences without a substantial loss of rigour. At the

438 Notes to page 95

other extreme, the different paralinguistic signs by virtue of which emotional attitudes are represented will also suffer a selective translation into speech.

4 It might be asked, however, Is not something important missing in this list of discourses, Is there not a discourse of emotions, a discourse of desire? However, although there is no denying the importance of emotions and desire (see chapters 6 and 7), I fail to see that they constitute a specific discourse. Emotions do not exist per se; they are always related to objects in the broad semiotic sense (whether these exist in perception, in memory, and/or in the dynamical unconscious). They are, further, bound up with the aesthetic and ethical norms of the individual and of the group to which he or she belongs. They are relational forces partly determining the relationship between the subject, him- or herself, others, and the environment and society at large. This is why it seems sensible to hold with Peirce that 'any emotion is a predication concerning some object, and the chief difference between it and an objective intellectual judgment is that while the latter is relative to human nature or to mind in general, the former is relative to the particular circumstances and disposition of a particular man at a particular time. What is here said of emotions in general, is true in particular of the sense of beauty and the moral sense. Good and bad are feelings which first arise as predicates, and therefore are either predicates of the not-I, or are determined by previous cognitions' (CP 5.247).

The situationality of emotive predication does not mean that emotional responses are private in the sense of being inexplicable to others. Rather, emotions are largely shared within a community. Thus, emotions, in addition to being species-specific, are related to traditions and habits just as much as, or more than, they are to situations. What we feel is to a great extent determined both by our common reactions to outer and inner stimuli (e.g., bodily sensations of pleasure and pain) and by shared aesthetic and ethical standards that we are brought up to honour or despise (cf. Habermas's idea about the 'softer' discourses of aesthetics and therapy). Furthermore, emotional predication has its own history in the individual person that both accounts for the wide variety of emotional responses to the same object and explains why certain individual responses, prima facie, do not make sense. Psychotherapies, e.g., psychoanalysis, attempt to explain the etiology of individual harmful emotional responses precisely by relating them to events and objects, to what actually happened in the life history of the patient, but also, more importantly, to the objects of his or her conscious and unconscious fantasies.

Emotions and desires are related to intellectual judgments in a complex way. Also intellectual predication has its own particular history in every individual. It seems, however, that except for vanguard discussions, for instance within scholarship and science, there is less individual tenacity concerning concepts. Explanations and argumentation concerning concepts offered by others are often accepted because they are (supposed to be) susceptible to public proof, and thus compelling to reason. Furthermore, often there is little at stake for most individuals in accepting definitions of intellectual conceptions, but quite a lot at stake in rejecting them (the individual may be accused of being a heretic, to be burnt, or just despised as stupid). A child may give up its own faulty intellectual understanding of a given phenomenon and, at the same time, be both unwilling and unable to discard the original emotional significance of it, even if the emotional significance is related to the discarded intellectual signification. With regard to the discrepancy between intellectual signification and emotional significance we all remain children to some degree; for instance, we never really give up our belief in the magical power of words, to wit, literature.

5 The Egyptian text(s) about *Sinue* are now commonly thought to be a kind of novella, but they have also been classified as autobiography.
6 Booth, however, has strong opinions on the ethical commitments of an author.
7 When first young *Maro* in his boundles Mind
A work t'outlast Immortal *Rome* design'd,
Perhaps he seem'd *above* the Critick's Law,
And but from *Nature's Fountains* scorne'd to draw:
But when t'examine ev'ry Part he came,
Nature and *Homer* were, he found, the *same*:
Convinc'd, amaz'd, he checks the bold Design,
And Rules as strict his labour'd Work confine,
As if the *Stagyrite* o'erlook'd each Line.
Learn hence for *Ancient Rules* a just Esteem;
To copy *Nature* is to copy *Them*.
    (Pope [1711] 1969: 41–2, vv. 130–40)
Here Pope states not only the classicist and enlightenment dream of a world transparent to reason, but also the idea of the coalescence of norm, reason, and nature.
8 *Robinson Crusoe*, due to the status of its protagonist as a cultural-hero, contains many descriptions of technical items and techniques of reproduction and survival.
9 The non-fiction novel, a problematic genre to the literary scholars and

historians of today, would have met with approval in antiquity and the Middle Ages.
10 Interestingly, this century is also the period during which aesthetics is recognized as an autonomous field of study; e.g., Addison (1734), Baumgarten (1750), and Kant (1790).

Chapter 3 Mimesis: Literature as Initiation and Model

1 There is an almost heroic and very laudable effort on the part of some linguists, e.g., Ann Banfield (1982) and Monika Fludernik (1993), to find linguistic criteria that distinguish literary from non-literary, or rather fictional from non-fictional, texts. I must admit, however, that I find this attempt vain. This is certainly not to say that literary texts do not use specific linguistic forms. In fact, one way of looking at literature is, as the Formalists did, to see it as a bag of tricks and devices; and among such devices, linguistics may, of course, describe linguistic peculiarities. My reservation is another one, and it is threefold: (1) Literature's use of linguistic forms is too diverse; it contains so many different grammatical forms that it defies univocal classification, because it includes the uses of poetry, narrative, and drama (Ann Banfield, for instance, investigates only narrative and Monika Fludernik only free indirect discourse). (2) The particular features described by linguists need not be present in a text that we, for other reasons, would not hesitate to call literary. (3) The features isolated by linguists as literary may well turn up in other kinds of writing, for instance, in autobiographies and diaries.
2 Here especially see the work of Käte Hamburger, *Die Logik der Dichtung* (1957, rev. ed. 1968). Although I find her conclusions erroneous (e.g., that lyrical poetry is not fictional), it is nevertheless a highly interesting and fine piece of literary scholarship.
3 Fictitious sign would normally be a misleading expression if only the sign-vehicle were thought of, but remember that a sign in Peirce is a dynamic relation between sign, object, and interpretant.
4 This is why professors of literature rightly warn their students not to rashly assume that what are valid presuppositions for action within their own culture are valid in the Sagas as well (although some presuppositions will be).
5 *Great Expectations* is, I suppose, the closest English literature of the 19th century has to offer in the widespread continental subgenre: the *Bildungsroman*.
6 For valuable discussions of fictionality see also Eco 1979, Searle 1979, and Pavel 1986.

7 Many signs in *Finnegans Wake* have to be translated into a natural language, such as English, to make sense.
8 The fictional worlds of interactive video games are, of course, another matter, but even here the player's influence is limited.
9 Most decent present editions of his work will contain not only the map but also the key that gives the actual equivalents of the fictional proper names.
10 Cf. the two versions of *Great Expectations*. Even if separateness and individuality of the universes represented in different fictional texts are most common, there are many examples of the effort, both collectively and by individual authors, to construct the individual texts as a part of the same universe. The *Iliad* and the *Odyssey* are supposed to refer to the same universe, and so are the tragedies. Thus, a common mythology ties the texts together. In our times some authors have created individual works that are parts of a chronicle of a given region; e.g., Hardy and Faulkner.
11 London: Hutchinson, 1992. Still, the fictional setting of Nazi Germany having won the war is fairly common in science fiction.
12 As William Amos informs us: 'It has been [Christopher] Isherwood's practice to obtain written declarations from his originals that they will not sue, and this precaution is now often insisted upon by publishers sensing possible trouble. For as Angela Thirkell's publisher once cautioned her, the stock prefatory 'all characters are imaginary' disclaimer is worthless, cutting no ice either with public or with lawyers' (Amos 1985: xiv).
13 Cf. the dirty underground picture of all the hybrid beings of the Disney family copulating.
14 The ancestry of this kind of text includes a kind of poem known in the Renaissance as a *macedoine*, which consists of lines taken from other poems and combined in such a way as to make up a poem.
15 The Protestant church considers all four books apocryphal, whereas the Roman Catholic church recognizes books 1 and 2 as canonical.
16 Indeed until the second half of the 12th century Purgatory did not exist as a Latin noun (purgatorium), only as an adjective, as in *ignis purgatorius* (purifying fire) and *loca purgatoria* (places of purification).
17 The recognition of Purgatory was, however, important for the authority of the Catholic church and for its grip on its members. Further, logically, the idea of Purgatory filled in a blank in the description of the fate of man. It mediates between the time of the human individual and eschatological time, the time span ending with the abolition of historical time, the Last Judgment, and eternal bliss, or damnation. The idea of Purgatory also mediates between a human understanding of sin and justice and divine justice and grace. Furthermore, the time that the individual person spent in Purgatory was made indirectly dependent on the deeds of the living,

because, it was taught, works of piety (prayers, alms, fasting, and sacrifices) could alleviate the lot of the souls in Purgatory by inspiring divine forgiveness. The ways just mentioned were all, to a great extent, controlled by the church. And thus the Church's privilege of granting indulgence we extended even to the dead souls in Purgatory (a power made part of the dogma; see also Dante's *Purgatory* II, 90–105). Because of controversies within Christianity, Purgatory was an important subject at three synods (in addition to Lyon 1274, Florence 1439 and Trent 1563). Nevertheless, in the end, the location and structure of Purgatory, the nature and intensity of the punishment suffered there, and the duration (other than that it was temporary) of the confinement was left to opinion. In fact, the Catholic church never completely made up its mind concerning these questions.

18 Furthermore, within our own surrounding world we act, in the very concrete sense of physical action. If we earnestly believed that indications and states of affair described in a fictional world were valid within our environment, we might well act to our disadvantage, because in that case the signs of the fictional text would, indeed, be misleading. This may be the reason that, according to Roman Jakobson (in Sebeok ed. 1960: 371), the Majorca storytellers introduced their stories by saying: 'Aixo era y no era' (it was and it was not).

19 Although this is generally true, written texts may certainly be much in need of commentary, as is evident from the helpful commentaries in scholarly editions of correspondence and other kinds of historical documents.

20 The difference is not that the archaeologist and detective deal with objects, whereas the reader and literary scholar deal with signs. Rather, archaeologist and detective discover additional (indexical) signs, while reader and scholar discover additional, or alternative, interpretants to the sign already at hand.

21 Dissimilarity and contrast are related to similarity on an abstract level, because similarity and dissimilarity are correlative concepts; they presuppose one another.

22 This acceptance is not so strange considering that deviant behaviour is a general feature of our own universe. Normal behaviour involves acting according to a norm, in the double sense of acting like most others and complying with certain standards and values.

23 Later the Russian Formalists restored this interface.

24 According to Eleanor Rosch (1975a), the robin is also an exemplar, because it is the bird that most North Americans spontaneously mention as the prototypical bird.

25 We read, for instance, in Amos (p. 221) that Oriane Duchesse de Guermantes in Proust's *Remembrance of Things Past* is an amalgam of Comtesse Adhéaume de Chevigné (1860–1936), Comtesse Henri Greffulhe (1860–1952), and Mme Émile Straus (1846–1926).
26 Even the pictorial representations of actual brain scannings are manipulated to conform to a standard representation of the brain see Posner and Raichle 1996).

Chapter 4   Self-representation and Analogy in Literature

1 Say a Japanese quartz-clock, to avoid all discussions about the possible difference in sounds made by a pendulum swinging to and fro. However, I also think that ascribing differences to the swinging to and fro of a pendulum is mistaken.
2 '[T]here are many attributes which are common to many animals, either identically the same (e.g., organs like feet, feathers, and scales, and affections similarly), or else common by analogy only (i.e., some animals have a lung, others have no lung but something else to correspond instead of it; again, some animals have blood, while others have its counterpart, which in them has the same value as blood in the former)' Aristotle 1961: 103, *Parts of Animals*, I, 5, 646b.
3 However, she misinterprets a metaphor that she considers as one of mere appearance as an attributional metaphor, namely, Herrick's 'the glorious lamp of heaven, the sun.' This metaphor is clearly an analogy, lamp : indoor space : : sun : the heavens. Gentner overlooks the fact that Herrick's metaphor, according to her own terminology, is a double metaphor. A lamp and the sun do not only have attributes in common – i.e., they look the same way; they also have the same place and function within a limited and an unlimited space respectively.
4 However, the relation between metaphor and analogy is obviously not symmetrical. While all metaphors, on my view, are analogies – i.e., metaphor is a subset of analogy – not all analogies are metaphors. It is, for instance, hard to see the metaphorical nature of $8 - 6 = 6 - 4$. In Mary Hesse, moreover, scientific analogies based on identity (cf. p. 188) are not metaphorical either.
5 Chapters 7, 8, and 9, of Turner's 1991 book offer a meticulous and rewarding inquiry into the different forms of metaphors.
6 The exact status of conceptual integration and blending seem not quite clear, however. Conceptual integration is defined as a cognitive operation, and in 'A Mechanism of Creativity,' Turner and Fauconnier claim that

conceptual integration 'interacts with other cognitive operations such as analogy, metaphor, mental modeling, categorization, and framing' (1997: 17). Earlier, however, they said that mapping (which is the core operation in conceptual integration) may be 'analogical, categorical, or metaphoric, [and may] connect generic roles or values through identity connectors' (Turner and Fauconnier 1995: 11). It is clear that conceptual integration, like analogy, need not be metaphorical.

However, it remains open whether, or in which way, they consider conceptual integration as something different from analogy (obviously, the application of the proverb may be analysed as an analogy, husband : cat : : wife & lover : mice). One way of looking at such distinctions may be to characterize categorization as an either/or operation (something is either X or Y, either animate or inanimate), blending as a both/and operation (something is, combines, or belong to both X and Y – e.g., a mobile home), and metaphor as a particular kind of blending that makes categories clash (Achilles is both a man and a lion).

7 In his own theory of literature, he has, both in his concept of modes and in his division of genres, worked out very elaborate classifications of such designs (e.g., Frye 1957).

8 The following exposition makes no effort to judge the relative age and authenticity of the variants because their very existence is a proof that saga was considered important, and the different versions can be seen as ongoing attempts to retell it in a consistent way and enrich its explanatory power and emotional impact.

9 To the Greeks, Klytaimnestra's murder of her husband can neither be justified nor excused. In *The Odyssey* she is judged as follows by Agamemnon:

... There is no being more fell,
more bestial than a wife in such action,
and what an action that one planned!
The murder of her husband and her Lord.
...
                       ... that woman,
plotting a thing so low, defiled herself
and all her sex, all women yet to come,
even those few who may be virtuous.
   (*The Odyssey* [trans. R. Fitzgerald] 1961: 199, XI, 393–402)

Thus, in Homer Klytaimnestra is certainly condemned, but without any full-fledged argumentation; i.e., the action itself is reckoned sufficiently foul to condemn her without any debate about pros and cons – at least by the one who speaks, Agamemnon. This is why in this case, as in most ancient mythical texts, the narrated, i.e., the narrative structure and its semantics, is in itself interpretation – and maybe consolation.

10 The mother is not the true parent of the child
   Which is called hers. She is a nurse who tends the growth
   Of young seed planted by its true parent, the male.
   So, if Fate spares the child, she keeps it, as one might
   Keep for some friend a growing plant. And of this truth,
   That father without mother may beget, we have
   Present, as proof, the daughter of Olympian Zeus:
      (*The Eumenides* [trans. P. Vellacott] 1956: 169–70, vv. 657–63)

11 ... mine goes to uphold Orestes' plea,
   No mother gave me birth. Therefore the father's claim
   And male supremacy in all things, save to give
   Myself in marriage, wins my whole heart's loyalty.
   Therefore a woman's death, who killed her husband, is,
   I judge, outweighed in grievousness by his.
      (ibid.: p. 172, vv. 737–42)

12 When I presented this part of the chapter as a lecture at the University of Toronto, Professor Mario Valdés, edits a comparative history of the Hispanic and indigenous literatures of Latin America, commented that all the literatures of this huge part of the world had fables. It seems that the fable has the same universality as the myth and the fairytale.

Chapter 5   Literature as Self-expression: Subjectivity and Imagination

1 To solve a riddle is to unveil a secret, which in turn, according to magical thinking, means the acquisition of great, sometimes superhuman, power (cf. Oedipus solving the riddle of the Sphinx).
2 This integration of expression of content, by the way, is the reason for New Criticism's claim that paraphrase *is* a heresy because it breaks up the interrelations and reciprocal reinforcement between the text levels. Certainly, paraphrase is heresy; not because (partial) translation of poetic texts is impossible – certainly it is not, but because the integrative nature of experiencing literature, and thus its significance, disappears.
3 The grammatical understanding of subject is similar to that of logic, but there is a distinction between the grammatical and the logical subject of a sentence. Whereas only Catullus in 'Catullus loves Lesbia' is considered a subject in grammar, both are considered subjects in logic (and both proper

names are indexical expressions). Further, in grammar there are different kinds of complications, such as empty subjects that are only grammatical but not logical; for instance, 'it' in 'it rains.'

4 Two famous ones being Descartes's *cogito* and Kant's transcendental I, both formally rather than experientially defined.

5 Only some main features of the psychoanalytic concept of the subject have been indicated here; for a fine extensive description see Andkjær Olsen and Køppe 1988: 5–88.

6 P.F. Strawson has succinctly pointed out the interdependence of the I and you and their changing places as utterers, interpreters, and also as objects of speech, and consequently the role of semiosis in the constitution of the subject: 'One can ascribe states of consciousness to oneself only if one can ascribe them to others. One can ascribe them to others only if one can identify other subjects of experience. And one cannot identify others if one can identify them *only* as subjects of experience, possessors of states of consciousness' (Strawson 1957: 100).

7 In fact the semiotic pyramid might be useful in showing the relationship of some of the central elements of Lacanian psychoanalysis. The distinction between addresser and utterer resembles that between ego and subject, the distinction between the immediate and dynamical object that between the objects a and the Thing. The interpreter would then be the other, while the interpretant would be the Other and the Law. The sign would be the sign or the letter, related to all the other elements of the model, and especially both to the Other and to the subject. Of course this analogy is by no means perfect, and would need a lot of work.

8 On the semiotic pyramid (cf. p. 55), the immediate interpretant is not placed with the utterer and interpretant, but is a separate element within semiosis. There are several reasons for this. First of all, no individual or group possesses or understands the sum of interpretive habits of a species as complex as *Homo sapiens* and the different cultures of mankind. Individuals and groups may be excluded from developing certain competences because they are disabled (the blind cannot scan the environment visually), because of the variety of different forms of intelligence, and because they are not given the means of accessing such habits (uneven distribution of information and education within a community). Second, interpretive habits are public and shared; they do not, with certain exceptions, belong to a single individual, but to a community or subcommunity. Thus, they are not only available to be used by individual persons; they can be appealed to, discussed, and criticized, and through discussion, or silently through altered conditions of living, they may be changed. Third,

such interpretive systems are only indirectly linked with specific events happening at a specific moment within a singular context. They are general dispositions to interpret and act.

9 The dynamical interpretant, the objective content and result of acts of interpretation, is a selection from the possibilities offered by the immediate interpretants chosen, or just processed, by the subject in a concrete situation (this is why on the diagram it is contiguous with the immediate interpretant).

10 The utterer in literature is, however, in itself a huge topic that has been studied by the different theories of point of view, by speech-act theory, by linguists, and by several psychological and sociological approaches to literature. Neither point-of-view nor speech-act theory will receive any systematic treatment here: as regards the first, point of view, a very large and fine scholarly literature already exists (Lubbock, Booth, Stanzel, Genette, and, last but not least, Dorritt Cohn); speech-act theory seems to cover indifferently non-fictional and fictional utterances. I am aware of interesting questions, e.g., about the so-called logical status of fictional discourse and the possibility of seeing fiction production as a specific kind of speech act, that of pretending (Searle 1979), and about the so-called unspeakable sentences specific to literature. These questions, however, will be discussed in passing in other contexts, not systematically.

11 There an important difference between seeing the interpretive work as a reconstruction and seeing it as a construction; see chapter 7.

12 This is in agreement with the understanding of the immediate relates of the sign – immediate object, immediate interpretant, immediate utterer, and immediate interpreter – as being signs themselves pointing towards the external aspects of semiosis that they are supposed to represent, by similarity or contrast.

13 And this in spite of the plain truth of Genette's claim that 'to tell a story and therefore to "report" facts (real or fictive), its one mood, ... strictly speaking can only be the indicative' (Genette 1980: 161). Nevertheless, it is a real utterer who reports, not what has happened, but a hypothetical state of affairs imagined by an individual or collective mind.

14 This difference should not be made too absolute, however, for intermediary forms exist; as, for instance, in the collaboration of playwrights. Further, such a distinction between elite and mass literature is itself historical.

15 Using the terms fear and anxiety interchangeably may seem a little frivolous, because whereas fear clearly demands an object – fear of living, fear of dying, fear of diving, fear of flying – anxiety does not immediately call for an object, i.e., a motive or cause. But although anxiety may, at first

glance, seem a general condition rather than something specifically determined by an object, in the last analysis, it too must be related to specific conditions of living.

16 The term desire, however, is troublesome. I have nevertheless chosen it, first, because it connotes something dynamical and forceful that makes the subject, if not actually act, at least fantasize consciously and unconsciously. It covers Freud's German concepts *Wunsch* (= wish) and *Begierde* (= desire, appetite). Second, I have chosen it because of Lacan's distinction between need, desire, and demand. Desire, according to Lacan, lies between the need, belonging to the real and related to the biological, to the concrete object that satisfies the body's cravings, and the demand, which is directed towards the other.

   A demand may be articulated in language. It is, in the last analysis, a request for, an insistence on, unconditioned love. In this radical form it cannot be satisfied, and although it is suppressed by the subject, it is nevertheless always active in the unconscious. In spite of a demand's absurdity, however, it may well be expressed in language, and this is why it is, according to Lacan, related to the symbolic order. At the same time, however, the demand for unconditioned love may reveal to the subject its whole past (see Lacan 1977: 254).

   Desire, related to memory and fantasy, wedges itself between the creatureliness of the need and the communicative appeal of the demand. Indeed, Lacan claims, a little playfully, that subtracting need from demand leave us with desire, i.e., that which cannot really be satisfied (ibid.: 311). I mentioned above that desire also translates Freud's 'wish.' To his conception of wish is related as well the so-called hallucinatory wish-fulfilment: a re-establishment in fantasy of an experience of satisfaction so forceful and sensuously rich that, as in a dream, it is taken to be real. Desire and wish-fulfilment are auto-communicative rather than directed to others (contrary to demand), and they are iconic – primarily, but not only, represented by visual signs and, according to Lacan, related to the order of the imaginary. According to the view on psychological development held by psychoanalysis, desire is related to the narcissistic phase, i.e., primarily to the period between six and eighteen months of age.

17 Freud first mentions sublimation, in letter 61 to Fliess, in connection with fantasies in hysteria. Sublimation is said to be 'protective structures, sublimations of the facts, embellisments of them, and at the same time serve for self-exoneration' (Freud 1966: I, 247).

18 Distinguishing between different kinds of desire is not in agreement with Lacan's idea that desire is singular (while the drives are plural). I have, however, chosen to see desires as forces that may compete and clash.

19 Here we are not concerned with the possible realizations as physical acts, but with the mental representation, consciously and unconsciously, of the scenarios of pleasure and pain that determine the search for gratification.
20 Despite the many features shared by the desire for power and the desire for recognition, their outcomes are different. The effect of pursuing the desire for recognition is usually either positive or at least harmless. Even if self-conceit and vanity are laughable and irritating, they are among the minor sins. Power-seeking and the display of force, however, are unfortunately not always linked with the mental sanity and equanimity that are the preconditions for power's beneficial execution.
21 Passage's translation of Horace is a fine verse translation in the old metres. And what is important here is that Passage is not shy; he translates the crude sexual passages as they are in Horace's text. The current synoptic Loeb edition should be avoided, at least as regards this satire; either it softens the translation, or it simply does not translate. For instance, will the reader of the Loeb English text remain innocent of the fact that the narrator to still his desires will call either a slave girl or a slave boy (see Passage's translation of v. 117, here p. 261).
22 One of my colleagues, Carsten Nicolaisen, was investigating images of power. As a part of his project he made contact with the local branch of the Danish Association for Sado-masochists, and he was invited to take photos at three consecutive meetings in the club. During one of these meetings the following happened: A female masochist provoked four male sadists. She was overpowered and chained to the cross. Her bottom was bared and beaten with a strap. Two things were surprising to my colleague. First, the delicate balance between a rather rough acting and a very controlled staging. The woman fought obstinately; she had, in fact, to be overpowered, and the lashes she then received were so cutting that in order to willingly submit to them, not to speak of enjoying them, you would have to be a masochist. On the other hand, what happened had nothing to do with assault. All five acted as according to a script, and without a doubt the female masochist was in charge. She allowed herself to be cast, and cast herself, in the role of victim. Second, my colleague was even more surprised by the conversation of the male sadists. While they were occupied with chaining the woman to the cross, they perceived some tools lying about, one of which was a wire-cutter. Seeing the wire-cutter, the men started talking about themselves as overpowering a wild beast that should have its claws cut and its eye teeth pulled out.

Sadomasochistic games are themselves attempts to stage and act out specific compulsions in order to relieve an instinctual pressure and pleasure by (partly) realizing fantasies. Naively, one might think that the staging and the very real bodily involvement in the fantasy would completely fill up the minds of the participants. Nevertheless, in the middle of this physically exhausting actualization of a fantasy, another fantasy materializes and is shared verbally among the sadists. My colleague's narrative, however, only elucidates the fact that people, also *privatissime*, each for him- or herself or together, fantasize while playing the game of rain and clouds. It also illustrates the metonymical sliding of desire constantly on the move. This insight is most often linked with to Lacan, but it is common property. Goethe lets Faust say:

> So tauml' ich von Begierde zu Genuss,
> Und im Genuss verschmacht' ich nach Begierde
> (Goethe 1808–32/1963: I, 3249–50)
> (Thus reel I from desire to fulfilment,
> And in fulfilment languish for desire)

It may seem strange that in situations in which one would think that the participants were, and should be, absolutely present, mentally as well as physically, there is strong evidence that many, most, perhaps all are only half-present. It might be, however, that it is our understanding of presence and absence that should be revised. It might be that the simultaneity of physical action, interaction with others, and the inner gaze at the private theatre of fantasy is an optimal form of presence, because body and mind and conscious and unconscious are playing in concord.

23 It should be mentioned that the ancient theory of the so-called 'maternal impression,' the idea that the images seen by the woman during intercourse influence the embryo, was thought valid by many medical writers of that time. Indeed, this theory died hard because it was also held by many Renaissance writers.

24 The great Marxist, but no lesser Aristotelian aesthetician, Georg Lukács, subscribes to the ancient Greek understanding of music as representation. He sees music as a mimesis of a mimesis. First, in his view, emotions arise in connection with representation of outer and inner states of affairs. From the beginning, they have no autonomous existence. Second, however, when they become mimed, it also becomes possible to represent them unrelated to concrete individual representations of states of affairs. And music may, as the discussions by Plato and Aristotle make clear, be instrumental in evoking emotions. When we are sad, we may play sad music, but we may also become sad by listening to such music (see Lukács 1963: II, 330–401).

25 These ideas of the working of mind can be traced back to Aristotle.

26 The obscure conception of primal repression may be conceived as an effect of this missing translation of certain elements of the primary semiotic systems into language; what has been primally repressed becomes, so to speak, beyond the reach of the individual's own speech.
27 The objective of the cure certainly is to bring the painful and malignant repetitions to a stop by making conscious and explaining that which works dumbly in the mind of the patient and determines his or her behaviour. And if the cure is successful, the compulsion to repeat certain specific actions and patterns of imagination is dissolved or at least attenuated. If the cure helps the patient to live less painfully, it is certainly very valuable; but even if treatment may liberate somebody from repeating some specific and painful experiences and fantasies, repetition generally cannot be escaped.
28 Dynamically, as well as topographically, such a regression is well known in schizophrenia, where words are treated as things.
29 Cf. also Anácreon:

> Life is lovely. But the lifetime
> that remains for me is little.
> For this course I mourn. The terrors
> of the dark pit never leave me.
> For the house of Death is deep down
> underneath; the downward journey
> to be feared, for once I go there
> I know well there is no returning.
> (trans. Lattimore 1949: 47)

Chapter 6   The Interpreters

1 According to Freud, 'the day-dreamer carefully conceals his fantasies from other people because he feels he has reasons for being ashamed of them. I should now add that even if he were to communicate them to us, he could give no pleasure by his disclosures. Such fantasies, when we learn them, repel us or at least leave us cold ... [T]he essential *ars poetica* lies in the technique of overcoming the feeling of repulsion in us which is undoubtedly connected with the barriers that rise between each single ego and the others' (Freud 1959 [1908]: vol. 9, 133).
2 Churches are examples of institutions. A given church possesses both a conceptual structure and spiritual, social, economic, and physical resources. On the one hand, it delimits physical and virtual spaces: churches,

burial grounds, convents, hospitals, schools, etc.; on the other, it indicates spiritual domains such as heaven, purgatory, and hell. It may possess much property and worldly power, and it defines and regulates the interaction between this world and the otherworldly provinces. In addition to real estate (e.g., the houses of worship) it will use sets of props and uniforms, each of which possess a ritualistic and metaphorical value that may be explained historically. The agents are its officers, the hierarchically organized clergy, and its clients/users are the congregations. The officers fulfil a number of functions: spiritual, administrative, social, etc. Both parties (supposedly) function according to norms operative on different levels and with complicated histories (e.g., the histories of dogmas within different creeds). These norms are supposed to regulate the mental and spiritual life and the social interaction of the religious community. Such norms are related to the core values of the creed (such as faith, hope, and love) and to ulterior goals such as the spiritual guidance and well-being of their congregations, the preaching of the word to the faithful, and the conversion of non-believers. The general goal of a church is to create a congregation that live in accordance with the commandments of its creed, works towards salvation, and avoids perdition. The interactions, both between the officers and between officers and congregation, follow pre-established patterns, frames, and scripts (e.g., rituals involving service, prayer, sacraments, confession). Furthermore, an important goal of a church will be to survive and grow as an institution because it thinks itself indispensable in regulating the transactions between what, according to the individual creed, is defined as the material and the spiritual. Churches are invested with different degrees of power, which, among other things, depend on their relations with other institutions. Most, if not all, are characterized by factions and internal strife, and they are constantly negotiating their faith, handed down by tradition, with the interpretive habits, the social and interpersonal action, and the values and norms of the surrounding community. A church will always be in a potential or actual state of change because its faith and practices are always, at least indirectly, challenged.

3 However, the ways in which narrators of historical epics and novels of later times see the past may often be influenced by the reconstructions of historians.
4 Often religious texts are written anonymously and hymns created by members of the priesthood.
5 Neither in the case of Hesiod nor in that of Virgil, it might be argued, is the technical knowledge imparted the most important.
6 The Catholic *Index librorum prohibitorum* existed until 1960; and it seems

more than doubtful that the fatwa on Rushdie's *The Satanic Verses* has been lifted effectively.
7   In the *Politics* Aristotle advocates that free men should learn to play music only on certain instruments and to a certain level of perfection. It is unseeming to reach to the level of perfection attained by professional musicians.
8   Readers have always read, or listened to, literature, not only to be entertained, but to learn something. This fact has been stressed in poetics from Aristotle and Horace to Schiller, and in some guise or another, this aspect still plays an important role in reflections on literature.
9   This is also seen in subliterary genres. Folklorists think that a good many folk tale have been rather obscene, and in fact specimens of this kind of tale have survived. However, the editing of the tales in the 18th and 19th centuries meant that most of them were completely bowdlerized, as were the classics for centuries, in the editions *ad usum delphini* meant for the young and tender.
10 Or rather, how to distinguish 'real' literature from ideology, since he certainly leaves us with the problem of deciding which literature is real and non-ideological and which is average, mediocre, and thus ideological. (However, in all fairness, such a distinction always creeps in dealing with literature, whether the critic be Marxist, liberal, or Catholic.)
11 Desire and fear are correlative; one rarely exists without the other. Fear may, however, be a dominant factor in interpersonal conflict, e.g., in the hero(ine)'s flight from / fight with a threatening enemy, as in thrillers in which hunters are on the verge of tracking down their prey.
12 In fairy-tales, the princess's father is the king, and is thus representative of, and the most powerful person within, the country.
13 Obviously ecological endeavours are also attempts to control nature, albeit by other means.
14 Eco's distinction between 'interpretation' and 'use' and semantic and critical interpretation may turn out to be less than waterproof (see Eco 1990: 44–63; also Eco 1992).
15 However the criteria differ, they do not contradict each other; they just focus on different relationships. The big difference is, that Propp analyses the tales from the point of view of the initially active hero, whereas Holbek see the folk tale as featuring two heroes (a hero and a heroine), who are taking turns in being active and passive. Although I personally find Holbek's model superior because it is able to integrate and explain more basic oppositions than the one by Propp, preferring one model to the other seems to depend on what seems relevant to the aims of one's own studies.
16 Or for a second, third, and fourth meaning, as in the famous fourfold

interpretation of the scriptures in the Middle Ages: literal, allegorical, tropological, and anagogic.

17 Because transcategorical linking is common to metaphor, allegory, and symbol I find it impossible to distinguish clearly between them. Analogy, which is the basic form underlying these tropes is a proportion between usually three or four elements). As a form it is not itself a trope. A metaphor is a semantically interpreted analogy that links elements from categorically different domains (e.g., Peter the Apostle is called the Rock; in whichever way this is interpreted, a person is described as a specimen of inorganic nature). A symbol, it seems to me, is a metaphor that has gained a certain generality, either within a limited text corpus (e.g., within that of an individual author) or within a culture at large. Finally, an allegory may be defined as a more or less extended and more or less consistent network of metaphors.

18 Furthermore, truth as a correspondence between propositions and reality is conceived not as something beyond discussion, but as something that has to be investigated and defended by arguments.

19 See the beautiful and concise description of the phenomenology of reading by George Poulet (1972).

20 It is not by accident that we have such traditional fields of literary research as topos research, the history of literary motives and themes, narratology, and even dictionaries of imaginary places (e.g., Manguel and Guadalupi), etc. Such studies testify to the existence of abstract cognitive models within the different dimensions of literature and to the fact that such literary models have a history.

21 The idea of such basic emotions has been common since Darwin (1872/1968), but already Hume (1739) made a comparable list of 'simple passions.'

22 There will, of course, always be models for the characters, or rather for the features ascribed to characters, but except for the *roman à clef*, in which it is an important point that the originals be recognized, models are of minor significance; and anyway the author is the primary model.

Chapter 7 Interpreting Literature

1 Within the last twenty years there have been many different approaches to the reader's role in interpretation: from reading as an almighty and unique act of meaning creation for which no common standards are available (e.g., Fish 1980), through reading as filling in the blanks of the text (e.g., Iser 1978), to rather strict demands on the competence of the reader (Riffaterre 1978 and Eco 1979).

2 Freud goes on to point out that this principle of evenly suspended attention is the counterpart to the demand that patients should without reservation communicate everything that comes to their mind. Freud gives two further alternative formulations of his principle, namely, that the therapist should abandon conscious influence on attention and give himself to 'unconscious memory,' and the more plain and technical advice, 'He should simply listen, and not bother about whether he is keeping anything in his mind' (ibid.).
3 Gadamer is right that text meaning always transcends the *mens auctoris*, although the intended meaning is an important part of the text.
4 For instance, *Edward III* has recently in earnest been added to the Shakespearean canon by receiving its own volume in the Cambridge Edition, because the older argument, that parts of the play have been written by Shakespeare, is now thought to warrant its publication as a Shakespeare play.
5 For instance, in the example from Andersen, the red-shoe clue might lead to scanning all his texts that mention footwear to look for contexts having to do with vanity, self-centredness, and the outlet or frustration of sexual desire. One might find a particular symbolism that together with other features (the red shoes are but a single clue in a complex pattern) would make it possible from the texts produced by Andersen to reconstruct a part of his (alleged) subjectivity. Such an interpretation will be symptomatic, focused on his psychical make-up. (This particular example may seem peculiar, even weird. It is, however, more sensible than it, prima facie, looks.)
6 Puis fierent il nud a nud sur lur broni
  Des helmes clers li fous en escarbunet.
    Ceste bayaille ne poet remanier unkes,
    Josque li uns sun tort i reconnuisset
      (*La Chanson de Roland* 1964/1937: 298)
7 Why, for instance, does such a discrepancy exist between the centrality and importance of the female characters in Attic tragedy and the role of women in Athens in the fifth century BC.
8 The process of secularization in Europe for the last three centuries being a case in point.

Bibliography

Addison, J. 1983 (1712). 'The Pleasures of the Imagination.' In Richard Steele and Joseph Addison, *Selections from The Tatler and The Spectator*, 364–405. Ed. A. Ross. London: Penguin Classics.
Adorno, Theodor W. 1970. *Ästhtische Theorie. Gesammelte Schriften 7*. Frankfurt a.M.: Suhrkamp Verlag.
– 1973. *Negative Dialektik. Gesammelte Schriften 6*, 7–412. Frankfurt a.M.: Suhrkamp Verlag.
Aeschylus. 1956. *The Oresteian Trilogy*. Trans. P. Vellacott. Harmondsworth: Penguin.
Aitchison, Jean. 1987. *Words in the Mind: An Introduction to the Mental Lexicon*. Oxford: Blackwell.
Althusser, Louis. 1971a. 'Ideology and Ideological State Apparatuses (Notes towards an Investigation).' In *Lenin and Philosophy and Other Essays*, 127–85. New York, London: Monthly Review Press.
– 1971b. 'A Letter on Art in Reply to André Daspre.' In *Lenin and Philosophy and Other Essays*, 221–7. New York, London: Monthly Review Press.
Amos, William. 1985. *The Originals: Who's Really Who in Fiction*. London: Sphere Books.
Andersen, Hans Christian. 1974. *The Penguin Complete Fairy Tales and Stories of Hans Andersen*. Trans. E.C. Hausgaard. Harmondsworth: Penguin.
Andkjær Olsen, O., and S. Køppe 1988. *Freud's Theory of Psychoanalysis*. New York: New York University Press.
Apollodorus. 1921. *The Library*. Trans. J.G. Frazer. Cambridge, Mass., London: Harvard University Press, Heinemann/Loeb.
Aristotle. 1926. *Art of Rhetoric*. Trans. J.H. Reese. Cambridge, Mass., London: Harvard University Press, Heinemann/Loeb.

- 1927. *The Poetics*. Trans. W. Hamilton Fife. Cambridge, Mass., London: Harvard University Press, Heinemann/Loeb.
- 1941a. *Posterior Analytics*. In *The Basic Works of Aristotle*, 110–87. Ed. Richard McKeon. New York: Random House.
- 1941b. *Topics*. In *The Basic Works of Aristotle*, 188–209. Ed. Richard McKeon. New York: Random House.
- 1941c. *Politics*. In *The Basic Works of Aristotle*, 1127–1324. Ed. Richard McKeon. New York: Random House.
- 1942. *The Student's Oxford Aristotle. Volume III, Psychology*. Trans. W.D. Ross. Oxford: Oxford University Press.
- 1961. *Parts of Animals*. Trans. A.L. Peck. Cambridge, Mass., London: Harvard University Press, Heinemann/Loeb.

Augustine. 1952a. (397–426). *On Christian Doctrine*. Trans. J.F. Shaw. In *Augustine: Great Books of the Western World*, vol. 18. Ed. Robert Maynard. Chicago, London, Toronto: William Benton, Encyclopaedia Brittannica Inc.
- 1952b (413–26). *The City of God*. Trans. Marcus Dods. In *Augustine: Great Books of the Western World*, vol. 18. Ed. Robert Maynard. Chicago, London, Toronto: William Benton, Encyclopaedia Brittannica Inc.

Auster, Paul. 1990. *The New York Trilogy*. Harmondsworth: Penguin.
Austin, J.L. 1962. *How to Do Things with Words*. Oxford: Oxford University Press.
Bakhtin, Mikhail. 1968. *Rabelais and His World*. Cambridge, Mass.: MIT Press.
- 1986. *Speech Genres and Other Essays*. Austin: University of Texas Press.
Balzac, Honoré de. 1989 (1835). *Le Père Goriot*. Ed. G. Gengembre. Paris: Magnard (Collection texte et contextes).
Banfield, Ann. 1982. *Unspeakable Sentences*. Boston, London: Routledge & Kegan Paul.
Barthes, Roland. 1975 (French 1973). *The Pleasure of the Text*. New York: Noonday Press.
- 1986. 'The Death of the Author.' In R. Barthes, *The Rustle of Language*, 49–55. Oxford: Blackwell.
Bascom, William. 1984 (1734). 'The Forms of Folklore.' In Alan Dundes, ed., *Sacred Narrative*. Berkeley: University of California Press.
Baumgarten A. 1974 (1734). *Reflections on Poetry*. Berkeley: University of California Press.
Bettelheim, Bruno. 1976. *The Uses of Enchantment*. New York: A. Knopf, Inc.
Bevan, W.L., and H.W. Phillott. 1969. *Mediaeval Geography: An Essay in Illustration of the Hereford Mappa Mundi*. Amsterdam: Meridian.
Black, Max. 1962. *Models and Metaphors*. Ithaca, NY: Cornell University Press.
- 1993 (orig. 1977). 'More about Metaphor.' In Ortony 1993: 19–41.
Blake, William. 1971. *The Complete Poems*. Ed. W.H. Stevenson. London: Longman.

Booth, Wayne. 1961. *The Rhetoric of Fiction*. Chicago: University of Chicago Press.
Bourdieu, Pierre. 1993. *The Field of Cultural Production*. Cambridge, UK: Polity Press.
Brooks, Cleanth. 1968 (1947). *The Well-Wrought Urn*. London: Methuen / University Paperbacks.
Brooks, Peter. 1984. *Reading for the Plot: Design and Intention in Narrative*. New York: Alfred A. Knopf, Inc.
Brown, G., and G. Yule. 1983. *Discourse Analysis*. Cambridge: Cambridge University Press.
Bruner, Jerome S. 1966. 'On Cognitive Growth.' In J.S. Brunes, R.R. Olver, and P.M. Greenfield, eds, *Studies in Cognitive Growth*, 1–67. New York: John Wiley.
- 1986. *Actual Minds, Possible Worlds*. Cambridge, Mass.: Harvard University Press.
Brunetière, Ferdinand de. 1924 (1892–5). *L'évolution des genres dans l'histoire de la littérature*. Paris: Hachette.
Bullinger, E.W. 1968 (1898). *Figures of Speech Used in the Bible Explained and Illustrated*. Grand Rapids, Mich.: Baker Book House.
Burgess, Anthony. 1984. 'On the Short Story.' *Les cahiers de la nouvelle / Université d'Angers* 2: 31–47.
Burkert, W. 1979. *Structure and History in Greek Mythology*. Berkeley: University of California Press.
Burroughs, William S. 1968 (1966). *Nova Express*. London: Panther Books Ltd.
Byron, Lord. 1986. *Byron: The Oxford Authors*. Ed. J.J. McGann. Oxford: Oxford University Press.
Børtness, Jostein. 1980. *Aristoteles om diktekunsten: En innføring*. Oslo: Solum.
Capote, Truman. 1965. *In Cold Blood*. New York: Random House.
Carroll, Lewis. 1962. *The Annotated Snark*. Ed. M. Gardner. Harmondsworth: Penguin Books.
- 1971 (1865). *Alice in Wonderland*. Ed. Donald J. Gray. New York: W.W. Norton.
Chanson de Roland. 1964 (publiée d'après le manuscrit d'Oxford et traduite par Joseph Bédier). Paris: L'édition d'art H. Piazza. *Song of Roland*. 1937. Trans. Dorothy L. Sayers. Harmondsworth: Penguin.
Coislinian Tractate. In *Readers' Encyclopedia of World Drama* (q.v.), col. 949–51.
Collected Ancient Greek Novels. 1989. Ed. B.P. Reardon. Berkeley: University of California Press.
Constructions of the Self. 1992. Ed. George Levine. New Brunswick, NJ: Rutgers University Press.
Darwin, Charles. 1968 (1859). *The Origin of Species*. Ed. J.W. Burrow. Harmondsworth: Penguin.

Deely, John. 1982. *Introducing Semiotics: Its History and Doctrine*. Bloomington: Indiana University Press.
- 1990. *Basics of Semiotics*. Bloomington: Indiana University Press.
Détienne, M., and J.-P. Vernant, eds. 1989. *The Cuisine of Sacrifice among the Greeks*. Chicago: University of Chicago Press.
Dinesen, Isak. 1991 (1957). *Last Tales*. Harmondsworth: Penguin.
Donald, Merlin. 1991. *Origins of the Modern Mind*. Cambridge, Mass.: Harvard University Press.
Donne, John. 1933. *The Poems of John Donne*. Ed. H. Grierson. London: Oxford University Press.
- 1967. *Selected Prose*. Chosen by E. Simpson, ed. H. Gardner and T. Healy. Oxford: Clarendon Press.
Dundes, Allan. 1964. *The Morphology of the North American Indian Folktales*. Helsinki: Academia Scientarum Finnica. FF Communications no. 195.
Dundes, Allan, ed. 1965. *The Study of Folklore*. Englewood Cliffs, NJ: Prentice-Hall.
- *Sacred Narrative*. 1984. Berkeley: University of California Press.
Eco, Umberto. 1979. *The Role of the Reader*. Bloomington: Indiana University Press.
- 1984. 'Dictionary vs. Encyclopedia.' In *Semiotics and the Philosophy of Language*, 46–86. Bloomington: Indiana University Press.
- 1990. *The Limits of Interpretation*. Bloomington: Indiana University Press.
- 1992. *Interpretation and Overinterpretation*. Ed. S. Collini. Cambridge: Cambridge University Press.
Eco, U., and Sebeok, eds. 1983. *The Sign of Three: Dupin, Holmes, Peirce*. Bloomington: Indiana University Press.
Ekman, Paul. 1994. 'All Emotions Are Basic.' In P. Ekman and R.J. Davidson, eds, *The Nature of Emotion: Fundamental Questions*, 15–19. Oxford: Oxford University Press.
Elam, Keir. 1980. *The Semiotics of Theatre and Drama*. London: Methuen.
Eliot, T.S. 1921. 'Prose and Verse.' In *The Chapbook. A Monthly Miscellany* (London), no. 22 (April), 3–10.
- 1932. *Selected Essays*. London: Faber and Faber.
- 1933. *The Use of Poetry and the Use of Criticism*. London: Faber and Faber.
- 1949 (1938). 'Preface.' In St.-John Perse, *Anabasis* (trans., with preface, T.S. Eliot). New York: Harcourt Brace Jovanovich.
- 1957. *On Poetry and Poets*. London: Faber and Faber.
Epstein, E.L. 1975. 'The Self-reflexive Artefact: The Function of Mimesis in an Approach to a Theory of Value for Literature.' In Fowler 1975: 40–78.
Erlich, Victor. 1965. *Russian Formalism*. The Hague: Mouton & Co.

Euripides. 1966. *Ten Plays*. Trans. M. Hadas and J. MacLean. New York: Bantam Books.
Fauconnier, Gilles. 1994. *Mental Spaces: Aspects of Meaning Construction in Natural Languages*. Cambridge, New York: Cambridge University Press.
Fielding, Henry. 1973. *Tom Jones*. Ed. S. Baked. New York: W.W. Norton.
Fish, Stanley. 1980. *Is There a Text in This Class? The Authority of Interpretive Communities*. Cambridge, Mass.: Harvard University Press.
Flaubert, Gustave. 1961 (1857). *Madame Bovary. Moeurs de province*. Ed. E. Maynial. Paris: Garnier.
– 1863. *Salammbô*. Ed. E. Maynial. Paris: Garnier.
– 1965. *Madame Bovary*. Trans. E. Marx Eveling and P. de Man. New York: W.W. Norton.
– 1973–91. *Correspondance*, I–III. Ed. Jean Bruneau. Paris: Gallimard (Bibliothèque de la Pléiade).
Fludernik, Monika. 1993. *The Fiction of Language and the Languages of Fiction*. London: Routledge.
Forster, E.M. 1927. *Aspects of the Novel*. London: Edward Arnold.
Foucault, Michel. 1970. *The Order of Things: An Archaeology of the Human Sciences*. London: Routledge.
– 1972 (French 1969, 1971). *The Archaeology of Knowledge and the Discourse on Language*. New York: Pantheon Books.
– 1977 (French 1975). *Discipline and Punish: The Birth of Prison*. New York: Vintage Books.
Fowler, R., ed. 1975. *Style and Structure in Literature*. Ithaca, NY: Cornell University Press.
Fox, James J. 1977. 'Roman Jakobson and the Comparative Study of Parallelism.' In D. Armstrong and C.H. van Schooneveld, eds, *Roman Jakobson: Echoes of His Scholarship*. Lisse: Peter de Ridder Press.
Freud, Sigmund. 1953 (1913*f*). 'The Claims of Psycho-Analysis to Scientific Interest.' In *The Standard Edition of the Complete Psychological Work of Sigmund Freud* (*S.E.*), vol. 13, 163–90.
– 1953–4 (1900*a*). *The Interpretation of Dreams*. In *S.E.*, vols. 2 and 5. London: The Hogarth Press.
– 1955a (1909*d*). 'Notes upon a Case of Obsessinal Neurosis' (The Rat Man). In *S.E.*, vol. 10, 151–249.
– 1955b (1920*g*). *Beyond the Pleasure Principle*. In *S.E.*, vol. 18, 3–66.
– 1958 (1912*e*). 'Recommendations to Physicians Practising Psychoanalysis.' In *S.E.*, vol. 12, 109–20.
– 1959 (1908*e*). 'Creative Writers and Day-dreaming.' In *S.E.*, vol. 9, 141–53.
– 1960 (1905*e*). *Jokes and Their Relation to the Unconscious*. In *S.E.*, vol. 8.

- 1961 (1923*b*). *The Ego and the Id.* In *S.E.*, vol. 19, 3–66.
- 1963 (1916–17). *Introductory Lectures on Psycho-Analysis.* In *S.E.*, vols. 15 and 16.
- 1964 (1937*b*). 'Construction in Analysis.' In *S.E.*, vol. 23, 255–70.

Freundlieb, Dieter. 1995. 'Foucault and the Study of Literature.' In *Poetics Today* 16 (Summer 1995): 201–44.

Friday, Nancy. 1973. *My Secret Garden.* New York: Pocket Books.
- 1975. *Forbidden Flowers.* New York: Pocket Books.
- 1980. *Men in Love.* London: Arrow Books.
- 1991. *Women on Top.* London: Hutchinson.

Friedrich, Hugo. 1956. *Die Struktur der modernene Lyrik. Von Baudelaire bis zur Gegenwart.* Hamburg: Rowohlt.

Frye, Northrop. 1957. *Anatomy of Criticism.* Princeton, NJ: Princeton University Press.
- 1963. *Fables of Identity.* New York: Harcourt, Brace & World Inc.
- 1966 (1951). 'The Archetypes of Literature.' In John B. Vickers, ed., *Myth and Literature*, 87–97. Lincoln: University of Nebraska Press (orig. pub. in *Kenyon Review*, 1951: 92–110).
- 1976. *Spiritus Mundi: Essays on Literature, Myth, and Society.* Bloomington: Indiana University Press.
- 1982. *The Great Code: The Bible and Literature.* London: Routledge and Kegan Paul.

Gadamer, Hans-Georg. 1960. *Wahrheit und Methode.* Tübingen: Max Niemeyer Verlag.

Gallie, W.B. 1964. *Philosophy and the Historical Understanding.* London: Chatto & Windus.

García Márquez, Gabriel. 1971 (1967). *One Hundred Years of Solitude.* New York: Avon Books.

Gebaur, G., and C. Wulf. 1992. *Mimesis: Kultur–Kunst–Gesellschaft.* Reinbek bei Hamburg: Rowolt.

Geertz, Clifford. 1997. 'Thick Description: Toward an Interpretive Theory of Culture.' In C. Geertz, *The Interpretation of Cultures*, 3–30. London: Hutchinson.

Gelb, I.J. 1952. *A Study of Writing.* Chicago: University of Chicago Press.

Genette, Gérard. 1972. *Figures III.* Paris: Éditions du Seuil.
- 1980. *Narrative Discourse.* Ithaca, NY: Cornell University Press.

Gentner, Dedre. 1983. 'Structure-Mapping: A Theoretical Framework for Analogy.' In *Cognitive Science* 7: 155–170.
- 1988. 'Metaphor as Structure-Mapping: The Relational Shift.' In *Child Development* 59: 47–59.
- 1989. 'The Mechanisms of Analogical Learning.' In S. Vosniadou and A.

Ortony, eds, *Similarity and Analogical Reasoning*, 199–241. Cambridge: Cambridge University Press.
Gentner, Dedre, B. Falkenhainer, and J. Skorsfad. 1988. 'Viewing Metaphor as Anaology.' In David H. Heilman, ed., *Analogical Reasoning*. Dordrecht: Kluwer.
Gentner, Dedre, with K.D. Forbus. 1991. 'Similarity-based Cognitive Architecture.' In *Sigart Bulletin* 2. 4: 66–9.
Gentner, Dedre, with D.L. Medin and R.L. Goldstone. 1993. 'Respects for Similarity.' In *Psychological Review* 100. 2: 254–78.
Gibbs, Raymond W. 1994. *The Poetics of Mind*. Cambridge, New York: Cambridge University Press.
Goethe, J.W. von. 1963 (1808–32). *Faust*. Ed. Erich Trunz. Hamburg: Christian Wegner Verlag.
– 1976. *Faust. A Tragedy*. Trans. W. Arndt. New York: W.W. Norton.
Goodman, Nelson. 1969. *Languages of Art*. London: Oxford University Press.
– 1972. 'Seven Strictures on Similarity.' In *Problems and Projects*, 437–50. Indianapolis: Bobbs-Merrill.
– 1978. *Ways of Worldmaking*. Indianapolis: Hackett Publishing.
Gorlée, Dinda. 1996. *Semiotics and the Problem of Translation. With Special Reference to the Semiotics of Charles S. Peirce*. Atlanta: Rodopi USA / Canada (Approaches to Translation Studies 12).
Grant, Robert M. 1965. *A Short History of the Interpretation of the Bible*. London: Adam & Charles Black.
Greek Lyrics. 1949, Trans. R. Lattimore. Chicago: University of Chicago Press.
Greimas, A.J. 1966. *Sémantique structurale*. Paris: Larousse.
– 1970. *Du sens*. Paris: Seuil.
Grice, Paul. 1971. 'Utterer's Meaning, Sentence-Meaning, and Word-Meaning.' In Searle, ed., 1971: 54–70.
– 1975. 'Logic and Conversation.' In P. Cole and J.L. Morgan, eds, *Syntax and Semantics*, vol. 3, *Speech Acts*, 41–58. New York: Academic Press.
– 1978. 'Further Notes on Logic and Conversation.' In P. Cole, ed., *Syntax and Semantics*, vol. 9, *Pragmatics*, 113–28. New York: Academic Press.
Habermas, Jürgen. 1971. *Knowledge and Human Interests*. Boston: Beacon Press.
– 1975. *Legitimation Crisis*. Boston: Beacon Press.
– 1979. 'What Is Universal Pragmatics?' In J. Habermas, *Communication and the Evolution of Society* (ed. Thomas McCarthy). Boston: Beacon Press.
– 1983. 'Interpretative Social Science vs Hermeneuticism.' In N. Haan et al., eds, *Social Science as Moral Inquiry*. New York: Columbia University Press.
– 1987. *The Theory of Communicative Action*, I–II. Boston: Beacon / Polity Press.

- 1987. *The Philosophical Discourse of Modernity*. Twelve Lectures. Cambridge, Mass.: MIT Press.
- 1993. *Justification and Application: Remarks on Discourse Ethics*. Cambridge Mass.: MIT Press.

Hamburger, Käte. 1957 (revised ed. 1968). *Die Logik der Dichtung*. Stuttgart: Ernst Klett Verlag.

Hardwick, Charles S., ed. 1975–87. *Semiotic and Significs: The Correspondence between Charles S. Peirce and Victoria Lady Welby*. Bloomington: Indiana University Press.

Hardy, Thomas. 1967. *Personal Writings: Prefaces. Literary Opinions. Reminiscences*. Ed. Harold Orel. London: Macmillan.

Harly, J.B., and D. Woodward, eds. 1987–98. *The History of Cartography*, I–II. Chicago: University of Chicago Press.

Harris, Robert. 1993. *Fatherland*. London: Arrow.

Hegel, G.W.F. 1977. *Phenomenology of Spirit*. Trans. A.V. Miller, foreword by J.N. Finlay. Oxford: Oxford University Press.

Heliodorus. See *Collected Ancient Greek Novels*.

Hernadi, Paul. Forthcoming. 'Why Is Literature?'

Herval, René. 1957. *Les véritables origines de 'Madame Bovary.'* Paris: Nizet.

Hesiod. 1973. *Theogony*. Trans. D. Wender. In *Hesiod and Theognis*. Harmondsworth: Penguin.

Hesse, Mary B. 1966. *Models and Analogies in Science*. Notre Dame, Ind.: Notre Dame University Press.

Heusden, Barend van. 1997. *Why Literature? An Inquiry into the Nature of Literary Semiosis*. Tübingen: Stauffenburg Verlag (Probleme der Semiotik, Band 18).

Hjelmslev, Louis. 1953 (1943). *Prolegomena to a Theory of Language*. Baltimore: Waverly Press (Danish orig., *Omkring Sprogteoriens Grundlæggelse*).
- 1954. 'La stratification du langage.' In *Essais linguistques* (1959), 36–68.
- 1959. *Essais linguistiques*. TCLC XII. Copenhagen: Nordisk Sprog og Kulturforlag.
- 1970. *Language. An Introduction*. Madison, Milwaukee: University of Wisconsin Press.
- 1973. *Essais linguistique*, II. TCLC XIV. Copenhagen: Nordisk Sprog og Kulturforlag.

Holbek, Bengt. 1986. *Interpretation of Fairy Tales*. Helsinki: Academia Scientarum Finnica. FF Communications no. 239.
- 1989. *Tolkning af trylleeventyr*. (Interpretation of Fairy Tales). Copenhagen: Nyt nordisk forlag Arnold Busck.

Homer. 1963. *The Odyssey*. Trans. R. Fitzgerald. New York: Anchor Press / Doubleday.

- 1974. *The Iliad*. Trans. R. Fitzgerald. New York: Anchor Press / Doubleday.
Horace. 1983. *The Complete Works of Horace*. Trans. C.E. Passage. New York: Frederick Ungar Publishing Co.
Hume, David. 1888 (1739). *A Treatise of Human Nature*. Ed. L.A. Selby-Bigge. Oxford: Clarendon Press, 1978.
Ibsen, Henrik. 1928–34. *Samlede verker* (Collected Works). Ed. F. Bull et al. I–XX. Oslo: Gyldendal.
- 1970. *The Correspondance of Henrik Ibsen*. Ed. Mary Morison. New York: Haskell House Publishers.
- 1986 (1873). *Emperor and Galilean*. In *Plays Five*, trans. M. Meyer. London: Methuen.
Iconicity: Essays on the Nature of Culture. Festschrift for Thomas Sebeok on his 65th Birthday. Ed. P. Bouissac et al. Tübingen: Stauffenburg Verlag.
Ignatius, Saint. 1997 (1548). *The Spiritual Exercises of Saint Ignatius*. Ed. P. Wolff. Liguori, Miss.: Triumph.
Ingarden, Roman. 1965 (1931). *Das literarische Kunstwerk*. Tübingen: Max Niemeyer Verlag.
Iser, W. 1978. *The Act of Reading*. Baltimore: Johns Hopkins University Press.
Jakobson, R. 1960. 'Linguistics and Poetics.' In *Selected Writings*, III (1987): 18–51. The Hague: Mouton (also in T. Sebeok, ed., *Style in Language* [Cambridge, Mass.: MIT Press, 1960], 350–77).
- 1965. 'Quest for the Essence of Language.' In *Selected Writings*, II: 349–59. The Hague: Mouton.
Jakobson, R., and M. Halle. 1956. *Fundamentals of Language*. The Hague: Mouton.
James I. 1965. *The Political Works of James I*. Repr. from 1616 ed. with intro. by C.H. McIlwian. New York: Russel & Russel.
Jauss, Hans-Robert. 1989. *Questions and Answers: Forms of Dialogical Understanding*. Minneapolis: University of Minnesota Press.
Johansen, J. Dines. 1970. *Novelleteori efter 1945* (Postwar Theories of the Short Story). Copenhagen: Munksgaard.
- 1985. 'Prolegomena to a Semiotic Theory of Text Interpretation.' *Semiotica* 57.3/4: 225–88.
- 1986a. '"Il ne faut pas oublier le pain": Meaning and Linguistic Form.' *Journal of Pragmatics* 9 (1985): 567–90.
- 1986b. 'The Place of Semiotics in the Study of Literature.' In Jonathan D. Evans and André Helbo, eds, *Semiotics and International Scholarship – Towards a Language of Theory*, 101–26. Dordrecht: Nijhoff.
- 1986c. 'Semiotics and Comparative Literature.' In *Sensus Communis: Festschrift für Henry Remak*, 23–38. Tübingen: Günter Narr Verlag.

- 1986d. 'Sign Concept, Meaning and Study of Literature.' In *Pragmatics and Linguistics*, 95–102. Odense: Odense University Press.
- 1987. 'Literature.' In Thomas Sebeok, ed., *Encyclopedic Dictionary of Semiotics*, I: 453–9. 3 vols. Berlin, New York, Amsterdam: Mouton de Gruyter.
- 1988a. 'What Is a Text? Semiosis and Textuality: A Peircian Perspective.' *Livstegn* (Bergen, Norway) no. 5: 7–32.
- 1988b. 'The Distinction between Icon, Index, and Symbol in the Study of Literature.' In M. Herzfeld and L. Melazzo, eds, *Semiotic Theory and Practice*, 497–504. Berlin: Walter de Gruyter.
- 1989. 'Hypothesis, Reconstruction, Analogy: On Hermeneutics and the Interpretation of Literature.' *Semiotica* 74.3/4: 235–52.
- 1990. 'The Triple Status of a Fictional Universe of Discourse.' In *Proceedings of the XIIth Congress of the International Comparative Literature Association*, vol. 5: *Space and Boundaries in Literary Criticism*, 77–82. Munich, 1988.
- 1991a. 'Literature and Development.' In P. Grzybek, ed., *Cultural Semiotics: Facts and Facets*, 63–72. Bochumer Beiträge zur Semiotik 26.
- 1991b. 'Literature: Collective Memory – Collective Fantasy.' *Face* 1 (Sao Paulo): 35–59.
- 1991c. 'Literary Theory: Parochial or Universal? In Gurbhagat Singh, ed., *Differential Multilogue: Comparative Literature and National Literatures*. Delhi: Ajanta Publications.
- 1992a. 'Desire: Representation and Repetition in Literature.' *Orbis Literarum* 47: 257–87.
- 1992b. 'Code and Reference: Bertrand Russell and Roman Jakobsen on Cheese. *Cruzeiro Semiotico* 14: 65–74.
- 1993a. *Dialogic Semiosis*. Bloomington: Indiana University Press.
- 1993b. 'Let Sleeping Signs Lie: On Signs, Objects, and Communication.' *Semiotica* 97.3/4: 271–95.
- 1996a. 'Iconicity in Literature.' *Semiotica* 110.1/2: 37–55.
- 1996b. 'Arguments about Icons.' In Vincent M. Colapietro and Thomas M. Olshewsky, eds, *Peirce's Doctrine of Signs: Theory, Applications, and Connections*, 273–82. Berlin, New York: Mouton de Gruyter.
- 1996c. 'Sign Structure and Sign Event in Saussure, Hjelmslev, and Peirce.' In Colapietro and Olshewsky, eds, *Peirce's Doctrine of Signs*, 329–38. Berlin, New York: Mouton de Gruyter.

Johansen, J.D., A. Helbo, P. Pavis, and A. Ubersfeld, eds. 1991. *Approaching Theatre*. Bloomington: Indiana University Press.

Johnson, Mark. 1987. *The Body in the Mind: The Bodily Basis of Meaning, Imagination, and Reason*. Chicago: University of Chicago Press.

Jolles, André. 1930. *Einfache Formen*. Tübingen: Max Niemeyer Verlag.

Jones, Ernest. 1949. *Hamlet and Oedipus*. London: Victor Gollantz.
Kafka, Franz. 1956. *The Trial*. New York: Random House / The Modern Library.
Kant, I. 1928 (1790). *The Critique of Judgement*. Oxford: Clarendon Press.
Kelly, M., ed. 1994. *Critique and Power: Recasting the Foucault/Habermas Debate*. Cambridge, Mass.: MIT Press.
Kermode, Frank. 1966. *The Sense of an Ending*. New York: Oxford University Press.
Kierkegaard, Søren 1992 (1846). *Concluding Unscientific Postscript to Philosophical Fragments*, I–II. Trans. H.V. and E.H. Hong. Princeton, NJ: Princeton University Press.
Köngäs Maranda, E., and Pierre Maranda. 1971. *Structural Models in Folklore and Transformational Essays*. The Hague, Paris: Mouton.
Kris, Ernst. 1952. *Psychoanalytic Explorations in Art*. New York: International Universities Press.
Lacan, Jacques. 1977. *Écrits. A Selection*. New York: W.W. Norton.
Lakoff, George. 1987. *Women, Fire, and Dangerous Things: What Categories Reveal about the Mind*. Chicago: University of Chicago Press.
– 1988. 'Cognitive Semantics.' In U. Eco, M. Santambrogio, and P. Violi, eds, *Meaning and Mental Representations*. Bloomington: Indiana University Press.
– 1993. 'The Contemporary Theory of Metaphor.' In Ortony 1993: 202–51.
Lakoff, G., and M. Johnson. 1980. *Metaphors We Live By*. Chicago: University of Chicago Press.
Lakoff, G., and M. Turner. 1989. *More than Cool Reason: A Field Guide to Poetic Metaphor*. Chicago: University of Chicago Press.
Lausberg, Heinrich. 1960. *Handbuch der literarischen Rethorik*, I–II. München: Max Hueber Verlag.
Lautréamont, Comte de. 1978. *Maldoror and Poems*. Trans. P. Knight. Harmondsworth: Penguin.
le Goffe, J. 1981. *La naissance du purgatoire*. Paris: Gallimard.
Lemon, L.T., and M.J. Reis, eds. 1965. *Russian Formalist Criticism*. Lincoln: University of Nebraska Press.
Levin, Samuel. 1962. *Linguistic Structures in Poetry*. The Hague: Mouton.
Levine, George, ed. 1992. *Constructions of the Self*. New Brunswick, NJ: Rutgers University Press.
Levison, Stephen C. 1983. *Pragmatics*. Cambridge: Cambridge University Press.
Lévi-Strauss, C. 1967. *Structural Anthropology*. New York: Basic Books.
Lorris, Guillaume de, and Jean de Meun. 1962 (ca. 1237–77). *The Romance of the Rose*. Trans. H.W. Robbins. New York: Meridian Books.

Lotman, Yu. M. 1967. 'Tezisy k probleme "Iskusstvo v modeliruyushchikh sistem."' *Trudy po znakovym sisteman* 3: 130–45.
Lotman, Yu. M., and B.A. Uspensky. 1978 (Russ. 1971). 'On the Semiotic Mechanism of Culture.' *New Literary History* 9.2 (Winter): 211–31.
Lubbock, Percy. 1965 (1921). *The Craft of Fiction*. London: Jonathan Cape.
Lukács, Georg. 1963. *Ästhetik*, I–II. Neuwid: Luchterhand Verlag.
Lüthi, Max. 1976. *Once upon a Time: On the Nature of Fairy Tales*. Bloomington: Indiana University Press.
Lydenberg, Robin. 1987. *Word Cultures: Radical Theory and Practice in William S. Burroughs' Fiction*. Urbana: University of Illinois Press.
Lyons, John. 1977. *Semantics 1–2*. Cambridge: Cambridge University Press.
Lyotard, Jean-François. 1984. *The Postmodern Condition: A Report on Knowledge*. Manchester: Manchester University Press (Theory and History of Literature, vol. 10).
Lyra Graeca, I–III. 1922–27. Trans. and ed. J.M. Edmons. Cambridge, Mass., London: Harvard University Press and Heinemann/Loeb.
Lämmert, Eberhart. 1955. *Bauformen des Erzählens*. Stuttgart: Metzler.
MacMaster, Graham, ed. 1972. *William Wordsworth*. A Penguin Critical Anthology. Harmondsworth: Penguin.
Manguel, A., and G. Guadalupi. 1987. *The Dictionary of Imaginary Places*. 2nd expanded ed. Toronto: Lester & Orpen Dennys.
Martinet, André. 1964. *Elements of General Linguistics*. Chicago: University of Chicago Press.
Master Metaphor List. 1991. 2nd ed., compiled by G. Lakoff, J. Esperson, and A. Schwartz. Cognitive Linguistics Group, University of California, Berkeley. Database containing a large systematic list (217 pp.) of different kinds of metaphors.
Meletinskij, Eleasar M. 1976. 'Perspectives et limites de l'étude structurale de folklore.' *Studia Finnica* 20: 94–102.
Melville, H. 1971 (1852). *Pierre or The Ambiguities*. Ed. H. Hayford et al. Evanston and Chicago: Northwestern University Press and The Newberry Library.
Mey, Jacob L. 1993. *Pragmatics: An Introduction*. Oxford: Blackwell.
Miller, George A. 1993. 'Images and Models, Similes and Metaphors.' In Ortony 1993: 357–401.
Minnis, A.J., A.B. Scott, and D. Wallace. 1988. *Medieval Literary Theory and Criticism c. 1100–c. 1375. The Commentary Tradition*. Oxford: Clarendon Press.
Montaigne, Michel de. 1965 (1588). *The Complete Essays of Montaigne*. Trans. Donald M. Frame. Stanford: Stanford University Press.

Morgan, Ted. 1988. *Literary Outlaw: The Life and Times of William S. Burroughs*. New York: Henry Holt and Co.
Morris, Charles. 1971. *Writings on the General Theory of Signs*. The Hague: Mouton.
Mumby, Dennis K. 1992. 'Two Discourses on Communication, Power and the Subject. Jürgen Habermas and Michel Foucault.' In Levine 1992: 81–106.
Murphey, Murray C. 1961. *The Development of Peirce's Philosophy*. Cambridge, Mass.: Harvard University Press.
Nelson, William. 1973. *Fact or Fiction: The Dilemma of the Renaissance Storyteller*. Cambridge, Mass.: Harvard University Press.
Nöth, W. 1990. 'The Semiotic Potential for Iconicity in Spoken and Written Language.' *KODIKAS/CODE* 13.3/4: 191–209.
Ogden, C.K. 1932 (1967). *Opposition*. Bloomington: Indiana University Press.
Ohmann, Richard. 1971. 'Speech Acts and the Definition of Literature.' *Philosophy and Rhetoric* 1: 19.
Olrik, Axel. 1908. 'Episke Love i Folkedigtningen.' *Danske Studier* 1908: 69–89 ('Epic Laws of Folk Narrative,' in Dundes 1965: 129–41).
Ortony, Andrew, ed. 1993. *Metaphor and Thought*. Orig. ed. 1977. Cambridge: Cambridge University Press.
Ovid. 1990. *The Love Poems*. Trans. A.D. Melville. Oxford: Oxford University Press (World's Classics).
Pavel, Thomas. 1986. *Fictional Worlds*. Cambridge, Mass.: Harvard University Press.
Peirce, Charles S. 1931–58. *Collected Papers of Charles Sanders Peirce* [CP]. Ed. Charles Hartshorne et al. 8 vols. Cambridge, Mass.: Harvard University Press.
– 1975–9. *Charles Sanders Peirce: Contributions to The Nation* [CN]. Ed. Kenneth Laine Ketner and James Cook. 4 vols. Lubbock: Texas Tech Press.
– 1977. *Semiotic and Signifies: The Correspondence between Charles S. Pierce and Victoria Lady Welby* [SS]. Ed. C.S. Hardwick. Bloomington: Indiana University Press.
– Unpublished manuscripts [MS], numbered and paginated by Institute for Studies in Pragmatism, Texas Tech University, Lubbock.
Perelman, C., and L. Olbrechts-Tyteca. 1969. *The New Rhetoric*. Notre Dame, Ind.: Notre Dame University Press.
Piaget, Jean. 1962. *Plays, Dreams and Imitation in Childhood*. New York: Norton.
Piaget, J., and B. Inhelder. 1969. *The Psychology of the Child*. London: Routledge and Kegan Paul.
Plato. 1924. *Meno*. In *Laches, Protagoras, Meno, Euthydemus*. Trans. W.R.M. Lamb. London: Heinemann (Loeb).

- 1941. *The Republic*. Trans. with intro. by F.M. Cornford. Oxford: Oxford University Press.
Plautus. 1916. *Amphitryon*. In *Plautus*, I. Trans. P. Nixon. London: Heinemann (Loeb).
Plutarch. 1864. *The Lives of the Noble Grecians and Romans*. Trans. J. Dryden, ed. A.H. Clough. New York: Random House.
Pope, Alexander. 1969. *Poetry and Prose*. Ed. A. Williams. Boston: Houghton Mifflin.
Posner, M.J., and M.E. Raichle. 1996. *Images of Mind*. New York: Scientific American Library.
Poulet, George. 1972. 'The Phenomenology of Reading.' *NLH* 2: 123–62.
Prendergast, C. 1986. *The Order of Mimesis: Balzac, Stendhal, Nerval, Flaubert*. Cambridge: Cambridge University Press.
Propp, V. 1968 (Russ. 1928). *Morphology of the Folktale*. Austin: University of Texas Press.
Quintilian. 1920–2. *Institutio oratoria*, I–IV. With English trans. by H.E. Butler. London, Cambridge, Mass.: Loeb Classical Library.
Ransdell, Joseph. 1986. 'On Peirce's Conception of the Iconic Sign.' In Bouissac et al., *Iconicity* (q.v.).
Readers' Encyclopedia of World Drama. 1969. Ed. J. Gassner and E. Quinn. New York: Thomas Y. Crowell.
Réage, Pauline. 1954. *Histoire d'O*. Paris: Jean-Jacques Pauvert.
Réage, Pauline. 1975 (1969). New ed., expanded. *Retour à Roissy*. Paris: Jean-Jacques Pauvert.
Richards, I.A. 1936. *Philosophy of Rhetoric*. New York: Oxford University Press.
- 1955. *Speculative Instruments*. New York: Harcourt, Brace & World.
Ricks, Christopher. 1972. 'Wordsworth: A Pure Organic Pleasure from the Lines.' In MacMaster 1972: 505–34.
Ricoeur, Paul 1978. *The Rule of Metaphor*. London: Routledge and Kegan Paul.
- 1984–8. *Time and Narrative*, I–III. Chicago: University of Chicago Press.
- 1991. *Reflection and Imagination: A Paul Ricoeur Reader*. Ed. Mario Valdés. New York: Harvester/Wheatsheaf.
Riffaterre, Michael. 1978. *The Semiotics of Poetry*. Bloomington: Indiana University Press.
- 1990. *Fictional Truth*. Baltimore: Johns Hopkins University Press.
Robin, R.S. 1967. *Annotated Catalogue of the Papers of Charles S. Peirce*. Amherst: University of Massachusetts Press.
Ronen, Ruth. 1994. *Possible Worlds in Literary Theory*. Cambridge: Cambridge University Press.
Roman de la rose. See Lorris, Guillaume de.

Rosch, Eleanor. 1973. 'Natural Categories.' *Cognitive Psychology* 4: 328–50.
- 1975a. 'Cognitive Representation of Semantic Categories.' *Journal of Experimental Psychology: General* 104: 192–233.
- 1975b. 'Cognitive Reference Points.' In *Cognitive Psychology* 7: 532–47.
- 1977. 'Human Categorization.' In Neil Warren, ed., *Studies in Cross-cultural Psychology*, 1: 1–49. New York: Academic Press.
- 1978. 'Principles of Categorization.' In E. Rosch and B.B. Lloyd, eds, *Cognition and Categorization*. Hillsdale, NJ: Erlbaum.

Rosch, Eleanor, and C.B. Mervis. 1975. 'Family Resemblances: Studies in the Internal Structures of Categories.' *Cognitive Psychology* 7: 573–605.
- 1981. 'Categorization of Natural Objects.' *Annual Review of Psychology* 32: 89–115.

Rosch, Eleanor, C.B. Mervis, et al. 1976. 'Basic Objects in Natural Categories.' *Cognitive Psychology* 8: 388–439.

Roth, Philip. 1973. *Our Gang* (Watergate ed.). New York: Bantam Books.

Rushdie, Salman. 1981/1982. *Midnight's Children*. London: Pan Books / Picador.

Russell, Bertrand. 1950 (1940). *An Inquiry into Meaning and Truth*. London: Unwin.
- 1948. *Human Knowledge. Its Scope and Limits*. New York: Simon & Schuster.

Ryan, Marie-Laure. 1991. *Possible Worlds, Artificial Intelligence, and Narrative Theory*. Bloomington: Indiana University Press.

Saussure, Ferdinand de. 1959 (1916). *Course in General Linguistics*. Trans. Wade Baskin, intro. J. Culler. Glascow: Fontana/Collins.
- 1967 (1916). *Cours de linguistique générale*. Ed. C. Bally. Paris: Payot.

Savan, David. 1976. *An Introduction to C.S. Peirce's Semiotics*, Part I. Toronto: Toronto Semiotic Circle: Monographs, Working papers, and Prepublications.

Schiffrin, Deborah. 1994. *Approaches to Discourse*. Oxford: Blackwell.

Schutz, Alfred, and Thomas Luckmann. 1973. *The Structures of the Life-World*. Evanston, Ill.: Northwestern University Press.

Searle, John R. 1969. *Speech Acts*. Cambridge: Cambridge University Press.
- 1979. *Expression and Meaning*. Cambridge: Cambridge University Press.

Searle, ed. 1971. *The Philosophy of Language*. Oxford: Oxford University Press.

Sebeok, Thomas. 1976. *Contributions to the Doctrine of Signs*. Bloomington, Lisse: Indiana University Press / Peter de Ridder Press.
- 1979. *The Sign and Its Masters*. Austin: University of Texas Press.
- 1991. *A Sign Is Just a Sign*. Bloomington: Indiana University Press.
- 1994. *Signs: An Introduction to Semiotics*. Toronto: University of Toronto Press (Toronto Studies in Semiotics).

Sebeok, ed. 1960. *Style in Language*. Cambridge, Mass.: MIT Press.

Segal, Hanna. 1991. *Dream, Phantasy and Art*. London: Tavistock/Routledge (New Library of Psychoanalysis 12).

Shakespeare, William. 1981 (1601). *Hamlet*. Ed. Harold Jenkins. London: Methuen (Arden Shakespeare).

Short, Thomas L. 1982. 'Life among the Legisigns.' In *Transactions of the Charles S. Peirce Society* 18.4: 285–310.

Shklovsky, Victor. 1965. 'Art as Technique.' In L.T. Lemon and M.J. Reis, eds, *Russian Formalist Criticism*, 3–24. Lincoln: University of Nebraska Press.

Smalley, Beryl. 1986. *The Study of the Bible in the Middle Ages*. Oxford: Blackwell.

Song of Roland. See *Chanson de Roland*.

Spenser, Edmund 1966 (1589). *The Faerie Queene*. Ed. P.C. Bayley. Oxford: Oxford University Press.

Stanzel, F.K. 1955. *Die typischen Erzählsituationen im Roman*. Wien: Wilh. Braumüller.

Sterne, Laurence. 1980 (1760–7). *Tristram Shandy*. New York: W.W. Norton.

Strawson, P.F. 1957. *Individuals*. London: Methuen.

Strindberg, August. 1958. *August Strindbergs Brev*. Ed. T. Eklund. Vol. 6. Strindbergselskapets Skrifter. Stockholm: Bonniers.

Sweetser, Eve E. 1990. *From Etymology to Pragmatics*. Cambridge Studies in Linguistics 54. Cambridge: Cambridge University Press.

Theognis. *See* Hesiod.

Thucydides. 1972. *The Peloponnesian War*. Trans. Rex Warner. Harmondsworth: Penguin.

Tinbergen, Niko. 1953. *Social Behaviour in Animals*. London: Chapman and Hall.

Todorov, Tzvetan. 1977. *Poetics of Prose*. Ithaca: Cornell University Press.

– 1990. *Genres in Discourse*. Cambridge: Cambridge University Press.

Tolstoy, Leo N. 1978 (1869). *War and Peace*. Trans. Rosemary Edmons. London: Penguin.

Turner, Mark. 1987. *Death Is the Mother of Beauty: Mind, Metaphor, Criticism*. Chicago: University of Chicago Press.

– 1991. *Reading Minds: The Study of English in the Age of Cognitive Science*. Princeton, NJ: Princeton University Press.

– 1996. *The Literary Mind*. New York, Oxford: Oxford University Press.

– 1997. 'Figure.' At <http://www.wam.umd.edu/~mturn/>.

Turner, M., and G. Fauconnier. 1995. 'Conceptual Integration and Formal Expression.' At <http://www.wam.umd.edu/~mturn/>.

– 1997. 'A Mechanism of Creativity.' At <http://www.wam.umd.edu/~mturn/>.

- 1998. 'Metaphor, Metonomy, and Binding.' At <http://www.wam.umd.edu/~mturn/>.
Tuten, Frederic. 1993. *Tintin in the New World. A Romance*. London: Marion Boyars.
Vernant, J.-P. 1989. 'At Man's Table: Hesiod's Foundation Myth of Sacrifice.' In Détienne and Vernant 1989: 21–86.
Vitacollona, Luciano. 1988. 'Text'/'Discourse' definitions. In J. Petöfi, ed., *Text and Discourse Constitution*, 421–39. Berlin, New York: De Gruyter.
Weitz, Morris. 1964. *Hamlet and the Philosophy of Literary Criticism*. London: Faber and Faber.
Wellek, René, and Austin Warren. 1942. *Theory of Literature*. New York: Harcourt, Brace & World.
Winnicott, D.W. 1971. *Playing and Reality*. London: Tavistock.
Wittgenstein, Ludwig. 1963. *Philosophical Investigations Philosofische Untersuchungen*. Trans. G.E.M. Anscombe. Oxford: Blackwell.
Woolf, Virginia. 1976. *Moments of Being: Unpublished Autobiographical Writings*. Ed. Jeanne Schulkind. Sussex, UK: The University Press.
Wordsworth, William. 1974. *The Prose Work of William Wordsworth*, I. Ed. W.J.B. Owen and J.W. Smyser. Oxford: Clarendon Press.
- 1979. *The Prelude 1799, 1805, 1850*. Ed. J. Wordsworth et al. New York: W.W. Norton (Norton Critical Edition).

Index

abduction, abductive 37, 187, 366, 390, 368, 371, 398
Abelard and Heloise 152
accommodation 345, 346
Addison, Joseph 440
address 291, 349
addressee 49–58, 82, 240, 358, 361, 365, 396, 422, 423
addresser 49–58, 82, 98, 229, 238, 310, 358, 396, 446
Adorno, Theodore W. 312
ad usum delphini 453
Aeschylus 219, 445
aesthetic distance 242, 429
aestheticism 18
aesthetic preferences 347–8
aesthetics 436, 438
Aethiopica 262
affect 268
Agathon 7
agency 234
Aitchison, Jean 10
Alcestis 9
Alcman 337, 373
Alice in Wonderland 323
allegorization 327, 334–8, 339, 424, 425, 427, 429

allegorize 155
allegory, allegorical 107, 108, 145, 155, 160, 190, 191, 339, 427, 454
alliteration 199, 202
Althusser, Louis 231, 231, 306, 307, 308, 312
American Psycho 394
Amos, William 441, 443
Amphitrion 8
An, A.M. 238
Anachreon 337, 373, 451
anagogic 454
analogue 164, 165, 224, 249, 299, 427, 431
analogy, analogical 33, 107, 145, 164, 165, 175, 176, 177, 181, 182, 185, 186, 188, 189, 190, 191, 192, 193, 194, 199, 200, 201, 202, 205, 210, 211, 212, 216, 218, 222, 224, 225, 226, 227, 229, 230, 267, 272, 324, 334, 335, 337, 372, 388–92, 394, 422, 423, 427, 443, 444
Anatomy of Criticism 401
Andersen, H.C. 148, 348, 382, 385, 387, 455
anecdote 4
answer 360

476   Index

Antony and Cleopatra 135
anxiety 249, 251, 447
Apollinaire, Guillaume 147
application, applicative 373, 408
appraisive 15–20
arbitrary 29, 40, 48, 58, 170, 200, 272
archetype 402
argument, argumentative 358–9, 368, 387, 404, 428, 432
argumentation 47
Aristophanes 7
Aristotle xiv, 4, 6, 7, 8, 16, 36, 104, 105, 108, 113, 114, 149, 159, 160, 162, 163, 164, 168, 169, 186, 188, 189, 190, 194, 200, 202, 204, 212, 221–2, 224, 266, 267, 273, 296, 309, 325, 443, 450, 453
artefact 15, 285, 345, 376, 381, 424, 426
Arthurian romances 107
l'art pour l'art 18
L'art, les caresses ou le sphinx 340
assimilation 345, 346
As You Like It 308
Augustine 84, 113, 155, 335, 336
Auster, Paul 113
Austin, J.L. 50, 437
author, authorship xii, xiii, 77, 381–5, 393, 394, 397
authority xiii, 290, 295, 312, 313, 319, 347, 348, 386
autonomy, autonomous 123, 360
axiology, axiological 15, 234
axis of combination 180
axis of selection 180

Babeltower 122
Bakhtin, Mikhail 277, 409
Balzac, Honoré de 159
Banfield, Ann 440
Barthes, Roland 265–6, 383

basic-level concept 59, 62, 158
basic-level image 331, 333, 334, 340
Baudelaire, Charles 273
Baumgarten, Alexander 449
beauty, beautiful 11, 16, 17
Beckett, Samuel 113, 224
belief 55, 294, 312, 353
Bettelheim, Bruno 258
Bevan, W.L., and H.W. Phillott 126
Beyond the Pleasure Principle 268
Bible 89
bienséances 170
Bildungsroman 440
biography, biographical 383, 385
Black, Max 165, 168, 200
Blake, William 203, 204, 230–3, 332, 333, 337
blended space 196, 197, 198
blending 196, 443–4
bonding 60
Book of Proverbs 376
Booth, Wayne 98, 239, 240, 439, 447
Bourdieu, Pierre 294, 347
bowdlerize 453
Brandes, Georg 18
Brooks, Peter 264
Brown, G., and G. Yule 74
Bruner, Jerome 91, 229–30, 232–3
Brunetière, Ferdinand de 4
Bullinger, E.W. 176
Bulwer-Lytton, E.G. 121
Burgess, Anthony 433
Burkert, Walter 101, 102, 179, 270
Burroughs, William 113, 138, 142, 143
Byatt, A.S., 122
Byron, Lord 7

Capote, Truman 136, 138, 142, 143
Carroll, Lewis 67

categorization, category, categorical 3, 10, 63, 193, 202, 205, 233, 337, 420
cathartic, catharsis 16
Cervantes, Miguel de 248
Chanson de Roland, La 455
charm 274
Chomsky, Noam 65, 434
Chrétien de Troyes 107
chronological-biographical 384
City of God 155
Clarissa 109
clue 398
code 62, 365
code model 66
co-factual 140
cognitive interests 89
cognitive science 58, 175, 434
cognitive semantics 62
cognitive studies 196
coherence 123
Cohn, Dorritt 447
Coislinian Tractate 105
collateral experience 70, 146, 157
collateral observation 116, 117, 361
collective memory 90, 92, 276, 294
combination rule 66, 68
comedy 6–9, 105, 161, 293, 381, 403
comic strip 141
cominterpretant 46–8, 52, 415
Commedia Divina. See *Divine Comedy*
commens 46
communicational interpretant 46
communicative 405
communicative action 80, 157, 366, 408, 421
communicative competence 81
communicative semiosis xi
community 55
comparison 200, 201, 221–4, 227
complementarity xiv

comprehensibility 80, 81, 82, 87
compulsion to repeat 451
consensus 84, 85
consensus-correspondence theory of truth 158, 160
constative 86
construction 362, 447
CONTAINERschema 61–2, 435
conte 6
contemplation 97, 99, 346, 371, 430
context xi, xiii, 30, 45, 49, 65, 72, 124, 135, 138, 163, 203, 310, 359, 361, 362, 363, 398, 404, 405, 410, 437
contextualization 358, 374, 380, 387, 388, 397, 400–7
contiguity 29, 41, 48, 58, 60, 124, 146, 159, 160, 422
continuity 40, 160, 199, 435
convention, conventional 13, 25, 29, 32, 40, 41, 42, 58, 68, 91, 119, 135, 152, 161, 166, 170, 171, 241, 299, 355, 356, 365, 381, 393, 400
conventionality 200, 422
conversation 395–6
co-reference, co-referentiality 133, 134
correlation 387
correspondence 123, 159, 160, 425
co-text 310
counterfactual 83, 134, 140, 225
coupling 182–3
co-variation 378
craft, craftsmanship 15
cross-universe transfer 388
culture-specific 58
cut-up technique 142

Dante 106, 143, 144, 171, 172, 442
Darwin, Charles 4, 43, 420, 435, 454
daydream, daydreaming 102, 250, 257, 262, 263, 270, 301, 417

478 Index

decoding 66
deduction, deductive 61, 368, 369, 371
Deely, John 434
Defoe, Daniel 240, 241, 393
deictic 70, 129, 146, 187, 225
demand 448
denial 244
Descartes, René 360, 446
designation 35, 37–8
desire 77, 79, 230, 231, 236, 238, 246, 248–59, 263, 264, 269, 276, 277, 278, 280, 281–4, 296, 301, 304, 305, 313, 314, 315, 316, 318, 319, 321, 325, 342, 344, 392, 397, 401, 416, 417, 424, 429, 430, 431, 432, 438, 448, 449, 453
diagram, diagrammatic 30–1, 42, 61, 147, 165, 178, 199, 197, 242, 248, 249, 259, 264, 272, 322, 327, 331, 338, 343, 420, 427, 431, 434, 436
diagrammatization 327, 332–4, 339
dialogue, dialogic xii, xiii, 25, 45, 46–58, 70, 71, 80, 81, 87, 89, 150, 171, 203, 237, 307, 372, 375, 378, 381, 384, 399, 410, 418, 420
dicent 358–9, 368
dichotomization 177
Dickens, Charles 5, 121, 122, 393
diegesis 149, 160
difference, differentiation 40, 41, 179, 272, 339, 380, 424, 426
differentia specifica 5, 7, 9, 204
Dinesen, Isak 61, 243
discourse xi, xii, 3, 12, 25, 74–89, 421, 437
discourse analysis 74
discursive formation 75
Disney 118, 148, 441
distinctive feature 15, 39, 63–4, 179, 272

Divine Comedy 106, 143, 144, 145, 248
Donald and Daisy Duck 118, 148
Donald, Merlin 233
Don Juan 7
Donne, John 228, 415
Don Quixote 234, 247, 248
doxa 163, 231, 301, 302, 406
Doyle, Conan 393
drama 6, 203, 204, 205, 220
dream 102, 257, 263, 270, 342
drive 235, 268
Dundes, Allan 206
dynamical 355, 364, 380
dynamical interpretant 44–7, 57, 82, 355, 356, 358, 372, 380, 447
dynamical interpreter 357
dynamical object 26–9, 36, 82, 116, 117, 132, 234, 239, 356, 446
dynamical utterer 49, 139, 357, 365

Eckermann, J.P. 433
Eco, Umberto 37, 388, 434, 440, 453, 454
education, educational 296, 298, 301, 305, 346
Edward III 455
effectual interpretant 46, 47, 415
effort 42, 44, 354, 355, 407
ego 446
Elam, Keir 150
Eliot, George 169
Eliot, T.S. 203, 204–5, 244
Ellis, Brett Easton 394
'Eloisa to Abelard' 152
embodiment 62
emotional interpretant 43–4, 60
Emperor and Galilean 150, 353
encoding 66
Encyclopaedia Britannica 125

encyclopedia, encyclopedic 89, 92, 106
energetic interpretant 43–4, 60, 62
entertainment, entertain 295, 296, 298, 347, 408
enumeration 275
enunciation 392, 398
epideictic 222–3, 296, 353
Epstein, E.L. 182
Erlich, Victor 161
Essais (Montaigne) 229
essentially contested concepts 14–20, 416
ethics 438
Euminedes 445
Euripides 8, 104
evenly suspended attention 374–5, 455
example 98, 222, 299, 300
exclusion 75, 77, 170
exemplar 164, 169, 205
exemplariness, exemplary 98, 225, 432
exemplification 162, 170
exemplum 107
existence 315
existential 256, 314, 318, 353, 385
existential analogy 221–7
experience 59, 117, 124, 141, 158, 163, 166, 185, 199, 205, 232, 233, 239, 247, 256, 257, 267, 285, 297, 300, 304, 312, 313, 315, 324, 325, 331, 381, 388, 392, 401, 403, 424, 426, 430, 432, 435, 436, 446
experiential universe 98, 156, 161, 167, 224, 371, 398
experiment 431
expression 11
expressiveness, expressive 86, 424, 429, 430

fable 113, 221, 222, 223, 224, 226, 297
face-to-face dialogue 55, 151, 399
Faerie Queene 108
fairy tale 206–11, 258, 297, 319, 381, 403, 453
fallibility, fallible 44, 158, 337, 357
falsity, false 106, 170
family resemblances 3
Father, The 244
Fatherland 134, 140, 160
Fauconnier, Gilles 443–4
Faulkner, William 441
Faust 264
Faust 450
fear 236, 238, 248–59, 264, 269, 296, 301, 314, 318, 319, 321, 342, 392, 397, 401, 416, 417, 429, 430, 432, 447, 453
feeling 42, 43, 61, 354, 355, 407
fiction, fictional xi, 11, 12, 32, 99, 103, 106, 107–9, 113, 115–46, 240, 252, 259, 264, 277, 278, 273, 284, 290, 298, 300, 304, 305, 305, 309, 311, 313, 342, 430, 435
fictional discourse 447
fictionality 97–9, 105, 115, 119, 159, 371, 384, 388, 391, 392, 423, 425, 428, 429, 430, 440
fictionalization 129
fictional universe 97, 115–46, 148, 154, 156, 161, 222, 226, 248, 287, 389, 398
fictional world 442
Fielding, Henry 246
figure, figurative 153, 154, 157, 160, 175, 176, 229, 336, 345, 379, 408
figures of addition 176
figures of change 176
figures of omission 176
final interpretant 44, 47, 48, 372

480 Index

Finnigans Wake 441
first-degree iconicity 179, 119
Fish, Stanley 404, 454
Flaubert, Gustave 5, 6, 118, 128, 129, 131, 165
Fliess, Wilhelm 448
Fludernik, Monika 440
folk tale 3, 101, 102
form, formal xii, 11, 15, 32, 33
Formalist 416
Forster, E.M. 169
Foucault, Michel xi, xiv, 74–80, 85–7, 89, 170, 228, 247
Fowler, R. 182
frame 71, 73, 452
Freud, Sigmund 50, 235, 254, 268, 269, 270, 274, 276–7, 345, 362, 374, 375, 448, 451, 455
Friday, Nancy 262
Friedrich, Hugo 433
Frye, Northrop 7, 89, 91–2, 205, 206, 274, 275, 401, 444
function, functional xi, 3, 10–14, 180, 416, 423

Gadamer, Hans-Georg 67, 360, 367, 399, 409, 455
Galen 434
Gallie, W.B. 14–20
García Márquez, G. 137, 142, 143
Gay, John 225, 226
Gebauer, G., and Wulf, C. 114
George Silverman's Explanation 5
Geertz, Clifford 300
Gelb, I.J. 103
generic space 197, 198
Genette, Gérard 447
genre xi, 4, 10, 13, 87, 205, 304, 339, 380
Gentner, Dedre 191, 192, 193, 195, 196

genus 10
Georgics 294
Gibbs, Raymond 193
Gilgamesh 377
Ginzburg, Carlo 371
Girl Who Tread on Bread 382
Goethe, J.W. von 264, 433, 450
Goffman, Erwin 150
Goodman, Nelson 166, 167, 193, 245
Gorgias 11
Gorlée, Dinda 64
Gosse, Edmund 150
grammar 65
Grant, R.M. 155
Great Expectations 121, 122, 393, 440, 441
Greenberg, Joseph 148
Greimas, A.J. 39, 206, 211
Grice, Paul 399, 437
Guilleragues, Vicomte de 119
Gulliver's Travels 126

Habermas, Jürgen xi, xiv, 55, 74, 75, 80–8, 90, 97, 158, 256, 354, 363, 366, 367, 369, 370, 397, 421, 437, 438
habit, habitual 29, 42, 43–4, 162, 163, 170, 171, 238, 354, 363, 365, 388, 389, 399, 403, 405, 406, 407, 409, 420, 423, 446, 452
Haggard, Rider 145
Hamburger, Käte 440
Hamlet 120, 289, 382, 389
Hardy, Thomas 127, 128, 129, 382, 441
Harley, J.B., and D. Woodward 125
Harris, Robert, 134, 135, 137, 143
Hecataeus 103
Hegel, G.F.W. 169, 253, 254
Heliodorus 262
Henry V 327

Hergé 141
hermeneia 202
hermeneutic circle 360
hermeneutics, hermeneutic xiii, 374, 409
Hernadi, Paul 248, 430
Herodotus 106
Herrick, Robert 443
Herval, René 129
Hesiod 275–6, 294, 452
Hesse, Mary 188, 189, 443
heterogeneity xii, 417
heterotopic 202
Heusden, Barend van 177, 430
Hippocrates 114, 434
historical context 373
historical discourse 90–4, 96, 100, 103, 105, 124, 148, 149, 155, 161, 167, 243, 159, 301, 302, 370, 407
historicity 13
history, historical 13, 385–6, 387
Hjelmslev, Louis xiv, 39, 118, 211, 434, 437
Holbek, Bengt 200, 206–11, 258, 259, 376, 379, 453
Homer, Homeric 103, 104, 105, 168, 212, 293, 295, 348, 333, 334
Horace 259–63, 288, 321, 449, 453
horizon 367
human condition xiii, 16, 286, 290, 299, 314, 322, 377, 427, 432
Hume, David 454
hybrid 130
Hyginus 212
hyperbolic 154
hypokatastasis 190
hypothesis, hypothetical 186, 225, 243

Ibsen, Henrik 20, 150, 224, 353, 384
icon, iconic 26, 29–35, 40–2, 45, 48, 63, 73, 114, 124, 147, 148, 164, 173, 179, 187, 197, 224, 249, 269, 272, 285, 299, 312, 322, 327, 328, 332, 339, 343, 427, 431, 432, 434, 436, 448
iconic exemplification 162, 173, 329, 330, 333, 346
iconicity 148, 149, 160, 173, 178, 179, 184, 200
iconization, iconizing 126, 326, 327, 338
ideal speech situation 82, 83
ideational representation 269
identification 322, 342, 343, 374, 422, 429
ideology 306–8, 311, 312, 318, 348, 386, 416
Ignatius, St 289, 346
Iliad 275, 283, 304, 305, 441
illocution, illocutionary 68, 69, 150
image 30–1, 147, 197, 204, 205, 327, 436
image-schema 62, 63, 331, 333, 420, 434
image-schematic level 59
imagination, imaginary 15, 115, 117, 123, 126, 145, 205, 290, 300, 305, 307, 322, 324, 325, 425, 427, 430, 431, 435, 448, 451
imaginization 327, 328–31, 339, 346
imitation, imitate 16, 17, 99, 114, 149, 160, 185, 348, 381
immanent rationality 367–8
immediate 355, 364
immediate interpretant 44–7, 56, 57, 58–63, 66, 81, 82, 237, 238, 355, 356, 357, 358, 372, 380, 420, 446, 447
immediate interpreter 308, 357, 358, 447
immediate object 26–9, 56, 82, 116, 132, 182, 357, 358, 446

immediate utterer 49, 239, 357, 365, 447
imperative 86
implied author 239, 397
inborn, innate 43, 62, 237, 254
In Cold Blood 138, 139, 140
indeterminacy 72
index, indexical 26, 29–38, 40–2, 48, 58, 63, 73, 114, 115, 119, 120, 124, 130–2, 135, 138, 139, 140, 148, 156, 160, 163, 200, 234, 237, 269, 285, 310, 332, 342, 369, 392, 420, 437, 442
Index librorum prohibitorum 452
induction, inductive 186, 187, 189, 222, 225, 299, 300, 368, 369, 371, 390
inference, inferential 32, 47, 73, 164, 176, 185, 187, 191, 368, 405, 420
information, informational 48, 58, 420
informational semiosis 58
Ingarden, Roman 181, 326
innate. *See* inborn
input space 196–8
inquiry 99
inquisitoriality 97, 98, 371, 430
instinct 43–4, 170, 254
institution xii, xiii, 13, 69, 73, 75, 77, 96, 100, 244, 290–303, 306, 380, 381, 404, 407, 408, 422, 425, 428, 430, 452
integrative 409
intention, intentional xiii, 66, 69, 361, 362, 398, 400, 403
intentional interpretant 46–7, 49, 372
interpellation 303, 306, 307, 344, 349, 423, 425
interpolation, interpolate 71, 389, 390

interpretant 42–8, 57, 81, 355, 365, 380, 418, 419, 440
interpretation xii
interpreter 45, 46, 49–58, 82, 237, 238, 240, 355, 365, 372, 380, 418, 419, 420, 422, 423, 428, 429, 446, 451
intersemiotic 71, 72
intertextuality, intertextual 3, 142, 143, 184, 185, 381, 383, 406
intimacy 304, 305, 313, 315, 316, 322, 324
intrasemiotic 72
intrasubjective 383
intrasystemic 179, 185
introjection 322, 342
invariance, invariant 376–7, 379
Ion 7, 313
Iphigenia in Aulis 104
Iphigenia in Tauris 8
irony, ironic 65, 240, 400
Iser, Wolfgang 326, 454
Isherwood, Christopher 441
isotopic 202

Jakobson, Roman xiv, 10, 64, 148, 149, 159, 177–81, 185, 200, 203, 436, 442
Jakobson, R., and M. Halle 64
James I, 93, 272
Jauss, H.-R. 106, 107
Johansen, Jørgen Dines 4
Johnson, Dr 241
Johnson, Mark 33, 40, 59–61, 62, 200, 330, 333, 420, 434, 435
Jolles, André 298
Jones, Ernest 389
Jonson, Ben 281
Joyce, James 5
Jungian 385, 402

Kafka, Franz 153, 154, 160, 320, 337
Kant, Immanuel 62, 85, 434, 436, 440, 446
Kelly, M. 75
Kermode, Frank 176, 177
Khnopp, Ferdinand 340
Kierkegaard, Søren 234, 235, 241, 242
King Lear 382
Köngas Maranda, E. 206, 333

Lacan, Jacques 235, 249, 287, 448
Lakoff, George 4, 34, 61–2, 158, 193, 194, 196, 200, 330, 420, 434, 435, 436
Lancelot Prose 107
language 63–73, 88
Lausberg, Heinrich 176
Lautréamont, Comte de 277
law 91
Law, the 446
le Goffe, Jacques 143
Le Père Goriot 159
letter writing 396
Lettres portugaises, Les 119, 430
Levison, Stephen C. 65
Lévi-Strauss, Claude 200, 216, 273
libidinal object 304
libido 269
licence 97, 99, 241, 303, 311, 313, 325, 371, 425, 428, 430
lie 424
lifeworld xii, 74, 97, 124, 141, 143, 154, 156, 161, 162, 163, 166, 167, 169, 226, 227, 228, 257, 300, 328, 387–90, 398, 403, 420, 421, 422, 423, 424, 425, 430, 432, 434
linguistic pragmatics xiv
linguistics, linguistic xii
LINKschema 59–61

Linnaeus 4
literal 157, 191, 192, 336, 379, 408
literal 454
literal similarity comparison 192
literariness 417
literary discourse 91
Locke, John 234
locution, locutionary 68
logical interpretant 42, 43–4, 60, 62
Lotman, Yu. M. 90, 164, 169, 200
Lubbock, Percy 447
Luckman, Thomas 253, 327
Lukács, Georg 450
Lyderberg, Robin 142, 143
Lyons, John 436–7
Lyotard, Jean-François 238, 239
Lyra graeca 337
Lyrical Ballads 279
Lüthi, Max 206

Macbeth 234, 283
Macbeth 283, 353
macedoine 441
MacMaster, Graham 205
Madame Bovary 120, 128, 129, 140, 148, 329–30, 331
Magic Mountain 141
Manguel, A., and G. Guadalupi 454
Mann, Thomas 141
Maranda, Pierre 206
Martin Chuzzlewitt 5
Marvell, Andrew 203, 204, 321
maxim 71, 225, 226
maximal unification 392
Medea 8
meditation 428, 429
Meletinskij, Eleasar M. 206
Melville, Herman 289
Memoirs of Captain Carleton 241

484 Index

Meno 410
mens auctoris 66, 455
Merry Wives of Windsor 240
metaphor, metaphorical 4, 33–5, 60, 124, 148, 153, 158, 160, 165, 176, 190, 191–202, 224, 272, 326, 336, 337, 339, 340, 346, 431, 443, 444, 452, 454
metonymy, metonymical 35, 158, 391, 450
Mey, Jacob 65
Midsummer Night's Dream 259
mimesis, mimetic, mime xii, 99, 114, 149, 165, 185, 230, 313, 302, 304, 405, 422, 423, 428, 450
minimal departure 374, 388, 397
Minnis, A.J., A.B. Scott, and D. Wallace 155
model 29, 30, 31, 50, 71, 162, 164–7, 168, 169, 170, 200, 246, 247, 299, 300, 301, 314, 322, 342, 346, 348, 355, 356, 365, 402, 422, 425, 426, 432, 446, 454
modelling 153
modernity 75
Moll Flanders 393
Montaigne, Michel de 229, 289, 419
moral, moral standards 91, 139
moralisatio 107
Morgan, Ted 113
motif 318–21
Much Ado About Nothing 382
Mukařovsky, Jan 200
Mumby, Dennis K. 75
myth 101, 297
mythical discourse 90, 92, 100

naming 275
Napoleon 130, 141

narcissicism, narcissistic 248, 254, 256, 274, 285, 348, 448
narrative 3, 4, 6, 100, 102, 203–21
nature 16
need 235, 315, 316, 401, 432, 448
negative analogy 188
Nelson, William 108
neutral analogy 188
New Criticism 383, 445
Nicolaisen, Carsten 449
non-committal 99
non-fiction novel 138, 439
norm 14, 55, 86, 98, 189, 234, 247, 299, 312, 321, 325, 353, 367, 374, 386, 432, 436, 452
nouvelle 6
Nova Express 142
novel 4
novella 6
novelle 4, 5–6
Nöth, Winfried 149, 177

object 355, 365, 380, 418, 419, 440
Odyssey 248, 441, 444
Oedipus 8
Ogden, C.K. 5
Ohmann, Richard 242
Olrik, Axel 206
omnipotence 274, 285, 288, 303, 344, 348
One Hundred Years of Solitude 141
oratory 12
Oresteia 149, 219–20
originals 168
Ortony, Anthony 200
Othello 382
Other, the 446
other-representation 174, 175, 177, 179, 267, 341, 407, 418–23, 426

Our Gang 139, 140, 142, 223
Ovid 241, 245–6

pain 251, 252
paper-doubt 360
parable 190, 191
parallelism 33, 180, 184, 185, 190, 199, 200, 201, 202, 211, 222, 272, 278, 332, 376
paraphrase 379, 445
Parcival 107
parody 381
Pascal, Blaise 436
Passage, C.E. 449
Passoa 241
pattern poem 147
Paul, St 144, 334
Pavel, Thomas 145, 440
Peer Gynt 20
Peirce, C.S. xi, xiii, xiv, 3, 25–63, 68, 116, 117, 120, 147, 158, 165, 174, 186, 187, 202, 204, 224, 228, 234, 236, 237, 247, 248, 249, 332, 353, 354, 355, 357, 360, 363, 366, 368, 373, 402, 407, 417, 420, 421, 430, 433, 434, 435, 436, 438, 440
percept 58–9, 61, 114, 115
perception, perceptual 58–9, 61, 62, 63, 71, 420, 426, 436
Perelman, C., and L. Olbrechts-Tyteca 223
perlocution, perlocutionary 68, 70
persona 116
persuasion, persuasive 387
Petersen, Clemens 20
phenomenology 58, 321
phoneme 38–9, 63–4, 66
phonology 64–5
Piaget, Jean 345, 346

Piaget, J., and B. Inhelder 62
Plato xiv, 11, 16, 104, 105, 114, 152, 189, 231, 232, 266, 309, 310, 325, 411, 429, 450
Plautus 8
pleasure 251, 252
Pleasure of the Text 265
plurifunctionality 100, 101
Plutarch 104
poet xiii
poetic 64, 99
poetic function 179, 272
poeticity 97–9, 177, 182, 233, 371
poetry 203, 205, 242, 430
polysemy, polysemic 68, 70, 233, 234, 358, 363, 408
Pope, Alexander 182, 183, 439
positive analogy 188
Posner, M.J., and M.E. Raichle 63, 443
possibility 30
potential space 343
Poulet, George 454
power 77, 79
practical certainty 372
practical discourse 90, 91, 93–6, 109, 219–20, 298, 301, 302, 428
practical interest 89
pragmatics, pragmatic 13, 45, 64–5, 73, 74
pragmatism 58
prediction 361, 363
Prendergast, Christopher 114
pretence, pretending 139, 241
primal repression 451
primary process 273, 276
probability, probable 159, 160, 161
Profitable Reading of Fiction 128
projection 195, 196, 201, 322, 342, 343, 427, 429

Index 485

proper name 130
property 30
proportion 181, 185, 187, 333, 454
proposition 358
propositional function 358
Propp, Vladimir 101, 179, 200, 206, 208, 209, 211, 259, 333, 379, 453
propriety 170
prototype 141, 164, 392
Proust, Marcel 169, 443
proverb 197, 444
psychoanalysis 102, 212, 235–7, 239, 244, 251, 252, 253, 254, 268, 269, 273, 276, 278, 285, 385, 390, 402, 417, 438
Purgatory 143–5, 171, 172, 441
purposive idea 269

quality, qualitative 30, 31, 147, 165, 173, 188
quasi-dialogue 399
question 360
Quintilian 36, 37, 99, 309

radial 10, 158, 205, 371
rational reconstruction 366, 398, 399
rationality 83, 85, 367, 421
Rat Man 276, 277
Réage, Pauline 121
reagent 35–7, 73, 237, 369
realism 150
reality, real 28, 29, 44, 63, 106, 114, 115, 129, 132, 307, 312, 320, 321
reason 430
reciprocity, reciprocal 55, 71, 86, 230, 231, 254, 299, 316, 333, 366, 383
recognition 205, 206
reconstruction 361, 362, 363, 364, 367, 372, 373, 387, 394, 397, 399, 408–10, 447

recontextualization 364
Red Shoes 382
reduccio 107
reduction 379
regulative 86
religious discourse 94, 95, 103
reparation 285, 286
repetition, repetitive 176, 177, 179, 181, 184, 199, 200, 201, 202, 212, 216, 227, 184, 185, 230, 231, 249, 264, 267, 268, 269, 270, 275, 276, 279, 280, 283, 284, 285, 288, 304, 323, 324, 377, 451
repetition compulsion 270
representation (*Vorstellung*) 268
representation 114–16
Republic 16, 104, 152, 310
rheme 358–9, 368
rhetoric, rhetorical 11, 64, 99, 126, 175, 176, 185, 190, 191, 199, 200, 202, 222, 223, 231, 309, 387, 417, 423
Richard III 132
Richard III 132
Richards, I.A. 163, 174, 227
Richardson, Samuel 109
Ricks, Christopher 205
Ricoeur, Paul 133, 151, 339
riddle 231
Rifattere, Michel 115, 454
rightness, right 80, 81, 82, 87, 98, 298, 366, 421, 423
Rimbaud, Arthur 197–9
rites of passage 252
Robin, R.S. 434
Robinson Crusoe 439
romance 3
roman à clef 224, 454
Roman de la rose 279–80
Rosalind 304, 305, 306, 308, 349

Rosch, Eleonor 4, 9, 442
Roth, Philip 136, 139, 142, 143
Rouault, Emma 119
rule xii, 45, 50, 62, 64, 66, 74, 91, 98
rule-governed, rule-breaking, rule-creating xii, xiii, 62, 68, 72, 73, 152, 299, 377, 355, 365
Rushdie, Salman 174, 453
Russell, Bertram 117
Russian Formalism 16, 161, 333, 405, 442
Ryan, Marie-Laure 388

Salammbô 131
Satanic Verses 453
Saussure, Ferdinand de xiii, 39, 402
schema, schemata 39, 62, 158, 175, 182, 345, 435
Schiffrin, Deborah 437
Schiller, Friedrich 453
Schleiermacher, F.D.E. 399
Schutz, Alfred 253, 299, 327
science fiction 145
Scott, Walter 241
script 71, 73, 452
Searle, John 50, 69, 134, 135, 139, 193, 341, 437, 440, 447
Sebeok, Thomas A. 114, 434
secondary process 270, 276
second-degree iconicity 180, 200, 272
Segal, Hanna 278, 279
self-expression 229, 230, 233, 243, 289, 422
self-reflexive, self-reflexivity 175, 176, 185, 203, 272, 304, 395, 405, 422, 424
self-representation 175, 176, 177, 203, 205, 229, 230, 243, 267, 341, 387, 407, 418–23, 426
semantics 64–5

semiotic competence 41, 48, 55, 62, 237, 251, 257, 355, 388, 401, 406, 408, 436
semiotic pyramid xi, 54–8, 81, 82, 182, 237, 364, 375, 446
semiotic-pragmatic xi, xiii
semiotization 236
Seneca 8
sensorimotor 62, 63, 355
sensus plenior 334, 427
sensus litteralis 334
Shakespeare, William 120, 132, 135, 184, 239, 245, 280, 282, 286, 304, 305, 378, 382, 409, 455
Sharpe, Ella 278
Sherlock Holmes 393
Shklovsky, Victor 161
short story 3, 6
Short, Thomas 42
Shortest Way with Dissenters 240
similarity, similar 29, 30, 40, 41, 48, 58, 60, 107, 124, 146, 147, 149, 153, 159, 160, 161, 176, 178, 179, 187, 188, 189, 191, 192, 193, 194, 200, 202, 211, 222, 227, 267, 271, 272, 279, 339, 376, 380, 400, 422, 424, 426, 435, 442
similarity-comparison view 190
simile 176, 190, 191, 193, 202, 272, 340
sincerity, sincere 98, 367
Sinue 439
situational 437
situationality, situational 49, 70, 71, 157, 363, 404
sketch 3
Smalley, Beryl 155
Snow Queen 382, 385, 387
Socrates 7, 410
Solon 104

488 Index

Song of Roland 389, 397
Song of Solomon 335
Sophocles 7
source domain 195
source-target model 196
species-specific 58, 63, 237, 438
speech act 64, 66, 69, 86, 114, 122, 241, 274
speech-act theory 68, 447
Spenser, Edmund 108, 109
Stanzel, F.K. 447
state apparatus 306
stereotype 392
stereotypical 346
Sterne, Lawrence 64
story 3
Story of O 121
strategic action 80, 157, 408, 421, 428
Strawson, P.F. 446
Strindberg, August 244
structuralism, xiv, 39, 383
structuration 376, 388
structure, structural 3, 10, 11, 12, 13, 15, 375, 376, 423
subject, subjective xii, xiii, 229, 233–41, 244, 245, 247, 249, 251, 257, 259, 305, 307, 312, 318, 320, 322, 324, 331, 343, 353, 368, 380, 385, 396, 397, 398, 400, 420, 421, 422, 424, 425, 427, 432, 438, 445, 446, 447, 455
subjective thematics 248–59
sublimation 250–1, 448
supplementation 358, 359, 380
surplus coding 98, 268, 272, 273
surplus meaning 179
Swift, Jonathan 126
symbol, symbolic 26, 29–35, 38–42, 66, 114, 118, 124, 162, 269, 285, 327, 328, 332, 339, 373, 432, 437, 448, 454
symptom, symptomatic 35, 37, 73, 310, 398, 405, 455
synecdoche, synecdochical 35
syntax 61, 64

tale 4
target domain 195
technical discourse 90–6, 100, 301, 302
technical interest 89
text 87–9, 433–4
text linguistics 74
'The Dead' 5
The Trial 153, 156
Theognis 286
Theogony 275–6
theoretical discourse 91–5, 99, 100, 105, 159, 301, 302, 428
Thespis 104
Thing 446
thing-representation 268, 270, 276
Thirkell, Angela 441
Through the Looking Glass 67
Thucydides 105, 106, 138, 303
timing 321
Tintern Abbey 248
Tintin 141
Todorov hypothesis 10–13
Todorov, Tzvetan 10–13, 97, 204
token 356
Tolstoy, Alexander 130, 136, 143
T-O map 125
Tom Jones 246
topos 185
trace 35, 73, 132
tradition 126, 185
tragedy 6–9, 16, 161, 206, 293, 403
tragicomedy 9

transformation 378, 387
transhistorical 385, 401
transindividual 385–6
transitional object 343, 344, 345
transitional space 353
translation 39, 42, 45, 71, 81, 123, 327, 354, 355, 356, 358, 359, 378, 379, 380, 407, 438
Trew law of Free Monarchies 93, 94
Trial 248, 337
Tristram Shandy 64
trope, tropical 202, 379
tropological 454
trustworthines 309
truth, true 44, 80, 81, 82, 87, 91, 98, 106, 116, 129, 132, 138, 139, 146, 155, 157, 158, 167, 170, 290, 366, 367, 421, 424, 425, 454
truthfulness, truthful 80, 81, 82, 87, 366
Turner, Mark 33, 194, 195, 197, 200, 443–4
Tuten, Frederic 137, 141
Tynan, Kenneth 139
type, typical 169, 356, 380
Tzara, Tristan 142

Ulysses 5, 170
Un coeur simple 5
understanding 80, 81, 83, 354, 362, 421
universal pragmatics 157, 158, 160, 298, 366
utterance 433
utterer 49–58, 82, 98, 117, 229, 230, 237, 238, 240, 242, 245, 289, 310, 355, 356, 380, 381, 393, 394, 398, 418, 419, 420, 422, 423, 428, 446, 447

Valdés, Mario 445
validity claim 80, 83, 84, 85, 91, 298, 366–7
value 55, 99, 157, 238, 290, 294, 299, 310, 312, 321, 353, 367, 374, 386, 432, 452
vates 347
Verne, Jules 145
verse 204
vicarious experience 297, 424
Virgil 171, 172, 294, 452
virtual 118, 153, 159, 162, 378
virtualization 85
Vitacollona, Luciano 74
Volpone 281–3
voyeuristic 348–9
vraisemblable 170

Warburton, Bishop 109
War and Peace 130, 140, 141, 331
Warren, Austin 181
Weitz, Morris 389
Wellek, René 181
Wells, H.G. 145
Weltzer, Johannes 266
Wessex 127, 129, 382
wheel map 125
Winnicott, D.W. 60, 343, 344, 345, 346
Winter's Tale 382
Wittgenstein, Ludwig 4
Wolfram von Eschenbach 107
Woolf, Virginia 285
word-presentation 268, 270, 276
Wordsworth, William 204, 242, 278, 279
world-making 166, 230, 246

Xenophanes 104